B⁺
6.06
1.75

HX
387
.B

Brandt
A documentary
history of
Chinese
communism

12,489
24558

DATE DUE

A documentary history of Chinese communi
HX387.B   24558

Brandt, Conrad
    VRJC/WRIGHT LIBRARY

A DOCUMENTARY HISTORY OF
CHINESE COMMUNISM

ORIGINALLY PUBLISHED BY HARVARD UNIVERSITY PRESS

A DOCUMENTARY
HISTORY OF
CHINESE COMMUNISM

By
CONRAD BRANDT
BENJAMIN SCHWARTZ
and
JOHN K. FAIRBANK

ATHENEUM, NEW YORK

1973

This study was made possible in part by funds granted by the Carnegie Corporation of New York to the Russian Research Center of Harvard University. That Corporation is not, however, the author, owner, publisher or proprietor of this publication and is not be be understood as approving by virtue of its grant any of the statements made or views expressed therein.

Published by Atheneum
Reprinted by arrangement with Harvard University Press
First published in 1952
All rights reserved
ISBN 0-689-70022-9
Manufactured in the United States of America by
The Murray Printing Company, Forge Village, Massachusetts
First Atheneum Printing January 1966
Second Printing January 1967
Third Printing March 1971
Fourth Printing March 1973

CONTENTS

ABBREVIATIONS

CC: Central Committee

CCP: Chinese Communist Party

CEC: Central Executive Committee

CI: Communist International (Comintern)

CP: Communist Party

CY: Communist Youth Corps (of China)

ECCI: Executive Committee of the Communist International

KMT: Kuomintang (The Nationalist Party of China)

Parentheses are used for original statements in parentheses, and for words inserted to complete grammatical structure;

Square brackets are used for expanded statements inserted editorially, and for notes of explanation;

Double square brackets are used for summarized passages or sections;

Italics are used for words underlined or italicized in the original, and for romanized Chinese words.

INTRODUCTION

THIS IS A STUDY of the Chinese Communist Party line, in its development over a period of thirty years, from 1921 to 1950. It is therefore a rather technical study of one major aspect of Chinese Communism, not a history of the movement as a whole, much less a history of the Chinese revolution. Yet no aspect of Modern China is more important for Americans to comprehend if they would attempt to gauge the strength of the ideological bond which now links the Chinese and Russian Communist states.

Is the new Central People's Government of the People's Republic of China at Peking a puppet of Moscow, a satellite in the fashion of Eastern Europe, or the minor end of a Moscow-Peking axis? Or is Chairman Mao Tse-tung a potential Chinese Tito, biding his time until he can escape the Russian embrace? Can the genuinely nationalistic aspirations of Modern China find satisfaction within the Soviet orbit? How strong is Moscow's influence over China's new rulers?

Such questions are of urgent concern to American policy today, but they are being asked and answered by the speculations of journalists and politicians, with little or no basis in the substantial facts of history. The recent American failure in China, so eloquently documented in the State Department's voluminous White Paper, suggests that the American people are too far away from Modern China and too much out of touch with the fundamental forces at work in the Chinese revolution to create and carry out an effective policy towards it. Chinese society, like Russian Communism, is after all very different from anything in the immediate experience of the American people. It is now evident that our easy and extensive influence in China over the last century has blinded us to our own ignorance of Asia and to our basic inability to decide the course of history there. Having, as representatives of the West, led the way in breaking down the old order in many parts of Asia, we have too easily assumed that our Western democratic order could become established in its place. The Chinese Communist rise to power has rudely upset this fond belief and faced us with the ominous question, can any part of Asia avoid following the example of China?

This volume is therefore designed as a tool for the preliminary understanding of Chinese Communism. It is a limited device which cannot dig very far below the surface, but a tool for systematic work, nevertheless. From a considerable mass of materials, mainly in Chinese (and some in Japanese and Russian), we have selected forty key documents which mark significant stages or aspects of the ideological development of the Communist movement in China. These documents are mainly the formal statements of the Party line, as worked out at one Party Congress or Central Committee Plenum after another, through all the vicissitudes of thirty years of revolutionary effort, frustration, failure, progress, and success. Many of them are milestones in one of the great revolutionary success-stories of history. They record the early effort of the Comintern to subvert the Kuomintang, during the uneasy alliance of the years 1923–7, the bald prevarications and denunciations by which the Stalinist line in China was justified after its ignominious failure in this effort, the persistent doctrinaire attempt of Li Li-san to base the Communist power on China's weak city proletariat, the eventual rise of Mao Tse-tung as an organizer of the peasantry in the hills of South China. These main outlines are by now well known in the West, as are the later phases of the story—the epic Long March, the Yenan period and the united front from 1937 to 1945, and the recent civil war. Yet the inner core of Marxist-Leninist doctrine which has underlain and inspired Chinese Communist performance has remained largely unstudied by non-Marxists.

The critical commentaries which we have interspersed among these documents are necessarily interpretations of history, no more perfect or final than the writings of historical workers in any new and un-trodden field. In them, we have attempted to give a connected running account of the major turns and developments in Chinese Communist strategy over the years. Together, these documents and commentaries, like the actors and chorus in a Greek drama, reveal some of the inside story of practical revolution, the aims and assumptions of the leaders, the doctrines and slogans they used, their tactics and organizational methods, up to their final conquest of power. Naturally, this story is highly superficial, if only because of the limitations of space. We have not been able in the scope of this volume to get far beyond the obvious signposts, we have not pursued the Russian connection exhaustively through Comintern channels nor at the Moscow end, nor have we tried to describe the great expansion of Chinese Communist power in the period since 1937. Yet the ideas and conceptions by means of which Marxism-Leninism has been applied to China form a continuous thread, which leads on into the future. This thread of ideas is the main subject of our survey.

ON UNDERSTANDING CHINESE COMMUNISM

In any revolution the doctrines of the revolutionists can be distinguished from the circumstances of the time which conduce to their acceptance. CCP ideology has been one thing, the condition of life in Modern China has been another, but the two have had a close interconnection. The CCP ideology is obviously of little meaning outside its specific historical context, for it has been painstakingly built up as an intellectual and emotional answer to practical human problems in Modern China. Thus Mao Tse-tung's élitist slogan that the Party must lead the People would have little appeal in the United States (just as political Communism in general has remained largely powerless here), because the American people do not consist mainly of peasants and do not acknowledge a need to be led by an élite. In short, in spite of the Marxist claim to universality, it is evident that Marxism-Leninism has had its success in China roughly in proportion as it has fitted into the Chinese scene, adapted itself to Chinese needs and conditions, and taken advantage of specific Chinese opportunities. This truism does not mean that the Communist doctrine, when once installed in power in China or any other country, may not move heaven and earth to follow its inner logic or the logic of Stalin, and try to remould the local scene and the people in it. But it does mean that the Communist rise to power in China can be understood only in terms of its Chinese context. Consequently, if the reader of this book is unacquainted with the Chinese scene and its peculiar conditions, he can hardly expect to understand the ideas of Mao Tse-tung or Mao Tse-tung's success.

In brief, Chinese Communism cannot be understood if it is looked at purely from an American point of view. Its success is intelligible only from a Chinese point of view. Yet a genuinely American point of view towards it is absolutely essential to any development of sound American policy in Asia.

We suggest that this dilemma can be resolved only by a conscious division of the subject into two stages or aspects. We must look at Chinese Communism first, in so far as we can, from the point of view of the Chinese people and of the Chinese Communist leadership, and then, secondly, from our own point of view as Americans. Since as Americans we are widely committed, in faith and tradition, to the legally established freedoms of our pluralistic society, we can expect in the end to feel a profound abhorrence for the concentrated monolithic power of the People's Democratic Dictatorship under Mao

Tse-tung and his élitist party. Any threat of despotism, however benevolent, is antithetic to our way of life; we cannot help feeling that the Communist system of "democratic centralism" lends itself to despotism almost without fail and that we are therefore menaced by the spread of Communist despotism in Asia. How to protect our own democratic tradition, which we esteem as far superior and preferable to the "democratic centralism" of Marxism-Leninism, is a very urgent practical problem; but we cannot deal with it in this volume.

On the other hand, before proceeding to our analysis of the CCP line and its history in China, it is essential that we make a brief effort to understand the point of view of the Chinese people towards the Communist movement in their midst. This involves a quick appraisal of the Chinese political tradition and the modern revolutionary process, and particularly an appreciation of the emotional and psychological temper of life amid the poverty, uncertainty, and modern chaos of China's once-great civilization.

THE SOCIAL CONTEXT OF THE CHINESE REVOLUTION

The first characteristic of Chinese life which must strike any observer is the material poverty of the people. Four-fifths of the population assiduously cultivating their small plots of land, where our broad farms are adequately handled by less than a third of the American population; at least three-fifths of the people illiterate and beyond reach of the printed word; almost no motor roads and fewer automobiles; mud-and-bamboo huts, rice and vegetables with barely a touch of meat, cotton clothes and straw sandals, a board for one's bed, and all the diseases man is heir to—these conditions are known to us intellectually but never directly experienced. Until recent times most peoples have been inured to such toil and hardship. They have been the norm in China for three millennia.

Such conditions become explosive only when the inherited social structure is undermined and the recurrent problems of everyday life can no longer be handled in traditional ways. Thus the peasant unrest which was mobilized in the great Taiping Rebellion of a century ago (1850–64) was handled eventually by the landlord-scholar-official class, who suppressed it as they had so often done before. But China's material poverty was not alleviated thereby, and the Chinese Empire entered the twentieth century with its ratio of people to land and the productive efficiency of its economy substantially unchanged and unimproved. The raw stuff of peasant rebellion has therefore been lying about in the countryside ever since, ready to be used by the application of modern ideals (a concern for the welfare of the individual and of the nation) and modern technology (science applied to life on the soil, political organization applied to the masses). Thus the innumerable peasant villages of the world's most populous nation have been steadily growing more ready for change, more available to the revolutionary organizer, without losing those hard material conditions of famine, disease, warfare, and early death which lend passion and violence to a revolutionary cause. Quite unlike America, Modern China has been a land where vast masses of intelligent but ignorant people have had little or nothing to lose by revolution.

A second characteristic of Chinese society has been its bifurcation into two groups—the mass of peasantry and the upper classes. It does not require a Marxist to make a class analysis of this social structure; the Confucian classics long ago divided the Chinese people into scholars, farmers, artisans, and merchants—an ideological device whereby the officials smuggled themselves into the top position under the category of "scholars", much as the CCP today assumes the top position by identifying itself with the "proletariat". The important thing about this bifurcated structure (illiterate farmers on the land; scholar-officials, merchants, and artisans in the towns) has not been its rigidity but its stability. Movement from class to class, up or down the social scale, has been feasible for many individuals in every generation; few aristocratic or hereditary sinecures have stood in the way of a healthy social mobility. Yet for all this lack of caste and nobility, China has been left by force of economic and cultural circumstance with a division at any given time into the rulers and the ruled, the peasant masses who were politically passive and the urban groups whose literacy, means, and technology made them part of the government superstructure. Some have called this the division between town and countryside. Certainly it is far more than a mere social arrangement, and inheres in the economic life of an agrarian-based community. In 1949 the CCP acknowledged this dichotomy (and also followed Marxist-Leninist dogma) when it announced that the Communist revolution that had thus far risen to power on the strength of village organization in the countryside would henceforth devote its main attention to the urban proletariat and their industrial production in the cities. In short, for a great variety of complex reasons, Chinese society has been structurally élitist. The men of learning, of wealth, of affairs, and power have always been a small minority, quite distinct from the ignorant, poor, and powerless mass of the Chinese people.

A third characteristic of the old order in China has been the importance of the role of ideology. Few people in history have had so long-continued and rigorous a training in intellectual orthodoxy, for the Confucian state which survived until 1912 was built upon a distinctive ethical system that played a recognized part as one of the institutions of government. Confucian morality began with the individual, his family, and the social order of his community. But it did not stop at the personal level—or perhaps we should say its personalistic ethic was elevated to the imperial plane: filial devotion to one's parents was coequal with loyalty to the Emperor. The ethical teachings of the sages were institutionalized, so that education cemented the social and political order and learning supported authority. Heterodox learning was therefore extirpated and a great value put on having correct ideas. It was recognized that moral prestige gave the government its sanction to rule and much of its power to do so, and that morality was equivalent to orthodoxy—hence the need of the Nanking government for Dr. Sun's *Three Principles of the People* as an ideology which could knit state and people together. This tradition of the moral universe, in which government is based upon ideological principles, has gone hand in hand with the Chinese tradition of government by an élite. The ideology has been created and preserved by the élite, the élite has been selected and controlled by the ideology. The peasant masses have been ruled by both.

THE KEYS TO POWER

From this situation, which we have tried to describe in simple terms, it has inevitably followed that the two primary keys to power in Modern China have been the peasants and the students. The former provide the raw materials of revolution—soldiers and the food to feed them—while the latter provide the leadership. As inheritors of the social prestige of the Confucian scholar class, from whose numbers the imperial bureaucracy had traditionally been drawn, the students of Modern China have had a major role of leadership thrust upon them. By circumstance as well as tradition, and despite their own youth and inexperience, the students and their professors have found themselves in a unique position of influence. A hard-earned mastery of Chinese writing has continued to be essential to the process of government, and they have inherited a near-monopoly. A grasp of Chinese culture and history, of the principles of politics and administration, have been equally in demand as the only possible basis for an intellectual leadership capable of saving China from the aggression of foreign powers.

Consequently, the modern student class, as the heirs of the Chinese cultural tradition, have been the natural exponents of modern Chinese nationalism.

Anyone taking a quick look at Chinese history will agree that nationalism has not yet by any means realized its full potentialities in Modern China. For 3000 years of recorded history, the Chinese people thought and acted as the centre of the known world. Ethnocentrism was inbred in their language and institutions, with the assumption that outer barbarian states, however strong in arms, were always inferior in the attributes of true civilization. Modern imperialist aggression, reminiscent of Mongol and Manchu invasions, has therefore been even more upsetting than before, because it has been accompanied by the modern breakdown of China's ancient culture. The previous invasions and revolutions during China's long history had destroyed neither the Confucian state nor the way of life on which it was based, whereas three short generations of contact with the West have destroyed the self-sufficiency of the Chinese farm economy, loosened the bonds of the ancient family system, eclipsed the classics and their Confucian ideology, eliminated the imperial government, and cast China into the melting-pot. This collapse of the Confucian state has obliged modern Chinese patriots to nurse their profound pride of culture while experiencing all the chaos and humiliation of a dislocated society.

We may imagine therefore that the sentiments of a modern Chinese patriot have not been confined to mere xenophobia or chauvinism. Contact with the dominant West has obliged him to look inward and search out the causes of China's modern weakness. During forty years of revolutionary effort Sun Yat-sen was sustained by the widespread urge for national strength and unity. The same urge sanctioned the rule of Chiang Kai-shek for twenty years. Yet a great deal more was recognized to be necessary than mere unity. Increasingly as time went on, the modern intellectuals realized that nothing less than a complete regeneration, a national rebirth, would save their country and its people. This movement for rebirth took many forms—the literary renaissance which modernized the written language, the modernization of scholarship and its application to current problems, experiments in rural reconstruction which brought college students for the first time into the peasant villages of the countryside, boycotts, strikes, and demonstrations against imperialism which revealed the strength of patriotic mass action. Out of this turmoil of revival, experiment, and re-creation, there gradually emerged one very generally accepted idea—that the salvation of China was inseparable from the fate of the peasant masses, who form eighty per cent of the population. Any gains made in the upper level of society, in the modern cities or among the literate few, could not be held as long as the countryside remained unregenerate: the competition of coolie labour from the rice paddies, the depredations of rabble armies employed by local warlords, the penury and low consumption standards of the masses, would continue to make a modern society, peace and order, and industrial development all impossible.

The implication of the above has been that nothing less than social revolution among the peasant masses—broad and deep changes in the economic and political institutions, a thorough revision of class relationships and cultural values—could meet the demands of China's crisis. Both Sun Yat-sen's *Three Principles of the People* and the writings and theories of many scholars and politicians have pointed in this direction. Even Chiang Kai-shek, though hardly in close contact with China's rice-roots, ushered in the penultimate phase of his career in 1943 by publishing in *China's Destiny* a strident call for the philosophical, social, intellectual, moral, political, and economic reconstruction of the nation. In a word, the revolutionary process has been recognized by most Chinese to have been going on for a long time, ever more deeply and with no end in sight.

In the long struggle to organize political power and take the leadership of the revolution, the programmes of action advanced by the leaders and would-be leaders of Modern China have run the gamut of Western experience. Many have been amazingly dependent upon Western inspiration: the garbled Christianity which the Taiping leaders purloined from Protestant missionaries, the simulacrum of the Japanese and Prussian constitutions by which the Empress Dowager tried unavailingly to save her dynasty, the Anglo-Saxon institutions so much admired by the ardent reformers of 1898 and their successors were all in turn abortive. The climax of this failure came in 1912 when the early Kuomintang sought to import parliamentary democracy, only to find themselves blocked and dominated by a military strong-man. Sun Yat-sen's disillusionment with representative government was bitter and intense, and prepared him for his acceptance of Soviet methods in 1923. Americans too often forget that, from that day to this, the Kuomintang and the Chinese Communist Party have both been protagonists of "democratic centralism" in the Leninist pattern. This opportunism in adapting Western political forms to Chinese uses is best illustrated in the career of Chiang Kai-shek, who rose to power with Soviet aid, consolidated his position as a reforming Methodist, and perpetuated it, when fascism was in flower, with Blue Shirts, a youth corps, and other trappings of the Axis.

Communism in China has therefore grown in fertile soil. Both the bankruptcy of the old order and the urgency of contemporary problems have called for strenuous measures, which Marxism-Leninism is doctrinally fitted to suggest and sanction. The overthrow of the state by bloody violence, dictatorship over the many by the few, an oppressive bureaucracy—the possibility of such developments is nothing new in Modern China, and therefore no great deterrent to the work of revolutionary conspiracy, organization, and action. The thing which sets Marxism-Leninism apart from other political importations in Modern China is the effectiveness with which it has finally (as of the middle of 1950) fitted into the Chinese scene. This can be understood only if a number of features are kept in mind.

NATIVE ELEMENTS CONTRIBUTING TO CHINESE COMMUNISM

In a country as old as China, almost everything has happened some time. It is not our object here by hindsight to suggest that the Communist victory in China was always on the cards, or that it fits the native pattern. In many ways it is antithetic to deep-seated Chinese values—the family tradition, the humane compromises of everyday life. It would be well to eschew all generalities about "the Chinese character" and "the lessons of Chinese history", for our knowledge falls far short of such a grasp. Nevertheless one can point to a number of circumstances and institutions in Chinese life which are unlike our own and which seem conducive to, or unusually compatible with, Marxist-Leninist concepts of party organization and party dictatorship.

In the first place, citizens of the United States or other Western nations have seldom lived through a time in which the government administration of the day was overwhelmed by its problems and literally went to pieces. Yet in China the immediate and obvious circumstance in the rise of the Communists has without doubt been the debility and collapse of the Kuomintang government. In the end this gave the CCP a rapid victory, almost by default. The themes of latter-day Nationalist corruption, strategic stupidity, administrative ineptitude, and general incompetence have been sufficiently elaborated in our press and official records; what needs to be more fully understood is the Nanking government's gradual bankruptcy of morale, which in turn sapped the morale of its erstwhile supporters and produced a general rout and debacle. Loss of morale cannot justly be attributed to Chiang Kai-shek as an individual, but perhaps it may

VERNON REGIONAL
JUNIOR COLLEGE LIBRARY

be traced to the power structure which he headed, and which had become conservative and anti-revolutionary. This sessile spirit affected the lower and higher echelons of the KMT party organization, the minor officials in the sprawling government agencies, and even the clerks, shopkeepers, and students in the cities. As the war-time and post-war inflation endlessly progressed, all these people were consumed by it in substance and finally in spirit. Spiralling prices made life increasingly precarious and hard, month after month and year after year. Malnutrition, disease, and depression followed, the government in power offered no way out, and Free China lost its feeling of support for, or tacit acquiescence in, the Generalissimo's régime. The morale, high spirits, and self-confidence of the Communists were progressively heightened by contrast, until in a social-psychological sense the Mandate of Heaven finally passed into the hands of Mao Tse-tung. This recognition that Mao possessed the future accounts in large part for the rapid collapse of the Kuomintang in Central and South China in 1948 and 1949, at a time when it could still muster large forces.

Already the Kuomintang's efforts at self-preservation had automatically estranged it from the intellectuals and upper strata who form China's vocal public opinion. No amount of searching and seizing, censorship and intimidation could maintain the Nationalist government's prestige as long as the conditions of daily life continued to deteriorate. In the meantime, over the span of three decades, the Chinese Communist movement had capitalized upon a number of elements favourable to strong party organization, to be found both in China's traditional institutions and in her modern circumstances.

One such feature of old China had been the institution of the secret society, which was likely to flourish in the declining years of a dynasty as the only available form of organized opposition to it. Secret organization had been necessitated in such cases, at least as early as the Han dynasty, by the fact that the imperial régime exercised a monopoly control over public association—meetings not under official auspices were presumed to be purposely or potentially subversive; societies, guilds, clubs, and firms were all expected to secure, and often pay for, official sanction. Against the hard and watchful surveillance of the official bureaucracy, the secret societies were obliged to perfect their methods of covert communication, espionage, and security. When the youthful Sun Yat-sen set out to overthrow the Manchus, his first act was to form a secret society, which grew by amalgamation with other societies until the demise of the Manchus allowed this

VERNON REGIONAL
JUNIOR COLLEGE LIBRARY

revolutionary organization to come above ground as the Kuomintang of 1912. Once the latter was routed by the militarist Yuan Shih-k'ai, Sun's immediate response in 1914 was to form another secret society, the Chinese Revolutionary Party, complete with all the oaths signed in blood and other paraphernalia of its kind.

More important than the cloak-and-dagger aspects of secret organization was the tradition of blood-brotherhood which sustained its morale. Members risked their lives in a common cause, on a basis of impersonal loyalty. Frequently, of course, this was reinforced by a superstitious or semi-religious creed of Buddhist or Taoist tinge as well as a fanatical and desperate hatred of officialdom, to which might be added the support of a territorial base among disaffected peasantry. The famous rebellion of the White Lotus Society in Honan late in the eighteenth century took many years to suppress. In South China the Triad Society, after failing to join the Taipings in the 1850s, played a shadowy but definite part in the plots of Sun Yat-sen and his colleagues. Thus the devotion of Chinese Communists to the CCP and their long record of sacrifice and martyrdom for the revolutionary cause are in a pattern partially inherited from the past—even though the Communists have always decried secret societies as such.

Party organization in modern times has also derived strength from the obvious fact of the impotence of the individual. The Chinese political dispensation being one of men, not of laws, the average citizen has not been able to rely as Americans do upon legal safeguards which protect him from arbitrary arrest and maltreatment at the hands of the local régime. Not only has the individual been insecure against the government, he has also lacked the usual democratic channels for orderly expression of political views and interests. Liberal modern journalists have had to be chary of criticism, and the freedom of the press has seldom been fully recognized. Faced with the cheapness of human life in a poor and overcrowded country, Chinese intellectuals have been hard put to answer the Communist argument that the individual can accomplish nothing alone and must join the Party to make himself effective.

The need of the individual for social integration in a community seems also to have strengthened the appeal of the Party as a focus for youthful loyalty. In former generations the extended family system, with its broad kinship ramifications and institutions of nepotism and family solidarity, gave young Chinese a ready-made group life. Modern times have seen the breakdown of the family's hold over its children, disesteem for arranged marriages and male domination, lessened respect on the part of the young for the aged, and the decline of the large-family pattern of living. Chinese boys and girls in such circumstances have lacked the security and some of the satisfactions which Chinese youth had customarily enjoyed, and the Party with its personal bonds and commitments has been a meaningful substitute, even for non-Communist sympathizers on the fringe. The same personal and social needs which produced the student movement, on May 4, 1919, and in successive years, have undoubtedly operated to draw energetic and idealistic young people into the CCP and its many subsidiary activities.

Added to this social circumstance has been the turbulent politics of the past generation, climaxed by the Japanese invasion of 1937 and widespread warfare. It is no accident that the CCP, after being dislodged from the mountains of South China, made its comeback in the North-west in war-time. While the destructive aggression of Japan smashed the modern façade of Nationalist China and forced the Kuomintang into the defensive in the backward regions of the South-west, the war of resistance gave Chinese Communism a new sanction for its revolutionary effort. Patriotic mobilization and sacrifice for war against Japan had an appeal for young China which the anti-landlord crusade of the Chinese Soviet Republic in Kiangsi had never had. As in other parts of Asia, the presence of an aggressor gave the Communists a golden opportunity to link their domestic revolution with national survival. Thus the political crises of the times, in the two decades since Japan's aggression began in 1931, have provided abundant opportunity for political organizers. Refugee migrations brought the intellectuals directly into the peasant villages of the interior, after 1937, and the juxtaposition of these key elements produced a natural chain reaction which could be guided and fostered by a party organization.

An important facet of the Chinese heritage has been revived and developed through this contact between the top and bottom strata of Chinese society—namely, the philosophy of benevolent moral leadership, by which the cultivated man (the Confucian *chün-tzu*, the gentleman or man of superior attainments) has felt it incumbent upon himself to set an edifying ethical example for the community. This ideal was closely associated with the supreme Confucian virtue of benevolence (*jen*, human-heartedness, unselfish love), which was supposed to animate the ruler in particular. The whole Confucian type of humanism, in short, has been a reservoir of sanctions and concepts from which the modern concern for the broad masses of the common people has been nourished. Confucian humanism was of course not the same as that of the European Renaissance, embedded as it was in the hierarchic Chinese society of status in which men had their various roles in society and norms of ideal conduct according to each role. The ancient idea of benevolent rule was at best paternalistic and often in fact despotic. But every ruler in China since before the unification of the empire in 221 B.C. has subscribed in some degree to the ancient thesis that his rule is for the benefit of the common people, since only by that means can its stability be assured. This traditional government of the ruler, by the officials, and for the people has not perished in modern times, and has provided the Chinese Communists with an ancient foundation on which to erect their claim to the Mandate of Heaven.

Of course a great deal more than tradition has gone into the modern movement of intellectuals to participate in, and ameliorate the life of, the common man in China. In many ways this general movement (of which the Communists have taken the leadership) has been the most revolutionary in Chinese history, since it aims to break down the old bifurcation between the ruling upper classes and the ruled masses. The CCP stands committed to this ultimate aim, although the hard circumstances of Chinese life and the dangerous potentialities of power concentrated in the hands of the Party may make this impossible; the effort may be abandoned by an oncoming generation of office-holders. In Russia, for example, egalitarianism is now distinctly out of favour. Yet it represents one of the great revolutionary driving forces in Asia —the idea that the benefits of modern science and enlightenment can and should be extended to all men. Christianity and other influences from the West have played their part in this aspect of the revolution. The fact remains that the Chinese Communist ideal of "Liberation" now capitalizes upon it and harnesses it for political purposes; and this can be done in China merely by extending, without contradicting, ancient philosophical virtues which form part of the cultural heritage, and also without having to stress the political and legal rights of the individual.

THE MECHANICS OF THIS VOLUME

In the following volume we have devoted our attention to the vicissitudes of Communist strategy and doctrine, rather than to the Chinese scene in which the Communists were acting. Of necessity we have excluded from our comments any effort to describe the depth and sweep of the modern revolutionary fervour, its emotional ebb and flow, and the idealistic exaltation which has so obviously been associated by devoted followers with the work and writings of revolutionary leaders—with Chiang Kai-shek in his day, and with Mao Tse-tung above all. We are here concerned less with the emotions of the struggle, with which the revolutionists are often intensely concerned, than with its ideology as expressed in concrete political acts and institutions—both the ideology proper as the general Marxist-Leninist framework of assumptions and view of world history, and the Party line as its expression at any given moment in policies applied to the practical circumstances of the day. This concentration seems appropriate because Marxism-Leninism is, after all, fundamentally a "science" devoted to the seizure and maintenance of power. Mao Tse-tung's rise to power, viewed technically in this light as a case-history of how to make a revolution, is every bit as dramatic and instructive as the life of Lenin and far more attractive in its detail than the backstairs rise of Stalin.

Nevertheless, as we proceed to trace the moves and countermoves of the Comintern's power game in China, the reader would do well to remember, as any successful revolutionist must remember, that the game is being played with human hearts and passions among all the sentiments, hopes, and fears of a period of social upheaval. This is not easy to realize when one is confronted with the esoteric terms and dogmas of the Communist mystique: the whole Marxist explanation of world history, so neat and hard, is not easily accepted by unbelievers, and hence the real implications of a class-analysis, the full venom of a charge of left-deviation, the deadly seriousness of a Central Committee decision may not be fully grasped by uninitiated Americans. Unfortunately we can no longer afford to ignore this special terminology and its inner meaning.

For analytic purposes we divide this documentary history into six chronological phases: the first is a prelude, before the CCP had really got into action, and the last is, at the moment, a postlude very close at hand and difficult to judge. In the intervening twenty-two years from 1923 to 1945, however, the history of Chinese Communism shows a thoroughly fascinating pattern of "withdrawal and return", if we may misuse Professor Toynbee's phrase. The phase of early co-operation and disastrous rupture with the Kuomintang (sec. II, 1923-7) was succeeded by a period of decline and disorientation (sec. III, 1927-31) during which the doctrinaire efforts of Li Li-san and others to seize power in the cities were in sharp contrast to the rice-roots experimentation of men like Mao Tse-tung in the countryside. In the next phase (sec. IV, 1931-4) the latter won out and maintained an embattled soviet régime in the South China hills. Up to this point the documentation of the movement is at best fragmentary, but we know that until the rise of Mao to power in the Kiangsi soviet, Chinese Communism had remained under direct and often heavy influence and inspiration from the Communist International (Comintern) in Moscow. In the next phase (sec. V, 1935–45) great changes occur, for the war against Japan brings rapid growth in CCP power and personnel, within a revived united front with the Kuomintang. We have divided this period into two parts (sec. V and VI) in order to trace, first, the development of the united front as a Communist strategy in Chinese domestic politics, and, second, the many problems of internal Party discipline and ideology which resulted from the patriotic fervour and great expansion of the period. In the last phase (sec. VII, 1945–50) the Party comes to power, returns in triumph to the cities, and meets the great problems of governing China.

Our *Chronology* is designed to record the development of Chinese Communism chiefly in its inner history, not in its worldly power and expansion. The *Documents* (numbered from 1 to 40) have been selected, as indicated above, from a wide variety of sources, several of them rare and hard to get, and some so rare that no Chinese text has been obtainable and we have had to rely on Japanese or Russian versions. Details of these origins are given in *Bibliography A*. Our *Commentaries* (lettered from A to X) may be read as a separate analytic summary, the inadequacies of which are quite apparent to us, but which we believe to be better than nothing. *Notes* have been inserted in the text whenever possible and appended only sparingly at the back, when essential to document our comments or supplement our translations. Each translation has of course been based on, or checked with, the original, in several cases with the discovery of gross errors which have been publicly current in Western books for decades past. In the process of translation we have found it necessary to establish a uniform rendering of a number of key terms. A *Glossary* of such terms, as well as Chinese names, is included in order to aid the work of future translators, and also provide reference to Chinese characters, which are omitted from the text.

It should be particularly noted that our selection of documents cannot be exhaustive, but is necessarily quite superficial. For this reason we have not tried to include items from Russian sources and Comintern publications which would illuminate the origin and background of some of the Chinese documents here presented. In our commentaries we have tried to indicate some of this important documentation on the side of the Russian influence in China, but this has not been our main object. Chinese Communism, we suggest, must be studied not in one volume of documents, but in several, and our space has been fully absorbed in the effort to show the structure and development of the CCP line in China, without attempting to trace the inner history of how it came into being. A good deal of Russian documentation found its way into Chinese translations. But we cannot in this present space represent the scope of the Russian and Comintern influence on Chinese Communism, except indirectly; certain tentative opinions on this subject are presented in our *Concluding Comments*. The reader will also note that for reasons of space we have had to condense some documents by selecting extracts from them; in such cases we have adhered to the full original text in our extracts, except where our summaries are enclosed in double brackets (see the table of *Abbreviations*).

ACKNOWLEDGMENTS

This project has been made possible by the foresight of the Russian Research Center at Harvard University, friends of the Center having made available the time of Messrs. Brandt, Chao, and Schwartz, as well as necessary facilities. For other assistance we are indebted to many persons: Mr. Boyd R. Compton of the Far Eastern Institute, University of Washington, Seattle, let us use his translations of documents nos. 29, 33, 34, and 35 from the volume *Cheng-feng wen-hsien*, on which he has been specializing. Messrs. Robert North and Chi Wen-shun of the Hoover Library let us have their translations of documents nos. 15 and 16. Professor H. Arthur Steiner of the University of California at Los Angeles let us use translations of documents nos. 1 and 37. We are indebted to Mrs. Adele Austin Rickett of Peking for her translation of no. 36. Finally the major task of translating Chinese materials, compiling the *Chronology* and *Glossary*, and handling the many procedural details to which a compilation gives rise has been performed by Mr. Chao Kuo-chün, and we are immensely indebted to him, as well as to the persons above mentioned whose contributions are more specifically acknowledged in *Bibliography A*. We have also received much assistance in checking translations from Mrs. E-tu Zen Sun. Naturally neither Mr. Compton, Mrs. Rickett, Mr. Chao, Mrs. Sun, nor any other of these translators should bear responsibility for our final versions of the documents, much less for the views and interpretations expressed in the commentaries or other parts of the volume. We also wish to acknowledge the helpful interest or assistance, in varying degree, of Dr. A. K. Ch'iu of the Chinese-Japanese Library; and of Professor Clyde Kluckhohn, Mrs. Helen Parsons and the staff of the Russian Research Center at Harvard; Dr. Arthur Hummel of the Library of Congress; Mrs. Mary Wright and the staff of the Hoover Library on War, Revolution, and Peace; Derk Bodde, Harold Isaacs, Michael Lindsay, Robert North, C. Martin Wilbur, and K. A. Wittfogel, among others. Finally it should be noted that the great part of the commentaries in which the essential story is told, as well as much of the translating, e.g. from Japanese, have been the work of Messrs. Schwartz and Brandt, as Fellows of the Russian Research Center at Harvard, the assistance of Mr. Fairbank having been mainly of an editorial and auxiliary nature.

A CHRONOLOGY OF THE
COMMUNIST MOVEMENT IN CHINA, 1918–50

(Revised 1963)

Note. Items in this chronology have been selected for their significance in the Chinese Communist movement. Events that have had an important bearing on this development, especially those that are not commonly known (such as pertinent meetings of the ECCI), are also included. The main point of an entry is *italicized*. Needless to say, many facts, especially in the early years, are obscure and fragmentary, and we have omitted many items of doubtful certainty, while also omitting in more recent years all but the major events. (For a "Chronology of Principal Events Affecting Sino-American Relations" in the same period, see U.S. Department of State, *United States Relations with China*, Wash. D.C., 1949, pp. xxxvii–xli.)

1918

Late in the year. A *Marxist study group* formed in Peking University under the leadership of Professor Li Ta-chao.

1919

March 2–6. *CI organized and First World Congress* held in Moscow.

May 4. The *May Fourth Movement begins*, with cultural renaissance, anti-imperialism, literary and social reforms as the major themes; starts in Peking and spreads to major cities.

1920

March. *CI delegate Voitinsky arrives in Peking* and establishes contact with Li Ta-chao, then proceeds to Shanghai to confer with Ch'en Tu-hsiu and other leading Chinese radicals. Local Communist groups established in various cities in China beginning in May, 1920.

July 19–August 7. *Second World Congress of the CI* is held in Moscow and Petrograd.

August. Chinese Socialist Youth Corps founded in Shanghai (was renamed Chinese Communist Youth Corps at its Third Congress, in February 1925).

September. *Conference in Shanghai* attended by Chang T'ai-lei, Chang Tung-sun, Ch'en Tu-hsiu, Shao Li-tzu, and others. Formation of CCP discussed and first party nuclei officially organized.

1921

June 22–July 12. *Third Congress of the CI*, Moscow.

July 1. *First National Congress of the CCP* convenes in Shanghai, then moves to the South Lake in Chekiang Province. Party formally established. Twelve delegates attend: Chang Kuo-t'ao, Ch'en Kung-po, Ch'en T'an-ch'iu, Ch'en Wang-tao, Chou Fu-hai, Ho Shu-heng, Li Han-chün, Li Ta, Liu Jen-ching, Mao Tse-tung, Pao Hui-seng, and Tung Pi-wu. Ch'en Tu-hsiu at that time is in Canton. Officers elected: Ch'en Tu-hsiu (Chairman of the CC), Chou Fu-hai (Vice-Chairman of the CC), Chang Kuo-t'ao (Chairman of Organization), Li Ta (Chairman of Propaganda). Maring (the pseudonym of H. Sneevliet) attends as delegate of the CI.

July. *The Secretariat of the Chinese Labour Union (Chung-kuo lao-tung tsu-ho shu-chi-pu) formed in Shanghai,* with Chang Kuo-t'ao as head.

October. *Hunan branch of the CCP set up, with Mao Tse-tung as Secretary.* Mao starts activity as *labour organizer.* Another Communist, *P'eng Pai,* begins to *organize peasants* in Hailufeng, Kwangtung Province.

Winter 1921–22. *Chinese Socialist Youth Corps formed in France* by Ch'en Yen-nien (the son of Ch'en Tu-hsiu), Chao Shih-yen (alias Shih Yang), Jen Cho-hsüan (alias Yeh Ch'ing), Li Fu-ch'un, Li Wei-han (alias Lo Mai), Wang Jo-fei, Ts'ai Ho-shen, and others.

1922

January 12. *Hongkong Seamen's Strike* launched by Kuomintang and by Communists such as *Su Chao-cheng* and *Lin Wei-min.* Successfully concluded on March 5.

January 17. *Chang Kuo-t'ao attends Conference* of Toilers of the East, Moscow and Petrograd. Ch'ü Ch'iu-pai also said to have attended.

May 1–6. *First Congress* of the All-China *Labour Federation* at Canton. About 170 delegates representing more than 100 unions.

May 1. *First Congress* of the CY of China.

July. *Second Congress of CCP* meets at Shanghai, resolves to make common cause with the KMT against imperialism and the warlords. CCP formally joins CI.

July. *European Headquarters of the CCP established in Paris.* Chou En-lai, Chao Shih-yen, Ch'en Yen-nien, Wang Jo-fei elected to Executive Committee.

August. *Special Plenum of the CC, CCP,* meets at Hangchow and resolves under pressure from the CI delegate, Maring, that CCP members should enter the KMT as individuals.

November 5–December 5. *Fourth World Congress of the CI,* Moscow. Radek advocates closer CCP-KMT collaboration.

1923

January 26. *Sun Yat-sen and A. Joffe,* a special envoy of the Soviet Foreign Ministry, issue a *joint manifesto* in Shanghai declaring China unripe for Communism and pledging Soviet support to the KMT.

February 7. *Suppression of CCP-led Peking-Hankow (P'ing-han) Railway Workers' Strike* by soldiers of General *Wu-P'ei-fu.* Communist union leader *Lin Hsiang-ch'ien* and thirty-five workers killed.

June. *Third Congress of the CCP* meets in Canton under supervision of CI representative Maring. Delegates split over question of future relations with KMT, *Chang Kuo-t'ao* and others advocating a more independent course. *Ch'en Tu-hsiu,* with Maring's support, reelected Secretary-General.

August. *Plenum of CC, CCP,* approves proposal of *Chang Kuo-t'ao* not to share control of left-wing trade-unions with the KMT.

September. *Michael Borodin arrives in Canton* to replace Maring as chief CI representative in China and to become personal adviser to Sun Yat-sen as well as adviser to the KMT.

1924

January 20. *First National Congress of the KMT* convenes in Canton with CCP participation. Adopts the Three Great Policies of Sun Yat-sen: admission of the Communists to KMT membership, alliance with the Soviet Union, and support of the workers and peasants. CCP leaders Li Ta-chao, T'an P'ing-shan, and Yü Shu-te elected to CEC of KMT as regular members; Chang Kuo-t'ao, Ch'ü Ch'iu-pai, Mao Tse-tung, Lin Tsu-han (Lin Po-ch'ü), Han Lin-fu, and Yü Fang-chou elected as alternate members.

June 16. *Whampoa Military Academy* established near Canton to train KMT army on Soviet model. Chiang Kai-shek becomes commandant of the Academy, Chou En-lai its chief political commissar.

June 7–July 8. *Fifth World Congress of CI,* Moscow.

1925

January. *Fourth Congress of the CCP* convenes in Canton. Resolves on harder line toward the KMT. Sets up two regional offices of the CC: one for North China, headed by Chang Kuo-t'ao, and one for Central China under Ts'ai Ho-shen.

March 12. *Sun Yat-sen dies* at Peking.

March 21–April 6. *Fifth Enlarged Plenum, ECCI*, Moscow.

May 1–7. *Second Congress of the All-China Labour Federation*, Canton, with 281 delegates representing 166 unions. Lin Wei-min elected Chairman of the CEC with Liu Shao-ch'i and Liu Wen-sung as Vice-Chairmen and Teng Chung-hsia as Secretary-General.

May 30. British Concession police in Shanghai fire on student demonstrators, killing thirteen. Incident sets off protest strikes and demonstrations known as *May Thirtieth Movement*.

June–July. *May Thirtieth Movement* leads to *general strike* in Shanghai and to the formation, under CCP leadership, of the Shanghai General Federation of Labour. Movement becomes nation-wide, lending national prominence to CCP leaders Li Li-san, Ts'ai Ho-shen, and Liu Hua. CCP membership increases fourfold in Shanghai alone. Agitation spreads to countryside. *Mao Tse-tung* begins to organize peasants in Hunan.

Autumn. *Sun Yat-sen University* in Moscow opens its doors to Chinese students with KMT and CCP sympathies. Karl Radek becomes rector, Pavel Mif vice-rector.

1926

January. *Second Congress of the KMT* meets in Canton. Left wing led by Wang Ching-wei predominates, helping CCP to retain KMT key posts. Four new CCP members added to KMT CEC.

March 20. *Chiang Kai-shek* stages *military coup* against CCP and left KMT in Canton, places Soviet advisers under house arrest. Beginning of Chiang's ascendancy in the KMT.

May 1–12. *Third Congress, All-China Labour Federation*, Canton. Six hundred delegates represent 540,000 members. Su Chao-cheng elected Chairman of the Federation.

May 15. *KMT CEC* passes resolution designed to *reduce CCP* influence inside KMT. Communists barred from higher KMT party posts, prohibited from criticizing KMT doctrine.

July. KMT armies launch *Northern Expedition* against warlords to reunite China. *Plenum of CC, CCP*, meets in Shanghai, demands that KMT relax its discipline and loosen its party structure.

November. Northern Expedition reaches Yangtze River. KMT government moves from Canton to Wuhan.

November 29–December 16. *Seventh Enlarged Plenum of ECCI* held in Moscow, with China the chief subject of discussion. Stalin upholds his policy of supporting Chiang Kai-shek and the KMT against mounting criticism from within the Soviet CP.

1927

January. CCP joins KMT left-wing government at Wuhan. T'an P'ing-shan becomes Minister of Agriculture and concurrently Minister of the Interior; Su Chao-cheng, Minister of Labour.

Late March–early April. Organized labour in Shanghai, largely under CCP leadership, launches a series of uprisings against the city's warlord garrison, paving the way for the entry of Northern Expeditionary forces under Chiang Kai-shek.

April 5. Wang Ching-wei returns from exile in Europe to assume the premiership of the Wuhan Government. From Shanghai, Wang issues a *joint manifesto* with Ch'en Tu-hsiu, pledging the left KMT and the CCP to continued close collaboration.

April 12. *Chiang Kai-shek stages a large-scale military coup in Shanghai*, shattering the power of leftist trade-unions and of all other organizations close to the CCP. Thousands killed or imprisoned. The CI withdraws its support from Chiang.

April 27–May 5. *Fifth Congress of the CCP held at Hankow* under the direction of newly arrived CI delegate M. N. Roy. CCP formally breaks with KMT right-wing under Chiang Kai-shek, but pledges continued collaboration with left-wing under Wang Ching-wei. Peasant associations in Hunan instructed to exercise restraint. CCP membership reported to be 50,000. *CC establishes a Political Bureau* consisting of Ch'en Tu-hsiu, Chang Kuo-t'ao, Chou En-lai, Ch'u Ch'iu-pai, Li Li-san, Li Wei-han, Su Chao-cheng, T'an P'ing-shan, and Ts'ai Ho-shen.

April 28. Soviet Embassy in Peking raided by troops of Marshal Chang Tso-lin. *Li Ta-chao and other CCP leaders* found on the premises are *summarily executed*.

May 20–26. *Eighth Plenum of the ECCI convenes in Moscow. Last open discussion of China question among Soviet party leaders.* Stalin silences Opposition, orders CCP to continue support of KMT left-wing under Wang Ching-wei.

June 11–12. CCP transmits *Eleven Proposals to CEC, KMT at Wuhan* spelling out measures to be taken in common fight against Chiang Kai-shek. *Wang Ching-wei decides*, after conferring with General Feng Yü-hsiang, to *expel the Communists*.

July 13. *CCP ministers withdraw from Wuhan Government*. T'an P'ing-shan and Ts'ai Ho-shen, hitherto the foremost advocates of collaboration with Wuhan, excluded from Political Bureau. CEC of left KMT formally expels CCP members.

Late July. *V. Lominadze replaces M. N. Roy* as CI representative in China. *Borodin*, after conferring with CCP leaders at Lushan, *returns to Russia.*

August 1. *KMT troops at Nanch'ang stage an insurrection,* led by CCP generals *Yeh T'ing and Ho Lung.* Rebels forced to evacuate within a week, flee toward seacoast. *Beginning of Chinese Red Army.*

August 7. *CC, CCP, holds emergency conference at Hankow, dismisses Ch'en Tu-hsiu from party leadership. Ch'ü Ch'iu-pai* replaces Ch'en as "opportunist," but resolves, at insistence of CI delegate *Lominadze*, to *continue support of left KMT.*

September–November. *Autumn Harvest Uprising* in Hunan, led by *Mao Tse-tung.* Brief *occupation of Swatow* by Yeh T'ing and Ho Lung (September 25–30). *First Chinese soviets* set up by P'eng P'ai in Hailufeng counties, Kwangtung.

November 10–14. *CC, CCP* meets at Hankow, *blames Mao Tse-tung* for failure of Autumn Harvest Uprising. *Mao dismissed from all important party posts. T'an P'ing-shan expelled from CCP.*

December 11–13. *Armed uprising in Canton ("Canton Commune").* CCP seizes control of city under direct orders from Stalin, sets up urban soviet. Commune led by *Yeh T'ing* and *Chang T'ai-lei*, acting under general direction of CI representative *Heinz Neumann.* General *Li Chi-shen* defeats the insurrectionists, of whom at least three thousand, including Chang T'ai-lei, lose their lives.

1928

January 1. *Chu Teh leads the "South Hunan Uprising"* of peasants, miners, and soldiers.

February 9–25. *Ninth Plenum, ECCI,* Moscow, announces a new line on China.

May. *Mao Tse-tung and Chu Teh join forces at Ching-kan-shan*, Hunan, and form the Fourth Red Army. Mao continues his organization of peasants with a moderate programme in opposition to recommendations from the Party.

June 18–July 11. *Sixth National Congress of the CCP convenes in Moscow.* The Congress urges a greater emphasis on agrarian re-revolution under the leadership of the proletariat, condemns the putchism (blind-actionism) of Ch'ü Ch'iu-pai, and elects Hsiang Chung-fa as Secretary-General. Chou En-lai elected head of Organization Bureau (later replaced by Li Wei-han); Li Li-san, Propaganda Bureau; Hu

Wen-chiang, Military Bureau (later Chou En-lai); Liu Shao-ch'i, Labour Bureau; P'eng Pai, Peasantry Bureau (later Lo I-yuan); and Ch'ü Ch'iu-pai, CI representative.

July–September. *P'eng Teh-huai* leads the Pingkiang (P'ing-chiang) Uprising in Hunan. *The Sixth World Congress of the CI* convenes during the same period.

Summer. *Liu Tzu-tan* (Liu Chih-tan) starts uprising in northern Shensi.

October 22. *Hsiao K'o*, commanding the Sixth Red Army, joins forces with Ho Lung, who commands the Second Red Army, under the Hunan-Hupei soviets.

1929

January. *Su Chao-cheng dies* in Shanghai of illness.

June. *Second Plenum* of CC, CCP, meets in Shanghai, resolving to support the Sixth Congress resolutions.

June 27. *Soviet Consulate in Harbin raided.*

July 3. *Tenth Plenum, ECCI*, Moscow.

August. *Mao Tse-tung and Chu Teh set up soviets in Kiangsi. Kian Uprising led by Lo Ping-hui.*

August 30. *P'eng Pai executed* in Shanghai by the KMT.

September. Various *Oppositionist Groups* led by Ch'en Tu-hsiu, P'eng Shu-chih, Liu Jen-ching, and others meet in Shanghai.

November 15. *Ch'en Tu-hsiu* and others *dismissed* from the CCP.

November. *Fifth Congress, All-China Labour Federation*, held secretly in Shanghai. Hsiang Ying elected Chairman of the Federation.

1930

February 8–28. *Enlarged Presidium Meeting, ECCI*, Moscow.

May. *Delegates from various soviet areas meet in or near Shanghai.* Conference passes: (1) resolution proposing establishment of Central Soviet Government in China; (2) Organic Law, Draft Land Law, and Labour Law of the Soviets.

May. *Ch'en Shao-yü* (alias Wang Ming), *Chang Wen-t'ien* (alias Lo Fu), *Ch'in Pang-hsien* (alias Po Ku), *Shen Tse-min, Wang Chia-hsiang, and twenty-three others return* from Moscow to China. P. Mif also comes to China as CI representative.

July 27–August 5. *Communist forces occupy Changsha.*

August–September. *Third Plenum of CC*, CCP, convenes in Lushan. Li Li-san is criticized by group led by Ch'en Shao-yü for his "putschist" policy.

November 16. *Letter from CI* to the CCP condemns the Li-san line.

November 25. *Li Li-san resigns* from the Political Bureau.

December. *First KMT Offensive* against the Communist forces in Hunan and Kiangsi checked within a month.

December. *Fu-t'ien Incident.* Twentieth Army led by Liu T'ieh-ch'ao revolts on the basis of Li Li-san line, but is soon suppressed.

1931

January 8. *Fourth Plenum of the CC*, CCP, convenes in Shanghai and *formally abandons the Li-san line.* Hsiang Chung-fa remains Secretary-General of the Party, but Li Li-san, Ch'ü Ch'iu-pai, Li Wei-han, and Ho Ch'ang are replaced by Ch'en Shao-yü, Chang Wen-t'ien, Shen Tse-min. Chou En-lai is re-elected. Plenum decides to hold Congress of Soviets in Kiangsi. Li Li-san publicly recants and soon goes to Moscow "to study".

January. *Various Chinese Opposition Groups hold a conference* in Shanghai upon the advice of Trotsky. A nine-man CEC is set up, including Ch'en Tu-hsiu (Secretary-General and Chairman of the Political Bureau), P'eng Shu-chih (Propaganda Bureau), Kao Yü-han (Organization Bureau), Liu Jen-ching (Special Agents), and Ts'ai Chen-t'e (Secretary).

February 2. *Lo Chang-lung*, Chairman of the All-China Federation of Labour, is *dismissed* from the CCP together with Wang K'o-ch'üan and others.

February 7. *Ho Meng-hsiung and twenty-two others executed* by the KMT in Shanghai.

May–June. *Second KMT Offensive* against the Kiangsi soviet by Chiang Kai-shek.

June 21. *Hsiang Chung-fa*, Secretary-General of the CCP is *arrested and executed* by the KMT in Shanghai. Other members of the CC arrested include Lo I-yuan, Yang Pao-an, and others.

June. *Ch'en Shao-yü elected acting Secretary-General*, CCP, replacing Hsiang Chung-fa. Other members of the Political Bureau are: Chang Wen-t'ien (Organization), Chou En-lai (Military), Shen Tse-min (Propaganda), Meng Ch'ing-shu [Mme. Ch'en Shao-yü], (Women's Bureau), Ch'in Pang-hsien, and others.

July–October. *Third KMT Offensive* against the Kiangsi soviet conducted by Chiang Kai-shek. Communist forces are commanded by Chu Teh with Liu Po-ch'eng as Chief-of-Staff.

Summer. *Ts'ai Ho-sheng*, dispatched by CC to Hongkong, *disappears* in Hongkong and is never heard of again.

Autumn. *Ch'en Shao-yü, Chou En-lai, Chang Kuo-t'ao*, and other dele-gates to the Soviet Congress arrive at *Juichin*, Kiangsi.

November 7. *First All-China Congress of the Soviets convenes* at Juichin. *The Chinese Soviet Republic is established with Mao Tse-tung as Chairman,* Chang Kuo-t'ao and Hsiang Ying as Vice-Chairmen, Chu Teh as C.-in-C.; Juichin is made the capital; 290 delegates also pass Consti-tution of the Soviet Republic, Land Law, Labour Law, and elect a sixty-one-man CEC with Mao Tse-tung as Chairman.

1932

February. *Chinese Soviet Republic declares war on Japan* and calls on all groups and classes in China to resist Japanese aggression.

May. *Hsü Hsiang-ch'ien and Chang Kuo-t'ao organize the Fourth Front Army* in northern Szechwan.

October 1. *Ku Shun-chang*, head of the Special Service Department of the CCP, *goes over to the KMT* after his arrest. Shortly afterwards, Ch'en Shao-yü, Chou En-lai, Ch'ü Ch'iu-pai, Chang Wen-t'ien, Ch'in Pang-hsien, and others flee from Shanghai.

October 15. *Ch'en Tu-hsiu, P'eng Shu-chih*, and other Chinese Trot-skyites are *arrested* by the KMT in Shanghai and sentenced to imprisonment. (Ch'en dies near Chungking on May 28, 1942.)

Autumn. *Ch'en Shao-yü, Chang Wen-t'ien, Ch'in Pang-hsien, Liu Shao-ch'i, and other members of the CC go to Juichin*, Kiangsi. Ch'in Pang-hsien succeeds Ch'en Shao-yü as Secretary-General of the CCP and Ch'en leaves for the Soviet Union as head of a delegation.

1933

April 15. *CCP issues "Manifesto on Anti-Japanese United Front".* Similar announcements are made on January 15 and March 4, 1933.

November. *Fifth KMT Offensive* against the Kiangsi soviets begins.

November. *People's government* set up at Foochow, Fukien, by Li Chi-shen (sen), Ch'en Ming-ch'ü, Ts'ai T'ing-k'ai, Chiang Kuang-nai, Ch'en Yu-jen (Eugene Ch'en), and others in opposition to the Nanking government and establishes liaison with the CCP, but is soon suppressed by Chiang Kai-shek.

1934

January 21. *Second All-China Soviet Congress* convenes at Juichin; Mao Tse-tung reports at length on the conditions and progress of the Chinese Soviet Republic. About 700 delegates elect a 172-man CEC of the Chinese Soviet Republic. *Mao Tse-tung is re-elected*

Chairman; Chang Kuo-t'ao and Hsiang Ying, Vice-Chairmen; Liu Shao-ch'i, Chairman of the All-China Labour Federation.

Fifth Plenum of the CC meets also at Juichin. Chang Wen-t'ien replaces Ch'in Pang-hsien as Secretary-General of the CCP.

October 16. *Communist forces start to evacuate Kiangsi,* the beginning of the 6000 mile *Long March.*

November 10. *Juichin occupied* by KMT forces.

1935

January. *Tsun-i Conference* held by CCP leaders in Kweichow. Mao Tse-tung formally assumes Party leadership as Chairman of CC and Politburo.

June 18. *Ch'ü Ch'iu-pai,* arrested by the KMT on February 23, is executed at Nanchang.

July 20. *First Front Red Army joins forces with Fourth Front Red Army* at Ko-kung, Szechwan, after many engagements with KMT troops.[41]

July. *Fang Chih-min,* arrested on January 24, is *executed* by the KMT at Nanchang.

July–August. *Mao-erh-kai Conference* in north-western Szechwan. Politically, the Conference decides on the anti-Japanese People's United Front and issues a proclamation on August 1, calling on all classes to fight against Japan.   Militarily, the Fourth Front Red Army is left in Szechwan under Chu Teh, Chang Kuo-t'ao, and Hsü Hsiang-ch'ien, while the major forces under Mao Tse-tung, P'eng Teh-huai, Lin Piao, Tso Ch'üan, Ch'en Keng, Chou En-lai, and the majority of the CC march towards the North-west.   Some reports say that Mao Tse-tung and Chang Kuo-t'ao have an argument on which course to follow.

July–August. *Seventh World Congress, CI,* Moscow, passes resolution proclaiming united front in China against Japan.

August–November. *Communist forces* led by Mao Tse-tung, Chou En-lai, and others *reach the North-west* and soon join forces with local Communist guerrilla units under Liu Chih-tan and Kao Kang in Northern Shensi.

December. CCP resolves to *set up anti-Japanese national united front.*

1936

August. CCP reiterates to the CEC of the KMT its *proposal of united front against Japan,* but gets no response.

September. CCP passes resolution *calling for a unified Democratic Republic.*

October. *Second and Fourth Red Armies* under Chu Teh and Lo Ping-hui *join the main forces in Kansu.*

December 12. *Sian Incident.* Communist mediation helps to effect the release of Chiang Kai-shek (December 25), who has been kidnapped by Chang Hsüeh-liang and Yang Hu-ch'eng. After Chiang's return to Nanking, a truce is finally reached between the CCP and the KMT.

December. Yenan becomes the headquarters of the CCP. In 1936, Mao Tse-tung is re-elected Chairman of the CC and its Political Bureau. (Some sources say Chang Wen-t'ien still holds the title of Secretary-General of the CCP in 1937.)

1937

February 10. *CCP asks the Third Congress of the KMT* to agree to a common programme calling for: (1) cessation of civil war; (2) democracy and freedom; (3) convocation of a National Assembly; (4) preparations for war against Japan; and (5) improvement of the people's livelihood. The CCP in turn offers to: (1) abolish its independent political régime; (2) abolish the designations "Soviet" and "Red Army"; (3) carry out democracy; and (4) discontinue land confiscations. No reply is given by the KMT.

March 3. *Shensi-Kansu-Ninghsia Soviet government* is set up, with Chang Kuo-t'ao as Chairman and Yenan as capital.

April. *Liu Chih-tan killed* in combat with KMT forces in Shansi.

July 7. *Sino-Japanese War begins* with "incident" near Peiping at the "Marco Polo" bridge.

August 15. *CCP announces its "Ten Great Policies for Resistance against Japan, and National Salvation".*

August 21. *Treaty of non-aggression signed between U.S.S.R. and the Nanking government.*

August. *Red Army is reorganized into the Eighth Route Army,* with Chu Teh and P'eng Teh-huai as C.-in-C. and Vice C.-in-C., respectively, and Lin Piao, Ho Lung, and Liu Po-ch'eng as Divisional Commanders.

September 22. *CCP's Manifesto on KMT-CCP Co-operation,* drafted on July 4 and handed over to the KMT on July 15, is made public by the Central News Agency of the Central Government.

September. *Eighth Route Army advances to northern Hopei and Shansi* to harass the Japanese rear by guerrilla warfare. *Victory at P'ing-hsing-kuan* in Shansi by forces under Lin Piao marks the first major victory in the anti-Japanese war. Name of Shensi-Kansu-Ninghsia

Soviet government *changed to Shensi-Kansu-Ninghsia Border Region government.*

Autumn. Communist and other forces in Kiangsi and Fukien are reorganized by the Central Government into the *New Fourth Army with Yeh T'ing and Hsiang Ying* as Commander and Deputy Commander, respectively. Later the New Fourth Army moves into Kiangsu and Anhwei to harass the Japanese rear.

December. *Shansi-Hopei-Chahar Border Region* is established.

1938

Spring. *Ch'en Shao-yü returns from Moscow* to Yenan.

April. *Chang Kuo-t'ao,* reportedly at odds with Mao Tse-tung over united front tactics, *escapes to KMT territory,* and *is expelled from* the CCP.

June. *"On Prolonged Warfare"* published by Mao Tse-tung.

July 6. *Seven CCP delegates*—including Chou En-lai, Ch'in Pang-hsien, Ch'en Shao-yü, Wang Jo-fei—attend the People's Political Council (1st Session) at Chungking.

November. *Enlarged Sixth Plenum of the CC, CCP, convenes at Yenan.* Mao Tse-tung gives a report, "On the New Stage", in which Japanese aggression and the Chinese Trotskyites such as Han Lin-fu's "Third Front" and Liu Jen-ching's "Lenin Front" are branded as the principal enemies of the CCP.

In 1938, Communist forces advance into Honan, Shantung, Suiyuan, eastern Hopei, and Chekiang.

1939

January. *The First People's Council* of the Shensi-Kansu-Ninghsia Border Region convenes and elects *Kao Kang Chairman. Lin Po-ch'ü is elected Chairman of the S-K-N Border Region government.*

Summer. Central *Government begins strict blockade* of Shen-Kan-Ning Border Region.

December 15. *A pamphlet, "The Chinese Revolution and the CCP",* is issued by Mao Tse-tung, explaining the necessity of a coalition of classes in the stage of anti-Japanese national democratic united front, with Communism as the final goal of the CCP.

1940

January 19. *"On the New Democracy"* is published by Mao Tse-tung, giving "new democracy" as the transitional stage towards Communism in China.

Spring. *Japanese forces* in North China *launch determined campaign* against Communist forces.

July 7. *CCP introduces "Three-Thirds" system* (one-third Communists, one-third KMT representatives, and one-third non-party members) into all political administrations in the Communist areas.

August. *Communist forces stage counter-offensive* against the Japanese with the "100 Regiments Offensive".

1941

January 5. *New Fourth Army Incident*. KMT forces under General Ku Chu-t'ung attack headquarters of the New Fourth Army, capturing its Commander, Yeh T'ing, and killing its Vice-Commander, Hsiang Ying. General Ku proceeds to disband the New Fourth Army whose remnants, under the command of Ch'en I, escape to northern Kiangsu and Shantung.

April 13. Conclusion of a *five-year neutrality pact between U.S.S.R. and Japan*.

June. *Chieh-fang jih-pao* (*Liberation* [*or Emancipation*] *Daily*), official newspaper of the CCP, begins publication at Yenan.

November 6–21. *Second People's Council* of the S-K-N Border Region convenes at Yenan. *Kao Kang and Lin Po-ch'ü are re-elected* Chairman of the Council and of the Border Region government, respectively; 219 elected delegates attend the Convention.

1942

February. *Cheng-feng Movement begins*. A movement to correct undesirable and erroneous tendencies in the CCP, Communist forces, and administrative units, it starts with a speech entitled "Correcting [unorthodox] tendencies in learning, the Party, and literature and art" given by Mao Tse-tung at the opening ceremony of the Central Party Academy at Yenan on February 1.

May 28. *Ch'en Tu-hsiu dies* near Chungking.

1943

February. *CCP launches "Increase Production" Movement*, emphasizing the role of labour-exchange groups and labour heroes, and putting armies, schools, and administrative organs on a self-supporting basis.

October 1. *CCP announces "Ten Proposals"*, to wit: (1) fight the enemy; (2) improve the army and administration; (3) unify leadership;

(4) support the government and love the people; (5) increase production; (6) "correct wrong tendencies"; (7) realize the "Three-Thirds" system; (8) reduce rent and interest; (9) investigate cadre workers (for incorrect acts); and (10) educate the masses about current affairs.

Liu Shao-ch'i becomes Secretary of the Central Secretariat, CCP.

1944

Winter. *CCP mobilizes people for "Meetings of Democracy",* designed to enhance administrative and productive efficiency through public discussion and self-criticism.

1945

February 7–12. *Crimea (Yalta) Conference.*

April 23–June 11. *Seventh Congress of the CCP convenes at Yenan,* hearing Mao Tse-tung's report, "On Coalition Government". The Congress, with Jen Pi-shih as Secretary, elects a CC of forty-four regular and thirty-three alternate members; also revises the Party Constitution, drafted by Liu Shao-ch'i, and resolves "to follow Mao Tse-tung's thought, as well as Marxism, for guidance in all work of the CCP".

August 14. *Surrender of Japan.* Communist forces expand their control to Manchuria (Lin Piao, Kao Kang, Ch'en Yün, Li Fu-ch'un, P'eng Chen, and others), Shantung (Ch'en I, Jao Shu-shih, and Su Yü), Hupei, Honan (Liu Po-ch'eng, Li Hsien-nien, Teng Tzu-hui, and Ch'en Keng), eastern Hopei, northern Shansi, Suiyuan, Chahar, and Jehol (Ho Lung and Nieh Jung-chen), while KMT forces take over key cities with the help of U.S. air and sea transport.

August 14. *Treaty of alliance between U.S.S.R. and the Central Government.*

August. *Li Li-san returns* from U.S.S.R. to serve as Political Adviser to Lin Piao in Manchuria.

August 26. *Mao Tse-tung flies to Chungking* in the company of U.S. Ambassador Patrick Hurley, for peace talks with Chiang Kai-shek.

October 11. *A joint statement is issued by Mao and Chiang,* pledging their desire for peace and unity.

End October. *Nationalist-Communist military clashes* break out in eleven provinces.

November 27. *General Marshall is appointed Special Envoy* of President Truman to China, after the resignation of Ambassador Hurley.

December. *Seven Communist delegates*—Chou En-lai, Yeh Chien-ying, Tung Pi-wu, Ch'in Pang-hsien, Wang Jo-fei, Wu Yü-chang, and Teng Ying-ch'ao (Mme. Chou En-lai)—*fly to Chungking* to attend the Political Consultative Conference with eight KMT and eleven "independent" delegates.

1946

January 10. Nationalist and Communist negotiators working with General Marshall as mediator reach *a cease-fire agreement.*

January 31. *The Political Consultative Conference* passes unanimous resolutions on major issues. The principal resolutions of the PCC call for: (1) reorganization of the State Council and Executive Yuan on a coalition basis to serve as the supreme organ of the government pending convocation of a new National Assembly; (2) nationalization of the armed forces; and (3) establishment of a reviewing committee to revise the 1936 draft Constitution.

March 12. *Nationalist forces occupy Mukden*, one day after the withdrawal from the area of Russian troops (whose withdrawal was postponed from December 1945 upon the request of the Nationalist government). General Marshall returns to the U.S. to report to President Truman.

April 15. *Chou En-lai declares state of hostilities to exist in Manchuria* on the ground that the Nationalists persist in attacking.

April 18. General Marshall returns to China.

June 23. *Mao Tse-tung demands U.S. cease all aid* to the Nationalists and withdraw U.S. forces from China.

August 4. Ch'in Pang-hsien, Yeh T'ing, Wang Jo-fei, Teng Fa, and four others are *killed in a plane crash* while flying from Chungking to Yenan.

October 11. *Nationalist forces occupy Kalgan*, CCP having asserted that the attack will mean irretrievable civil war.

November 15. *The Communists boycott the National Assembly at Nanking*, summoned by Chiang Kai-shek.

December. CCP promulgates regulations on "*Compulsory Purchase of Excess Land* from the Landlords".

1947

January 7. *General Marshall returns* to the U.S., admitting the failure of his mission in China.

February 11. *CCP delegation headed by Chou En-lai* is ordered to leave Nanking by the Nationalist Government.

March 19. *Nationalist forces occupy Yenan*, Chinese Communist capital since 1936.

October 10. *CCP announces its New Land Law*, generally abolishing land rights of landlords, who are given an amount of land like the average peasant.

October 27. *Nationalist Government outlaws the Democratic League*, composed of third-party groups largely sympathetic to the CCP.

December 25. Mao Tse-tung calls for the formation of a *Cominform in the Far East.*

1948

January 1. *Seventh Plenum (1st Session) of the CC, CCP* convenes; Mao predicts CCP victory in the civil war.

April 1. *Mao Tse-tung*, in a speech before the Congress of Cadre Workers of the Shansi-Suiyuan Liberated Area, warns *against ultra-leftist tendencies.*

April 22. *Communist forces re-occupy Yenan.*

July 15. *CCP approves the position of the Cominform regarding the Yugoslav Communist Party.*

August 1–22. *Sixth Congress of the All-China Labour Federation* convenes in Harbin with 504 delegates; Ch'en Yün is elected Chairman of the Federation, with Liu Ning-i, Li Li-san, and Chu Hsüeh-fan as Vice-Chairmen.

August 19. *North China People's Government is formed*, with Tung Pi-wu and Po I-po as Chairman and Vice-Chairman, respectively, and its seat at Shih-chia-chuang, Hopei.

November 1. *Communist forces occupy Mukden.* Later Lin Feng is elected by a Council of People's Delegates to be Chairman of the North-east Administrative Council, with Kao Kang as Chairman of the North-east Central Bureau of the CCP.

1949

January 15. *Communist forces occupy Tientsin.*

January 31. *Communist forces occupy Peiping.*

March 1. All-China Students' Congress convenes in Peiping, following which the *All-China Students' Federation* is established.

March 16–23. *Seventh Plenum* (2nd Session) of the CC, CCP, convenes at Shih-chia-chuang. It resolves: (1) to shift the Party's central task from rural areas to urban areas; (2) to call on Party members to learn wholeheartedly industrial, productive, and managerial techniques; and (3) to rally the working class, peasantry, revolutionary intelligentsia, co-operative petty bourgeoisie, and national bourgeoisie to build a "new democratic" China.

March 27. *All-China Women's Congress* inaugurated in Peiping, following which the *All-China Federation of Democratic Women* is established.

March. *The Politburo, the CC of the CCP, the General Federation of Labour* and other national organizations (youth, women, students . . .) move their headquarters to Peiping.

April 11–18. *The New Democratic Youth League* (started in October 1946) holds its *First Congress* in Peiping, with Liao Ch'eng-chih as its head.

April 20. *During the crossing of the Yangtze by the Communist forces*, the British ship, H.M.S. *Amethyst*, accused of firing on Communist units, is damaged by Communist guns near Chinkiang.

April 23. *Communist forces occupy Nanking.*

May 11. *All-China Federation of Democratic Youth* formed at closing session of All-China Youth Congress.

May 25. *Communist forces occupy Shanghai.*

June 15–19. *First Plenary Session of the Preparatory Committee of the People's Political Consultative Conference.*

July 1. Mao Tse-tung publishes his *"On the People's Democratic Dictatorship"*, in commemoration of the 28th Anniversary of the CCP.

July 2. First All-China Conference of Writers and Artists, following which the *All-China Federations of Writers and Artists* is established.

July 16. *The Sino-Soviet Friendship Association* is organized in Peiping with branches in major cities.

August 1. *A one-year trade pact* is concluded between Soviet Russia and the North-east Administration, to export agricultural products from Manchuria in return for machinery, petroleum, and other manufactured goods.

August 2. British ship *Amethyst escapes to Hongkong.*

August 7. *U.S. Department of State issues its "White Paper"* on United States relations with China.

August 26. *Communist forces occupy Lanchow.*

August 27. *North-east People's Government is formed* with Kao Kang as Chairman and Li Fu-ch'un, Lin Feng, and Kao Ch'ung-min as Vice-Chairmen.

September 21. *The People's Political Consultative Conference*, with 510 regular and seventy-seven alternate delegates and seventy-four invited delegates, convenes in Peiping to elect the Central People's Government.

September 27. *Organic Law of the PPCC* and *Organic Law of Central People's Government adopted* by the PPCC.

October 1. *The Central People's Government of China is established,* with Mao Tse-tung as Chairman; and Chu Teh, Liu Shao-ch'i, Soong Ching-ling (Mme. Sun Yat-sen), Li Chi-shen, Chang Lan, and Kao Kang as Vice-Chairmen. Chou En-lai is appointed Premier of the State Administrative Council and Minister of Foreign Affairs. Peking is made the capital.

October 1. *U.S.S.R. recognizes the Central People's Government,* followed by Eastern European countries. General N. Roshin, former Soviet Ambassador to the Nationalist Government, becomes Ambassador at Peking. Wang Chia-hsiang is appointed Chinese Ambassador at Moscow.

October 9. *Mao elected Chairman of the National Committee, PPCC.*

October 14. *Communist forces occupy Canton.* General Yeh Chien-ying is appointed Governor of Kwangtung Province and Mayor of Canton.

November 30. *Communist forces occupy Chungking.* Nationalist Government moves to Taipeh, Taiwan (Formosa).

November 24–December 5. *Congress of the Asiatic and Australian Labour Federation* convenes at Peking with more than 120 persons representing fourteen countries. Liu Shao-ch'i presides and gives the opening address.

December 4. The State Administrative Council decides to set up *six Regional Military and Political Committees* for China: (1) North-east People's Government, headed by Kao Kang, administering Heilungkiang, Liaotung, Liao-hsi, Kirin, Sungkiang, and Jehol provinces; (2) East China MPC, headed by Jao Shu-shih, administering Shantung, Kiangsu, Anhwei, Chekiang, Fukien, and Taiwan provinces; (3) Central and South China MPC, headed by Lin Piao, administering Honan, Hupei, Hunan, Kiangsi, Kwangtung, and Kwangsi provinces; (4) North-west MPC, headed by P'eng Te-huai, administering Shensi, Kansu, Chinghai, Ninghsia, and Sinkiang provinces; (5) South-west MPC, headed by Liu Po-ch'eng, administering Szechwan, Kweichow, Yunnan, and Sikang provinces; (6) Suiyuan MPC, including Suiyuan and Inner Mongolian Autonomous government. Four provinces in North China, Hopei, Shansi, Pingyuan, and Chahar, are directly administered by the Central People's Government.

December 16. *Mao Tse-tung arrives in Moscow.*

1950

January 1. *New Year's Manifesto is issued by the CC, CCP,* listing five major tasks for the Chinese people in 1950 as: (1) transform war economy to peace economy; (2) heal the war damages; (3) overcome post-war financial and economic difficulties; (4) rebuild production in industry, agriculture, and other fields; and (5) reconstruct transportation and communications in the whole country.

January 5. *Great Britain recognizes the Chinese People's Government,* followed by Norway, Pakistan, Ceylon, Denmark, Sweden, Finland, Afghanistan, Israel, Switzerland, and India.

January 9. *Chou En-lai,* Foreign Minister of Chinese People's Republic, cables United Nations, demanding the ouster of Nationalist delegation.

January 20. *Chang Wen-t'ien is appointed chief delegate to the United Nations* and to the Security Council of the U.N. by the People's government at Peking.

January 21. *Chou En-lai,* Premier and Minister of Foreign Affairs of the People's Government, *arrives at Moscow.*

Feburary 14. *Sino-Soviet Friendship Pact and Trade Agreements signed at Moscow.*

February 20. *Mao Tse-tung and Chou En-lai leave Moscow for Peking.*

April 17–24. *Communist forces occupy Hainan Island.*

May 1. *Liu Shao-ch'i,* in his *May Day speech,* deliberates on the "five favourable conditions and six important tasks" in the Chinese revolution.

SELECTED DOCUMENTS
WITH
CRITICAL COMMENTARIES

SELECTED DOCUMENTS WITH CRITICAL COMMENTARIES

SEC. I. THE EMBRYONIC PERIOD (1921–3)

COMMENTARY A. THE SECOND CONGRESS: THE "BLOC WITHOUT"

The earliest public statements of the CCP are the *First Manifesto on the Current Situation* and the *Manifesto of the Second Congress* of June–July 1922. A documentary history of Chinese Communism must begin with these, because earlier Party meetings—notably the First Congress of July 1921—apparently issued no declarations whatever. The record now available thus begins almost two years after the foundation of the Party.

As indicated in our *Chronology*, the actual formation of the CCP at a meeting in Shanghai in July 1921 had followed more than a year of preparation. As early as 1918 Marxist study groups had been formed among intellectuals in Peking and elsewhere. In September 1920 a small conference at Shanghai had been attended by Ch'en Tu-hsiu, influential dean of the college of letters at Peking University, where the movement of May 4, 1919 had originated. A varied group of intellectuals participated in this early activity—Mao Tse-tung, Tung Pi-wu, and some others who are in power today, Chang Kuo-t'ao who fled to the Kuomintang in 1938, Ch'en Kung-po and Chou Fu-hai, who eventually wound up as puppets under Wang Ching-wei at Nanking, and other individuals like the philosopher Chang Tung-sun or Shao Li-tzu, a KMT leader, whose careers have been outside the ranks of Communism but who are now co-operating with the new régime at Peking. The intellectual and social ferment of the time which brought such men together, under Ch'en Tu-hsiu as first chairman of the CC of the CCP, awaits serious and more penetrating study. In our concentration in this volume upon the ideological development of Chinese Communism, we pass over this personal and historical background.

The chief significance of the manifestos of June–July 1922 lies in their call for a "democratic united front of workers, poor peasants, and petty bourgeoisie" (see document no. 2, p. 64). To form this united front, the Communists proposed to convoke a conference between themselves and the other "revolutionary elements"—

principally those inside the KMT (see document no. 1, p. 63). Some historians of Chinese Communism have interpreted this move as laying the foundation of the CCP-KMT bloc as it took shape in 1923.[1] This interpretation is erroneous in that it fails to make the vital distinction between the "bloc without" and the "bloc within" —that is, between a two-party alliance and a system of dual party membership under which the individual members of one party *enter* the other. It was only in this latter form, as a "bloc within", that the Communists became allies of the KMT; but this did not begin until August 1922—that is, one month after the Second Congress. Before that, the CCP line—as laid down in the two manifestos below— betrayed no inclination whatever towards a "bloc within" the KMT.

The *First Manifesto on the Current Situation*—whose line coincides with that of the Second Congress—expresses an attitude of benevolent criticism towards the KMT. It admits that the KMT deserves to be called a revolutionary party, but hastens to add that this is merely a relative matter. It lauds the KMT government at Canton for its liberal labour policy, but chides it for its inclination to make deals with the Northern militarists (see pp. 58–9). It is true that the KMT leader at Canton, Sun Yat-sen, was by no means free of this inclination; and when he went to Peking two years later to negotiate with the Northern régime he still met with Communist opposition on this score.[2]

In August 1922, the Comintern delegate Maring proposed to a special plenum of the CCP Central Committee that a Communist bloc be formed inside, instead of alongside, the KMT. Prominent CCP leaders—including Ch'en Tu-hsiu, the Secretary-General—opposed this plan on the ground that it would cost the Party its class independence.[3] Maring countered this objection by advancing the novel view that the KMT was, in fact, a multi-class party—a view clearly in conflict with Marx's concept of parties as organs of single, indivisible class interest. Many of the CCP leaders were too good Marxists to reconcile themselves easily to such irreconcilables; they still believed, with all the orthodoxy of new converts, that "the struggle for democracy is a struggle of one class" (see document no. 1, p. 58). Maring therefore had to invoke the discipline of the Comintern to force the adoption of his plan.

Raised thus into official Comintern dogma, the multi-class theory defined the KMT as a "bloc of four classes"—that is, as a bloc of the bourgeoisie, petty bourgeoisie, workers, and peasants. By contrast, the Second CCP Congress still had omitted the bourgeoisie from the projected united front (see document no. 2, p. 64). It was only *after* the August plenum of 1922 that the Communists proposed to make the KMT "the central force of the national revolution" (see document no. 4, p. 71). As of June 1922, they still believed that to "act jointly" with the KMT was sufficient to assure the triumph of the national revolution (see document no. 1, p. 62). As though to avoid any mis-understanding on this point, the Second Congress opened its *Manifesto* with the reminder that such joint action was not to be construed as a proletarian surrender to the capitalists. On the contrary, the workers were to use the lull in the class struggle to lay the groundwork for the establishment of soviets (see document no. 2, p. 65). Half a year later, however, by early 1923, Communist strategy had changed to such an extent that the Soviet representative, A. A. Joffe, was quite willing to agree with Dr. Sun on the unsuitability of the soviet system to Chinese conditions (see document no. 3).

When seen with the hindsight of this new perspective, the CCP line *prior* to August 1922 soon appeared to have been symptomatic of the "infantile disorder of 'leftism'".[4] In November 1922 Karl Radek upbraided the Chinese Communist delegation to the Fourth Comintern Congress for their all-too-literal approach to Marxism-Leninism. "Get out of the Confucian study chambers of Communism!" Radek ex-horted the Chinese delegation, which included Ch'en Tu-hsiu. It was the task of the CCP to "bring the workers into a rational relationship with the objectively revolutionary elements of the bourgeoisie". The Chinese Communists, Radek said, simply had to grasp the fact that "neither the question of Socialism nor that of the Soviet republic are now on the order of the day".[5]

The full extent of the CCP's "leftism" prior to August 1922 may be measured by the length of time which elapsed before the demands of the Second CCP Congress regained doctrinal sanction from the Comintern. The chief plank of the Second Congress—support of the KMT in the form of the "bloc without"—was resuscitated by the (Trotskyist) left opposition in Russia after mid-1925, on the ground that the "bloc within" had fulfilled its function of gaining the CCP a foothold among the masses. But through this identification with "Trotskyism", the "bloc without" became anathema to Stalin, and remained taboo in Comintern doctrine until redeemed in the days of the anti-Japanese united front after 1935 (see document no. 21). Similarly, the class strategy of the Second CCP Congress coincided with "Trotskyism" in its failure to embrace the bourgeoisie as a revolutionary ally (see document no. 2, p. 64). Such failure became

"Trotskyist" heresy after the "bloc of four classes" was raised into Comintern dogma; and it remained heresy until Chiang Kai-shek's coup of April 1927 forced the Comintern to drop the bourgeoisie from the revolutionary bloc (see Commentary E, p. 90). Lastly, the demand of the Second CCP Congress that the workers prepare to set up soviets (see document no. 2, p. 65) later assumed such a deep "Trotskyist" hue that Stalin could only revive it, slowly and cautiously, after the total break-up of the CCP-KMT alliance in mid-1927.

The Second CCP Congress thus marks not the beginning but the end of an era in Chinese Communist history. It marks the end of a period of youthful purism and isolation; for after August 1922, purity of dogma yielded to practical compromise, and cliquish aloofness to mass work in the KMT. This transformation was wrought by an outside force—by the first impact of Comintern discipline on the CCP leadership. Thus it was not on its own initiative that the young Chinese Party set out on the road which led to the heights of the "Great Chinese Revolution" of 1925–7 and thence, in mid-1927, into an abyss of terror and destruction.

1. FIRST MANIFESTO OF THE CCP ON THE CURRENT SITUATION (June 10, 1922)

For thousands of years China has endured feudal economic conditions. Agriculture has been the basis of China's economy. Hence, China has been socially disunited and has lacked organizational strength and (so has lacked) interest in the country's political life. Not until the second half of the nineteenth century did the development of world capitalist production raise before the capitalist governments the problem how to use the boundless (extent of) China as a market. China, which had previously been inaccessible to alien influence for thousands of years, was now subjected to oppression by other states. During the period when the annexationist aspirations of capitalist states were asserting themselves, China's masses attempted to resist the conqueror by direct action. After the popular revolt was crushed, China began to feel the yoke of foreign enslavement more than ever and to discover at the same time the mercenary and sinful nature of her own government.

In the process of the struggle the Chinese popular masses learned the truth that the country's defence from foreign enslavement was impossible without a decisive change of the entire political system of the country. The struggle headed by K'ang Yu-wei [leader of the Reform Movement of 1898] was one of the manifestations of the aroused self-consciousness of China. But the 1911 revolution, which offered the popular masses an opportunity to participate directly in the political reconstruction of the country, was the most significant event in the period of struggle against the old régime. Under the conditions of China's political and economic oppression by foreign states, the popular masses of China, in their political development and in the growth of their power to organize, had to go beyond the phase of minor reform for the correction and improvement of the state administration and reach the point of revolution, which launched slogans and demands for democratic power. The revolution [of 1911] cast aside China's traditional monarchy, which had existed for thousands of years, and opened a new era in China's political history.

The revolution of 1911 had two historical tasks: first, the overthrow of the Manchu dynasty and, second, the liberation of China from foreign oppression and the transformation of China into an independent state. In this second objective the 1911 revolution aimed to create, within a framework of racial and national independence, favourable conditions for the industrial development of China. The 1911 revolution expressed the transition from the political system of feudalism to a democratic régime, from manual labour and an artisan economy to capitalist production.

The revolution in China—under the definite conditions of its historical environment—did not consummate a victory. The democratic party [presumably, the Kuomintang], which expressed the demands of liberal social strata, resorted to a compromise with the counter-revolutionary class of feudal lords. The first error of the democratic party was its reconciliation with Yüan Shih-k'ai [military leader and president of the Chinese Republic, 1912–16] in spite of the fact that in view of the forced "abdication" of the dynasty under exceptionally unfavourable financial conditions, the position of the head of the reactionary classes was extremely difficult. The leaders of the revolutionary government issued an order to the revolutionary troops to quarter themselves in Nanking instead of ordering them to cross the Yangtze for a further offensive against North China.

The revolutionary government handed the reins to Yüan Shih-k'ai, the organizer of the "Pei-yang" military party, which united all the feudal lords, the counter-revolutionary warlords, and military commanders.

After Yüan Shih-k'ai's unsuccessful attempt [in 1915–16] to restore the monarchy in China, authority passed momentarily into the hands of the democratic party, which was (however) incapable of holding it and turned it over to the reactionary Tuan Ch'i-jui, the new head of the "Pei-yang" military party. For a second time the conciliatory policy of the democratic party led it to defeat.

Under present conditions, when Hsü Shih-ch'ang, the President of the Peking (government) [September 1918–June 1922], has left the capital and power is in the reactionary hands of Ts'ao K'un and Wu P'ei-fu—the present leaders of "Pei-yang" military party—a third democratic party defeat can be averted only if the democratic elements of the country renounce completely the policy of conciliation and compromise, and take the path of revolutionary struggle. Democratic power can triumph in China only through revolutionary seizure of power.

The result of the revolution's defeat has been a strengthening of the world imperialist yoke in China and of the reactionary régime of her own militarists. The so-called republican rule is in the hands of militarists who, under conditions of a semi-feudal economy, use it to join their own actions with those of the world imperialists, who are concluding an agreement with the Chinese military clique regarding loans for their military needs and for the state's self-preservation. The foreign states are making use of the opportunity to invest their capital in China, thus acquiring, by means of a system of financial enslavement, "spheres of influence" in China and special rights and privileges.

But the maintenance of civil war in China is of first importance to the world imperialists, for it delays China's progress, prevents China from developing her own industry, saturates the Chinese market with goods of their own foreign manufacture, and also prevents the Chinese bourgeoisie from utilizing the country in the interests of domestic exploitation. Under these historical conditions the development of Chinese industry is hindered by unequal competition on Chinese territory between Chinese and foreign capital, which has insured its own dominance through measures of economic pressure (a tariff system, etc.), by the civil war, by local disturbances, by the looting of the population by the officials, and by every type and form of oppression.

The socio-economic conditions in China affect the middle, intermediary classes with particular force. The owners of small enterprises are being deprived of property; artisans fill the ranks of the army of the unemployed; peasants sell their land to landlords for absurd sums of money because they are unable to conduct their own economy, owing to the continuously rising cost of living.

These conditions will remain unchanged so long as power remains in the hands of the feudal-lord government, in the hands of militarists; so long as power is not seized from their hands; and so long as a democratic government is not established.

Democratic government means a democratic party government. We have in mind the creation of power on the basis of a total reorganization of the entire political system of administration. Basically, this demand entails the overthrow of the authority of the reactionary, counter-revolutionary elements and groups by revolutionary methods, by a democratic party, or by a bloc of democratic groupings which will organize power to conform to the historical requirements of their own country and with consideration for the realities of the new international environment.

As a result of the compromise achieved [in February 1912] by Yüan Shih-k'ai on the one hand and Sun Yat-sen and Sung Chiao-jen [the KMT leaders] on the other (both men were leaders of the KMT), a cabinet was formed composed of members of the KMT party, headed by Chao Ping-chün,[1] Yüan Shih-k'ai's puppet, in the role of Prime Minister. What were the results of the activities of this so-called Kuomintang Cabinet? During the second year of the republic (1913), Sung Chiao-jen, who wanted to form a cabinet composed exclusively of KMT party members, was assassinated. Even if Sung Chiao-jen had not been assassinated, he would have suffered the same fate as that suffered by the entire movement against Yüan Shih-k'ai. The assassination of Sung Chiao-jen and the dismissal from Kiangsi province of General Li Lieh-chün [a KMT member, then commanding the expeditionary forces against North China] were caused by that movement. Both these occurrences were practical evidence of the impossibility of a coalition between the KMT and Yüan Shih-k'ai.

After the rout of the KMT, "power was seized" [sic] by the party of "progressives" [presumably the Progressive party, or Chin-pu-tang, first organized by Liang Ch'i-ch'ao] and Hsiung Hsi-ling was commissioned to form a cabinet. The party of "progressives" served as a tool in the hands of Yüan Shih-k'ai. Its participation in the government merely discredited the party to the very limit.

After Yüan Shih-k'ai's fall [d. June 6, 1916], the struggle against the counter-revolutionary government ended in the restoration of constitutionalism, the election of Li Yüan-hung [vice-president, 1913] to the presidency, and the convening of the parliament. All this was, however, not accompanied by actually removing the power of Yüan Shih-k'ai's adherents and friends, who were firmly installed in their seats. The leaders of the democratic party were proud of the victories they had won and of the fact that the republic was restored.

After the collapse of Chang Hsün's plans [July 1917] for returning the Manchu dynasty to the throne, the democratic elements entered the government along with the reactionary military, with General Feng Kuo-chang as President and Marshal Tuan Ch'i-jui as Prime Minister (leader of the Anfu clique). All this was called a "republic".

The postulate must be clear to everyone that the political struggle is not a struggle between individuals for power, but a manifestation and expression of class struggle—the social struggle of the proletariat against the bourgeoisie in the period of revolution and, in the period of bourgeois revolution, the struggle of the bourgeoisie against the feudal lords and the system of feudal economy. The postulate must also be clear that only such freedom is precious as is achieved in the process of hard struggle and at the price of human blood, in distinction from those methods of struggle which are used by our class enemies.

The struggle for democracy is a struggle of one class, a struggle which aims to overthrow the dominance of another class; it is the replacement of one system by another, and in no event can it be regarded as a struggle of one individual or one group for the overthrow of another individual or group.

A real democratic party must possess two characteristic elements: (1) its principles must be correlated with the concepts of democracy; and (2) its actions must consist in an active struggle against feudalism in the form of the military. Of all the political parties existing in China, only the KMT can be characterized as a revolutionary party, yet it possesses only a relative amount of democratic and revolutionary spirit. The programme of this party has not yet been fully elaborated. But its three principles, "of the people, for the people, and by the people" [evidently an oblique reference to Sun Yat-sen's Three People's Principles], in conjunction with plans for the industrial development of China [cp. Sun's *International Development of China*, 1922 (1919)] reflect the democratic spirit of the KMT. In addition to this party's participation in the revolutionary struggle through its parliamentary members, the KMT has offered a number of other proofs of its democratic spirit, namely: the Canton government [headed by Sun Yat-sen, 1921–2] has not been restricting the labour movement; it has abolished police regulations in regard to "public order and national security"; and it has abolished the law by which workers were deprived of the right to strike. Not infrequently, however, this party's actions have been contradictory in nature. On occasion the KMT manifests a friendly attitude even with respect to . . . [periods as in original] monarchists, and an inclination for a rapprochement "for tactical reasons" with the "Pei-yang" military clique. If the KMT, as a party, wishes to play a definite role in the revolutionary struggle for the consolidation of democracy in China, it must renounce once and for all every policy of vacillation, compromise, and endless zigzags.

With respect to the present situation, the view is very popular that the convening of the old parliament [at Peking] and the restoration of Li Yüan-hung as President [June 1922] are cardinal events which assure the solution of the political problems confronting China. This point of view cannot stand criticism and is in complete contradiction to the facts. Is there any basis for asserting that parliament will be able to realize its "legal power" when there is a dominance of a feudal power of the "Pei-yang" party type, a power which pursues the idea of a monopolistic military control over the government and appraises itself as a group of "relatives" who fell heir to the "Pei-yang" military clique? The account of past experience has testified plainly that Li Yüan-hung during his presidency in the recent past (1915–17) [this should be 1916–17] did not manage to resolve a single political task or any problem as a whole. What reasons are there for asserting that Li Yüan-hung will be able to organize a democratic government when —in the face of all the unfavourable historical circumstances—Li Yüan-hung's term of office, as such, has already expired? So long as the military dominates in China and over China, the organized struggle against democracy will not end, nor will the struggle end among the militarists themselves.

This thought can be illustrated by examples: the war between Fengtien and Chihli (Fengtien—the military party of the Mukden satrap, Chang Tso-lin; Chihli—the military party with its actual leader General Wu P'ei-fu and its nominal head, Marshal Ts'ao K'un) can by no means be regarded as concluded: it will flare up again. If Chang Tso-lin is victorious, then struggle will inevitably go on within the ranks of the Fengtien party. Chang Tso-lin will fight against his own colleague and "co-partisan", General Sun Lieh-chen, the present military governor of Kirin province in Manchuria; and the latter in turn will battle with General Wu Chun-sheng, the present governor of Heilungkiang province in Manchuria. If the Chihli party is victorious, then wars will be inevitable between the members of this party —between Wu P'ei-fu and Ts'ao K'un or Feng Yü-hsiang, the present military governor of Honan province, known as "the Christian general". If the [rival] Anfu party wins and manages to take power away from the Chihli party, a clash between the Fengtien and Anfu parties will be inevitable. And within the Anfu party itself, "Little Hsü" [General Hsü Shu-cheng], the soul of the Anfu party, a pro-Japanese, will immediately after victory over the Chang Tso-lin party declare war upon his worst enemy, General Lu Yung-hsiang, commander of the troops of Chekiang province. Besides the aforementioned eventualities guaranteeing and conditioning [*sic*] military developments in China, the struggle for the positions of military governor (*tu-chün*) and military command posts in the provinces of Shensi, Szechwan, Hunan, and elsewhere will not cease.

The military is the cause of civil war in China. So long as the military exists and rules, the creation of a so-called "good government" will be out of the question. In the present circumstances no government in China can be stable and firm, and the life and property of Chinese citizens are subject to destruction every time the militarists clash.

You kind advocates of good government, after the appearance of the first issue of your magazine *Endeavor* [presumably *Nu-li*]—the weekly organ of the liberal professorial staff of Peking National University—and as soon as the helpless and powerless Hsü Shih-ch'ang (Peking president, who was seated at the helm by the Anfuists and resigned under Wu P'ei-fu's pressure) was exiled from Peking [June 1922], you found it possible to feel satisfied and reconciled, and addressed a wire to the South proposing that the offensive against the North be discontinued. This bourgeois pacifism, this opportunist policy, this broken line of compromises is indeed an obstacle to giving life to your own lofty slogans and cries of "struggle", "endeavour", "combat the sons of evil". Considering the conditions prevailing in Tientsin and Paoting [in Chihli province], nominally the staff headquarters of the Chihli party's Marshal Ts'ao K'un, do you really believe that a "good government" can be organized under existing conditions? Do you count on carrying out your three principles and the six concrete aims of your programme under military dictatorship? (The programme of the Peking professors has been announced in the group's declaration and published in the first issue of *Endeavor*.) After the fall of the Manchu dynasty, Chang Ping-lin [a scholar-revolutionist] tried his best to reach a compromise with Marshal Tuan Ch'i-jui, head of the Anfu clique. All these efforts and honourable intentions ended in the triumph of reaction. Aren't you also proceeding along the same path and don't you think that you will fall heir to the inglorious reputation of your predecessors?

Members of the KMT! You were originally revolutionary fighters for the triumph of democracy. You should also conduct a revolutionary struggle now for democracy and prefer to perish in this struggle than to vanish from the socio-political arena in consequence of a policy of compromise. During the first year of the existence of the Chinese Republic [1912] you were deceived by Yüan Shih-k'ai, who tried his best to demonstrate his loyalty to the republic. You were cruelly deceived also by Tuan Ch'i-jui, when he proposed the restoration of parliament and of the constitution [1916–17]. Do not let yourselves be deceived now by all this talk about restoring parliament, abolishing the *tu-chün* system, demobilizing provincial troops, for the sake of concluding another compromise with the military of North China. Does the present constitutional parliament differ in any way from the parliament of the fifth and the sixth year of the Republic [1916–17]? Aren't the hopes for abolishing the *tu-chün* system and for demobilization merely hopes that the tiger may shed its own skin? Does the title of "troop commander" as distinct from or other than *tu-chün*—a phenomenon which can be observed in the provinces of Yunnan, Szechwan, and Hunan—differ essentially from the *tu-chün* institution and the conditions which existed prior to the nominal abolition of the *tu-chün?*

Is there any hope whatever for a troop demobilization at a time when war between militarists is at its height? "Little Hsü (General Hsü Shu-cheng, an active Anfuist) said: "I am an advocate of disarmament, but wait until my soldiers are adequately trained and equipped, so that I may disarm the soldiers of my adversaries." General Chang Shao-cheng said: "War is raging now in Shansi province. The situation is extremely critical in Fengtien and Honan provinces. It is imperative that someone control affairs in the provinces. If Generals Wu P'ei-fu and Ts'ao K'un should actually put the demobilization scheme into effect, imagine what would become of the provinces."

The military's incapacity for disarming itself is most convincingly expressed in these cited views of two ranking militarists. All that is left for you to do is to fulfil completely your historical mission of struggle for the triumph of the democratic revolution and watch out that you are not deceived again by political charlatans.

Workers, peasants, students, soldiers, policemen, and merchants! So long as the authority of the military is not overthrown, there will be no hope of disarming the provincial armies and abolishing the *tu-chün* system. So long as the authority of the military is not overthrown, there will be no hope of reducing the demands for national funds, which are used to cover war expenses and further to disrupt the entire national and local financial system. So long as the authority of the military is not overthrown, all conditions will be present to allow the military to secure new loans from foreigners and thus bring about an intensification of foreign influence in China. So long as the authority of the military is not overthrown, there will be no hope that the military will cease imposing heavy imposts on the citizens of China; there will be no hope that looting may cease, no hope that order may be restored in all regions of China. So long as the authority of the military is not overthrown, there will be no hope of a broad development of education in China and of industrial progress in our country. So long as the authority of the military is not overthrown, there will be no hope that the struggle among militarists for the expansion of their own spheres of influence may cease. Peasants and merchants are always war victims. These wars will be inevitable and endless if they are not stopped by the people themselves.

For all of us, the only way by which we can liberate ourselves from the hard yoke of the military is to join the democratic struggle against the relics of the past—a struggle for freedom and peace. The government opposition game, played by the bourgeoisie, the intelligentsia, and the politicians, cannot be trusted. We all want peace, but real peace rather than false peace. We welcome a war to achieve the triumph of democracy, to overthrow the military and the militarists and to liberate the Chinese people.

The CCP, as the vanguard of the proletariat, struggles for working-class liberation and for the proletarian revolution. Until such time as the Chinese proletariat is able to seize power in its own hands, considering the present political and economic conditions of China's development and all the historical processes now going on in China, the proletariat's urgent task is to act jointly with the democratic party to establish a united front of democratic revolution to struggle for the overthrow of the military and for the organization of a real democratic government.

The concrete aims of the present political struggle cannot be limited to a fight for the publication of data on government finances or for surveillance over the activity of the parliament or of local organs of administration.

Our most immediate aims are as follows:

(1) Revision of the system of tariffs forcibly imposed on China by world capitalism; abolition of consular jurisdiction [extra-territoriality]

and of the entire system of privileges for foreigners; the estimation of railway subsidies made to China by foreign capital and the immediate transfer of all railways to the hands of the state.

(2) Abolition of the régime of the military and of the mercenary bureaucrats; confiscation of the property of the militarists and distribution of their large landholdings among the poorest peasants.

(3) General suffrage.

(4) Freedom of assembly, speech, and press; annulment of laws for the safeguarding of "public order" by police; freedom to strike.

(5) Restricted taxation on land.

(6) Compulsory education.

(7) Prohibition of child and woman labour; laws pertaining to sanitary conditions in factories and shops; laws on workers' insurance.

(8) Abolition of all tariff surtaxes and of the *likin* system [provincial transit taxes on domestic trade].

(9) Revision of the entire Law Code with immediate abolition of the death penalty and physical torture.

Equality of the rights of men and women.

Introduction of a progressive income tax.

Under the rule of feudal militarists, none of this minimum programme can be carried out by the methods of compromise, petition, or requests. The CP takes the initiative in calling a conference, to be participated in by the revolutionary elements of the KMT and revolutionary socialists, to discuss the question of creating a united front for struggle against warlords of the feudal type and against all relics of feudalism. This struggle along a broad united front is a war to liberate the Chinese people from a dual yoke—the yoke of foreigners and the yoke of powerful militarists in our country—a war which is just as urgently needed as it is inevitable.

The Central Committee of the Chinese Communist Party.

2. MANIFESTO OF THE SECOND NATIONAL CONGRESS
OF THE CCP (July 1922) [résumé]

The proletariat's support of the democratic revolution is not (equivalent to) its surrender to the capitalists. Not to prolong the life of the feudal system is absolutely necessary in order to raise the power of the proletariat. This is the proletariat's own class interest. It would be no liberation for the proletariat if a successful democratic revolution brought it only some minor liberties and rights. The successful demo-cratic revolution develops the capitalist class, at present in its infancy —capitalist opposition to the proletariat being left to the future. When that stage is reached, the proletariat must launch the struggle of the second phase: (the struggle) for the dictatorship of the prole-tariat allied to the poor peasants against the bourgeoisie. If the organization and fighting power of the proletariat has been [suffi-ciently] strengthened, the struggle of this second phase will carry the victory of the democratic revolution to its completion.

The CCP is the party of the proletariat. Its aims are to organize the proletariat and to struggle for (the establishment of) the dictator-ship of the workers and peasants, the abolition of private property, and the gradual attainment of a Communist society. At present the CCP must, in the interest of the workers and poor peasants, lead the workers to support the democratic revolution and forge a democratic united front of workers, poor peasants, and petty bourgeoisie. In the interest of the workers, the CCP struggles to secure, within this united front, the following objectives:

(1) The quelling of internal disorders, the overthrow of military cliques, and the establishment of internal peace.

(2) The removal of oppression by international imperialism and the complete independence of the Chinese nation.

(3) The unification of China proper (including Manchuria) into a genuine democratic republic.

(4) The achievement of a genuine democratic republic by the libera-tion of Mongolia, Tibet, and Sinkiang.

(5) The establishment of a Chinese Federated Republic by the unification of China proper, Mongolia, Tibet, and Sinkiang into a free federation.

(6) The unlimited right to vote for (all) workers and peasants, re-gardless of sex, in all assemblies and municipal assemblies, and absolute freedom of speech, assembly, publication, association, and strike.

(7) Legislation for workers, peasants, and women (as follows):

(*a*) Better treatment of workers. Abolition of the contracting system. The eight-hour working day. Provision of employees' clinics and sanitary installations in factories. Factory insurance. Protection for female and child labour. Protection for the unemployed.

(*b*) Abolition of heavy poll and transport taxes. Establishment of a national—municipal and village—land-tax.

(*c*) Abolition of *likin* and all extraordinary taxes. Establishment of a progressive income tax.

(d) Passing of legislation limiting land-rents.

(e) Abolition of all legislation restricting women.

(f) Improvement of the educational system.

The above seven items are all in the interest of the workers, peasants, and petty bourgeoisie and are prerequisites for their liberation from their present oppression. If we ourselves put up a concerted struggle for liberation, the workers and poor peasants will flock to the banner of (our) Party and the petty bourgeoisie will also link up with us. However, the workers must not become the appendage of the petty bourgeoisie within this democratic united front, but must fight for their own class interests. Therefore it is imperative that the workers be organized in the Party as well as in labour unions. Ever mindful of their class independence, the workers must develop the strength of their fighting organization (in order to) prepare for the establishment of soviets in conjunction with the poor peasantry and in order to achieve (the goal of) complete liberation. The CCP is a section of the CI. The Party calls the Chinese workers and peasants to rush to its banner for the (coming) struggle: it asks the oppressed masses of all China to fight in common with the workers and poor peasants under the Party banner; and it hopes that the revolutionary masses of the whole world will march forward shoulder-to-shoulder. Only an alliance of the world proletariat and the oppressed peoples can lead to the liberation of the world.

SEC. II. THE PERIOD OF EARLY CCP-KMT CO-OPERATION (1923–7)

COMMENTARY B. SUN YAT-SEN AND THE COMMUNISTS—THE "BLOC WITHIN"

The following three documents illuminate, from three different angles, the political and ideological background of the KMT-CCP alliance. The first document, the Sun-Joffe manifesto of January 26, 1923, stakes out the common ground on which Russian bolshevism and Chinese nationalism built their alliance. The second document— Sun Yat-sen's marginal comments on a letter accusing the Communists of undermining the KMT—contains the KMT leader's interpretation and defence of his twin policies of "Alliance with Russia" and

"Admission of the Communists" (December 1923). The last document, the Manifesto of the Third Congress of the CCP (June 1923), represents the first declaration, on the part of the Chinese Communists, of their motives and tasks in the KMT alliance.

The Sun-Joffe manifesto marked the opening of the negotiations which were to end with the successful conclusion a year later of the KMT-CCP alliance at the first KMT Congress in January 1924. These negotiations were continued during the summer of 1923 between Joffe and Liao Chung-k'ai, a vigorous leader of the KMT left-wing (assassinated on August 20, 1925). On the basis of these negotiations, Sun agreed to adopt the Soviet system of party, government, and army organization. It may appear paradoxical that Sun's acceptance of this system as the best method for accomplishing the Chinese revolution should have followed so shortly after his explicit rejection, in the Sun-Joffe Manifesto, of "Communism or even the Soviet system", as unsuitable to Chinese conditions. But Sun was no more guided by the rules of logic than any other political leader; and his acceptance of the Soviet system while declaring his anti-Sovietism is quite in tune with the leitmotif of his thought: the elimination of foreign influence by the use of foreign methods. The Russians, on their part, were quite willing not to quibble with Sun about ultimate ends; their faith in historical inevitability made any such discussion superfluous, and for their purposes it was quite sufficient to agree on the immediate need for completing the Chinese nationalist revolution.

In the autumn of 1923, Soviet advisers, headed by Michael Borodin, thus began the work of refashioning the KMT organization and the Cantonese armies after the Soviet pattern. But this transferral of the Soviet form, coupled as it was with the policies of "Alliance with Russia" and "Admission of the Communists", could not but affect the substance of KMT thought. Thus Sun Yat-sen's marginal comments on the accusation raised against the CCP in December 1923 express a need—political at least and intellectual at most—to bolster his practical arguments for the Soviet alliance with an ideological synthesis of the Three People's Principles and Soviet Communism.

In these comments, Sun announced, for the first time, the oft-repeated formula that "essentially, there is no difference between the Principle of People's Livelihood and Communism". It seems futile to suggest, as some commentators have done,[1] that Sun thought of early pastoral rather than modern Communism in this statement, for its aim was clearly to reconcile his KMT subordinates to collaboration with present-day bolsheviks, not with primitive shepherds. Sun even carried this synthesis of his own teaching and bolshevism one step further by interpreting the Russian revolution as an application, by stages, of his own Three People's Principles (People's Rights or Democracy, People's Livelihood, and Nationalism—see document no. 5 p. 73). In performing this *tour de force*, he did not make it clear whether the Three People's Principles were absolute truths at which the Russian revolution had arrived independently or whether the bolsheviks were somehow indebted to him for their insight.

If it be thought, however, that Sun submitted to Communist hegemony by this ideological compromise, it is well to recall one phrase in his comments which allows no difference of interpretation. "If Ch'en disobeys our Party," he said of the Communist leader, "he will be ousted." This is as clear a statement as could be desired of how Sun envisaged the relationship between the CCP and the KMT. It was to be the relationship of subordinate to master, of auxiliary to main force. This was the view which Sun bequeathed to his disciple Chiang Kai-shek, who, to be sure, applied it with a thoroughness that went far beyond Sun's intentions. For in 1923, when the CCP was still small and very young, Sun could well believe that the Communists, entering the KMT as individuals, would observe its discipline and eventually submerge in its ranks. This belief was part of his faith in the goodwill of the Soviet leadership, which he trusted would use the discipline of the Comintern to reinforce the hold of the KMT over its Communist members. In so far as the Comintern did (between 1925 and 1927) oppose all attempts to take the CCP out of the KMT, Sun's expectation was not altogether unjustified. But he failed to appreciate, at least sufficiently, that Moscow's eagerness to ally itself with the KMT was prompted by the desire to have and to hold it —and, eventually, to transform it in its own image.

The Soviets, for their part, had never made any secret of their motives for giving support to nationalist movements in dependent countries. At the Second Congress of the Comintern in 1920, Lenin had fully spelled out, in his "Thesis on the National and Colonial Question", the tactic of "temporary agreements or even alliances" with bourgeois-democratic movements in such countries. The purpose of this tactic was to widen Communist influence among the masses and thus provide a basis for the future hegemony of the proletariat. In laying down this policy, Lenin made the important reservation that the Communists should in no circumstances abandon their organizational independence and their full freedom of action and agitation. It was this precept which the Trotsky-Zinoviev opposition accused the Stalinist leadership of having violated by subordinating the CCP's independence to KMT discipline. The basic ambiguity of Lenin's "National and Colonial Thesis" lay in its failure to specify the nature and duration of "temporary agreements or even alliances". Yet it was precisely in this ambiguity that the KMT and the CCP found the possibility of collaboration. Their alliance was based on the expectation, secretly held by each partner, that at some point in the future, each would be in a position to devour the other. Each partner was fully confident that it would be the devourer.

As noted above (Commentary A), the decision to have individual CCP members enter the KMT was taken at a Plenum of the CCP Central Committee, in August 1922, after some pressure had been brought to bear on it by Maring, a delegate of the Comintern. The original impetus for this move apparently came from Dr. Sun himself, who hoped to control the Communists more easily as members than as allies of the KMT.[2] This new policy of the "bloc within" was not given official CCP formulation until June 1923, when the Third CCP Congress officially proclaimed its purpose to make the KMT "the central force of the national revolution". In this context, it should be remembered that, in the summer of 1922, the fortunes of Dr. Sun's party had stood at a new low. The leader himself was a refugee in Shanghai, expelled from his capital at Canton by local warlord troops. Although he found it possible to return to Canton in February 1923, the KMT remained—as the Manifesto of the Third Congress points out—without any firm support from either the masses or an armed force of its own. Yet the Communists realized that, for all these deficiencies, the KMT possessed immeasurable potential strength in the revolutionary tradition surrounding its leader, Sun Yat-sen. They realized that this tradition only needed organization—which they could give—and military aid—as proffered by the Russians—in order to finish the unfinished Chinese revolution. It was precisely because the KMT was organizationally infantile that the Communists undertook to make it "the central force of the national revolution". For if the organizational apparatus, the mass basis, of the new KMT came under their control, its role of revolutionary leadership would fall to them also.

The Communists gained admittance to the KMT (in January 1924) by pledging individual allegiance to its principles and submission to its discipline. Under a system of dual party membership, designed for the occasion, they bound themselves to keep faith, simultaneously, with Dr. Sun's platform, negating the class struggle, and with their own platform enjoining (in the words of the Third Congress) "a two-fold struggle within the national . . . as well as . . . the class movement". Dual party membership thus involved adherence to two organizations built on the principle of democratic centralism—a reconciliation of irreconcilables by the alchemy of politics. To Dr. Sun's eclectic mind, the inter-penetration of two democratic centralisms presented no more of a problem than the formerly attempted fusion of Western constitutionalism with traditional Chinese institutions. To the Communists, on the other hand, the process of thinking simultaneously in mutually exclusive categories was a "dialectical" habit; and conscious deceit need not be imputed to them. Thus the basic contradictions inherent in dual party membership were left for history to resolve; and history resolved them by the "dialectic" peculiar to itself —the naked power struggle.

By the spring of 1927, the KMT and the CCP had both achieved the primary objective of their alliance: a position, attained by the help of the other, from which each could make its bid for total power. The KMT now possessed, by courtesy of the Russians, a party apparatus and a party army; and by courtesy of the Communists, a foothold among the broad masses. The Communists in return had, by courtesy of the KMT armies, extended their sway over vast workers' and peasants' organizations in South and Central China, recently liberated from warlord rule. Thus each had won a lever by which to hoist the other into oblivion. By armed power Chiang Kai-shek could check—and hope to suppress—the mass movement. By control of the mass movement the Communists could undermine—and hope to conquer—the KMT leadership. In the China of 1927 the odds in this contest favoured armed power. The mass organizations built by the Communists in the course of the "Great Revolution" of 1925–7 were smashed within weeks by the peasant troops of the KMT military. The alliance ended, as both partners had expected, in the dictatorship of one; but it was the Communists who suffered the vengeance of their intended victims.

The legacy of Dr. Sun thus contained, in its very eclecticism, the germ of discord among his heirs. In so far as it enjoined supremacy of the KMT, unification of the country, and abolition of the unequal treaties, it was duly fulfilled by Chiang Kai-shek. But in so far as it enjoined social reforms and identified the People's Livelihood with Communism, its fulfilment was left to the CCP. Thus the Communist régime ruling China today can also, by the use of judicious emphasis, claim the role of executor of Sun's will.

3. JOINT MANIFESTO OF SUN YAT-SEN AND A. A. JOFFE
(January 26, 1923)

(1) Dr. Sun is of the opinion that, because of the non-existence of conditions favourable to their successful application in China, it is not possible to carry out either Communism or even the Soviet system in China. M. Joffe agrees entirely with this view; he is further of the opinion that China's most important and most pressing problems are the completion of national unification and the attainment of full national independence. With regard to these great tasks, M. Joffe has assured Dr. Sun of the Russian people's warmest sympathy for China, and of (their) willingness to lend support.[1]

(2) In order to eradicate misunderstandings, Dr. Sun has requested M. Joffe to reaffirm the principles enunciated by Russia in its Note to the Chinese government of September 27, 1920. M. Joffe accordingly reaffirmed these principles, and categorically declared to Dr. Sun that Russia is willing and ready to enter into negotiations with China on the basis of Russia's abandonment of all treaties, and of the rights and privileges (conceded by China) under duress, secured by the Tsarist government from China. Among the above-mentioned treaties are included the treaties and agreements concerning the Chinese Eastern Railway. (The administration of this railway has been specifically dealt with in article VII of the said Note.)

(3) Dr. Sun holds that the Chinese Eastern Railway question in its entirety can be satisfactorily settled only by a competent Sino-Russian Conference. But the key to the current situation lies in the fact that a *modus vivendi* ought to be devised for the administration of the said railway at present. Dr. Sun and M. Joffe are of the same opinion that the administration of this railway should be temporarily re-organized after an agreement has been reached between the Chinese and Russian governments, but (on condition) that the real rights and special interests of either party are not injured. Dr. Sun also holds that the matter should be discussed with Chang Tso-lin.

(4) M. Joffe categorically declares to Dr. Sun (and Dr. Sun is entirely satisfied with regard to this point): that it is not, and never has been, the intention or the objective of the present Russian government to carry out imperialistic policies in Outer Mongolia, or to work for Outer Mongolia's independence from China. Dr. Sun therefore does not deem the immediate evacuation of Russian troops from Outer Mongolia to be urgently necessary or to the real advantage of

China. This is due to the fact that, the present Peking government being weak and impotent, after the withdrawal of the Russian troops it would most likely be unable to prevent the activities of the Russian Whites from causing fresh difficulties for the Russian government, thereby creating a situation even graver than that which exists at present.

4. MANIFESTO OF THE THIRD NATIONAL CONGRESS
OF THE CCP (June 1923)

The Chinese people are doubly oppressed both by foreign powers and by warlords, and the nation's existence, as well as the freedom of its people, are in an extremely precarious state. Not only the workers, peasants, and students, but also the peaceful and moderate merchants feel (oppressed).

The farcical confusion of the present Peking régime; the increasing oppression and destruction of trade unions and students' federations by the Northern warlords' régime; the unruliness of soldiers and bandits in Shantung and Honan; the threats by foreign powers to retract, on various pretexts, benefits granted by the Washington Conference; the atrocities committed by the Japanese sailors at Shasi and Changsha; the powers' forced cotton exports from China; the Kwangtung fighting engineered by Wu P'ei-fu and Ch'i Hsieh-yüan; disorders in Szechwan fostered by Wu P'ei-fu and Hsiao Yao-nan; civil war looming between the Chihli and Mukden factions, and imbroglios among the various cliques within the Chihli faction:[1] all these show how internal and external troubles have again beset the people. There is no salvation unless the people muster up their own strength in a national movement for self-determination. (All) this also demonstrates that the national revolutionary movement led by our Party with the slogans "down with the warlords" and "down with international imperialism" is on the right path.

The KMT should be the central force of the national revolution and should assume its leadership. Unfortunately, however, the KMT often suffers from two erroneous notions. Firstly, it relies on foreign powers for help in the Chinese national revolution. Such requests for help from the enemy not only cost the [KMT] to lose the leadership of the national revolution but also make the people depend on foreign power, thus destroying their confidence and spirit of national independence; secondly, (the KMT) concentrates all its efforts on military action, neglecting propaganda work among the people. Consequently, the KMT loses its political leadership, because a national revolutionary party can never succeed by relying solely on military action without winning nationwide popular sympathy.

We still hope that all the revolutionary elements in our society will rally to the KMT, speeding the completion of the national revolutionary movement. At the same time, (we also) hope that the KMT will resolutely discard its two old notions of reliance on foreign powers and concentration on military action, and that it will pay attention to political propaganda among the people—never missing an opportunity for (such) propaganda in order to create a true central force for the national welfare and a true leadership for the national revolution.

Considering economic and political conditions at home and abroad, and the sufferings and needs of (those) classes of Chinese society (workers, peasants, industrialists, and merchants) which urgently need a national revolution, the CCP never forgets for one moment to support the interests of the workers and peasants. It is our special task to do propagandistic and organizational work among the workers and peasants. Still more central is our task to lead the workers and peasants into joining the national revolution. Our mission is to liberate the oppressed Chinese nation by a national revolution, and to advance to the world revolution, liberating the oppressed peoples and oppressed classes of the whole world.

Long live the national revolution of China!

Long live the liberation of the oppressed peoples of the world!

Long live the liberation of the oppressed classes of the world!

5. SUN YAT-SEN'S COMMENTS ON AN ACCUSATION AGAINST THE CP (presented to him in December 1923)

[*Note:* the accusation itself is not reproduced here; Sun's comments were in his own handwriting.]

This draft [of the KMT constitution] was prepared by Borodin at my request and checked by myself. The original was in English and was translated into Chinese by Liao Chung-k'ai. Ch'en Tu-hsiu had no part in this and no suspicions should be cast (on him).

The reason that the Russian revolution succeeded but ours did not is because our Party members still do not understand the "Three People's Principles". Essentially, there is really no difference between the Principle of People's Livelihood (*Min-sheng chu-i*) and Communism.

VERNON REGIONAL
JUNIOR COLLEGE LIBRARY

The Russian revolution, in its beginning stage, only carried out the Principles of People's Rights and People's Livelihood. After fighting with the foreign powers for six years, it then discovered that the Principle of Nationalism (*Min-tsu chu-i*) really required the utmost effort and attention.

The allegation [that the Three People's Principles are obsolete] is due to the bigotry and excessive adoration for the Russian revolution on the part of the young Chinese students. The reason why they attacked and criticized our Party is because they wanted to monopolize Russian friendship and prevent Russia from dealing with our Party [the KMT]. Thus they hoped to monopolize Russian aid and to compete with our Party as an independent unit. But the Russian revolutionary party are learned and experienced people, who were not fooled by these youngsters but saw through their tactics. Consequently, they [the Russian revolutionaries] disagreed with them, corrected them on our behalf, and ordered them to join the KMT for the purpose of acting in unison with us. In case of non-compliance [the "youngsters"] would be disavowed. (The Russian revolutionaries) also explained (to the Chinese Communists) that the Principle of Nationalism is a timely remedy [for the ills of China] and not an obsolete relic of the past. Thus many of them were enlightened and joined our Party. If Russia wants to co-operate with China, she must co-operate with our Party and not with Ch'en Tu-hsiu. If Ch'en disobeys our Party, he will be ousted.

The Chinese revolution has never been welcomed by the foreign powers, which have often helped our opponents in attempts to destroy our Party. The capitalist countries will never be sympathetic to our Party. Sympathy can only be expected from Russia, the oppressed nations, and the oppressed peoples. It was not Ch'en Tu-hsiu's but Russia's idea to befriend us. If we suspect Russia because of our suspicions of Ch'en Tu-hsiu, we shall fall into Ch'en's trap and help him to realize his plan [to monopolize Russian friendship]. . . .

COMMENTARY C. THE CCP AND SUN YAT-SEN'S LEADERSHIP

The *Fourth Manifesto on the Current Situation* was issued by the Party immediately before the summoning of the Fourth CCP Congress in Canton in January 1925. It was issued in response to Sun Yat-sen's call for the establishment of a national assembly and his expressed intention of negotiating with the Peking government regarding the establishment of a provisional national government.

In spite of Sun's alliance with the Communists, his main immediate aim, as in the past, had continued to be the achievement of national political unity. When the second conflict arose between the Mukden and Chihli warlord cliques in September 1924, he felt that the time had come for the Northern Expedition. In this he was opposed by the CCP and Borodin, who maintained that such an expedition would be premature and that the immediate task of the Nationalist government at Canton was the consolidation of its position in the South. The discussion of military affairs in the Fourth Manifesto would suggest that perhaps a third unexpressed ground of opposition was the CCP's distrust of the military leaders of the Nationalist army. This distrust was later made much more explicit in certain articles by Ch'en Tu-hsiu in the CCP organ *Hsiang-tao* (*The Guide Weekly*).

In November 1924, however, when Sun called for the establishment of a national assembly and for negotiations with Peking on the setting up of a provisional government, the CCP could not afford to oppose these slogans. At the same time, there is every reason to suppose that it regarded any flirtation with the Peking government with genuine misgivings. Hence its assertion that the recent changes in Peking "simply reflect—as in the past—conflicts between the Mukden and Chihli cliques and between Anglo-American and Japanese imperialism".

Thus the Fourth Manifesto approves in general terms the slogan of a national assembly and a provisional government, but makes certain minimum demands of any proposed assembly which are so sweeping in nature that they could hardly prove acceptable to the Peking militarists. For example, the demand for the abolition of certain military ranks (see paragraph (5) (c) below) would be particularly repugnant to them.

This document suggests how the tensions and mutual suspicions which were later to split the KMT and the CCP asunder were already present during Sun's lifetime when the CCP was nominally following his leadership.

6. FOURTH MANIFESTO OF THE CCP ON THE CURRENT SITUATION (January 1925)

(1) The political changes in Peking simply reflect, as in the past, conflicts between the Mukden and Chihli cliques and between Anglo-American and Japanese imperialism.

(2) In its plans to dismember China, imperialism has passed from a policy of partition (up to the Washington Conference [1921–2]) through a period of joint control (up to the London Conference of 1925), to the present policy of independent action.

(3) Only a national assembly can serve to meet this crisis. A national assembly preparatory conference should be summoned immediately in Peking and the support of all classes, as well as of all military forces which have no definite ties to imperialism [this refers to Feng Yü-hsiang's forces], should be obtained. This assembly should serve as a provisional government until a legal government is established.

(4) This Party will support such a provisional government (even) if it should not become a government of the left, provided that it does not deprive the masses in general of their opportunities to participate in political affairs and on the condition that it suppress all anti-revolutionary military activities.

(5) In the interests of our total national liberation and on behalf of the special interests of our oppressed soldiers, peasantry, workers, small merchants, and intelligentsia, our Party hereby presents the provisional national government and national assembly with the following minimum demands. At the same time, our Party recognizes that the support of these demands is the responsibility of our whole people and of its representatives—particularly the responsibility of the KMT.

(*a*) The unequal treaties must be abolished. Of first importance is the return of control of the customs and the establishment of uniform, national customs rates, for this constitutes the only key to the political liberation of our people from foreign domination.

(*b*) The present police regulation for the maintenance of public peace and the present penalties against striking must be abolished. Absolute freedom of assembly, association, speech, and the freedom to strike must be guaranteed, for these constitute the only key to the internal political liberation of our people.

(*c*) The highest rank in our peace-time standing army should be that of brigadier-general (*Li-chang*). Such ranks as those of high inspecting commissioner (*Hsün-yüeh-shih*), military governor (*Tu-chün*), military superintendent (*Tu-li*), commissioner (*Tu-pan*), commander-in-chief (*Tsung-ssu-ling*), military inspectors (*Chien-yüeh-shih* and *Hu-chün-shih*), garrison commander (*Chien-shou-shih*), army commander (*Chün-chang*), and divisional commander (*Shih-chang*) should be abolished.

(*d*) The source of the curse of militarism in China has been an extremely small number of high-ranking officers. Henceforth, the brigade command should adopt a committee system of organization. It should make public all military expenditures and improve the living standards and education of the men now in service. After their discharge soldiers should be provided with land, farming tools, or other means of earning a livelihood.

(*e*) A top limit should be placed on all forms of taxation. All supplementary taxes and other forms of squeeze above and beyond the legitimate land-tax should be abolished. An equilibrium should be established between the price of farm products and the prices of manufactured commodities which arc necessities of life. The formation of trade associations (peasant associations, etc.) and armed self-defence units should be accelerated. These are urgent demands of the peasantry at this time.

(*f*) The eight-hour day, time off on New Year's day, Sundays, holidays, and days of commemoration, a minimum wage law, abolition of the piece-work system, improvement of hygienic conditions in the factories, facilities for supplementary education, establishment of a system of accident insurance, age limits on child labour, and maximum working hours for young workers, pre-natal and post-natal care for women workers are all urgent minimum demands of the workers.

(*g*) Top limits should be placed on taxes on urban dwellings, and new housing facilities for workers should be constructed.

(*h*) The property of the ringleaders in the recent war should be confiscated and used to compensate the population of the battle areas in the North-east and South-east for their losses and to help the sufferers from the floods in the North.

(*i*) The *likin* duties in various areas and other forms of pernicious impositions do not furnish the national treasury with any great income and constitute a distinct burden to small merchants and others. They should therefore be abolished.

(*j*) Salt taxes and rice taxes should be abolished.

(*k*) Import duties should be increased, the income of nationally-owned enterprises should be readjusted and taxes should be levied on inheritances and urban ground-rent in order to compensate the treasury for its loss of revenue from *likin* and other pernicious impositions, and in order to subsidize landless peasants and to provide funds for the spread of education.

(*l*) In order to protect the security of the intelligentsia and students, funds allocated for education must not be diverted to other uses.

Certain types of revenue should be earmarked to provide free tuition scholarships in primary schools, to improve the quality of primary school education, and to spread education among the masses.

(*m*) Women should be granted complete political, legal, economic, educational, and social equality.

COMMENTARY D. MAO TSE-TUNG IN HUNAN: A SIDE-CURRENT

The next document is a revolutionary classic. Written in February 1927, it is the earliest of Mao's writings now available in the United States. It was also the first to win its author widespread attention, having been published in three Chinese journals as well as in a Russian translation.[1]

This *Report* cannot, of course, be taken as a complete expression of Mao's political outlook since it deals with specific events and a very limited subject. However, the vigour of its style and the broad sweep of some of its statements combine to make it one of the clearest portraits of "Maoism" in its formative stage. Here is the impassioned championship of the poverty-stricken peasant masses, the ruthless realism, the self-confidence and faith in mass action which have distinguished Mao's leadership up to now.

The first passage that invites comment is Mao's attack on the "erroneous decisions of the revolutionary régime in regard to the peasant movement" (see p. 80). Mao refers here to the restraints placed on peasant "excesses" by the National government at Wuhan, a coalition of the left KMT and the Communists. Only two months before, in December 1926, the Executive Committee of the Communist International, at its Seventh Plenum, had ordered the Chinese Communists to enter this government, on the ground that it provided "a very effective way to reach the peasantry".[2] The Communists actually did not follow this order until March 1927—that is, a month after Mao submitted his *Report*. But this Communist accession to key cabinet posts (including the Ministry of Agriculture) at Wuhan did not bring any change in the agrarian policy that had been criticized by Mao. After the break-up of the Wuhan coalition in July 1927, Moscow hastily discovered that "opportunist" CCP leaders had sabotaged its instructions to unleash the peasant movement in full force. It thus sought to obscure the fact that by committing the CCP to full support of the Wuhan government it had itself precluded giving a free rein to the peasants, whose rebellion threatened the political and financial existence of that government. That the demand to support both

Wuhan and the peasants was impossible to carry out has since been admitted by M. N. Roy, the Comintern delegate, then in charge of its enforcement.[3]

Mao Tse-tung has, of course, never openly criticized the Comintern's policy of supporting Wuhan as a "bloc of workers, peasants, and petty bourgeoisie". The bankruptcy of this line in July 1927 enabled him, on the contrary, to bolster his orthodoxy by openly stating his opposition to the Ch'en Tu-hsiu leadership which, as the executor of an unsuccessful line, had emerged in Stalinist hindsight as the tool of petty-bourgeois opportunism. But even though Mao was thus vindicated on the rebound by the dialectics of Comintern infallibility, the fact remains that, at the time, he stood in effect opposed to the Comintern's chosen instruments in China. According to his own account, his disagreement with the Party leadership on agrarian policy began as early as 1925 but "did not come to a climax until 1927".[4] His report on the Hunan peasantry thus dates from the period of his most intense opposition to the prevailing Party line. Yet it was given a stamp of official approval by being printed, without comment, in Communist publications. This contradiction can be understood only by a closer examination of the "Maoist" implications of the *Report*.

Superficially, Mao's investiture of the peasantry in the role of leading class force of the revolution does not seem to contradict the Comintern's own view of the agrarian question as the "central part of the present situation". However, the Comintern had also been quite specific as to which class was to solve the agrarian question. In its "Thesis on the Chinese Situation", the Seventh ECCI Plenum of December 1926 had declared unequivocally that "the proletariat is the only class . . . in a position to carry on the radical agrarian policy which is a condition for the . . . further development of the revolution".[5] At the same Plenum Stalin had explained, in support of this view, that in China revolutionary peasant committees were insufficient to "permeate this ocean of peasantry" and that therefore the Communists could influence the peasants only through the "national revolutionary power" (that is, the Wuhan government) and through the revolutionary army. "The part of initiator and guide of the Chinese revolution", Stalin concluded, "must inevitably fall into the hands of the Chinese proletariat."[6]

Mao Tse-tung's answer to this viewpoint is silence. Nowhere in his *Report* does he give the Chinese proletariat so much as a passing nod. This may be readily explained by the narrow scope of his subject.

But the fact remains that no previous writer of the Marxist-Leninist school had ever conceived of the peasantry as anything but an *auxiliary* to the revolutionary proletariat of the cities. In 1905—the very year in which he "discovered" the peasantry—Lenin had declared that the urban proletariat would "infallibly constitute the kernel of our . . . Party", whose main task he defined as the infusion of "political consciousness into the peasant movement". Again, on the eve of the October revolution of 1917, Lenin had stated categorically that "only the revolutionary proletariat can carry out the programme of the poor peasants".[7]

In Mao Tse-tung's *Report*, on the other hand, the "revolutionary vanguard" of the bourgeois-democratic revolution turns out to consist of the poor peasantry (see pp. 86–8). Mao is very specific as to the distribution of merit in this revolution. Allotting it a total value of ten points, he calculates that "the urban dwellers and the military units rate only three points, while the remaining seven points should go to the peasants in their rural revolution" (see p. 83). "Urban dwellers" presumably include various layers of the bourgeoisie, while "military units", still engaged in the Northern Expedition at the time, rate a sizeable share of the three points left over by the peasantry. Hence the share allotted to the proletariat turns out to be minimal.

"Maoism" can thus be reduced to a simple syllogism. The "revolutionary vanguard", in Marxist-Leninist parlance, invariably stands for the urban proletariat. The "revolutionary vanguard" in Mao's *Report* stands, on the other hand, for the poor peasantry. By implication, the urban proletariat is thus equated to the poor peasantry. Precisely this equation constitutes the theoretical basis of Mao's rise to power. Having lost control of the urban workers (the proletariat in the orthodox sense of the word), the Chinese Communists, under Mao, eventually found a new "proletariat" in the poor peasantry as organized and led by themselves.

Thus it may be said that Mao has given a new twist to Leninism, in so far as Leninism is a Marxist dogma enjoining the hegemony of the urban proletariat. But Leninism is more than dogma: it is also a way of seizing or holding power under any particular conditions. As such, it demands singleness of purpose and multiplicity of means, hardness of will and suppleness of principle, and a keen perception of the "objective" realities which the "subjective" will of the Party bends towards its own ends. In this sense Mao is a Leninist in the best tradition; and his *Report* is a classic of Chinese Leninism.

7. MAO TSE-TUNG: REPORT ON AN INVESTIGATION OF THE PEASANT MOVEMENT IN HUNAN (February 1927)

I. AGRARIAN REVOLUTION

Seriousness of the Peasant Problem

On a thirty-two-day (January 4–February 5, 1927) inspection tour of five *hsien* [districts or counties] of Hunan—Hsiangtan, Hsiang-hsiang, Hengshan, Liling, and Changsha—I have collected a considerable body of materials by listening carefully to reports made by experienced peasants and comrades in the peasant movement at informatory meetings held both in county-seats and villages. Many aspects of the peasant movement directly contradict what we have learned from the gentry in Hankow and Changsha. Some unique incidents have never been seen or heard of before. These conditions, I think, prevail in other provinces too; thus various arguments against the peasant movement must be controverted immediately and the erroneous decisions of the revolutionary régime [i.e. the Wuhan government] in regard to the peasant movement must be quickly corrected. Only thus can the revolution benefit in the future. The further development of the peasant movement is a tremendous prob lem. Within a short time, hundreds of millions of peasants will rise in Central, South, and North China, with the fury of a hurricane; no power, however strong, can restrain them. They will break all the shackles that bind them and rush towards the road of liberation. *All imperialists, warlords, corrupt officials, and bad gentry will meet their doom at the hands of the peasants* [underlining in original]. *All revolutionary parties and comrades will be judged by them. Are we to get in front of them and lead them or criticize them behind their backs or fight them from the opposite camp?* Among these three alternatives every Chinese can choose freely, but the current situation demands a quick decision. The following are the results of my inspection and my opinions are presented in detail for reference by revolutionary comrades.

Let's Organize. The Hunanese peasant movement, as regards the well-organized counties in central and southern Hunan, can be divided into two stages: the first being that of organization, from January to September 1926. Within this stage, there was a secret period from January to June and an open period from July to September, when the revolutionary armies were engaged in the ousting of Chao [Chao Heng-hsi, then governor of Hunan]. In that stage, the total membership of the Peasant Associations did not exceed 300,000 or 400,000;

and the masses under their direct command totalled just a little over 1,000,000. There were few instances of conflict inside the villages; hence there was only a little criticism from the different classes in this regard. Because members of the Peasant Associations served [the revolutionary army] as guides, scouts, and coolies, some officers spoke even favourably of them. The second, or revolutionary, stage lasted from October [1926] to January of this year. The membership of the Peasant Associations jumped up to 2,000,000 and the number of people under their direct command increased to 10,000,000. (When joining a Peasant Association, the peasants usually put down one name for the whole family; thus 2,000,000 members means 10,000,000 people.) About half of the entire peasantry in Hunan is organized. In such places as Hsiangtan, Hsianghsiang, Liuyang, Changsha, Liling, Ninghsiang, Pingkiang, Hsiangying, Hengshan, Hengyang, Leiyang, Chenhsien, Anhwa, etc., almost the entire peasantry has been incorporated into the Peasant Associations and take orders from them. After organizing themselves extensively, the peasants began to take action. Thus, within four months, an unprecedented agrarian revolution broke out.

Down with the Village Bosses (t'u-hao) and Bad Gentry, All Power Belongs to the Peasant Associations. After the peasants organized themselves, action ensued. The major targets of their attack were the *t'u-hao*, bad gentry, and illegitimate landlords, as well as the old patriarchal ideology, corruption of city officials, and undesirable village customs. This attack was like a hurricane: only those could survive who bent to its force. As a result, privileges of the feudal landlord class, thousands of years old, were totally swept away. Their prestige and prerogatives were altogether abolished. After the overthrow of the gentry's power, the Peasant Associations became the only organs of power and [the slogan] "all power to the Peasant Associations" became literally true. Even such trifles as quarrels between married couples were referred to the Peasant Associations for settlement. No problem could be solved independently of the Peasant Association membership, whose every word passed for a command. In the villages the Peasant Associations became the authority for everything [seeing to it that], "whatever was promised, was done". Outsiders could comment only favourably, not critically, on the Peasant Associations. Bad gentry, *t'u-hao*, and illegitimate landlords were deprived of their right of free speech; [so] nobody dared to voice objections. Under the Peasant Association régime, the top-layer *t'u-hao* and bad gentry fled to Shanghai; the second layer fled to Hankow; the third layer to Changsha, and the fourth layer to the county-seats [*hsien* cities], while the small fry of the fifth layer and below surrendered to the Peasant Associations in the villages.

"I contribute ten dollars, so please let me join the Peasant Association," pleaded the small-fry bad gentry.

"Ha! Who cares about your bloody money?" answered the peasants.

Many middle and small landlords, as well as rich and middle peasants who formerly opposed the Peasant Associations, now begged for admission to them. I met a number of those people in the places I visited, and they said: "I beg the commissioner from the capital [Changsha] to endorse me!"

At the time of the Manchu dynasty, when the population census was made, there were two kinds of census, one regular and another subsidiary. Decent people were registered in the regular census and bad elements such as bandits, etc., were registered in the subsidiary census. At present the peasants in some localities have threatened those who opposed the Peasant Associations with the remark: "You will be registered in the subsidiary census!"

Those who were afraid of being registered in the subsidiary census tried by various means to gain admission into the Peasant Associations, not resting till their names were included in the rosters. Often the Peasant Associations refused categorically and threw them out; then they spent their days in suspense, like homeless wanderers. Such a condition is called "*Ta ling*" [lit., a lone wanderer] in the local slang. Thus, the so-called "peasant society" that was despised by most people four months ago has become a thing of glory today. Those who knelt before the gentry now kneel before the power of the peasants. Indisputably, the situation before last October and that after it belong to two [different] worlds.

Very Bad and Very Good. The peasant revolt in the countryside awakened the gentry from their sweet dreams. When the news reached the cities from the villages, the urban gentry protested tumultuously. On first arriving in Changsha, I met people of different backgrounds and heard a lot of gossip. From the middle social strata to the KMT right wing the general comment was: "very bad". Even some revolutionary [-minded] people did not object to this comment, especially when they used their imagination as to the conditions in the countryside. Some progressive elements only remarked apologetically: "Though this is bad, it is inevitable during the process of revolution." All in all, nobody entirely denied the epithet "bad". But as pointed out previously, it is actually the rising up of the vast peasant masses to accomplish their historic mission; it is the rising up of the democratic forces in the countryside to overthrow the feudal forces in the villages, which is the true goal of the national revolution. Sun Yat-sen devoted forty years to the national revolution; what he wanted but failed to achieve has been accomplished by the peasants in a few months. The patriarchal, feudal *t'u-hao* and bad gentry, together with the illegitimate landlords, were not only the foundation of the dictatorial régime of the past several thousand years, [but also] the tools of the imperialists, warlords, and corrupt officials. This is a great achievement unprecedented in the past forty years or several thousand years. This is "very good"—not in the least "bad", and not at all "very bad". To give credits where they are due, if we allot ten points to the accomplishments of the democratic revolution, then the achievements of the urban dwellers and the military units rate only three points, while the remaining seven points should go to the peasants in their rural revolution. The comment "very bad" *is obviously an argument to serve the interests of the landlords and crush the peasants: it is obviously an argument of the landlord class, which tries to preserve the old feudal order by obstructing the establishment of a new democratic order: it is obviously an anti-revolutionary argument.* No revolutionary comrade should blindly repeat such remarks. If you are a person of firm revolutionary ideology and visit the countryside, you will experience a satisfaction never felt before; tens of thousands of slaves—the peasants—are overthrowing their man-eating enemy. The action of the peasants is entirely correct; their action is "very good!" "Very good" is a slogan of the peasants and other revolutionary groups. All revolutionary comrades should realize that the national revolution requires a tremendous change in the villages. The Revolution of 1911 did not achieve such a change, and therefore it failed; now there is such a change, and it is one of the major factors in the accomplishment of the revolution. Every revolutionary comrade should support this movement; otherwise he is against the revolution.

The Problem of "Excesses". Another group of people say: "Peasant Associations should be organized, but their actions are too excessive." This is the argument of the middle-of-the-road group. But what are the facts? The peasants in the villages have indeed been "disorderly". The power of the Peasant Associations being supreme, the landlords have been prohibited from speaking up and their prestige is wiped out. This is like stepping on the landlord after striking him down. The phrase is coined, "All landowners are *t'u-hao* and all gentry are bad." In some places those who owned fifty *mou* of land or more were automatically called *t'u-hao* and those who wore long gowns were all branded as bad gentry. Their "names being recorded in the subsidiary census", *t'u-hao* and bad gentry were fined, required to make contributions, and had their sedan chairs smashed. Some people forced their way into the homes of *t'u-hao* and bad gentry who were hostile to the Peasant Association, and killed their pigs and commandeered their grain. The ivory beds of the daughters and daughters-in-law of the *t'u-hao* and bad gentry were stepped upon by the dirty feet of the peasants. On the slightest provocation men were paraded down the streets, wearing tall paper hats [such as are worn by criminals *en route* to punishment]. "Vile gentry! Now comes our day!" Actions were unrestrained; things were turned upside down, and terror swept some of the villages. This is what some people called "excesses", "going to the other extreme" or "unspeakable". This kind of comment appears superficially correct, but actually it is erroneous.

First, the above-mentioned incidents were the result of oppression by the *t'u-hao*, bad gentry, and illegitimate landlords, who bore down on the peasants with their power and privileges. Thus [the peasants'] tumultuous resistance is only a reaction. Their resistance is most intensive and disorderly where *t'u-hao*, bad gentry and illegitimate landlords have wreaked the worst damage. The peasants' eyes make no mistakes. Who is bad and who is not bad; who should be punished most severely and who should be punished lightly: the peasants judge this most clearly; only very seldom do they hand out undeserved verdicts. So even Mr. T'ang Meng-hsiao [General T'ang Sheng-chih, militarist supporter of the Wuhan government] once said: "When the peasants attacked the *t'u-hao* and bad gentry in the villages, they were right in nine out of ten cases."

Secondly, revolution is not a dinner-party, nor literary composition, nor painting, nor embroidering. It cannot be done so delicately, so leisurely, so gentlemanly, and so "gently, kindly, politely, plainly, and modestly" [quoted from the *Analects* of Confucius]. Revolution is insurrection, the violent action of one class overthrowing the power of another. An agrarian revolution is a revolution by the peasantry to overthrow the power of the feudal landlord class. If the peasants do not apply great force, the power of the landlords, consolidated over thousands of years, can never be uprooted. There must be a revolutionary tidal wave in the countryside in order to mobilize tens of thousands of peasants and weld them into this great force. The excesses described above result from the tremendous revolutionary enthusiasm of the peasants. In the second [revolutionary] stage of the peasant movement, such acts are very necessary. In this second stage, an absolute peasant power must be established, no criticism of the Peasant Associations should be allowed; the gentry's power must be totally liquidated, the gentry knocked down, even trodden upon. All excesses in the second stage have a revolutionary significance. In fine, every village should be in a state of terror for a brief period; otherwise, counter-revolutionary activities in the villages cannot be suppressed, and the gentry's power cannot be overthrown. To correct wrongs one must go to the other extreme, without which they cannot be righted. The argument of this group [against peasant "excesses"] appears superficially different from that of the former group; but in reality it is based on the same viewpoint, being an argument for the interests of the privileged landlord class. This kind of argument retards the development of the peasant movement and serves to sabotage the revolution. We cannot but oppose it firmly.

II. THE VANGUARD OF REVOLUTION

The "p'i-tzu" movement

[i.e. the movement of rural "undesirables"—paupers, gamblers, loafers, et al.].

The KMT right wing claims: "The peasant movement is a *p'i-tzu* movement—a movement of peasant loafers." This argument was widely circulated in Changsha. When I visited the villages, the gentry told me: "Peasant Associations are all right, but their present leadership is unacceptable and should be replaced." This comment has the same meaning as that of the [KMT] right wing, namely, that the peasant movement is all right (it being already in existence, no one dares to say otherwise), but that the present leaders of the peasant movement are not all right, especially those in the lower units, all of whom are allegedly *p'i-tzu* who used to go around in worn-out shoes, carry broken umbrellas, wear blue gowns, and gamble. In brief, all those who used to be despised and trodden down by the gentry, who had no social standing, and were deprived of their right to speak, are now raising their heads. They are not only raising their heads, but are holding power in their hands. They have become kings of the village Peasant Associations (the lowest units of the Peasant Associations), which they have turned into deadly weapons. They put their muscular, sunburnt hands on the heads of the gentry. They bind the bad gentry with ropes, put tall paper hats on them, and parade them through the villages. Their crude curses are heard every day by the gentry. They give orders to all, standing above all, where previously they stood below. Hence this is called "abnormal".

Revolutionary Vanguard or Revolutionary Heroes. An issue or a person can be viewed from two opposing angles; thus two contradictory arguments can be arrived at. "Very good" and "very bad" is one example; "*p'i-tzu*" and "revolutionary vanguard" is another. As recounted above, the peasants have fulfilled a long unfulfilled revolutionary mission, performing the major task in the national revolution. But is this revolutionary mission, this major revolutionary task, carried out by all the peasantry? No. The peasantry is divided into three sub-classes: rich, middle, and poor peasants. Their conditions differ, and so do their concepts regarding the revolution. During the first stage, rich peasants (those with cash and grain surpluses) picked up the news that [the Nationalist revolutionary army] had been routed in Kiangsi, that Chiang Kai-shek had been wounded in the foot and flown back to Kwangtung, that Yochow had been reoccupied by Wu P'ei-fu, and that the Peasant Associations would not last long nor would the Three People's Principles [*San-min chu-i*] expand, since they had never existed before. When managers of the village Peasant Associations (many of them *p'i-tzu*) approached the rich peasants with the membership list, saying: "Please join", some of the rich peasants replied blandly: "Peasant Association? I have lived and tilled the land here for many decades but have never heard of any Peasant Association; yet I still eat my rice. I advise you not to start such a thing." "To hell with the Peasant Association; heads will roll and troubles flow," sneered other rich peasants. But believe it or not, the Peasant Associations have lasted several months already and even dared to oppose the gentry. Some gentry in the adjacent districts who refused to turn in their opium pipes were arrested and paraded through the villages by the Peasant Associations. Some big gentry in the cities were even killed (such as Yen Yung-ch'iu of Hsiangtan or Yang Chih-tse of Ninghsiang). On the anniversary of the October revolution, at anti-British rallies, and at the general celebration of the victory of the Northern Expedition [of 1926–7], more than 10,000 peasants raised banners of various sizes, amidst poles and hoes, and paraded in great strength. Then the rich peasants began to feel perturbed. At the celebration of the victory of the Northern Expedition, they heard that Kiukiang had fallen, that Chiang Kai-shek had not been wounded in the foot, and that Wu P'ei-fu had finally been defeated. Also the slogans "Long live the Three People's Principles", "Long live the

Peasant Associations", and "Long live the peasants" appeared clearly on colourful handbills.

"Long live the peasants; do these men deserve that?" The rich peasants were deeply disturbed. The Peasant Association thus assumed an important role. Its members said to the rich peasants: "Your names will be registered in the subsidiary census!" and "In a month, the membership fee for new-comers will be ten dollars!"

Under such conditions and threats the rich peasants gradually began to join the Peasant Association. Some paid the membership fee of fifty cents or one dollar (the stipulated fee is ten cents), and some were admitted only through the good offices of a third party. Some die-hards still refused to join the Peasant Associations. When rich peasants enrol in the Peasant Associations, they usually put down the name of a sixty- or seventy-year-old family patriarch because they were still afraid of being conscripted. They did not work enthusiastically for the Peasant Associations even after joining, but remained passive. As to the middle peasants (those having no surplus cash or grain, nor debts, but barely maintaining a living), they adopted a wavering attitude, thinking that they would not benefit much from the revolution. They had rice in the pot and were not disturbed by creditors knocking at their door at midnight. On the basis of "precedent" they brooded: "Will the Peasant Associations survive?" "Are the Three People's Principles going to last?" Their consolation was: "Probably not!" They held that everything would be decided by the will of Heaven. "Organizing a Peasant Association—who knows whether the will of Heaven favours it or not?" In the first stage, when members of the Peasant Associations entered the households of the middle peasants with the Peasant Association roster and said: "Please join!" they answered "Do not rush me!" Only when the Peasant Associations became very powerful in the second stage did the middle peasants begin to join up. They are better than rich peasants as Peasant Association members, but rarely become active, and retain their wavering attitude. Only one group in the countryside has fought hard and relentlessly from the very start: the poor peasants. Out of the secret stage into the open stage, it was they who fought, who organized, and who did the revolutionary work. They alone were the deadly enemies of the *t'u-hao* and bad gentry, whose bastions they attacked unreservedly. They alone were capable of doing the destructive work. They asked the rich and middle peasants: "We joined the Peasant Association long ago, why do you hesitate?" The rich and middle peasants answered sarcastically: "You have not a single tile above you, nor a needle-sized [strip of] land beneath you—naturally you joined the Peasant Association!"

It is true that the poor peasants have nothing to lose. They are the outcasts or semi-outcasts of the village, and some of them are literally "without a single tile above and without a strip of land below". Why shouldn't they join the Peasant Association? According to an investigation made at Changsha, the poor peasants constituted seventy per cent, the middle peasants twenty per cent, and the rich peasants ten per cent [of the total] peasantry. The poor peasants can be further classified as very poor and poor. The very poor—twenty out of the [total] seventy per cent—are entirely without occupation, having neither land nor capital; with nothing to live on, they have to become soldiers, or hired hands, or beggars or bandits. The remaining fifty per cent constitute the poor [peasants] who are partially without occupation, but who have a little land or capital, though not enough to meet their expenses. Thus they suffer all year long—handicraftsmen, tenants (except rich tenants), and owner-tenants. (The percentage of poor peasants may be less in other *hsien* than Changsha, but the difference is slight.)

This multitudinous mass of poor peasants is the core of the Peasant Associations, the vanguard in the overthrowing of feudal forces, accomplishing the not-yet-accomplished revolutionary mission. Without the poor peasant class (in the words of the gentry: without the *p'i-tzu*), no revolutionary conditions would exist as they do now in rural areas; and the *t'u-hao* and bad gentry could never be overthrown to complete the democratic revolution. The poor peasants (especially the very poor) secured the leadership of the Peasant Associations because they were the most revolutionary. During the first and second stages [of the peasant movement], the chairmen and committee members in the lowest units of the Peasant Associations (village Peasant Associations) were almost entirely poor peasants. (In the village Peasant Associations of Hengshan, fifty per cent of the cadres came from the very poor peasant class, forty per cent from the poor peasant class, and ten per cent from poor educated elements.) *This leadership by the poor peasants is very essential. Without the poor peasants, there will be no revolution.* To reject them is to reject the revolution; a blow at them is a blow at the revolution. Their revolutionary course is faultless from beginning to end. They have cost the *t'u-hao* and bad gentry "face". They have thrown the big and small *t'u-hao* and bad gentry to the ground and have trampled on them. Many "excesses" of theirs during the revolutionary period have been a revolutionary necessity.

Some *hsien* magistrates, *hsien* Party headquarters, and the Peasant Associations of certain *hsien* in Hunan have already committed a number of errors. Some even dispatched soldiers to arrest the lower cadres of the Peasant Associations at the request of landlords. In the prisons of Hengshan and Hsianghsiang *hsien*, many chairmen and committee members of the village Peasant Associations are imprisoned. This error is extremely grave. Unintentionally, it strengthens the position of the reactionaries. The mere fact that the illegitimate landlords rejoiced and that the reactionary atmosphere thickened when the chairmen and committee members of the village Peasant Associations were arrested is sufficient to expose the mistaken nature [of the arrests]. We should oppose such anti-revolutionary slogans as "*p'i-tzu* movement" and "lazy peasant movement", while taking special care not to help the *t'u-hao* and bad gentry (even unintentionally) by attacks on the leading class of the poor peasants. As a matter of fact, though some of the poor peasant leaders have indeed been "gamblers without gainful occupation", the majority of them have since reformed. They themselves now prohibit gambling and clean up banditry. Where the power of the Peasant Associations is strong, local gambling is completely prohibited and banditry disappears. In some localities it is safe to leave articles unattended on the roadside and doors unlocked at night. According to [my] investigation in Hengshan, eighty-five per cent of the poor peasant leaders are now reformed, able, and hardworking people. Only fifteen per cent still retain some of their bad habits. These can only be called "a few undesirable elements", but one should never imitate the slander of the *t'u-hao* and bad gentry by branding them as "*p'i-tzu*". As regards these "few undesirable elements", Peasant Association discipline should be improved by mass propaganda and individual training among them, under the slogan "strengthen the discipline of the Peasant Associations!" Indiscriminate arrests by soldiers, which cost the faith of the poor peasant class and strengthen the position of the *t'u-hao* and bad gentry, should definitely be avoided. This point deserves the utmost attention.

COMMENTARY E. THE BREAKDOWN OF THE UNITED FRONT STRATEGY

The following document is a Japanese summary of the political and agrarian platforms adopted by the Fifth Congress of the CCP, which convened in Hankow in late April and early May 1927. Although far from complete, this summary is presented here as a substitute for the original text, which is apparently unavailable in the United States.

The extract from the *Manifesto of the Fifth Congress* entitled "Re-orientation of the Revolutionary Movement", is an interpretation, in terms of Marxist class analysis, of Chiang Kai-shek's estrangement from the Communists, which began in early 1926 and ended in an open break after his occupation of Shanghai (April 12, 1927). According to this analysis, Chiang, as the representative of the bourgeoisie, led his class into an alliance with feudalism and imperialism in order to suppress the mass movement of workers and peasants, which was still supported by the petty bourgeoisie and its political organ, the Wuhan government. The rival Nanking government established by Chiang on April 15, 1927, was thus a "counter-revolutionary" alliance between "bourgeois-feudal" KMT elements and the imperialists, while Wuhan stood for a "purified" KMT, uniting the workers, peasants, and petty bourgeoisie.

This analysis, by classes, of the Wuhan-Nanking rift invites a number of observations. First of all we must note that Chiang actually used his military power not only to smash the labour move-ment in Shanghai and elsewhere, but also to extort financial aid from the upper bourgeoisie. How, then, can he be said to have "repre-sented" the bourgeoisie or to have been its "hireling"? The class analysis resolves such contradictions by imputing a sense of *long-range* interest not only to the class itself, but also to the agent who "repre-sents" it in violation of its short-range interests. It is precisely this imputation of long-range perspective to political action which renders the class analysis so dubious as a theory of motivation.

Furthermore, the claim that Chiang became an "ally of the imperial-ists" by winning foreign support at Shanghai necessarily raises doubt as to the purity of the anti-imperialism practised at Wuhan. For it was there that Borodin guided strenuous efforts to obtain recognition from the Japanese.[1] Similarly, Wuhan was no less dependent than Nanking on the support of "feudal" warlords; in fact, its chief military prop, General T'ang Sheng-chih, had joined the revolution much later than Chiang, whom he soon followed in taking a stand against the mass movement.

But whatever the merits of defining the Wuhan-Nanking rift in class terms, it was only by such a definition that the Comintern could reaffirm the continuity and infallibility of its line. The Comintern leadership had backed Chiang Kai-shek to the last, flouting the protests of the Trotsky-Zinoviev opposition. Chiang's defection therefore left it in sore need of a dialectical alibi. Such an alibi could be readily found in the Theses of the Seventh ECCI Plenum (December 1926), provided that Chiang's break with the united front were interpreted as a betrayal by the bourgeoisie. Had not the Theses predicted the transition from the "bloc of four classes" (bourgeoisie, petty bourgeoisie, workers, and peasants) to the "bloc of three classes" (the same minus the bourgeoisie)? To be sure, the Theses had also stated that "certain strata of the big bourgeoisie may, for a certain period, continue to march with the revolution".[2] But this hazy prediction could easily be forgotten—the more easily since neither "strata" nor "period" had ever been specified. Thus the Stalinist leadership could treat Chiang's defection as a "progressive" step, purifying the "revolutionary KMT" and facilitating its conversion into an "organ of the revolutionary democratic dictatorship of the proletariat and peasantry". The coup of April 12, 1927, the actual beginning of the end of the "Great Chinese Revolution", was hailed by Stalin himself as the beginning of the end of Chiang Kai-shek.[3]

How did this interpretation of the political consequences of Chiang's defection affect Communist agrarian policy, as laid down by the Fifth Congress in May 1927? The Congress gave the usual Party-line analysis of agrarian misery in China, blaming foreign imperialism and the "compradore class" for the poverty of the Chinese countryside. On this basis it proclaimed the nationalization of land and abolition of private property as a "basic principle" of the Party's agrarian programme (see p. 96). But this "basic principle" was, of course, a hollow phrase as long as it remained Communist policy to subordinate the peasant movement to the exigencies of retaining both the KMT coalition and the services of the landowning army officers. We have the word of no less an authority than Mao Tse-tung that the Fifth Congress "failed to pass an adequate land programme". So as not to disrupt the Second Northern Expedition—that is, Wuhan's campaign in the spring of 1927 against the Northern warlord Chang Tso-lin—all land belonging to officers of the revolutionary army was declared not subject to confiscation. Since almost all these officers came from landowning families, this was a long step towards abandoning confiscation altogether. The same effect was achieved by defining large estates as those exceeding 500 *mou* (approximately 83 acres)—a figure fantastically large for China and apparently accepted at the insistence of the KMT. In the same vein, the Central Committee of the CCP refused to submit to the Congress a land redistribution scheme drafted by Mao Tse-tung in accordance with his *Report on the Peasant Movement in Hunan*[4] (see document no. 7 above).

The Fifth Congress met under the spiritual guidance of the Indian Comintern delegate, M. N. Roy; it is therefore quite possible that its resolutions partially reflected Roy's views, which were, at that time, somewhat to the left of the official Comintern line as enforced by Borodin.[5] In any event, it is obvious that such demands as the vesting of local authority in village councils and the establishment of a people's army (see pp. 96–7) could be given only limited effect as long as the Party remained committed to full support of the Wuhan government and its military supporters. It was not until June 1, 1927, that Stalin instructed the CCP to combat peasant excesses by means of the peasant unions rather than by KMT troops and to form a separate Communist army. He also called for the cashiering of "unreliable" KMT generals, a thorough reshuffle of the KMT Central Executive Committee, and land confiscations without official sanction (officers' land remaining exempt, however). He thus demanded, at one and the same time, an offensive "from below" against the Wuhan government and the closest collaboration with that government in purging the KMT party and army leadership. In order to achieve this collaboration, Roy showed the Stalin directive to Wang Ching-wei, the Chairman of the left KMT at Wuhan. In this manner Wang learned of the methods by which the CCP was to win the "leading role" in the KMT —that is, the objective which had been set for it by the Eighth Plenum of the ECCI (May 1927). From Wang's point of view, however, the "leading role" in the KMT belonged to the KMT. He therefore took steps leading to the suppression of the mass movement and the expulsion of the Communists from the Wuhan KMT (June–July 1927). In this he had the enthusiastic support of all but a handful of his generals—the "revolutionary generals" whom the Comintern now had to reconvert, in short order, into "feudalists". Thus the "bloc of three classes"—like the "bloc of four classes" before it—disintegrated amid bloodshed and mutual recriminations.

The successive Communist partnerships with Chiang Kai-shek and Wang Ching-wei broke up because, contrary to Stalin's expectation, the KMT leaders could not be squeezed out and flung aside (as Stalin had put it) "like lemons".[6] Why Stalin, a past master in the art of appraising an adversary's strength, erred so dismally in his estimate of the KMT is a question which opens a wide range of speculation. Only three partial reasons may be suggested here. First of all, Stalin has repeatedly admitted that his information from China was insufficient. Secondly, he was doubtless confused, if not outright deceived, by the Marxist cant which KMT leaders (including extreme rightists) intoned for his benefit. Thirdly, Stalin's tactical line, in 1927, was at least as much a function of his struggle with Trotsky as of far-off events in China. He could not afford to move with the actual situation if he thereby gave the impression of capitulating to Trotsky. Thus to admit, after the disaster at Wuhan, that the CCP should leave the KMT would have been to put Trotsky in the right. The CCP had been cast out of the KMT in fact; but Stalin could, and did, order it to remain in the KMT in name. For in the Russian intra-Party struggle Chinese events figured not as such, but only as signs of History, confirming one exegete against the other, and aiding his bid for power.

8. RESOLUTIONS OF THE FIFTH NATIONAL CONGRESS OF THE CCP (May 1927) [résumé]

(1) *Reorientation of the Revolutionary Movement*

The manifesto of the congress declares that we (the Communists) formed the united front and participated in the Northern Expedition because of its anti-imperialist nature; but in the course of this Northern Expedition, Chiang Kai-shek's class, the bourgeoisie, turned the victory to its class advantage by bearing down on the masses who constitute the vast majority of the nation. Chiang Kai-shek is not only the leader of the bourgeoisie but also the ally of the feudalists. We must therefore oppose him with all our strength, for the following reasons:

Class differentiation and imperialist intervention being the distinguishing characteristics of the present revolutionary stage, we cannot easily vanquish imperialist interventionism unless we make clear the meaning and lessons of class differentiation. As the class struggle becomes more accentuated, the anti-imperialist struggle will advance all the more independently of the class struggle. When the bourgeoisie offered indirect opposition to imperialism, the proletariat gave its utmost support to the united front; but now the bourgeoisie has openly discarded the anti-imperialist struggle and declared war against the proletariat. Behind the bourgeoisie stand the feudal reactionaries, the warlords, and the imperialists, who have already concluded a counter-revolutionary alliance in order to suppress the national revolution.

(2) *On the Agrarian Question* [résumé]

The economic life of the Chinese village is still based for the most part on feudal relations. The bulk of the land is in the hands of landlords who live on the produce of their tenants. The rents are not fixed and tenant rights are not granted for long terms. On the average, the tenant receives only about fifty per cent of his produce. In addition, the peasants are constantly summoned together at the convenience of the landlords, militarists, and bureaucrats, who hold all the political power in the village, and are made to disgorge all sorts of taxes and imposts. Furthermore, a considerable portion of the land is held in common by the village or owned by temples.

In addition, primitive capitalist modes of exploitation have also penetrated into the village so that the peasants are exposed to a double type of exploitation. Since the rents extracted by the landlords constitute the bulk of the tenants' produce, the peasants have no remaining surplus, hence no possibility of improving their methods of production. This is the main cause of the primitive state of our agriculture. It is a form of "serfdom". The peasants produce only for consumption and all surpluses are expropriated by the landlord. However, on this foundation of feudal relations a whole superstructure of capitalist exploitation has been erected. In general, the peasant pays his rent in kind, so that all surplus agricultural products are concentrated in the hands of the feudal landlord. Thus while remaining a landlord he simultaneously becomes a commercial capitalist. However, the fact that he remains essentially feudal prevents him from developing into a full-fledged capitalist; that is, he does not convert the surplus agricultural produce which he has accumulated into productive capital but prefers to engage in land speculation and usurious activities. It is this non-development of our economy which has prevented the development of communications and which accounts for the localized nature of our economy. It is because of this that our country is divided into a number of separate markets completely isolated from each other. These markets are completely monopolized by the landlords and the disposal of surplus agricultural products is completely in their hands. Thus by artificially boosting prices, the landlords exploit not only the peasants but also the urban proletariat and the petty bourgeoisie. This situation creates a hotbed of usury. Usury becomes the only channel of credit and the only method of capital accumulation, but the capital thus accumulated is again diverted to land speculation and the dictatorship of the landlord class is still further reinforced.

Furthermore, the existence of a surplus population in the village makes possible the maintenance of feudal, militaristic, exploitative organizations which are organically connected with the imperialist powers. The imperialists are bending every effort to obtain markets for their own products and cheap raw materials for their own industry. Among these raw materials, labour is the most important and the surplus population of the countryside provides an inexhaustible reservoir of cheap labour. The constantly increasing number of peasants alienated from the soil lowers the cost of labour to practically nothing, thus strengthening the basis of imperialism.

Peculiar Characteristics of the Chinese Agrarian Revolution. Thus, a native militarism which is consuming the very vitals of our national life and a foreign imperialism which is impeding the development of our rural economy have been grafted on to the feudal structure of the village. A prime condition for the success of our struggle against these two enemies is the total destruction of feudal relations in the village. A fundamental change in our system of landownership is a basic principle of the national revolution, and no democratic development can be expected without such a change. In order to achieve success in this struggle, the peasants must be made to participate actively and consciously; and by destroying feudal exploitation in agriculture, the energies of the peasantry will be won for the revolution. The agrarian revolution, the destruction of feudalism, are prime prerequisites for the establishment of democracy. In the normal evolution of human society the bourgeoisie generally liberates the peasantry from the shackles of feudalism. In China, however, due to the intervention of imperialism, the bourgeoisie has been unable to develop enough strength to resist the feudal system. On the one hand, the bourgeoisie has developed from the feudal landlord class and still maintains close connections with that class. On the other hand, it has developed as a compradore class closely tied to imperialist exploitation. Thus the Chinese bourgeoisie cannot fight in the vanguard of the agrarian revolution. On the contrary, it stands in a hostile relation to that revolution. Not only can it not struggle for democratic freedom, it actually opposes that struggle. The succession (to power) of Chiang Kai-shek is a prime proof of this fact. In view of these facts, the peasantry must seek its allies, in its struggle against feudalism and its supporters, among the petty bourgeoisie and the proletariat. It must be led by the proletariat and supported by the petty bourgeoisie.

The proletariat and urban petty bourgeoisie suffer from pre-capitalist and feudal forms of exploitation in the form of swollen prices of living necessities and restrictions on the free development of commerce. Like the peasantry, these two classes stand in a hostile relationship to the feudal system and require an agrarian revolution in their own interests.

For a basic solution of the agrarian question, a new land division based on the principle of equality is essential. This can be accomplished only when land is nationalized. The Party must lead the peasantry in its struggle for the equal distribution of land. It thus cannot be denied that the nationalization of land and the abolition of private property must be a basic principle of our Party's agrarian programme.

Trends in the Agrarian Movement. Our experience in Kwangtung, Hunan, Hupei, and other provinces has demonstrated that the peasant movement must be based primarily on the poor peasants (tenants, semi-tenants, and small landholders) and must be organized by them.

At the present stage, the basic aims of the movement must be destruction of patriarchal, feudal power, and the establishment of peasant government in the villages. Hence, in this struggle, the problem of arming the peasants is of crucial importance. As a result of this general trend many landlords have already taken action to carry out a practical solution of the agrarian problem.

Agrarian Programme of the National Revolution. On the basis of a concrete analysis of the objective forces and subjective forces which have made themselves manifest in the peasant movement, the Fifth Congress has arrived at the following conclusions. It feels that a solution of the agrarian problem at the present stage of our revolution requires the following measures:

(*a*) Village communal land, school land, temple property, land belonging to the Christian Church, and land held by groups should be confiscated in its entirety, and apportioned to peasants who are actually tilling the soil.

(*b*) Land of small landlords should not be confiscated.

(*c*) The confiscated land should be subject only to one graduated land-tax to be paid to the state. No additional taxes of any kind should be imposed. The rent on land which has not been confiscated should not exceed the land-tax on land which has been confiscated. The tenants on land which has not been confiscated should have the right of tenancy in perpetuity.

(*d*) All political privileges and special political authority of the landlords and landed nobility should be abolished, and a system of rural economy should be established in which all authority is vested in the village people's council. This people's council should be based on the oppressed classes of the village.

(*e*) A people's army shall be established to disarm the armed forces of reaction in the village and to defend the village government and the results of the revolution.

(*f*) A struggle should be carried on to protect the peasants against usury.

SEC. III. THE PERIOD OF REORIENTATION (1927–31)

COMMENTARY F. FROM COALITION TO ADVENTURISM
THE AUGUST 7 CONFERENCE

The August 7 (1927) Conference was held at Hankow or Kiukiang, and attended by only some twenty-two delegates. It stands out in Chinese Communist annals as an act of redemption which restored the Party, after "opportunist" deviations, to its bolshevik destiny. In point of fact, the accomplishments of the Conference were somewhat more modest. Ch'en Tu-hsiu, who had led the Party since its foundation, was removed from his post of secretary-general and replaced by Ch'ü Ch'iu-pai. An Emergency Politburo was set up to direct Party affairs pending the convocation, within six months, of a national Party congress (which actually did not convene until July 1928, and then in Moscow). Most important of all, a new line was laid down which marked the transition of the CCP from a governmental to an insurrectionary party. This line was new in so far as it gave the first doctrinal formulation to the state of affairs that had arisen from Wuhan's break with the Communists (July 15, 1927; see Commentary E). Expelled from the left KMT and outlawed in everything but name, the Communists had no other means of survival than conspiracy and rebellion. On August 1, 1927, Communist-led troops at Nanchang had raised, for the first time, the banner of military revolt.

But the August 7 Conference gave only partial acknowledgment to the new situation. In blatant disregard of reality, it asserted the necessity of continued work within the KMT, stating its case in the words of the Eighth ECCI Plenum of May 1927—words which had gathered the dust of three eventful months (see document no. 9, p. 115). How could the Chinese Communists, in open rebellion against KMT authority, still insist that it was up to them to "reorganize the KMT" (see document no. 10, p. 122)? The answer is to be found not in China but in Moscow, where Stalin needed the alleged KMT alliance as a shield to hide the ugly facts which belied his infallibility.

The question of Russian influence on the August 7 Conference appears very simple at first glance. As a consequence of the debacle at Wuhan, the old Comintern delegation had been recalled and replaced by a new group under the leadership of Lominadze. Ch'ü Ch'iu-pai, the leading figure at the August 7 Conference, has stated quite unequivocally that it was "convened by telegraphic order of the Comintern and under the guidance of the Comintern delegate".[1] Here the question is usually allowed to rest.

However, it is quite possible to accept the substance of Ch'ü's account without eliminating a number of questions as to the scope of Comintern "guidance". According to another participant at the Conference, it was convened by Ch'ü Ch'iu-pai himself for the specific purpose of removing the Ch'en Tu-shiu leadership.[2] This version appears to contradict Ch'ü's; but the contradiction is more apparent than real.

There are good grounds for assuming that while the Kremlin issued a general directive for the reorientation of the CCP, it did not foresee the specific conditions under which this reorientation took place, nor the specific personnel changes involved. In mid-July, Bukharin, pronouncing the CCP leadership responsible for the Wuhan debacle, had called for the election of a new Central Committee by an extraordinary conference of the CCP.[3] Such a conference never took place, nor was a new Central Committee elected, because expulsion from the KMT coupled with fierce repression left the CCP apparatus in a shambles. The August 7 Conference was thus only a caucus of the old Central Committee; for by Ch'ü's own admission it lacked the quorum to constitute of a regular conference.[4] The fact that hardly any account the Conference jibes with any other may also be taken to support the claim that it was held in haste and under pressure.[5]

There can be no doubt that the line adopted by the August 7 Conference was a faithful expression of Stalin's views; but this does not make it a foregone conclusion that either Stalin or any of his henchmen chose the men to implement his views. To be sure, such names as Ch'ü Ch'iu-pai and Li Li-san were familiar to a handful of experts in Moscow. But, on the other hand, Comintern records of this period abound in confessions of ignorance on Oriental affairs; in fact, Bukharin has frankly admitted that while the Kremlin knew the political leaders—Communist and non-Communist—of Western Europe, it possessed no such information on the Far East.[6] In this light it does not appear very likely that Lominadze—a novice in Chinese affairs and a new-comer to the Chinese scene—was so familiar with Chinese Communist personalities as to take a direct hand in the replacement of the Ch'en Tu-hsiu leadership. It appears safer to assume that Lominadze carried general instructions to reform the Party leadership, but that the details of this reform remained to be worked out by the CCP leaders themselves. Thus there is nothing intrinsically unlikely in the claim that the Ch'ü Ch'iu-pai group, which emerged victorious from the Conference, had engineered the Conference with a view to its own ends.

Two days after the Conference, a joint plenum of the CC and C.C.C. (Central Control Commission) of the CP of the Soviet Union resolved that the "Right deviation in the leadership of the Chinese brother Party has now been liquidated and the policy of the leadership corrected." The same resolution went on to admonish the CCP that it still had to "reform the leadership" and "appoint new leaders from among members possessing actual revolutionary experience".[7] It appears, then, that at this point Moscow was quite aware that the personnel changes effected on August 7 were not quite the deep-going transformation which official Party history has since made them out to be.

In fact, none of the men who rose to prominence through the August 7 Conference can be said to have lacked "actual revolutionary experience". On the contrary, all these men were rich in such experience, accumulated in the service of that very leadership whose "opportunism" they now condemned. The *Circular Letter* of the August 7 Conference gives a very detailed list of the crimes of "opportunism". But for excellent reasons it fails to specify all the criminals.

The capital offence of "opportunism" was, according to the new line, its failure to give full support to the agrarian revolution. It is perfectly true that during the Wuhan period the CCP leadership exerted itself to restrain the rebellious peasants. The reasons for this policy have been discussed above (see Commentary D, pp. 77–8). What remains to be noted here is the implementation of this policy by some of the very men who now posed as its opponents. On the Party level, the orders to restrain the peasant rebellion in 1927 had been issued by Ch'ü Ch'iu-pai, then head of the Peasant Bureau of the CCP Central Committee. Similarly, the "cowardly and irresolute leading organ" which cancelled an impending attack on Changsha in late

May (see document no. 9, p. 113) turns out to have been Li Wei-han (Lo Man), a member of the CCP Politbureau and chairman of the Hunan Provincial Council, a close ally of Ch'ü at the August 7 Conference.[8]

Even the role of Mao Tse-tung during the latter part of the Wuhan period is not entirely clear. On the basis of Mao's *Report on the Peasant Movement in Hunan* (see no. 7), it may be safely assumed that he remained inwardly opposed to the agrarian policy pursued by the Communist leadership. Yet it was Mao who became, in May 1927, the first president of the National Peasant Federation,[9] whose "opportunistic" directives are heavily censured by the *Circular Letter* (pp. 111–12). In this case Mao may be presumed to have given his formal approval to directives which were probably contrary to his convictions. Such action may be regarded as merely good Party discipline; but it should also be noted that throughout the critical years of his rise to power, Mao proved a master in the art of sham compromise—the art which the Chinese describe as "open respect, hidden rebellion".

The practices of "opportunism" were not, of course, limited to the peasant rebellion. The *Circular Letter* also contains an indictment of the "opportunist" labour policy which prevailed in the Wuhan period (pp. 106–9). Here again it turns out that this policy could not have been implemented without the collaboration of two men—both future Party leaders—who played important parts at the August 7 Conference. Certainly no labour directive of the Wuhan government could have been carried out without at least the formal approval of Li Li-san, then head of the Labour Bureau of the CCP Central Committee and secretary of the equivalent bureau in the KMT.[10] The *Circular Letter* specifically includes the Labour Federation of Hupei in its indictment (see p. 108): but it prudently refrains from mentioning that Hsiang Chung-fa—a member of Ch'ü's caucus on August 7—had been chairman of that Federation.

Thus it was only the most conspicuous Party leaders—Ch'en Tu-hsiu, T'an P'ing-shan, and their closest associates—who were now settled with full responsibility for the line that had failed. But in the summer of 1927 their guilt was still painted in relatively light colours. In condemning the CCP leaders, Moscow still made generous allowance for their immaturity and inexperience and for the "objective" difficulties on the Chinese scene. It was only as the failures of the new line provoked the old leaders' outspoken dissent that their "opportunism" assumed the dark colours in which Party historians have painted it ever since.

The indictments drawn up by the August 7 Conference form part of a practice which is standard in the Communist household. If a policy fails, its executors—not its originators—are sought out for blame. This practice is far more than an expedient; it is a necessary corollary of the Marxist-Leninist faith. A dogma which posits historical foreknowledge in a chosen élite can only grapple with the surprises of History by taking them out of History; it can account for the unforeseen only by deriving it from a "subjective" will to upset—or sabotage—History's chosen, predicted course. The Party line being the line of History, deviations are conceivable only as personal vagaries, and acts of chance become acts of rebellion. We have here arrived at one of the back doors through which morality, banned from the halls of scientific socialism, has staged a stealthy come-back.

In its positive programme the August 7 Conference accurately reflected the new line laid down by the Kremlin. This new line seems to have been a response to a number of urgent needs—to explain away the disastrous failures which had gone before, to meet the attacks of Trotsky without giving him credit for prophetic foresight, and to achieve tangible successes in China.

The first need was met by proclaiming that the recent alliance with the "national bourgeoisie" had been an inevitable stage of the Chinese revolution and that, having sloughed off the "national bourgeoisie", the revolution would now pass into a new "higher" stage based on an alliance of peasants and workers with the support of the vacillating petty bourgeoisie. If any gross errors had been committed in the "first stage", they had been committed by the leadership of the Chinese Party which had wilfully misinterpreted the unfailingly correct line of the Comintern.

Trotsky's attacks were met by proclaiming that even now—after the break with Wuhan—the time was not yet ripe for the establishment of Soviets and that the Kuomintang was still an effective instrument through which the Party could carry on its revolutionary work. Besides meeting the need of countering Trotsky, this stubborn desire to retain the symbol of the Kuomintang alliance may have reflected a genuine feeling on the part of the Stalinist leadership that the Party could make itself effective only through some established, indigenous political structure.

Furthermore, in contradiction to Trotsky who was proclaiming the definite recession of the revolutionary wave in China, Stalin now proclaimed that the revolution was passing to a new higher stage. Here too, however, in addition to the need for countering Trotsky's views, it is quite possible that Stalin genuinely believed that success was attainable in China. Had not the Party gained effective control of the masses in the past and had not Trotsky himself felt that China was ripe for Soviets? In all this the Kremlin lightly overlooked the devastating effects of the catastrophes which had befallen the Party and the total disillusionment of the urban proletariat.

Finally, in contradiction to Trotsky who held that the bourgeois revolution had already attained its consummation, Stalin stubbornly maintained that in spite of the defection of the "national bourgeoisie", the revolution was still bourgeois-democratic in nature.

In terms of strategy the new line implied a call for armed insurrection. Since the "sham" Kuomintang was now a coalition of feudal classes and national bourgeoisie, it was the clear task of the real Kuomintang, now assumed to be led by the Communist Party, to overthrow the sham Kuomintang régime in order to consummate the bourgeois-democratic revolution. Since the revolution was now rising to a new higher tide, the presumption was clear that the objective and subjective forces were in existence to assure the success of armed insurrection in town and country. Such, in brief, are the main assumptions which underly the resolutions in document no. 10.

9. CIRCULAR LETTER OF THE CC [CCP] TO ALL PARTY MEMBERS (August 7, 1927) [extract]

I. INTRODUCTION

[[The following is a summary of the first five paragraphs of this letter, pp. 149–52: The revolution has been at a critical stage since April 1927. Workers' and peasants' organizations have suffered suppression by the Nanking KMT under Chiang Kai-shek and the Wuhan KMT under Wang Ching-wei. It is generally expected that the white terror will increase in intensity. We call upon the masses to resist. We must once more point out that the counter-revolutionary forces of the KMT have actually betrayed the true principles of the KMT, which, as founded by Sun Yat-sen, was itself revolutionary. As the vanguard of the Chinese proletariat, the CCP now has a great mission to fulfil.]]

In the recent resolution of the ECCI it was pointed out that the leadership of our Party had committed grave errors of opportunism. The ECCI called on the entire Party to criticize itself thoroughly and correct such mistakes. [p. 153] The mistakes mentioned here are neither individual nor incidental but rather result from the grievously erroneous opportunist line carried out by the leadership of our Party. If this opportunist line is not abandoned and if the past mistakes remain uncorrected, then of course the future tasks of the Party cannot be correctly formulated and there will be even less chance of carrying on the revolutionary struggle and meeting the stupendous duties now facing us. In order to correct these mistakes, however, we must know how these errors were committed so that every Party member will learn the lessons of the past. If the Party does not correct the mistakes of the leading cadres it will be impossible to advance even one step along the path of the revolution. . . .

[p. 154] Our strength is derived not only from our Party's class characteristics, but also guaranteed by the struggle of the masses and the poor peasants who form the foundation of our Party. As the resolution of the ECCI states, "the CCP is carrying on a heroic struggle. The broad masses of the CCP are carrying on a truly revolutionary struggle among the lower social strata of workers, peasantry, and urban paupers." However, errors of opportunism have been committed by the Party's leading cadres. Their constant vacillation, their irresolution at critical moments, their false, unrevolutionary theories which were contradictory to Communism, and their unrevolutionary conduct, are not only in complete contradiction to the resolutions and instructions of the CI, but also in total conflict with the revolutionary activities of the Party masses.

[[The following passage, pp. 154-5, hails the strikes and insurrections led by the CCP in Shanghai, Kwangtung, and Hunan during the past few years.]]

[p. 155] Another glorious page in the history of the Chinese revolutionary movement was written by the comrades who led the peasant movement in Hunan. A political régime of the peasant associations was set up by the peasant masses and led by CP members. Land that belonged to the big landlords was confiscated by spontaneous action on the part of the peasants and redistributed among peasants in the villages; the local militia [p. 156] of the gentry were disarmed; peasants' armed groups were organised; and the feudal, reactionary forces were thoroughly suppressed. The peasant movement developed on a large scale, permitting the conclusion of a revolutionary—but not opportunist—alliance with the lower masses of the KMT to organize peasant revolts against the reactionary régime at Changsha. (If the Party's central organ had not retreated so shamelessly at the crucial stage, such revolts would undoubtedly have been victorious.) Such are the achievements of the Party members in Hunan. Such are the best methods for solving the land problem.

[[The following passage, half a page, continues to laud at length the effort of the Party rank and file and of the masses, but attacks the Party leading cadres as rightist, opportunist, and wavering.]]

II. THE NATIONAL REVOLUTION AND CLASS STRUGGLE

[[The following is a summary of pp. 157–62: (1) The Party's leading organ at that time did not understand correctly the nature of the Chinese revolution, and failed to abide by the Leninist theory and practice of the CI. (2) The Chinese revolution is a bourgeois-democratic revolution with its major inclination towards socialism. To maintain that, during this stage, the national anti-imperialist revolution forms a separate element in conflict with the class struggle and social revolution is erroneous and unbolshevik. The CI has always rejected this kind of interpretation as undesirable opportunism. (3) The national bourgeoisie in China, unlike the compradore class in the big cities, is being hard pressed by foreign capital and therefore has to fight an economic battle against the imperialists. However, the national bourgeoisie, stunned by the large-scale revolutionary movement of the working class, finally came to ally itself—like the landlord and compradore classes—with the ruling power of foreign capital. (4) The class struggle of the working class against the bourgeoisie, and of the peasant masses against the feudal landlords is not only compatible with, but necessary to, the anti-imperialist, national revolution. The wavering petty bourgeoisie should be won over by the resolute, revolutionary actions of the proletariat and of the CCP.]]

[p. 163] Here we have an evaluation of the various dynamic forces of the Chinese revolution, which should have determined the revolutionary strategy of the CCP. However, the Party's leading cadres, in theory and especially in practice, had an opposite viewpoint in evaluating the strength of the various classes in the Chinese revolution. This (erroneous evaluation) caused the wavering and hesitant opportunism of the Party leadership. In the menshevik manner the CC separated the national liberation movement and the class struggle as conflicting elements, and seemed to think that the development of the class struggle would be detrimental to the national revolution. The CC wanted the Party, the working class, and the peasantry to limit their class demands and refrain from staging revolutionary struggles against the Chinese bourgeoisie and the landlords. The directive letter of June 19 [1927] sent by the CC to the Shanghai (Party) Committee declares that "one of the major characteristics of the Chinese revolution is its anti-imperialist nature. . . . In recent months we have neglected anti-imperialist activities." The CC seemed to imply that the emphasis on attacking feudalism had led to unfavourable consequences. The CC upbraided the CP members for going too far and instructed the revolutionary peasants led by our Party to retreat. In the same directive, it was added that "on the one hand, the anti-imperialist movement has declined and, on the other, the workers' and peasants' movement, at least from the point of view of the petty bourgeoisie, has reached its climax. (Our Party's) activity in arming the workers and peasants, confiscating the land, and calling for non-capitalist development has aroused the distrust of the petty bourgeoisie, who think that the CP is about to turn [p. 164] against the KMT and carry out a class revolution instead of a national revolution." Thus the CC at that time deemed class struggle one thing and national revolution another. The directive also stated that "the petty bourgeoisie does not realize that land confiscation is a prerequisite to the national revolution but seems to think that the CCP's confiscation of land is aimed at a revolution like the [Russian] October revolution to expand the power of the workers and peasants. The petty bourgeoisie, as a result, cannot but raise this issue and call for a check on the workers' and peasants' movement or a break with the CP. Under these conditions, can (the CCP) accept the policy of the petty bourgeoisie? If we did, we would destroy our own strength, forfeit the leadership of the proletariat, and surrender to Chiang Kai-shek and it would mean a capitalist future. Can we then insist on the confiscation of land and the arming of workers and peasants? The result of such insistence would be an immediate split [with the leftist KMT], leading to the immediate destruction of the revolutionary bases. If we cannot successfully cope with this difficult situation by appropriate methods, it will mean the victory of the bourgeoisie. Should we give up the policy of arming the workers and peasants and the confiscation of land? This, of course, is undesirable. For example, in the fight against Hsü K'o-hsiang [a militarist who turned against the Communists at Changsha on May 21, 1927] we have already decided on a policy of land confiscation and of arming the peasants. This was an independent policy but a dangerous one. If we carry on independently then there will be a split with the KMT. And though this would be a defeat with glory, the split would still be disadvantageous to us. [p. 165] We should seek a new path, on which the impasse in which we now find ourselves can be overcome, thus expanding and deepening the revolution and leading it to final victory." This directive concluded with instructions to the Party members in Shanghai "not to regard the national revolutionary movement solely as a workers' problem, but to carry on anti-imperialist propaganda among all classes", which would mean to carry on propaganda on behalf of the Shanghai bourgeoisie. This is indeed an unheard of, unrevolutionary, un-Communist course, and clearly shows that the views of the (Party's) leading organ regarding the basic problems of the revolution, as well as on the nature of the revolution for national liberation, are entirely erroneous.

The opportunism of the CC regarding this problem reflects the influence of the bourgeoisie on Communists. The whole revolutionary policy has been turned upside down. The CC's policy had nothing in common with the directives and resolutions of the CI, nor with the struggle of the working class and the revolutionary peasantry.

Whoever insistently defends those opportunists or stands for a continuation of such opportunism will sever himself forever from Communism.

III. THE CCP AND THE WORKERS' MOVEMENT

[p. 166] The CCP is the vanguard of the proletariat, the most advanced, most revolutionary, and most class-conscious section of the proletariat. The work of the CCP should always be based on the basic interests of the working class and should aim at a change of the entire social structure by revolutionary methods. Since the CP takes the welfare of the working class as its point of departure, it should raise demands which are objectively tenable in the stage of the bourgeois-democratic revolution, before (the revolution) reaches its socialistic stage. One of the major tasks of the CP is to organize the working masses and to lead their struggle, fight resolutely for the elevation of the living standards of the working class, for wage increases, the establishment of an eight-hour working day, complete freedom in organizing workers and class unions, an unlimited right to strike, and for the elimination of the conditions of enslavement among workers who possess no rights or privileges whatsoever.

The workers can raise those demands in the course of the democratic revolution, but (they) must do so by means of an independent struggle of the proletarian masses. The CCP should spread and encourage the class struggle of the proletariat and help every workers' struggle against the bourgeoisie. The CI has repeatedly instructed the CCP to fight for the improvement of the material conditions of the working masses, and for the betterment of living conditions in the factories and in society, for [p. 167] the immediate abolition of the laws which oppress the workers, and for the realization of such rights as the eight-hour working day, increase of wages, and recognition of workers' rights to organize unions and to strike. At the same time, the CI points out it is necessary to arm the workers speedily, boldly, and resolutely, especially those elements which are most class-conscious and best organized. This course is considered absolutely essential by the CI. Such directives of the CI are in keeping with the struggle of the workers themselves in the industrial areas and the actions of the rank and file Party members. But the leading organ of our Party has developed a different course. It has simply hindered and minimized the class struggle and the revolutionary actions of the workers. Instead of spreading and promoting strike movements, the CC, together with the leaders of the KMT, decided on an arbitrary method of mediation and ruled that the final authority belonged to the government. Under the government of a coalition of classes, led at this first stage by the bourgeoisie, this kind of policy actually served merely to protect the interests of the bourgeoisie and greatly obstructed the workers' movement. Our CC did not protest against the resolution of the CEC of the KMT which prohibited strikes in enterprises without the permission of the government, and demanded that the unions stop fighting for the demands of the workers but rather undertake the responsibility for maintaining labour discipline. The Central government [in Ssu Mei's version the text here reads, "the CC"] seemed to think that the restriction of the workers' movement would preserve the alliance with the bourgeoisie [Ssu Mei says, "petty bourgeoisie"], but did not understand that the irresolution shown in protecting the interests of the working class would only hasten the [petty] bourgeoisie's turn to the right. The CC used every method possible to restrain the economic struggle of the workers and to prevent them from struggling for their direct welfare, (but failed to realize that) if these demands were not met, the leadership of the working class in the revolutionary movement would never be secured. The CC decided on such a policy at that time because its evaluation of the alliance with the petty bourgeoisie was erroneous. Also erroneous was its concept of the interest of the national revolution.

The spontaneously developing workers' movement has established powerful labour unions with a mass foundation and is entirely under the influence of CP members. There have also come into existence armed workers' guards, the extensive organization of labour, the youth corps, etc. The working class, discovering its own strength, rose in direct struggle against the bourgeoisie, which had become counter-revolutionary and retarded production, deliberately inviting industrial depression and financial chaos. When the unions arrested a few factory and shop owners, the whole bourgeoisie came out and shouted (about the workers') "excesses". Joining in this cry were not only the intellectual elements of the petty bourgeoisie, but also the CC of our Party. In some documents, the CC criticized those "excesses" severely. The CC did its best to enjoin the workers from taking over factories even when their owners deliberately closed them down. (The CC instructed them) not to close any shops even when their proprietors raised prices deliberately; and to refrain from arresting anyone even if he was discovered to be counter-revolutionary.

[p. 169] The working class was surging towards the realization of a true democratic dictatorship of the workers and peasants, but the CC used every means possible to prevent the workers' movement from progressing along the revolutionary path.

Not only did the CC fail to take measures to arm the workers, but, encountering the active opposition of the bourgeoisie, it disarmed (itself) voluntarily, and dissolved the workers' guards at Hankow. It also voluntarily disbanded the labour youth corps in order to preserve the alliance with the petty bourgeoisie.

The CC of the KMT instructed the labour unions to assume responsibility for the maintenance of strict workers' discipline. Anyone disobeying the regulation was to be handed over to the government for punishment. The unions could only administer punishment to the workers. Yet the CC of our (Party) did not raise a single word of objection to all this, and when the Labour Federation of Hupei accepted these instructions, the CC [of the CCP] acquiesced. Every independent expression of the working class was branded by the CC as "excessive" and "infantile", and it was not aware that its own remarks were those of the counter-revolutionary bourgeoisie.

The Party's leading organ adopted an entirely erroneous policy, not only with regard to the workers' economic struggle, but also with regard to political activities. [p. 170] The workers in Hankow played a historic role when they retrieved the British concession there. Yet this action was not only not led by the Party's leading organ, it was even criticized by the CC after the event. Recently, the CC showed an inclination to disband voluntarily the secret unions in Shanghai and make the workers join the "yellow unions" of Chiang Kai-shek. Fear of the masses and distrust of the strength of the masses were reflected in intra-Party affairs. The majority of the leading cadres of the Party are composed of representatives of the intellectual elements and the petty bourgeoisie. Only upon the insistence of the ECCI were a few workers admitted to the directing organs (of the Party). In many unions, the directing Party members are not workers but students and intellectuals. When the Party school was about to be established the CC insisted on reducing the number of workers [on the candidates list], maintaining that the cultural level of the workers was too low and their political consciousness undeveloped and un-awakened. As a matter of fact, the political consciousness of the workers in Shanghai is higher than that of the Party leadership. Our Party should cut itself off once and for all from such unproletarian, unrevolutionary, thorough opportunism.

IV. THE CCP AND THE AGRARIAN REVOLUTION

The question of agrarian revolution is the crux of the bourgeois-democratic revolution in China. The CI has repeatedly explained itself concerning this question. [p. 171] The CI gave clear and definite instructions to our Chinese Party indicating ways of solving the land problem (in China). The resolution of the Eighth Plenum of the ECCI [May 1927] also reiterated the previous directives (of the CI). This resolution pointed out: "Only by relying on the agrarian revolution in the rural areas and by satisfying the needs of the urban working class and guaranteeing their political rights can the masses be brought into the struggle. Demands such as those for the abolition of rental payments to the gentry, redistribution of land, confiscation of the land of the landlords, temples, and bureaucrats, cancellation of usurious debts of the poor peasants, prohibition of exploitive contracts, drastic reductions in taxes, and the shifting of the tax burdens to the shoulders of the rich should be carried out on a nationwide scale, particularly in areas under the rule of the Wuhan government. These demands should succeed in arousing the masses to oppose the landlords, the bourgeoisie who have betrayed the revolution, and the warlords of North China." Agrarian revolution consists of confiscation and nationalization of land—this is the major content of the internal social economy in the new stage of the Chinese revolution. The main thing at present is to employ the "mass-type" revolutionary methods to solve the land problem (and allow) the tens of millions of peasants to solve this problem by rising from below. The CC should be the vanguard of this movement and direct it. In the government, the CP should carry out such a policy so that the government itself will act to support the agrarian revolution. [p. 172] Only thus can the present government be turned into the centre of political organization of the workers' and peasants' movement, and the organ of the dictatorship of the workers and peasants.

But the work of the leading Party organ was directly contrary to this revolutionary course. The peasant movement in Hunan which had turned into a powerful agrarian revolution, and the revolts of the peasant masses in other provinces against the landlords and gentry were not directed nor guided by the CC, but were carried out against its orders and directives. In general, these movements were only initiated by the lower strata of the masses themselves. The peasant movement in various areas was led only by the lower Party cadres and Party members, and the CC often obstructed or even reversed the revolutionary movement of the peasants. The Party's leading organ did not pay any attention to the significance of the land problem in the Chinese revolution. Before the Fifth National Congress (of the CCP) [April–May 1927], the Party's leading organ paid only the least possible attention to the land problem. At the Special Conference at Hankow in December 1926, which was an important conference (convened) to decide the tasks of the Party after the success of the Northern Expedition, not a single word was mentioned on the stand to be adopted by the Party *vis-à-vis* the land problem. At the various provincial conferences of the peasant associations (such as those held in Hunan in December 1926 and in Kiangsi in January 1927), the Party did not define its stand on the land problem. Only in the provincial conference of the peasant associations in Hupei in March of this year [1927] did the Party touch on this issue.

[p. 173] At the Fifth National Congress of the Party, a resolution on the peasant question was passed, but the Party leaders, comrades Ch'en Tu-hsiu and T'an P'ing-shan, stated that the task of the moment was to extend but not to deepen the revolution, and that consequently land confiscation should be postponed until some future date.

The land committee of the CEC of the KMT convened for three weeks, and the Communist members headed by T'an P'ing-shan changed their stand on the land question twice, on both occasions acting according to the opinion of the KMT representatives. Finally (the CP members) drafted a proposal which laid down some principles for the solution of the land problem but which did not call for immediate action. When the CEC (of the KMT) refused to make public this resolution, not a single CP member of the committee protested.

The seventh enlarged plenum of the Hunan provincial committee of the CP even resolved that rent reduction should only be demanded when the rent exceeded fifty per cent [of the principal crops]—at a time when the peasant associations in Hunan had already begun their active struggle and even carried out, in practice, a redistribution of land. The leading organ of our Party verbally admitted some of its mistakes, but the policy of obstructing the agrarian revolution was maintained to the very end. Our Party actually followed the footsteps of the petty-bourgeois leadership of the KMT and vigorously opposed the "excesses" of the peasant movement.

The course adopted by the leading organ of the Party was, in actuality, opposed to agrarian revolution. [p. 174] Thus the circular of the propaganda bureau of the CC on June 1 [1927] declared that "we must remember that the Party's peasant policy is to check firmly any excesses (committed) against the small landlords, revolutionary militarists, and petty bourgeoisie". Another circular dated June 14 also stated that, "The failure to check the unorganized actions on the part of the peasants to solve the land problem by themselves has led to many excesses. Such a condition must be corrected." There was even one school of opinion which maintained that the excesses in the Wuhan area were fomented by the agents of Chiang Kai-shek. This is simply an imitation of the Wuhan (government) militarists, because they too have stated that the excesses were instigated by Chiang Kai-shek's agents. Thus the leaders of the CP would even defend the oppressors of the peasant movement. One directive of the National Peasant Federation declared: "Chiang Kai-shek, bad gentry, and village bosses are utilizing a few peasants to harm the welfare of the families of officers, to spread rumours and manufacture an internal split. They deliberately carry out leftist agitation in order to suppress the peasant movement later." One of the responsible leaders of the CCP announced on one occasion that "irresponsible arrests cause anxiety to the petty bourgeoisie, who get the impression that the KMT government has become the prisoner of the CP. This impression must be eradicated."

In this manner, the great peasant revolt in Hunan not only frightened the bourgeoisie, landlords, and warlords, but also the leadership of the CP. At a time when the CP members and the masses in various areas fought relentlessly [p. 175] for the development of the (peasant) movement, with an admirably brave spirit of sacrifice, the CC, frightened by the intimidation and wavering of the leaders of the KMT, failed to produce a revolutionary platform for the solution of the land problem. (The CC) also took an extremely opportunist position regarding the question of achievement of political power by the peasants. The CC did not take into consideration the revolutionary fighting experience of the peasant masses in drawing their conclusions, but wishfully relied on a system of village self-government which was rigid, impractical, and harmful to the revolution. In fact, the spontaneous upsurge (of the peasants) has given the revolutionary political power to the peasant associations, which have confiscated land of the big landlords, reduced rent, disarmed the militia corps (*min-t'uan*) and the gentry, and punished the counter-revolutionary elements in rural areas.

The CC did not aid and develop this form of revolutionary political régime, but agreed to the rigid organization of rural self-government as proposed by the CEC of the KMT. What is the real meaning of this rural self-government? The answer can be found in the directive of the National Peasant Federation which states: "Establish self-governing bodies in the rural areas in order to consolidate the victory secured by the peasants and eliminate the anarchic conditions prevailing in the villages."

The CC strongly opposed the redistribution of property, the imposition of fines [on the landlords] and the arrest of village bosses (*t'u-hao*). As early as May 26 [1927][1] the CC announced that "infantile acts of the poor peasants are estranging us from the petty bourgeoisie". [p. 176] Although the CC did not dare to oppose openly the slogan of land confiscation, all its actions were predicated on the abandonment of such a line. The May 26 resolution stated that "naturally, we cannot abandon the platform passed by the Fifth National Congress, but we should realize that the land problem in China should pass through a propaganda phase. We must solve the most urgent question concerning the land problem, namely, the question of village administration. Consequently, we must: (1) spread propaganda regarding the land problem, especially among the soldiers, and (2) organize self-governing bodies in the villages, as well as in the *hsien*." If this resolution is taken together with the fact that the CC did not raise the slogan of land confiscation but, on the contrary, resolutely opposed land redistribution, it becomes clear that the CC had adopted a policy of opposition towards the confiscation of the land of the big landlords.

This policy produced very undesirable effects on the activities of the Party during the Hunan coup. After the counter-revolutionary coup at Changsha [the coup of Hsü K'o-hsiang against the CCP on May 21, 1927], peasant forces which had mobilized at the suggestion of the CP members in Hunan began to attack the counter-revolutionaries in Changsha. Had the armed attack of the peasants not been obstructed by the cowardly and irresolute leading organ of the Party, Changsha, surrounded as it was by 100,000 armed peasants, would have been easily captured. At the last moment, on the eve of the attack (by the peasant army) on Changsha, the leader of the Hunan Party headquarters, a member of the Central Political Bureau, ordered the cancellation of the attack on the ground that military action against Changsha would lead to a national political imbroglio and that instructions from the CC should be awaited. [p. 177] On the next day a letter from the CC arrived stating that the attack should be postponed, and that the peasant forces should undergo further consolidation pending solution of the incident by the National government [at Wuhan]. When the order for the cancellation of the attack was dispatched to all units of the peasant armies, the majority of them withdrew, but two units which had, by some accident, not received the order, stormed the city and attacked the counter-revolutionary forces. Outnumbered, they too had to withdraw after a vigorous struggle. The general retreat (of the peasant armies) resulted in the victory of the counter-revolutionaries and led to several days of counter-revolutionary persecutions throughout Hunan province. The hesitation on the part of the CC during the peasant revolt was tantamount to the betrayal of the revolution and entirely inexcusable. It is indeed a black spot in the annals of our Party.

Why did the CC obstruct the insurrection? The reasons can be found in the resolution of May 26 [1927] (which says) : "The task that confronts the Party at present is neither to overthrow the enemy nor to surrender completely. There is still a middle way which must be found. At present it is undesirable [for our Party] to have any direct armed conflict [with the KMT]. Our duty is to wait for opportunities and to consolidate our strength and be ready for the unavoidable attack." Such an attitude of shameful hesitation did not help the peasant movement by waiting for future opportunities but actually helped to provide the counter-revolutionary elements at Changsha with such opportunities. The degree to which the CC had yielded to a policy of capitulation at the time of the Changsha incident can be seen from its decision to support the circular telegram of T'ang Sheng-chih. [General T'ang first pretended to be leftist and later turned against the CCP. This refers to a telegram sent by T'ang to the National government at Wuhan.] The CC showered T'ang Sheng-chih with praises, thus creating illusions and spreading the impression that the Changsha incident occurred against the wishes of T'ang. [p. 178] Although the CC sometimes protested to the National government against the suppression of peasants' and workers' organizations by the Changsha authorities and demanded punishment for the counter-revolutionary traitors, its actual wavering and hesitation helped the counter-revolutionary elements in the Hunan coup to consolidate their power.

This moribund policy (of the CC) should have taught us a bitter lesson. The opportunist line of the CC on the peasant problem was pushed so far that its instructions, adopted at a critical moment, smacked of downright betrayal of the mass movement.

The actions of T'an P'ing-shan, CP representative in the government [T'an served in the left KMT government at Wuhan as Minister of Agriculture and of Interior], were equally shameful. The Ministry of Agriculture stubbornly refused to support the agrarian revolution and attempted to harness the peasant movement as a branch of bourgeois reformism. In a directive issued by the Ministry of Agriculture in May, it was stated that "infantile acts of the peasants must be corrected, particularly acts of elements which have deviated from the correct policy and have endangered the welfare of the great majority of peasants; such acts must be punished. As regards the struggle against counter-revolutionary elements and the punishment of bad gentry and village bosses, they must be carried on in accordance with the provisions of law. They must be handed over to the authorities in accordance with Party and government instructions, and no spontaneous action should be taken against them." This directive as well as all other activities of the Ministry of Agriculture were a concrete manifestation of the unrevolutionary and conciliatory line of our Party on the land problem at that time. If the entire Party proceeds in the spirit of this line, then our Party will never be Communist or revolutionary. Fortunately the activity of the masses and the lower Party cadres are in striking contrast to this policy of the CC. Thus, even though hamstrung by the leading organ, our Party can still furnish the peasant masses with correct leadership.

V. THE CCP AND THE KMT

[[The following is a summary of pp. 179–90, which criticize the "submissive and opportunist" line of the Party leadership towards the left KMT at Wuhan as being contrary to the directives of the Eighth Plenum of the ECCI (held May 20–26, 1927). We do not translate these quoted directives, which are already available in English.

[[(2) The CC, like the KMT hierarchy, has been full of petty-bourgeois prejudices and illusions. As a result, it was not the CCP that led the KMT at Wuhan but the upper strata of the left KMT who dominated the leaders of the CCP, both politically and ideologically. The Party and youth organizations of the CCP in the KMT, as well as other Communist directing groups in the KMT, were unwisely dissolved by the leading organ of the CP.

(3) The erroneous policy of the CC was based on the theory that at that time it was necessary to retreat temporarily in order to retain the alliance with the left KMT. One of the eleven resolutions of the Enlarged Meeting of the CC dated June 20 [1927] declared that "since the KMT is an anti-imperialist coalition party of the petty bourgeoisie, workers, and peasants, the leadership of the national revolution naturally belongs to the KMT". Other resolutions yielded to the KMT the authority to control workers' and peasants' organizations, the mass movement, and workers' guards, and prohibited any excessive actions. This was no longer a compromise with opportunism but total liquidationism. It not only abandoned the independent policy of the CP, but liquidated the entire revolutionary movement of the masses.

(4) The Party should learn its lesson from the mistakes of the Party's leadership. The Party must remember that all its strength and its future lie in the masses of workers and peasants and in their confidence, strength, and organization. The Party must keep in mind that in the future the alliance with the KMT should be an alliance with the leftist and revolutionary KMT, i.e. an alliance with its masses and its lower organs. There should be no more illusions about the traitorous KMT leaders in the Wuhan government.]]

VI. THE PARTICIPATION OF CP MEMBERS IN THE NATIONAL GOVERNMENT

[[The following is a summary of pp. 190–7:

The resolution of the *Eighth Enlarged* Plenum of the ECCI [May 1927] pointed out that "the CCP should continue to work in the central and local organizations of the KMT, but must criticize its ally and insist on a correct governmental policy". The CP members in the Wuhan government, especially T'an P'ing-shan, were guilty of yielding to the reactionary Wuhan government and of abandoning the struggle of the masses of workers and peasants.

"The stand taken by the CC contradicted both the policy of the CI and the basic requirements of the Communist programme which has as its aim a resolute revolutionary struggle to turn the Wuhan government into a democratic dictatorship of workers and peasants. Our ties with the masses must be strengthened and maintained. Only in this way can the CCP work through the KMT."]]

VII. THE PROBLEMS OF ARMING (THE WORKERS AND PEASANTS) AND
THE PROBLEM OF RELATIONS WITH THE ARMY

[[The following is a summary of pp. 197–200: the leading organ of the Party tried to deal with the generals and officers in the KMT army instead of engaging in agitation among the men and the junior officers. The leading cadres of the Party did nothing about the urgent task of arming the workers and peasants, but adopted a conciliatory attitude towards reactionary generals like T'ang Sheng-chih and Chu P'ei-te.]]

[p. 200] VIII. PROBLEM OF THE PARTY AND OF THE RELATIONS WITH
THE CI

One of the reasons why the CC was so deeply caught in its opportunist line was the irregular conditions existing within the Party. The CC was not supervised by, or responsible to, the masses. Nor did it present the Party's policy to the rank and file for discussion. The Party's organization was entirely based on a patriarchal system and all policies were decided by the top leadership which considered its opinion binding, indisputable, and infallible. Under these conditions, intra-Party democracy became an empty phrase. Even at places where the Party could perform a very great public function, the so-called intra-Party democracy was entirely a formality. Within the Party there was neither group life nor public opinion. The Party masses did not have any supervisory or persuasive functions *vis-à-vis* the Party leadership. Under these conditions within the Party, the CC naturally carried out its instructions by dictatorial means, and it did not really wish to realize intra-Party democracy.

The relation between the Party and the CI was also not in accordance with accepted organizational procedure. There has never been a case in the history of the CI where the instructions and resolutions were actually rejected in such a critical situation. This was no longer merely a simple breach of discipline, but a criminal act against the Chinese and international Communist movement. The Chinese revolution does not merely have a national significance, but also forms a major sector in the world revolution. [p. 202] The fate of the world revolution will be decided by the fate of the Chinese revolution. The CCP not only carried out an erroneous policy, a policy that brought the revolution to defeat, that voluntarily liquidated the revolution and capitulated to the enemy, but also would not admit its errors or obey the instructions of the CI. Not only that, but it also deliberately ignored its obligations to, and the discipline of, the CI, even maintaining that it was not necessary to transmit to the whole Party the resolutions of the CI, (thus depriving) the members of the opportunity to express their views after studying those resolutions.

Therefore, recently the CI had to criticize openly the policy of our CC, and had to expose it to the entire CCP membership and other branches of the CI in the various countries.

IX. CONCLUSION

The CI has severely criticized the opportunist line of the CC, which has in reality betrayed the (Chinese) revolution. We agree that this criticism is entirely just and that the policy of the ECCI regarding the Chinese problem is entirely correct. We welcome the recent instructions of the CI which have made possible the unmasking of the past mistakes of the (Party) leadership and have saved our Party (from destruction). We positively agree that, in the past, the leadership of the CC carried out an opportunist, unrevolutionary policy and that it is necessary to carry out a thorough revision of our policy on the basis of the lessons of the past. [p. 203] In this letter, we have analysed past mistakes from a correct Communist viewpoint, and the analysis is based firmly on the ground of Leninism and the views of the CI. The entire Party and all Party members should give the utmost attention to an examination of these problems, and be instructed to discuss in detail the past policy of the Party. The resolutions of the ECCI on the Chinese question (July 1927) and this letter should form the basis of discussion. If Party members do not learn from the lessons of the past, they cannot progress, or correctly lead the Chinese revolution.

Certain conclusions should be drawn from the discussions: (We) should not only criticize the past Party leadership and expel the opportunist elements from the directing organs of the Party, but also re-examine all Party work from a Communist and revolutionary viewpoint, examine the actual direction of mass work, and prove in action that the CCP is truly the vanguard of the Chinese labouring class, capable of leading them, and that it will guide them to victory.

The Party should establish close ties with the unions and the peasant associations and guide them, and shift the centre of Party work in this direction. The Party should establish a close relationship with the CY and give more assistance to its work. The delegates of the CC of the CY have proved themselves recently to be politically stronger than the CC of the CCP. [p. 204] The CC of the CY fully supported our proletarian stand and entrusted the CC to carry it out, but the leaders of the CC of the CCP, fearing that their opportunist policy might be shaken, tried to silence the voice of the CY and deprive it of its right to pass political resolutions. This failed because the CC of the CY stood firmly on the policy of the CI from beginning to end. The Party should recognize the political significance of the work of the CY and (establish) close liaison with it. Finally, the Party should, in spite of (the present) severe political oppression, effect real intra-Party democracy[2] in order to encourage the discussion of Party policies among the Party masses. Collective activities in Party head-quarters on all levels should be inaugurated by secretaries of lower Party organs in order to realize collective guidance. Also every precaution should be taken to preserve Party organs from the reactionaries. Strictly secret organs must be established, but at the same time they should be fighting, underground units of the Party.

Under (the present) trying circumstances and in a revolutionary crisis[3] we should undertake to reorganize our forces, correct the serious mistakes of the past, and find a new path. We are firmly convinced, however, that our Party possesses adequate strength to effect such reforms in a resolute, revolutionary manner. We should call on all the Party members to bend all their energies to help the Party to realize these reforms. We are firmly convinced that the fighting determination of our comrades and their devotion to the [p. 205] revolution will enable us to overcome all difficulties and resolutely set the Party on the correct course. Our Party under the direction of the CI will assuredly win the final victory.

10. RESOLUTIONS OF THE AUGUST 7 EMERGENCY CONFERENCE
(August 7, 1927) [résumé]

I. THE PARTY'S NEW POLICY

In its basic direction, the Chinese revolution is going over from the stage of the bourgeois-democratic revolution into the stage of the socialist revolution. The basic content of the Chinese revolution at present is the agrarian revolution, while the working class is demand-ing liberation from a system of unprecedented oppression. The tendency to consider that the national revolution (consists of a struggle) against imperialism, a class struggle, and a social revolution, as (three) antagonistic elements, is an incorrect tendency and one of the earmarks of opportunism. The backwardness of China's economy and the corrupting influence of feudalism in the villages have made it possible for foreign capital to exploit the Chinese masses. Because the feudal class and the imperialist powers depend upon each other, in order to liberate China we must make every effort, at the same time (that we oppose imperialism), to oppose the régime of the land-lords and evil gentry. Furthermore, if we wish to destroy the feudal system, we must do everything to carry forward an ever more drastic agrarian revolution. By increasing the participation in it of the peasant masses, we shall carry forward the movement to overthrow the domination of the landlords and gentry. By broadening the scale of the national movement, we shall consolidate the victory of the national movement.

In the first stage of the revolution, the Chinese bourgeoisie partici-pated in the struggle against foreign capitalism. However, as the workers' and peasants' movement began to develop at a more rapid tempo, as revolutionary demands began to arise and as the influence of the CP gradually began to increase, the bourgeoisie abandoned the national revolutionary front and went over to the counter-revolution-ary camp. Accordingly, it is one of the necessary prerequisites for success in the revolution for national liberation that the proletariat fight for the fulfilment of its own just class demands.

The petty bourgeoisie can for the most part still participate in the revolutionary movement. They tend to vacillate between the bour-geoisie and the proletariat. However, as the struggle increases in intensity, as the ultimate victory of the proletariat and the peasantry becomes more apparent, they are bound to join in the battle. Thus the vanguard of the proletariat must not only do everything in its power to consolidate its own camp and to carry on its own valiant struggle, but must also lead the petty bourgeoisie.

II. THE ORGANIZATION OF THE PARTY

Since the split between our Party and the KMT we have modified the organization of our Party. At an emergency meeting of the CC, an Emergency Politburo consisting of seven permanent members and five alternates was elected. This Central Emergency Political Bureau shall prepare to summon a National Party Congress within the next six months. In the interim the Central Emergency Political Bureau shall perform all the functions of the CC. During the past several months the CC has been located in Wuhan. Now we shall establish a southern bureau in Canton.

During the period in question, the Central Emergency Political Bureau shall secretly publish our political organ and carry on country-wide propaganda. It shall establish a special propaganda committee under its own jurisdiction to prepare other types of propaganda material.

The most urgent organizational problem now facing us is the formation of solid, hard-fighting secret Party organs. All sections of the Party must be reorganized on the basis of this principle. Party branches on all levels must be organized on the lines outlined below in the shortest possible space of time. In each branch committee a standing committee of five to seven men shall be elected to act as the leading Party organ and perform all Party functions. Every Party branch shall maintain extremely close and secret relations with higher level and lower level branches and must maintain strict secrecy and discipline. Party branches on all levels should avail themselves of every possibility of carrying on public activities and do everything possible to increase the Party's strength. Party cells should be formed immediately in all unions. Such cells need not consist of more than five to seven men, and shall be completely subordinate to their respective Party committees in matters of organization and political guidance. They must submit to all resolutions passed by Party organs and all tasks imposed by the Party. Any Party member, no matter what his position, must be severely punished if he is derelict in the duties of his position. All branches must immediately shift over to a secret mode of operation and must be reorganized with this end in view.

A second vital problem facing us is the transformation of our Wuhan Party branch into a secret organization. We have several thousand members in Wuhan, but most of them have no experience in carrying on secret organizational activities. The CC must therefore help the Hupei provincial committee to carry out the reorganization. The composition of branch committees on all levels below the provincial committee shall be scrutinized by the other superior organs. All opportunists shall be eliminated and worker-members shall be given places on the local committees and given important posts of responsibility, thus strengthening our organizational structure. In our present secret phase of operation, the centralization of authority is imperative. It is necessary to eradicate the errors of opportunism which have recently pervaded the Party. The centralization of authority does not mean the elimination of democracy. On the contrary, problems of Party policy must be discussed in detail by all Party branches.

Drastic revisions are required in the matter of our relations with the

CY. The principle of the exchange of representatives between local branches on all levels and the CY must be vigorously implemented. The representatives of the Party branches shall have the right to vote and shall participate in the discussion of policy, guiding the rank and file of the CY membership.

III. THE LABOUR MOVEMENT

The crux of the labour movement at this time is the conflict between the true labour unions and the sham labour unions. At the present time, the Nanking and Wuhan governments have already become representatives of the feudal class and the bourgeoisie and tools of the counter-revolution. This does not prevent them, however, from hanging out the false signboard "KMT" or from claiming to protect the workers and peasants and maintaining labour unions. The actual state of affairs has, however, already been unmasked beyond the shadow of a doubt.

The following points concerning the labour movement deserve particular attention:

(1) When labour unions are organized by the proletarian masses (their leadership) shall be elected from the masses under the guidance of this Party until such time as they are absorbed into the All-China General Federation of Labour.

(2) In the unions, workers shall hold the positions of leadership. All leaders who are creatures of the counter-revolution shall be prevented from penetrating our genuine labour unions.

(3) Our Party must lead the masses and carry on a political struggle to obtain freedom of assembly, organization, and speech, and freedom to strike for the workers. The most pressing demands of the proletariat at the present time are economic demands. If the economic struggle is led by the CP, the results will serve to intensify the political struggle. Attention must be paid to the arming of the workers and to military training for street battles. We must prepare to co-ordinate battles with peasant uprisings, thus leading to the overthrow of the counter-revolutionary régime.

The labour movement is the basic function of the Party. We must remedy the erroneous tendency which has prevailed hitherto to consider it only a part of our general activities. We must bend our total efforts to lead the workers. Accordingly we must liquidate the labour union departments in our Party branches on all levels, and set up separate labour union committees to guide our Party members in the labour unions directly.

IV. THE AGRARIAN MOVEMENT

Unorganized, sporadic uprisings by the peasants are immediately crushed by the militarists. At the present time, therefore, the preparation by the Party of systematic, planned peasant insurrections, organized on as wide a scale as possible, is one of the main tasks of the Party. We should take advantage of the harvesting period this year to intensify the class struggle in the villages. The slogan of these peasant insurrections should be the transfer of political power in the villages into the hands of the peasant associations. The land of large and middle landlords should be confiscated and distributed to poor peasants. Small landlords should be forced to lower their rents (this is based on the strategy of neutralizing the small capitalists and small landlords whose power is much larger than their numbers would indicate). If our programme of agrarian revolution is carried out within a fixed period, we may proceed to the universal slogan of "land to the tillers", carry out the nationalization of land, and proceed to the redistribution of land.

The land revolution is the crux of the agrarian problem and this is, in turn, the central problem of the bourgeois-democratic revolution in China. The only way to draw the masses into the struggle is to carry out the agrarian revolution in the villages. We must, accordingly, absolutely eliminate the rents exacted by the rich gentry and redistribute their land. All land of temples, bureaucrats, and landlords must be confiscated and usurious debts which poor peasants cannot pay should be wiped off the records, and all harsh contracts should be annulled. Demands for the reduction of taxes and the shift of the tax burden on to the shoulders of the rich peasants must be met on a national scale. The confiscation of land and the nationalization of land are an integral part of the agrarian revolution. This is the vital socio-economic class content of China's revolution. The thoroughgoing liquidation of the agrarian problem by the peasant masses themselves, comprising tens of millions, is a movement which must be led by our Party.

V. THE PARTY AND THE KMT

Under present conditions, unless we achieve hegemony within the KMT, we shall not be able to achieve the hegemony of the Chinese proletariat. We must reorganize the KMT and make it a genuine mass organization of the urban and agrarian toiling masses. We must bring into it, on a broad scale, labour union factory committees, peasant committees, peasant associations, savings associations of small artisans, soldiers' organizations, peasant soldiers, the Red Spear Society (excluding counter-revolutionary elements), and workers' militia units. Only thus shall we finally set China's democratic revolution on the road to victory and be able to resist the treachery of various factions within the KMT and its treacherous military men. The Party must immediately unmask the agreement between Chiang Kai-shek and the imperialists and all other vacillating policies, and must take all appropriate concrete measures in the fields of propaganda, agitation, and organization.

VI. OTHER PROBLEMS

Observations on the problem of the Wuhan government troops and the arming of the workers and peasants: most of the troops of the Wuhan government are mercenary troops and differ in no essential from the troops of other Chinese warlords. Furthermore, most of their commanders are landlords and bourgeoisie. Accordingly, in formulating a policy concerning these troops, we must of course focus our attention on the rank and file. There is no need to pay any attention to their reactionary commanders. The essential point is that we carry on large-scale activities among the men and the non-commissioned officers. The scattered armed units of peasants and workers now in existence can become a real supporting force in the revolution only when they have been rebuilt on a single, uniform plan and transformed into a well-organized, solid force. We must do everything possible to get hold of arms and arm the worker and peasant masses.

In the matter of the relations of the Party to the CI—unless we are able to carry out the resolutions of the CI during the present crisis, our discipline will be totally shattered. On the other hand, the utterly incorrect policies pursued by our Party till now, and the actions which led to the defeat of the revolution, must be severely condemned. We must maintain close connections with workers' and peasants' unions, lead them and shift the centre of gravity of party activities in this direction. We must also maintain close ties with the CY and do everything possible to aid it in its activities.

COMMENTARY G. THE SIXTH CONGRESS AND THE DOCTRINE OF PREPARED INSURRECTION

The Sixth National Congress of the CCP was held in Moscow from July to September 1928, at a time when the CCP had suffered a number of set-backs (failures in the Nanchang uprising, the Swatow insurrection, the Autumn Harvest insurrection in Hunan, and the Canton Commune) and when an examination of strategy and the mapping of major programmes were in order. Two explanations are generally offered for the fact that the Sixth Congress met in Moscow: first, that safety required these comprehensive discussions of the various issues confronting the Chinese revolutionary movement to be held only outside of China because of the KMT "white terror". Secondly, it has been stated that the Sixth Congress was held in Moscow to meet the wishes of the Communist International, which held its Sixth World Congress there during the same period. The CI at that time was particularly interested in eliminating Trotskyist influences both inside and outside the Soviet Union.

No complete list of those who attended the CCP Congress is now available, but by piecing together bits of information, we find these persons listed among the CCP leaders who attended (alphabetically arranged): Chang Kuo-t'ao, Chang Wen-t'ien (aliases: Lo Fu and Ssu Mei), Chou En-lai, Ch'ü Ch'iu-pai, Ho K'o-ch'üan (alias K'ai Feng), Hsiang Chung-fa, Hsü T'e-li, Li Li-san (alias Pai Shan), Li Wei-han (alias Lo Man), Lin Tsu-han (Lin Po-ch'ü), Liu Po-ch'eng, Shen Tse-min, Ts'ai Ch'ang (Mme. Li Fu-ch'ün), Tso Ch'üan, Wang Chia-hsiang, and Yeh Chien-ying.

The Congress, after reviewing the events of the Chinese revolution since the Fifth National Congress of April–May 1927, passed resolutions on the political question, the peasant movement, the agrarian problem, the workers' movement, propaganda, etc. (for details, see *Bibliography A* under document no. 11). Ten policies (see below, document no. 11, sec. II, 4 (1)) and a Party Constitution of fifteen chapters and fifty-three articles were adopted (the latter was revised at the Seventh National Congress in April 1945, see below, document no. 37). The Congress resolved that the "crux of the Chinese revolution and the fundamental and central tasks of the CCP at the moment [are] to drive out the imperialists in order to bring about the real unification of China, and to carry out a thorough agrarian revolution, abolishing the private ownership of land by the landlord class" (see document no. 11, sec. II, 3 (2)). The Congress also resolved formally to work for the overthrow of the KMT government and condemned the policy of Ch'en Tu-hsiu as an opportunist, rightist deviation and that of his successor, Ch'ü Ch'iu-pai, as a putschist, leftist deviation. Ch'en was attacked by the Congress for having adopted a too conciliatory line towards the left KMT government at Wuhan, and Ch'ü was reprimanded for his "ill-prepared, ill-directed putschism", which had led to failure in a number of uprisings from August to December 1927 (for the definition of putschism or "blind-actionism", see below, document no. 11, sec. II, 13 (1), (2), and (3)). At the conculsion of the Congress, Hsiang Chung-fa was elected Secretary-General, replacing Ch'ü Ch'iu-pai, and a new Central Politburo was set up (for members elected to various posts, see *Chronology*, under July–September 1928).

Like the August 7 Conference before it, the Sixth Congress staunchly maintained as many of Stalin's previous theoretical positions as possible in the face of Trotskyist attack. In its historic perspectives, the revolution in China was still a bourgeois-democratic revolution aimed at eliminating feudalism and imperialism. In its class analysis, the Congress reiterated the line already adopted before the Canton Commune—namely, that the "national bourgeoisie" had gone over to the "feudal camp" and that the Kuomintang was now a coalition of "feudal classes" and bourgeoisie, with the latter in a subordinate position. The formula for the revolution was still Lenin's 1905 formula of the "Democratic Dictatorship of Workers and Peasants". Even the emphasis on the agrarian problem as the "main content" of the bourgeois-democratic revolution was not new, although it was now treated in extensive detail.

The only innovation in the "theoretical" sphere was the new "estimate of the revolutionary situation" (which first appears in the Resolutions of the Ninth Plenum of the ECCI of February 1928) in terms of the imagery of waves. After the Canton insurrection it was no longer possible to speak of a continuing rising wave. On the other hand, the Kremlin could not accept the Trotskyist view that the wave had definitely receded. Hence, the formula that China was now in a "trough between two waves". During the period of the trough, it is the duty of the CCP *to prepare* for armed insurrections. No indication is given, however, of the length of the trough or of when the time would come for passing over from preparation to action. We are not surprised that the post-Congress Li Li-san leadership of the Party was inclined to seize upon any circumstance unfavourable to the enemy as a sign that the new wave had finally arrived. The formula of "preparation for insurrection" thus allowed the Kremlin a free hand in attacking the "putschism" of the previous Party leadership even while calling for insurrection in the future.

This ambiguity is evident, for instance, when the Political Resolution points out "the lack of a general revolutionary rising tide at the present time" (sec. IV, 10 (2)) and warns against "putschism" and "playing with insurrection" (sec. IV, 13), but at the same time asserts that "the Party must prepare for armed insurrections in view of the inevitable arrival of a new revolutionary rising tide" (sec. IV, 11–12). In the two years following the Sixth Congress when Li Li-san (who had played a very active role in it) took the view that a new revolutionary rising tide had indeed arrived and ordered the peasant armies in the Soviet areas to attack urban cities in co-ordination with insurrections by the workers (see below, document no. 14 and Commentaries H and I), he met disastrous failure and the "Li Li-san line" was severely condemned as putschism. Yet the contemporary resolution of the Sixth World Congress of the CI also stated in 1928 that "in China, the future growth of the revolution will place before the Party as an immediate practical task the preparation for the implementation of armed insurrections as the sole path to the completion of the bourgeois-democratic revolution and to the overthrow of the power of the imperialists, landlords, and national bourgeoisie—the power of the KMT."[1]

The Sixth Congress's emphasis on the agrarian problem has constantly been cited by orthodox Communists as the peculiar feature of this Congress which foreshadowed the whole subsequent development of Chinese Communism. It is true that much more attention is devoted to this subject than in previous pronouncements. From the First Congress of 1921 to the Fifth in 1927, the CCP hierarchy under Ch'en Tu-hsiu had never considered the peasantry a decisive factor in the Chinese revolution. Mao Tse-tung's feat in organizing millions of peasants in Hunan had not won him any key position in the Party leadership. On the contrary, as Mao proceeded to organize peasant armies and carry out agrarian reforms he was several times reprimanded by the Central Committee for "deviations", and was once dismissed from his position as an alternate member of the Central Politburo, in November 1927.[2] The fifth Congress of 1927 had still maintained that (1) the peasant movement could play only a minor and subsidiary role in the Chinese revolution and that (2) nationalization of land and the abolition of private property must be a basic principle of the CCP agrarian programme. But by 1928 circumstances had changed. The as yet minor activities being carried on by Mao Tse-tung, Chu Teh and others in the hinterland were at this time the only positive development in the whole bleak landscape of Chinese Communism—a fact which could not be ignored.

This does not mean, however, that the 1928 formula of the

"Democratic Dictatorship of Workers and Peasants", which implied relatively great attention to the peasantry, was a new development. The notion that the agrarian question was the central content of the bourgeois-democratic revolution had already been advanced as early as the Seventh Plenum of the ECCI in November 1926. What is more important, the notion that the "content" of the revolution is agrarian by no means implied that the peasantry was to be the *central class* of the revolution. On the contrary, it was constantly reiterated that the peasantry must be under "proletarian hegemony". Lenin's original formula of "Democratic Dictatorship" had definitely contemplated a régime in which the peasantry would be represented by peasant parties while the workers would be represented by Social Democrats. Now, however, China was to have a "Democratic Dictatorship of Workers and Peasants" in which the peasantry as a whole was to have no separate political expression of its own. It is furthermore made amply clear in document no. 11 (which is generally ignored in discussions of the Sixth Congress) that "proletarian hegemony" can be achieved only to the extent that the Party recaptures its hold on the urban proletariat. Thus while the agrarian problem is the central problem of the revolution, the Party's recapture of its own class bases is in a real sense a task which has priority, even though both may be pursued simultaneously. Many points in the Resolution on the Peasant Movement, though ambiguous, ostensibly served as guiding principles in much of the succeeding period—e.g. the policies towards the middle and rich peasants (sec. II, 3 and 1), the emphasis on guerrilla warfare as a "major form of struggle" (sec. IX, 1), the organization and functions of the peasant associations (sec. VIII, 1), and the role assigned to women and youth in the rural areas (sec. V and VI).

11. POLITICAL RESOLUTION [OF THE SIXTH NATIONAL CONGRESS OF THE CCP] (September 1928)

I. CHINA AND THE WORLD REVOLUTION

1. *The Development of World Revolution*

(1) *The October revolution of Soviet Russia is the first stage of the world revolution*

The world revolution of the last ten years can be divided into three major stages. The outcome of the imperialist war in Europe was the victory of the dictatorship of the proletariat in the Russian October revolution. This marks the beginning of the first stage of the world revolution. At that time there was also a deep revolutionary crisis in Western Europe (Germany, Italy, Austria-Hungary, etc.).

(2) *The revolution failed in the various countries of Western Europe because of the betrayal by the social democratic parties*

Because the Communists—*the vanguard of the proletariat* [emphasis as in original]—were *immature and weak at that time, and the Communist Parties were not united and consolidated*; because the social democratic parties were agents of the bourgeoisie and numerous workers were still under the leadership of these reformist parties: *for these reasons the direct revolutionary action of the masses suffered great set-backs.* Only the Russian revolution succeeded. As a consequence of the defeat of the working class, the bourgeoisie of various countries in Europe and America continued to oppress the working class, consolidated their political power, and temporarily and partially *stabilized the capitalist economy.*

(3) *The second stage of the world revolution and the partial stabilization of capitalism*

The second stage of the world revolution shows a partial and temporary stabilization of capitalism: world finance, trade, and production have equalled or exceeded the pre-war level; the capitalists have launched a general offensive against the proletariat; drastic economy measures of rationalization [*chieh-sheng chu-i*, although the English word "nationalization" is incorrectly inserted in the original Chinese text] were carried out in the capitalist productive organizations, causing a further deterioration in the workers' living conditions; and the rights won by the workers in the previous stage (such as eight-hour day, higher wages, and political freedom) were lost.

(4) *Meanwhile, the major conflicts within international imperialism grow sharper*

Although on the one hand world capitalism has gone through a period of stabilization, recovering and even increasing its productive capacity beyond the pre-war level, the major conflicts within international imperialism, on the other hand, grow ever sharper. The relationship of the capitalist world to socialist Soviet Russia deteriorates day by day: the struggle between the working class and bourgeoisie in the capitalist countries, and that between the imperialist powers and the toiling masses of the colonies and semi-colonies, also grows ever sharper, resulting in many armed uprisings and riots (China, Java, India, Morocco, Syria, etc.). Also, due to the uneven development of capitalism, the conflict among the imperialist powers grows more intense day by day, entailing the danger of a second imperialist world war.

(5) *The third stage of the world revolution means the new and old conflicts of imperialism will all grow sharper*

The sharpening of these conflicts [mentioned in the previous paragraph] marks the beginning of the third stage of the world revolution. The characteristics of the third stage of the world revolution are: a leftward tendency and revolutionary activity on the part of the working class; uprisings by tens of millions in the Eastern colonies to join the struggle against imperialism; Soviet Russia's increasing impact on the stability of capitalism and its increasing importance as a revolutionary centre for the workers' movement in various countries and the oppressed peoples throughout the world.

(6) *Revolutions, insurrections, an anti-Soviet war, and war among the great powers are the prospects of this stage*

The third stage of the world revolution will (see) another round of open, decisive upsurges by the working class and insurrections in the colonies, accompanied by the danger of an anti-Soviet war and the possibility of many large-scale conflicts between the imperialist powers.

2. *The International Significance of the Chinese Revolution*

(1) *The world revolutionary situation further increases the international significance of the Chinese revolution*

The Sixth Congress of the CCP, evaluating the present international situation, *considers the approach of highly important world-historical events in the nature of a much sharper class struggle, to be inevitable.* Therefore, the international significance of the Chinese revolution, one of the major components in the world revolutionary process, is further enhanced. The struggle of the Chinese labouring masses; (their) opposition to the imperialists and their political and economic rule; (their aim) to weaken imperialist power; (their) demand for the liberation of hundreds of millions of Chinese people and (their) demand to be emancipated from unprecedented oppression and exploitation: (all these) combine to lessen the imperialists' pressure on Soviet Russia, and on the workers of other countries, thus helping to push the advance of the proletarian world revolution.

(2) *The socialist revolution in China will be even more important a component in the socialist world revolution than the present democratic revolution*

The first stage of the Chinese revolution—the bourgeois-democratic one—helps the socialist world revolution, of which it is a major component. The second stage, in the future—the proletarian socialist revolution—will be even more a direct component in the world socialist revolution. At the same time, the Chinese revolution will affect neighbouring countries—large colonies like India, Indo-China, Java, and Korea—arousing the teeming masses of those oppressed nations to political struggle; it will fundamentally shake the foundations of imperialist Japan and England and deal a heavy blow to capitalism in the U.S.A. Therefore, the completion of the Chinese revolution will be the prelude to the victory of the world proletarian dictatorship.

II. THE NATURE OF THE CHINESE REVOLUTION AND ITS SOURCE OF POWER

3. *The Nature and Tasks of the Chinese Revolution*

(1) *The present stage of the Chinese revolution is bourgeois-democratic*

The Sixth Congress of the CCP agrees entirely with the evaluation of the Chinese revolution by the *Seventh, Eighth, and Ninth Plenums of the ECCI* [November 29–December 16, 1926; May 20–26, 1927; February 9–25, 1928, respectively]. The nature of the present stage of the Chinese revolution is bourgeois-democratic; it is erroneous to think of the present stage of the Chinese revolution as having already passed over into the socialist revolution. It is also erroneous to regard the present Chinese revolution as a "permanent revolution", because: (*a*) the real unification of China has not yet been accomplished and she has not yet been emancipated from imperialism; (*b*) the private landownership system of the landlord class has not yet been over-thrown, and all semi-feudal remnants have not been liquidated; and (*c*) the present political power is the governmental power of the landlords, warlords, compradores, and national bourgeoisie, an alli-ance of reactionary forces dependent on the political and economic strength of international imperialism; therefore, the immediate goal of the (Chinese) revolution is to solve these problems. The core of the Chinese revolution at present and the fundamental and central tasks are:

(2) *The two major tasks of the revolution at present are the overthrow of imperialism and the agrarian revolution*

(*a*) To drive out the imperialists and to accomplish the real unification of China; and

(*b*) to abolish completely and popularly (i.e. through the people) the private landownership system of the landlord class and to carry out the agrarian revolution in which the Chinese peasants (small owners) will destroy all the semi-feudal bondage in the land system.

These two tasks do not yet exceed the scope of the capitalist mode of production—but they can only be accomplished by overthrowing, through the revolutionary method of armed insurrection, the rule of the imperialists and that of the landlord-warlord-bourgeois KMT and *by setting up a democratic dictatorship of workers' and peasants' Soviets under the leadership of the proletariat.*

(3) *To carry out, successfully, the overthrow of imperialist rule and the agrarian revolution, it is necessary to abolish, first, the régime of the gentry and the bourgeoisie and to set up a democratic dictatorship of workers and peasants*

(*c*) Therefore, the third task of the Chinese revolution at the present bourgeois-democratic stage is already the struggle to establish the rule of councils of workers', peasants', and soldiers' deputies (Soviets). This is the best method of inducing the vast toiling masses to participate in political rule and to realize the democratic dictatorship of workers and peasants.

(4) *The present bourgeois-democratic revolution in China can only succeed by opposing the national bourgeoisie. The workers and peasants are the revolution's only source of power*

The national bourgeoisie of China betrayed the revolution and joined the counter-revolutionary camp of the imperialists, gentry, and landlords. They were once (before the spring of 1927) a force that could weaken the imperialists and undermine the warlord system, but they have now come to strengthen and unify the imperialists and the warlord system. *Therefore, the sole source of power (of the Chinese revolution) lies, at the present bourgeois-democratic stage, in the Chinese proletariat and peasantry.*

China's anti-imperialist, bourgeois-democratic revolution, which completely transforms the (existing) land system, can only be accomplished in opposition to the national bourgeoisie, which is one of the most dangerous enemies obstructing the success of the revolution.

4. The Programme of the Chinese Revolution at the Present Stage

(1) Ten great demands of the Chinese revolution

At the present stage, the major slogans of the Chinese revolution are:

(a) Overthrow the rule of imperialism.

(b) Confiscate enterprises and banks of foreign capitalism.

(c) Unify China and recognize (the principle) of national self-determination.

(d) Overthrow the warlord-KMT régime.

(e) Establish the régime of councils of workers', peasants', and soldiers' deputies (Soviets).

(f) Realize the eight-hour day, higher wages, unemployment relief, social security, etc.

(g) Confiscate the land of all landlords—land should belong to the peasants.

(h) Improve the livelihood of the soldiers and allot them land and work.

(i) Abolish taxes imposed by the (KMT) government, warlords, and local administrations; institute unified, progressive taxes.

(j) Unite with the proletariat of the world and the Soviet Union.

These *ten great demands* are the *present* major slogans of the CCP for winning the masses, preparing armed insurrections, and overthrowing the régime of the gentry and the bourgeoisie.

5. The Source of Power of the Chinese Revolution and its Transition to a Socialist Future

(1) The Chinese revolution has a socialist future

The proletariat and the peasantry now constitute the sole source of power of the Chinese revolution, and the leadership of the proletariat has already been established in the stage of the bourgeois-democratic revolution. (The proletariat can support and guide the peasantry in the agrarian revolution and the struggle against the imperialists.) This will therefore open the path of the Chinese revolution towards a non-capitalist, that is, socialist, future.

(2) *The transformation of the democratic into a socialist revolution is deter-mined by the strength [li-liang] of the struggle*

World capitalism is at present in a frightened state of depression. There have been ten years of socialist construction in a country under proletarian dictatorship, the Soviet Union, whose political and economic power is growing; this will help the Chinese proletariat to win the revolution for a socialist future, and guarantee its victory.

At the same time, *the democratic dictatorship of workers and peasants in the form of Soviet rule will be the starting-point of transformation to the dictatorship of the proletariat. Only the struggle*, the *strength*, the *solidarity and organizational strength* of the proletariat and only the comparative ratio of *class strength* can decide when the bourgeois-democratic stage of the revolution will end, and how it will be transformed into the process of socialist revolution of the proletariat.

III. EXPERIENCES OF PAST STRUGGLES

6. *The Objective Causes for the Failure of the Chinese Revolution*

(1) *When the national united front entered the left-KMT period, the central (government) of Wuhan also turned reactionary*

Between the Fifth and Sixth Congresses of the CCP [May 1927 to September 1927], the Chinese revolution underwent many important incidents. The success of the Northern Expedition, the weakening of imperialist power, the rapid revolutionization of the vast labouring masses, the extensive development and growth of the workers' and peasants' movements in semi-secrecy, *the beginning of the deepening of the agrarian revolution*—these [developments] were followed by serious set-backs in the revolution, losses of (previous) revolutionary gains, the suppression of the CCP, and the oppression of the mass movement.

The development of the Chinese revolution brought a class differen-tiation which so frightened the Chinese bourgeoisie that they surren-dered to the counter-revolutionary imperialist camp. The first stage —that of the *all-inclusive national united front*—now passed over to the second stage—*the period of the left-KMT* (the so-called Wuhan period). After the bourgeoisie left the revolutionary camp to become a counter-revolutionary force, and after Chiang Kai-shek's betrayal, the Wuhan central (government) of the left-KMT fell more and more into vacilla-tion and reaction. The vacillation of the Wuhan central (government) became increasingly obvious, especially during the military coup of Hsü K'o-hsiang at Changsha [May 21, 1927]. Opposing the agrarian revolution, the Wuhan central (government), on May 21, openly declared war against the masses of workers and peasants and became the counter-revolutionary centre. At the same time, the revolution was under attack from the imperialists, warlords, gentry, and bourgeoisie; thus the entire counter-revolutionary mission of the KMT was openly accomplished.

(2) *The failure of the Nanchang Insurrection marked the end of the Left-KMT Period*

The Nanchang insurrection, a Communist-led attempt to preserve the gains of the revolution by military force, ended in failure. The reason for this failure lay in the overwhelming strength of the enemy and also in the tactical errors of the directing organ. *The failure of the Nanchang insurrection ended the second stage of the Chinese revolution—the period of the left-KMT.* Then the Canton commune began *the third stage of the Chinese revolution, the period of the Soviets.*

(3) *The objective causes of the failure of the Chinese revolution*

Despite its impressive development in the initial stage, the Chinese revolution finally failed. At this historical stage, it did not have sufficient strength to overcome the numerous difficulties of the period. Among the objective difficulties and causes (of failure), these should be mentioned.

(4) *The first (cause) is the powerful strength of the imperialists*

(*a*) The imperialists, the arch-enemy of the Chinese revolution, were very strong and are the organizers and controllers of all reactionary forces. By means of their political and economic power and some puny concessions to the national bourgeoisie, they *split* the national united front through coercion and bribery—using the traditional methods of bribing the warlords, of suppressing the revolution by forceful gunboat "diplomacy" and economic blockade. By using their powerful strength (in the form of banks, corporations, warships, and troops), they became one of the most serious obstacles to the development and success of the Chinese revolution.

(5) *The second (cause) is the betrayal of the revolution by the national bourgeoisie*

(*b*) The national bourgeoisie betrayed the revolutionary united front. In the initial stage, the bourgeoisie participated in the revolution. This sowed the seed of its [the bourgeoisie's] inevitable betrayal and withdrawal from the revolutionary front. The betrayal of the national bourgeoisie temporarily weakened the revolutionary forces and strengthened the counter-revolutionary alliance.

(6) *The third (cause) is the powerful army led by the landlords*

(*c*) The Chinese army is mercenary, which is one of the characteristics of Chinese warlordism; therefore, the reactionary group possesses a numerically superior military force—the kind of force which often determines victory or defeat. The revolution (itself) once utilized this type of army. But the officers of such an army are usually the spokesmen of the landlord gentry. The soldiers (in such an army) are men who have been unproductive and who have little contact with workers or peasants. The army was then an obedient tool of the gentry, the feudal landlords, and the bourgeoisie.

(7) *The fourth (cause) is the uneven development of (the movement of) workers and peasants*

(*d*) The development of the revolutionary movement (has been) uneven. The peasant movement had just begun to develop when the Chinese proletariat was engaged in other struggles (such as the May Thirtieth movement [1925] or the March uprising in Shanghai [1927]). (Even though) the Chinese working class was weakly organized, dispersed, and not particularly powerful, still it very early entered the arena of political struggle and was beset repeatedly by the reactionaries without receiving timely support from the peasantry. The Chinese working class failed under these attacks, without being able to hold on long enough for the peasant movement to develop on an extensive mass scale. Furthermore, the revolution also developed unevenly according to place. The peasants of Kwangtung, Hunan, and Hupei in the South had already begun to overthrow the régime of the landlords and gentry and to confiscate and even redistribute the land in some localities, while the peasants in the North were only beginning to participate in the liberation struggle. This naturally made it even easier for the bourgeoisie and feudal gentry to carry out their own reactionary mission.

(8) *The vacillation of the petty bourgeoisie*

(*e*) The overwhelming majority of the upper strata of the urban petty bourgeoisie are closely related to the feudal land (system) and also linked with foreign capital. These petty-bourgeois elements wavered and (then) betrayed the revolution. During the rapid advance of the anti-imperialist movement and the agrarian revolution, the petty bourgeoisie vacillated more and more, and finally surrendered to the reactionary camp of the gentry bourgeoisie.

7. The Mistakes of Opportunism

(1) *Misunderstanding of the nature of the revolution and incorrect interpretation of the united front policy*

But objective difficulties were not the only forces determining the inevitable failure of the Chinese revolution. The Sixth Congress of the CCP holds that: the principal reason for the failure of the revolution was the opportunist policy of the directing organ of the vanguard of the proletariat—the CP, which, at a critical juncture of the revolution, (adopted) a non-bolshevik, opportunist policy, thus, in an objective sense, betraying the interests of the struggling, toiling masses. This opportunist policy was, first of all, due to the CC's *erroneous conception of the nature of Chinese revolution and the tasks of the united front.* The independence of the CP was not preserved; no class criticism was made of the revolutionary ally; the revolutionary forces were not mobilized nor were the masses prepared to foil the reactionary plot of our temporary allies. On the contrary, at times (the CC) obstructed the development of the mass movement to suit its erroneous notion of the united front. Thus the then leading organ of the CCP doomed the Chinese revolution to inevitable failure.

(2) *A dependent, uncritical, and conciliatory policy hampered the class struggle and the agrarian revolution, and willingly surrendered the leadership of the revolution*

The leadership of the CCP at that time did nothing to develop the agrarian revolution and the class struggle of the masses, but engaged in intrigues with the (left KMT) leaders, ignoring the class conflict. It did not try to win over the army, nor did it arm the workers and peasants. It proved incapable of exploiting its participation in the (Wuhan) régime in order to fight for the interests of the masses. At the critical juncture therefore it was encircled by the enemy instead of breaking through (this) encirclement—as a matter of fact, it actually forfeited the leadership of the proletariat. This was the highest expression of opportunism which manifested itself most shamefully during the May 21 [1927] incident [at Changsha]. Lastly, the leadership of the CCP failed to carry out the directives of the CI—thus causing the eventual failure of the heroic struggle of the workers and peasants.

The Sixth Congress of the CCP admits that it was entirely correct for the CI to by-pass the CC and call directly on the CCP membership (and on the) masses, in order to demand a thorough change in the Party line and a reshuffling of the Party leadership.

8. *The August 7 Conference and the Enlarged Conference of November* [*1927*]

(1) *The August 7 Conference as the beginning of Bolshevization*

The Emergency Conference of August 7 [1927] based itself on the CI's directive to correct thoroughly the opportunist errors of the preceding period; therefore, it was a turning-point in the history of the CCP, and of great significance—[it posed] the task of *bolshevizing the Party*. The August 7 Conference criticized the errors of opportunism in a frank bolshevik spirit, raised the central slogan of the agrarian revolution, and designated the overthrow of the reactionary KMT central government as the aim of the proletariat and peasantry, mapped out the general strategy of armed insurrection, and began to liquidate the opportunist elements in the leadership by mobilizing the Party membership (and the) masses; thus reorganizing the old leadership, it rescued the Party from the mire of opportunism and (put it back) again on the revolutionary path.

(2) *The errors of the August 7 Conference vis-à-vis the KMT and its inadequacy vis-à-vis the agrarian question do not lessen its significance*

It is true that the August 7 Conference still harboured some wishful thoughts about the left KMT and that it did not deal thoroughly with the agrarian question. But these defects can never diminish its great historical significance. (Therefore), the Sixth Congress of the CCP wholeheartedly supports the major resolutions of the August 7 Conference.

(3) *The November Conference continued (the task) of bolshevization but did not adequately prevent adventurism*

The Enlarged Conference of November [1927] continued the work of bolshevization. It mapped out a more detailed and thorough agrarian policy, raised the slogan of the democratic dictatorship of workers' and peasants' Soviets, and resolutely decided on an overhauling of the Party and the induction of worker-comrades into responsible positions. The Sixth Congress holds, at the same time, (that) the November Conference was very correct in pointing to the necessity of well-prepared, well-co-ordinated armed insurrections. But in evaluating the Chinese revolution, the resolution of the Enlarged Conference of November erroneously chose the term "permanent revolution". This permitted the possibility of interpreting the revolution as continuously ascending, and thus resulted in false tactics. Notions about the bolshevik policy of insurrection also remained unclarified for a long time, entailing inaccuracies of judgment and tactics, and under-estimation of the enemy's strength—which can all become the basis of adventurist tendencies. Consequently the already discovered adventurist tendencies in the Party were not effectively checked. (Such ultra-leftist tendencies are extremely harmful.)

9. *The Significance of the Nanchang Insurrection, the Autumn Harvest Uprising, and the Canton Commune*

(1) *These insurrections were definitely not all adventurism*

The Sixth Congress of the CCP holds that the Nanchang insurrection, the Autumn Harvest uprising, and especially the Canton Commune definitely did not constitute adventurism from the point of view of policy.

(2) *The errors of the leadership in the Nanchang insurrection*

The Nanchang insurrection was a military action against the central KMT (government), and (as such) it was a correct move. The objective cause of its failure was the overwhelming superiority of the enemy. As to the tactical errors of the leadership at that time, they were:

(*a*) lack of a clear programme;

(*b*) lack of determination in the agrarian question;

(*c*) lack of co-ordination with the peasant movement and failure to arm the peasants;

(*d*) failure to destroy the old régime and replace it by the workers' régime; and

(*e*) sundry military blunders. These mistakes were the subjective causes of the failure of the Nanchang insurrection.

(3) *The Autumn Harvest uprising won over the peasant masses; but the mechanical application of the policy leads to playing at insurrections and military putsches*

In many places the Autumn Harvest uprising deepened the Party's influence among the peasant masses and introduced the slogan of the agrarian revolution into the mentality of broad peasant masses. The many peasant struggles that followed and even the establishment of Soviet areas, were generally due to the effect of the Autumn Harvest uprising. But the mechanical application of the Autumn Harvest policy led in some places to playing at insurrections and military putsches.

(4) *The Canton Commune opened the Soviet period, but its failure made it a rearguard action*

The Sixth Congress of the CCP supports the (statement) of the Sixth [*sic*, evidently a copyist's mistake for Ninth] ECCI meeting that the Canton Commune has world historical significance. The Canton Commune was a necessary, heroic attempt, a struggle to retain revolutionary gains, and to deepen the revolution and *to set up directly a soviet régime*. But objectively speaking, the Canton Commune became "a rearguard fight" in the stage of revolutionary failure.

The Sixth Congress holds that the Ninth ECCI meeting correctly pointed out the errors in the insurrection: inadequate work among the workers, peasants, and the reactionary armed units; incorrect attitude towards the masses in the yellow unions; inadequate preparatory work by the Party and the CY; weak political manœuvring of the masses (lack of large-scale political strikes, etc.). The Sixth Congress holds that these errors were one of the causes for the failure of the insurrection. But the Canton Commune has a great significance, and the Congress specially calls on the Party headquarters on all levels to make a careful study of the rich experiences (accumulated) in the heroic struggle of the Cantonese proletariat.

(5) *The Party's failure to change its policy in time after the Canton Commune and to put up an adequate fight against adventurism was due to over-estimation of the collapse of the revolution's enemies*

That the Canton Commune was, objectively speaking, "a rearguard fight" in the stage of revolutionary failure, was not taken into account by the leadership of the Party. Because the revolution had suffered a severe set-back, the direction of (Party) work should have been resolutely shifted from direct armed insurrection on a large scale to better day-by-day organization and mobilization of the masses. Attention should have been concentrated on overcoming adventurist tendencies, further strengthening the Party's leadership in the anti-imperialist movement, and further doing away with arbitrary dictatorialness [in method] regarding the working class and the masses.

The leadership did not then fully understand this, and obviously made inadequate efforts in this direction—under-estimating the power of the imperialists and the reactionaries, considerably over-emphasising the success of the peasant movement, and also under-appraising the degree of failure suffered by the revolution. The plans of the uprisings in Hunan and Hupei, etc., were erroneous in that they did not evaluate the situation in this light.

IV. THE PRESENT SITUATION IN THE REVOLUTIONARY MOVEMENT AND THE GENERAL LINE OF THE CCP

10. *The Situation after the Revolutionary Rising Tide* [Kao-ch'ao] *Has Passed*

(1) *The passing of the revolutionary rising tide*

The first wave of the movement of workers and peasants led for the most part by the CCP has now passed because the workers and peasants have suffered serious defeats, their revolutionary organizations have suffered severe blows (trade unions, peasant associations, CP headquarters), their best cadres have been slaughtered and their vanguard has suffered tremendous losses.

(2) *The absence of a revolutionary rising tide at the present stage and the uneven development of the workers' and peasants' revolution*

In the present situation, there is, generally speaking, *no revolutionary rising tide (involving) the masses on an extensive scale. The present situation is characterized by an uneven rate of development in the Chinese revolutionary movement.* The *peasants'* guerrilla warfare has unevenly advanced [lit., "has advanced by rising up here and falling back elsewhere"] and is still only in a scattered, decentralized condition. The *armies* of the warlords have begun to show signs of disintegration; at the same time, the urban *workers' movement* has suffered great reverses, and the fighting power of the *working class* has been weakened—because, compared with other revolutionary forces, it has received the heaviest blow from the gentry, the landlords, and the bourgeoisie.

(3) *The imperialists are following a policy of partition (of China)*

Because the Chinese revolution has failed, because the insurrection of the workers and peasants has been suppressed, and because the national bourgeoisie has betrayed the revolution of national liberation: (for these reasons) the power of the imperialists in China is *better consolidated and stronger* than in 1925–7. Japanese aggression in North China and the dispatch of (Japanese) troops to Tsinan *actually mark the beginning of the partition of China* (among the imperialists).

(4) *At present the imperialists are stronger than the Chinese revolution*

The objectives of the partition policy (of the powers) are: (1) to achieve colonial, economic exploitation by non-economic force, so as to completely destroy the revolution in China, and (2) to step up the struggle for markets. As the powers (thus) redouble their efforts to secure the China market, conflicts among the imperialist powers intensify.

(5) *There will be a war in the Pacific for the partition of China, but at present the conflict among the powers has not reached such an intensive degree*

There is, therefore, the danger of an imperialist war in the Pacific, and the coastal provinces of China will become the battleground. The major causes of this war will be the fight over the China market and demands for re-allocating (spheres of influence) to suit the new relationship between the imperialist powers. At the same time, although there are extremely great conflicts within the imperialist camp (such as that between Japan and the U.S.A.), *the imperialists are at present still much stronger than the Chinese revolution* and are forming again an alliance to oppose the revolutionary united front in China. *Whenever their political and economic rule is slightly endangered, they will jointly oppose the Chinese revolution.*

(6) *Although there is conflict between the Chinese gentry and the bourgeoisie, they still join forces in suppressing the revolution*

The bourgeoisie's turning to the reactionary camp enables the reactionary forces to consolidate and strengthen the forces of the imperialists, warlords, and landlords. Consequently, (they) are able to deal a severe blow to the working class.

Although there are many, many conflicts in the reactionary camp (between the bourgeoisie and the landlords, the bourgeoisie and the imperialists, and between the various groups and cliques within the landlord class, etc.), which lead to armed clashes and warlord imbroglios, yet the imperialists, gentry, landlords, bourgeoisie, and national bourgeoisie form a united front to oppress the Chinese toiling masses whenever their revolutionary struggle explodes.

II. *Why a Revolutionary Rising Tide is Inevitable*

(1) *The reactionary régime in China does not have the ability to destroy the revolution and a new revolutionary rising tide is inevitable*

None the less, there are many indications showing that a new, extensive revolutionary tide is inevitable.

There are several prime forces accelerating and reinforcing the advance of a new (revolutionary) rising tide:

(*a*) *none* of the *conflicts* underlying the revolution *can be resolved* [by the counter-revolution]; (*b*) the *imperialists* will never be willing to *abandon* lightly their *privileges* in China, such as concessions, leased territories, and tariff control; the reactionaries led by the bourgeoisie cannot achieve real centralization and unification; (*c*) there is *hardly any solution for the industrial and economic crisis*; it is difficult to improve even slightly the livelihood of the working class; and there are many other difficulties (inherent) in a colonial status (such as) the aggravation of the periodical agricultural crisis, leading to a steady rise of prices for raw materials and foodstuffs, and the daily growth of the labour reserve army, (all these) resulting in severe oppression of the industrial and working class; (*d*) the reformist devices of the bourgeoisie cannot solve the agrarian problem; there is no unused land from which to make concessions to the poor peasants, rich peasants, and tenants, because in China the small landlords constitute an absolute majority and refuse to accept even rent reductions; and (*e*) there are continuous conflicts within the ruling class and imbroglios among the warlords. In the future, these imbroglios are not only possible but inevitable—although on the surface the Nanking government has unified China.

(2) *The international situation can help the growth of the (revolutionary) rising tide*

(Another) force helping the growth of the revolutionary rising tide is the daily sharpening conflict among the imperialist powers. This will help to unleash the Chinese revolution. (The same is true for) the growth of the international proletarian movement and the development of the national revolutionary movement in the colonies adjacent to China (such as India).

(3) *There are signs of a new rising tide, but they should not be over-estimated*

The Sixth Congress holds that signs of a preliminary, weak new revolutionary rising tide are already noticeable. First of all, there is the symptomatic revival of economic *mass strikes*. The working masses are rapidly losing their illusions about the KMT and are spontaneously organizing themselves from the bottom up. All this shows the deepening of the workers' class consciousness. Furthermore, the *anti-imperialist movement* is also developing, awakening not only the working masses but also some of the revolutionary urban petty bourgeoisie to join (the revolution).

As regards the peasant struggle, the *bases in the Soviet régime* preserved until the present time (in the Southern provinces) and their few *revolutionary armies of workers and peasants* will become an ever more *important element in the new rising tide*.

The Sixth Congress also holds that the signs mentioned above should not be over-estimated, because even taken together they do not make up a true rising tide, the number of people (now) participating in the struggle is still insufficient, and at present the urban working class has not yet overcome its set-backs.

(4) *The prospect of a revolutionary rising tide in one or more provinces and a Soviet régime is possible*

The degree of consolidation of the reactionary régime in different regions is uneven; therefore, the revolution, in a general new rising tide, may succeed first in one or more provinces. At present, there is no revolutionary rising tide, and no such successes are possible; but such a prospect is possible. In this respect, the important role of urban leadership and the rising tide of the proletarian masses will show their decisive power, and will decide how to turn the slogan "all power to the council of workers', peasants', and soldiers' deputies" into a slogan of direct action.

12. *The Task of Winning Over the Masses*

(1) *In the new (revolutionary) rising tide, the KMT régime and the imperialists should be overthrown by armed insurrection*

The new rising tide of the future requires still more preparation for armed insurrections, and even actual insurrections as immediate practical tasks for the Party—this is the only way to accomplish the bourgeois-democratic revolution and the overthrow of the political régime of the imperialists, gentry, bourgeoisie, and the KMT.

(2) *At present, only the advocacy of armed insurrection on a national scale is necessary to prepare for a new revolutionary rising tide*

Now is the time to rally and consolidate the proletarian forces;

armed insurrection on a national scale remains for the time being a propaganda slogan. (We) should now make the masses realize, in leading them in everyday struggles, that if the KMT-warlord régime is not overthrown, the living conditions of the masses can never improve. Propaganda among the masses should also be carried on continuously.

(3) *To win over the masses is the present general line*

At present, the first revolutionary wave is over, due to repeated failures: *a new (revolutionary) wave has not yet arrived, and the forces of the reaction are still stronger than those of the workers and peasants. The general line of the Party is to win over the masses.* The Party should *use all its power to intensify the rallying and unifying of the proletarian masses and rally them around the main slogans* of the Party; it should engage in stupendous organizational work, in order to consolidate the revolutionary unions and peasant associations. (The Party) must do its very best to lead (the masses) in daily economic and political struggles in order to expand the mass organizations of workers and peasants. Finally, it is necessary to intensify the (work of) explaining to the proletariat the past experiences of the revolution.

(4) *The Party must intensify its leadership in everyday struggles*

The Party should exploit every conflict between workers and capitalists in the factories, between peasants and landlords in the villages, and between soldiers and officers in the military camps. However small these clashes may be, they should be exploited to agitate and penetrate deeper into these class conflicts in order to win the vast masses of workers and peasants to our side. The Party must exploit all the imperialists' brutal deeds in China and all slaughter and suppression of the masses by the reactionaries (naturally not calling for armed insurrection on every occasion), in order to widen the resistance of the masses, and to be in the position of sole leader of the revolutionary movement when the (revolutionary) rising tide begins.

(5) *To prepare for armed insurrection, (we) must win over the masses*

The task of winning over the masses is the task of preparing for armed insurrection—*because the fulfilment of this task is a prerequisite for a new revolutionary rising tide and for the possibility of turning the propaganda slogan of armed insurrection into that of direct practical action.*

13. *The Danger of Opportunism and Putschism*

(1) *The danger of the Party's alienation from the masses lies in putschism and dictatorialness* [min-ling chu-i]

Winning over the masses depends on the realization, by the Party, of a policy based on correct calculation; (it depends on) the *liquidation of ultra-leftist errors and sentiments* (putschism, military adventurism, individual terrorism) within the Party and of the KMT-style erroneous tendency to issue [arbitrary] orders to the masses.

The major dangers are putschism and dictatorialness; they both alienate the Party from the masses.

(2) *Putschism means military adventurism by a few, ignoring the masses and the strength of the enemy*

Putschism, in theory, means a few individuals wishing to attack an obviously far superior enemy by continual military actions, blind and impetuous measures which forsake and ignore the masses. Of course, it sometimes is also due to an over-estimate of the rate and degree of disintegration in the counter-revolutionary camp, and to neglecting all the prerequisites of insurrection, which is light-heartedly undertaken without serious preparations. A putsch in practical action is an insurrection by a few "Party men" without the necessary day-by-day economic and political preparation, a brutal struggle that relies entirely on military strength, in the nature of a military adventure. Naturally, such a putsch usually forces the masses into military insurrection, often resulting in unorganized, sporadic acts of terrorism. This will lower the Party's prestige among the masses and end in the unrequited loss of the vanguard units of the workers and of Communism.

(3) *Putschism is an unproletarian concept*

Putschism represents class-alienated elements, rural and urban paupers (unemployed, bankrupt petty bourgeoisie, some of the revolutionary intelligentsia), and mercenary soldiers who recently joined the revolution; it is an expression of their ideology and (way of) action. It thus shows the influence of the petty bourgeoisie on the working class, and contrasts with the characteristics of discipline and organization among the proletariat.

(4) *The Party should induce the paupers and semi-proletariat to join the revolution under the leadership of the proletariat*

At the same time, the Communist Party must not look down on the paupers; they are a great and powerful force in the revolution. The task of the Party is to carry on maximum organizational work among these pauper masses and raise their political consciousness, especially regarding the urban and rural semi-proletarian class. The Party must do its utmost to absorb these pauper elements into the general revolutionary movement under the leadership of the industrial proletariat. But the Party must also constantly increase its efforts to oppose the influence of petty-bourgeois ideology on the working class and the Communist Party.

(5) *The so-called socialism of the peasant petty bourgeoisie must also be opposed*

Beside putschism, there are other dangerous tendencies. Elements in some Party units, in dealing with some problems, hold views that make the Party incline towards the bankrupt peasants, urban paupers, and the lumpenproletariat, and alienate it from its proletarian base. For example, there are erroneous notions regarding the relationship between the working class and the peasantry, which falsely conceive of socialism as equalization of property (in villages, equal distribution of land; in the cities, of goods). Also a tendency to burn down cities has appeared in some peasant uprisings, and leadership by the urban proletariat (of the urban and rural petty bourgeoisie) has been held in low esteem. These tendencies in the Party should be firmly opposed.

(6) *"Dictatorialness" alienates the masses from the Party*

Furthermore, working merely through dictatorialness is also a dangerous tendency, alienating the Party from the masses. The attitude of the Party towards the working class would become the gentry-like KMT method of dealing with the masses. Dictatorialness means the direction and compulsion of the masses by dictatorialness without educating or convincing them. Formerly, under opportunism, (the Party), on behalf of the KMT, ordered the masses *not to act*. Now, under putschism, the masses are *ordered never to remain inactive* in order to oppose the KMT.

(7) *Dictatorialness and the task of winning over the masses cannot co-exist*

Even in the workers' movement such methods have been used, with orders being issued everywhere. Appointments by order of union leaders or leading organs have generally been a top-to-bottom working method. Consequently, cadres were not raised from the masses. Even in Party membership drives and in carrying on the labour movement, a method of approaching a few workers' leaders in order to influence *their masses* was adopted. As a result, genuine mass work was confronted with tremendous obstacles.

A similar tendency exists in Party organizational matters, resulting in the unusual shrinkage of intra-Party democracy (not entirely due to secrecy), the bureaucratization of the Party organization and the mere issuing of orders to the membership and to the masses. If such dictatorialness is not resolutely and utterly liquidated, the Party cannot become a fighting party capable of leading the masses. Dictatorialness and the winning over of the masses cannot co-exist.

(8) *A correct policy towards the petty bourgeoisie will save the Party from being endangered again by opportunism*

Past experiences should enable the Party to conquer ultra-leftist sentiments and KMT-style dictatorialness. At present an incorrect tendency regarding the question of the petty bourgeoisie may still arise.

Among the tasks of the Party, the urban petty bourgeoisie is to be induced to participate in the anti-imperialist, anti-warlord movement. Among the tasks of the Party, the peasant masses who own private property (owner-peasants) should also be induced to join the struggle for the confiscation of the landlords' land and against taxation by warlords. (But) misunderstandings of this policy may lead to an even more undesirable tendency; when the movement against rich peasants is not emphasized, *too great concessions* to the rich peasants in the villages, or interference with the revolutionary movement of the workers and urban paupers for the sake of compromise with shopkeepers and the petty bourgeoisie, will result in subjecting this movement to the leadership of the petty bourgeoisie and actual loss of the [revolutionary] leadership (by the Party) in the name of preserving the united front.

(9) *Alliance (is necessary) with the petty bourgeoisie and the rich peasants against all reactionary forces: but it is also necessary to lead the labouring people against all exploiters*

When the interests of the workers and shop employees clash sharply with those of urban shopkeepers and petty bourgeoisie, or when poor and middle peasants clash with rich peasants in the villages, the Communist Party should always stand for the labourers against the exploiting class.

(10) *The erroneous tendency to neglect the anti-imperialist movement*

The Chinese revolution being a semi-colonial revolution, the anti-imperialist struggle has a major function (in it). It is a serious mistake to neglect the anti-imperialist *movement* which is developing by not assuming its leadership. Furthermore, class relations in the new stage of the Chinese revolution (Soviet stage) are entirely different from what they were in the May Thirtieth period [1925]. The deeper penetration of the revolution calls for greater attention to the *anti-imperialist and the anti-militarist struggle* of the future, which will result in direct mass action a dozen times more drastic (than the present). We must not neglect these future prospects. It is a serious error to neglect the anti-imperialist movement and the anti-imperialist struggle of the vast lower strata while wanting to strengthen the opposition to the reactionary classes inside the country.

(11) *It is also a seriously erroneous tendency to neglect the role of the peasant revolution*

Furthermore, in the process of intense class differentiation (attendant upon) the class struggle, and in the process of a thoroughgoing agrarian revolution, the most reliable ally of the proletariat in the general revolutionary front of China is no other than the peasantry. Therefore, neglect of the leadership of the peasantry by the proletariat and of the revolutionary role of the peasantry, as well as "tailism" [*Wei-pa chu-i*] which follows peasant petty-bourgeois ideas, are all very dangerous tendencies.

The above-mentioned tendencies—such as putschism, dictatorialness, the doctrine of equalization of property, conciliationism, neglect of anti-imperialism, and of the revolutionary role of the peasantry —are all unbolshevik paths.

(12) *Both anti-putschism and anti-dictatorialness are a continuation of anti-opportunism*

The bolshevization of the CCP was assured by opposition to the opportunist leadership and to opportunist tactics. Now (we) must continue the anti-opportunist struggle, *especially against ultra-leftist defections*. These so-called "leftist" dangerous tendencies are only another aspect of the opportunist petty-bourgeois ideology which has affected the working class and the Communist Party.

V. THE TASKS OF THE PARTY

14. *The Problem of Work inside the Party*

At present the major tasks of the Party, after its fighting strength has been weakened by losses due to defections, are to *strengthen its fighting power* and to proletarianize itself:

(*a*) Revive destroyed Party cells and Party headquarters on all levels. *Special attention should be paid to the establishment and development of Party cells in big industrial establishments and factories*, for they are the major places of assembly for the working-class masses.

(*b*) Actively recruit Party members among workers, continue to promote worker-comrades and "actives" to the leading organs of the Party, and make sure the leading organs possess the characteristics of the working class. Attention, of course, should also be paid to the correction of any bias and false tendencies in these matters.

(*c*) Realize true *democratic centralism*; maximum democracy within the Party should be guaranteed within the limits of secrecy; decide important issues through collective discussion and collective decisions; (but) at the same time oppose the tendency towards extreme democracy, because it can destroy Party discipline, encourage an attitude of irresponsibility, and damage confidence in the Party leadership.

(*d*) Resolve all intra-Party disputes and liquidate tendencies towards regionalism and "clique-ism", because these tendencies damage Party unity and lower its fighting power. Abolish the so-called *"punishment"* system; a comrade who commits mistakes in work should be corrected and re-trained through work, unless he insists on upholding his mistakes with a system or a line. If a comrade can correct himself after committing an error, he should be given work to demonstrate his having reformed.

(*e*) Intensify the training of Party members and of the masses, raise their political level, systematically propagate Marxism-Leninism, and study the lessons of past stages of the Chinese revolution.

(*f*) Intensify propaganda for correct concepts of armed insurrection, and for the general task of setting up the régime of councils of workers', peasants', and soldiers' deputies (Soviets).

15. *The Relations between the Party and the Working Class and the Question of the Labour Movement*

(*a*) The major task of the Party is to *win over the majority of the working class*, to secure their active support for the vanguard of the proletariat, the Communist Party, and to induce them to believe in the Communist Party and consciously accept its leadership. Full attention should be paid to the labour movement, especially to industrial workers. Only thus can the leadership of the working class over the peasantry be strengthened.

(*b*) In order to accomplish this task, some old false notions concerning the relationship between Party and (working) class should be *corrected immediately*. Such false notions seem to hold that the Party is *a special force standing ahead of the* (working) *class*, and is in a position to help and *command that class*; what is not realized is that the Party is only *the most conscious and the most advanced element of the working class itself*.

(*c*) Firmly oppose *compulsion and orders* imposed on our own class, (such as) the method of compulsory strikes and compulsory armed uprisings. The Congress holds that such methods are contrary to the interest of the proletariat and of the Communist Party, and *will ruin the Chinese revolution*.

(*d*) The utmost effort should be made to revive revolutionary unions. Party members should join unions that have a real mass following in order to achieve the goal of winning over the working masses, even if these unions are reactionary.

(*e*) Work systematically with every effort in various organizations in order to have the working masses discard their illusions about the KMT. Give the masses a detailed explanation of the lessons of the Chinese revolution and the policies and tasks of the CCP.

(*f*) All these are necessary for winning over the masses and should be carried out in the course of the struggle. The leadership of the masses in their daily economic struggles should be greatly strengthened.

16. *The Major Tasks of the Party in the Peasant Movement*

(*a*) The central slogan of the peasant movement is *the confiscation of the landlords' land for disposition by the councils of peasants' deputies (Soviets)*.

(*b*) The tactical line is (as follows): *the arch-enemy being the gentry landlords, the basic strength of the proletariat in the villages lies in the poor peasants and the middle peasants. They are solid allies. It is wrong to step up the struggle against the rich peasants intensely, because that would confuse the major conflict between the peasants and the landlord class. This, however, does not mean that the class struggle against the rich peasants and the semi-landlords is to be abandoned.*

(*c*) *Support the guerrilla warfare of the peasants and further its penetration (among the masses) and consolidation.* Lead the peasants into organized struggle and into the struggle for the conscious establishment of *Soviet régimes and the carrying out of the agrarian revolution. Co-ordinate the peasant movement in rural areas with the struggle of the working class in the cities.*

(*d*) It is not only possible but necessary *to organize revolutionary armies of workers and peasants* in the present guerrilla areas. Because of singular political circumstances, this task is now the *central issue* in the peasant movement, *deserving special attention by the Party. The success with which this task is carried out may give an impetus to the growth of a new revolutionary rising tide—(it may be) one of the major sources of power determining the new revolutionary rising tide.*

(*e*) Pay more attention to the mass organizations of the peasants (such as peasant associations, peasant committees, and secret societies of peasants). Consolidate the guiding role of the proletariat in the peasant organizations.

(*f*) Support and give leadership to the peasant masses' partial demands in refusing to pay taxes, rent, and debts, and in demanding rent reduction, etc., so as to organize the vast peasant masses.

17. *The Party's Task in the Soviet Areas*

In the past, the error of neglecting the development and expansion of revolutionary areas was committed in many of the Soviet areas. There was also an erroneous tendency to supplant the Soviet by the Party.

Henceforth our tasks are:

(*a*) *To expand the Soviet bases*, and to capture and consolidate new areas which will serve as bases for further expansion.

(*b*) *To develop*, with maximum effort, *a regular revolutionary army of workers and peasants*—the Red Army.

(*c*) *To carry out fully the Party's agrarian programme.*

(*d*) To set up Soviet régimes and to induce the broad masses to participate in their administration.

(*e*) To liquidate resolutely counter-revolutionary plots and to wipe out completely the political and economic power of the ruling class.

(*f*) To protect commodity transactions in business and to overcome any tendency towards equalization of property (i.e. the tendency to split up for equal distribution the property of the petty bourgeoisie.

small merchants, artisans, etc.). Such a procedure will accentuate economic disruption and upset the Soviet régime. But (we) should realize that sabotage by shopkeepers and the petty bourgeoisie is possible; and proper preventive measures should be taken. There must be a correct economic policy.

(g) To guarantee, to the highest possible degree, co-ordination with neighbouring cities and the workers' movement.

(h) When the Soviet régime can be extended to the urban centres, the livelihood of the working class must be thoroughly improved. Every means must be used to induce the working masses to participate actively in the Soviets and to realize the leadership of the proletariat in the Soviets.

18. *The Anti-imperialist and the Anti-warlord Struggles*

(a) Fight actively for the leadership of the anti-imperialist and anti-militarist struggles. Induce the vast working masses and the petty-bourgeois masses to participate (in these struggles). Expose the guilt of the national bourgeoisie which supports the imperialists. Co-ordinate the struggle against imperialism with that against the warlords and the KMT government. Actively lead the masses of soldiers and poor petty bourgeoisie to fight a harsh struggle against the warlords.

(b) In (the course of) the anti-imperialist movement, fight openly or secretly for the existence of the revolutionary unions. Boldly demand freedom for the mass movement, and show initiative in translating this freedom into action.

(c) Utilize the slogans against the imperialists. Those against the oppression of warlords, and the slogans for maximum tax and surtax reductions. By fighting against usury (through the establishment of credit, producers' and consumers' co-operatives), alienate the vast majority of people who do not exploit others—such as the labouring petty bourgeoisie, small business men, handicraftsmen, part of the petty-bourgeois intelligentsia, the workers, and the lumpenproletariat —from the KMT and the national bourgeoisie.

(d) Support the economic demands of shop employees, artisans, apprentices, and coolies. Organize the poor petty bourgeoisie of the cities, propagandize them, and co-ordinate their organizations with the proletariat. Make them understand that it is necessary, after the victory of the revolution, that society should organize them for collective production.

19. *On the Question of (Our) Relationship with Other Parties*

(1) *The various groups of the KMT are all reactionary*

(*a*) The Sixth Congress of the CCP agrees completely with the resolution of the CC's November Conference [1927] on KMT groups and with that of the Ninth ECCI Meeting, to the effect that all KMT groups are reactionary, that they represent various sections and cliques of compradores, landlords, gentry, national bourgeoisie, and a sector of the petty bourgeoisie allied with the ruling class. Wang Ching-wei's left group, Chang Fa-k'uei, Ch'en Kung-po, and others too, are counter-revolutionary; during the period of the Nanchang insurrection and the Canton commune, this group became totally fascist. Their superficial, fancy, leftish talk was only a front to camouflage their surrender to the gentry bourgeoisie and (their) policy of murdering and oppressing the workers and peasants.

(2) *The general objective of our Party is to prepare for the overthrow of the various groups of the KMT*

(*b*) The major task of (our) Party *vis-à-vis* the KMT is to prepare for the *overthrow* of its régime. At the present time, before the arrival of the revolutionary rising tide, (the task of the Party is) *to win the masses* and to rally them around the CCP. At the same time, every possible attack should be made continuously on the counter-revolutionary record of crime of various KMT groups and every possible blow should be dealt to the régime of the gentry, the landlord, and the bourgeois cliques, taking advantage of every opportunity to destroy the enemy's power. These are the methods (to be used) at the present stage in preparation for the overthrow of the KMT.

(3) *Oppose parties like the Third Party which dull the class consciousness of the workers and peasants*

(*c*) The Congress also supports the Ninth ECCI Meeting's evaluation of the so-called "Third Party" of Teng Yen-ta and T'an P'ing-shan. [T'an had left the CCP in November 1927.] During the present conditions of polarization of class forces and intensification of the class struggle, a "political party" like that, lacking a mass basis, is bound to become a counter-revolutionary tool of the gentry, land-lords, and bourgeoisie, *spreading dope among the masses to dull (their) class consciousness* by such demands as that for a *"revival of the mass movement and the worker-peasant policy by the KMT"*. They actually endeavour to weaken the struggle of the workers and peasants against the KMT.

Therefore, the task of the CCP *vis-à-vis* the so-called "Workers' and Peasants' Party", the "Third Party", etc., is to criticize their vacillations, hesitations, and compromises in the anti-imperialist and mass movements, and to scold them as spies of the ruling class.

20. *The Military Question and the Soldiers' Movement*

The high significance of military power in the Chinese revolution, the great necessity of preparing for military techniques in armed insurrection, and the coming of a new revolutionary rising tide oblige the CCP to pay special attention to the military question and to the soldiers' movement.

The tasks of the Party are (as follows):

(*a*) To extend the movement against warlord wars; to break up the armies of the warlords; to bend all efforts towards winning their soldiers for the revolutionary camp; to raise such slogans as "soldiers should get land or work", "improve the livelihood and treatment of the soldiers"; and to stir up mass struggles of the soldiers.

(*b*) To establish revolutionary armies of workers and peasants in the Soviet areas; to expand the regular army of the revolution; and to consolidate the Party's leadership of the army.

(*c*) To intensify the military training of workers and Party members as much as possible and to establish, with utmost effort, secret military units for the workers' self-defence (pickets, etc.).

(*d*) To train military personnel in the Party, and to raise the most reliable officers from workers and Party members.

(*e*) To intensify (Party) work among workers (in establishments) connected with military affairs (such as munition factories, etc.), and among transport and communications workers. Systematically coordinate the above work with that in the armies.

(*f*) To begin systematic work of sabotage among the imperialists' naval and land forces stationed in China. Special attention should be paid to the soldiers' movement among the Indian and Indo-Chinese soldiers.

21. *The Problem of Liaison between the CCP and the Communist Parties of Other Countries*

In order to tighten liaison with brother parties in other countries, the Sixth Congress holds that it is necessary:

(*a*) To exchange regular reports on the work of each party and the development of the revolutionary movement.

(*b*) To have responsible delegations sent by the CC to the major brother parties in other countries so as to settle details regarding closer co-ordination and practical questions (connected with) the support of the Chinese revolution by other branches of the CI.

(*c*) To ask the CCP's delegation to the Sixth CI Congress to bring up for serious discussion the question of inadequate support to, and participation in, the Chinese revolutionary movement by the brother parties of other countries.

(*d*) To tighten liaison with the Japanese Communist Party (so as) to oppose, in unison, Japan's military intervention in China, to sabotage Japanese army units stationed in China, to stir up Japanese soldiers to join the revolution, and to decide jointly on practical methods for carrying on the labour movement in the Japanese enterprises in China (such as the South Manchuria Railway [Company]).

(*e*) To request the Communist parties of England, France, and the U.S.A. to step up (their) anti-militarist activities, to send an adequate number of agents to China for sabotage work among the (foreign) troops stationed there, to intensify propaganda for support of the Chinese revolution in the various countries, and to expose the aggressive plots of their respective imperialist government.

(*f*) Furthermore, a practical method of co-ordination should be worked out, with the Communist Parties of each country concerned, in regard to the relationships between the labour movement of Indo-China and the Indo-Chinese Communist Party, between the Chinese workers' movement in the Dutch East Indies (the Malay archipelago) and the Indonesian Communist Party (Communist Party of Java), and between the Mongolian question and the Revolutionary Party of Mongolia.

(*g*) To tighten (our) liaison, through the WFTU and the world relief organization [International Workers' Aid], with the unions and labour masses of the world, so as to enable them to give stronger support to the Chinese revolution and the mass organizations, and especially to spread propaganda against the unprecedented white terror in China.

22. The Sixth Congress of the CCP entirely accepts the resolution of the Ninth ECCI Meeting on the China question, which also is the basis of this resolution. These two resolutions are to be regarded simultaneously as the principles by which all policy is to be guided during this period.

12. RESOLUTION OF THE SIXTH NATIONAL CONGRESS [OF THE CCP] ON THE PEASANT MOVEMENT (September 1928)

I. THE DEVELOPMENT OF THE PEASANT MOVEMENT AT PRESENT

(1) *The increasing sufferings of the peasant masses.* In the villages the *living conditions of the peasant masses are deteriorating daily.* [Emphasis as in original Chinese text.] On the one hand, there is ceaseless warfare among the warlords and economic depression and stagnation in the country. On the other hand, because of the temporary victory of the counter-revolution of the bourgeoisie, landlords and gentry, the direct oppression and exploitation of peasants in the villages has been further aggravated. Thus, *the class contradictions in the village have been drastically intensified,* while the peasant movement *advances to wider and higher demands and more intensive fighting.*

(2) *The intensification and unbalanced development of the peasant movement.* In the last few months, peasant riots and guerrilla fighting in many provinces have proved the growing intensification of the peasant movement. The setting up of local Soviet administrations, the confiscation and redistribution of the land of the landlords, and the elimination of gentry rule in the villages have been *expanded in scope and area,* to include the northern part of China and Manchuria. One especially distinguishing feature of the peasant movement at present is *its local and unbalanced nature.* On the one hand, this is due to objective causes such as the vastness of the economic circumstances, etc. On the other hand, it is due to the *looseness and disorganization* of the peasant masses and the *lack of centralized leading organs* of the CCP within the peasant movement.

(3) *Differences in demands made in various localities in the peasant struggles.* In the recent struggles, there are obvious differences in the demands being made by the peasant masses in various parts of the country. In Southern and Central China, landless peasants constitute the majority of the rural population, and the major aspect of the struggle centres on opposing landlords, struggling for possession of land, and fighting for political power. In Northern China (Honan, Shantung, Chihli, Manchuria, etc.) the majority of the peasants are small landowners. *The direction of their struggle generally centres on the opposition to warlords, bureaucrats, and gentry, exploitation through exorbitant taxes, and labour conscription,* and aims at the overthrow of the political power of the warlords. This is another form of the struggle to destroy feudal land relations. Of course, the struggle of tenants against landlords for the

possession of land also exists in the North, but at present, on the whole, it is mainly a fight of peasant owners to retain their land ownership.

II. THE CLASS DIFFERENTIATION IN THE VILLAGES AND THE TACTICAL LINE OF THE CCP

(1) *The more advanced the peasants' struggle, the more glaring the class contradictions.* The experience of the peasant movement in the past teaches that in the *struggle against warlords, landlords, gentry, and other forms of feudalistic exploitation,* it may be possible for the whole peasantry to *form a united front politically.* However, when the movement advances and develops, *a class conflict arises extremely rapidly between the rural proletariat and rural bourgeoisie,* between poor and rich peasants, especially *at the time of land redistribution* after the victory of the revolt.

(2) *The characteristics of Chinese rich peasants and [our] tactics concerning them.* In the course of the peasant movement, the attitude of the rich peasants often has been *defeatist, neutral, or hostile,* and they finally have *joined the anti-revolutionary camp.* This is due to the characteristic of the Chinese rich peasants *who employ [both] capitalist and pre-capitalist, semi-feudal modes of exploitation.* They usually engage in exploiting hired labourers in agricultural, as well as in industrial and commercial, enterprises; or at the same time rent out a part of their land to exploit the tenants in the usual cruel manner, or else exploit the poor peasants through usury. The Party must anticipate that the peasants will *inevitably continue to differentiate into sub-classes* and that the *rich peasants will inevitably join the anti-revolutionary camp. Therefore (the Party) should prepare, at the beginning of the peasant movement, for the struggle at the next stage.*

In places where the rich peasants have already become reactionary forces, the struggle against rich peasants should be carried on simultaneously with the struggle against warlords, landlords, and gentry.

As long as the rich peasants have not yet lost their revolutionary potentialities, as long as they struggle against the oppression of warlords and bureaucrats, the *CCP should endeavour to absorb rich peasants into the struggle against warlords, landlords, and gentry.* Where the rich peasants waver between revolution and counter-revolution, the Party, so far as the struggle of poor peasants and hired farm hands is not handicapped, should not intensify the struggle against the rich peasants, thus driving them all the more quickly into the counter-revolutionary camp and making them aggressive enemies of the revolution. The task of our Party at the present stage is to neutralize this type of rich peasant in order to reduce the strength of the enemy; but the struggle of the poor peasants and hired farm hands should be carried on simultaneously, *and no concession should be made to the rich peasants for the sake of the united front.*

(3) *The alliance with the middle peasants is the main condition guaranteeing the success of the agrarian revolution.* The *main forces* of the agrarian revolution are the poor peasants and rural proletariat struggling under the leadership of the working class, and the *alliance with middle peasants is the chief factor guaranteeing the success of the revolution.* The CCP platform of confiscating the land of all landlords for distribution among landless peasants or peasants with small landholdings *will win the support of the numerous middle peasants,* because the middle peasants are themselves a part of the masses oppressed by the landlords and other feudal exploiters.

(4) *The tactical line of the CP at the present stage of the revolution.* At the present stage of the revolution, the major tactic of the CP should be to create a united front which shall *embrace the overwhelming majority of the peasant masses* from hired farm hands to middle peasants who *are exploited by the feudal remnants.* Under all circumstances, special attention should be paid to the *work among poor peasants, preventing the rich peasants from seizing the leadership in peasant organizations,* and *consolidating the ideological and organizational leadership of poor peasants and hired hands.*

III. THE PROBLEM OF EQUAL DISTRIBUTION OF LAND

(1) [*The CCP*] *should support the slogan of equal distribution of land but should also criticize it.* In the areas where there are many unemployed and poor peasants, a movement for "equal distribution of land" is bound to arise. If this slogan is *supported by the majority of the peasant masses, the CP should support it.* For it is a slogan that leads to the *complete liquidation* of all feudal remnants and gives a direct blow to the system of private property.

At the same time, however, this slogan is an *illusion of petty-bourgeois socialism.* The Party must criticize it in order to make the peasants understand fully that under the present capitalist system *real equality is absolutely impossible.* Only after the *victory of the proletarian revolution will a truly socialistic reconstruction be feasible.*

(2) "*Equal distribution of land*" *should not be applied forcibly in the areas where middle peasants constitute a majority.* In areas where middle peasants and small landowners constitute the majority of the rural population, "*equal distribution of land*" *will decidedly contravene the interests of the numerous middle peasants and it is emphasized that it should not be enforced.*

IV. THE RURAL PROLETARIAT

(1) *The rural proletariat must have their own organization and platform.* The proletariat and semi-proletarian classes are the foundation of the Party in the village. *To organize the village proletariat* (hired farm hands), to map out a clear platform and to *lead them in their class struggle* will be the *urgent tasks* of the CCP in the villages. The peasant movement in the southern provinces is already led by the poor peasants. In the peasant organization in these areas, *cells* of hired farm hands should be *organized* so that the *leadership of hired farm hands* in the peasant organizations can be *strengthened.* In the areas where a rich-peasant-economy and landlord-economy already exist, it is better to set up an *independent organization* of the rural proletariat (the union of hired farm hands). (The union) should also join the peasant associations and establish liaison with the *hsien* workers' union. If no independent organizations (for the hired farm hands) are set up, there should at least be *strong cells of hired farm hands* within the peasant organizations of mixed elements. Workers in the handicraft industries may join the hired farm hands' union. *Work should also be strengthened among the immigrants* to Manchuria and Inner Mongolia because they are all landless peasants from various provinces migrating there as farm workers.

V. THE FUNCTIONS OF WOMEN IN THE PEASANT MOVEMENT

In the struggle of the peasant movement towards victory, it is very important to absorb peasant women into the struggle. They participate directly in the economy of the village, constitute an important element among the hired farm hands, and play a very important role in the life of the peasants. Therefore it is imperative that they join the movement. The experiences of the peasant movement in many areas in the past show that peasant women are the bravest participants among the struggling peasants. Scorning to absorb the peasant women into the movement will definitely result in the failure of the agrarian revolution. The main task of the Party is to recognize peasant women as extremely active participants in the revolution and to absorb as many as we can into all the revolutionary organizations of the peasants, especially the peasant associations and Soviets.

VI. THE FUNCTIONS OF YOUTH IN THE PEASANT MOVEMENT

During the past periods of struggle, the peasant youth has played a tremendous role in the agrarian revolution. In the local Soviets, in peasant guerrilla forces and other peasant movements, there are always a great many young peasants participating. From now on their role should be strengthened. In the various forms of peasant struggle, the special welfare of the young peasants should be considered and helped to be achieved. Young peasants should be absorbed into active participation in the peasant associations and Soviets. The peasant associations should, through their Peasant Youth Department, assist the work and development of the Youth Vanguard and Youth Labour Corps. In the Soviet areas (the Party) should do its utmost in assisting the village youth to achieve their own platform.

VII. PUBLICIZE THE LAND POLICY (OF THE PARTY) AND LOCAL DEMANDS

The task of the CCP in the near future is to bring the vast peasant masses under its influence. The Party should *popularize* its *land policy and co-ordinate it with the special conditions of various localities*. In the areas where the movement is weak or suffering a temporary set-back, the Party should support the *various local demands of the peasants* (such as rent and interest rate reductions, resisting taxes, etc.) and lead these movements to higher stages.

VIII. PEASANT ASSOCIATIONS AND OTHER PEASANT ORGANIZATIONS

(1) *The (CCP) should do its best to enlarge and consolidate the organization of peasant associations*. In the last few months, in the peasant movement in Southern and Central China, the organization and leadership of peasant associations have shown signs of decomposing. This is because the mode of peasant struggle has shifted to a more radical guerrilla warfare, thus lacking a close liaison with the broad masses. Peasant associations in the provinces of Central and Southern China have been revolutionary organizations with a long history, leaving a deep impression among the peasant masses. The CCP should *work for the expansion and consolidation of the peasant associations, rally the hundreds of thousands of peasants, and lead their struggle to prepare for the coming of a new revolutionary rising tide* [Kao-ch'ao]. The peasant associations should *retain their characteristics as broad organizations of the peasants* and use the slogan of agrarian revolution to mobilize the peasant masses. In the villages ruled by reactionary forces, the peasant associations should take the form of *illegal organizations*, leading the peasants in various forms of struggles—ranging from resistance to rent and tax collection, or the killing of gentry and landlords, to the preparation for armed revolt. The organization of the peasant associations should be as democratic as possible. The practice of appointment of the executive

members of the peasant associations by the Party should be corrected, making the peasant associations true organizations of the masses.

(2) *The peasant associations and the Soviets.* Since the peasant associations serve as executive organs leading the masses in revolt, they naturally should become the core of the new régime of "peasant deputies' committees" (Soviets) after the victory of the revolt. After the establishment of the Soviet régime, all political and economic power in the villages should be *concentrated in the hands of the Soviets*.

(3) *Tactics concerning the Red Spear Society, the Big Sword Society, etc.* In many places, the Red Spear Society, the Big Sword Society, etc., are very powerful among the peasant masses. Their leadership is usually in the hands of the gentry, landlords, and rich peasants. But these organizations do possess the *characteristics of being close to the masses and against the warlords*, thus performing, objectively, revolutionary functions. Our Party must continue to strengthen its work among the lower strata of the masses in order to *seize the leadership* in these organizations. Also it must propagate the major slogans of our Party among the poor and middle peasants in these organizations in order to make the Party the nuclear force in these organizations and gradually change their nature.

(4) *Organizing peasant associations and other organizations.* In addition, it is necessary to further the organization of peasant associations. If, in some places, the peasant associations are not supported by the masses, then other names or temporary organizations can be used. Or if it better suits local conditions, peasant organizations already in existence should be utilized (such as the Anti-Warlord League, Tax Resisting League, etc.).

IX. GUERRILLA WARFARE

(1) *The Party must actively lead the guerrilla warfare, which will be the chief instrument of struggle.* In places where the class struggle has reached an intensive stage, every minor struggle for livelihood leads to armed conflict. Thus guerrilla warfare has become the *chief instrument of struggle* in these places. Therefore the CP must actively and resolutely lead these struggles, giving them better *organization* and *closer liaison with the masses as a whole*.

(2) *The major tasks of guerrilla warfare and the realization of the slogans of the agrarian struggle, etc.* The major tasks of guerrilla warfare are: first, the immediate realization of the slogans of the agrarian struggle (such as the confiscation of the land of the landlords for distribution among the peasants, killing of oppressive gentry and landlords, setting

up of peasant delegates', committees and village Soviets, etc.) in order to mobilize more peasant masses to join the fighting front of the revolutionary struggle; second, the *setting up of the Red Army.* The brave young fighters, particularly those of proletarian and of semi-proletarian background, should be gradually absorbed, during the course of guerrilla fighting, into the guerrilla units in order to expand them gradually into a worker-peasant revolutionary Red Army; third, *weakening the strength of the reactionary elements* (through such methods as the confiscation of the firearms of the village guards, of police forces, etc.).

(3) *The weaknesses of guerrilla warfare: looseness, lack of close liaison with the masses, destruction of cities and villages, wanton killing and destruction.* In the course of guerrilla warfare in the past many weaknesses and undesirable tendencies were discovered. These weaknesses and tendencies will hamper or even destroy the effectiveness of guerrilla warfare, and therefore must be corrected. First, the conduct of guerrilla warfare separated from the masses has the effect of making them misunderstand the meaning of guerrilla warfare, or even respond to the propaganda of the landlords that guerrilla warfare is banditry. Hence, from now on, guerrilla warfare must *begin with the spontaneous demand of the masses, and must be carried on simultaneously with propaganda and agitation work.* Second, the tendency to destroy cities and kill, burn, and rob purposelessly. This tendency is only a reflection of a lumpenproletariat and peasant mentality which *may hamper the development of the Party among the peasant masses or even among the proletariat.* Therefore, every effort should be made to erase this erroneous concept within the Party. Of course, our Party should actively lead the peasant masses in their struggle to liquidate the landlords and gentry and to weaken the anti-revolutionary forces. What is opposed by the Party, however, is purposeless killing and burning which are irrelevant to our revolutionary mission. "Burning and killing for their own sake" and not for the real benefit of the revolution is objectionable. Third, looseness and lack of organization. From now on, (we) must direct the peasant associations in a planned, organized, and centralized manner.

(4) *When guerrilla warfare develops into local revolts, the Party must take into consideration the objective conditions, and the subjective strength, and lead with suitable tactics.* The resolution of the Ninth Plenary Session of the ECCI states that "the spontaneous guerrilla warfare of the peasants in various provinces and districts . . . can be a starting-point in the nationally victorious mass revolt only on the condition that it is

carried on in alliance with a new revolutionary tide among the proletariat in the cities". Past experience has proved this to be an extremely valid statement. In the increasingly intensified class struggle at present, the *setting up of a Soviet régime in one* hsien *or several* hsien *is possible*. It is not necessary that guerrilla warfare should turn into local revolts. Only when, during the process of struggle, the vast peasant masses are mobilized, when there arises a genuine demand on the part of the masses for a political régime of their own, and when the reactionary forces in the area are actually tottering, can guerrilla warfare develop into local revolts. Therefore when the guerrilla forces have brought a large area under their control, have secured the participation of a large number of people, and the conditions are ripe for producing a *hsien* or municipal local revolt, the Party must consider carefully *its objective conditions and subjective strength, and proceed with the revolt well prepared, well organized, well planned, employing suitable tactics and under the leadership and with the co-operation of the workers of the* hsien *or municipality*. After the success of the revolt, the slogan of the mass struggle should be put into effect, and all the reactionary forces should be liquidated in order that still greater numbers of peasants and workers may be mobilized and the policies of the Soviet régime be realized. Particular attention should be paid to the extension of the revolt to the adjacent areas.

(5) *The Party should lead the spontaneous revolts of the peasants*. At present, when the suffering of the peasant masses is increasing daily, spontaneous revolts easily occur. The Party must give genuine leadership to spontaneous revolts. It should particularly intensify its work among handicraft workers and shop employees in the *hsien* cities or towns, to enable them to *understand the significance of the peasant revolt and help to lead such spontaneous revolts until* the establishment and the expansion of the Soviet régime.

X. TACTICS REGARDING MILITIA CORPS [*min-t'uan*] AND BANDITS

(1) *The Party should publicize the land policy among the militia corps and bandits, establish cadres (within them) and absorb their members*. In their social basis the *min-t'uan* and bandits are related to poor peasants. In some places the poor peasants, unable to make a living, are forced to become bandits; furthermore, most of the members of the *min-t'uan* are employed in this way [by the landlord gentry] in order to make a living. Therefore the Party should strengthen its work among them, *publicize the land policy, establish secret Party organization and cells*, etc.

These armed masses should be absorbed and alienated from the hegemony of the gentry and landlords.

XI. WORKING-CLASS LEADERSHIP OF THE PEASANTRY

(1) *The consolidation of working-class leadership among the peasantry is a prerequisite to the success of the agrarian revolution.* A *close liaison* between the peasant movement and the workers' movement and the consolidation of the *ideological and organizational leadership* of the working class and the CP in the peasant movement are prerequisites to the success of the agrarian revolution. Therefore the liaison between the peasant movement and the workers' movement must be tightened and proletarian members should be drawn into the peasant movement and its leading organs. To achieve this purpose, constant intercourse should be maintained between the workers' organizations and the peasant associations, and propaganda should be directed at the vast peasant masses regarding the significance and aims of the working-class struggle, in order to make them realize that liberation can be achieved only under the leadership of the proletariat. *Work should also be done among the unemployed workers who have returned to the villages from the cities.*

XII. PARTY WORK IN THE VILLAGE

(1) *The main task of the village Party headquarters is to consolidate the leading role of the working class in the peasant movement.* To secure and consolidate the leading role of the working class in the peasant movement is the main task of the village Party headquarters and the general policy in all practical work. In all peasant struggles and work, the Party cell should strive to secure its leading role. In propaganda and agitation work, the Party cell should explain the functions of the CP and its present tasks.

(2) *The Party organization in the villages should be composed of proletarian and semi-proletarian elements.* The organization of the CP in the village should be expanded among the rural proletariat and the progressive elements of the semi-proletariat (handicraftsmen, hired farm hands, poor peasants). If all the revolutionary masses are absorbed into the Party organization, then the peasant organizations (peasant associations) would be replaced by the Party organization. The revolutionary peasant masses must be gathered into the peasant associations or the Soviets. *The past tendency of replacing the peasant associations and the Soviets with the Party and accepting petty-bourgeois* [three characters are missing here in the original text after the word "bourgeois"] *peasants should be rigorously corrected.* The Party should never directly command

the masses but *should only influence the peasant associations and the Soviets through the functions of the Party cells and the Youth Corps.*

In order to carry out this work, the Party must mobilize some active elements to work in the villages. The peasant committees of the central and provincial Party organizations should particularly strengthen their work.

COMMENTARY H. LI LI-SAN—FIRST PHASE

The Second Plenum of the Central Committee of the Chinese Communist Party, held in June 1929, marks the rise of Li Li-san's rule within the Party. At the same time, it marks an ebbing of the fortunes of the Communist movement in China. The Party had made little progress since the Sixth Congress of September 1928 in the basic task of winning over the city proletariat, while the guerrilla activities of Mao Tse-tung and Chu Teh were still in their initial stage. In view of this bleak situation, it is most likely that the Plenum was called to reinforce the position of the Party leadership and to underwrite its policies by emphasizing their identity with the policies of the Sixth Congress—a Congress which enjoyed a peculiar odour of sanctity due to the fact that it had been held in Moscow under the very shadow of the Comintern.

It is worthy of note that this claim of identity of policy between the Sixth Congress and the Second Plenum of June 1929 did not arouse any objection in Moscow at the time. It was only after the more spectacular failure of the CCP policy in 1930 that a wide discrepancy was found between the Li Li-san line and the line of the Sixth Congress. This is all the more remarkable in light of the fact that this document produced by the Second Plenum already contains one of the major "theoretical errors" of which Li Li-san was later to be accused, namely, an exaggeration of the imminence of a world revolutionary crisis. It would thus appear that it was only *after* the CCP leadership's tactical errors had become glaringly apparent that its theoretical errors were given close attention.

In spite of its official optimism, based on the *a priori* assertion of the Sixth Congress of the Comintern and the Sixth Congress of the CCP that the Chinese revolution was now in a stage of "uprising", a close reading of the document gives us some insight into the actual difficulties which the CCP faced in its attempt to win over the urban proletariat. There is constant reference not only to the "white terror", but also to the effectiveness of "bourgeois reformism"—that is, to the efforts of the KMT to build up its own "yellow trade unions". This document makes it quite obvious that these yellow unions were enjoying considerable success at this time, a year after the Sixth Congress, while the CCP still considered it the basic task of any Communist Party to have a concrete foundation among the urban proletariat. The CCP has to postulate a "Reviving Struggle in the Workers' Movement", whether such a postulation accords with the facts or not. The Plenum does call for a vigorous leadership of the peasant movement, and an expansion of guerrilla activities. At the same time, the bare statement that "certain Soviet areas as well as the Red Army under command of Chu and Mao are still in existence", indicates that the CCP's activities in the rural area were still far from flourishing.

The resolution of July 1929 is also notable for its frequent references to intra-Party opposition and its discussion of the issues involved in the struggle between the leadership and the "right opposition" of Ch'en Tu-hsiu. Finally, this document gives a good account of the rather complicated "class analysis" which constituted the theoretical aspect of the official Communist line on China at that time.

13. RESOLUTIONS AND SPIRIT OF THE SECOND PLENUM
OF THE CC (Circular no. 40 of the CC) (July 9, 1929)

To all Party headquarters of various levels, all comrades:

The Second Plenum of the CC—[the first plenum to meet] since the Sixth National Congress [of September 1928]—met a few days ago. This Plenum, convened one year after the Sixth Congress at a time when both the revolutionary movement throughout the world and the struggle of the masses in China are on the upsurge, undertook the great historical task of solving the many serious tactical problems now facing us. More than half of the members of the CC and six other comrades attended the Plenum, which lasted six days. Under the guidance of the line [laid down by] the Sixth National Congress and the directives of the CI, and imbued with the spirit of the Party's hard struggle during the past year, and that of internal Party unity, the Plenum successfully accomplished its significant task. The Plenum passed various resolutions and issued manifestos on political affairs, organizational matters, the workers' movement, and on the reports of the activities of the Political Bureau [Politburo]. Its major accomplishments are: a more accurate analysis and explanation of political principles, a more concrete policy for action relative to political tactics, a clearer conception of our tasks and methods to be employed in matters of organization and the workers' movement, and in particular, an expression of satisfaction with the line of activity of the Politburo during the past years, along with more practical and detailed directions regarding future activities.

The following is a report on essential points covered:

The Plenum Is of the View that the CC Has Correctly Applied the Policies Decided Upon by the Sixth Congress and Recognizes That the Party Has Made Progress in its Efforts to Consolidate Its Position

Regarding the reports on the activities of the Politburo, the Plenum is of the view that in matters of general policy the spirit of the Sixth Congress has been followed and that the policies decided upon by the Congress have been correctly applied. In its activities during the past nine months, the Plenum recognizes that our Party, in the midst of constant and bitter struggle within and without, achieved further consolidation politically and organizationally. This proves, on the one hand, the correctness of the policy of the Sixth Congress, and demonstrates on the other, that these principles have been correctly applied to our actual struggles. The Plenum notes that at times the CC has reacted rather slowly to political change; and although its analysis of the political situation has been in principle entirely correct, yet some of the interpretations may have been too mechanical or exaggerated, resulting in certain incorrect political ideas on the part of some comrades. A more correct interpretation of these principles must be attempted. The Plenum is satisfied with the CC's directives on tactics to various Party units and with its supervision of the trade union movement, especially with its detailed instructions to the major urban centres regarding the [annual] May First [May Day] and May Thirtieth movements. Accordingly, the Plenum instructs the Politburo to apply the experience of the May Thirtieth movement [see *Chronology* under May 30, 1925] in Shanghai to its work in the August First [Anti-imperialist-war Day] movement and to map out a more comprehensive plan on a national scale. As to work in the peasant movement, in the Soviet districts, in the soldiers' movement and in the Red Army as well as among the guerrilla forces, the Plenum is of the view that there has been a lack of positive direction from the CC concerning these activities. Not enough attention has been paid to the anti-imperialist movement. There is not enough co-ordination among the various movements in different areas. Particular attention should be paid by the CC to work in the key districts of Wuhan and Canton.

The Plenum recognizes the considerable progress made by the CC on organizational and propaganda work, but also notes certain defects.

The Plenum Accepts the CC's Policy Regarding the Intra-Party Political Struggle.[1]

The Plenum accepts the anti-rightist line adopted by the CC as its major policy in the intra-Party political struggle. At the same time, leftist inclinations should be checked. The principle adopted by the CC in dealing with non-political disputes within the Party is that educational methods should be used. When educational methods are found to be inadequate, organizational disciplinary measures are to be adopted as a last resort, such as the CC's decisions on the Kiangsu affair and the Shun-chih affair.[2] The Plenum considers these decisions correct and unavoidable, and approves the dismissal of comrades X and Y from the CC. It agrees with the CC that the serious attention of the entire Party must be called to the activities of the Trotskyite Opposition in the CCP, which have the possibility of temporary expansion, and are anti-revolutionary. These decisions concerning the political struggle within the Party serve as a powerful guarantee of the consolidation of the Chinese Party.

The Plenum Instructs the CC on the Direction of Work in the Various Departments

The Plenum points out that in the future the CC must give more detailed and practical directions to various Party units. During the past year the CY has been carrying on its struggle in accordance with the correct line of the Sixth Congress and the CC is directed by the Plenum to render more help to the CY in the future. The CC Committees on Peasantry and on Women should further strengthen their own activities. The Party organizations in the Labour Federation should concentrate their efforts on the union movement among railway, maritime, and mine workers, and on their relations with, and guidance of, the Red unions in the various areas. Party organizations in the Relief Commission must begin to work for the establishment of independent mass organization and mass activities on the part of the Commission itself. The Plenum calls particular attention to the inadequacy of measures to counteract the mass movement engineered by the KMT. In propaganda work, emphasis should be laid on the movement for theoretical criticism. The CC is called upon by the Plenum to improve its own division of labour and collective leadership, its inter-departmental relations, communications between the CC and local units, and the relations between the CCP and the CI and other Communist Parties. Extension and improvement of these activities strengthen the Party's leadership among the masses and make it more possible for the Party to win over the masses and hasten the upsurge of the revolutionary tide.

The Deepening of the World Revolutionary Crisis and the Development of the Chinese Revolutionary Movement Emphasize the Urgency of the CCP's duty of Winning Over the Masses

The major developments throughout the world in the past year fully prove the absolute correctness of the prediction of our Party and of the Sixth Congress that the world revolutionary crisis would deepen. First, the danger of an imperialist war is more imminent. Second, due to the consolidation and development of the Soviet Union, the hostile schemes of the imperialists against the Soviet Union are becoming ever more aggressive. Third, the class struggle of the proletariat in various countries and the revolutionary movement in the colonies are daily growing more intense. In preparing for the World War, the imperialists are further hastening their conspiracy to divide up China and to increase hostilities among the warlords. The intensification of the world revolutionary crisis also stimulates the development of the Chinese revolution. In the present political situation in China, the Plenum discerns three basic contradictions:

First, international imperialism is the real ruler of China's total political and economic life. With the growing aggression of imperialism in China, the basic conflict of interests among the imperialists themselves has also deepened in the past year. It is important to note that in the triangular struggle among imperialist England, Japan, and the United States, England and Japan are tending to draw closer to each other in order to oppose America. Basically, however, there is not the slightest difference in their aggressive policy towards China. It would be a grave error to cherish illusions that American imperialism will help Chinese national capitalism to develop independently or to over-estimate the influence of American imperialism and to assume that it has secured control of the Nanking government.

Second, as far as the present Chinese economy is concerned, the feudal classes still have a solid foundation even though their power is daily approaching a state of collapse. Aided and utilized by the imperialists, the warlords and the feudal and semi-feudal upper strata still form one of the major factors in political transformations in

China. It is therefore groundless for the Trotskyite Opposition to assert that the present political régime in China is in the hands of the bourgeoisie and that the Chinese revolution is already socialist in nature. It is also false to maintain, however, that the Chinese bourgeoisie since turning against the revolution has identified itself with the compradore class, reconciled itself with the feudal forces, and completely given up its own national democratic reformist platform. Thus there still exists in the ruling camp the basic contradiction among the bourgeoisie, the imperialists, and the feudal class. However, it would be equally wrong to exaggerate this contradiction, to fancy that the bourgeoisie may still demand the overthrow of imperialist and feudal rule and retain certain revolutionary functions. In their common struggle against the Chinese revolution, they will remain allies. Because of the sharpening of the contradictions among the imperialists in China, because of the contradictions among the ruling class, because of the intensified fighting of the warlords for territory, war is becoming an inevitable, commonplace phenomenon within the ruling class, hastening it on the way to destruction. As a result, the exploitation of the worker-peasant masses by the ruling class becomes ever more cruel, the sufferings of the masses grow ever more intense, and the struggle of the masses inevitably grows sharper. Furthermore, as imperialist oppression and exploitation grow in intensity, the anti-imperialist movement on the part of the masses is gradually reviving.

Third, the conflict between the reactionary ruling class and the revolutionary struggle of the masses is the most serious contradiction in the present political situation of China. At present, the workers' struggle is beginning to revive, the agrarian revolution is developing, certain Soviet areas as well as the Red Army under the command of Chu [Teh] and Mao [Tse-tung] are still in existence, revolts of troops still occur frequently and these troops then join the agrarian uprisings. The anti-imperialist movement is gradually reviving—all these factors indicate that the whole revolutionary movement is on the upswing. In these circumstances, the Plenum notes certain characteristic trends: (1) the trend from small-scale struggles to large-scale strikes; (2) from mere resistance to the bourgeois offensive to the struggle for freedom and the anti-KMT movement; (3) a comparative decrease in the influence of the reformists and the yellow [union, i.e. KMT union] leaders; (4) an increase in the influence of the Party and Red unions, although these should not be overestimated. In all of these (facts), indications of a new revolutionary rising tide can be discerned. It is therefore equally incorrect to maintain that the upsurge of the revolutionary tide is very remote or to maintain that it is imminent. The Plenum calls on all our comrades to be firm in their faith that only our struggle, and our effort to win over the masses, will determine whether the revolutionary tide is to arrive sooner or later.

In View of the Present Political Situation, the Plenum is Convinced that our Party must Resolutely Carry out Fifteen Political Tasks

Present political conditions lend urgency to the Party's general mission of winning over the broad masses and preparing for armed insurrections. The present basic tasks of the revolution, as pointed out by the Party and the Sixth Congress of the CI, are indubitably correct. They are to drive out the imperialists, unite China, consummate the agrarian revolution, liquidate feudal elements, overthrow the political régime of the gentry, capitalists, and KMT, and set up a Soviet régime of workers, peasants, and soldiers. As a result of the Party's work in the past year, its political influence and position of leadership among the masses have grown to some extent. However, the influence of the KMT's reformism has not been totally eradicated, and the masses' strength for struggle is still weak. The Party's roots among the masses are still not strong enough. Therefore, to win over the great body of the masses, the following tasks must, in the opinion of the Plenum, be carried out:

(1) Anti-imperialist struggle must be strengthened in co-ordination with the anti-world-war movement and the "support-the-Soviet-Union" movement. It must be understood that the overthrow of imperialist rule and the thorough accomplishment of the agrarian revolution are inseparable tasks. This does not mean, however, that there is no independent anti-imperialist movement outside the agrarian revolution. It simply means that the movement must be closely co-ordinated with the workers' movement, the anti-KMT, and the anti-militarist struggle.

(2) The CCP must resolutely lead the struggle against the gentry, the compradore class, the capitalist class, and KMT rule and must mobilize the struggle of the masses in all its forms in the march towards our general goal.

(3) We must spread the anti-warlord struggle. Our general line is [not?] to adopt the principle of defeatism [the text seems erroneous here in omitting a negative]. At present, the suffering of the masses resulting from the wars between the militarists should be utilized to

stir up the struggle for daily bread in order to co-ordinate it with the general political struggle.

(4) We must increase our leadership in the agrarian revolution. We must broaden and deepen that revolution. The agrarian revolution can be completed, however, only after the victory of the [general, political] revolution. It would be extremely erroneous, however, to think that an agrarian revolution [cannot?] exist without a total national armed insurrection of the workers and peasants [the text seems to omit a negative here also].

(5) We must continue our determined fight against bourgeois reformism. The deceitfulness of the reformist theory should be exposed in the course of the struggles of the masses. At the same time offensives on the ideological level are also essential. It is true that at present the influence of reformism has diminished considerably, but it would be wrong to assume that reformism has ceased to be a major enemy of the revolution. On the other hand, it would be an even more serious mistake to suggest that reformism has a good chance of succeeding.

(6) The strengthening of our leadership in the daily struggle of the masses remains at present the major task in our fight to win over the masses. However, under present conditions, (we) should not limit ourselves to the slogans of the daily economic struggle but should advance resolutely from minor struggles to large-scale strikes, from economic struggle to political struggle. Furthermore, these struggles should be co-ordinated in a planned manner with our over-all struggle for freedom.

(7) We must strengthen our activities in our own workers' movement as well as in the yellow [i.e. non-CCP or KMT] unions. If the Party has no solid foundation in the working class, particularly among the workers in the important industries, and if there are no unions led by the Party, then the Party will not obtain the leadership of the revolution. However, it would be a mistake to regard the Red unions as the sole centre of activity and to neglect work in the yellow unions. At present, the major and central task in the workers' movement is to strengthen our activities among workers in such heavy industries as railways and mining.

(8) We must strengthen our leadership of the peasant movemen and carry on our activities in a well-planned way. In the present stage of the rural struggle, it is still a mistake to oppose rich peasants unconditionally. Nevertheless the class struggle of hired farm hands and poor peasants against the rich peasants should not be relaxed. Special attention should be paid to the organization of hired farm

hands. As a result of the present famine in China, especially in North China, objectively speaking there is a great possibility for the flourishing of the peasant struggle. Therefore the Party must resolutely oppose in the rural areas all rightist deviations such as the stress on peaceful development, the movement towards legalism, evasionism, etc., and at the same time correct the remnants of leftist deviations.

(9) We must lead the guerrilla warfare, expand the Soviet areas, and organize the Red Army: the present situation in the rural struggle can easily lead to armed conflict. Therefore in leading the guerrilla warfare we must turn it into an organized, mass-based action. The Party should carry out our land policy in the Soviet areas to mobilize the broad masses. Soviet areas should be enlarged and at the same time the Red Army should be organized and expanded. Whether the Red Army forces should be concentrated or dispersed, must be decided by objective circumstances.

(10) We must strengthen our movement among soldiers: without the participation of vast numbers of soldiers, the final victory of the Chinese revolution can neither be achieved nor be assured. In the past, various Party units neglected the movement among soldiers on the ground that it was the particular duty of the agents in the military forces. As a matter of fact, agitation and propaganda work among the soldiers are the duty of every Party member. At present in our movement among soldiers, it would be wrong to rely on "putschism" or to deny the need for a daily economic struggle among the troops of the warlords. The Party should also conduct agitation and propaganda work among the troops of the imperialists stationed in China.

(11) We must consolidate our Party organization and expand the Party's foundation among the proletariat: especially among the workers in the railways, merchant marine, mining and metal industries, munition factories, municipalities, textile industry, etc. Party cells should be set up to strengthen the Party's power in leadership and in struggle.

(12) We must strengthen our propaganda and education activities: we must spread propaganda on Party policies, with particular emphasis on Communist ideology, intensify education in Marxism-Leninism, interpret our basic theories and tactics in the course of our struggles, and co-ordinate all our agitation and propaganda slogans to heighten the political standards of our Party members. At the same time, however, the undesirable political "chatter-box" type within the Party should be discouraged.

(13) We must increase the influence of the Party among the urban poor. Special attention should be paid to the students' movement: in the anti-imperialist fight for liberation, the poor people in the cities, particularly the students, are powerful allies of the working class. It is a mistake to maintain that the Chinese students have lost their revolutionary function. At the same time, however, we must guard against the vacillating tendencies of the bourgeoisie. The movement of the urban poor against exorbitant taxes should be directed by the Party into channels which will lead it to opposition to KMT rule.

(14) We must pay attention to work among our youth and women. The constant deterioration in the living conditions of young workers and peasants, the rapid increase in the number of women workers in light industries, the importance of peasant women, and the significant role of youth in the worker-peasant struggle, all call for special effort on the part of the Party in its work among youth and women, especially the work of aiding the CY.

(15) We must accelerate the militarization of our Party members, and we must set up organizations for the military training of the masses: if the Party does not carry out this task with iron resolution, it cannot be said to be determined in its policy of preparing for armed insurrection. Among the masses of workers, peasants, and youth, the Party must develop organizations such as local militia, village corps, Red guards, etc., to carry on military training.

The Plenum Points Out the Major Tactical Line of the Party

In order to accomplish the above fifteen tasks and reduce the difficulties which face us, the Plenum feels that the Party must fight resolutely to carry out the following major tactical line both within and outside the Party:

(1) We must strive to engage in public activities, but at the same time we must co-ordinate them with secret activities. Inasmuch as the status of the Party has been illegal, the Party must seize every opportunity to use public [i.e. open, non-secret] means to do work in propaganda and agitation, to summon the masses to struggle publicly and to organize them publicly in order to be able to win over the broad masses to the influence of our Party. Simultaneously, the secret work of the Party in Party organizations and cells should be strengthened to consolidate the Party's leadership. The development of public activities will facilitate the expansion of the secret activities of the Party. However, public activities are carried on in the midst of continuous struggles under conditions of daily oppression in our

drive towards a revolutionary rising tide. It does not mean, therefore, that we minimize our slogans, or that we beg the KMT for public status.

(2) One particular difficulty encountered in carrying out the Party's tactical line is the presence of rightist tendencies in the Party. This is not only a remnant of opportunism within the Party, but a reflection of the defeatist sentiment and incorrect ideas of certain sections of the masses. Thus, the rightist inclinations to stress peaceful development, the movement to obtain legal status, and the movement to stress open [*kung-k'ai*, i.e. public, non-secret] activity have repeatedly arisen within our Party. Of course, this is not to say that matters have yet reached a drastic stage or that the rightists constitute a dangerous clique. However, the Party must fight the rightist tendency resolutely, from both the subjective and objective points of view, in order to prevent its possible development.

(3) On the other hand, it is also a grave mistake to assume that all the "leftist" dangers have been eliminated or that "leftist" deviations are not dangerous. The present grave leftist danger which manifests itself as an unwillingness to engage in public activities, an unwillingness to carry on daily and partial struggles, unwillingness to join yellow unions with large memberships, putschism and impatience, etc., must all be liquidated by the Party to correct the Party's alienation from the masses.

The Plenum Points Out Progress and Weakness in Organization, Defects in Activities, and the Correct Organizational Line of the Party

In view of the present organizational condition of our Party, the Plenum notes that although circumstances have remained difficult during the past year, the Party, through relentless struggles inside and outside the Party, has made considerable progress and extricated itself from its disorganized state. Generally speaking, the shaky condition of the Party has gradually been overcome but there still exists some weakness both in organization and in activity. These weaknesses, especially the weak proletarian basis of the Party, the low political standard of Party members, the inadequacy of worker cadres, the remnants of opportunism and putschism, may easily foster the growth of various incorrect political concepts, particularly rightist notions within the Party. However, we should not because of these weaknesses overlook the considerable progress which has been made. Basing ourselves on this progress, we should patiently and relentlessly eliminate weaknesses and defects in Party organization, and strengthen the bolshevik character of our Party. The Plenum considers the following to be the correct line of Party organization:

(1) To enlarge the proletarian base of the Party. The Party should first of all penetrate the ranks of the industrial workers. Attention should be paid to the possibility of raising both the quantity and quality of Party membership. We must at the same time improve the old Party base and develop a new Party base.

(2) Cells are the basis of the Party, the nucleus of mass organization. The Party should therefore carefully organize central cells in various industries, develop cell life to make it possible for every member to work in the Party cells.

(3) The major organizational task of local Party headquarters is to plan activities, carry out a correct policy of democratization within the Party, strengthen Party discipline, publish factory bulletins and other propaganda materials, take care of the distribution of propaganda materials, intensify the training of cadres, particularly the worker cadres, etc.

(4) The higher units of the Party should devote their energy to the guidance of political activities and should stress inspection activities.

(5) The Party should regard the assistance of the CY as a part of its own work. Within the Party, particular attention should be paid to secret work. By strengthening its base among the masses, the Party will eliminate the phenomenon of betrayal by Party members.

(6) The Party organizations and mass organizations should be separated and their relationship clearly defined. The Party should have its Party organizations carry on activities within the mass organizations.

The Plenum Resolutely Opposes Incorrect Ideas on Organization Inside the Party and Demands the Elimination of the Activities of the Oppositionists Within the Party

The Plenum recognizes that, since the Sixth Congress, Party life has shown a new spirit—a fighting spirit on behalf of the correct line. However, some comrades still advocate peace within the Party, and call for absolute democracy, thus undermining the principle of democratic centralism. Some comrades still show signs of liquidationism or formalism in organizational matters. The Party is now operating in the atmosphere of the white terror. The Party itself is still infected with non-proletarian sentiment, particularly the tendency towards cliques and sectarianism which can easily be utilized by the international oppositionists to split the Chinese Party. Therefore, the

Plenum deems it not only necessary for the Party to apply correctly the political line, but also to call for an enforcement of iron discipline within the Party. A resolute fight must be waged by the whole Party against various incorrect deviations. Incorrect ideas on organizational problems must be resolutely opposed. And the activities of the oppositionists within the Party must be eliminated by ideological argument and organizational discipline, and their leaders and active elements must be purged from the Party.

The Plenum Points Out the Characteristics of the Reviving Struggle in the Workers' Movement and Outlines Our Central Tasks in the Workers' Movement in the Future

The Plenum notes that under the present reactionary rule, the living conditions of the workers are reducing them to the position of slaves and beasts of burden. As a result, the struggle of the workers is constantly increasing. As the workers' struggle begins to revive, certain characteristics of this struggle become more visible: as the political consciousness of the workers increases, the masses of the yellow unions are tending to turn to the left. The workers' movement is thus bound to gather momentum in the future. The reactionary forces—imperialists, KMT, and bourgeoisie—are all intensifying their attacks on workers, especially by means of reformism and yellow unions that serve as the most damaging obstacle to the development of the workers' struggle. The policy on the workers' movement decided upon by the Sixth Congress, which based itself on the experiences of the previous year, is undoubtedly correct. The Party has not, however, fully carried out its tasks in this area, although considerable progress has been made. A number of rightist and leftist errors have not been fully corrected, the work among the industrial workers is still being neglected, and our unions still lack a foundation among the broad masses. Accordingly, the Plenum proclaims our policy and central tasks in the workers' movement in future to be the following: (1) Actively develop the workers' movement in major industries, particularly in the railway, maritime, and mining industries. (2) Lead the working masses to fight resolutely against reformism. (3) Participate in those yellow unions which have a mass following in order to develop the struggle of the masses, spread Party propaganda, organize cadre cells, and win over the masses. We shall thus be able to eliminate the yellow (union) leaders and change the nature of the unions. (4) Stimulate and broaden the economic and political struggle of the workers and reinforce their fighting strength. (5) Develop and expand, from the bottom up, union organizations which have a class nature and are mass-based. (6) Utilize all possible opportunities to engage in open activities in order to expand the activities of our Red unions. (7) Employ correctly the strategy of factory committees. (8) Intensify our activities among young workers and women workers. (9) Lead the fight of unemployed workers. (10) Lead the struggles of the rural workers and organize their unions. (11) Intensify and spread political propaganda among the working masses. (12) Pay attention to the military organization and training of the workers. The Plenum is of the view that Red unions must play an important role in accomplishing these tasks. The Party must rally the masses round itself, oppose resolutely the slogan of worker-capitalist co-operation, expose the deceit of the yellow (union) leaders, continue relentlessly the fight against the imperialists, the KMT, and the warlords, ally itself with the international proletariat, oppose the Second International, support the agrarian revolution of the peasants, fight for an eight-hour working day, lead with greater effort the daily economic struggles of the masses, pay attention to activities in heavy industries and strategic areas, and draw non-Party workers into the unions. Only in the process of carrying out these tasks can the National Labour Federation secure for itself a solid and broad foundation. Only thus can the Party rally round itself the broad masses of workers.

Comrades, the above are the spirit and resolutions of the Second Plenum of the CC! The unanimous decisions of the Plenum are a weapon in our struggle to advance in the spirit of the Sixth Congress and under the guidance of the CI, to conquer the enemy and win over the masses, to accelerate the revolutionary rising tide. The Politburo, in accordance with the instructions of the Plenum, calls on all our comrades to carry out all these resolutions relentlessly in the spirit of the Sixth Congress, and to convert the resolutions of the Plenum into perfect instruments for realizing the spirit of the Sixth Congress and the mission of the Chinese revolution! The Central Committee, July 9, 1929.

Addendum: To all Party headquarters of various levels, all comrades:

All the resolutions of the Plenum will be distributed soon after this circular. After receiving them, Party units of all levels should hold meetings to discuss them and pass resolutions after discussion. Procedure of the meeting should be as follows: The provincial (Party) committee should hold a plenary session or ask responsible comrades of key areas to participate in the provincial executive committee discussion meetings. In the local Party units, if it is a key area, the inspector, who is a member of the provincial executive committee, should call a joint meeting of responsible comrades of adjoining *hsien* in a key city. In the meeting of Party units of ordinary districts, every effort should be made to get a representative from the Party head-quarters in a key city to participate. In the areas where a member of the provincial executive committee is stationed, the local Party unit should ask the active members to meet for reports and discussion. In the cells each should discuss, in a planned manner, the tactical line adopted at the Plenum, beginning from the joint meeting of secretaries of the cells. The contents of the discussions should be co-ordinated with the local conditions, working experience, and tactics in struggle. Resolutions should be passed in accordance with the local working conditions, and should not merely answer the Plenum's resolutions in terms of general principles. The resolutions of the various Party units should not be too long and do not necessarily have to be more than one. The primary purpose is to enable the lower Party units, up to the cell, to discuss these resolutions in a more systematic and practical way.

The Central Committee

COMMENTARY I. THE LI LI-SAN LINE

By the early months of 1930 the Li Li-san leadership of the CCP found itself confronted with a most desperate situation. The Sixth Congress of the Comintern and the Sixth Congress of the CCP, both meeting in Moscow, July–September 1928, had burdened the Chinese Party with a series of tasks which simply could not be fulfilled. While it had been decreed that the "content" of the Chinese revolution was the agrarian revolution, it had been stressed with equal vehemence that the agrarian revolution could be consummated only under "prole-tarian hegemony". It had further been made amply clear that the CCP could achieve such a hegemony only when it had recaptured the leadership of the urban proletariat. In a real sense, then, Li's first task was the re-establishment of the Party's former close relations with the city workers. At the same time, however, it was decreed in advance that China stood on the brink of a new revolutionary surge, and the CCP was charged with the task of preparing for it. This insistence on the imminence of a rising revolutionary tide in China may well have been the result of Stalin's need to place himself at the opposite pole from Trotsky, who was stubbornly maintaining the view that the revolutionary tide had ebbed in China. Whatever may have been the case, Li Li-san was obliged to prepare the ground for armed insurrections.

Since a revolutionary wave was imminent, it was not unreasonable to assume that any sign of weakness on the part of the enemy, any conflict among warlords, was to be taken as a symptom of the new revolutionary tide. If Li failed to act at such a time on the ground that his preparations were still inadequate, he could always be accused of "passivity" by his numerous enemies. On the other hand, if he acted and failed, he could always be accused of "adventurism".

Actually, the situation which confronted Li was the very opposite of a revolutionary surge. Like his predecessor, Ch'ü Ch'iu-pai, Li was confronted with an intractable fact which refused to yield to the directions of the Comintern—namely, the obdurate indifference of the urban proletariat. If at this time the CCP had made itself the mouth-piece for the economic grievances of the workers, it might still have regained control of segments of the working class. But the policy of the Comintern called for political strikes and preparation for armed insurrection. This made inevitable the complete alienation of the urban workers from the Party.

Nor was the Comintern willing to allow Li to rest in this uncomfortable state. On the contrary, he was subject to constant pressure from Moscow, which was still seeking successes in China in spite of the fact that that country no longer seems to have occupied a central place on the Comintern's horizon. As late as October 1929, the Central Committee of the CCP received a letter from the ECCI announcing "the beginning of the revolutionary tide"—an announcement which was equivalent to a call for action.

The early months of 1930 were indeed marked by a "rising tide", but not in the urban centres. It was at this time that the Soviet areas of South China began to emerge as a powerful independent force in the Communist movement. From the point of view of the Party leadership this new force represented both an opportunity and a problem. If it could be harnessed to the purposes of the Party it could be used to support the CCP's lagging fortunes in the cities. Otherwise, it would merely serve to accentuate the lack of co-ordination between the peasant movement in the village and the labour movement in the city, against which the Ninth Plenum of the ECCI in February 1928 had issued such stern warning. It would mean that the Party might become completely dominated by "a peasant mentality".

It is in the light of these circumstances and of the constant pressure from Moscow that we must view the resolution of June 11, 1930 (document no. 14); for however ambitious he may have been to become the "Stalin of China" and however ruthless and despotic he may have been in his relations with others, there can be little doubt that Li Li-san hoped to achieve his ambitions on the basis of what he regarded to be the Comintern line.

While some of the notions in this rather desperate document may not have been directly inspired from Moscow, it would be most difficult to prove that they contradicted any major premise of the Moscow line as it existed at the time. The attempt to portray this document as a catalogue of monstrous errors did not begin until several months later, and contemporaneous Comintern literature fails to betray any awareness of these errors. Particularly worthy of note in this document are those points which were later to be the object of such vehement attack. We find here, first of all, a laborious effort to prove that success in the Chinese revolution and in the world revolution are mutually interdependent. This analysis was quite plausible in terms of the current Comintern doctrine of the "Third Period", which assumed that world capitalism had achieved a definite though precarious stabilization in the "Second Period" of the mid-1920s but would soon collapse, though at an uneven pace. Behind this analysis there actually lay the desperate desire to enlist the aid of the Soviet Union itself so as to ensure success in the Chinese revolution. What Li contemplated here was probably something in the nature of the aid later to be received from the U.S.S.R. by the Spanish Loyalists in 1937–8. Moscow, of course, ignored this appeal, but we find no hint at the time that it was a monstrous error of "semi-Trotskyism".

We also find here the first guarded references to the strategy later to be used in the attack on Changsha on July 27, 1930, namely, the use of the peasant Red Army to seize urban centres. (Presumably, such an attack would be neatly co-ordinated with an insurrection of the proletariat within the cities.) Far from opposing this strategy, we find that an ECCI letter of July 23, 1930, actually endorses it. It suggests that the Red Army be strengthened so that "in the future according to political or military circumstances, one or several political or industrial centres can be occupied".[1] The putschist nature of this strategy was discovered only after the spectacular failure at Changsha. Finally, we find the prophecy that a successful bourgeois-democratic revolution in China would soon be transformed into a socialist revolution. This too was later to be cited as a proof of Li's Trotskyist proclivities, although similar prognostications can be found throughout Comintern literature of the period.

However, the failure at Changsha set in motion the forces which were to undermine Li Li-san's position. Like the Canton insurrection of December 1927, the Changsha attack was an event which aroused world-wide attention, and thus forced Moscow to reconsider its position in China. In China itself there were hostile forces within the Party eager to take advantage of Li Li-san's discomfiture. Ho Meng-hsiung, Lo Chang-lung, and those elements close to the Communist labour movement deeply resented the disastrous policies which were wrecking it. Wang Ming and the ambitious "returned student" faction, fresh from their studies at the Sun Yat-sen University in Moscow, were an even more formidable source of danger, supported as they were by Pavel Mif, former director of the University and now Comintern representative in China. The latter, deeply resentful of Li's iron hold on the Chinese Party machine, was to be the chief architect of the "anti-Li Li-san line".

In the autumn of 1930, the Kremlin sent Ch'ü Ch'iu-pai back to China to examine the situation and suggest changes. To Ch'ü, who had lost his position of leadership in China, this might have represented an opportunity to regain power. To our surprise, however, we find that the Third Plenum of the Party, finally called at Ch'ü's behest in September 1930, actually reconfirmed the authority of Li Li-san, who was loyally supported by his staunch confederate, Chou En-lai. Ch'ü Ch'iu-pai was effectively silenced. There are many factors which may account for this unexpected turn in events. One may have been the divided nature of the opposition. Another may have been the formidable power of the personal machine which Li had built for himself. Document no. 15 would suggest that perhaps an even more important factor was the indecisive nature of the instructions which Ch'ü Ch'iu-pai brought back with him from Moscow. The Kremlin found itself, after all, in a somewhat embarrassing position. What elements of Li Li-san's behaviour could it attack without incriminating itself?

Thus Li Li-san and Chou En-lai were able to seize the bull by the horns and thrust upon their opponents the burden of proving the existence of divergences between their own line and the line of the Kremlin. They were indeed willing to admit that the Party had possibly committed certain tactical errors; that it had perhaps "made an excessive and incorrect evaluation of the speed and degree of development of the revolution" (document no. 15); but had not the ECCI itself stated in its July letter that "the new rising tide in the

Chinese revolution has undoubtedly become a fact"? Furthermore, Li and Chou were now quite willing to make any readjustments of policy which the Kremlin would require. Document no. 15, based on a report of Chou En-lai, accurately delineated the effective strategy employed by the Li Li-san leadership at the Third Plenum. The foreword at the beginning of the document was added by Chou En-lai at the time of the Fourth Plenum, when he was forced to do humble penance for having helped to frame this strategy.

In spite of Li Li-san's temporary success, however, the forces working against him grew in strength. Pavel Mif, the Comintern representative, was infuriated by the manner in which the Third Plenum had been conducted, almost behind his back. He was determined to impress the Kremlin with the fundamental nature of Li Li-san's errors and to press the fortunes of his own protégés, the "returned student" faction. It would appear that in Moscow the perennial need to dissociate the Kremlin from failure and find a scapegoat for it finally moved the Kremlin itself to turn on Li Li-san. In the ECCI letter of November 16, 1930, it was finally proclaimed that Li Li-san himself had been the fountain-head of all the errors committed in China and that he had wilfully misinterpreted the un-failingly correct line of the Kremlin.[2]

The result was, of course, the immediate loss of power by Li Li-san, soon followed by his carefully prepared recantations in Moscow. In China, however, the immediate result of Li's fall was a desperate struggle for power, particularly between the Ho Meng-hsiung-Lo Chang-lung factions and the "returned student" faction. But this was an uneven struggle, since the latter group enjoyed the patronage of Mif. The Fourth Plenum (see document no. 16), held in January 1931, marked the definite victory of Mif and his young protégés. The anti-Li Li-san line as finally formulated was in the main the work of this group, who used it as a bludgeon to beat not only Li Li-san but all the factional opponents of the new upstart leadership.

Since Li Li-san had on the whole acted on premises set down in Moscow, the attempt to prove that the Li Li-san line had been "an anti-CI line" (document no. 16) involved formidable difficulties. It was necessary to scrutinize all Li Li-san's past pronouncements (document no. 14 proved to be the most fruitful from this point of view) for fancied divergencies from the Comintern line or for resemblances, no matter how far-fetched, to Trotsky's doctrines. The result was the tortuous scholastique of the anti-Li Li-san line.

At the heart of this scholastique, however, there lay a kernel of reality. After Changsha it would appear that Moscow abandoned, for a time at least, the concept of using the power of the Red Army to seize urban centres in order to overcome "the uneven development of the peasants' and workers' movement". It was apparently decided that the Soviet areas were too valuable an asset to be sacrificed so recklessly. Nevertheless this shift was a shift from the Kremlin's own past views, which it now attempted to attribute to Li Li-san himself. It must further be pointed out that neither Moscow nor the new Chinese leadership had renounced the recapture of the urban proletariat as a basic Party aim. Finally, it must be noted that the Comintern at this time chose as the instruments of its policy not the seasoned leaders of the Soviet areas, but Mif's protégés of the "returned student" faction.

14. LI LI-SAN: THE NEW REVOLUTIONARY RISING TIDE AND PRELIMINARY SUCCESSES IN ONE OR MORE PROVINCES
(June 11, 1930)

. . . Resolution on present political tasks adopted by the [CCP] Politburo on June 11, 1930. . . .

I. THE CHINESE REVOLUTION AND THE WORLD REVOLUTION

(1) Recent developments in international affairs—the greater intensity of the armament race among the powers since the Naval Conference [at London in April 1930], the growing conflict between Italy and France, and the manipulation by England, Japan, and America of warlord warfare in China—indicate that the danger of an imperialist war has become still more imminent. The imminence of a concerted imperialist attack on the Soviet Union is (also) demonstrated by Japan's constant plots to stir up trouble through the use of White Russians, by Briand's designs to form a United States of Europe so as concertedly to attack the Soviet Union, by the United States' instigating countries on the American continent to sever diplomatic relations with Soviet Russia, and by mobilization of the armies of Russia's small neighbour countries like Poland and Lithuania at the instance of the English and French imperialists. The reason for (all) this is that the capitalist countries of the whole world are in a state of serious depression, in an insoluble crisis produced by the incurable basic conflicts (in capitalism). On the other hand, the rising tide [kao-ch'ao] of strikes by the working class of all countries, the growing struggle of the unemployed, and especially the great achievements in socialist construction on the part of the Soviet Union: (all these) have

further bolstered the determination of the working class (to advance) towards a socialist revolution. The Social Democrats and other leftist groups are daily losing their hold on the masses, (while) the prestige of the CI and of the CPs of all countries increases day by day. What deserves our special attention is the intensification of the revolutionary movement in the colonial areas of the whole world. The revolutionary rising tide in India, the insurrections in Indo-China, unrest in other colonial areas, and the rapid development of the Chinese revolution—all these are shaking the foundation of the imperialist world rule. Therefore, the imperialists are ever more anxious to try to initiate an attack on Soviet Russia in order to save themselves from the crisis. Thus a war of aggression against the Soviet Union becomes the principal danger of the present. The general severe economic depression and precarious political situation of the world show plainly that unprecedented world incidents and a world revolution loom in front of us. Such an international situation is undoubtedly advantageous to the development of the Chinese revolution—and more favourable to it than the period of the first Great Revolution (1925–7), from which it differs completely.

(2) From the standpoint of imperialist world rule, China focuses most sharply all the basic conflicts among the imperialists: China is the spot where the conflict among the major imperialists—England, Japan, and the U.S.A.—is the most intense; it is one of the areas where the capitalist world and the socialist Soviet Union have direct contact; it is an area where the anti-imperialist colonial revolution has penetrated the deepest. At the same time, the conflict between the Chinese proletariat and bourgeoisie can easily be stepped up—for instance, every one of the present workers' economic struggles is rapidly being converted into a severe political struggle, or even armed conflict. Thus, the various forms of conflict among the imperialists, now focused in China, are likely to sharpen, resulting in incurable economic and political crises, in ceaseless imbroglios among warlords, in the collapse of the ruling class's foundations, and in the increasing turning of the working class and the broad toiling masses towards revolution to seek their own emancipation. Thus China is the weakest link in the ruling chain of world imperialism; it is the place where the volcano of the world revolution is most likely to erupt. Therefore, with the present aggravation of the global revolutionary crisis, the Chinese revolution may possibly break out first, setting off the world revolution and the final decisive class war of the world.

(3) China is the largest colony of the world, which means she is the largest market, investment outlet, and supplier of raw materials for the imperialists of the world. China thus forms an integral part of the imperialists' economic system. The loss of China by the imperialist rulers would mean the inevitable end of the imperialists, especially that of imperialist England, Japan, and America. Therefore all the imperialists are bound to use every possible means for the cruel suppression of the Chinese revolution; and the Chinese revolution is bound to fight it out very cruelly with the imperialists. But, due to the objective fact that the outbreak of the Chinese revolution may set off a world revolution, we shall be able, when the cruel war comes, to mobilize not only tens of hundreds of millions of the masses in our (own) country to engage in an intense struggle, but also to call on the world proletariat and on the toiling masses of the colonies to fight the last battle with the imperialists. In this final decisive battle (we) shall undoubtedly be able to achieve complete victory.

(4) Misunderstanding of this situation is the chief source of liquidationist and rightist thoughts. Ch'en Tu-hsiu once said: "It is only possible for the Chinese revolution (to succeed) after the outbreak of the world revolution." Some rightist comrades claim that "although the revolution is now progressing, there will be no way of coping with the imperialists in the future"; and some maintain that "the prerequisite of preliminary success is to start (insurrections) in provinces where the imperialists are weak". (These comrades) do not understand that the Chinese revolution may break out first and set off the great world revolution, and that it will struggle heroically alongside the world revolution, for the objective conditions that will make its success possible. We must explicitly point out the error of this pessimistic rightist concept.

II. A NEW REVOLUTIONARY RISING TIDE IS DRAWING NEARER EVERY DAY

(5) As a consequence of the effect of the basic crisis of imperialism, especially the continuous fighting among the warlords during the past two years, the Chinese political and economic situation has now reached an extraordinarily serious state: financial chaos, bankruptcies, increasing crises of unemployment, soaring prices, and growing deterioration of the livelihood of the masses. The rural economy has suffered unprecedented destruction, with famine and war spread over the whole country, exposing tens of thousands of people to hunger, cold, displacement, and death. Most areas of the South are in a cruel

war between the peasants and landlords. No clique of the ruling class is able to save the critical situation or to unify the country; further deterioration and collapse are inevitable. On the other hand, the toiling masses of workers and peasants have no choice, in such unendurable circumstances, but to wage the revolutionary struggle with determination. This completely explains how the objective conditions for revolution have matured, and serves to answer the lies of the liquidationists (to the effect) that "the bourgeoisie is being stabilized". The revolutionary struggle of the broad masses surges rapidly forward: the strike wave spreads out; the economic struggles turn into political ones; broad worker masses, shaking themselves free from the deceptions of the KMT's yellow unions, turn to struggle against them and the KMT; and (the workers) free themselves from legal forms of peaceful petitioning and (proceed to) direct action or even to armed conflict. All this demonstrates that the political consciousness of the worker masses is proceeding rapidly towards the revolutionary rising tide. This situation became clearer after the extensive, serious political struggles of Red May—May 1 and 30 of this year [1930]. Especially the rural struggle has undoubtedly developed into an extremely wide rising tide, not only destroying the rule of the landlords, the bourgeoisie, and the KMT in the villages, but also establishing Soviet régimes in many areas, in opposition to the imperialist-KMT régime which rules the whole nation. After the First All-China Congress of Soviet Areas' Delegates [May 1930, in Shanghai], [the rural struggle] will (now) expand even more rapidly. In addition, (there are) the vigorous development of the Red Army, and the conversion to the revolutionary camp, as well as spontaneous mutinies, of the soldiers in the warlord armies; this over-all situation shows that a new revolutionary rising tide in China is directly ahead.

(6) Thus, while the ruling class continues to weaken and collapse, the mass struggle is daily approaching a revolutionary rising tide. This shows clearly that the future of the warlords' strife may well turn into the victory of the national revolution and the final death of the warlords' rule. Only a victorious revolutionary upheaval of the masses of workers and peasants can completely eliminate the warlords' wars and achieve unification and peace in China. Therefore, the immediate task of the CP is to call on the broad masses to oppose the warlords' wars by revolutionary struggle, to prepare resolutely for the concerted general uprising of all revolutionary forces in order to overthrow the warlords' rule, and to eliminate completely the warlords' wars, (thereby) winning the victory of the revolution.

(7) The major signs of the revolutionary rising tide are the heightened political struggle of the revolutionary vanguard and of the general and even the backward masses, and the outbreak of great political strikes in the major cities. But serious rightist or even liquidatiionst concepts will inevitably result if (one) considers only the superficial unevenness in the development (of the revolution) in the cities and countryside, and neglects (to consider) the workers' struggle, the sharpening of class antagonisms, the rapid growth of revolutionary spirit and determination on the part of the broad masses, and the bankruptcy of the ruling power of the ruling class; that is, the conditions under which every incident may lead to the outbreak of a great revolutionary struggle. The major reason why the workers' strike movement has not yet turned into a revolutionary rising tide decidedly does not lie in a lag of revolutionary consciousness on the part of the workers, nor in their lack of desire for revolution; rather it lies in the fact that the ruling class, about to collapse, is waging a last-ditch battle in the cities, using all possible methods—white terror and trickery—to suppress the workers' struggle. Thus the urban struggle is more intense and cruel than that in the countryside; this is why we must redouble our efforts in city work for the ultimate victory in the revolution. But the major handicap in our present work are rightist ideas of doubt and pessimism regarding the workers' struggle. The elimination of such waverings is the major prerequisite for speeding the arrival of the rising tide in the workers' struggles.

(8) Generally speaking, not every struggle of the worker masses will turn into a revolutionary upsurge; other essential factors must accompany it. In the present Chinese situation, (such factors) are the extensive spread of peasant uprisings, the rapid expansion of the Red Army of workers and peasants, a growing awakening among the [KMT] soldier masses and the mutinies on their part, and the serious crisis of the ruling class. In fact, one great workers' struggle in an industrial or political centre may immediately lead to the formation of a revolutionary upsurge—(that is), to a directly revolutionary situation. Furthermore, the outbreak of a great struggle in the key cities would, under present conditions, mean that the ruling class is not only unable to hold the rural areas, but also incapable of suppressing or controlling the revolutionary struggle in the cities. This would mean that objective conditions are ripe for armed insurrection. Therefore we may say that the upsurge of the revolutionary rising tide will inevitably be followed by armed insurrection. We should, therefore,

actively prepare from now on for armed insurrection. Attention should be paid not only to political preparatory work—(such as) mass propaganda for armed insurrection and for the necessity of seizing political power, but also to hastening organizational and technical preparations. If we do not understand the objective situation clearly, (we) will undoubtedly commit grave rightist errors in our tactics, (such as) ignoring the necessity of preparing for armed insurrection, and will undoubtedly become the "tail" of the masses or even an obstacle to the revolution.

(9) The basic economic and political crisis in China is everywhere becoming more intense and there is no fundamental difference in it (as regards locality). Therefore, the great workers' struggle breaking out in key cities will lead to a national revolutionary rising tide, and the great struggle itself will signify the arrival of the national revolutionary rising tide. So the revolutionary upsurge may break out first in this or that province, but there cannot be a single revolutionary rising tide in one or more provinces apart from the national revolutionary rising tide. Therefore, when the Party prepares for the national revolutionary rising tide, it must pay serious attention to co-ordination and mobilization on a national scale; the concept that a national revolutionary rising tide can be pushed by establishing local régimes in one or more provinces is undoubtedly extremely erroneous.

III. PRELIMINARY SUCCESSES IN ONE OR MORE KEY PROVINCES AND
THE ESTABLISHMENT OF A NATIONAL REVOLUTIONARY RÉGIME

(10) In industrially backward China, economic centres completely controlling the national industries have, generally speaking, not yet been formed. Furthermore, under the control of a few commercial centres trading with the imperialists (such as Shanghai, Hongkong, Tientsin, Wuhan, and Dairen), political régimes of local warlords have come into existence. The nation's ruling class is in general in a condition of vacillation and collapse, but to a different degree in different areas. Therefore, during the national revolutionary rising tide, the revolution may win preliminary successes in one or more key provinces (judging from present circumstances, the objective conditions of Wuhan and its adjacent provinces are more mature). For the present, while the new revolutionary rising tide approaches day by day, (our) general tactical policy is to prepare (ourselves) for (winning) preliminary successes in one or more provinces and for setting up a national revolutionary régime.

(11) Preliminary successes in one or more provinces are inseparable from the national revolutionary rising tide. "These successes cannot be attained without the condition of a revolutionary rising tide" (resolution of the Sixth Congress). Therefore, in order to prepare for preliminary successes in one or more provinces, attention must be paid to the co-ordination of work on a national scale. The present expansion and intensification of the warfare among warlords will undoubtedly provide a favourable situation for preliminary successes in one or more provinces. To fight actively for the attainment of such successes is at present the main task of the Party. But (we) must realize that after the revolution has succeeded in one or more provinces, the various groups of reactionaries, provincial warlords, and especially all the imperialists, will temporarily forget their own differences and unite to suppress the revolution. In the first Great Revolution [1925–7], the revolutionary government in Kwangtung could exist as a local régime for more than one year and consolidate its power. It is impossible for such a situation to reoccur in the present Soviet stage of the revolution. Preliminary successes in one or more provinces will at once give rise to cruel war—not only civil war to liquidate the reactionaries, but also international war to resist all imperialist oppression. Therefore, only with the preparation for a national revolutionary rising tide to achieve preliminary successes in one or more provinces can the revolutionary government rapidly mobilize tens or hundreds of millions of the masses of the nation to wage resolutely a decisive fight against the reactionary forces and obtain the support of the world proletariat—especially that of the Russian proletariat, which has already met success—so as to vanquish the reactionary forces and win national victory. Thus preliminary successes in one or more provinces are the beginning of national victory, a step towards more intensive struggle in the national revolution. There can never be any "local régimes" or "regional governments" [ko-chü or p'ien-an]; every provincial (Party headquarters) should actively prepare for successful insurrection in that province in co-ordination with the general situation. Thus, in preparing for preliminary successes in one or more provinces, special attention must be paid to heightening (our) national activities, as well as to their co-ordination with the struggle of the international proletariat. Especially more propaganda about the Chinese revolution (must be spread) among the international proletariat.

(12) The great struggle of the proletariat is the decisive force in the winning of preliminary successes in one or more provinces. Without

an upsurge of strikes of the working class, without armed insurrection in key cities, there can be no successes in one or more provinces. It is a highly erroneous concept to pay no special attention to urban work, and to plan "to use village (forces) to besiege the cities" and "to rely on the Red Army alone to occupy the cities". Henceforth, the organization of political strikes and their expansion into a general strike, as well as the strengthening of the organization and training of the workers' militia to set up a central force for armed insurrections, are the major tactics in preparing for preliminary successes in one or more provinces. Particular attention should be directed to (the fact that) the ruling class will (stage) a final struggle in the cities. This cruel struggle will be even fiercer than that in the rural areas; therefore, (we) must redouble our efforts in urban work, set up strong bases in the key cities—especially among workers of important industries—awaken the will of the broad masses to struggle to the death. These are the most grave tasks for the present and the tactical problems that must be solved first.

(13) In view of the present objective economic and political conditions of China, a rising tide of proletarian struggles unaccompanied by peasant uprisings, soldiers' mutinies, powerful assaults by the Red Army, and a (whole) combination of various revolutionary forces, also will not lead the revolution to victory. Also it will be unattainable if one of the above four revolutionary forces is lacking. The liquidationists who look down on the peasantry and (want to) liquidate the Red Army, are undoubtedly (spreading) reactionary ideas, attempting to weaken the ally of the proletariat and to destroy the fighting power of the revolution. The great revolutionary role of the peasantry has even a higher significance in China; the birth of the Red Army in the agrarian revolution is a special feature of China, which can never be understood by the Trotskyite liquidationists. It is also entirely false to adopt a wait-and-see attitude, maintaining that the present workers' struggle in the cities has not (yet) reached the rising tide (stage) and that a conservative policy should be adopted in the rural areas, and the expansion of the Red Army should be stopped. Granted that the workers' struggle has not yet reached a revolutionary high tide, and peasant uprisings, soldiers' mutinies, and the Red Army's expansion are still inadequate; still we should specially emphasize the intensifying of the workers' struggle while working for the development of peasant uprisings, the outbreak of soldiers' mutinies, and the vigorous expansion of the Red Army.

IV. THE REFORMIST AND LIQUIDATIONIST FACTIONS

[[The following three sections, nos. 14, 15, and 16, are devoted to attacks on the "reformist" group headed by Wang Ching-wei of the KMT and the "liquidationist" group headed by Ch'en Tu-hsiu. Party members are called upon to eliminate the influence of these persons among the masses.]]

V. PREPARE FOR THE TRANSFORMATION OF THE REVOLUTION

(17) The major tasks of the present revolution are the overthrow of imperialist rule, and the destruction of feudal forces by agrarian revolution. These are undoubtedly the characteristics of a democratic revolution. The unfounded assertion of the liquidationists, that the present task of the democratic revolution is finished, is a reactionary concept trying to make us slacken (our efforts in) the task of democratic revolution and our (work) of mobilizing the masses against the imperialists and for the agrarian revolution. But at present the proletariat is the only class leading the revolution—the bourgeoisie having become part of the reactionary alliance; thus the complete victory of the democratic revolution is inseparable from the overthrow of bourgeois rule and will inevitably result in the consolidation of proletarian leadership and the successful establishment of a Soviet régime. These (factors) assume in advance that the victory of the democratic revolution will transform (itself) into a victory of socialism.

(18) When the revolution has (won) preliminary successes in one or more provinces, the imperialists, gentry, and bourgeoisie will oppose it by every means (such as) armed attack, economic sabotage, and organizing counter-revolutionary coups. This cruel war will be one against the imperialists, landlords, and compradores, as well as against the bourgeoisie. At that time, the revolutionary government, in order to win the national revolution, will not only confiscate the banks, businesses, and factories of the imperialists, but also the factories, businesses, and banks of the Chinese bourgeoisie, so as to weaken the (power of) these counter-revolutionary weapons. It will also be necessary to organize and control production in order to cope with the grave economic blockade. At the same time, politically, it is necessary to have a centralized, dictatorial régime in order to meet the persistent counter-revolutionary attacks. This will necessitate an advance from the dictatorship of workers and peasants to that of the proletariat. A revolutionary transformation is primarily a transformation of class relationships. The dictatorship of the proletariat is already

in the nature of a socialist régime. Therefore the beginning of revolutionary victory and the establishment of a revolutionary régime will be the beginning of a revolutionary transformation. There will be no interim stage.

(19) It is a grave error to assume that the revolution can begin to be a revolutionary transformation only after victory on a national scale. For if the revolutionary government at that time does not carry out a class policy, (if it does not) confiscate the factories, businesses, and banks of the bourgeoisie, (if it does not) pre-empt the counter-revolutionary weapons of the bourgeoisie, then not only will the deepening of the revolution stop, but victory on a national scale will also be obstructed. This is a suicidal policy during a revolution. Therefore, the theory that the revolutionary transformation must have several stages is undoubtedly an extremely dangerous rightist notion. On the other hand, it is also erroneous to assume that "a revolution is still a democratic revolution on the eve of its victory, but that the régime set up after the victory of the revolution is a purely socialist régime". This neglects the process of revolutionary transformation (no matter how brief this process, it must be gone through), and ignores the fact that, when counter-attacking the cruel onslaught of the imperialists, the gentry, and the bourgeoisie, it is necessary to have the slogan and policy of democratic revolution for the mobilization of tens and hundreds of millions of the masses to overcome this counter-revolutionary attack.

(20) The dawn of victory for the revolution will mean a more cruel class war. On top of an all-out counter-revolutionary armed attack, the imperialists, gentry, and bourgeoisie will try every means to induce the petty bourgeoisie who remain in the revolutionary camp to turn against the revolution. Therefore, in the process of revolutionary transformation, new vacillations and betrayals are inevitable. Therefore we must never harbour any illusions about peaceful transformations of the revolution, but should henceforth utilize our correct policy of strengthening the leadership of the proletariat, establishing independent organizations for hired farm hands, consolidating the alliance with the poor peasants, eliminating the influence of the rich peasants, and winning over the middle peasants, in order to lessen the difficulties during the revolutionary transformation in the future. Such a correct, firm policy has definitely an important significance in the smooth realization of the future revolutionary transformation and should never be neglected by us.

(21) Another factor decisive for the victory and transformation of

the revolution is the mighty support from the already successful proletariat of the Soviet Union, and especially the outbreak of proletarian revolutions in capitalist countries. Because of China's semi-colonial nature, the victory of socialism in the Chinese revolution will be inseparable from the world revolution. The unprecedentedly fierce struggle of the Chinese revolution against the imperialists will inevitably heighten the world revolutionary upsurge; on the other hand, without a revolutionary rising tide of the world proletariat, it would be difficult to assure the continued success of the Chinese revolution. Therefore, it is at present our grave duty—and one of the main factors in the preparation for the victory and transformation of the revolution —that (we should) intensify propaganda for the Chinese revolution among the world proletariat, and, in particular, strengthen the alliance (with the latter) in the struggle.

VI. THE TASKS AND TACTICAL LINE OF THE PARTY

(22) At present, when the revolution is rapidly developing and the great revolutionary tide is approaching, the Party should not only pay attention to winning over the broad masses and organizing their struggle so as to hasten the arrival of this great revolutionary tide, (it should) also pay attention to the task of organizing armed insurrections on a national scale to capture political power when the great revolutionary rising tide arises. Therefore, it is necessary to step up the organization of the masses for the political struggle and the propaganda for seizing political power by armed insurrection. The general tactical line of the Party at present is to pay attention to hastening the national revolutionary upsurge, to organizational and technical preparations for armed insurrection, and to plans for preliminary successes in the provinces adjacent to and centring round Wuhan.

(23) The continued spreading of the warlords' warfare results in uprooting, bankruptcy, death, and destitution for the masses. The whole rule of the KMT is shown not only to have fallen into the lowest depths of despair, but also to have completely lost the confidence of the broad masses. (Therefore), the masses can be mobilized only by resolutely carrying out the line of opposition to the warlords' warfare, and under the central slogan of opposing warlords' war. If the Party fails actively to raise such a slogan, but in its place proposes some partial economic demands, the masses will feel frustrated and will not rise enthusiastically to struggle. The masses said long ago: "Whenever the insurrection comes, notify us, (and) we will come."

The Party should now boldly tell the masses: "The time for insurrection is approaching. Let all of you organize." It has been a grave shortcoming that in the past the Party paid much too little attention to the struggle against the warlords' warfare. Now the Party must resolutely raise the slogans of opposing imperialism, the KMT, and especially the warlords' warfare, and must organize sympathetic strikes (even general strikes), local uprisings, and soldiers' mutinies, and summon the Red Army to attack relentlessly in order to carry out the general line of converting the war of the warlords into a war to liquidate the warlords.

To carry out this line, it is, first of all, necessary to pay attention to the international mission of the Chinese revolution. The outbreak of the Chinese revolution will spur the imperialists not only to suppress the Chinese revolution in unison, but also to attack the Soviet Union with greater vigour. (Therefore), armed protection of the Soviet Union should become one of the central slogans of the revolution. Attention should be paid, at the same time, to co-ordination with the revolutionary struggles of the proletariat in capitalist countries and colonies and to the strengthening of propaganda for the Chinese revolution among the revolutionary masses of the world. On the other hand, the danger of an imperialist war is moving closer day by day. Henceforth, it is also an urgent task to engage in extensive propaganda and agitation for the anti-imperialist war, as well as to hasten the mobilization of a widespread movement against imperialism and in support of the revolutionary movement in colonial areas.

In the struggle against the warlords, (we) must, at the same time, give stronger support to the resolution of the councils of (workers', peasants', and soldiers') deputies in the Soviet areas: the fight-for-the-Soviet-régime movement. (We) must tell the broad masses that complete emancipation will come only after the overthrow of the warlords' régime and the establishment of a Soviet régime. The movement, in order to arouse the determination of the broad masses to struggle for the Soviet régime, should be carried into every factory, every school, and every village.

(24) The crux of the question in this line is the organization of political strikes. We (should) not only pay attention to the strengthening of political propaganda in economic strikes and convert every economic struggle into a political one, but also resolutely raise political slogans (opposing, for instance, the stationing of troops in factories, White Russian (Guards), arrests of workers, yellow unions, and demanding freedom to organize unions and to strike). Slogans should

concentrate on opposing the warlords' warfare, so as to organize extensive political strikes among the masses. Without resolute political struggles, economic gains are definitely hard to win. Only resolute political slogans can heighten the courage of the masses to struggle. (We should take care that, in our tactics, every political slogan for agitation, every political struggle, is co-ordinated with economic demands.) The lessons of the organizing of the May First and May Thirtieth movements are that, in general, political propaganda and agitation are inadequate. (We did) not boldly raise political slogans in organizing the strikes of the May First and May Thirtieth (movements), but mobilized the masses mostly by economic slogans. This was the major reason why, in various districts, large-scale strikes could not be organized. It was a very grave rightist error, showing not only a tendency to "tail" the masses, but also the serious error of obstructing the struggle of the masses.

(25) General organizational weakness is a most serious weakness in the present workers' movement. We must pay the utmost attention and spend our greatest efforts on expanding the Red unions and establishing factory committees. But (we must) realize that such efforts can only yield greater results under resolute political battle-slogans. (We) must resolutely begin a movement to fight for the freedom to organize unions and to strike. The masses can be rallied around us in increasing numbers only by struggling openly for the Red unions, and against the yellow unions as well as the KMT. If (the Party) limits itself to narrow, secret work, it will be difficult for the mass organizations to develop on a large scale and consolidate themselves.

(26) At present it is our urgent duty to establish and expand the military organizations of the working masses (Red storm troops and pickets) [ch'ih-se hsien-feng-tui and chiu-ch'a-tui], and to intensify their military training. Not only must we propagate, in the struggle, the need for organizing (workers') pickets, but also (we) must use the slogan of preparing for armed insurrection to mobilize the broad masses to join the (workers') pickets and the Red storm troops. Only thus can military mass organizations be rapidly expanded; (only thus can) the pickets and Red storm troops become the central units of the insurrection.

(27) One of the major tasks in the execution of the present general line is the resolute organization of local uprisings. The aim of local uprisings is to capture cities and to establish local Soviet régimes. (This) is the highest stage of peasant uprisings, whose future is

inevitably linked with (the uprisings) in key cities to complete the success of a nationwide insurrection. The rural struggle has, at present, reached a rising tide and conditions for local uprisings, in general, are undoubtedly mature. The Party should unhesitatingly mobilize the broad masses, under the slogan of local uprisings, to accomplish this task. The most serious obstacle to the accomplishment of this task is the "guerrilla" concept of the past, which (advocates) attacking, instead of occupying, cities and lacks the resolution to establish local Soviets in the cities. This is a reflection of the peasant mentality and has nothing in common with (our) present line. When a local uprising succeeds, a local Soviet régime should be immediately established and the masses should be immediately mobilized to carry out resolute attacks and substantial expansion (of the régime).

(28) The vigorous expansion of the Red Army is an even more pressing task of the present, especially in the Soviet areas. Without the co-ordination of a large and mighty Red Army, a nationwide victory for the revolution cannot be won in a China ruled by warlordism. At present, our Party—especially those Party units in the Soviet areas—should mobilize the broad masses to join, support, and concentrate their armed strength in the Red Army. In order to break down the localism and conservatism of the peasant mentality, (we) must tell the broad masses that the agrarian revolution can be assured of victory only if the régime of the KMT, gentry, and bourgeoisie is completely overthrown and if the revolution is carried to victory on a national scale. Such a mentality is at present the most serious obstacle to the vigorous expansion of the Red Army. The second grave obstacle is the failure to understand the general development of the revolutionary situation, and a stubborn adherence to the military concept of guerrilla warfare, in opposition to the expansion of the Red Army and its expansionist tactics. This (attitude) is due to complete ignorance of the fact that military tactics, equipment, troop designations, and organization should all change with the general political line. To obstruct a change in Party tactics by clinging to an old military viewpoint is a serious rightist mistake.

(29) The strategy and tactics of the Red Army should not only consist of resolute attacks on the major forces of the enemy, assaults on key cities and lines of communication (of the enemy), and a complete change from the guerrilla tactics of the past, but also should turn the warlord's warfare into a revolutionary war to liquidate the warlords, and carry out, in a co-ordinated and organized fashion,

under the general plan, the military task of preliminary successes in one or more provinces. The over-all aim of this task [of the Red Army] is the seizure of political power and the establishment of a national revolutionary régime in co-ordination with armed uprisings in key cities. The guerrilla tactics of the past have become entirely incompatible with this line and must undergo a fundamental change. Another serious task of the Red Army at present is to intensify political training along class lines. An absolute majority of the Red Army being at present made up of peasants, special attention should be paid to their political training along class lines in order to consolidate the leadership of the proletariat and eliminate thoroughly the erroneous tendencies (in) the peasant mentality.

(30) Under the present over-all line, the mission of the soldiers' movement is not only to incite the soldiers in the warlords' armies to mutiny and to bring them over to the Red Army, but to organize the soldiers' anti-warlord mutinies as a central strategy. That is to say, not only to incite small-scale, scattered mutinies, but also to raise the banner of anti-warlord warfare and of the liquidation of warlords in an organized and planned manner, and in co-ordination with other revolutionary forces. Thus, after a mutiny, the tactic of resolute attacks should be adopted to rout the warlord troops. The past practice of fleeing after the uprising must be effectively corrected.

(31) The gravest obstacle to the execution of this general line is the rightist ideas which are absolutely incompatible with it. The Party must, as a prerequisite to executing this general line, resolutely fight against all wavering, rightist ideas, especially "tailist" tendencies. The liquidationists, with their systematic liquidationist philosophy, have, in fact, turned from an intra-Party opposition group into a class enemy. The Party must carry out a more resolute struggle within its ranks and especially among the masses against (the liquidationists). But the rightist ideas hidden inside the Party have also become a great danger at present because they superficially support the Party line, but in every actual tactic have shown doubts, vacillation, sabotage, and inaction. Without overcoming all these rightist ideas, it will be impossible to carry out the Party line and policy to the full.

(32) Youth and women are an important factor in the revolutionary struggle. We must resolutely oppose the tendency to neglect the youth and women's movements, because it is a grave political error. The positive role of youth and women can be witnessed in any struggle at present; and the Party should actively draw them into the revolutionary camp. The Party must, by all available means, assist the

reorientation of the work of the CY, and oppose the tendency towards Bohemianism within the (CY) corps.

VII. THE ORGANIZATIONAL PROBLEM OF THE PARTY

(33) The present inadequate organizational strength of the Party (especially in the cities), which is the major weakness of the revolution, has shown itself clearly in every struggle. However, it is a grave rightist concept to doubt (the correctness) of the present Party line and (the existence) of a revolutionary situation because of this weakness in (Party) organization. But it is also a serious error to overlook this weakness in Party organization and not to struggle actively for the strengthening of the Party organization. Therefore, it is (our) over-all task to pay special attention to the strengthening of Party organization in order to carry out the present general line.

(34) A number of serious weaknesses indeed stand out in (our) present Party organization: first, its slow expansion among the workers —thus, the proletarian basis (of the Party) is not rapidly expanded. (Secondly), only a few cadres possessing the characteristics of workers have been inducted into the Party. (Thirdly), the defective life in Party cells (which) are incapable of functioning as leading nuclei among the masses. As a result, the correct Party policy cannot be conveyed to the masses in its entirety. On the other hand, the backward mentality of the masses is often reflected [in the Party cadres], resulting in a wavering (attitude) towards the Party policy. The chief reason is that the struggle against rightism by the (Party) cells is totally inadequate; in many localities such a struggle has not even reached the cells, where many wavering rightist elements still occupy leading positions, obstruct the execution of all (Party) tactics, and first of all prevent the cells from having a proper life. For better cell life, for the development of Party organization, and for the actual and correct execution of the Party line and policy, it is requisite to wage a resolute struggle in the (Party) cells against the right, to intensify cell education, and to train cadres in the cells. Party headquarters on all levels are asked to give serious attention to this question.

(35) The danger of petty-bourgeois romanticism is also manifest in the present Party organization: (Party) work and inspections are not carried out in an organized, systematic fashion, but often in feverish spurts. This does great harm to the efficiency of (Party) work, and particularly the negligence of security is directly threatening the very existence of the Party. The recent important arrests (of CP members) in several provinces were chiefly due to negligence of security work.

This grave, bloody lesson should arouse the utmost attention of the entire Party to struggle resolutely with the tendency of petty-bourgeois romanticism. This should be one of the major tasks in the consolidation of Party organization.

15. CHOU EN-LAI (SHAO SHAN): REPORT TO THE THIRD PLENUM
(September 24, 1930) [extract]

I. THE INTERNATIONAL SITUATION AND THE CHINESE REVOLUTION. . . .
[we omit sections 1, 2, and 3; see under *Bibliography A*]

4. [p. 2] *The World Revolution and the Chinese Revolution*

In some countries the economic crisis has already been transformed into a political crisis. In some countries the economic crisis has only begun. Although these developments have been uneven, they will undoubtedly affect all China. At the same time, the crisis in China makes it impossible for the imperialists to reach stability. It also accelerates the development of the world revolution. It can clearly be seen that the uneven development of the world revolution makes possible the victory of revolution in some countries ahead of others. This is a clear answer to the mistake of the right-wing of the CI, represented by Bukharin and others. They talk strangely about "organized capitalism", "U.S.A. exceptionalism", and "Indian decolonization", etc. It also answers the pessimistic forecasts that the Soviet Union will collapse under the pressure of its present drastic development. Moreover, it answers the doubts concerning the characteristics of the post-war "third period" raised by Chinese rightists, who maintain that the victory of the Chinese revolution may not stir up a world revolution. These rightist slogans have been all smashed by facts.

II. THE NEW RISING TIDE OF THE CHINESE REVOLUTION AND THE COMINTERN LINE

1. *The ever-expanding conflicts among warlords within the context of the national economic and political crisis*

On the foundation of the Chinese political and economic crisis, there has been an expansion of civil wars among the warlords. This is a characteristic of present Chinese conditions. There is no need to repeat in detail the story of the bankruptcy of Chinese agriculture, the accelerated decline of industry, the stagnation of commerce, the destruction of, and interruption in, railways, and the exorbitant prices of foodstuffs. At the same time, the KMT has failed completely in its domestic and foreign policies during the last three years, and the window-dressing of peace and unification has gone to pieces. . . .

2. *The Political Struggle of the Masses develops against the Background of Peasant Warfare*

(1) The deep penetration of the agrarian revolution has made possible the enlargement of the Soviet areas, which have extended as far as regions near the Yangtze river and into South China. According to present statistics, more than 300 *hsien* have established Soviet régimes, and more than 50,000,000 people are under their control. . . .

(2) The soldiers in the warlord armies have been made revolutionary, and they are inclined towards agrarian revolution. . . .

(3) The city paupers are becoming more revolutionary daily and we note above all a rising upsurge in the workers' struggles during the past year. . . .

This state of affairs proves that the Chinese revolutionary situation is growing more acute daily and that the promotion and development of the revolutionary movement is taking place under the leadership of the CCP and the banner of the Soviets. . . .

4. [p. 3] *The Characteristics of the New Revolutionary Upsurge and the Comintern Line*

In the new upsurge of the Chinese revolution, there is one feature considered of prime importance by the CI. It is the existence of the uneven development of the revolution in the national economic and political crisis. In a divided China ruled by the imperialists, China's economic development retains many local characteristics and political changes occur at different times, some earlier, some later. Furthermore, revolutionary experience varies, some people having more and some less. These conditions have determined the uneven development of the Chinese revolution. While the workers at present have not yet taken up arms to overthrow the reactionary régime, the peasant warfare in villages to overthrow the KMT rule is spreading. Peasants in the North suffer more than those in the South, but the peasant masses have not established their Soviet régime, nor have they redistributed the land. This shows, in degree and in speed, the unevenness of the revolutionary developments.

In this respect, there has been some difference in the evaluations made by the CI and the CC. The CC has realized this unevenness, but has not paid attention to it, and has thus been unable to solve its present problems. In evaluating future perspectives it took a certain possibility in the future as a basis for action at the present time. Therefore, it made exaggerated and incorrect evaluations of the speed and degree of development of the revolution and sporadic practical mistakes occurred. This is what the CI wants to correct.

The resolution of the CI states: "The new rising tide in the Chinese revolution has undoubtedly become a fact." This refutes the arguments of the opportunists. As of today, however, the forces of the Chinese workers and peasants have not yet been concentrated sufficiently to attack the rule of the imperialists and the KMT, and there is as yet no revolutionary objective situation on a national scale. In other words, the situation has not yet (ripened) to (the point of) armed insurrections on a national scale. Nevertheless, the CI is not of the view that this is simply a prospect in the remote future. . . .

Do the errors of the CC lie in a difference in line from the CI? Absolutely not. There is no difference in line. The present task of the CCP is to win over the broad masses, concentrate their revolutionary strength, organize the revolutionary war, actively prepare for an armed insurrection, overthrow the imperialist and KMT rule, and establish the Soviet régime. All these objectives do not differ in the slightest from the instructions of the CI, with which there is complete harmony. Only because of an over-estimation in degree and in speed of the present revolutionary development, the CC made sporadic tactical mistakes. . . .

III. THE MAIN TASKS AND THE BASIC STRATEGY OF THE PARTY

1. *The Party should carry on a twofold task to organize the revolutionary war and prepare actively for the armed insurrection*

During the course of organizing the revolutionary war, the Party, in accordance with the CI directives, must carry on a twofold task. On the one side we must consolidate the existing Soviet areas, centralize the scattered Soviet areas, concentrate and strengthen the leadership of the Red Army, mobilize even more peasant masses, and establish a central Soviet government to advance towards the key industrial cities. In other words, we must advance on a consolidated basis and expand with deep penetration. In the past the CC work in this respect was inadequate. It only stressed the development and expansion of the Red Army, but neglected its consolidation and strengthening.

Especially in regard to the Soviet areas, the direct guidance of the CC has been inadequate. This task becomes even more important today. It can now be seen that in the two attacks on Changsha [in July and September, 1930] the direction of the Red Army was not centralized, there was no co-ordination among units, our rear was not consolidated, the masses were not mobilized to the maximum limit, there was no work among the enemy soldiers, and above all the CC exercised no direct command. . . .

Secondly, we must mobilize the struggle of the urban worker masses, intensify the work of propaganda and organization, and mobilize greater numbers of the masses to prepare actively for armed insurrections. This is the other side of our task. . . .

2. [p. 4] *The central problem in the Soviet areas*

According to the instructions of the CI, the central problems are as follows:

(1) *The establishment of Soviet bases.* . . .

(2) *The Soviet Delegates' Conference and the Central Government.*

The Soviet Delegates' Conference of last May [1930, in Shanghai], which promulgated laws and was attended by the leaders of the Red Army and of the masses, did not resolve to establish a government. Because the conference was not publicly convened in the Soviet areas, it was only a preparatory meeting in nature. At that time the CC had too mechanical a concept, maintaining that the central government must be located in Wuhan or at least in Changsha or Nanchang, instead of emphasizing the problem of centralizing the proletarian leadership, of unifying the command, and of unifying and carrying out the laws. It did not realize that by doing so it would provide more incentive for the masses of the Soviet areas and influence the worker-peasant masses of the whole country much more. This is the main function of establishing a provisional central government. Of course, it is better to establish it in key cities than in small cities, but that is a question of secondary importance. In regard to this question, the CC understood the situation in theory, but was defective in its application.

(3) *The Diplomatic Policy towards the Imperialists.*

The CP will not vacillate in its anti-imperialist policy, especially it will not vacillate in its struggle at the present stage of the democratic revolution, when anti-imperialism is one of the two main tasks. . . .

(4) *The Land Problem.*

The CC and the CI lines are fundamentally the same: the fruits of land confiscation should go to the poor peasants and the hired farm hands, and some benefits should accrue to the middle peasants, but they should never go to the rich peasants. Although the concept of equal redistribution of land may be construed as the point of view of petty-bourgeois socialism, this was the only way to liquidate the feudal forces completely. . . .

[p. 5] The question of nationalization of land should be popularized but cannot be put into effect immediately, for as yet there is no victorious political régime on a national scale. We cannot construe the Soviet ownership of land as nationalization . . . we definitely cannot say that the Chinese peasants have already rid themselves of the idea of private ownership. Thus the prohibition of free sale of land is an unnecessary slogan at present, and it only serves to increase the worries of the peasants. Of course, the nationalization of land is the most thorough form of the bourgeois-democratic revolution, and also one of the requisites for the revolutionary transformation. . . . Therefore, the anti-rich peasant line is very important and cannot be neglected, even when the rich peasants have the same amount of land as the poor peasants.

Also, we must prevent (any) leftist error towards rich peasants and a disregard of our relationship with the middle peasants. . . .

(6) *Economic Policy.*

At the present stage of the democratic revolution, the principle of economic policy will still be to permit free trade and free business under Soviet laws and under the principle of production supervised by workers. This is to enable the Soviet régime to utilize economic activities so as to concentrate its attention on the organizing of the revolutionary war and on external expansion. But at the same time it should be noted that, in time of civil war, the industrialists and business men will ally themselves with the reactionaries under the reactionary régime. . . .

(7) *The question of the Red Army.*

It is late to talk about the strengthening of the Red Army today, since we already had the Red Army one year ago, but it was not entirely a true Red Army. Although the Red Army grew out of guerrilla forces, it must be different from the latter. The Second Plenum [of the CC, CCP, in June 1929] brought up this point, but inadequately. The tactic of vigorous expansion of the Red Army in the past has overcome the "guerrilla fixation". But that is not enough. We must make the Red Army the major force in the internal war. It should become a strong and centralized Red Army under proletarian organization and leadership. This can clearly be seen from the lesson of the two attacks on Changsha. The directives from the CI are:

(*a*) The main component of the Red Army should be the poor peasants, hired farm hands, coolies or their sons, who have benefited from the agrarian revolution.

(*b*) The important cadres should be workers. The disorganized peasant consciousness should be corrected.

(*c*) The Party should establish its absolute prestige and confidence among the Red Army; the influence of Trotskyists, liquidationists, and other factions should be eliminated; and the lumpenproletarian-peasant attitude of neutrality should also be liquidated. Only thus can success be achieved. . . .

3. [p. 6] *The Work in Non-Soviet Areas*

(1) Urban work: The CI's instructions show that we should set up a policy of general strikes in key cities to develop the work on a national scale. . . . In the course of the daily economic struggle, many economic strikes have been transformed into political strikes, so that the two have become inseparable. The central strategy of the Party is to carry on organized political strikes. Doubts that the CC has carried on political strikes under its leadership are not based on facts . . . at the same time we want to point out that the application of this tactic of organizing political strikes has sometimes been too mechanical. It is necessary skilfully to co-ordinate this central tactic with the daily struggles. We sometimes were mechanical and unco-ordinated in applying this tactic. . . . Thus the resolution of the CI states, "the carrying out of proletarian leadership requires that the Party must continuously develop the struggle of the strike movement, and organize and lead the economic struggles of the Chinese proletariat". The Party should co-ordinate political and economic struggles, develop political strikes as much as possible, and map out a programme of political general strikes for various areas or several key industrial cities. In organizing political strikes, in addition to the anti-warlord and anti-KMT slogans, it must also raise economic demands close to the life of the workers in general and (close) to the most backward elements of the working class.

Incidentally, (when) the CC in the past planned the Wuhan insurrection, the Nanking insurrection and the Shanghai general strike, the CI objected. The CI was not objecting to the principle, but was instructing us how to prepare for it, opposing its being done immediately today or tomorrow. . . .

(2) To intensify the anti-imperialist struggle. . . .

(3) To carry out an independent revolutionary movement of the masses. . . . In the independent revolutionary movement of the masses under our leadership, (we) must not neglect the utilization of the united front in the lower (social strata). . . .

(4) [p. 7] To develop the peasant war extensively. . . .

IV. PROBLEMS OF THE PARTY

1. *The progress of the Party and weaknesses in Organizational Work* . . . .

The CCP is weak in organization and its proletarian cadres are inadequate. The industrial workers in the Party number only a little more than 2,000. Though the political influence of the Party is great, the organizational power (of the Party) is unable to consolidate this influence. Therefore, the CI has pointed out that the Chinese Party should devote itself to the task of reinforcing its own subjective strength.

2. [p. 8] *The Central Tasks in Organization*

(1) To enlarge the proletarian foundation.

Though there are 120,000 Party members, the industrial worker members only number a little more than 2,000. This percentage is too small; its leadership role is indeed too weak.

(2) To consolidate the work of the Party cell.

(3) To strengthen the cadres, particularly by bringing in worker cadres. To strengthen the leadership of the Party headquarters at various levels.

(4) To strengthen the nuclear functions of the Party cell and of the Party and CY in unions and among the masses.

3. *Self-criticism within the Party and a resolute struggle against rightist deviation.* . . .

The CC has engaged in sharp self-criticism after examining its own work. During this period the directive work of the CC was carried on collectively and, therefore, the responsibility fell on the group as a whole. When we mentioned in our criticism that Comrade [Li] Li-san should shoulder more responsibility than others, we did not mean that other comrades of the CC were free of blame. The responsibility for slowness in the execution of, and conveyance of, CI instructions is to be shared by all of us. For instance, concerning the question of the mutinies at Nanking and Chinkiang, I myself committed mistakes

Summarizing the work of the recent three months, we accept the criticisms of the CI, and point out that Comrade Li-san should shoulder more responsibilities in ideological (matters), but we must not tolerate irritating remarks by other comrades such as those made by Comrade (Ho) Meng-hsiung about "Li-sanism". In the examination of our past activity, we should also carry on self-criticism on a collective basis. . . .

. . . In general, the rightist line displays the following tendencies:

(*a*) A tendency to under-estimate the revolutionary situation; a tendency not to believe in the arrival of a revolutionary high tide or the post-war "third period".

(*b*) A tendency to tremble before the cannon and machine-guns of the imperialists and to try to find a way out by surrender to, or compromising with, the imperialists.

(*c*) A tendency to belittle greatly the significance of the peasant war, to speak of the invasion of Changsha as a tribal action, and of the Red Army as hoodlums and bandits.

(*d*) A pessimistic estimate of our subjective strength, which is considered insufficient for leading any struggle.

(*e*) A wavering attitude towards political strikes. . . .

V. THE TRANSFORMATION OF THE REVOLUTION

1. [p. 9] *The Characteristics of the Chinese Revolution*

The transformation of the revolution is a somewhat theoretical question which occupies an important place in the CI resolution. It also points out the problems which may be solved in China in the future. The resolution of the CI clearly points out the characteristics of the immediate Chinese revolution:

(1) After the failure of the last Great Revolution [1925–7], the bourgeoisie no longer takes part in the revolution. It becomes reactionary and forms one of the objects which we want to overthrow. It is necessary to disarm it politically.

(2) The Chinese agrarian revolution is entirely under the leadership of the proletariat. The peasants, rallying round the proletariat in the agrarian revolution, are the strong foundation of a worker-peasant alliance.

(3) The Chinese revolution opposes the feudal class and also opposes the capitalistic control of the imperialists. This is the characteristic of the Chinese revolution in the overthrow of the world capitalistic system.

(4) The Chinese revolution is developing under a Soviet régime. This form of political power was not decisive in Russia in 1905. [This sentence is blurred in the original.] In China, however, it has been instrumental in putting political power into the hands of the proletariat, and has become the strongest political expression of the broad worker-peasant labouring masses.

(5) By means of their political hegemony, the Communists constitute an absolute majority. This is already true in the present peasant war in various areas, not to mention the future. Any group that favours the National Assembly [of the KMT government] will not be permitted to participate [in the revolutionary régime]. The masses will not allow them to participate.

These excellent internal conditions enable the Chinese revolution, on its victorious path, to contemplate the perspective of socialistic, non-capitalistic development.

The instructions of the CI further pointed out that the transitional process must go through a great many preparatory stages so as to gradually and fundamentally transform (the revolution) into a socialist revolution. . . .

. . . The democratic revolution is still the central slogan at present. The preparation for the transformation must have, as its point of departure, the thorough realization of the democratic revolution. The rightist drawing of a clear line of demarcation between the two stages of revolution is incorrect, but we definitely cannot say that the transformation is already the main task at present. Another more dangerous mistake is the idea that as soon as we have won the industrial cities, the revolution will immediately take on a socialistic character. This idea is very detrimental to the thorough realization of the democratic revolution for the whole country.

This indicates that the resolution [of the CC] of June 11 [1930] concerning the explanation of this point is too mechanical. But its spirit in opposing the two [above-mentioned] mistakes is correct.

Finally, the Party should elaborate on the correct theories of Marxism-Leninism concerning the revolutionary transformation and oppose the nonsensical theory of Trotsky that the Chinese revolution is already a socialist revolution. At the same time, we must also oppose the reactionary nature of the Three People's Principles of the KMT and the deceitful claim that the KMT will lead China towards a non-capitalistic development. On the theoretical front, we must defeat all reactionary groups, and fight for the victory of Marxism-Leninism in China!

16. RESOLUTION OF THE ENLARGED FOURTH PLENUM OF THE
CC, CCP (January 1931)

(1) The resolution of the CI of July 1930 concerning the Chinese question,[1] in addition to its previous resolutions, has provided the CCP with clear directives concerning the task of a broad attack against the imperialists, feudalism, and the KMT counter-revolution through the use of our real revolutionary mass organization and by the mobilization of all our revolutionary forces. However, precisely at the critical moment when the revolutionary rising tide was swelling, the leadership of the CCP, then under the domination of Comrade Li Li-san's line, disregarded these directives of the CI and launched (us) on to a risky path of putschism and a line in conflict with that of the CI. Everybody is now aware of the havoc wrought by the anti-CI line of Comrade Li-san. It is impossible to enumerate all the gravely evil consequences of Comrade Li-san's anti-Leninist and adventurist line as they manifested themselves in practice. The Fourth Plenum has, however, pointed out some of the main evil effects; they are: weakening of the Party's influence over, and ties with, the masses; the drastic reduction in ability of the Party to mobilize the masses; the weakening of the activities of all mass organizations; the set-back in our labour movement, and the fact that in the leadership and organization of the strike movement we have not only failed to advance but have repeatedly lost ground; and the fact that, as a result of the leadership of Li-san, the Party did not under the conditions of a revolutionary rising tide use every means to consolidate the Party, the CY, and the mass organizations, but on the contrary has in practice liquidated the mass organizations and the CY and loosened the Party structure. Furthermore, Li-san carried on systematic oppression against those who supported the CI line, bringing life in the Party to a completely abnormal state. The fact that the Party has so generally deteriorated and is now so weakened has made it possible for Trotskyists and Ch'en Tu-hsiu-ists, on the one hand, and rightists within the Party, on the other, to avail themselves of this opportunity to become more active. At the same time, many people have started insurrections based on purely putschist methods without making an estimate of the objective situation and without proper preparation. These tendencies have caused the Party to lose prestige among the masses, brought physical injury to our most active members, and destroyed our organizations in the key districts of the country. The task of expanding the anti-imperialist movement has been completely

forgotten. The Party's leadership paid almost no attention to the expansion of the daily struggle in the peasant movement in non-Soviet areas. The Party's tasks of leadership in the non-Soviet rural areas, of developing and gradually intensifying the struggle of the peasant masses in order to bring them to a level where they could directly aid and participate in the Soviet movement have been completely abandoned. Finally, the clumsiest mistake resulting from Comrade Li-san's position has taken place within the Soviet areas. This had a very bad effect on the consolidation and development of the Red Army. There was a premature, adventurous, and dogmatic instruction to seize big cities when we had no consolidated rear, had not made necessary preparation, and had an insufficient base in the masses. The Changsha debacle was a result of these mistakes. On the other hand, there has been no sufficiently resolute struggle against Comrade Li-san's former theory of an alliance with the rich peasants. Nothing has been done about the organization of poor peasant associations, unions of hired farm hands, and unions of coolies. Owing to the negligence of the local Party headquarters, and as a result of Li-san's policy, the rich peasant elements have been able to infiltrate into the directing organs and have seized the fruits of agrarian revolution for their own interests. The collective farm and all other premature socialistic measures proposed by Li Li-san would in fact have, inevitably, further consolidated the interests of the rich peasants. The order prohibiting free business transactions and the buying and selling of land made the Soviet economic condition even more difficult. These mistakes were detrimental to the alliance between us and the middle peasants, and dampened the enthusiastic participation of the great majority of the peasant masses in the Soviet movement. Li Li-san's leadership completely neglected the task of establishing a strong Soviet base, and completely neglected the establishment of a strong Soviet political régime. In addition, a directive was issued to abolish guerrilla warfare. All of these were considered as belonging to stages past. Thus, our front was in a greatly weakened condition while the warlords invaded the Soviet areas. These are the main reasons why the Red Army suffered serious set-backs. At the same time, there has been no extensive work to help the Soviet movement; this is particularly obvious in regard to the preparatory work of calling an All-China Soviet Congress.

In surveying the results of the Li-san line, the Enlarged Fourth Plenum particularly wishes to point out that, from the Sixth Congress [July–September 1928] until June 1930, the CC made many mistakes concerning the problem of rich peasants, the yellow union problem, and the reorganizationalist problem, etc.; nevertheless, under its correct over-all line, the Party had achieved great results, a great part of which, however, have been dissipated as a result of the Li-san line.

(2) The mistakes of Comrade Li-san are not isolated nor incidental mistakes, but rather are based on a systematic anti-Leninism embodying many incorrect concepts. These erroneous concepts are, in essence, a repetition of Trotsky's theory. The Li-san line denies the unevenness of development of the world revolution by emphasizing the perspective of a general revolutionary upsurge. This means the denial of the possibility of the separate victory and consolidation of the Chinese revolution. The Li-san line completely fails to understand the nature and stages of the Chinese revolution. Li substituted Trotsky's point of view, denying the place of the bourgeois-democratic stage of the revolution in Lenin's theory of the transformation of the revolution. As a result he entirely misunderstood the tasks of the present stage of the Chinese revolution. He denied the unevenness of the development of the revolution in China and disregarded the unique characteristics of the Chinese political and economic environment. Thus, the Li-san line denies the possibility of a preliminary success in one or several provinces. The Li-san line has no understanding of the Party's function as the organizer of the revolution, nor the relationship that should exist between the vanguard of Communism and the worker and peasant masses. The Li-san line distorted and in effect rejected the Marxist-Leninist theory of armed insurrection and tried to build a foundation in theory for a policy of adventuristic putschism, and in effect forced the Party along this course. Thus we have a statement by Li-san on this subject to the effect that "workers are only willing to carry on insurrection, but not strikes". In summary, the Li-san line is contradictory to the line of the CI, a policy of opportunism under the camouflage of "leftist phrases", and an opportunistic passivism in regard to the task of organizing the masses in a practical and revolutionary way. The historical root of the Li-san line is the opportunism and the putschism which had arisen before the Sixth Congress [of 1928] and which has not yet been eradicated from the Party. Comrade Li-san, basing himself upon this absolutely incorrect line, carried out a struggle against the CI line, disobeyed CI discipline, and adopted the arguments used by the leftist and rightist rebels against the CI by saying that the CI did not understand the Chinese situation and could not lead the Chinese revolution.

The Fourth Plenum firmly condemns the anti-Leninist line of the [CCP] Politburo from June to August 1930 and its hostile attitude towards the CI, which is absolutely intolerable, and particularly points out that all the serious set-backs suffered by the Party are a result of the failure of Comrade Li-san and other comrades supporting him to heed the directives and previous warnings of the ECCI. The fourth Plenum also points out that the credit for correcting the erroneous line and mistakes of the CC belongs entirely to the CI.

(3) The CI requests that the Party completely expose the "theory" of Comrade Li-san and totally eradicate the effects of all his anti-CI policies. The present situation in China and the attack on the Soviet areas by the imperialists, the KMT, and the warlords make it more necessary than ever for the Party to carry out a thorough shift from the semi-Trotskyite Li-san line to the line of the CI directives and resolutions. Judging the Third Plenum of the CCP [September 1930] from this point of view, the present Enlarged Fourth Plenum points out that the Third Plenum did not fulfil this task. The political resolutions of the Third Plenum amply prove this point. (*a*) The political resolution of the Third Plenum pointed out only the individual mistakes of Comrade Li-san, and even this was done in a mild tone. In the resolution we find no hint of the fact that Li Li-san's line was an absolutely incorrect line and was contradictory, in principle, to that of the CI; (*b*) this resolution reproduces without change the famous resolution of June 11 [1930, see document no. 14, above] which involved an anti-CI policy; (*c*) the political resolution of the Third Plenum also lent its approval to the political line and work of the Politburo from June to August [1930], even though the semi-Trotskyite Li-san line was dominant in the work of the Political Bureau during this period; (*d*) obviously, many practical mistakes emerged from this incorrect and compromising viewpoint included in the political resolution and some articles in other resolutions of the Third Plenum.

The resolutions passed by the Third Plenum prove that the Party did not realize at that time the full extent of the incorrectness of the Li-san policy and did not realize that this policy is completely contradictory in principle to the only correct line of the CI. Naturally, the resolution did not establish the principles necessary for bringing about a thoroughgoing change in the over-all policy of the Party. These resolutions could not furnish the foundation for the exposure of the "theory" of Comrade Li-san and for the complete overcoming of these incorrect theories in practice.

Other documents relating to the Third Plenum have committed even greater mistakes and have further confused the corrections demanded by the CI in the Party line of the CC [of the CCP]. For instance: (a) In the *Letter to All Comrades*, from the Third Plenum, the wording was even milder than that in the *Political Resolution* [of June 11, 1930], which left the Party members entirely unaware of the difference between the CI line and the semi-Trotskyite Li-san line; (b) the article on "The Significance of the Third Plenum", written by Ch'ü Ch'iu-pai, which appeared in the first issue of *True Words* [*Shih-hua*] together with the resolutions of the Third Plenum, did not mention one word concerning Li Li-san's mistakes, and said nothing regarding his putschist line; (c) the notices of the CC after the Third Plenum not only failed to expose Comrade Li-san's line, but, on the contrary, tended to construe it as a correct line and as the line of the CI. The generally compromising line of the Third Plenum later led to a situation in which there was not the slightest evidence of a real change of policy in local Party units. During this period, the Northern Bureau (of the CCP), the Southern Bureau (of the CCP), and the provincial committee members of the Kiangsu [original characters *Chiang-nan*, i.e. *Kiang-nan*, are presumably a misprint] and other Party organizations, all passed incorrect resolutions.

The Enlarged Fourth Plenum must further point out that the leadership of the Party adopted an inexcusably disrespectful attitude towards the CI representative. This attitude is reflected in the following fact: A few comrades of the [CCP] Politburo and the CI representative previously agreed on a revision and rewording of the political resolutions of the Third Plenum (among other things, an evaluation of the Li-san line and of the work of the Politburo from June to August [1930] was included). Although this had been agreed upon, nothing was included in the political resolution. In addition, the CI representative was not informed beforehand, and consequently he could not correct the compromising tendency of the Politburo towards the Li-san line in time. The Fourth Plenum is of the view that the compromising viewpoint of the Third Plenum made it possible to recognize the CI line only in words, and to display disrespect towards the CI representative—the major responsibility in this respect should be assumed by Comrade [Ch'ü] Ch'iu-pai.

(4) The supplementary resolution of the [CCP] Politburo on November 25 [1930] was in complete agreement with the recent letter [November 16, 1930] of the CI; it pointed out the compromising line of the Third Plenum, gave a correct evaluation of the work of the

Politburo from June to August, and condemned the Li-san line as anti-CI and anti-Leninist. It thus went a step closer to the CI line; yet the second article of the resolution did say that the Third Plenum generally accepted the CI line, consequently the significance of this resolution was obliterated and its political significance greatly reduced.

Circular no. 96 [of the CC] corrected the mistakes of the Politburo and those of the November 25 resolution, but it still contained errors. This circular did not announce the bankruptcy of the Li-san line, but mentioned instead a crisis in the Party—the Party, in fact, had just entered into the process of correcting Li-sanism and begun to take a correct path. Furthermore, this circular pointed out that the struggle against the Li-san line was a struggle on two fronts. This shows that its understanding of the twofold struggle was not correct. True, the Li-san line did use leftist terms to cover up its actual rightist opportunism. But the anti-Li-san line definitely does not cover the entirety of the two-front struggle. The rightist opportunists can and already have found other means of expressing themselves (such as Kuo Miao-ken and others). It must be remembered that although it is exceedingly important to struggle against the putschism of the Li-san line, the immediate danger of the Party at present is still the rightist tendency. Moreover, it must be firmly remembered that the Party can stand on the ground of the CI line and carry on the revolutionary attack only when the Party struggles against opportunism, putschism, and compromise-ism are finally won. All these points were not covered in Circular no. 96, thus disarming the Party in the struggle against the rightists. For these rightists are very active in distorting the CI line under the false banner of anti-Li-sanism, carrying on a struggle against the Li-san line on rightist grounds, denying the danger of a rightist tendency, blurring the necessity for an anti-rightist struggle, and attempting to induce some of the lower level organs to use incorrect methods of struggle in opposing Li Li-sanism. For example, they deny the necessity of shifting to practical work in the Party, and demand extreme democracy; they raise the arbitrary slogan of dismissing the whole Politburo and all the leading comrades who have committed some mistake, attempt to change the fight for principle into a fight between groups and individuals, and refuse to engage in self-criticism, etc. In addition, this circular charges that the Politburo, until recently, had actually been continuing and strengthening the Li-san line. It is true that the CC could not lead the struggle against the Li-san line owing to the vacillation of its viewpoint after the Third Plenum, but the explanation offered by

Circular no. 96 regarding the process of the shift to the CI line by the CC is an incorrect one. This has caused the Party more trouble in carrying on its struggle, under the leadership of the CC, against the Li-san line both in the theoretical and practical spheres.

(5) The Enlarged [Fourth] Plenum completely agrees with the recent letter of the CI, and with a view to implementing all the directives of the CI proposes to the whole Party the following urgent tasks:

(a) To overcome the Li-san line and the compromising attitude towards it in theory and practice. The Fourth Plenum stresses that to carry out this task, we must carry out all the directives of the CI in practice and that Party work as a whole must undergo a sweeping change. We should not confine ourselves to merely verbal struggles against Li Li-sanism. The Fourth Plenum calls on the whole Party to unite, to carry out resolutely the many urgent tasks confronting it.

In order to carry out this task, the Fourth Plenum deems it necessary to disqualify those CC members who were belatedly elected by the Third Plenum and who supported Comrade Li-san, and to bring into the CC comrades who support the CI line in the struggle against Li-sanism, and to re-examine the membership of the Politburo so as to secure a correct leadership for the Party.

(b) To bring about a determined change in cell activities. One of the important elements of this change is to carry out a struggle against opportunism in concrete activities, oppose passivity and fight against discontented elements who have fomented various anti-Party, detrimental tendencies and who themselves reflect these tendencies.

(c) To revive the organizations of the Party and of the CY which have been destroyed, to improve the work of the mass organizations, above all of the unions, with special emphasis on activities in factories, and to consolidate and strengthen the activities of the Party cells. The Party must take full advantage of every opportunity for utilizing legal [front] organizations. At the same time the Party must use all means to develop and strengthen its leadership in the anti-imperialist movement.

(d) To bring new cadres into the Party, especially the more active elements among the workers, to assume leading positions.

(e) To mobilize the entire Party to fight against the imperialist and the KMT warlord invasion of the Soviet areas, to convene the Soviet Delegates' Congress and to organize the working class and the peasants against the planned invasion of the *Soviet Union*. This is a most important task.

(6) The Enlarged Fourth Plenum authorizes the new Politburo, on the basis of this resolution, to issue instructions and to assign detailed work to the various Party units to supplement the resolutions of the Third Plenum.

(7) The Fourth Plenum is of the view that the Seventh Congress of the Party should be called [not called until April 1945] and that the new Politburo should be authorized to make the necessary preparations in order to assure the fulfilment of the following points: that there be qualified delegates from various areas; that the Congress be ready to make a careful summation of the experiences of the Soviet movement; that it be ready to make a careful summation of the experiences of Party work in industrial centres; and that it pass resolutions on the Party constitution and other documents.

(8) The Fourth Plenum points out that the Third Plenum of the CY accepted the compromising line of the Third Plenum of the Party and reflected it in its own resolutions; the CC of the CY until recent times had shown irresolution in correcting their past Li-san line, and essentially did not carry out the line of the International Youth in its activities. The Fourth Plenum considers that the reorganization of the CC of the CY, carried out by the Political Bureau, was entirely correct, and that the CC of the CY, after its reorganization, has worked according to the CI line. The Fourth Plenum at the same time authorizes the convocation in the near future of the Fourth Plenum of the CC of the CY.

(9) The Enlarged Fourth Plenum has been in entire harmony with the directives of the CI, has corrected the political line of the Party, solved intra-Party problems, and regenerated the Party's leadership in order to guarantee the execution of this line. The Fourth Plenum sincerely hopes that the rank and file of the whole Party will unite like one man, overcome co-operatively all difficulties in the bolshevik spirit, and carry out its present important historic mission. This promises new successes for the Party and guarantees a new victory for the working masses in the continuing and inevitably ascending development of the rising tide of the Chinese revolution.

SEC. IV. THE PERIOD OF THE KIANGSI SOVIET
(1931–4)

COMMENTARY J. THE SHIFT TO THE HINTERLAND

The proclamation of a Chinese Soviet Republic at Juichin, Kiangsi, in November 1931, was the apogee of a movement which had sprung from the breakdown of legal Communism in mid-1927. When the CCP had ceased to be a governmental party, some of its peasant organizers—notably Mao Tse-tung, the future chairman of the Soviet Republic—had sought to save the Communist cause by rural insurrection. In September 1927, after the failure of the Communist drive on Swatow, the Comintern had finally adopted the slogan of Soviets, hitherto anathematized as "Trotskyism". The Soviet slogan merely gave doctrinal sanction and recognition to the attempts of the Chinese Communist guerrillas to establish bases in the countryside. The only such bases which proved capable of weathering the counter-attacks of the KMT were the ones established by Mao Tse-tung and his military helpmate, Chu Teh, on the mountainous Kiangsi-Hunan border. It was here that the groundwork for the later Soviet Republic was laid.

But although the guerrilla activities of the Mao-Chu team were henceforth recognized in Comintern doctrine as an important side-current, they were valued—by both the Comintern and the CCP leadership—only as a peasant war supporting urban revolution. Thus the so-called Canton commune of December 1927 represented the first (and unsuccessful) attempt to establish an urban Soviet in China. As Communist strength in the cities waned under KMT repression, peasant troops were used in attempts to bring Soviet government to the cities, as in the ill-fated attack on Changsha in the summer of 1930. It was only after the total failure of this strategy, and the subsequent disgrace of its protagonist, Li Li-san, that the Mao Tse-tung leadership emerged as the dominant force in Chinese Communism.

The Chinese Soviet Republic, proclaimed in November 1931, was officially designated a "democratic dictatorship of the proletariat and peasantry", according to Lenin's formula of 1905. As applied to the Chinese Soviet districts, however, this formula was a disguise rather than a description of existing facts. The slogan of the "democratic dictatorship" as advanced by Lenin had stood for a coalition government of workers and peasants—that is, for a coalition between his own Social Democrats and the Social Revolutionaries.[1] But the Chinese Soviet government did not make the slightest pretence of being anything but a Communist one-party dictatorship. There was not—as in the later "New Democracy" period—even the semblance of a coalition.

Another reason why the Chinese Soviet Republic was not exactly a "democratic dictatorship of workers and peasants" was that it lacked the workers. Tucked away in the mountainous hinterland, the Soviet Republic contained hardly any industrial workers; therefore its "proletariat" consisted almost entirely of village artisans, handicraftsmen, and farm hands. For this reason, the labour legislation of the Soviet Republic—designed for industrial rather than rural workers —can be taken only as a statement of objectives. Yet the Soviet Constitution, in deference to Marxian orthodoxy, weighted Soviet representation in favour of the "workers" (see document no. 17, p. 221), a provision difficult to reconcile with the Marxian claim that dogma can be only "superstructure" over concrete fact.

In the field of practical policy, the distinguishing characteristic of the Soviet Republic was the radicalism of its agrarian reforms. The Soviet Land Law decreed confiscation, without compensation, of all lands belonging to "feudal lords and landlords, militarists and *t'u-hao* [village bosses], gentry and other big private landowners" (see document no. 18, article 1). The confiscated lands were to be distributed among the middle and poor peasantry.[2] Expropriated *t'u-hao* could also be allotted land, provided that they tilled it by their own labour and that they took no part in any "counter-revolutionary action" (article 3).

In evaluating the radicalism of agrarian reform in Soviet Chain, certain reservations should be made. First of all, the Soviet régime was less "radical" than the preceding Li Li-san leadership, in that it abandoned all attempts at collectivization. Under the guiding spirit of Li Li-san, a conference of Soviets' delegates at Shanghai had authorized collectivization in May 1930.[3] The first draft of the Land Law of 1931 still contained a clause permitting *voluntary* collectivization.[4] But the law as finally passed did not mention the subject at all.

Furthermore, the scrupulous regard shown by the Land Law of 1931 for the property rights of the middle peasants left nothing to be desired from the "bourgeois-democratic" standpoint. Article 5 stipulated that the middle peasants could be exempted from the programme of egalitarian land distribution if the "majority" of them so desired. The final version of the Law made no mention at all of land nationalization, which had still been cited as an ultimate objective in the first draft.[5] Lastly, even the "religious feelings" of the peasantry were given due consideration in the article providing for expropriation of temple and monastery land (article 6).

Of course it is highly doubtful that the majority opinion or the religious feelings of the peasantry were paid as much respect in practice as they were on paper. But, on the other hand, official Party reports of the period clearly indicate that the practice of land reform exceeded the letter of the law less often than it fell short of it.

According to these reports,[6] landlords and rich peasants in many Soviet areas managed to retain political authority by declaring themselves for the Soviets. Being thus in a position to control the implementation of land reform, they would either escape expropriation entirely or allot themselves the best land in the process of distribution. The land hunger of the rural paupers thus remained unsatisfied; and their continuing demand for land caused repeated redistributions, which had to be stopped by decree in order to save crop production.

It is quite apparent that the Soviet government at Juichin exerted only tenuous control over the scattered mountain areas under its nominal jurisdiction. The radical measures on its statute books had little effect wherever local authority lay with "Soviets" under the management of the gentry. In addition, the Soviet Land Law allowed much leeway in its enforcement by requiring "direct support" or "voluntary support" by the peasant masses (see articles 5 and 6). It would be unrealistic to dismiss this concern for popular approval as sheer propaganda. Under constant attack by KMT forces, the Soviet Republic could not, if it wished to survive, alienate too many of its people.

In October 1934, the Soviet Republic finally succumbed to the determined "extermination campaign" of Chiang Kai-shek; and the Red Army, with its followers, set out on the "Long March" to the borderlands of the North-west. Speaking in 1936, with the benefit of nearly two years' hindsight, Mao Tse-tung ascribed the Soviet's defeat to two basic errors: to its final adoption of positional, instead of guerrilla, tactics of defence, and to the lack of a united front with the Fukien rebels who rose against Chiang Kai-shek in November 1933.[7] Thus by 1936—one year before the united front against Japan was sealed (see document no. 21)—Mao felt convinced that the only strategy which could have saved the Soviet Republic was the very strategy which, after 1937, saved Communist North-west China from the Japanese.

17. CONSTITUTION OF THE SOVIET REPUBLIC (November 7, 1931)[1]

The First All-China Soviet Congress hereby proclaims before the toiling masses of China and of the whole world this Constitution of the Chinese Soviet Republic which recites the basic tasks to be accomplished throughout all China.

The accomplishment of these tasks has already begun in the existing Soviet districts. But the First All-China Soviet Congress holds that the complete realization of these tasks can come only after the overthrow of the rule of imperialism and the KMT and the establishment of the rule of the Soviet Republic throughout all China. Then alone will this outline Constitution of the Chinese Soviet Republic find more concrete application and become a more detailed constitution of the Chinese Soviet Republic.

The First All-China Soviet Congress calls upon all Chinese workers, peasants, and toilers to proceed to struggle, under the guidance of the provisional government of the Soviet Republic, for the realization of these basic tasks:

(1) It shall be the mission of the Constitution of the Chinese Soviet Republic to guarantee the democratic dictatorship of the proletariat and peasantry in the Soviet districts, and to secure the triumph of the dictatorship throughout the whole of China. It shall be the aim of this dictatorship to destroy all feudal remnants, eliminate the influence of the imperialist powers in China, to unite China, to limit systematically the development of capitalism, to carry out economic reconstruction of the state, to promote the class-consciousness and solidarity of the proletariat, and to rally to its banner the broad masses of poor peasants in order to effect the transition to the dictatorship of the proletariat.

(2) The Chinese Soviet régime is setting up a state based on the democratic dictatorship of the workers and peasants. All power of the Soviet shall belong to the workers, peasants, and Red Army soldiers and the entire toiling population. Under the Soviet régime the workers, peasants, Red Army soldiers, and the entire toiling population shall have the right to elect their own deputies to give effect to their power. Only militarists, bureaucrats, landlords, the gentry, *t'u-hao* [village bosses], monks—all exploiting and counter-revolutionary elements—shall be deprived of the right to elect deputies to participate in the government and to enjoy political freedom.

(3) In the Chinese Soviet Republic supreme power shall be vested in the All-China Congress of Soviets of Workers', Peasants', and

Soldiers' Deputies. In between Congresses, the supreme organ of power shall be the All-China CEC of the Soviets; the CEC shall appoint a Council of People's Commissars, which shall conduct all governmental affairs, and promulgate orders and resolutions.

(4) All workers, peasants, Red Army soldiers, and all toilers and their families, without distinction of sex, religion, or nationality (Chinese, Manchurians, Mongolians, Moslems, Tibetans, Miao, Li as well as all Koreans, Formosans, Annamites, etc., living in China) shall be equal before the Soviet law, and shall be citizens of the Soviet Republic. In order that the workers, peasants, soldiers, and toiling masses may actually hold the reins of power, the following regulations concerning Soviet elections shall be established: All the above-mentioned Soviet citizens who shall have attained the age of sixteen shall be entitled to vote and to be voted for in the elections of the Soviets. [They] shall elect deputies to all congresses of workers, peasants, and soldiers (Soviets); they shall discuss and decide all national and local political questions. The method of electing deputies [is as follows]. The workers shall elect their deputies in the factories; the artisans, peasants, and urban poor shall elect deputies according to their place of residence. Deputies to the local Soviets shall be elected by these basic units (i.e. factory districts) for a definite term; they shall participate in the work of one of the organizations or commissions attached to the town or village Soviets and shall periodically submit reports to their electors concerning their activities. The electors shall have the right at all times to recall their deputies and demand new elections. Since only the proletariat can lead the broad masses to socialism, the Chinese Soviet régime grants special rights to the proletariat in the elections to the Soviets by allowing it a greater number of deputies.

(5) It shall be the purpose of the Soviet régime to improve thoroughly the living conditions of the working class, to pass labour legislation, to introduce the eight-hour working day, to fix a minimum wage, and to institute social insurance and state assistance to the unemployed as well as to grant the workers the right to supervise production.

(6) In setting itself the task of abolishing feudalism and radically improving the living conditions of the peasants, the Soviet régime of China shall pass a land law, and shall order the confiscation of the land of all landlords and its distribution among the poor and middle peasants, with a view to the ultimate nationalization of the land.

(7) It shall be the purpose of the Soviet régime of China to defend

the interests of the workers and peasants and restrict the development of capitalism, with a view to liberating the toiling masses from capitalist exploitation and leading them to the socialist order of society. [The Soviet government of China] shall announce the abolition of all burdensome taxation and miscellaneous levies introduced during the counter-revolutionary régime and shall put into effect a single progressive income tax. It shall harshly suppress all attempts at wrecking and sabotage on the part of either native or foreign capitalists; it shall pursue an economic policy which shall be beneficial to the workers and peasant masses, which shall be understood by these masses and which shall lead to socialism.

(8) The Soviet régime of China shall set itself the goal of freeing China from the yoke of imperialism. It shall declare the complete sovereignty and independence of the Chinese people, shall refuse to recognize any political or economic privileges for the imperialists in China, and shall abolish all unequal treaties and foreign loans contracted by the counter-revolutionary governments. No foreign imperialist troops, whether land, sea, or air, shall be allowed to be stationed on any territory of the Chinese Soviets. All concessions or territories leased by the imperialists in China shall be unconditionally returned to China. All custom houses, railways, steamship companies, mining enterprises, factories, etc., in the hands of the imperialists shall be confiscated and nationalized. It shall be permissible for foreign enterprises to renew their leases (for their various businesses) and to continue production, provided they shall fully comply with the laws of the Soviet government.

(9) The Soviet government of China will do its utmost to bring about the culmination of the workers' and peasants' revolution in its final victory throughout the whole of China. It declares that it is incumbent upon the entire toiling masses to participate in the revolutionary class struggle. The gradual introduction of universal military service and the change from voluntary to compulsory military service shall be worked out especially. The right to bear arms in defence of the revolution shall be granted only to workers, peasants, and the toiling masses; all counter-revolutionary and exploiting elements must be completely disarmed.

(10) The Soviet government of China guarantees to the workers, peasants, and toilers freedom of speech and the press as well as the right to assembly; it will be opposed to bourgeois and landlord democracy, but is in favour of the democracy of the workers and peasant masses. It breaks down the economic and political prerogatives of

the bourgeoisie and the landlords, in order to remove all obstacles placed by the reactionaries on the workers' and peasants' road to freedom. The workers, peasants, and toiling masses shall enjoy the use of printing shops, meeting halls, and similar establishments by the power of a people's régime, as a material basis for the realization of these rights and liberties. Furthermore, under the Soviet régime, all propaganda and other similar activities by reactionaries shall be suppressed and all exploiters be deprived of all political liberties.

(11) It is the purpose of the Soviet government of China to guarantee the thorough emancipation of women; it recognizes freedom of marriage and will put into operation various measures for the protection of women, to enable women gradually to attain to the material basis required for their emancipation from the bondage of domestic work, and to give them the possibility of participating in the social, economic, political, and cultural life of the entire society.

(12) The Soviet government of China shall guarantee to all workers, peasants, and the toiling masses the right to education. The Soviet government will, as far as the conditions of internal revolutionary war allow, begin at once to introduce free universal education. Above all, the Soviet government shall defend the interests of labouring youth and give them every opportunity of participating in the political and cultural revolutionary life with a view to developing new social forces.

(13) The Soviet government of China guarantees true religious freedom to the workers, peasants, and the toiling population. Adhering to the principle of the complete separation of church and state, the Soviet state neither favours nor grants any financial assistance to any religion whatsoever. All Soviet citizens shall enjoy the right to engage in anti-religious propaganda. No religious institution of the imperialists shall be allowed to exist unless it shall comply with Soviet law.

(14) The Soviet government of China recognizes the right of self-determination of the national minorities in China, their right to complete separation from China, and to the formation of an independent state for each national minority. All Mongolians, Tibetans, Miao, Yao, Koreans, and others living on the territory of China shall enjoy the full right to self-determination, i.e. they may either join the Union of Chinese Soviets or secede from it and form their own state as they may prefer. The Soviet régime of China will do its utmost to assist the national minorities in liberating themselves from the yoke of imperialists, the KMT militarists, *t'u-ssu* [tribal headmen], the princes, lamas, and others, and in achieving complete freedom and autonomy. The Soviet régime must encourage the development of

the national cultures and of the respective national languages of these peoples.

(15) The Chinese régime offers asylum to Chinese and foreign revolutionaries persecuted for their revolutionary activities; it will assist and lead them in recovering their strength so that they may fight with increased vigour for the victory of the revolution.

(16) All foreign toilers living in districts under the jurisdiction of the Soviet régime shall enjoy equal rights as stipulated by Soviet law.

(17) The Soviet régime of China declares its readiness to form a united revolutionary front with the world proletariat and all oppressed nations, and proclaims the Soviet Union, the land of proletarian dictatorship, to be its loyal ally.

18. LAND LAW OF THE SOVIET REPUBLIC (November 1931)

The peasant struggle launched under the leadership of the proletariat continues to develop and each day rises to new heights. Despite the violent resistance of the imperialists and militarists, the Soviet movement grows and expands. In one area after another the Chinese peasantry, armed and organized in the ranks of the Red Army, casts off the centuries-old yoke of feudal barons and landlords, the *t'u-hao* [village bosses] and the gentry; it confiscates and redistributes the land of these oppressors; it demolishes the feudal order of society, destroys the power of the KMT, and builds up the workers' and peasants' Soviet régime—a régime which will consistently and finally accomplish tasks in the anti-imperialist and agrarian revolutions.

The First All-China Congress of Soviets of Workers', Peasants', and Soldiers' Deputies ratifies the confiscation of the lands of the landlords and of other big private landowners. In order to establish uniform regulations for the confiscation and distribution of land, the First [All-China Soviet] Congress, in defence of the interests of the basic peasant masses and in order to safeguard the further development of the revolution, has passed the following agrarian law which will best secure the solution of the agrarian question.

Article 1: All the lands of the feudal landlords, *t'u-hao*, gentry, militarists and other big private landowners, shall be subject to confiscation without any compensation whatever, irrespective of whether they themselves work their lands or rent them out on lease. The Soviets will distribute the confiscated lands among the poor and middle peasants. The former owners of confiscated lands shall not be entitled to receive any land allotment. Hired farm hands, coolies, and toiling labourers shall enjoy equal rights to land allotments, irre-spective of sex. Independent workers living in villages who have lost their previous work shall likewise be entitled to a portion of the land, subject to the consent of the peasant masses. Aged persons, orphans, and widows, who are not in a position to work and who have no relatives on whom to depend, shall be given social relief by the Soviet government, or be taken care of after the land redistribution.

Article 2: The Red Army is the front rank fighter in the defence of the Soviet government and in the overthrow of the rule of imperialism and the government of landlords and capitalists. Therefore, each Red Army man must be given a plot of land, and the Soviet government must see to it that his land is tilled, whether or not his home is in the Soviet district or in an area ruled by the reactionaries.

Article 3: It is a peculiar feature of the Chinese rich peasant that he is at one and the same time a landowner and a usurer; therefore, his land shall also be subject to confiscation. If a rich peasant, after his land has been confiscated, does not participate in any counter-revolutionary activities and works his land by the use of his own labour power, he may be assigned land, but not of the best quality.

Article 4: All the property and lands of all counter-revolutionary organizations and of the military organizations of the white army, as well as of the active participants in counter-revolution, shall be confis-cated. However, exceptions to this rule shall be permitted in the case of poor and middle peasants who have been drawn into the struggle against the Soviets because of their ignorance. [These] shall be granted pardons by the local Soviets, but their leaders shall without fail be dealt with according to the provision of the present law.

Article 5: The First [All-China Soviet] Congress recognizes the principle that an egalitarian distribution of land is the most thorough method of destroying all feudal agrarian relations and the shackles of the private ownership of land by the landlords. However, the local Soviet governments shall on no account carry out this measure by force or by an order issued by higher authorities, but shall explain this procedure to the peasantry from every angle. This measure may be put into operation only with the direct support and at the desire of the basic masses of the peasantry. Thus, if the majority of the middle peasants so desire, they may [be allowed] not to participate in the redistribution [of land].

Article 6: All lands belonging to religious institutions or to temples and all other public lands shall be unconditionally delivered into the possession of the peasants by the Soviet government. However, in disposing of these lands, it shall be essential to obtain the voluntary support of the peasants, so that their religious feelings may not be offended.

Article 7: The well-to-do peasantry seek to have the land distributed according to the means of production. The First [All-China Soviet] Congress considers this to be a counter-revolutionary effort on the part of the rich peasants to hinder the development of the agrarian revolution and to further their own ends, and it must be strictly prohibited. The local Soviets, in conformity with the local conditions in each village shall choose the method [of land division] most advantageous to the poor and middle peasants, i.e. either division on a mixed principle according to the number of consumer workers in each family, or division of the land among the middle and poor peasants, as well as hired farm hands, in equal portions according to the number of consumers, and among the rich peasants according to the labour power supplied by them (i.e. in localities where egalitarian distribution shall take place according to the number of consumers, every rich peasant capable of working shall receive as much land as is allotted to one consumer). In dividing up the land, not only the area of the land assigned but also the quality of its soil (especially its productivity) shall be taken into consideration. Furthermore, in dividing up the land it shall be essential to introduce all possible land reforms in order to create the necessary conditions for destroying feudal remnants like state-owned uncultivated land, scattered land holdings, or demarcating lines running across fields.

19. MAO TSE-TUNG: REPORT TO THE SECOND ALL-CHINA SOVIET
CONGRESS (January 22, 1934) [extract][1]

1. *The Present Situation and the Success of the Soviet Movement*

Comrades! Two years have elapsed since the meeting of the First All-China Soviet Congress. The events of the past two years have shown a further decline in imperialist-KMT rule and a vigorous and triumphant development of the Soviet movement.

We have now arrived at an era when the Chinese revolution has taken a more acute turn and when the whole world is itself passing through a transitory period leading to a second, new phase of war and revolution [we omit 17 lines on the world situation]. . . . As part of the general world revolution, the Chinese revolution has further deepened due to the growing national crisis, the collapse of the

KMT economy, and the success of the Soviet movement, thus pushing the Chinese revolution into the very foreground of the world revolution.

The key factors in the present Chinese situation are: widespread civil war; a life-and-death struggle between revolution and counter-revolution; a sharp antagonism between the Soviet régime of workers and peasants and the landlord-bourgeois KMT régime; the struggle for national salvation by the Chinese people against the partition schemes of the Japanese and other imperialists; and, finally, the struggle between the imperialists who are actively preparing for a Pacific war and an attack on the Soviet Union, and the toiling masses of China and the East to prevent an imperialist war and to protect the Soviet Union [we omit 19 lines comparing the Chinese Soviet and KMT régimes]. . . .

The growing contrast between the two régimes [i.e. the Soviet and the KMT] cannot but lead the desperate struggle between them to assume more and more violent forms. The decisive, historical stage of the struggle is now drawing near. Now that five "suppression" campaigns have ended in failure, the KMT is launching its sixth campaign against us. Accordingly, the Soviet régime is now faced with the historic task of organizing and leading all of the revolutionary masses both in the Soviet districts and other parts of the country to fight in this decisive war; of mobilizing the broad worker-peasant masses to join the Red Army; of improving the political education and technical level of the Red Army; of enlarging the local armed forces and guerrilla units; of developing extensive guerrilla warfare; of strengthening, concentrating, and unifying leadership of the Soviet [central government] over the Red Armies in all Soviet districts; increasing the tempo and improving the quality of Soviet work in every field; of strengthening the financial and economic activities of the Soviet government to assure the filling of the material needs of our revolutionary war; of developing the class struggle among the working masses; of organizing the revolutionary enthusiasm of the working masses into a struggle to smash the enemy; of developing the agrarian struggle of the peasants; of mobilizing the broad peasant masses to fight for the acquisition and protection of the land; finally, calling upon all proletarian, peasant, and labouring masses of the Soviet districts and throughout China to fight to the utmost and at all costs in the revolutionary war. This is the way to smash the sixth offensive of the imperialists and the KMT, to save China from being colonized, and to attain victory in the Soviet revolution on a national scale.

2. The imperialist aggression and the Soviet government leadership in the anti-imperialist movement

The greatest events which have transpired in China since the inauguration of the Provisional Soviet Central government have been the attacks of the imperialists and the fourth, fifth, and sixth "surrounding-and-exterminating" offensives [of the KMT] waged upon the revolution by counter-revolutionaries [we omit 16 lines]. . . .

In the past two years the Provisional Soviet Central government has repeatedly circulated statements denouncing the predatory wars waged by the Japanese imperialists and the traitorous capitulation of the KMT. On April 14, 1932, the Provisional Central government formally declared war on Japan, issued mobilization orders for war against Japan, and called on the whole nation to wage a national revolutionary war and to oppose the imperialists and the KMT who are now enslaving China. The Provisional Central government and the Revolutionary Military Council have more than once announced their readiness to conclude an agreement with any armed unit for a joint anti-Japanese and anti-imperialist military fight on the following conditions: (1) Immediate cessation of the offensive against the Soviet districts. (2) Guarantee of civil rights for the masses such as freedoms of speech, of publication, of assembly, of association and freedom to strike. (3) Arming of the masses and creation of anti-Japanese volunteers. The T'ang-ku Agreement concluded between the KMT and Japan [May 30, 1933], and direct negotiations between China and Japan which have taken place since then are actions betraying the national interest and repeatedly repudiated by the Provisional Central government on behalf of the whole nation in statements recently made public. The Soviet government has supported the anti-Japanese struggle of the masses in every part of the country. To speak only of the anti-Japanese strike of the textile workers in West Shanghai [1932], the Soviet aided them with $16,000 [Chinese currency]. In addition, the masses of the Soviet districts have also made contributions to the Volunteers in the North-eastern Provinces as well as to the [participants in the] other anti-imperialist struggles.

In the Soviet territories, imperialist privileges have been abolished and imperialist influence wiped out. Imperialist Protestant pastors and Catholic priests have been ousted by the masses; estates of the people seized by imperialist missionaries have been returned;

missionary schools have been turned into Soviet schools. In short, the Soviet districts in China are the only ones liberated from the imperialist yoke. . . . [14 lines].

3. *The Imperialist-KMT Offensive Repulsed* . . . [6 pp.].

4. *Fundamental Policies of the Soviet in the Past Two Years* . . . [2 lines]

The Soviet régime has grown out of guerrilla warfare and from many isolated and small districts beyond the boundaries of which lies the world of the enemy. The enemy has been bent on its efforts to effect destruction and oppression of the Soviet areas. Yet the Soviet government has been victorious. It has been able to defeat the enemy and has gathered strength through its repeated victories over the enemy. This has been the environment in which the Soviet areas have developed . . . [13 lines].

This very environment has determined the tasks of the Soviet. It must do its best to mobilize, organize, and arm the masses, to attack the enemy without let-up, and to crush the enemy's offensive. Its task is to wage revolutionary war, to concentrate all of its strength on the development of the revolutionary war which will crush the enemy and overthrow the imperialist rule that has acted as the supporter and director of the dictatorship of the enemy. Our aim in defeating imperialism and the KMT is to liberate the Chinese people, to emancipate the 400,000,000 Chinese from the slavery and oppression of the Japanese and other imperialists, to free the hundreds of millions of our toiling compatriots from the oppression of militarists, bureaucrats, gentry and landlord bourgeoisie, to enable the Chinese people to establish under the leadership of the CCP, a bright, happy new socialist society, following the example of the workers and peasants of the Soviet Union. This is the basic task of the Soviet areas.

The various policies and activities can be understood only in terms of this environment and these goals. They are: to consolidate the now already firmly established democratic dictatorship of workers and peasants; to expand this dictatorship to the whole country; to mobilize, organize, and arm the Soviet areas and the masses throughout the country to fight in a determined revolutionary war to overthrow the imperialist and KMT rule and to consolidate and develop the worker-peasant dictatorship; to prepare the present democratic dictatorship of workers and peasants for its turn towards the socialist proletarian dictatorship in the future. All these form the point of departure of the Soviet policies . . . [12 lines].

(a) *The Armed Masses and the Red Army* . . . [5 pp.]

(b) *Soviet Democracy*

The Soviet (government) of the democratic dictatorship of workers and peasants is the government of the masses themselves, directly depending upon them. It must maintain the closest relation with them in order to function efficiently. It has already been the organizer and leader of the revolutionary war and the mass life, possessing great strength. Its enormous strength is incomparable to any form of bourgeois form of state in history. But its strength depends entirely on the people and can never for one moment alienate itself from them. It needs a strong power to cope with its class enemy but towards its own class basis—the masses of workers and peasants, paupers, civil employees, revolutionary intellectuals—it employs no force but broad democracy.

The wide democracy of the Soviet is, first of all, manifested in its elections. The Soviet gives the right to vote and to be elected to all formerly oppressed and exploited masses regardless of sex. This right of the masses of workers and peasants is unprecedented in Chinese history. The experience of the elections in the past two years tells us that the Soviet has been very successful in its elections. (1) Registration of electors: The names of the electors are written on a big red paper differentiating them from those who have no suffrage and whose names are written on white paper. An election meeting, with no exploiters participating in it, takes the place of the general mass meeting of the past. (2) Proportional representation: The proportions of social composition are as follows: one [representative] from every thirteen workers and their family members; one out of [every] fifty peasants and poor people; all the city and village Soviet councils are formed in this way. An appropriate ratio between workers and peasants is thus maintained in councils and executive committees at various levels from the village to the Central government. This method guarantees the leadership of the workers and the worker-peasant alliance in the Soviet régime. (3) Electoral unit: In order to guarantee that the majority of the electors participate in the elections, and that the workers elect their delegates to the Soviet, the election units for the peasants are villages, while workers form an independent unit, according to the election act proclaimed by the CEC of the Soviets in September 1933. This makes the election very convenient for the masses. (4) The number of electors who participate in the elections: The development of the election movement has enabled the mass of electors to realize clearly the effect of elections on their own lives. Many who in the past were inactive during the elections are now enthusiasts. In many districts, in the two elections in 1932 and the election in the latter part of 1933, more than eighty per cent of the electors voted. In other districts, only those who were sick, or in child-birth confinement or on watch duty were absent in voting. (5) The electoral list: In the elections in the latter part of 1933, an electoral list of candidates was adopted. This enabled the elector to make up his mind on the candidates before the voting took place. (6) The election of women: In the majority of city and *hsiang* [village] Soviets, women delegates constitute more than twenty-five per cent. In some places such as the upper Ts'ai-ch'i *hsiang*, there are forty-three women delegates among a total of seventy-five—about sixty per cent; and in the lower Ts'ai-ch'i *hsiang*, sixty-nine out of ninety-one delegates are women—which is sixty-six per cent. The broad masses of labouring women are participating in the management of state affairs. (7) Work report: Before the election takes place, the electors have the chance to hear reports about the past work of the city or *hsiang* Soviet in a preparatory meeting. They are led to give criticisms of this past work. This was more universally practised during the autumn election of 1933. All these have helped the masses to familiarize themselves with the Soviet election [procedure], which is the primary step in exercising the right of state administration, and have thus guaranteed the consolidation of the Soviet power.

Next, the Soviet democracy is also manifested in the city and *hsiang* councils, which form the foundation of the organization of the Soviet and enable the Soviet to keep in touch with the masses. Two years' progress has now resulted in better council organization. The characteristics of this organization are as follows: (1) The delegates are scattered evenly to live among the people so that they will have the closest possible contact with them (usually one delegate leads, and lives with, thirty to seventy people). This guarantees that the council does not become alienated from the masses. (2) The three to seven *hsiang* or city Soviet delegates elect one person from among them as chief delegate, who, under the supervision [literally, leadership] of the *hsiang* or city Soviets, is responsible for assigning and guiding the work of each delegate, passing on the communications of the presidium to the delegates, and summoning meetings of the people under his jurisdiction for the settlement of minor questions. This gives closer liaison between the presidium of the *hsiang* or city Soviet and the delegates, as well as effective leadership to the village work. (3) There are various permanent or temporary committees under the city or *hsiang* councils such as [committees on] culture, irrigation, sanitation, food, Red Army families defence, etc., which number several tens and draw the active elements among the masses into committee work. Also there should be certain committees in each village. In this way, the Soviets form a network in which the broad masses can directly participate. (4) Election for city or *hsiang* Soviets twice a year (for *hsien* or provincial Soviets, once a year). This makes it easier for the Soviets to keep in touch with the opinions of the masses. (5) Any delegate who commits serious errors may lose his seat through the proposal of ten or more electors, seconded by more than one-half of the whole electorate or through the resolution of the council meeting . . . [5 lines].

The city and *hsiang* Soviets are the base of the Soviet government organs above them; they are all formed by the Soviet Congresses of workers', peasants', and soldiers' deputies, and their executive committees. Government workers are also appointed by election. If any one is found to be incompetent, he may be recalled by public opinion. The solution of all problems is based on public opinion. So the Soviet régime is truly the régime of the broad masses.

Secondly, the democratic nature of the Soviets is further shown by the fact that the revolutionary masses are given the right of free speech, free association, free assembly, freedom of publication, and freedom to strike. The Soviet gives them all facilities such as meeting places, paper, printing shops, and other material needs, while the KMT in the areas under its control is suppressing all these freedoms by fascist terrorism. The Soviets eagerly foster all anti-imperialist and anti-KMT assemblies, associations, speeches, and publications. What is not permissible is the freedom of the suppressors and exploiters to commit counter-revolutionary acts. Moreover, to consolidate the dictatorship of workers and peasants, the Soviet must solicit the supervision and criticism of the broad masses. Every revolutionary citizen has the right to expose the errors or shortcomings of any Soviet functionary in his work . . . [4 lines]. Finally, the democratic nature of the Soviets also can be found in the division of administrative districts. All the administrative districts from province down to *hsiang* are now smaller than before. This enables the Soviets on various levels to have a thorough knowledge of the demands of the masses and makes the opinions of the masses quickly reflected in the Soviets . . . [5 lines].

(c) The Soviet Attitude towards the Landlord-bourgeois classes

The Soviet is not democratic towards the exploiters—landlords and bourgeois who have been overthrown by the revolutionary masses. . . . The Soviet maintains a different attitude towards them. Although overthrown, they still have a deep root and their remnants have not yet been wiped out. They have a superior knowledge and a better knowledge of techniques. They are constantly thinking of the restoration of their power. Particularly in the course of the civil war, they are always seeking to support the attacking enemies through anti-revolutionary activities. Hence, the Soviet has to curb and suppress them everywhere.

First of all, the Soviet rules the exploiting elements out of political power. In the Soviet constitution the landlord-bourgeois classes and counter-revolutionary elements are all deprived of the rights of election and military service. . . . Secondly, all landlords and bourgeoisie are deprived of the freedom of speech, publication, assembly, and association. . . . Thirdly, anti-revolutionary activities are suppressed by the revolutionary forces and revolutionary courts . . . [2 pp.].

(d) *The Soviet Labour Policy* . . . [8 pp.]

(e) *The Agrarian Revolution*

The Chinese Soviet and Red Army have grown up from the development of the agrarian revolution, which liberates the broad peasantry from the brutal oppression and exploitation by landlords and the KMT militarists. The principle of the land policy of the Soviet is to wipe out completely feudalistic and semi-feudalistic oppression and exploitation. In any village of the KMT districts, past or present, one finds atrocious impositions of land rents (sixty to eighty per cent), horrible usury (thirty to 100 per cent), and horribly onerous taxes (there are above 1700 different kinds of taxes throughout the country). Consequently, the land is concentrated in the hands of landlords and rich peasants. The overwhelming majority of the peasantry have lost their land and are obliged to live in extreme misery. This relentless exploitation has deprived them of their means to combat catastrophe. The whole country is, thus, constantly exposed to floods and droughts. The catastrophe-stricken area in 1931 covered 809 *hsien*, totalling a population of 44,000,000. The exploitation has also deprived the peasantry of their productive power. Much land has deteriorated or been uncultivated. Yet with their meagre production they have to compete with the dumping of imperialist agricultural products. All these [factors] have led the Chinese rural economy to a state of complete bankruptcy, which has given rise to a violent fire of agrarian revolution.

The power of the agrarian revolution in the Soviet districts has wiped out all feudalistic remnants. The peasant millions, awakening from their long dark age, have confiscated land and other properties from all the landlords and fertile land from the rich peasants, abolishing usury and onerous taxation. They have eliminated everything which stands in the way of the revolution and built up their own régime. For the first time, the Chinese peasant masses have broken their way out of the hell [they live in] and made themselves their own masters. This is the fundamental situation that differentiates the rural districts under the Soviet from those under the KMT.

The First All-China Soviet Congress proclaimed the land law [see document no. 18], which has since served as the correct guide for the proper solution of the land problem in this country. There have been numerous arguments over questions of class analysis in the villages owing to the accentuation of the class struggle. Based on the experiences of the agrarian revolution, the People's Council has passed a "resolution on the various problems of the struggle for land" resolving correctly certain questions regarding [the status] of landlord, rich peasant, middle peasant, and village loafers, etc. Undoubtedly, this will promote the further development of the village struggle. As to the methods of partition [i.e. redistribution of land] in connection with its distance, fertility, infertility, [relation to] forests, waters, etc., it is now of urgent necessity to work out definite programmes based on the experience in all areas, which may serve as a guide for the partition of land in the new Soviet districts.

The land inspection movement mobilized by the Central government is directed to wipe out thoroughly any feudalistic remnants and to guarantee that the real benefits resulting from the agrarian revolution will go to the hired farm hands and poor and middle peasants. According to statistics of July, August, and September 1933, 6988 landlord families and 6638 rich peasants' families in the Central Soviet district of Kiangsi, Fukien, and Kwangtung had 317,539 *piculs* [of grain] worth of land confiscated from them after investigation. The cash confiscated from the landlords and the [extraordinary] taxes [imposed on] the rich peasants totalled 60,916 *yüan*. The new enthusiasm of the peasant masses was further strengthened and the Union of Hired Farm Hands and the Poor Peasant Association have now become the pillars of the Soviet in the villages! This is the result of only three months' work, indicating that the Soviet government has to pay still closer attention to the class struggle in the villages. These results also show that the land inspection movement has been an effective means of developing further struggle in the village and of annihilating the feudalistic remnants in the rural districts.

Our class line in the agrarian revolution is to depend upon the hired farm hands and poor peasants, to ally with the middle peasants, to check the rich peasants, and to annihilate the landlords. The correct practice of this line is the key to the success of the agrarian revolution and the foundation for all other policies of the Soviet government in the villages. Hence, the Soviet government should deal severely with all erroneous tendencies to infringe upon the middle peasants (mainly the well-to-do middle peasants) or to annihilate the rich peasants. At the same time, it should also not permit the error of making a compromise with the landlords and rich peasants. It is by this way that we shall lead the agrarian revolution in the correct direction. In the past two years we have gained much experience in our mass work in the agrarian revolution. The particular points to be borne in mind are as follows:

(1) The majority of agricultural workers, poor and middle peasants should be mobilized to the fullest extent possible for the struggle against landlords and rich peasants in the [land] redistribution and inspection movements. The land redistribution and inspection work should be done with the full concurrence of the masses. The disposition of each class must be passed upon by a mass meeting. To conduct these tasks solely through the activities of a few Soviet functionaries involves the danger of lowering the fighting spirit of the masses.

(2) When landlords' property other than land and surplus traction animals and farm implements of the rich peasants are confiscated, the greater part of them must be allotted to the poor masses. If they are given over to the use of only a few, the spirit of the masses will be depressed, which would benefit the exploiting elements who resist [confiscation].

(3) The [re]distribution of land should not be left in an unsettled state over a long period of time. What is needed is a proper distribution within a rather short period, which will definitely determine the peasants' property status. Unless after a [land] distribution the masses demand [another], there should be no other redistribution, [because this] would antagonize the [land-holding] peasants and affect their positive [attitude] towards production; also it would be utilized by the exploiting elements to obstruct the development of agrarian struggle.

(4) The aim of the land inspection movement is to disclose the exploiters but not to disturb the exploited. Accordingly, the inspection should not be carried from house to house and from one piece of land to another. It should be done through the mobilization of the broad masses to expose the hidden landlords and rich peasants.

(5) Those anti-revolutionary elements who work to hinder [land] redistribution and inspection movements should be seriously dealt with. They should be severely punished by mass judgment or with concurrence and undergo imprisonment or even face the death penalty. Otherwise, the agrarian revolution will be handicapped.

(6) Class struggle should be promoted while clashes between families and localities should be avoided. The landlords and rich peasants are always thinking of replacing the class struggle by family or local conflicts. . . .

(7) The development of the agrarian revolution depends upon the class-consciousness and organizational strength of the broad masses in the villages. The Soviet functionaries must, therefore, carry on an extensive and intensive propaganda in the villages and work to strengthen the organizations of hired farm hands and poor peasants.

The aim of the agrarian revolution is not only to solve the land problem of the peasants but also to encourage them to increase the productivity of their land. Because of the capable leadership of the Soviet government, and the higher morale of the peasant masses themselves, agricultural production has been restored in most places, and in some places even increased.

On this foundation, the living conditions of the peasantry have been much improved . . . [2 lines].

In the past, the peasants would live on tree-bark or grain husks for several months a year. This situation no longer prevails, and there is no more starvation in the Soviet districts. The life of the peasantry is improving year by year. They are no longer in rags. They now eat meat more regularly. It is no longer a luxury to them as in former times. In the past, most of the peasants dressed in rags, but now they are generally improved, some 100 per cent, some 200 per cent. [[Sections are omitted from pp. 61 to 92 of Chinese original on financial and economic policy, culture and education, marriage, nationalities, military measures, and economic reconstruction.]]

Reconstruction of Soviets. The inauguration of the Central Soviet government which established the supreme leading organ of the Soviet movement in China has had a vital significance. It has in the past two years scored glorious successes in the fight against imperialism and the KMT. Nevertheless, many weaknesses are to be found in the organization and work of the Central government. The functions of the CEC and the people's commission must be differentiated, the organization and work of the presidium of the CEC should be improved and strengthened, and commissions should have a sufficient working staff, their work method improved; more commissions should be created, if necessary, so that the Central government can fulfil its role as the supreme leading organ of the revolution.

[As an important link with the Central government, as well as with local Soviets, the provincial Soviet government, which is the highest organ in the local government, has been lax in its work in certain respects, a defect which must now be overcome.]

The village and town Soviets constitute the basic structure of the Soviet system, and for this simple reason merit the utmost attention. Congresses [of workers', peasants', and soldiers' deputies] should be established in places where they do not yet exist, and their work strengthened. Presidia should be set up, committees moved into the villages, positive worker and peasant elements drawn into the Soviets, relation between a delegate and a number of inhabitants established; each village should have a chief delegate, permitting him to call a conference of the delegates and inhabitants to discuss the work in the village . . . [11 lines].

The provincial Soviets should direct maximum attention to the work in new Soviet territory, setting up or strengthening the work of the revolutionary committee. In regard to organization and work, the revolutionary committee differs radically from a Soviet and its functions (such as arming the inhabitants, waging mass struggle, clearing out the counter-revolutionaries, etc.) should be strengthened, as a transitional step to the setting up of a Soviet régime.

Soviet democracy has progressed far but not far enough. A struggle should be waged against bureaucratism and dictatorialism, which create a division between the Soviets and the masses. Persuasion should replace dictatorialism vis-à-vis the masses. Soviet functionaries should pay close attention to all demands and suggestions of the masses and never neglect them. Soviet functionaries, especially the worker and peasant inspection commissions, should draw in the broad masses for the critical examination of the work of the Soviet functionaries and lead the struggle in criticizing evil functionaries, and even punish them in accordance with Soviet laws, thus maintaining good relations between the Soviets and the masses. In the Soviet elections the significance of the election should be explained to the masses, more electors should be drawn in and alien class elements, corruption, and waste, as well as bureaucrats, eliminated. More active workers and peasants should be elected to manage state affairs and more workers inducted into the Soviets in order to strengthen the workers' hegemony in the Soviet régime. In order to get close to the masses the Soviets must establish an intimate connection with the labour unions, the poor peasant unions, representative organs of women workers and peasant women, co-operatives, etc., and mobilize the masses through these organizations to carry out the work of the Soviet.

In order that all the work of the Soviets may be adapted to the needs of the revolutionary war and to improve the speed and quality of the work of the Soviet, any laxness among the Soviet functionaries should be stamped out, the functionaries aroused to enthusiasm and consciousness that they work for the democratic dictatorship of the workers and peasants . . . [3 lines]. Slogans should be put forward: "Subordinate all work to the revolutionary war", "For greater speed and better quality of work", all to be brought before the functionaries of the Soviets. In this respect the responsible leaders of the Soviets, especially the worker and peasant inspection commissariat, must win over the Soviet functionaries by persistent persuasion and education.

The Soviets should enforce the following laws: labour [7 lines: eight-hour day, minimum wages, etc. . . .]; land law [6 lines: confiscation of land of the landlords, land inspection, etc. . . .]; culture and education . . . [2 lines]; and finally, all the laws and orders against the counter-revolutionaries [5 lines: security police and Soviet courts should draw the broad masses into the struggle against the reactionaries. . . .]

Anti-Imperialist-KMT Area Work. . . . The Soviets must strengthen their leadership of the anti-imperialist struggle throughout the whole country as well as of the revolutionary struggle of the workers and peasants in the KMT territory. Passivity on the part of the Soviets in this direction means connivance at the aggression of imperialism, prolongation of KMT reactionary rule, and a limitation on the development of the Soviets territorially. . . . By utilizing the concrete facts of the KMT's surrender to imperialism, the Soviets may arouse the national consciousness and class consciousness of the masses [in the KMT regions] to a sharp struggle against imperialism and its lackey, the KMT. The Soviets should call on the masses to organize and arm themselves, to fight for the independence of China, to drive imperialism out of China especially in the North-east, Jehol, Chahar, and North China where Japanese imperialism still marches on with bayonets. A people's revolutionary army and volunteers should be organized, and the existing volunteers be alienated from the reactionary influence of the KMT in a determined fight against Japanese imperialism. The Soviets must give all possible material and moral support to every anti-imperialist strike of the workers and every anti-imperialist struggle of the peasants and petty bourgeoisie.

The Soviets should aid in every way possible the revolutionary struggle of the workers against capital, of the peasants against the landlord, and of the revolutionary masses against the imperialists and the KMT in the white areas . . . [10 lines].

The Soviets or the revolutionary committee and the partisans must observe the fundamental policy of the Soviets and refrain from making indiscriminate attacks on the *t'u-hao* without any regard to class distinctions. In addition, the opposition of the reds to the whites, the flight of the masses, the salt question, the refugee problem, etc., should be dealt with on the class principle and in accordance with the principle of the mass line. The causes of the opposition of the reds to the whites and the flight of the masses have to be removed, and the work in the borderland must be improved—factors that can play a decisive role in changing the white into red districts . . . [peroration, 8 lines, followed by singing of the "Internationale"].

SEC. V. THE YENAN PERIOD—THE UNITED FRONT (1935-45)

COMMENTARY K. THE UNITED FRONT AGAINST JAPAN

In a sense we distort the record by dating the "Yenan period" from 1935, because the city of Yenan was not actually occupied by the Communists until December 1936, becoming their capital early in 1937. On the other hand, the CCP vanguard, after the Long March from Kiangsi, became established in North-west China in November 1935, and in that year the Comintern put forward the united front as a world-wide Communist policy.[1]

The following three documents (nos. 20, 21, and 22) appeared within two and a half months after the outbreak of the Sino-Japanese War in July 1937. They are included in this volume as illustrations of the CCP line during the early war period.

The united front between the KMT and the CCP began with the CCP's statement on KMT-CCP co-operation of September 22, 1937 (see document no. 21). As early as 1932, following the Japanese invasion of Manchuria on September 18, 1931, the CCP had announced its willingness to come to an agreement with all anti-Japanese groups, but it is not certain that agreement with the KMT was actually intended at this time. As late as April 1932 the CCP seems still to have advocated a "united front from below", i.e. a united front to be set up after the forcible overthrow of the KMT régime. This is still another disputed point awaiting investigation. At any rate, similar proposals were made repeatedly between 1933 and 1936, without eliciting any response from the KMT. The united front was actually born only after the Sian incident of December 1936 when Chiang Kai-shek was eventually released by his kidnapper Chang Hsüeh-liang on the advice of the CCP. From this time until the fall of Hankow in October 1938, the relations between the two parties were, at least superficially, quite friendly. After the spring of 1939, when 300 Communist guerrillas were alleged to have been massacred in Shantung, KMT-CCP relations again deteriorated. The conflict broke out into the open when the New Fourth Army was attacked by KMT forces in January 1941—the commander, Yeh T'ing, being captured and his Communist deputy being killed in action. From then on, hostilities continued intermittently.

The united front against Japan remained, however, nominally in force; and the "ten great policies" of the CCP remained its basic programme (see document no. 20). Emphasis was laid on agrarian reforms, i.e. on reduction of rent and interest rates, which were to be carried out by peasant associations and popularly elected local administrations. In July 1940 the CCP introduced the "three-thirds system" by which one-third of the officials in all governmental agencies were to be Communists, the remaining two-thirds to be divided between KMT members and non-party personnel. This measure proved to be an effective device for enlisting non-Communist support in the areas of North China.

The theory revived by Mao after 1935 to reconcile Communist and KMT principles was that the CCP, for the time being, aimed only at the accomplishment of the bourgeois-democratic revolution, which was also the goal of Dr. Sun's Three People's Principles. This had earlier been CCP doctrine in the period 1923–7 (see Sec. II above). But Mao also continued to point to Communism as the ultimate goal of the CCP. In his speech to the Congress of Delegates of Soviet Areas on March 3, 1937, Mao had spoken quite frankly on the Party's stand *vis-à-vis* the united front:

"Our answer to the question [whether the CCP programme agrees with the Three People's Principles] is yes. . . . The CCP will never forego its socialist and Communist ideals, which will be realized by the transition from the bourgeois-democratic stage of the revolution. The CCP has its own Party Constitution and programme. Its Party Constitution, being socialistic and Communistic, differs from the *Three People's Principles*. Its programme for democratic revolution [i.e. for the "bourgeois-democratic" revolution to overthrow "feudalism", achieve national unification, etc.], more complete than (that) of any other political party in the country, does not basically contradict the programme of the *Three People's Principles* proclaimed by the First and Second Congresses of the KMT."[2]

In another speech of this period, Mao said:

"We believe in revolutionary transformation and maintain that the democratic revolution (will) transform (itself) in the direction of socialism. There will be several stages of development in the democratic revolution, all under the slogan of the democratic republic, not under the slogan of the Soviet. . . . The solid ally of the proletariat is the peasantry; next comes the petty bourgeoisie. The bourgeoisie is competing with us for the leadership (of the revolution). . . . We believe in revolutionary transformation, but not in the Trotskyite permanent revolution, nor in semi-Trotskyite Li-sanism. We maintain that socialism should be reached through all the necessary stages of the democratic republic. We are opposed to 'tailism', and also to adventurism and impatience. To maintain that the bourgeoisie should be eliminated because of its transitional nature and to accuse the revolutionary groups (in the semi-colonial areas) of defeatism and collaboration with the bourgeoisie are Trotskyite words with which we cannot concur. The present alliance between the bourgeoisie and the revolutionary group is a necessary bridge to socialism."[3]

From Mao's own statements one can thus see that: (1) The united front with the bourgeoisie, though desirable and even necessary, is only transitional. The final goal remains socialism and Communism. (2) During this transitional stage, the KMT is regarded as a competitor in the struggle for leadership of the masses and of the revolution. (3) The nationalism of the Chinese people is given considerable weight and in fact skilfully exploited.

With these points in mind, one can understand more easily the CCP's insistence after 1937 on retaining control of its own territorial bases, maintaining its own armed forces, emphasizing the anti-Japanese national united front, and adopting a moderate war-time policy towards all rural classes including the landlords, as well as the eventual open conflict with the KMT after 1946. It is evident that Mao and the CCP leadership had learned from their experience during and after the first united front of 1923–7.

20. THE TEN GREAT POLICIES OF THE CCP FOR ANTI-JAPANESE RESISTANCE AND NATIONAL SALVATION (August 15, 1937)

Struggle for the mobilization of all possible strength in order to win the victory of the war of resistance

I. OVERTHROW OF JAPANESE IMPERIALISM

Sever diplomatic relations with Japan, expel Japanese officials from the country, arrest Japanese spies, confiscate the property of Japanese imperialists in China, repudiate Japanese loans, abrogate Japanese treaties, and take back Japanese concessions.

Fight to the bitter end for the protection of North China and the coastal areas.

Fight to the bitter end for the recovery of Peiping, Tientsin, and the north-eastern (provinces).

Drive the Japanese imperialist out of China.

Oppose any wavering or compromising.

II. TOTAL MILITARY MOBILIZATION OF THE NATION

Mobilize the navy, army, and air forces of the whole nation to wage a national war of resistance.

Oppose a passive, purely defensive strategy of resistance; adopt an active strategy of holding the initiative.

Hold regular national defence conferences to discuss and decide on national defence plans and strategy.

Arm the people and develop anti-Japanese guerrilla warfare to supplement the regular forces.

Reform political work in the army to achieve cohesion and unanimity between commanders and fighters and between army and people. Develop the active enthusiasm of the troops.

Render aid to the North-eastern People's Revolutionary Army and the North-eastern Volunteer Army [anti-Japanese guerrilla forces, some led by CCP members]. Harass the enemy's rear.

Ensure equal treatment for all military units fighting in the war of resistance.

Set up regional military zones over the whole country, mobilize the whole populace to participate in the war, in order to transform the mercenary system of military service into a proper conscription (system).

III. TOTAL MOBILIZATION OF THE ENTIRE NATION

Everyone, except traitors, should have freedom of speech, publication, assembly, association, and of armed resistance in the anti-Japanese fight for national salvation.

Abolish all old laws and regulations prohibiting patriotic popular movements and promulgate new, revolutionary laws and regulations.

Release from prison all patriotic and revolutionary political prisoners and permit political parties to function.

All the people of China should be mobilized and armed to participate in the war of resistance. Those who have strength should contribute their strength; those who have money, money; those who have weapons, weapons; and those who have knowledge, knowledge.

Mobilize Mongolians, Moslems, and other minority groups for a common struggle against Japan on the basis of the principles of self-determination and self-government.

IV. REFORM OF POLITICAL MECHANISM

Convene a National Assembly truly representative of the people; enact a truly democratic constitution; draft a programme for fighting against Japan and saving the nation; and elect a national defence government.

The national defence government should contain the revolutionary elements of all parties, groups, and popular organizations, and should exclude pro-Japanese factions.

The national defence government should adopt a system of democratic centralism which is democratic as well as centralized.

The national defence government should carry out a revolutionary policy of fighting against Japan and saving the nation.

Ensure local autonomy; oust corrupt officials and set up governments of integrity.

V. ANTI-JAPANESE FOREIGN POLICY

Within the bounds of territorial integrity and national sovereignty, anti-aggression, and mutual assistance pacts should be concluded with all countries opposed to Japanese aggression.

Support the peace camp and oppose the aggressors' camp of Germany, Japan, and Italy.

Fight against Japanese imperialism in alliance with the workers, peasants, and common people of Korea, Taiwan [Formosa], and Japan.

VI. THE WAR-TIME FINANCIAL AND ECONOMIC POLICY

Financial policy should be based on the principles of financial contributions by the wealthy and confiscation of traitors' property for anti-Japanese expenditure. The principles underlying economic policy should be the reorganization and expansion of production for national defence, development of the rural economy, assuring the self-sufficiency in agricultural products during war-time, encouragement of national commodities [native products of China], improving the quality of native products, thorough elimination of Japanese goods from the market, punishment of traitorous merchants, and prevention of speculation and hoarding.

VII. IMPROVEMENT OF THE WELFARE OF THE PEOPLE

Improve the treatment of workers, peasants, civil servants, teachers, and anti-Japanese soldiers.

(Give) preferential treatment to the families of soldiers fighting against Japan.

Abolish exorbitant and miscellaneous taxes [*Tsa-shui*, i.e. surtaxes of a burdensome and unreasonable nature].

Reduce rent and interest rates.

(Give) unemployment relief.

Adjust foodstuff distribution (equitably).

(Carry on) famine relief and rehabilitation.

VIII. THE ANTI-JAPANESE EDUCATIONAL POLICY

Change the old educational system and curriculum and institute a new system and curriculum with a view to fighting the Japanese and saving our country.

Institute general, compulsory, and free education to raise the national consciousness of the people.

Institute military training for students in the whole country.

IX. WIPE OUT TRAITORS, PUPPETS, AND PRO-JAPANESE GROUPS IN ORDER TO CONSOLIDATE THE REAR

X. (ACHIEVE) NATIONAL SOLIDARITY AGAINST JAPAN

On the cornerstone of all-out co-operation between the KMT and the CCP, build an anti-Japanese, national united front of all parties, groups, classes, and armies in the country to lead the fight against Japan and to cope with the national crisis by sincere unity.

21. THE CCP's PUBLIC STATEMENT ON KMT-CCP CO-OPERATION
(September 22, 1937)

[Published by the KMT Central News Agency on September 22, but drafted by the CCP on July 4 and handed to the KMT on July 15, see document no. 22, fourth paragraph.]

Beloved Compatriots! The CC of the CCP respectfully and most sincerely issues the following manifesto to all fathers, brothers, aunts, and sisters throughout the country:

At the present juncture, with the country facing extreme danger and the fate of the nation in precarious balance, we have reached an understanding with the KMT of China on the basis of peace, national unity, and joint resistance against foreign aggression, in order to save our fatherland from extinction. We are (thus) determined to overcome the national emergency by concerted effort. What a profound significance this will have on the future of the great Chinese nation! For we all know that, at present, when (our) national existence is so seriously endangered, the aggression of imperialist Japan can only be overcome by the internal unity of our nation. The foundation for national solidarity has already been laid, and the premise for national independence and emancipation established. The CC of the CCP offers congratulations on the bright and shining future of our nation.

However, we know that in order to transform this glorious future into a new China, independent, free, and happy, all our fellow countrymen, every single zealous descendant of Huang-ti [the legendary first emperor of China] must determinedly and relentlessly participate in the concerted struggle. The CCP avails itself of this opportunity to propose to all our compatriots the following general objectives for our common struggle. These are:

(1) Struggle for the independence, liberty, and emancipation of the Chinese nation by sincerely and swiftly preparing and launching the national revolutionary campaign of resistance, with a view to recovering the lost territories and restoring the integrity of our territory and of our sovereign rights.

(2) Realize democracy based on the people's rights, convoke the National Assembly [*Kuo-min hui-i*, frequently promised by the KMT

since 1935] in order to enact the Constitution and decide upon the plans of national salvation.

(3) Realize the happiness and comfortable livelihood of the Chinese people. First of all it is necessary effectively to eliminate famine and drought, stabilize the people's livelihood, develop a national defence economy, relieve the sufferings of the people, and improve their living conditions.

These are the urgent needs of China and the aims of (our) struggle. We trust that they will receive the whole-hearted support of the entire people. The CCP wishes to make a unanimous effort, with these general principles as an objective, hand in hand with our compatriots of the whole country.

The CCP fully realizes that in implementing this lofty programme, numerous obstacles and difficulties will have to be overcome. The first source of obstruction and sabotage will be that of Japanese imperialism. In order to deprive the enemy of all pretexts for conspiracy, and dispel misunderstandings on the part of (our) friends who have doubts, it is necessary for the CC of the CCP to declare frankly its sincerity in regard to the cause of national emancipation. Therefore the CC of the CCP again solemnly proclaims to the whole country:

(1) The *San-min chu-i* (Three People's Principles) enunciated by Sun Yat-sen are the paramount need of China today. This Party is ready to strive for their thorough realization.

(2) (This Party) abandons all its policy of overthrowing the KMT by force and the movement of sovietization, and discontinues its policy of forcible confiscation of land from landlords.

(3) (This Party) abolishes the present Soviet government and practises democracy based on the people's rights in order to unify the national political power.

(4) (This Party) abolishes the designation of the Red Army, reorganizes it into the National Revolutionary Army, places it under the control of the Military Affairs Commission of the National government [i.e. at Nanking], and awaits orders for mobilization to shoulder the responsibility of resisting Japanese aggression at the front.

Beloved Compatriots! The sincere, honest, fair, and conciliatory attitude of this Party has been previously clearly manifested to the entire people in both words and action, and has received the commendation of the people. In order to secure true unity with the KMT, consolidate national peace and unity, and carry out the anti-Japanese national revolutionary war, we have decided to translate immediately into action those of our words which have not yet been formally realized—such as the abolition of the Soviet area, and reorganization of the Red Army—in order that there may be a unified and united national force for resisting the aggression of the foreign enemy.

The enemy has penetrated into our country! The moment is critical! Compatriots, arise, and unite! Our great Chinese nation, with its long history, is unconquerable. Rise and struggle for the consolidation of national unity and the overthrow of Japanese imperialist oppression. Victory will belong to the Chinese nation.

Long live the victory of the anti-Japanese war!

Long live the independent, free, and happy new China!

22. MAO TSE-TUNG: URGENT TASKS OF THE CHINESE REVOLUTION SINCE THE FORMATION OF THE KMT-CCP UNITED FRONT (September 29, 1937)

The Formation of a United Front between the Two Parties

As early as 1932 the CCP issued its famous proclamation proposing to form—under three conditions—an anti-Japanese alliance with any group within the KMT which would be willing to suspend the civil war against the Chinese Soviets and Red Army and resist Japan. This was because after the September Eighteenth incident [of 1931 in Manchuria] the opposition to the Japanese invasions had become the primary task of the Chinese revolution. However, our plan was not successful.

In August of 1935 the CCP and the Central Government of the Chinese Soviets called on all parties, groups, and the whole Chinese people to organize an anti-Japanese army and government for national defence to offer joint resistance to Japanese imperialism. In December of the same year, the CCP made public its resolution to organize an anti-Japanese national united front. In May 1936, when the Red Army turned back from Shansi [Communist forces had advanced northward to fight the Japanese, but had been forced back by Yen Hsi-shan, then Governor of Shansi], the Central Soviet government and the Revolutionary Military Committee of the Red Army again made public a manifesto calling on the Nanking government to stop the civil war and co-operate in fighting Japan. In August of that year, the CC of the CCP again sent its now famous petition to the CEC of the KMT, asking the KMT to cease fighting, organize a united front between the two parties, and jointly resist Japanese imperialism. In September of the same year, the CCP made public its resolution supporting the establishment of a united democratic republic in China. Not only were there these declarations, letters, and resolutions, but the CCP also frequently sent its representatives to negotiate with the KMT. However, all these efforts were still of no avail. It was only after the Sian incident [December 12, 1936] that the plenipotentiaries of the CCP finally obtained, with the chief of the KMT [Chiang Kai-shek] at the end of 1936, an agreement important in the political scene of the time, namely, the cessation of civil war by both parties and both armies, and the peaceful settlement of the Sian incident. This was an epic event in the history of China, and henceforth was established the indispensable premise for the formation of a united front of the two parties.

On February 10 of this year [1937], on the eve of the Third Plenum of the CEC of the KMT, the CC of the CCP took concrete steps to set up a united front. It sent a telegram to the KMT Plenum offering systematic and specific suggestions. In this telegram the KMT was asked to give the CCP five guarantees, involving the cessation of civil war, democratic rights (the setting up of) a National Assembly, speedy preparation for the war of resistance, and the improvement of the living conditions of the people. In return the CCP promised to abolish its independent political régime, change the name of the Red Army and of the Soviet areas, practise democracy, and cease the confiscation of land. This was also an important political step, because without this step the formation of the united front between the two parties would have been delayed, which would have produced an entirely adverse effect on the speedy preparation for the war of resistance.

Later more detailed negotiations were held between the two parties. The CCP presented even more specific suggestions, on such questions as a common political programme for both parties, freedom for the mass movement, release of political prisoners, change of the name of the Red Army and Soviet areas, etc. While the issues of the promulgation of a common political programme, freedom for the mass movement, recognition of the Soviet areas and other [items] still remained unsettled, the designation of the Red Army as the Eighth Route Army of the National Revolutionary Army (also called the Eighteenth Army Group in the anti-Japanese battle order) was ordered, about one month after the fall of Peiping and Tientsin. After certain regrettable delays the CC's manifesto on KMT-CCP cooperation, drafted on July 4 and handed to the KMT on July 15, as well as an announcement on the legal status of the CCP by Chiang Kai-shek, agreed upon previously by him were belatedly made public through the Central News Agency on September 22 and 23 respectively, at a time when the war situation at the front was extremely grave. This manifesto of the CCP and the speech of Chiang Kai-shek, announcing the formation of the united front of the two parties, laid the essential groundwork for the great mission of the two parties' joint efforts for national salvation. This manifesto will not only form the guiding principle for the solidarity of both parties, but will also serve as the basic guiding principle for the solidarity of the whole nation. Chiang's speech recognized the legal status of the CCP in the nation and pointed out the necessity of co-operation to save the country. While this is all to the good, we have been somewhat disappointed to find that the KMT still retains its egotism and still fails to engage in proper self-criticism. Nevertheless, the united front of the two parties has been formed, and this has opened a new era in the revolutionary history of China. Its great political significance should be clearly understood by the whole nation. Henceforth (the united front) will have an extensive and profound effect on the Chinese revolution and will assure the defeat of Japanese imperialism.

The Effect of the Formation of the Two-Party United Front

Ever since 1925 the relationship between the KMT and the CCP has been a decisive factor in the Chinese revolution. As a result of the co-operation between the two parties on major policies, the Great Revolution of 1925–7 was successfully guided to the point where we were able to achieve, within two or three years, the revolution for nationalism, democracy, and people's livelihood which Sun Yat-sen had been unable to accomplish in forty years, and which was an achievement unprecedented in history. The establishment of the revolutionary base in Kwangtung and the victory of the Northern Expedition were both the results of the formation of the two-party united front. However, because a certain group was unable to adhere to the revolutionary doctrine, the two-party united front was wrecked at the very moment when the revolution was about to be consummated, resulting in the failure of the Chinese revolution. Since then, political power has been monopolized by one class and one party, and a wide gap has been created not only between the KMT and the CCP, but also between the government and the people. Foreign aggression utilized this opportunity, thus inaugurating a tragic chapter of humiliation in our history. All this was the result of the breach of the two-party united front.

Now the reunion of the two parties is about to usher in a new era in the Chinese revolution. There are, it is true, certain people who still do not understand the historical mission and the great destiny of this united front, who still think that this united front is merely an expedient, an absolutely temporary measure. However, the wheel of history will, through this united front, push the Chinese revolution forward on to a new era. The united front will have a decisive influence in determining whether or not China can be liberated from such grave national and social dangers. Of this we already have new and tangible evidence. First, as soon as the proposal of a united front was brought up by the CCP, the whole nation immediately supported it. This clearly reflects the trend of public opinion. Second, when the Sian incident was peacefully settled, and the two parties and two armies ceased fighting, an unprecedented degree of solidarity was immediately reached among all parties, groups, classes, and armed forces in the nation. Though this solidarity is far from adequate from the viewpoint of our needs in the war of resistance—in particular, the question of co-operation between government and people remains basically unsettled—the serious conflict existing between the provinces and the Central government was nevertheless modified as a result of the truce between the two parties. The third and most obvious evidence is the mobilization for a war of resistance on a national scale. We are not satisfied with the present state of the war since it is still limited to a war waged exclusively by the government and the army, in spite of its national scope. We pointed out long ago that Japanese imperialism could not be defeated by warfare of this type. Nevertheless, a movement of national resistance such as we have not seen during the past hundred years has begun, and this would not have been possible without internal peace and the two-party united front. If the Japanese bandits could seize the four provinces of the North-east without firing a shot when the united front was broken, then today when the two-party united front is re-established, the Japanese bandits will have to pay in blood to obtain any further territory in China. It is reported that the Japanese daily expenditures for war have amounted to anywhere from 20,000,000 to 25,000,000 dollars. In this manner, if China can hold on for one year, the financial resources of Japan will be drained dry, because she will have to spend 7.2 billion dollars in one year, and, needless to say, there will be huge increases in the future. Fourth, we have the international effect. The worker and peasant masses and Communist Parties throughout the world support the united front proposed by the CCP. Now that co-operation has been achieved between the KMT and the CCP, this reaction will increase, particularly in the form of active assistance from the Soviet

Union and her people. China and the Soviet Union have already concluded a non-aggression pact, and in future it will proceed one step further, to the stage of more concrete opposition to the Japanese bandits. From the above evidence we can conclude that progress in the realization of the two-party united front will lead China to a bright and great future. In a word, it means that the historical mission of national liberation will be accomplished in the future on the basis of the development of the united front. The result will be the defeat of Japanese imperialism and the establishment of a united, democratic republic in China.

But this great mission cannot be achieved if we stop at the present stage in the united front. The two-party united front still requires improvement, for the present united front is not yet a strong and solid one.

What Do We Mean by a Strong and Solid United Front?

Is the anti-Japanese national united front merely a united front of the two parties—the KMT and the CCP? No, it is a united front of the whole nation. The two parties constitute only a small part of this united front. The two parties are undoubtedly the leading elements within this great united front, but they are still only a fraction. The anti-Japanese national united front is a united front of all parties, groups, classes, and armed forces, a united front of all Chinese patriots, of workers, peasants, students, and soldiers. At present, of course, the united front is still limited in scope to the two parties. The vast majority of workers, peasants, soldiers, petty bourgeoisie, and other patriotic fellow countrymen are not yet awakened, their enthusiasm is not yet activated, and they are not yet organized or equipped with arms. This is the most serious situation at present. Its seriousness has led to our inability to win battles at the front. The grave situation in North China as well as on the Kiangsu and Chekiang fronts can no longer be hidden by censorship, and it is futile to attempt to hide it. The question is how to save this dangerous situation. The only way to overcome this situation is to carry out the will of Sun Yat-sen, that is, to "awaken the people". The will drawn up by Dr. Sun on his death-bed explicitly states that, from forty years' experience, he knew without doubt that this was the only way to achieve the goal of the revolution. Why has there been a stubborn refusal to carry out this will? Why is there still no resolute effort to carry out this will when times are so critical? Everyone knows that "control" and "suppression" are in contradiction to the idea of "awakening the people". Is there anything more unreasonable than sitting on the stool without making use of it at a time when the whole populace desperately wishes to excrete? War waged only by the government and the army will never defeat the Japanese imperialists. We have already vigorously warned our fraternal party in power on this question as early as April of this year, pointing out that without a rising of the masses to struggle, we would simply have a repetition of the case of Abyssinia. (In "The Tasks of the anti-Japanese National United Front at the Present Stage.") The CCP has not been alone in this. Many progressive elements in various places as well as many enlightened members of the KMT have pointed this out. Yet the policy of control remains unchanged. The result is the isolation of the government from the people, of the army from the people, and of officers from men. Unless the united front is implemented by the people, the grave situation at the fighting front will inevitably deteriorate rather than improve.

Why has the policy of control remained unchanged? It is because there are today no openly promulgated political programmes agreed upon by the two parties in the united front to replace the policy of control. The policies at present are the policies of ten years ago. In the whole field from governmental institutions, army system, and policies on mass movements, to financial, economic, and educational policies, they have remained on the whole unchanged during these ten years. Something has, however, changed, and changed drastically. That is, the cessation of the civil war and the unanimous resolve to fight Japan. The civil war between the two parties has ceased and the national war of resistance has begun. This is the very drastic change which has taken place in the Chinese political situation since the Sian incident. Nevertheless, many things mentioned above still remain unchanged. There results a lack of consistency between the changes made and the things unchanged. The past policies were adapted only to a policy of surrender to the foreign powers and suppression of the internal revolution. The same policies are employed now to meet the attack of the Japanese imperialists. Their unsuitability is everywhere evident and their weakness manifest. It would be a different matter if we did not wish to undertake the anti-Japanese war. But since we wish to, and have undertaken it, our future will be unthinkably precarious if no new policies are adopted, especially since we are already faced with a grave situation. To resist Japan we need a strengthened united front which means the mobilization of the people of the whole country to participate in the united front. To resist Japan we need a solid united front, which means the necessity of common policies. Common policies should be the guiding principle of the united front. It will also serve as a binding force of the united front, binding tightly, as with a cord, all the organizations and individuals from all the parties, groups, classes and armies that participate in it. Only thus can solidarity be achieved. We are opposed to the old form of control because it is unsuitable to the national revolutionary war. We welcome the establishment of a new system of control to replace the old, that is, by promulgating common policies to set up a revolutionary order. For only thus can the needs of the war of resistance be met.

The Fight for the Realization of the Three People's Principles and the Ten Great Policies

What should our common policies be? They are the Three People's Principles of Dr. Sun Yat-sen and the Ten Great Policies for Anti-Japanese Resistance and National Salvation announced by the CCP on August 15 [1937, see document no. 21 above].

The Declaration on KMT-CCP Co-operation issued by the CCP [see document no. 20 above] states that: "The Three People's Principles of Dr. Sun Yat-sen are necessary for China at the present time and our Party is willing to fight for their complete realization." Some people are puzzled by the CCP's willingness to carry out the Three People's Principles of the KMT. For instance, Mr. Chu Ch'ing-lai of Shanghai, one of those who raised the question, has maintained (in a certain periodical in Shanghai) that Communism and the Three People's Principles are incompatible. This is the point of view of formalism. Communism is to be implemented in a future stage of the revolutionary development. Communists do not wishfully envisage the realization of Communism at present, but are striving for the realization of the historically determined principles of national revolution and democratic revolution. This is the basic reason why the CCP has raised the slogans of an anti-Japanese national united front and a united democratic republic. As to the implementation of the Three People's Principles, the CCP agreed to it during the first united front formed ten years ago at the First National Congress of the KMT [January 1924], and they were indeed carried out on a national scale between 1925 and 1927 by every faithful Communist and every faithful KMT member. Unfortunately in 1927 the united front was shattered, resulting in the suspension of the Three People's Principles during the past decade. However, as far as the CCP is concerned, all the policies carried out by it during the last ten years have been in harmony with the revolutionary spirit of Dr. Sun Yat-sen's Three People's Principles and the three great policies [i.e. alliance with Soviet Russia, alliance with the Communists, and support of the workers and peasants]. The CCP has never ceased its firm resistance to imperialism; this is the principle of nationalism (*Min-tsu chu-i*). The Soviet system of people's representative councils is nothing else than the principle of democracy (*Min-ch'üan chu-i*) and the agrarian revolution is without a doubt the principle of people's livelihood (*Min-sheng chu-i*). Why, then, has the CCP announced the abolition of the Soviet and the cessation of land confiscation? This we have explained before. It is not that these measures are undesirable, but that armed invasion by Japanese imperialists has brought about changes in class relations in China, thus making imperative and making possible the alliance of all classes in the fight against Japanese imperialism. Furthermore, a democratic united front is being formed internationally, to fight against the danger of fascism. Therefore, the formation of a national, democratic united front in China is today a necessity in China. It was on these grounds that we proposed the slogan of a democratic republic to replace the slogan of the Soviet. The implementation of the slogan of "land to the tillers" was precisely the policy suggested by Dr. Sun Yat-sen. If we have today suspended this policy, it is entirely in order to rally a greater number of people to fight Japanese imperialism and not because the land problem does not need to be solved in China. We have already clearly explained our point of view concerning the objective reasons and time factors involved in this change of policy. Because the CCP, basing itself on Marxist principles, has consistently stood for and advanced the common policies developed in the first united front between the KMT and the CCP, i.e. the Three People's Principles, and has never betrayed the revolution, therefore the CCP was able, at a critical time when powerful bandits were converging on our territory, to make a timely proposal of a national, democratic united front, a measure that will save us from being conquered, and, furthermore, to carry out this measure without reservation. The question is not whether the CCP believes in and implements the Three People's Principles, but whether the KMT believes in and is implementing the Three People's Principles. We are now faced with the problem of reviving the spirit of Dr. Sun Yat-sen's Three People's Principles on a national scale, of implementing them in concrete policies and programmes, and of carrying them out honestly, concretely, and unhesitatingly. This is what the CCP ardently prays for day and night. It was with this in view that the CCP proposed on August 15, [1937] the Ten Great Policies for Anti-Japanese Resistance and National Salvation immediately after the Marco Polo Bridge incident [July 7, 1937]. These Ten Great Policies are compatible with Marxism and also compatible with the true, revolutionary Three People's Principles. This is our preliminary platform in the Chinese revolution at the present stage, i.e. the stage of the anti-Japanese national revolutionary war. China can be saved only by carrying out these policies. If policies contrary to the spirit of these policies continue unchanged, there will some day be a historical disaster. The disaster will take the form of the enslavement of the Chinese race by a foreign power.

These policies can be carried out only with the consent of the KMT, because the KMT is at present still the largest party in power. They cannot be carried out throughout the whole country without its consent. We believe that the wiser members of the KMT and their leader will one day consent to these policies. For if they do not consent, then the Three People's Principles will remain empty words, the revolutionary spirit of Dr. Sun Yat-sen will not be revived, Japanese imperialism will not be defeated, and enslavement of the country will be inevitable. The more intelligent members and leader of the KMT will certainly not allow this to happen, nor will the whole nation sit by and wait to become slaves without a country. Furthermore, Mr. Chiang Kai-shek pointed out in his statement of September 23 [1937] that "it is my opinion that we faithful followers of the revolution should not lay stress on personal differences and prejudices. For the sake of the realization of the Three People's Principles at this critical hour, (we should) let bygones be bygones and work for consolidation with the entire people in order to preserve the existence of our nation." This is entirely correct. Our urgent tasks at present are to work for the realization of the Three People's Principles, to forget personal and clique differences and prejudices, to revise old practices adopted in the past, to carry out immediately a revolutionary policy compatible with the Three People's Principles, and to begin working anew with the people. This is the only solution today. If delayed further, it will be too late for regret.

However, to carry out the Three People's Principles and the Ten Great Policies, we must have instruments of implementation. This brings up the question of government and army reforms. The present government is still a one-party dictatorship under the KMT and not a government of the national democratic united front. The realization of the Three People's Principles and the Ten Great Policies is not possible without a government of the national democratic united front. The present army system still rests on the traditional basis. It is impossible to defeat the Japanese imperialists totally with an army based on such a system. At present our troops are fighting the sacred war of resistance at the front and we have nothing but the highest respect for all the Chinese troops, especially those that are fighting at the front. But the military system is not suited to the task of completely defeating the Japanese bandits, nor does it allow for the unhindered implementation of the Three People's Principles or of a revolutionary platform. To perform these tasks successfully it is necessary that the system be reformed. This has been proved by the lessons learned in the war of resistance during the last three months. The principles of the reform should be based on the principle of co-operation between officers and men, and co-operation between the army and the people. The present military system is in basic contradiction to these two principles. The troops are devoted and brave, but the limitations of the system make it impossible for them to develop their potentialities. This must be speedily reformed. (We are) not saying that fighting should be stopped and resumed only after the reform of the system. Both can be carried on simultaneously. The central task facing us is to reform the political spirit and political work in the army. A model to be followed is the party army in the days of the Great Revolution [1925-7]. Generally speaking, that was an army in which there existed co-operation between the officers and the men and between the army and the people. It is imperative that this spirit be revived. China should learn from the lessons of the Spanish civil war. The Republican army of Spain was created under very difficult circumstances. Many conditions in China now are more favourable than those of Spain but (we) lack a strengthened and solid united front, a united front government that can carry out all our revolutionary policies and a large number of troops organized under a new army system. China should correct these defects by herself. The Red Army at present has only a partial and not a decisive influence on the anti-Japanese front; but its political, military, and organizational merits are worthy of adoption by the friendly armies in the country. The Red Army did not, at the beginning, possess its present characteristics. There have been many reforms, chiefly the political liquidation of feudalism and the carrying out of the principle of co-operation between officers and men and co-operation between army and people. This point is worthy of consideration by the friendly armies of the country.

KMT comrades now in power: We are today shouldering together with you the historical task of assuring the survival of our country. You have formed an anti-Japanese united front with us; this is all to the good. You have begun a policy of resistance; this is also to the good. We cannot, however, acquiesce in your continuation of other old policies. Our united front should be developed, should be strengthened, and should be reinforced by the people. (We) should consolidate it and carry out common policies. Reforms of political and military systems must be resolutely carried out. The formation of a new government is imperative. Only such a government can carry out a revolutionary policy and reform the army on a national scale. These suggestions of ours are based on the urgent needs of our time. Many members of your party have also felt such a need, and it is high time that it be implemented. Dr. Sun Yat-sen was resolved to reform the political and military systems, thus laying the foundation for the Great Revolution. This duty now falls on your shoulders. All KMT members who are faithful and patriotic will not consider our proposal superfluous. We firmly believe that this proposal meets the objective needs. We especially hope that Mr. Chiang Kai-shek will take up this task of reform.

Our race and nation now stand at a critical hour of survival. May the KMT and the CCP work in close harmony! May all our fellow countrymen who do not want to be slaves rally together on the foundation of KMT-CCP solidarity! The realization of all necessary reforms in order to overcome numerous difficulties—such is the urgent task now facing us in the Chinese revolution. The accomplishment of this task will certainly bring about the defeat of Japanese imperialism. If we devote our effort (to this task) our future is indeed bright.

COMMENTARY L. PROPAGANDA IN THE UNITED FRONT PERIOD

The next document (no. 23) illustrates the platform and propaganda techniques of the CCP during the early stage of the Sino-Japanese war. The upsurge of Chinese nationalism is skilfully exploited and given explicit expression in the first paragraph, which states that "the highest interests of the Chinese working class are identical with the highest interests of the Chinese nation and the Chinese people". The amiable relationship between the CCP and its "bourgeois" rivals during this period can be seen from such standard pronouncements as "the primary task of the CCP is to establish a democratic republic based on national independence, democratic liberty, and the people's welfare". This phraseology of course bears a close and hardly unintentional resemblance to Sun Yat-sen's Three People's Principles, i.e. Nationalism, Democracy (or People's Rights), and People's Livelihood.

On the other hand, the CCP continues to state in no uncertain terms that it is itself "the Marxist-Leninist Party of the Chinese working class" and that "only a Communist society will completely realize the final liberation of the Chinese nation and the Chinese people". The Party "must steadfastly maintain its political and organizational independence, expand and reinforce the Party forces . . . and retain as well as develop our traditional spirit of relentless struggle". The resulting mixture of "bourgeois" (i.e. liberal) and Communist slogans during the united front period produced that apparent doctrinal ambivalence which allowed the CCP to be many things to unorganized Chinese liberals outside it, while remaining disciplined within. Thus all the liberal freedoms in the KMT areas were consistently championed by the CCP, in the face of increasing KMT disregard or suppression of them, and a special appeal was made to the "petty bourgeoisie", the student and clerical classes of the cities. Note in this document how "democratic republic" is used instead of the term "Soviet" (used during the Kiangsi period) or "people's democratic dictatorship" (used recently). Also the expression "vanguard of the Chinese nation and Chinese people" has come to be used as frequently, at least in public pronouncements as the expression "the vanguard of the proletariat", so as to fit into the united front. Such propaganda techniques, geared to the specific aspirations of various segments of the Chinese people at a specific time, have constituted an important factor in winning over the Chinese populace and defeating the KMT.

23. PROPAGANDA OUTLINE ISSUED BY THE CC [CCP] ON THE SEVENTEENTH ANNIVERSARY OF THE CCP (June 24, 1938)

(1) The CCP is the Marxist-Leninist Party of the Chinese working class. Its historic mission is the final liberation of the Chinese nation and the Chinese people, for it is only by liberating the whole of mankind that the working class can liberate itself. The highest interests of the Chinese working class are identical with the highest interests of the Chinese nation and the Chinese people.

(2) For the final liberation of the Chinese nation and the Chinese people, the primary tasks of the CCP are to establish a democratic

republic based on national independence, democratic liberty, and the people's welfare, to win a thorough victory in the democratic revolution and to direct the Chinese revolution along the road to Communism. Only a Communist society will completely realize the final liberation of the Chinese nation and the Chinese people.

(3) The past seventeen years of the CCP have been filled with relentless struggle for national independence, democratic liberty, and the people's welfare. The basic goal of this struggle was clearly defined by the CCP as early as 1922. While there have necessarily been certain changes in some policies of the CCP during the course of these seventeen years due to changes in internal and external conditions, the basic direction of its struggle remains the same.

(4) After the September Eighteenth incident [Japanese seizure of Mukden, etc., in 1931] the CCP was the first to raise the slogan of a holy national war of self-defence to drive the Japanese bandits out of China and to preserve our territorial and sovereign integrity. After six years of hard struggle the national war of resistance finally began on July 7 of last year. The CCP pointed out at a very early stage that the expansion and consolidation of the anti-Japanese united front was the key to final victory in the war of resistance, and made itself the initiator and organizer of such a united front.

(5) Since their occupation of Hsü-chou [Suchow, key rail centre in northern Kiangsu, occupied May 19, 1938], the Japanese bandits have been advancing towards Wuhan in major force. The CCP points out that our most urgent tasks at present are to defend Wuhan, to defend our whole country, to employ every means to weaken the enemy and to strengthen our own forces, to overcome all difficulties and wavering sentiment, and to vanquish the enemy by prolonged warfare.

(6) The CCP has become strong and powerful in its seventeen years of heroic struggle for the final liberation of the Chinese nation and Chinese people. The correctness of its basic policy has been proved by the revolutionary history of China in the past seventeen years. It has won great prestige among the people of our whole nation and has become a vital factor in the political life of the country. In the past year, on the various national resistance fronts, the comrades of our Party have demonstrated that they are indeed the vanguard of the Chinese nation and the Chinese people. Our comrades must continue their effort in this direction in order to obtain final victory in the war of resistance.

(7) Consequently, the CCP must, in the face of all difficulties, stand

firm in the anti-Japanese national united front; at the same time it must steadfastly maintain the Party's political and organizational independence, expand and reinforce the Party forces, threefold, a hundredfold, greatly strengthen Marxist-Leninist training within the Party, and retain and develop our traditional spirit of relentless struggle—this will be the guarantee of the final liberation of the Chinese nation and the Chinese people.

COMMENTARY M. THE SIGNIFICANCE OF MAO'S NEW DEMOCRACY

At first glance Mao Tse-tung's *On the New Democracy* appears to be a theoretical justification of the whole united front strategy followed by the CCP in the period of its attempted alliance with the KMT against Japan from 1935 on.[1] Actually the work appeared precisely at the time (in early 1940) when ominous cracks were beginning to appear in the structure of this precarious KMT-CCP alliance. Mao's constant attacks on anti-Communists, on those within the KMT who were calling for "a one-party dictatorship", betray a genuine anxiety concerning the future course of the alliance. It is thus probable that *On the New Democracy* was written not simply in order to provide the united front strategy with a theoretical framework, but also to prepare the Party for the possible disintegration of the alliance in the future. *On the New Democracy* not only points out the "bourgeois-democratic" nature of the Chinese revolution at its present stage, but also re-emphasizes the fact that the CCP has its own ultimate aims and its own separate destiny. Viewed in this light *On the New Democracy* may be considered an integral part of the whole movement launched in the early 1940s to rally and consolidate the forces of the CCP, to restore the Party to the sharp outlines which had been somewhat blurred by the impact of the united front, and to make articulate the Party's doctrinal positions in terms of its minimum and maximum aims. The formulation of a clear-cut Party line was a vital step in the process of consolidation.

The peculiar and original feature of *On the New Democracy* is the fact that it is presented to us not simply as a more detailed statement of the united front line which had been elaborated at the Seventh Congress of the CI in 1935, but as a genuinely new contribution to Marxist-Leninist theory—a contribution which had originated in China and which presumably placed its author, Mao Tse-tung, in the ranks of the great theoreticians of Marxism. Within the context of the world Communist movement as it had developed under Stalin's sway, this represented a somewhat bold and original gesture. Moscow, it is true, had in previous years taken pains to provide special theoretical analyses of the Chinese situation, which had always been presumed to have its "historic peculiarities". This had been done during the period of the first united front and also during the Soviet period. But the main elements of these theories had always originated in Moscow. With the shift to the united front strategy in 1935, we find no further inclination in Moscow to provide a special line for China. Whether this reflected the reduced importance of China in the Kremlin's strategy or whether it was simply felt that Wang Ming's application of the general united front line to China (at the Seventh ECCI Plenum in 1935)[2] provided the Chinese Party with an adequate theoretical framework, China no longer received special treatment.

The presumption is thus legitimate that the gesture to create a new theory re-emphasizing "the historic peculiarities of the Chinese revolution" originated with Mao Tse-tung himself. It was a gesture with profound implications. It suggested that innovations within the Marxist-Leninist tradition could originate not only in Moscow but in other sectors of the world Communist movement as well; that the tradition is still capable of further "original" developments which rank in importance with those of Marx, Engels, Lenin, and Stalin. Viewed in this light, the *New Democracy* is an accurate reflection of the spirit of Chinese Communism during the Yenan period, for it was in this period that the movement most boldly asserted its own personality in all spheres of activity, developed its own ingenious techniques, and most vigorously asserted its national character.

While the claims made for the *New Democracy* are original, however, can the same be said for the positive content of the theory? Does it really represent an original development within the body of Marxism-Leninism-Stalinism? We should note that by 1940 the highly developed scholastique of Marxism-Leninism allowed little room for strikingly original developments within its own premises, and most of Stalin's own "innovations" have been *ad hoc* manipulations of elements already supplied by Lenin. Even within this narrow sense of "originality", however, a candid examination of the *New Democracy* in the light of previous Communist theory hardly justifies the broad claims which have been made for it. Mao Tse-tung's real "innovations" in the Chinese Communist movement appear to lie in the realm of practical political action more than in the realm of Marxist theory.

For example, the concept of China as a "semi-colonial and semi-feudal" country had been elaborated as early as the Second Congress of the CCP in 1922. The concept of the "bourgeois-democratic" nature of the present stage of the Chinese revolution was a commonplace of Kremlin literature. The notion that the Chinese revolution would not tread the path of the older democracies because it was occurring in the period of the world revolution can also be found throughout Comintern literature. The notion that the Chinese revolution would not follow the path of the Russian revolution because of the differentiating factor of imperialism, and that as a result of imperialism in China the national bourgeoisie (identified usually with the Kuomintang) could still play a revolutionary role, had been one of Stalin's main defences against Trotsky in 1927. The concept of a state form which is neither a "bourgeois dictatorship" nor a "proletarian dictatorship", but a "united dictatorship of several classes", had been used by the Stalinist leadership in 1927 to justify the entry of the Chinese Communists into the Wuhan government. The stress on the problem of the peasantry does indeed accurately reflect the peasant-based nature of Chinese Communism in 1940, but it was not a new element of theory. The Seventh Plenum of the ECCI in 1926 had already announced the centrality of the peasant problem. The Kremlin had, of course, always added the vital reservation that the peasant movement must be under "proletarian hegemony" (cf. commentary D above). But Mao, who finds it difficult in 1940 to hide the Party's isolation from the urban masses, uses vaguer language: "Without the workers," he states, "the Chinese revolution will not be able to succeed, for it is they who are the most revolutionary section of the people." Essentially, his statement adds nothing new in the realm of theory. Finally, the attempt to equate Sun Yat-sen's Three People's Principles with the basic tasks of the "bourgeois-democratic" period had been a favourite topic of discussion during the period of the first Kuomintang-Communist alliance.

Not only does the *New Democracy* not contain any essential theoretical novelty, but it fails to reflect the striking developments which had actually occurred within the Chinese Communist movement. While the theory of the *New Democracy* is basically similar to the theories used to justify the first CCP-KMT alliance of 1923–7, the realities which it supposedly reflects are entirely different. In 1940 the Chinese Communist Party already possessed its own territorial base, its own armed force, and its own growing peasant mass base. It confronted the Kuomintang as an independent force with its own effective sources of power. Why, then, did the *New Democracy* lay such little stress on these truly original developments? (They are mentioned briefly in sections 7 and 8 of the Chinese text, but in a minor key.) Mao Tse-tung, we suggest, deliberately avoided emphasizing these developments because they were precisely the features of Chinese Communism which were arousing the resentment and mistrust of the Kuomintang. So long as the CCP intended to maintain the united front, any emphasis on its own political and military independence was clearly inappropriate.

In brief, then, the *New Democracy* is a Marxist-Leninist scaffolding which conceals as much as it reveals. In spite of the claims made for its theoretical originality, it actually fails to depict Mao Tse-tung's genuinely original accomplishments, which lay in the field of active statesmanship. It is rather in the area of political action, and in his writings which directly illustrate political action, that we must seek Mao's true originality.

At the same time, the claims made for the *New Democracy* as a theoretical innovation, and the claims made for its author as a theoretician, represent a unique phenomenon in the world Communist movement. It is a phenomenon which Moscow has till now countenanced, but Moscow's future attitude towards this phenomenon may provide us with a valuable clue to the whole future drift of Soviet-Chinese-Communist relations.

24. MAO TSE-TUNG: ON THE NEW DEMOCRACY
(January 19, 1940) [extract]

1. *Whither China?*

Since the war of resistance (against Japan) began [July 1937] a buoyant and inspiriting mood has prevailed among our countrymen. All believed that the nation had found a way out and the former worried looks disappeared. But recently the atmosphere of compromise and reports of anti-Communism have increased daily and a state of bewilderment has again been created. (Such a bewilderment) especially confronts the writers and artists and young students who are more sensitive. Thus, the questions "What to do?" and "Whither China?" again stand before us. . . .[1]

2. [p. 2] *We Must Establish a New China.* . . .

We Communists of China have for years been struggling not only for the political and economic revolutions, but also for the cultural revolution. The aim of all our efforts is the building of a new society and a new nation of the Chinese people. In such a new society and new nation, there will be not only a new political organization and a new economy, but a new culture as well. . . .

3. [p. 3] *China's Historical Characteristics.* . . .

[p. 4] What, then, is the content of the so-called old politics and the old economics of the Chinese nation and its old culture?

Down from the dynasties of Chou and Ch'in [i.e. since *c.* 1000 B.C.] China has been a feudal society. Its politics were feudal politics, its economy a feudal economy, and consequently its culture, as the reflection of the corresponding forms of politics and economics, has also been feudal. . . .

[p. 5] What, then, is the content of the new politics and new economy of the Chinese nation, and what can be its new culture?

The progress of the Chinese revolution must be divided into two stages: (1) the democratic revolution; (2) the socialist revolution. These stages are different in nature. The above-mentioned democracy does not have the meaning of the old democracy, but is a new type of democracy, or new democracy.

Hence we can conclude that the new politics of the Chinese nation are the politics of new democracy, the new economy of the Chinese nation is the economy of new democracy, and the new culture is the culture of new democracy. . . .

4. *The Chinese Revolution is a Part of the World Revolution*

The historical characteristic of the Chinese revolution is that it is divided into two steps, that of democracy and that of socialism. The first step is not democracy in the general sense, but a new and specific kind, of a Chinese type—i.e. new democracy. . . .

[p. 6] Evidently, if the nature of the present Chinese society is colonial, semi-colonial, and semi-feudal, then the progress of the Chinese revolution must be in two steps. The first step is to turn the colonial, semi-colonial, and semi-feudal society into an independent democratic society; the second step is to push the revolution forward to build up a socialist society. The present phase of the Chinese revolution carried out by us is the first step.

The beginning of the first step of the Chinese revolution can be traced back to the Opium War [1839–42] when the Chinese society began to change from a feudal society to a semi-colonial, semi-feudal society. . . .

[p. 7] But a change took place in the Chinese bourgeois-democratic revolution after the outbreak of the first imperialist World War and the establishment of a socialist state on one-sixth of the land surface of the globe, i.e. after the Russian revolution of 1917.

Before that time, the Chinese bourgeois-democratic revolution was within the orbit of the old bourgeois-democratic world revolution and was a part of it.

From then on, the Chinese bourgeois-democratic revolution changed and came within the orbit of the new bourgeois-democratic revolution. From the standpoint of the revolutionary front, it is a part of the world proletarian-socialist revolution. . . .

[p. 9] As to the first stage or the first step in this colonial and semi-colonial revolution—according to its social nature, it is fundamentally still a bourgeois-democratic revolution in which the objective require-ment is still basically to clear away the obstacles in the way of capitalist development; nevertheless, this revolution is no longer the old type led solely by the bourgeoisie for the building of capitalist society and a state of the bourgeois dictatorship, but a new type of revolution wholly or partly led by the proletariat, the first stage of which aims at the setting up of a new democratic society, a new state of the joint dictatorship of all revolutionary classes. The fundamental character of this revolution will not change until the (arrival of the stage of) socialist revolution, even though, during its progress, it may pass through a number of stages in accordance with the possible changes in the conditions of enemies and allies.

This kind of [new democratic] revolution, because it is a great blow to the imperialists, is bound to be opposed and not tolerated by the imperialists; on the other hand, it is permitted by the socialist country and the socialistic international proletariat.

Therefore, it is inevitable that this revolution will become a part of the proletarian-socialist world revolution. . . .

[p. 13] From the above, it is clear that there are two kinds of world revolutions. One is a world revolution of the bourgeois and capitalist category, which ceased to prevail after the outbreak of the first im-perialist World War, and especially after the Russian revolution of 1917. Since then a world revolution of the second category has been born. It is the proletarian-socialist world revolution, in which the proletariat of the capitalist countries is the main force; and the oppressed nations in the colonies and semi-colonies are their allies. As to those classes, parties, or individuals of the oppressed nations, participating in the revolution, whatever classes, parties, or individuals they may be and whether or not they are subjectively conscious of the fact, inasmuch as they stand against imperialism—their revolution is bound to become a part of the proletarian-socialist world revolution, and they themselves are bound to become allies of the proletarian-socialist world revolution. . . .

[p. 14] This first stage of the Chinese revolution (it is again divided into several minor stages), according to its social nature, is a bourgois-democratic revolution of the new type. Although it is not a proletarian-socialist revolution of the newest type, certainly it already forms a part, an important part, of it and has been a great ally of it. The first step, i.e. the first stage of the revolution, is certainly not meant to, and certainly cannot, build up a capitalist society under the dictatorship of the Chinese bourgeoisie, but is meant to set up a new democratic society of the joint dictatorship of all revolutionary classes. After the first stage is accomplished, the development [of the Chinese revolution] will be carried forward into the second stage, namely, the building up of Chinese socialist society.

[p. 15] This then is the most fundamental characteristic of the present phase of the Chinese revolution, the new revolutionary process of the past twenty years (1919–40), (since the May Fourth [1919] movement). This is the living and concrete content of the Chinese revolution of today. . . .

5. *The Politics of New Democracy.* . . .

[p. 18] It is very clear in China that those who are really capable of leading the people to the overthrow of imperialism and feudalism will be trusted by the people, because imperialism and feudalism, especially imperialism, are the two deadly enemies of the people. Today those who are capable of leading the people to defeat Japanese imperialism and put democracy into practice are the saviours of the people. If the Chinese bourgeoisie is capable of fulfilling this duty, it certainly deserves every praise. Otherwise, the responsibility on the whole cannot but fall on the shoulders of the proletariat.

Therefore, no matter what the circumstances, the Chinese proletariat, peasantry, intelligentsia, and other petty-bourgeois elements are the main force upon which the fate of China depends. These classes either have awakened or are awakening, and are bound to be the basic parts of the state and government framework in the democratic Republic of China. The democratic Republic of China which we are aiming to construct now can only take the form of dictatorship of all anti-imperialist and anti-feudal people, i.e. a new democratic republic. In other words, [p. 19] a republic of the Three People's Principles in the true revolutionary sense as put forward by Dr. Sun

Yat-sen including the Three Great Policies [i.e. alliance with the Soviet, with the Communists, and for the interest of the workers and peasants].

Such a new democratic republic differs, on the one hand, from the old, western-type bourgeois-democratic republics that are under the dictatorship of the bourgeoisie; that kind of republic is out of date; it differs, on the other hand, from the newest, Soviet-style republic, which is under proletarian dictatorship. This kind of republic has already arisen in the Soviet Union and will be established in every country. It will no doubt be the final form of control for the completion of the nation and of government power in all progressive countries. Nevertheless, in a certain historical period, the Soviet-style republic cannot be fittingly put into practice in colonial and semi-colonial countries, the state form of which must be of a third form, namely, that of the new democratic republic. Being the state form of a certain historical period, it is a transitional form; but it is all the same an inevitable and necessary form of state.

Hence the forms of state in the world can be fundamentally classified, according to their social nature, into the following three categories:

(1) Republics of a bourgeois dictatorship.
(2) Republics of a proletarian dictatorship.
(3) Republics of a joint dictatorship of several revolutionary classes.

[p. 20] To the first category belong the old democratic countries. Today, after the outbreak of the second imperialist war, there is no breath of democracy among the capitalist countries. All have already changed or are just changing to bloody and putrid military dictatorships of the bourgeoisie. Certain countries with a joint dictatorship of landlords and bourgeoisie may be classified in this category.

The second category [of republics] is fermenting in the various capitalist countries, after having already achieved realization in the Soviet Union. It will become the ruling form of the world in a certain period.

The third category is the transitional form of the state in the revolutionary colonies and semi-colonies. There may be some different characteristics among different colonies and semi-colonies, but the state and governmental formations are basically alike, i.e. a new democratic republic of the joint dictatorship of several anti-imperialist classes. This form of state of the new democracy in present-day China is a form of anti-Japanese united front. It is anti-Japanese, anti-imperialist, and it is a coalition of several revolutionary classes in a united front. . . .

[p. 22] The state form—the joint dictatorship of several revolutionary classes; the governmental form—democratic centralism; this is the politics of new democracy, a republic of new democracy, a republic of the anti-Japanese united front, a republic of the Three People's Principles, which includes the famous Three Great Policies of Dr. Sun Yat-sen, and a Chinese Republic that is *res publica* in name and in reality. At present our country is a republic nominally, but there is no reality in it. To realize the meaning of the name is the task of today.

This is the internal political relationship which a revolutionary and anti-Japanese China ought, and must in no way fail, to establish. This is the only correct course for our work of national reconstruction at the present time.

6. *The Economy of New Democracy*

[p. 23] In such a republic as that mentioned above, our economy must be the economy of the new democracy, just as the politics is the politics of the new democracy.

Big banks, big industries, and big business shall be owned by this republic. "In order that private capital may not manipulate the livelihood of the people, all native-owned or foreign-owned enterprises, either monopolist or of a dimension too large for private efforts to manage such as banks, railroads, airlines, etc., will be managed and controlled by the state. This is the essence of restriction of capital." This was a slogan statement made by the KMT in the declaration of its First National Congress [January 1924]. This is the correct course for the economic constitution of the new democratic republic; at the same time, however, the state will not confiscate other capitalist private property and will not forbid the development of capitalist production that "cannot manipulate the people's livelihood". This is because the Chinese economy is still in a very backward state.

It [the new democratic republic] will adopt certain necessary measures to confiscate the land of big landlords and distribute it among peasants without any, or with very little, land, in order to realize Dr. Sun's slogan, "The tiller should own his land" and to liquidate the feudal relations in rural areas. This is not to build up socialist agriculture, but to turn the land into the private property of the peasants. The rich peasant economy will also be allowed to exist in the rural areas. This is the policy of "the equalization of landownership", the correct slogan of which is, "The tiller should own his land". . . .

7. [p. 24] *Refutation of the Theory of Bourgeois Dictatorship*

(Can we) go the road of a capitalist society under the dictatorship of the bourgeoisie? [p. 25] True, this is the old path traversed by the Western bourgeoisie. But the international as well as national environments do not allow China to do so. . . .

The modern history of China is a history of imperialist aggression, of imperialist obstruction of China's independence, and of China's development of her capitalism. . . .

8. [p. 30] *Refutation of Left Doctrinairism*

Is it possible for China to traverse the road of socialism, of proletarian dictatorship, if she is not to take that of capitalism, of bourgeois dictatorship?

This, too, is not possible.

Unquestionably, the present revolution is the first step and it will in the future develop into the second step, i.e. socialism. Only when she arrives at [p. 31] the period of socialism can China be called really happy. Yet the present is not the time to practise socialism. Socialism is out of the question before the tasks of the present revolution, the tasks of anti-imperialism and anti-feudalism, are fulfilled. The Chinese revolution can only be achieved in two steps: the first being that of new democracy; the second, that of socialism. Moreover, the period of the first step will be a considerably long one and can never be accomplished overnight. We cannot isolate (ourselves) from the actual conditions before us. We are not utopians.

9. [p. 33] *Refutation of the Obstinate Elements*

[p. 35] Everybody knows that, regarding the social system and programmes for action, the CP has a present programme and a future programme, a maximum and minimum programme. At present, it is the new democracy; in the future, it is socialism; these two organic components are guided by the ideological system of Communism. Is it not utterly absurd, then, to raise the cry that Communism must be "packed-up" when the principles of the minimum immediate programme of the CP are fundamentally and consistently the same as the political principles of the Three People's Principles? . . .

[p. 36] The basic political programmes of both the Three People's Principles and Communism for the period of the Chinese bourgeois-democratic revolution are consistent with each other. . . .

10. [p. 38] *The Old and the New Three People's Principles* (*San-min chu-i*)

[p. 39] First, the revolutionary, or new, genuine Three People's Principles must be for alliance with the Soviet Union. The facts of today are extraordinarily clear. If there is not a policy of alliance with Russia, of co-operation with the socialist state, then there must be a policy of alliance with imperialism, of co-operation with imperialism. Did not this sort of thing happen after 1927? . . .

[p. 41] Secondly, the revolutionary, new or genuine Three People's Principles must be for alliance with the Communists. . . .

[p. 42] Thirdly, the revolutionary, new or genuine Three People's Principles must be for the policy [of supporting] the peasants and workers. Those who cast aside the policy of [supporting the] workers and peasants, not sincerely helping the workers and peasants, and forsaking (the task of) "awakening the people" as inscribed in Dr. Sun's will, are preparing failure for the revolution, or for themselves. Stalin once said: "The question of the colonies and semi-colonies is in essence a peasant question." That is to say, the Chinese revolution is in essence a revolution of the peasantry; the present war of resistance [against Japan] is in essence a war of resistance of the peasantry. The politics of new democracy is in essence (the politics of) the transfer of power to the peasantry. The new, genuine Three People's Principles are in their essence the principles of a peasant revolution. The content of popular culture is in essence (the question of) the elevation of the cultural (level) among the peasantry. The anti-Japanese war is in essence a peasant war. (We are now all following the practice) "go up to the hills". Everything that we do is for the peasantry: our holding of meetings, conducting of various affairs, teaching, editing, writing, staging of dramas are all being done in the hills. Everything in this war, [p. 43] in all our daily life, is in essence given by the peasantry. Here the phrase "in essence" means "fundamentally", and certainly does not mean the overlooking of other elements. Stalin himself has explained this point. It is the common knowledge of every primary schoolboy, that eighty per cent of the Chinese population consists of peasants. The percentage has become even higher since the occupation of our large cities by the Japanese. Therefore, the peasant question becomes the fundamental question of the Chinese revolution, and the force of the peasantry is the main force of the Chinese revolution. Besides the peasantry, the second (largest) section of the Chinese population consists of workers. China has several millions of industrial workers. Without them, China would not be able to live on, for it is they who are the producers in the industrial economy. Without the workers, the (Chinese) revolution would not be able to succeed for it is they who are the leaders of the revolution and have the highest revolutionary spirit. Under these conditions the revolutionary, new or genuine Three People's Principles must adopt the policy of (aiding) the workers and peasants. If there is such a Three People's Principles which does not adopt this policy, does not truly protect and assist them, does not endeavour to "awaken the people", then it is bound to decay. . . .

11. [p. 46] *The Culture of New Democracy*

A given culture is the ideological reflection of the politics and economics of a given society. In China, there is the imperialist (form of) culture, which is the reflection of the control or the partial control, politically and economically, by the imperialists over China. This kind of culture, besides being advocated through the medium of the cultural institutions run directly by the imperialists, is also advocated by some shameless Chinese. . . .

[p. 47] As to the new culture, it is the ideological reflection of the new politics and economics, and it serves the new politics and economics. . . .

12. [p. 48] *The Historical Characteristics of China's Cultural Revolution*

[p. 49] In the field of culture or ideology, the May Fourth movement [1919] marked the dividing line between the two historical periods. . . .

[p. 50] But the situation after the May Fourth movement is quite different. From this time on, an entirely new cultural force was born in China, the cultural thought of Communism under the leadership of the CCP, i.e. the Communist world view and its theory of social revolution. . . .

[p. 51] Before the May Fourth movement, the new culture of China was of the nature of the old democracy, a part of the capitalist cultural revolution of the world bourgeoisie. After May Fourth the new culture has come to possess the nature of the new democracy, a part of the proletarian-socialist cultural revolution.

Prior to the May Fourth movement, China's new cultural movement, the cultural revolution, was under the leadership of the bourgeoisie, who at that time still had a leading function. After May Fourth, however, the cultural thought of this class [p. 52] fell behind even its political thought, and had no more leading function whatsoever. At the most, it can serve as an ally in the revolutionary period to a certain degree; as to the leadership of the alliance, it falls on the shoulders of proletarian cultural thought. This is a fact, as solid as iron and one which no one can deny.

The culture of the new democracy is the anti-imperialist and anti-feudal culture of the masses, or, in terms of present-day China, the culture of the anti-Japanese united front. It can only be led by the cultural thought of the proletariat, i.e. Communist thought; it cannot be led by the thought of any other class. The culture of the new democracy, in short, is "the proletarian-led anti-imperialist and anti-feudal culture of the masses".

13. *The Four Periods*

The cultural revolution ideologically reflects and serves the political and economic revolutions. In China the cultural revolution, like the politics, is in the form of the united front.

The united front in the cultural revolution has undergone four periods during the past twenty years: (1) the two years between 1919 and 1921; (2) the six years from 1921 to 1927; (3) the nine years from 1927 to 1936; (4) the three years from 1937 up to the present. . . .

14. [p. 59] *Partial Views Concerning the Question of the Character of the Cultural Movement.* . . .

[p. 60] A national culture with a socialist content must reflect a socialist politics and economics which we do not have at present. Therefore we cannot have a national (socialist) culture, for the time being. . . .

Therefore the essence of the new culture is still that of the new democracy [p. 61], not of socialism. But, undoubtedly we should now expand the propaganda of Communist thought and speed up the study of Marxist-Leninist teachings; for, without the two, not only the guiding of the Chinese revolution to the future socialist stage, but the very success of the democratic revolution of the present day itself, will be impossible. However, it still holds true that the fundamental nature of our national culture at present is not that of socialism but that of new democracy, because it is the anti-imperialist and anti-feudal culture of the people, not the anti-capitalist culture of the proletariat. We must separate the propagation of a Communist ideological system and the Communist social system from the practical application of the programme of new democracy; and also separate the Communist methods of observation, study, and work from the programme of national education of the new democracy. To mix up these two different approaches would undoubtedly be wrong.

From the above we can know that the content of the new Chinese culture at the present stage is neither the cultural domination of the bourgeoisie, nor the socialism of the proletariat, but is the anti-imperialist and anti-feudal new democracy under the leadership of proletarian cultural thought, or the new Three People's Principles.

15. *A National, Scientific, and Popular Culture*

This new democratic culture is national in character. It stands against [p. 62] imperialist oppression; it stands for the dignity and independence of the Chinese nation. It belongs to our own nation, and bears the characteristics of our own nation. It unites with the socialist culture and new democratic culture of other nations, establishes with them relations of mutual absorption and mutual development, all new cultures of the world, but it can never unite with the imperialist culture of other nations, because it is a revolutionary, national culture. China should absorb on a great scale the progressive culture of foreign countries as a raw material for her own cultural food. Such absorption was not sufficient in the past. This refers not only to the socialist and new democratic culture, but also to the ancient cultures of foreign countries, which are useful to us; for instance, the cultural heritage of the capitalist countries in their earlier period of growth. These foreign materials we must treat as we treat our food. We submit our food to the mouth for chewing and to the stomach and intestines for digestion, add to it saliva, pepsin, and other secretions of the intestines to separate it into the essence and the residue, and then absorb the essence of our nourishment and pass off the residue. It should never be indiscriminately and uncritically absorbed. The thesis of "wholesome Westernization" is a mistaken viewpoint. To absorb blindly foreign materials has done China much harm. The same attitude is necessary for the Chinese Communists in the application of Marxism to China. [p. 63] We must unify appropriately the general truth of Marxism and the concrete actuality of the Chinese revolution, i.e. we must adopt the national form before we can make Marxism useful and not apply it subjectively and dogmatically. Subjective and formal Marxists are only playing with Marxism and the Chinese revolution, and there is no place for them in the revolutionary ranks of China. Chinese culture must have its own form, i.e. a national form. A national form and a new democratic content—this is our new culture of today.

This new democratic culture is scientific. It opposes all forms of feudal and superstitious thought and stands for the "search for truth from concrete facts", it advocates objective truth and the unity of theory and application. In this respect, the scientific thought of the Chinese proletariat may form an anti-imperialist, anti-feudal, and anti-superstitious united front with the materialist and natural scientific thought of the Chinese bourgeoisie that are still progressive in character. However, it should never unite with reactionary idealism. We Communists may work in a united front for political action with people who profess religious or idealistic beliefs but should never approve the (philosophy of) idealism or religion themselves. During the long period of its feudal society, China built up for herself a glorious ancient culture; therefore, as a necessary precondition for developing a new culture and raising national self-confidence, we must comb through the process of development of the ancient culture, absorb all the democratic essence, and throw away the feudal rubbish it contains. But this should never be unconditional absorption. We must first carefully differentiate the rubbish of the old feudal ruling class from those elements that are more or less democratic and revolutionary in character. The new politics and new economics of present-day China are developed from the old politics and old economics and so is our new culture from the old culture. Therefore we should respect our own history and should not be isolated from it. But to respect our history is to give it proper [p. 64] place among the sciences, to respect its dialectic development, but not to negate our present with a view to praise everything in the old (including) the poisonous elements of feudalism. Therefore, it is important for us to lead the people and the young students, in the main, not to look backward, but to look forward.

This new democratic culture is popular in character. It should serve the toiling masses of the workers and peasants who represent more than ninety per cent of the whole population; and must gradually become their own culture. We should, from the viewpoint of standards, (both) differentiate and co-ordinate knowledge (required) for educating revolutionary cadres and for educating the revolutionary masses, and differentiate and co-ordinate the elevation of culture and its popularization. Revolutionary culture is a powerful revolutionary weapon of the people. Before the (outbreak of) the revolution, culture paves the way for it by spreading revolutionary thought. During the revolution it is a necessary and important front in the general revolutionary front, and revolutionary cultural workers are commanders of various grades on this cultural front. "Without revolutionary theories, there is no revolutionary movement." From that we can see how important the revolutionary cultural movement is to revolutionary practice. And this cultural movement and revolutionary practice are the movement and practice of the people. Therefore, all progressive cultural workers should have their own cultural troops in the anti-Japanese war, and these troops are nothing more than the people and the masses. Cultural workers or cultural thought that are isolated from the masses and the people are merely "commandants of castles in the air" or [p. 65] "troopless commanders", and their fire can never reach the enemy. To achieve our objective, the language must be reformed under certain conditions, and the words we use must be in close touch with the masses. We must understand that the masses are the boundlessly rich resources of our revolutionary culture.

This national, scientific, and popular culture is the anti-imperialist, anti-feudal culture of the people, the culture of new democracy, the culture of new Three People's Principles, the culture of the Chinese nation.

The combination of new democratic politics, new democratic economics, and new democratic culture is the Republic of New Democracy. It is truly a republic in name and in reality. And that is the New China we aim to build.

The New China stands before every one of us. We should be ready to receive it.

The mast of the ship New China is appearing on the horizon. We should clap our hands to welcome it.

Raise both your hands! The New China is ours!

COMMENTARY N. THE MODERATE LAND POLICY

The next document is included in this volume to illustrate the CCP's war-time land policy, which constituted the basis of its programme and a main reason for its popularity during the war. Carried out under the slogan of the "anti-Japanese national united front", this was the mildest land programme yet applied by the CCP. Many of its provisions—such as the reduction of rent and interest rates—resemble those still in effect as of mid-1950 in the "new areas" of China (those south of the Yangtze river and those which came under the control of the CCP after the general offensive of later 1947). One of the major features of its application during the years of the Sino-Japanese war was that maximum rent was fixed at 37.5 per cent.

The war-time land policy was intended to attract support for the war effort from all rural classes. Thus the civil, political, and property rights of the landlords were guaranteed, as well as those of the peasants. Receipt of rent and interest by the landlords was also guaranteed, after the enforcement of rent and interest reductions (see document no. 31, sec. 1 and 2). The drastic land policy of the Kiangsi Soviet period, providing for total confiscation of landlords' property without compensation and for allotment of poor land to the rich peasants (see document no. 18), was dropped after the Sino-Japanese war began.

Moderation remained the general rule until the period 1946–8 when the circumstances and demands of the civil war led to a more vigorous, and in some areas very harsh, treatment of landlords. This was based on a series of promulgations such as the draft law of December 1946 for compulsory government purchase of landlords' excess land in the Shensi-Kansu-Ninghsia Border Region, and the new Agrarian Law of October 10, 1947. Two directives of the CC, dated 1933, on "How to differentiate (rural) classes" and "Decisions on certain questions in the agrarian struggle", were re-issued in May 1948 to serve as guidance in classifying landlords, rich peasants, middle peasants, poor peasants, and hired farm hands. A period of readjustment ensued in 1948–50, with a renewed emphasis in the new areas on rent reduction rather than expropriation and a continued stress on increase of production. In June 1950 the Central People's government promulgated a Land Reform Law which abolished the "land ownership system of feudal exploitation by the landlord class", but called for rather moderate treatment of rich and middle peasants. This new land law also put special emphasis on the protection of landlords' enterprises in commerce and industry as well as on enterprises for the commercial handling of crops.

It cannot be too often reiterated in this volume that our concentration upon the political and ideological development of Chinese Communism prevents an adequate treatment of the CCP programme of agrarian reform, particularly the reform of landlord-tenant relations, which has necessarily had a great and often predominant importance in the eyes of the common Chinese peasant.

25. DECISION OF THE CC ON LAND POLICY IN THE ANTI-JAPANESE
BASE AREAS (January 28, 1942)

(Passed by the Central Political Bureau, January 28, 1942)

Since the beginning of the war of resistance [1937], the land policy carried out by our Party in various anti-Japanese bases has been a land policy based on the anti-Japanese national united front, i.e. a land policy involving reduction of rent and interest rates on the one hand, and the guarantee of rent and interest collections on the other. Since its implementation in various base areas [i.e. "Liberated Areas" mainly in North China and under the domination of the CCP], this policy has secured the support of the broad masses, rallied people of different classes, and sustained the war of resistance in the enemy's rear. In the areas where rent and interest rate reductions have been carried out more extensively, more rigorously, and more thoroughly, together with the guarantee of rent and interest collections, the enthusiasm with which the local people have participated in the anti-Japanese struggle and in democratic reconstruction (also) has been higher than elsewhere; furthermore, in these areas conditions of work are being kept up on a normal level, life is more stable and orderly, and the bases are generally more firmly consolidated. But in many base areas this policy has not yet been carried out extensively, rigorously, or thoroughly. In some bases rent and interest rate reductions have only been carried out in certain limited areas, and in other areas the rent and interest rate reductions are only taken as propaganda slogans, unaccompanied by any concrete rule of implementation, not to speak of actually carrying out the policy. Sometimes, laws on rent and interest rate reductions are promulgated by the local governments as a pure formality without being strictly observed, thus resulting in ostensible but not actual reduction. In these areas, the enthusiasm of the masses cannot be developed and consequently they cannot be effectively organized to form an active base for the struggle against the Japanese. In these areas, it is impossible to consolidate the anti-Japanese bases, which have become soft and weak spots and cannot survive enemy attacks. In a number of other places, on the other hand, leftist mistakes have been committed. Though these mistakes have occurred in only a small number of districts and have generally been corrected on the basis of directives from the CC, it is still necessary that the attention of comrades in all areas be called to it. At a time when the war of resistance is advancing to a more trying stage, the various bases must be called upon to mobilize the broad masses more extensively and to heighten their morale for the struggle against the Japanese, for the struggle for production, and for the rallying of all anti-Japanese classes to engage in relentless, sustained warfare in the enemy's rear. As the result of a careful study of experiences in various areas, the CC has arrived at certain conclusive decisions on the matter of land policy. The detailed rules for carrying out the land policy are attached herewith as an appendix transmitted together with these resolutions, for adoption in the various areas. It is hoped that the comrades of all areas will study these decisions and carry them out diligently.

(1) Recognize that peasants (including hired farm hands) constitute the basic strength of the anti-Japanese war as well as of the battle of production. Accordingly it is the policy of the Party to assist the peasants, reduce feudal exploitation by the landlords, carry out reductions of rent and interest rates and guarantee the civil liberties, political rights, land rights, and economic rights of the peasants, in order to improve their living conditions and enhance their enthusiasm for the anti-Japanese war and for production.

(2) Recognize that most of the landlords are anti-Japanese, that some of the enlightened gentry also favour democratic reforms. Accordingly, the policy of the Party is only to help the peasants in reducing feudal exploitation but not to liquidate feudal exploitation entirely, much less to attack the enlightened gentry who support democratic reforms. Therefore, after rent and interest rates' are reduced, the collection of rent and interest are to be assured; and in addition to protecting the civil liberties, political, land, and economic rights of the peasants, we must guarantee the landlords their civil liberties, political, land, and economic rights in order to ally the landlord class with us in the struggle against the Japanese. The policy of liquidating feudal exploitation should only be adopted against stubbornly unrepentant traitors.

(3) Recognize that the capitalist mode of production is the more progressive method in present-day China and that the bourgeoisie, particularly the petty bourgeoisie and national bourgeoisie, represent the comparatively more progressive social elements and political forces in China today. The mode of production of the rich peasants bears capitalist characteristics; they are the capitalists in the rural areas and are an indispensable force in the anti-Japanese war and in the battle of production. The petty bourgeoisie, national bourgeoisie, and rich peasants not only want to resist the Japanese but are also demanding more democracy. Therefore the policy of the Party is not to weaken capitalism and the bourgeoisie, nor to weaken the rich peasant class and their productive force, but to encourage capitalist production and ally with the bourgeoisie and encourage production by rich peasants and ally with the rich peasants, on the condition that proper improvements are made in the living conditions of the workers. Nevertheless, part of the income of rich peasants does represent

feudal exploitation which is resented by the middle and poor peasants. Thus when rent and interest rates are reduced in rural areas, the rent and interest (payable) to rich peasants should also be reduced. After such reductions, the rich peasant should be guaranteed his right to collect rent and interest as well as his civil, political, land, and economic rights. Landlords who partly employ capitalist methods in cultivating their land (so-called managing landlords) [i.e. landlords who employ hired farm hands] should be granted the same treatment as rich peasants.

(4) The above three basic principles constitute the point of departure of our Party's anti-Japanese united front and our land policy. The experiences of the past four years prove that only insistence on these principles can consolidate the anti-Japanese national united front, correctly settle the land problem, and rally all the people to support our movement of national resistance to isolate completely the Japanese bandits. Any extreme leftist or rightist tendencies will not achieve this purpose.

(5) In the rural united front, contradictions between the landlord and the peasant which manifest themselves in the form of opposition or obstructionism on the part of the landlord to peasant demands for democracy or better livelihood, etc., must be settled appropriately in accordance with the above principles. The reasonable demands of both sides should be satisfied, but both sides should bow to the overall interests of national resistance. In settling rural disputes, the working members of the Party and government should base themselves on the above basic principles and follow a policy of adjusting the interests of both sides. They should not take a one-sided stand either for the landlord or for the peasant.

(6) The three-thirds system [government by personnel drawn one-third from the CCP, one-third from the KMT, and one-third from non-party elements] in political administration is a reasonable political formula for adjusting the internal relationship among various anti-Japanese classes. This system must be carried out resolutely, strictly, and extensively in councils and governments of various levels. The view that such a system is only an expedient measure for appeasing non-Party elements is erroneous.

(7) Government regulations should include arrangements for both sides and not be partial. On the one hand legislation should provide for the reduction of rent and interest rates by the landlord without delay. He must not resist the implementation of these laws. On the other hand, it should also be stipulated that peasants are obliged to

pay rent and interest. They must not resist collection. On the one hand, the government should stipulate that title to land and title to property still belong to the landlord who has the right to sell, mortgage, hypothecate, and otherwise dispose of his land in accordance with existing legal provisions. On the other hand, legislation should provide that the livelihood of the peasants be taken into consideration when the landlord makes these dispositions (of his land and other properties). All contracts concerning land and debt should be concluded at the free will of both parties. When a contract expires, either party is free to abrogate it.

(8) Expenses for fighting the Japanese are to be borne by all classes except paupers and are to be paid to the government according to the principle of progressive taxation. There should be no unfairness in applying this principle, nor any refusal to pay.

(9) The implementation of laws regarding reductions of rent and interest rates is a prerequisite for an increase in agricultural production, which is the major production in the anti-Japanese bases. The officers of the Party and the government should do their utmost to promote and develop agricultural production. Government should extend to the peasants large amounts of agricultural loans, in order to solve their difficulties in obtaining credit.

(10) The task of the Peasant Association for National Salvation, in the matter of rent and interest rate reduction, is mainly to assist the government in carrying out the laws concerning the reductions of rent and interest rates. After the rent and interest rates have been reduced, its major task is to assist the government in mediating rural disputes and increasing agricultural production. It shall not, however, substitute its own decisions for government laws and orders, nor take the place of the administration. In its task of settling rural disputes, methods of mediation, rather than that of arbitrary decision, should be used. In the task of developing agricultural production, all members of the peasant associations should be mobilized to become models and leaders.

(11) Reduction of rent and interest rates and the protection of the peasant's civil, political, land, and economic rights are the first aspect of our Party's land policy. But many sectors within the anti-Japanese base areas have not yet carried out rent and interest rate reductions on any extensive, rigorous, or thorough basis, either because of resistance on the part of the landlords or because of the indifferent attitude or bureaucratism of the cadres within the Party and the government. Officers of the Party and the government in the various base areas

must, therefore, strictly check their own work, dispatch agents to inspect the results in the villages, investigate and study the situation carefully, summarize the experiences of various areas, praise the examples of correct achievement, and criticize cases of bureaucratism. One must realize that there generally exists a wide gap between the promulgation of laws and slogans and the implementation of such laws and slogans. If bureaucratism is not punished harshly and rightist tendencies are unopposed, we shall not be able to implement our laws and slogans.

(12) The guarantee of rent and interest collection and the protection of the landlord's civil, political, land, and economic rights are the second aspect of our Party's land policy. But certain leftist mistakes of neglecting this factor have occurred in various bases, either because of a misunderstanding of our Party's land policy on the part of the peasants, or because of the partial or complete misunderstanding of our Party's policy by cadres of our Party and government. We must therefore explain clearly the Party's policy, both within the Party and among the peasant masses in order to avoid the repetition of these mistakes, and to enable them to understand that the land policy of the Party in the anti-Japanese national united front differs in certain basic respects from the land policy of civil war days. They must be made to realize that they cannot limit their view to their own immediate narrow interests, but must merge their immediate interests with their future interests, and local interests with national interests. After the reduction of rent and interest rates, and the realization of the peasant's civil, political, land, and economic rights, peasants should be advised to pay rent and interest as well as to protect the civil, political, land, and economic rights of the landlord. Similarly, the landlord should be advised not to limit his view to immediate, narrow interests but to take into consideration future interests and the national welfare in the matter of rent and interest reductions as well as in the matter of the protection of the peasant's civil, political, land, and economic rights.

APPENDIX

Since conditions in various base areas differ and since there are different conditions existing even within a given area, no single set of rules can be applied uniformly as detailed provisions for the solution of the land problem. The CC has laid down certain broad general principles on land policy for uniform application. In this appendix some concrete provisions, based on these general principles, are presented for adoption in the various areas. The provisions in this appendix, if applicable to local conditions, should be decisively implemented. If adjustments have to be made, due to their incompatibility with local conditions, such adjustments may be made; but they must be reported to the CC and approval must be obtained therefrom.

I. ON RENT AND TENURE

(1) In the areas where rent has not been reduced, rent should, in principle, be reduced by twenty-five per cent, i.e. a reduction of twenty-five per cent from the pre-war rate for rent. No matter whether it be public land, private land, rented land, or shared land, and no matter whether it be cash rent, rent in kind, unfixed rent, or fixed rent, this rule applies to all. For land shared under various forms, it should not uniformly be ruled that the landlord is to obtain no more than forty or sixty per cent, but there should be a twenty-five per cent reduction of the former percentage in rent, based on a consideration of the labour, animal power, tools, fertilizer, seed, and grain contributed by the two parties. In guerrilla areas or places near enemy [Japanese military] strongholds, rent reduction may be less than twenty-five per cent. It may be a twenty per cent or fifteen per cent or ten per cent reduction, to be decided in accordance with the general goal of increasing the enthusiasm of the peasants for the struggle against the Japanese and rallying different classes for the war of resistance.

(2) All rents are to be collected after the harvest, and those who rent out land shall not collect the rental from the tenants in advance, nor shall additional payments be demanded.

(3) The payment of fixed rent ["iron rent", *t'ieh-tsu*] may be postponed or reduced if all or a part of the produce is destroyed by natural or man-made disasters.

(4) Rent in arrears for many years is to be exempted from payment.

(5) Public grain and public levies are to be paid according to a progressive schedule by both parties (landlord and tenant). The land-tax is to be paid by the owner of the land.

(6) If disputes arise regarding a cash rent contract, due to the depreciation of the paper currency, the government should summon the two parties concerned for discussion and mediation and may convert the entire or a part of the payment of the cash rent into payment in kind.

(7) If a mediation organ such as a rent commission is set up,

peasant, landlord, and government should all have representatives on it; but the final power of decision shall rest with the government.

(8) Permanent tenancy, when stipulated in the rent contract or based on [local] custom, should be maintained. If the system of permanent tenancy does not prevail in an area, however, no compulsory enforcement of such tenancy should be carried out. Both parties shall instead be encouraged to sign long-term contracts, for example, for five years or more, to enable the peasants to increase production with a feeling of security.

(9) In areas where there is no permanent tenancy or when a contract expires, the landowner has the right to dispose of the land in accordance with the stipulations of the contract including the right to re-rent, mortgage, sell, cultivate it himself, hire labourers to cultivate, etc. However, during war-time, any landowner who wishes to take back the land from a tenant must consider the livelihood of the peasants and must inform the tenant three months before the harvest. If the tenant is too poor, Government should call on the two parties to renew the tenancy or return only part of the rented land.

(10) When a landowner, at the expiration of the rent contract, wants to re-rent his land, mortgage, or sell it, the original tenant has the priority, if other conditions are equal, in renting, buying, or taking the mortgage on the land in question.

(11) When a landowner sells land rented out on the basis of permanent tenancy or before the contract expires, the original tenant has the right to continue his tenancy and the new owner cannot rent out the land to another party until the contract has expired.

(12) If a tenant gives up cultivating the land for two years without reason or deliberately refuses to pay rentals even though capable of doing so, the owner of the land has the right to take the land back.

II. ON THE PROBLEM OF INDEBTEDNESS

(1) The policy of reduction of interest rates on debts contracted before the war is a necessary policy to meet the needs of the debtors as well as to rally the creditors in the fight against Japan. One and one-half per cent [per month] is to be the rate in calculating interest. If the total payment of interest exceeds the amount of the original capital of the loan, interest is to stop; [only] the capital is to be repaid. If payment of interest is double the amount of the capital, payment on both capital and interest are to be suspended. As to the interest rate for loans contracted since the war, it can be freely decided locally in accordance with local social and economic conditions. The

government should not stipulate too low an interest rate, for it may result in a slowdown of credit and harm the people's welfare.

(2) Creditors are not to cancel loan contracts because of the reduction of interest rates, and debtors are not to refuse to pay interest after the reduction. The creditor has the right to sue for overdue debts in accordance with law.

(3) If a debtor is unable to pay either the interest or capital on debts newly contracted since the war, the creditor has the right to dispose of the collateral according to contract. All disputes are to be adjudicated by the government. When one collateral is used to cover several loans, the income from selling the collateral is to be distributed proportionally according to the priorities of the contracts. If the collateral is land, the same provision applies.

(4) If land is mortgaged but not yet sold, the party that mortgages it may redeem the land by paying the original mortgage price according to contract, and there must be no confiscation of the land or change of contract. If the mortgage has turned into a sale, the land cannot be redeemed. Disputes arising from the depreciation of paper currency, when the mortgaged land is redeemed, are to be settled by the government.

(5) When a debtor is unable to fulfil his contract signed since the war as a result of natural and man-made disasters as well as other irresistible causes, he may ask the government to mediate for a certain reduction of interest or for the payment of capital without interest.

(6) Disputes arising as a result of the repayment of a loan in depreciated paper currency are to be suitably settled by the government.

III. ON THE SETTLEMENT OF CERTAIN SPECIAL TYPES OF LAND PROBLEMS

(1) Land belonging to the most criminal and notorious traitors is to be confiscated and managed by the government and then rented out to the peasants to farm, as a measure of punishment. If members of a traitor's family have not participated in any treacherous activities, or if the case is minor in nature, this provision is not applicable.

(2) Land belonging to those who are forced to become traitors is not to be confiscated, in order to show leniency and encourage their repentance. If there is no one to look after the land in question, the government will manage it and rent it to peasants, and return the land to the owner when the person in question returns to fight the Japanese.

(3) Land belonging to a landlord who has fled from a given area is not to be confiscated, no matter where the landlord in question may be. If there is no one to look after the land, the government will

manage it on his behalf, get persons to till the land, receive his rentals in custody, and pay the land-tax and public grain for him. When the owner returns, the land will be handed back to him together with the rentals that are his due.

(4) "Black land", i.e. land that has evaded taxation or the title deeds of which are not taxed, is not to be confiscated, but the owner shall be ordered to pay taxes and public grain levies that are in arrears. If the obligations are not met within the stipulated time-limit, the government shall settle the case in an appropriate manner.

(5) Clan land, and society land, are to be managed by a control commission organized by the clan or society concerned. The income from such land will be used for the benefit of the clan or the society, or the local community.

(6) School land shall be reserved as a source of educational funds, to be managed by an educational fund committee set up by the government or the local inhabitants.

(7) Land that belongs to a religious group (Christian, Buddhist, Moslem, Taoist, or other sects) will undergo no changes.

(8) Uncultivated public land is to be distributed by the government to families of Red Army personnel, refugees, and poor peasants for cultivation, and the land ownership goes with it. Within a stipulated period it may be exempted from taxation *in toto* or in part.

(9) Uncultivated private land, no matter whether it had been under cultivation or not, should be made available first to the owner. If the owner is unable to cultivate it and leaves it unattended, the government may advertise for persons to till it and, within a stipulated time, exempt or reduce the taxation [on the land]. The ownership of such land still belongs to the original owner, but the tiller has a right to permanent tenancy.

COMMENTARY O. THE CCP-KMT ALLIANCE—FINAL PHASE

At the Seventh CCP Congress held in Yenan between April 23 and June 11, 1945, a main item of the agenda was Mao Tse-tung's report *On Coalition Government*. Negotiations between the CCP and the Nationalist government at Chungking concerning a solution of the Communist problem by "political" means and eventually by the incorporation of the CCP in a coalition régime had been under way since early 1944.[1] Mao's report of April 1945 summed up the theoretical basis on which the CCP approached the coming post-war problem of its relationship to the recognized National government of the KMT at Chungking. This basis was, of course, flexible. It would permit the CCP either to enter a coalition with the KMT, as was agreed at Chungking in January 1946, or to form a coalition with minor parties excluding the KMT, as was done at Peking in 1949.

The theme of Mao's report, one of the key documents of CCP history, is that since China is still "in the stage of bourgeois-democratic revolution", it needs "a new democratic government of a coalition nature embracing all parties and non-partisan representatives". This announcement in 1945 of the CCP's continued willingness to share political power with other parties and groups had a great effect on the various political elements in KMT China who were opposed to the KMT tutelage and had become increasingly conscious of its undesirable aspects. After the defeat of the KMT in 1949, in spite of the fact that nearly all effective political power now lay in the hands of the CCP, the "people's democratic dictatorship" could still be interpreted as a coalition made up of an alliance of four classes—workers, peasantry, petty bourgeoisie, and national capitalists, under the leadership of the working class, while the Central People's Government set up at Peking was also in form controlled by a coalition of the CCP and other parties or groups. "Coalition" has been a potent and persuasive slogan.

Another salient feature of this document *On Coalition Government* is the great importance attached to the peasantry. Thus Mao says: "The CCP—which has a resolute agrarian policy, fights for the interests of the peasants, and looks upon them as its allies—naturally becomes the leader of the peasants. . . ." Such statements try to reconcile the orthodox Marxist role of the CCP as the leader of the proletariat with the practical necessity of leading the Chinese peasantry. The central feature of the agrarian policy advocated by Mao, "the tiller should own his land", is a phrase borrowed or inherited from Sun Yat-sen, and in 1950 still remains in essence the immediate goal of the CCP's land programme.

Other basic points outlined in *On Coalition Government* are the call for "a new democratic economy which is managed partly by the state, partly by private capital, and partly by co-operatives", and the statement that "all religions are allowed to exist in the Communist areas". How long the admittedly transitional period represented by these policies will last before being supplanted by the next, socialist, stage has not been stated specifically. But Mao Tse-tung, in his report on *The Present Situation and Our Tasks* made to the Central Committee on December 25, 1947, stated that "the capitalist economy, which is an integral part of the national economy, must be allowed to exist for a long time, even after the revolutionary victory on a national scale is achieved". The length of "a long time" thus remains a question for the future.

26. REPORTS ON THE SEVENTH NATIONAL CONGRESS OF THE CCP (April 23–June 11, 1945)

The Convocation of the Seventh National Congress of the CCP

New China News Agency dispatch:

The CCP convened its Seventh National Congress in the latter part of April [1945] at Yenan. This is one of the most important events in the history of modern China. The tasks of this Congress were: to rally all the people of the country together on the eve of a Chinese general offensive, to cope with the critical current situation resulting from the erroneous policies of the KMT government, to defeat and completely annihilate the Japanese aggressor, and to establish an independent, free, democratic, united, and prosperous new China.

There were 544 regular delegates and 208 alternate delegates, a sum total of 752 in attendance at the Congress, representing a total membership of 1,210,000. The Congress elected Mao Tse-tung, Chu Teh, Liu Shao-ch'i, Chou En-lai, Jen Pi-shih, Lin Po-ch'ü, P'eng Teh-huai, K'ang Sheng [pseud. of Chao Yung], Ch'en Yün, Ch'en I, Ho Lung, Hsü Hsiang-ch'ien, Kao Kang, Lo Fu [pseud. of Chang Wen-t'ien], and P'eng Chen to the Presidium; Jen Pi-shih (was elected) Secretary-General of the Congress and Li Fu-ch'un Deputy Secretary-General. The four major items on the agenda of the Congress were: the political report by Comrade Mao Tse-tung [*On Coalition Government*], the military report by Comrade Chu Teh, the report on the revision of the Party Constitution by Comrade Liu Shao-ch'i, and the election of the Central Committee. All events and resolutions of the Congress will be published in the future.

The political report by Comrade Mao Tse-tung, leader of the CCP, is the central item of this Congress. The whole report consists of 60,000 words and is entitled *On Coalition Government*. Comrade Mao Tse-tung points out in his report that the formation of a coalition government is the (only) solution for the current situation in China (but not the so-called National Assembly which was illegally convoked by the KMT alone and is resolutely opposed by the people). The report describes two opposite lines [of policy] in China's anti-Japanese war—the line of oppressing the Chinese people and of passive resistance which is followed by the KMT, and that of awakening and rallying the Chinese people to a people's war. It also explains in detail the general platform of the CCP in the stage of the New Democracy and the concrete platform of the CCP in the present stage. The CCP will fight determinedly for the formation of a coalition government and for the realization of a democratic platform throughout the whole nation. The first step in this fight will be the convocation at Yenan at the earliest opportunity, of a Convention of People's Delegates of Liberated Areas, in order to discuss the integration of activities in various Liberated Areas, the strengthening of anti-Japanese activities in Liberated Areas, support of the people's anti-Japanese democratic movement in the KMT areas, aid of the popular underground movement in the occupied areas, and promotion of co-operation among all people by formation of a coalition government.

The CCP was formed in 1921. Six National congresses have been held in the past as follows: the First National Congress in July 1921; the Second National Congress in May 1922; the Third National Congress in June 1923; the Fourth National Congress in January 1925; the Fifth National Congress in April 1927; and the Sixth National Congress in July 1928. From the Sixth Congress to the present, seventeen years have elapsed. Due to the long interval of struggles it has not been possible until today for the Seventh Congress to convene. At the convocation of this Congress, the CCP's strength, solidarity, and prestige among the people are at an all-time high. At present the CCP has not only a total membership of 1,210,000, but also controls the Eighth Route Army, the New Fourth Army, and other anti-Japanese regular troops numbering 910,000, (in addition to) 2,200,000 people's militia. [The CCP controls] nineteen Liberated Areas covering nineteen provinces in North-west, North-east, North, Central, and South China, with a total population of 95,500,000. These figures are constantly increasing as a result of the rapid spread of the anti-Japanese war in the Liberated Areas. Therefore, the CCP and the Liberated Areas led by it have in fact become the nucleus of the people's struggle for national salvation and liberation from Japan. The present CCP Congress will undoubtedly produce a very great effect on the future development of China's anti-Japanese war as well as on internal politics. [End of dispatch.]

New China News Agency dispatch:

The Seventh Congress of the CCP was convened by Comrade Jen Pi-shih some time in the latter part of April. Comrade Mao Tse-tung delivered the opening address, which was followed by speeches of Comrades Chu Teh, Liu Shao-ch'i, Chou En-lai, Lin Po-ch'ü, and Ōkano Susumu,[1] leader of the Japanese CP. The texts (of the speeches) are as follows [only those of Jen Pi-shih and Mao Tse-tung are translated here]:

Comrade Jen Pi-shih declared the Congress opened and said: "Since the formation of our Party, twenty-four years have elapsed. In these twenty-four years our Party has gone through innumerable difficult, trying struggles—through the three periods of the Northern Expedition, the Agrarian Revolution, and the anti-Japanese War. The main accomplishment of our Party's heroic struggle in the past twenty-four years is that the principles of our Party have obtained the support of the vast masses of China. The Chinese people, in their struggle for their daily bread, have realized that the anti-imperialist, anti-feudal programme pushed by our Party since its founding day, as well as the course of the New Democracy set by our leader, Comrade Mao Tse-tung, and other detailed policies—are all to the interest of the people. The Chinese people realize that only the CCP can liberate them from their sufferings. They regard our Party as the steersman of a ship in a storm. They put their hope in our Party, and in our Party's leader, Comrade Mao Tse-tung. In the course of fighting over twenty-four years, our Party has produced its own leader in Comrade Mao Tse-tung. The ideas of Comrade Mao Tse-tung have a firm hold on the vast masses of China, forming an unconquerable force. Comrade Mao Tse-tung has not only become the symbol of the Chinese people, but also the symbol of the fight for freedom of other oriental nations. During the next two or three years, there will be changes of historical significance in China and (elsewhere) in the East. At the moment all our countrymen as well as all peoples in the orient and some peoples elsewhere in the world have their eyes upon us, to see what policy we shall adopt at this critical juncture, to drive out the Japanese aggressor for ever and build up a new China—the China of the New Democracy. (Thus) our Congress is meeting at a fitting moment. I now formally declare the Congress to be opened.

The Opening Address of Comrade Mao Tse-tung

Comrades! The Seventh National Congress of the CCP, convened (here) today, is a Congress shaping the destiny of 450,000,000, a congress for the overthrow of the Japanese aggressor and the building of a new China, a Congress to rally the whole nation and the peoples of the world to win the final victory.

19

The present moment is bright. In the West the war against fascist Germany is approaching its successful conclusion. In the East, the war against fascist Japan is also approaching victory. We are on the eve of victory.

Before us and the people of China there is light; but there is also darkness. The Japanese aggressor remains to be defeated. Even when he is defeated, there still remain two perspectives for China: (that of) an independent, free, democratic, united, and prosperous China or (that of) a semi-colonial, semi-feudal, divided, poor, and weak China.

What is our task? To rally all possible forces in our country and in the world to defeat the Japanese aggressor, to build an independent, free, democratic, united, and prosperous new China, and to fight for a bright, and against a dark, future. This is our task.

Is it possible for us and the Chinese people to accomplish this task? I think it is. First, besides other political parties in China, there is an experienced, strong CP of 1,210,000 members. Secondly, besides other areas in China, there are also the powerful Liberated Areas with a population of 95,500,000, with 910,000 regular troops and 2,200,000 people's militiamen. Thirdly, (we have) the support of the vast masses of the nation. Fourthly, (we have) the support of the vast masses of the world. Under these conditions it is entirely possible to defeat the aggressor and build a new China.

We need a correct policy. The crux of this policy is to defeat the aggressor and build a new China by rallying all possible strength in our country and in the world.

Since the foundation of the CCP in 1921, twenty-four years have passed. Through the three historical stages of Northern Expedition, the Agrarian Revolution, and the heroic anti-Japanese War, rich experiences have been accumulated (by our Party). At present our Party has become the centre of the Chinese people's fight against Japan and for national salvation. We should be modest and careful, not haughty or impatient, and devote ourselves heart and soul to the service of the Chinese people. (We) now fight for the defeat of the Japanese aggressor by rallying all the people together; in the future, (we) shall fight for the building of a New Democratic nation by rallying all the people together. If we can carry out the above, if we adopt a correct policy, and if all of us devote our efforts to it, the accomplishment of our task is assured.

> Down with Japanese imperialism!
> Long live the Chinese people's liberation!
> Long live the CCP!

Long live the Seventh Congress of the CCP!

[We pass over speeches by Chu Teh, Liu Shao-ch'i, Chou En-lai, and two others, and a long military report by Chu Teh.]

The Seventh National Congress of the CCP Successfully Concluded—New China News Agency, Yenan, June 13 [1945] telegram:

The Seventh Congress of the CCP was successfully concluded on the 11th [of June]. The Congress opened on April 23; thus it lasted exactly fifty days. The proceedings of the Congress went entirely according to plan: a political report by Comrade Mao Tse-tung on April 24, a military report by Comrade Chu Teh on the 25th, a report on the revision of the Party Constitution by Comrade Liu Shao-ch'i on May 14 and 15, and the election of a new CC on June 9 and 10. The rest of the time was used by various delegations and sub-groups of delegates for lengthy discussions of the reports of Comrades Mao Tse-tung, Chu Teh, and Liu Shao-ch'i, and for preparatory work on the draft Constitution and the election. There were twenty-two plenary sessions, which made it possible to achieve a high degree of democracy. The Congress passed two short resolutions and the new Party Constitution on the basis of the three reports. The resolution on the political report, passed on May 31, reads: "The Congress is entirely satisfied with Comrade Mao's political report, *On Coalition Government*, and deems it imperative that the tasks pointed out in the report be carried out in the practical work of the Party." The resolutions on the military report and on the new Constitution (respectively) were passed in June before the Congress closed; their full texts will be made public at a later date. Comrade Mao Tse-tung pointed out in his closing speech that the Congress had been very successful, and asked the delegates to carry its spirit of democracy and co-operation into the various sections of the Party, to propagate the line (laid down by) it to the Party and people, and to rally the entire people for a firm stand until final victory in the anti-Japanese war for national independence and freedom, coalition government and the prevention of civil war. Comrade Mao Tse-tung said: "A correct political line, in addition to solidarity, will surely result in success." On the same day Comrades Chu Teh, Wu Yu-chang, and Hsü T'e-li also delivered speeches, congratulating the Congress on its success, unprecedented in Party history, and setting forth—on the basis of the historical experience (gained in) four revolutionary stages since the 1911 Revolution—the various conditions necessary to the victory of the Chinese people. [End of telegram.]

New China News Agency, Yenan, June 13 [1945] telegram:

The Seventh National Congress of the CCP elected forty-four regular and thirty-three alternate members to the Central Committee. The names of the regular CC members are as follows:

Mao Tse-tung, Chu Teh, Liu Shao-ch'i, Jen Pi-shih, Lin Tsu-han [Lin Po-ch'ü], Lin Piao, Tung Pi-wu, Ch'en Yün, Hsü Hsiang-ch'ien, Kuan Hsiang-ying* [i.e. deceased],[2] Ch'en T'an-ch'iu,* Kao Kang, Li Fu-ch'un, Jao Shu-shih, Li Li-san, Lo Jung-huan, K'ang Sheng [pseud. of Chao Yang], P'eng Chen, Wang Jo-fei, Chang Yün-i, Ho Lung, Ch'en I, Chou En-lai,* Liu Po-ch'eng, Cheng Wei-shan, Chang Wen-t'ien [Lo Fu], Ts'ai Ch'ang [Mme Li Fu-ch'un], Teng Hsiao-p'ing, Lu Ting-i, Tseng Shan, Yeh Chien-ying, Nieh Jung-chen, P'eng Teh-huai, Teng Tzuhui, Wu Yü-chang, Lin Feng, T'eng Tai-yüan, Chang Ting-ch'eng, Li Hsien-nien, Hsü T'e-li, T'an Chen-lin, Po I-po, Ch'en Shao-yü [Wang Ming], and Ch'in Pang-hsien [PoKu].*

The names of the alternate members of the CC are as follows:

Liao Ch'eng-chih, Wang Chia-hsiang, Ch'en Po-ta, Huang K'o-ch'eng, Wang Shou-tao, Li Yü, Teng Ying-ch'ao [Mme Chou En-lai], Ch'en Shao-min [a woman member], Liu Hsiao, T'an Cheng, Ch'eng Tzu-hua, Liu Ch'ang-sheng, Su Yü, Wang Chen, Sung Jen-ch'iung, Chang Chi-ch'un, Yün Tse [Wu-lan-fu], Chao Cheng-sheng, Wang Wei-chou, Wan I, Ku Ta-ts'un, Tseng Ching-pin, Ch'en Yü, Ma Ming-fang, Lü Cheng-ts'ao, Lo Jui-ch'ing, Liu Tzu-chiu, Chang Tsung-hsün, Ch'en Keng, Wang Ts'ung-wu, Hsi Chung-hsün, Hsiao Ching-kuang, and Liu Lan-t'ao.

The list includes three members [now] in KMT prisons (Ch'en T'an-ch'iu,* Liao Ch'eng-chih, and Ma Ming-fang); three women (Ts'ai Ch'ang, Teng Ying-ch'ao [Mme Chou En-lai], and Ch'en Shao-min) and one Mongolian (Yün Tse [Wu-lan-fu]).

All the regular and alternate members of the CC were elected by a majority of delegates to the Congress. [End of telegram.]

New China News Agency, Yenan, 13th [June 1945] telegram:

The Seventh National Congress of the CCP has been called the "Congress of Solidarity" and "Congress of Victory". These two epithets sum up its effect on the future of China. The Seventh Congress adopted a policy of solidarity towards the overwhelming majority of the Chinese people (including the KMT and all the democratic groups in its army), a policy that meets the needs of the overwhelming majority of the Chinese people. So the documents of the Seventh Congress have secured not only the general support of all classes in liberated and occupied areas, but also have won wide sympathy in regions ruled by the KMT. Although the people in the KMT areas do not have freedom to express their sympathy openly, their voices penetrate the censorship of the KMT in support of the policy of the CCP. This is a true public opinion poll of China. The Congress of the CCP also expresses its desire for co-operation with the KMT on a democratic basis. (In this) it is the opposite of the KMT [Sixth] Congress [which met in Chungking, May 5–21, 1945], which talked hypocritically of political settlements while intriguing for an anti-democratic, "absolute" unification. Its aim is obviously to (instigate) a large-scale civil war. (In contrast), the Congress of the CCP frankly criticizes the mistakes of the KMT régime and points publicly to the danger of civil war, while also doing its best to form a coalition government with the KMT. Its aim is obviously to prevent a civil war and to achieve internal peace in order to step up the fight against Japan. On the problem of fighting Japan, the two Congresses also took opposite stands. The Congress of the KMT talked little about the anti-Japanese war and suppressed interpellations on war problems, because the KMT régime puts all its hope for winning the war on the United States, a voluntary retreat of the Japanese, and peace by conciliation, while eagerly preparing for civil war. The Congress of the CCP, on the other hand, exerted great efforts in discussing how to organize and arm the people more extensively and efficiently, and how to use the powerful forces of the people to recover, in co-ordination with the Allied forces, the occupied areas and large cities in North, Central, South, and North-east China which have suffered the longest under enemy occupation.

During the discussions at the Congress, the above points were the central themes of speeches delivered by Comrades Chou En-lai, P'eng Teh-huai, Ch'en I, Kao Kang, Chang Wen-t'ien, K'ang Sheng, Ch'in Pang-hsien, P'eng Chen, Nieh Jung-chen, Yang Shang-k'un, Ch'en Yün, Li Chih-chung, Lu Ting-i, Liu Po-ch'eng, Chu Jui, Ku Ta-ts'un, Li Fu-ch'un, Wu-lan-fu [Yün Tze], Lin Piao, Ma Feng-wu, Liu Lan-po, Chang Ting-ch'en, Fu Chung, and Yeh Chien-ying. Comrade Ōkano Susumu, representative of the Japanese Communist Party and Comrade Boku Ichiu, Vice-President of the Korean Revolutionary Academy for Political and Military Cadres, were also invited to speak at the Congress, and reported on the revolutionary movements in Japan and Korea, voicing their hope for an independent, democratic China. Because of the policy of solidarity adopted by it, the Congress firmly believes that the anti-Japanese war in China and democratic reforms will undoubtedly come to a successful conclusion. At the same time, the Congress declares that serious difficulties may still lie ahead of the Chinese people and the Party, and that the people should be mentally prepared for such difficulties. But nothing will prevent the Chinese people from achieving victory, whatever the obstacles.

The effect of the Seventh National Congress on the Party can also be expressed by the phrases "Congress of Solidarity" and "Congress of Victory". The solidarity of the Seventh Congress is built on the Mao Tse-tung line and on Mao Tse-tung's thought as guiding principles, and is based on extensive self-criticism and intra-Party democracy. The new Party Constitution, passed by the Seventh Congress, fully illustrates this point. A preamble has been added to the new Party Constitution wherein it is resolved that "the CCP guides all its work by Mao Tse-tung's thought which integrates Marxist ideology with the practical experiences of the Chinese revolution, and opposes any tendency towards narrow formalism or empiricism". "The CCP should not whitewash mistakes and shortcomings in its work. By means of criticism and self-criticism it should check constantly for mistakes, educate members and cadres, and correct its mistakes in due time."

The new Party Constitution also enumerated the rights of a Party member as follows: "(1) The right to participate in Party meetings, in discussions on Party policy and other practical problems; (2) The right to elect and be elected to Party posts; (3) The right to make suggestions and statements to any Party organ up to the CC; and (4) The right to criticize any Party member at Party meetings." This kind of spirit was also demonstrated by the discussions and elections at the Congress. The three reports to the Congress were fully discussed by various delegate-groups as well as by the [full] delegation and at the plenary sessions, many comments being made on the contents of the reports and on the practical work of the Party. The speakers also engaged in criticism and self-criticism in regard to past mistakes of the Party. Even those unable to attend because of illness presented their opinions in writing. As a result, there was an unprecedented unanimity of opinion within the Party.

The election of the new CC proceeded as follows: The various sub-groups of delegates presented preliminary lists of candidates to the Presidium, which prepared a (unified) preliminary list based on them. This list was presented again to the various sub-groups of delegates for discussion, and for preliminary election by secret ballot.

On the basis of the outcome of this preliminary election, the Presidium prepared a formal list of candidates to the Congress for election by secret ballot. The voting delegates at the (final election) may present a new list or add new names to the (final) list (prepared by the Presidium). The high degree of centralization cemented an unprecedented solidarity of the Party. This organizational line of strong intra-Party solidarity, together with the correct political and military lines that rally the overwhelming majority of the people together, are the root of the Congress's firm belief in final victory. Therefore, after the conclusion of the Congress, (we) can predict new high points in solidarity and democracy within the Party, the Chinese people, and the nation, and in the anti-Japanese war of the Chinese people. At these high points all difficulties and obstacles will be swept away; the enemy of the Chinese people, Japanese imperialism, and its accomplices, will go under; and an independent, free, democratic, united, and prosperous China will emerge on the continent of Asia. [End of telegram.]

27. MAO TSE-TUNG: ON COALITION GOVERNMENT
(April 24, 1945) [extract]

(A political report by Chairman Mao Tse-tung to the Seventh National Congress of the CCP on April 24, 1945.)

1. [p. 1] *The Basic Demands of the Chinese People*

Comrades! The long awaited Seventh National Congress of our Party is now opened. On behalf of the CC, I am going to make a report to you . . .

. . . a decisive victory has been scored in the sacred and just war against fascist aggressors throughout the world; the time is near for the Chinese people to defeat the Japanese invaders in collaboration with our Allies; but China, still hard pressed by the Japanese invaders, is not yet united and a grave crisis still exists in China. In such circumstances, what should we do? Indubitably, what China urgently needs is the establishment, through uniting all political parties and groups and non-partisan leaders, of a democratic, provisional coalition government, so that democratic reforms may be instituted, the [p. 2] present crisis overcome, all anti-Japanese forces mobilized and united for the defeat of the Japanese invaders in effective collaboration with our Allies, and the Chinese people liberated from the hands of the Japanese. This being done, the National Assembly, on a broad democratic basis, will have to be summoned to establish a regular democratic government, of a similar coalition nature, embracing more broadly all parties and groups and non-partisan representatives. This government will then lead the liberated people of the entire nation to build an independent, free, democratic, unified, prosperous, and strong new nation, in short, to build a new China after defeating the aggressors through unity and democracy.

We deem that only by so doing can the basic demands of the Chinese people be reflected. Hence, my report is mainly devoted to a discussion of these demands. It also treats with emphasis the problem of coalition government, as that problem has been regarded with great concern by the Chinese people and the Allied press. . . .

2. [p. 3] *The International and Domestic Situation.* . . .

What is the present international situation?

Contrary to the expectations of all Chinese and foreign reactionaries, the three great democracies—Britain, the United States, and the Soviet Union—remain united. Disputes among these democracies did, and may in the future, exist; but, after all, unity reigns supreme; this all-decisive condition, finally demonstrated at the Crimea [i.e. Yalta] Conference [February 1945], was created in the most important transition period in the history of the world—in the 1940s. . . .

[p. 4] The people, and only the people, are the motivating force in creating this world. The Soviet people have created a mighty force which was the [p. 5] major military force in defeating fascism. The great efforts of the peoples of the four great powers, Britain, the United States, China, and France, and the peoples of the other anti-fascist nations have made possible the defeat of the fascists, after which the peoples of these nations will build a world of stable and lasting peace. The United Nations Conference in San Francisco which is to be convened on April 25 [1945] will be the starting-point of this peace.

War has educated the people. They will win the war, the peace, and progress. This is the rule in the new world situation at present. . . .

The defeat of the fascist aggressor nations and the emergence of a general peace do not mean that there will be no more struggle. Widely scattered remnant fascist forces will continue to make trouble; the anti-democratic forces existing in the anti-fascist camp will continue to oppress the people. Therefore, after the realization of international peace, the [p. 6] struggles between the anti-fascist masses and remnant fascist forces, between democratic and anti-democratic forces, will go on in most parts of the world. . . .

[p. 7] What is the present domestic situation in China?

The prolonged war in China has exacted and will continue to exact huge sacrifices from the Chinese people, but at the same time it has steeled and will continue to steel the heroically struggling Chinese people. It has awakened and united them to an extent unparalleled not only in ancient China but also in the great struggles of the Chinese people during the last hundred years. Confronting the Chinese people are not only powerful national foes, but also powerful internal reactionary forces that actually help the national foes. This is one side of the picture. But, on the other hand, the Chinese people are not only awakened to an unprecedented extent, but they also have established strong and extensive Liberated Areas in China and are in the midst of a powerful, ever-rising nationwide democratic movement. These are the favourable internal conditions. . . .

3. [p. 8] *The Two Lines in the Anti-Japanese War*
The Key to the Chinese Problem

[p. 9] . . . Speaking of summing up experiences, we may see clearly that there exist in China two different guiding lines: one of which helps to defeat the Japanese aggressors, but the other, while incapable of defeating the Japanese aggressors, in some respects actually helps them to undermine the anti-Japanese war.

The passive policy adopted by the KMT government towards the war with Japan and its reactionary policy of oppression towards the people have resulted in [p. 10] military defeats, the loss of large parts of territory, a financial and economic crisis, the oppression of the people, hardships in the people's livelihood, and the undermining of national unity. These policies hamper the mobilization and unification of all the people's anti-Japanese forces for effectively waging the war, and impede the people's awakening and solidarity. But the movement of the people's awakening and unity has never been halted, it has been developing in a circuitous manner under the double oppression of the Japanese aggressors and the KMT government. The two lines—the KMT government's line of oppressing the people and carrying on a war of passive resistance, and the Chinese people's line of awakening and unity for the prosecution of a people's war— have been clearly existing in China for a long time. Here lies the key to all the Chinese problems. . . .

[p. 15] The People's War

. . . While I am making this report, our regular forces have been expanded [p. 16] to the strength of 910,000 men, while the people's militia have increased to over 2,200,000. Our regular forces are still numerically smaller than the existing KMT army (including central and provincial troops) by hundreds of thousands, but considering the number of Japanese and puppet troops they are engaging, the vast battlefields they have to cover, their fighting power, their support from the people, the people's militia, and the self-defence corps, their political quality, and their internal unity and solidarity, our regular forces have become the mainstay of the anti-Japanese war.

This army is powerful, because all who have joined it are conscientiously disciplined. They have come together to fight not for the selfish interests of a few or clique but for a just people's war, for the interests of the broad masses and the entire nation. The sole aim of this army is to stand closely by the people and whole-heartedly to serve the Chinese people. . . .

[p. 18] In the liberated areas, all anti-Japanese people in labour, peasant, youth, women's cultural, and other organizations, under the leadership of a democratic government, are engaging themselves heartily in various work to help the army, such as mobilizing people to join the army, transporting supplies for the troops, giving preferential treatment to the families of [p. 19] soldiers, and solving material difficulties for the troops. Of greater importance in this respect is the mobilizing of guerrilla units, people's militia, and self-defence corps to attack the enemy, lay mines, do reconnaissance work, to clean out traitors and spies, carry and protect the wounded, all of which directly help the operations of the army. At the same time, all the people in the Liberated Areas are ardently performing constructive work in political, economic, and cultural fields and public hygiene. Of the greatest importance in this respect is (the fact) that all the people are mobilized for the production of foodstuffs and daily necessities; all government organizations and schools, except in a few special cases, join in the productive work in their spare time for self-sufficiency. . . .

Two Battle-fronts

[p. 21] In recent years practically no serious fighting has occurred on the KMT battle-front, the sword of the Japanese aggressors being chiefly pointed at the Liberated Areas front. By 1943, sixty-four per cent of the Japanese forces invading China and ninety-five per cent of the puppet government forces were contained on the Liberated Areas front; only thirty-six per cent of the Japanese forces and five per cent of the puppet troops were contained on the KMT battle-front.

In 1944, when the Japanese aggressors launched an operation for the possession of a transcontinental communication line, the KMT's chaos [p. 22] and weakness were at once revealed and vast territories in Honan, Hunan, Kwangsi, and Kwangtung provinces were lost to the enemy within a few months. It was only then that some changes in the proportion of the enemy forces on the two battle-fronts took place. But even as I am making this report, out of 40 divisions of 580,000 enemy troops in China (not counting those in Manchuria), 22½ divisions of 320,000 men, or about fifty-six per cent are being used on the Liberated Areas front; only 17½ divisions of 260,000 men, or about forty-four per cent, are used on the KMT front. The distribution of the burden against the puppet troops remains entirely unchanged....

Liberated Areas of China

[p. 23] The Chinese Liberated Areas, with a total population of 95,500,000, are placed as far north as Inner Mongolia and as far south as Hainan Island. There are operations of the Eighth Route Army, the New Fourth Army, and other people's forces practically everywhere that the Japanese have reached. The vast Chinese liberated area includes nineteen large Liberated Areas, extending over the provinces of Liaoning, Jehol, Chahar, Suiyuan, Shensi, Kansu, Ninghsia, Shansi, Hopei, Honan, Shantung, Kiangsu, Chekiang, Anhwei, Kiangsi, Hupei, Hunan, Kwangtung, and Fukien. Of these provinces, the Liberated Areas cover the major part in some cases and a smaller part in others, with Yenan as the directive centre. Within the vast liberated territory, the Shensi-Kansu-Ninghsia Border Region west of the Yellow river, with a population of 1,500,000, is only one of the nineteen Liberated Areas, and the smallest of the lot in point of population, with the exception of the East Chekiang and Hainan areas....

KMT Controlled Areas

The leading ruling clique in the KMT has persisted in maintaining a dictatorial rule and carried out a passive policy against Japan while it has upheld a policy of opposing the people within the country. In this way, the KMT armies have shrunk to half their former size and the major part of them has almost lost its combat ability; in this way, a deep chasm exists between the KMT government and the people, and a serious crisis of poverty, discontent, and revolts among the people is engendered; thus the ruling clique of the KMT has not only greatly reduced its role in the war against Japan, but, moreover, has become an obstacle to the mobilization and unification of all the anti-Japanese forces in the country.

Why did this serious situation come into existence under the leadership of the major ruling clique of the KMT? Because this ruling clique represents the interests of China's big landlords, big bankers, and the big compradore class. This reactionary and extremely small stratum monopolizes all the important organs of military, political, economic, and cultural bodies under the KMT [p. 25] government. They place the preservation of their own vested interests in the first place and the interests of the war against Japan in the second place. . . .

The Danger of Civil War

[p. 31] Up to the present, the main ruling clique in the KMT has persisted in its reactionary policy of dictatorship and civil war. There are many indications that they have prepared, and, particularly at present, are preparing to start [p. 32] civil war once the Japanese aggressors are sufficiently driven out of China by the troops of a certain ally. They also hope that some Allied generals will pursue the same duties in China as General Scobie did in Greece. They cheered the slaughter of the Greeks by Scobie and the reactionary Greek government. . . .

Negotiation

To defeat the Japanese aggressors, to build a new China, and to prevent civil war, the CCP, after coming to an agreement with the other democratic groups, proposed before the [third session of the Third] People's Political Council in September 1944 the immediate ending of the KMT dictatorship and the setting up of a democratic coalition government. Undoubtedly this demand was very timely, for within a few months it got the response of the broad masses.

Many negotiations were conducted between us and the KMT government to discuss the way to end the one-party dictatorship, to form a coalition government, and to effect the necessary democratic reform. However, all our proposals were rejected by the KMT government, which was unwilling not only to end the one-party [p. 33] rule and to set up a coalition government, but also to effect any urgently needed democratic reform, such as the abolition of the secret police, the rescission of reactionary decrees that deprived the people of their freedom, the release of political prisoners, the recognition of the legal status of the various political parties and groups, the recognition of the Liberated Areas or the withdrawal of the troops blockading and attacking the Liberated Areas. This is why political relationships in China are in such an extremely serious situation.

Two Future Courses

Viewing the situation as a whole and analysing the above international and domestic situations, I urge you not to think that all our undertakings will be successful and perfectly smooth. No, far from it; the fact is, two possibilities, two future courses, one good and the other bad, are coexistent. Persistence of dictatorship and prevention of democratic reform; emphasis on the policy of oppressing the people instead of fighting the Japanese aggressors; the possibility of another civil war which will drag China to her former dependent, unfree, undemocratic, disunited, poor, and weak state, even if the Japanese aggressors are beaten—this is one of the possibilities, one of the future courses. It still exists, and will continue to exist even though there is a favourable international situation, a growth in the awakening of the people at home, or a development of the people's organized strength. Those who hope for the materialization of this probability are the anti-popular group in the KMT in China and the imperialist-minded reactionary elements in foreign [p. 34] nations. This is one side that must be noted, must not be ignored.

But, on the other hand, viewing the same situation as a whole and as analysed above, we grasp, with more confidence and courage, the other possibility, the other future course, that is, to overcome all difficulties, to unite the entire nation, to abolish the dictatorship, to effect democratic reform, to consolidate and expand the anti-Japanese forces, to beat the Japanese aggressors completely, and to build up a new, independent, free, democratic, united, and prosperous China. Those who hope for the materialization of this possibility are the broad masses, the CCP, and the other democratic elements and groups in China, as well as all nations who consider us their equals, the progressive elements and the masses in foreign nations. . . .

4. [p. 35] *The Policy of the CCP.* . . .

[p. 37] Our General Programme

This common programme may be divided into two parts: general and specific. We will first deal with the general programme, and then with the specific part.

Under the over-all premise of annihilating the Japanese aggressors and of building a new China, the fundamental views of us CCP members are, at the present stage, identical with those held by the overwhelming majority of the Chinese populace. These are, firstly, that China should not have a feudalistic, fascist, anti-popular system of government exclusively controlled by big landowners and big bourgeoisie, because such a system has been proved to be entirely bankrupt by the chief ruling cliques of the KMT in their eighteen years' rule. Secondly, China cannot, and therefore should not, attempt to build a state along the old-type democratic lines entirely ruled by the liberal bourgeois dictatorship. For in China, the liberal bourgeoisie has so far proved itself to be weak economically and politically, while on the other [p. 38] hand there has been born in China a politically powerful new factor that leads the broad masses of the peasant class, the petty bourgeoisie, the intellectuals, and other democratic elements —the awakened Chinese proletariat and its leader, the CCP. Thirdly, in the present stage, while the task of the Chinese people is still to oppose imperialistic and feudal oppression, while the requisite social and economic conditions are still lacking in China, the Chinese people cannot, and therefore should not, attempt to build a socialist state system.

Then, what is our proposal? We want to build, after annihilating the Japanese aggressors, a system of government based on the support of the overwhelming majority of the people, on the united front and the coalition of democratic alliance [of parties and groups]. We call this the New Democratic system of government. . . .

[p. 39] The New Democracy we uphold demands the overthrow of external national oppression and the doing away of the internal feudalistic, fascist oppression. After removing these oppressions we are not in favour of setting up an old democratic political system. Instead, we want to set up a political system based on the united front and the alliance of all democratic classes. These views of ours are entirely in accord with Dr. Sun Yat-sen's. In the manifesto of the First National Congress of the KMT [1924], Dr. Sun said: "The so-called democratic system in modern nations is often monopolized by the bourgeoisie, becoming an instrument with which to oppress the common people. But the KMT's principle of democracy [*min-ch'üan chu-i*] is the common property of all common people, and not the privilege of a small minority". . . .

The formation of the governmental structure of this New Democracy should be based on the principle of democratic centralization, with various grades of [p. 40] people's congresses making decisions on the major political policies and electing the government. This system is at once democratic and centralized, that is to say, it is centralization on a democratic basis, and at the same time is democracy under centralized direction. This system alone can give expression to broad democracy by investing supreme power in the various grades of people's congresses; at the same time, it permits the state affairs to be managed in a centralized manner, with the various grades of government doing the work entrusted to them by the various grades of people's congresses and safeguarding all the necessary democratic activities of the people.

The problems of the New Democratic state and government include the problem of a federal union. The various races in China should, in accordance with their own will and the principles of democracy, form a Union of Democratic Republics of China, and set up a central government based on that union.

Troops and other armed forces form an important part of the New Democratic state authority. Without them, the nation is without protection. Like all other governmental authorities, and completely different from the old-time troops and police who belong to a few and are tools for oppressing the people, all armed forces of the New Democracy belong to the people and protect them.

Our views on the New Democratic economy also conform to the principles laid down by Dr. Sun Yat-sen. On the question of land, Dr. Sun maintained that "the tiller should own his land". On the question of industry and commerce, Dr. Sun said in the manifesto mentioned above: "All native or foreign enterprises that are either of the nature of monopolies or in a scale beyond the means of private resources, for instance, banking, railways, shipping, etc., should be operated and managed by the state, so that private capital may not control the livelihood of the people. This is the essence of the regulation [p. 41] of capital." Our views on economy in the present stage are in complete accord with those of Dr. Sun Yat-sen.

Some people suspect that the Chinese Communists are opposed to the development of individuality, the development of private capital, and the protection of private property. These fears are unfounded. Imperialistic and feudal oppression has cruelly fettered the development of individualism and private capital, and has caused destruction to the property of the broad masses. The task of our New Democratic system is precisely to remove these fetters and check these destructions, to safeguard the free development of the people's individualism in their common life, to promote the free development of a private capitalist economy that benefits instead of controlling the people's livelihood, and to protect all honestly acquired private property.

According to Dr. Sun's Principles and the experience gained in the Chinese revolution, China's economy in the present stage should be managed partly by the state, partly by private concerns, and partly by co-operatives. Here "state" is not one "monopolized by a few", but a New Democratic state "owned by the ordinary people".

The New Democratic culture should also belong to the common people, that is to say, should be national, scientific, and popular in character and should decidedly not be monopolized by a few.

Such is the general, or basic, programme advocated by us Chinese Communists in the present stage—the stage of the bourgeois-democratic revolution. In [p. 42] contradistinction to the future, or ultimate, programme of our socialist or Communist system, this is our minimum programme. . . .

The carrying out of this programme does not yet advance China to socialism. This is not a question of being subjectively desirous or undesirous of making this advance; it is due to the fact that the objective political and social conditions of China do not permit such an advance.

We Communists never conceal or disguise our political planks. Our future, or ultimate, programme is to push China forward to socialism and Communism; this is definite and beyond question. The very name of our Party and our Marxian world outlook definitely point in this boundlessly bright, beautiful, and most ideal direction. When we joined the Party, we had in mind two clearly defined objectives: to struggle for the new bourgeois-democratic revolution at present, and to strive for the materialization of the future proletarian socialist revolution. We must resolutely disregard the ignorant and base enmity, false accusation, and vituperation from the enemies of Communism, and deal determined blows to them. But to the well-intentioned sceptics we [p. 43] should explain [our cause] in a friendly and patient manner. Such things are very clear, definite, and not the least bit ambiguous. . . .

[p. 44] Some people do not understand why the Communists, far from being afraid of capitalism, actually promote its development. Our answer is simple: to replace the oppression of foreign imperialism and native feudalism with the development of capitalism is not only an advance, but also an unavoidable process; it benefits the bourgeoisie as well as the proletariat. What China does not want is foreign imperialism and native feudalism, (but) not native capitalism, which is, on the contrary, too weak. Strangely enough, some spokesmen of the Chinese bourgeoisie dare not advocate openly and directly the development of capitalism, but talk about it in a very roundabout manner. On the other hand, some people maintain that we should not allow capitalism to develop broadly in China; they talk of advancing directly to socialism, and (say) that *San-min chu-i* and socialism can be established "in one stroke". Obviously, such phenomena reflect at once the weakness of China's liberal bourgeoisie and the deceitfulness of the big landlords and big bourgeoisie towards the people. We Communists, according to our Marxist understanding of the law of social development, clearly realize that, under the conditions of China today and the rule of the New Democratic state, private capitalist economy, in addition to state economy, the individual economy of the labouring people, and co-operative economy, must be given facilities for extensive development, if the state, the people, and the [p. 45] forward development of our society are to be benefited. No empty talk and deception can possibly mislead the sober thinking of the Chinese Communists. . . .

Some people wonder if the Communists, once in power, will establish a dictatorship by the proletariat and a one-party system, as they have done in Russia. Our answer is that a New Democratic state of a union of several democratic classes is different in principle from a socialist state of a proletarian dictatorship. China, throughout the period of her New Democratic system, cannot and should not have a system of government of the character of a one-class dictatorship or a one-party autocracy. We have no reason not to co-operate with political parties, social groups, or individuals outside the CP, who adopt a co-operative, but not a hostile, attitude. Russian history has created the Russian system. There the social system in which man exploits man has been abolished; the newest form of democracy—the socialist political, economic, and cultural system has been established; all anti-socialist political parties have been thrown out by the people, who support only the Bolshevik Party. To the Russians, such a system is completely necessary and rational, but even in Russia where the Bolshevik Party is the only political party, the governmental authority is invested in a union of workers, peasants, and intellectuals, or in an alliance of Party members and non-Party members; it is also not one in which only workers or the bolsheviks can work in the governmental organs. Chinese history will create the Chinese system. A special type, a New Democratic type of state with a union of several democratic classes will be produced, which will be entirely necessary and rational to us and different from the Russian system.

[p. 47] This also answers another question, which is this: You Communist (Party) members advocate the setting up of a coalition government, because, at present, there is no democratic election system and a coalition government is necessary for national unification and for waging the anti-Japanese war; but in the future too, when there will be a democratic election system, why not let the majority party in the National Assembly set up a one-party government instead of still wanting to organize a coalition government? Our answer is this: China's historical conditions prescribe a coalition government. I have mentioned above that matters have been changed by the appearance of a new factor, the CCP, which represents not only the proletariat, but by virtue of its programme and actual struggle, also the broad peasant class, the petty bourgeoisie, the intellectuals, and other democratic elements. Any government that excludes from itself the CP will not be able to achieve a single worthy thing; this is the basic characteristic of China in the historical stage of New Democracy. . . .

[p. 48] Our Specific Programme

[p. 49] We consider the following demands as the appropriate and minimum ones:

The Chinese people demand the mobilization of all forces for the annihilation, in concert with the Allied nations, of the Japanese aggressors and for building up an international peace; they demand the abolition of the KMT one-party dictatorship and the setting up of a democratic coalition government and a united supreme command; they demand national unification and the punishment of the pro-Japanese, fascist, and defeatist elements that impair national solidarity and oppose the people; they demand the punishment of those reactionary elements that instigate civil war, and an assurance of internal peace; they demand the punishment of traitors and Japanese spies, and the prosecution of officers who have surrendered to the enemy; they demand the abolition of reactionary secret police organizations and activities that are used for suppressing the people, and the concentration camps; they demand the rescission of the reactionary laws and regulations that suppress the people's freedom of speech, of publication, of assembly, of association, of thought, of belief, and of person, so that the people may acquire their full right; they demand the recognition of the legal status of all democratic parties and groups;

they demand the release of all patriotic political prisoners; they demand the withdrawal of all troops now surrounding and attacking the Liberated Areas, and employment of these troops on the anti-Japanese front; they demand the recognition of all anti-Japanese forces and popularly elected governments in the Liberated Areas; they demand the consolidation and expansion of the Liberated Areas and their armed forces at the expense of enemy-occupied areas; [p. 50] they demand that the people in enemy-occupied territory be given assistance in organizing underground forces for an armed revolt; they demand that they be armed for the defence of the nation; they demand the political and military reform of KMT-directed troops that always lose to the enemy, always oppress the people and discriminate against non-KMT forces, and the punishment of the generals responsible for the defeats; they demand the improvement of the conscription system and the living conditions of the rank and file; they demand preferential treatment for the families of anti-Japanese soldiers, that they may be relieved of their worries for their families at the front; they demand special privileges for the bereaved families of soldiers who fell for their country and for disabled veterans, and employment and assistance for veterans; they demand the development of the war industry for better waging the war; they demand the just distribution of Allied military and financial aid to all anti-Japanese forces; they demand the punishment of corrupt and grafting officials, and the realization of honest government; they demand better treatment for the middle and lower classes of government employees; they demand the right of democratic self-government for the people; they demand the abolition of the oppressive *pao-chia* [local security] system; they demand relief for war refugees and famine-stricken areas; they demand the setting apart of large funds for the extensive relief of the people in enemy-occupied areas when these areas are recovered; they demand the abolition of oppressive and burdensome taxes, and the imposition of a consolidated progressive tax; they demand agrarian reforms, reduction of rent and interest, proper protection for the rights of tenants, low-interest loans to poor peasants, and organization of the peasants for the development of agricultural production; they demand the prohibition of bureaucratic capitalism; they demand the abolition of the present system of economic control; they demand the checking of unrestricted inflation and the rise of commodity prices; they demand assistance to small industries by extending them loans and facilities in purchasing raw materials and in sales; they demand the improvement of the living conditions of workers, relief for the unemployed, and the organization of workers for the development of industrial production; they demand the abolition of party-regimented education and the promotion of [p. 51] national, scientific, popular culture and education; they demand the assurance of the livelihood of teachers and academic freedom; they demand the safeguarding of the interests of youth, women, and children, relief for needy students, the organization of youth and women for war and social work, freedom of marriage, equal status for both sexes, and education for youth and children; they demand better treatment for the racial minorities in China, according them the right of self-determination and of forming a union with the Han [Chinese] people on a voluntary basis; they demand protection for the interests of overseas Chinese and assistance for returned overseas Chinese; they demand protection for foreigners fleeing to China from the oppression of the Japanese invaders, and assistance to them in their anti-Japanese struggle; they demand the improvement of Sino-Soviet relations, etc.

To achieve these demands, the most important thing is to put an end at once to the KMT dictatorship and set up a nationally supported, democratic, unified, provisional central coalition government that includes all anti-Japanese political parties and representatives of non-party elements. Without this prerequisite it will be impossible to institute serious reform on a national scale—that is, in KMT-controlled areas.

Only these [demands represent] the voice of the broad [masses of the] Chinese people, and also of the wide public of the Allied countries. . . .

[Sections 1, 2, 4 and 5 omitted; see *Bibliography A*.]

(3) [p. 57] *The Freedom of the People*. . . .

Freedom is to be won by the people, not to be given as a favour. In Liberated Areas, the people already have won their freedom and those in other areas can and should fight for theirs. The more freedom the Chinese people get, and the greater the strength of the organized democratic forces, the more probable will be the setting up of a unified provisional coalition government. Once this coalition government is established, it will in turn give the people full freedom with which to consolidate the foundation of this coalition government. Then, and only then, after annihilating the Japanese aggressors, will it be possible to conduct free, unrestricted elections all over the country, to create a democratic National Assembly, and to set up a unified regular coalition government. Is it not clear that without the people's freedom, there can be no popularly elected National Assembly or government?

The most important freedoms of the people are the freedom of speech, press, assembly, association, thought, belief, and person. In all China, [these freedoms] are thoroughly realized in the Liberated Areas only. . . .

(6) [p. 64] *The land problem*

Why do we call the present stage of the revolution a "bourgeois-democratic revolution"? Because the target of the revolution is not the bourgeoisie in general, but imperialist and feudal oppression; the programme of the revolution [p. 65] is not to abolish private property, but to protect private property in general; the results of this revolution will clear the way for the development of capitalism; "Land to the tiller" means the transfer of land from the hands of feudal exploiters to the hands of peasants to become their private property, to enable the peasants to be free from their feudal land relationship, agriculture to advance from its antiquated backwardness to the modern level, and industry to obtain a market, thus creating the possibility of changing the nation from an agricultural to an industrial (economy). So, the policy of "land to the tiller" is a bourgeois-democratic policy, not a proletarian and socialist one. It is the policy of all revolutionary democratic groups, not of the Communists alone. Under the conditions present in China, the Communists act differently from the others only in that we take the policy seriously: [we] not only talk about it, but also act upon it. Who are the revolutionary democratic groups? Besides the proletariat, who are the most thorough revolutionary democrats—the peasants form the largest revolutionary democratic group. The overwhelming majority of the peasants, with the exception of those rich peasants who cling to the tail [i.e. remnants] of feudalism, are actively demanding "land to the tiller". The urban petty bourgeoisie is also a revolutionary democratic group. They will be benefited by the development of agricultural productivity, made possible by the policy of "land to the tiller". The liberal bourgeoisie is a vacillating class; they also support the policy of "land to the tiller", because they need a market; but many of them fear the policy because most of them have some connection with landownership. Those who are resolutely opposed to the policy of "land to the tiller" are the anti-popular groups within the KMT, because they represent the class of big landlords, big bankers, and big compradores. As there is no political party in China representing exclusively the peasant class, and as political parties representing the liberal bourgeoisie lack a resolute agrarian policy, the Chinese Communists [p. 66] who have a firm land programme and who really fight for the interest of the peasants, securing the broadest masses as their allies, as a result have become the leaders of the peasants and all revolutionary democrats. . . .

[p. 68] The peasants are predecessors of the Chinese worker, and millions of them in future will go to the cities and into factories. If China needs to build up a powerful national industry and many modern cities, then she has to undergo the lengthy process of transforming the rural population into an urban population.

[p. 69] The peasants are a market for China's industry. They alone can supply it with the richest food and raw materials, and absorb the vast quantities of industrial products.

The peasants are the source of our armies. The soldiers are peasants in military uniform. They are the mortal enemies of the Japanese aggressors.

The peasants, at the present stage, are the main foundation of democracy in China. Chinese democrats can achieve nothing if they do not rely on the 360,000,000 peasants for support.

The peasants, at the present stage, are the main foundation of China's cultural movement. Divorced from the 360,000,000 peasants, are not the illiteracy elimination campaigns, the universal education, the popular literature, and the national health campaigns all empty phrases?

I said "main foundation" because naturally I would not ignore the political, economic, and cultural importance of the remaining 90,000,000 people, particularly the working class, politically the most conscious of all classes of the Chinese people and able to lead all democratic movements. This must not be misunderstood.

To understand all this thoroughly is necessary not only for the Chinese Communists, but for all democratic groups as well.

The peasant's enthusiasm in production will be increased once land reforms—even preliminary reforms such as reduction of rent and interest—are carried out. By degrees, when the peasants are organized on a voluntary basis into agricultural production co-operatives or other co-operatives, their productive power will develop. Such agricultural production co-operatives at present can only be collective, mutual-aid labour organizations such as the labour-exchange brigades, mutual-aid groups, and worker-exchange groups, built on the peasant's individual economic basis (based on the peasant's private property), but the development of productive power and the increase in productive capacity already is astonishing. This system, universally adopted in the Liberated Areas, should be extended to other areas in the future. . . .

The broad revolutionary intellectual elements of China should realize the necessity of merging with the peasants, who need them and are waiting for their help. They should enthusiastically go to the villages, exchange their student's clothes for the coarse garb of the peasants, start willingly from the bottom, understand the peasants' demands, help to awaken the peasants and organize them, and fight for the completion of the extremely important task in China's democratic revolution—the rural democratic revolution.

After annihilating the Japanese aggressors, land belonging to them and to the principal traitors should be confiscated and distributed among those peasants having little or no land. . . .

(7) [p. 71] *The industrial problem*. . . .

[p. 72] Generally speaking, a China without independence, freedom, democracy, and unity cannot be an industrial China. Independence can be gained through the annihilation of the Japanese aggressors; freedom, democracy, and unity can be attained by abolishing the KMT one-party dictatorship, setting up a democratic coalition government, realizing the people's freedom, the people's unity, and the people's army, instituting land reforms, and liberating the peasants. Without independence, freedom, democracy, and unity, there cannot be a truly large-scale national industry. And without an industry, there will be no consolidated national defence, no well-being for the people, no prosperity and strength for the nation. This key point has been proved by the history of the 105 years after the Opium War of 1840, particularly the history of the eighteen years of KMT rule. China can be prosperous and strong, and not poor and weak, only if she is not colonial or semi-colonial but independent, not semi-feudal but free and democratic, not divided but unified. . . .

[p. 73] Having secured the New Democratic political conditions, the Chinese people and their government will have to take concrete steps to build up light and heavy industries gradually and within a certain number of years, so that China may be raised from the position of an agricultural nation to that of an industrial nation. China's independence, freedom, democracy, and unity of New Democracy cannot be consolidated if they are not built on a solid economic foundation, on the foundation of a progressive agricultural industry far more advanced than it is, on the foundation of large-scale industries that weigh heavily in the nation's economic scale, with corresponding [advancement in] communications, and commercial and financial enterprises.

We Communists are willing to struggle for the objectives mentioned above in co-operation with all anti-Japanese democratic parties and groups, and industrialists. The Chinese working class will play a great role in the fulfilment of this task. . . .

[p. 74] Under the New Democratic system of government, a policy of readjusting the relations between capital and labour will be adopted. On the one hand, the interests of workers will be protected. An eight- to ten-hour-day system, according to varying circumstances, will be adopted, as well as suitable relief for the unemployed, social security, and the rights of labour unions. On the other hand, reasonable profits of state, private, and co-operative enterprises will be guaranteed. In general, this will enable both labour and capital to work jointly for the development of industrial production.

Large amounts of capital will be needed for the development of industries. Where will it come from? It can only come from two sources: mainly from dependence on the accumulated capital of the Chinese people, and at the same time from borrowing foreign aid. We welcome foreign investments if such are beneficial to China's economy and are made in observance of China's laws. What is beneficial to both the Chinese people and peoples abroad is that China, after winning a firm internal and international peace, and having her thorough political and agrarian reforms, shall be able to develop fully, on a large scale, light and heavy industries and a modernized agriculture. On this basis, [we] shall be [p. 75] able to absorb vast amounts of foreign investments. A politically backward and economically impoverished China will be greatly disadvantageous not only to the Chinese people, but also to peoples abroad. . . .

(8) *The problems of culture, education, and the intelligentsia.* . . .

[p. 76] To wipe out illiteracy in eighty per cent of the nation's population is a necessary condition to building up a new China.

Suitable and determined measures should be taken to wipe out all subservient, feudalistic, and fascist culture and education.

Positive reform and relief measures should be undertaken in dealing with the ignorance of health rules, diseases and epidemics caused by imperialistic and feudalistic oppression, which have ravaged the spirit and body of the Chinese people; public health work should be extended. . . .

The aims of China's national culture and education should be New Democratic, that is to say, China should build up her own national, scientific, and popular new culture and education.

[p. 77] Towards foreign culture, the policy of exclusion is erroneous. Progressive foreign culture should be absorbed as much as possible for the reference of China's cultural movement. But it would also be wrong to follow it blindly. Foreign culture should be critically absorbed on the basis of the practical needs of the Chinese people. Similarly, ancient Chinese culture should neither be totally repudiated nor blindly followed, but should be critically accepted to facilitate the promotion of China's New Democratic culture. . . .

(9) *The problem of racial minorities.* . . .

[p. 78] The CCP is in complete accord with Dr. Sun's racial policy . . . to assist the broad masses of the racial minorities, including their leaders who have connections with the people, to fight for their political, economic, and cultural emancipation and development, as well as for the establishment of their own armed forces that protect the interests of the masses. Their languages, customs, habits, and religious beliefs should be respected. . . .

(10) [p. 79] *The foreign relations problem.* . . .

The CCP enthusiastically approve in particular the decisions of the Crimea [Yalta] Conference, which calls for the ultimate defeat of fascist Germany, the extirpation of fascism and its causes, the wiping out of the last vestiges of fascism in liberated Europe, the establishment of internal peace in the various countries, and the setting up of democratic systems chosen by the people of the various nations. . . .

[p. 80] The basic principles in the CCP's foreign policy are the establishment and consolidation of friendly relations with all nations on the basis of the thorough annihilation of the Japanese aggressors, the maintenance of world peace, mutual respect for national independence and equality, and the mutual promotion of national and popular interests and friendship, as well as the solution of all war-time and post-war problems such as the co-ordination of action in the war, peace conferences, trade, foreign investments, etc. . . .

We maintain that the KMT government must end its hostile attitude towards the Soviet Union and immediately improve the Sino-Soviet relationship. The [p. 81] Soviet Union was the first nation to abrogate the unequal treaties and to sign equal new treaties with China. During the First KMT National Congress, summoned by Dr. Sun Yat-sen himself in 1924, and the subsequent Northern Expedition, the Soviet Union was the only nation that assisted the Chinese war of liberation. After the war of resistance broke out on July 7, 1937, the Soviet Union was again the first to come to the aid of China in her fight against the Japanese aggressors. The Chinese people express their thankfulness to the Soviet government and its people for this help. We believe that the final, thorough solution of Pacific problems is impossible without participation of the Soviet Union.

We believe that the great efforts, sympathy, and help to China by both the governments and peoples of the two great nations, Great Britain and the United States, especially the latter, in the common cause of fighting the Japanese aggressors, deserve our thanks.

But we request the governments of all Allies, especially the British and the United States governments, to pay serious attention to the voice of the overwhelming majority of the Chinese people, so that their foreign policy may not go against the will of the Chinese people, and so as to avoid impairing our friendship or losing the friendship of the Chinese people. We believe that any foreign government that helps the Chinese reactionaries to stop the Chinese people's pursuit of democracy will be committing a grave error.

The Chinese people welcome the foreign governments' announcement that they will abrogate their unequal treaties with China, and sign new equal treaties to deal with the Chinese people on equal terms. But the signing of equal treaties does not mean that China has really attained equality with other powers. China cannot [p. 82] attain true equality with other powers by depending on the good graces of foreign governments and foreign peoples alone; she must depend on the effort of her people to build up, politically, economically, and culturally, an independent, free, democratic, united, prosperous, and strong New Democratic nation, otherwise there will only be nominal independence and equality, which would be non-existent in practice. In other words, the present policy taken by the KMT government will never give China true independence and equality. . . .

The Task in the Liberated Areas

[p. 88] . . . In the Liberated Areas, on the one hand, the army should carry on the work of supporting the government and loving the people while, on the other hand, the government should lead the people in giving the armed forces support and granting preferential treatment to the families of soldiers, so that relations between the army and the people may be further improved.

In their work in the popularly elected "three-thirds system" governments [see *Glossary* under *San-san chih*], that is, regional coalition governments in the various Liberated Areas, and [p. 89] in their social work, the Communists should continue to follow their old policy by closely co-operating, on the basis of their New Democratic common programme, with all anti-Japanese democratic elements, irrespective of class, political affiliation, and faith.

Similarly, in their military work, the Communists should collaborate with all anti-Japanese democratic elements who are willing to co-operate with us, in and out of the armed forces of the Liberated Areas, for the great objectives of annihilation of the Japanese aggressors, the defence of a democratic China, and the building up of a powerful people's army.

To strengthen the anti-Japanese resistance and the productive enthusiasm of the workers, peasants, and the labouring masses, the policy of a suitable, resolute reduction of rent and interest, and better treatment of workers and government employees should continue to be followed. Cadre workers in the Liberated Areas must learn hard how to do economic work. . . .

[p. 90] In carrying on all kinds of work in the Liberated Areas, we should pay special attention to encouraging the local populace to handle their own local affairs; thus the more capable elements should be absorbed and trained on a large scale to be local cadre workers. The great task of rural democratic revolution could not be accomplished if outsiders would not thoroughly mix with the local populace, if [they] would not help the local cadre workers with ardour, diligence, and sincerity, if they would not love them as they love their brothers and sisters. . . .

[p. 91] In accordance with the principle of religion, all religious groups are allowed to exist in the Liberated Areas. The government will protect them, be they Protestant, Catholic, Mohammedan, Buddhist, or any other religious organizations, as long as their members observe its laws and decrees. Everyone is free to believe in any religion or not, and no compulsion or discrimination against him is allowed.

5. [p. 92] *All Members Unite and Struggle for the Realization of Party Tasks*

[p. 93] . . . The universal truth of Marxism, as a reflection of the actual struggles of the world proletariat, becomes a useful weapon available to the Chinese people only when it is wedded to the concrete actuality of the revolutionary struggles of the Chinese proletariat and the broad masses. This is exactly what the CCP has put into practice. The development and progress of our Party is effected through the process of determined struggles against all kinds of dogmatism and empiricism that are in contradiction to this universal truth [of Marxism]. Dogmatism deviates from the concrete actuality, while empiricism mistakes partial experiences as universal truth; both these opportunist concepts are contradictory to Marxism. In its twenty-four years of struggle our Party has overcome and is overcoming such erroneous thoughts, greatly consolidating the Party ideologically. Our Party now has about 1,210,000 Party members, the overwhelming majority of whom joined the Party during the anti-Japanese war. Among these members, as well as among some who joined the Party before the anti-Japanese war, there still exist various incorrect concepts. The work of correcting unorthodox tendencies in the past few years has greatly eliminated these incorrect ideas, with excellent results. This work should be continued, [p. 94] and the ideological education inside the Party should be greatly expanded, with the spirit of "learning from the past as a warning for the future, and curing the ills to save the patient". All key Party workers on the various levels throughout the land should all understand that the close union of theory and practice is one of the salient features by which our Communists are distinguished from all other political parties. Therefore the mastery of ideological education is the principal factor in consolidating the Party and carrying on its great political struggles. If this mission is not accomplished, then all the Party's political tasks cannot be fulfilled.

Another salient feature by which we Communists can be distinguished from all other parties is the very close relationship between us and the broadest masses of the people. We begin by devoting ourselves to serving the Chinese people earnestly and wholeheartedly and are not to be severed from the people for a single moment, setting out always from the viewpoint of the interests of the people and not from the interests of one's own small group or oneself, and holding ourselves responsible to the people as well as to our leading organs. Communists must always be ready to uphold the truth, because all truth is in conformity with the people's interests. Communists must always be ready to rectify errors, because any error is against the people's interests. The experience of our twenty-four years has told us that all correct tasks, policies, and working style

[*Tso-feng*] are in conformity with the demands of the people in a particular time and place, and they are never separated from the people. All erroneous tasks, policies, and working style do not conform to the people's demands and are separated from the people. Dogmatism, empiricism, dictatorialness, tailism [*Khvostism*], sectarianism, bureaucratism, militarism, and arrogance in one's working attitude are undesirable and bad because they alienate the people. Anyone who makes such mistakes must correct them because these mistakes sever us from the masses. This Congress should call on the whole Party to be alert and watch every comrade in every link of Party work, not to be estranged from the people. The Party should educate every comrade to love the people, to listen to them carefully, to mix with them wherever he goes, instead of overriding them, to enlighten and heighten the consciousness of the masses in accordance with their degree of consciousness, and to help them, under the principle of genuine volition, to organize themselves step by step for all necessary struggles that are feasible under the particular circumstances. Dictatorialness is wrong in all kinds of work because its impetuosity tends to suppress the people's degree of consciousness and violate the principle of volition of the masses. Our comrades must not assume that what is understood by them is also similarly understood by the masses. We must go into the masses to find out whether they have understood and whether they are willing to take action. If we do this we shall be able to avoid dictatorialness. Tailism is also wrong in all kinds of work, because it lags behind the consciousness of the masses, violates the principle of leading the masses to progress forward, and suffers from the mistake of inertness. Our comrades must not assume that the people do not understand what they themselves have not yet understood. Many times the people advance ahead of us. They are anxious to go forward, but our comrades, instead of leading them on, keep reflecting the views of some of the backward elements and mistaking these views to be the views of the broad masses and so become their "tail". In short, every comrade should be taught to understand that everything a Communist says or does is judged by its conformity with the major interests of the broad masses or whether it is supported by [p. 96] them. Every comrade should be taught to understand that as long as we rely upon the people, have confidence in their inexhaustible creative power, trust them and unite as one with them, no difficulty will be too great to be overcome and no enemy will be able to crush us, but on the contrary we shall be able to crush our enemies.

Yet another salient feature by which we can be distinguished from members of other parties is our serious self-criticism. . . .

[p. 97] Comrades! When our Congress concludes, we are going to the battlefields, to fight for the defeat of the Japanese aggressors and the building up of a new China, following the resolutions of this Congress. To attain this end we must unite with the people of the whole country. Let me repeat: we must unite with anyone who favours the defeat of the Japanese aggressors and the building up of a new China, irrespective of his class, political affiliation, social group, or personal background. To achieve this goal, we must, under the organization and discipline of democratic centralism, keep the Party more efficiently and powerfully united than ever. We must unite with any comrade who is willing to abide by the Party's platform, constitution, and resolutions. In the period of the Northern Expedition our Party had not more than 50,000 members; most of them were later on dispersed by the then enemy. In the Agrarian revolutionary period [we had] not more than 300,000 members; the majority of them were again later on dispersed by the then enemy. Now we have over 1,200,000 members, and this time we shall never allow the enemy to disperse us again. If we can absorb the experiences of these three periods, adopt a humble instead of an arrogant attitude, stand together in a greater solidarity within the Party, and are more closely united with all the people of the whole country outside the Party, then [p. 98] it is certain that we shall not be dispersed by the enemy, but shall instead resolutely, thoroughly, and completely exterminate the Japanese aggressors and their faithful running dogs, and, after exterminating them, shall build up an independent, free, democratic, united, prosperous, and strong China. . . .

SEC. VI. THE YENAN PERIOD—IDEOLOGY AND PARTY AFFAIRS (1935–45)

COMMENTARY P. THE INDOCTRINATION OF PARTY PERSONNEL

Though written by different men, documents nos. 28 and 29 have a common purpose—to set before the actual or prospective Party member a model of ideal Communist behaviour. While Ch'en Yün's article was written before the official beginning of the *Cheng-feng* movement for the "correction of [unorthodox] tendencies" (see *Commentary T* below) it reflects the aim of that movement to reassert the basic Leninist conception of Party organization.

In world Communist literature these articles represent nothing new. Whole sentences and paragraphs are reminiscent of passages found in similar hortatory literature published by Communist parties elsewhere. There is, to be sure, a certain Chinese flavour which expresses itself in the unabashed use of moralistic phrases, some of which are reminiscent of the Confucian classics and out of keeping with the Marxist prejudice against moral valuations. But in other respects there is nothing unique. The chief significance of these documents lies in the fact that the Party chose to re-emphasize its basic principles during this period, in an evident determination to maintain its Leninist foundations in the midst of all the changes brought about by the war-time shift to the united front.

What do these two primers convey to the Party follower? The Communist Party, we learn, is the Party of the proletariat. It is from this fact that it derives its infallibility and its exclusive mission to redeem mankind; for the industrial proletariat, according to Marx, is the class destined by History for this task. But since by 1939 the Party no longer had much contact with China's industrial proletariat, Ch'en and Liu did everything possible to conceal this embarrassing fact. Their first expedient is simply to ignore it. "The Chinese Communist Party", Ch'en informs us, "is organized by the awakened and progressive elements of the proletariat." Their next expedient is to admit "the weakness of Party work in the urban workers' movement", and to call for more vigorous efforts to gain control of the urban proletariat. This blandly overlooks the fact that, while such exhortations are a conventional feature of CCP literature during the whole period from the early thirties until the late forties, at no time during these years does the CCP seem to have diverted any significant portion of its energies from the task of winning a peasant base to the task of recapturing a city base. Finally, Ch'en and Liu use the expedient of confusing the rural proletariat with the proletariat proper, in spite of the fact that neither Marx nor Lenin accepted such an identification. Lenin provides for the absorption of "rural proletarians" into the Party, but always on the condition that the Party has a solid base in the urban proletariat. "Only the industrial proletariat", Lenin states, "led by the Communist Party can liberate the toiling masses of the countryside from the yoke of capital."[1] However, having concealed the Party's doubtful foundations by these expedients, Ch'en and Liu are now free to ignore this anomaly.

In spite of the fact that during this period the Party rank and file were made up almost entirely of persons drawn from the peasantry and the intelligentsia, Ch'en and Liu disingenuously echo the usual Communist doctrine that all evidences of human frailty and disharmony within the Party are due to infection by non-proletarian elements. How then can one distinguish truly proletarian elements from non-proletarian elements in a party in which few actual proletarians are to be found? This can be done only by making a total inversion of certain Marxist presuppositions. Instead of deducing ideological tendencies from class affiliations, it now becomes necessary to deduce class affiliations from ideological tendencies. Elements within the Party which "are capable of dedicating themselves to Communism and the proletarian mission" are *ipso facto* true representatives of the proletariat. Elements which introduce disharmony into the Party or are disloyal to the Party's principles represent non-proletarian classes. Thus purity of belief becomes the criterion of class purity. Those who stray from the correct line can be freely bracketed with the exploiting classes, whatever their actual class origins may have been. Ultimately, of course, this holds true for all Communist Parties everywhere. But where a Party still enjoys actual ties to the industrial centres and draws a substantial portion of its membership from the proletariat, it is still possible to point to the existence of an actual "proletarian core" as evidence of the legitimacy of the Party's claims.

The experience of the Chinese Communist movement in its Maoist development thus makes it amply clear that the Leninist formula of Party organization and the Leninist strategy of political action can both be maintained in an environment where the industrial proletariat is practically non-existent. This suggests that a Communist Party is a political instrument which derives its dynamism not from any organic tie with the industrial proletariat, but from the fact that it is a tightly organized, highly disciplined community—or élite corps—of believers which bases itself and rises to power on the dynamism of mass discontent. The mass basis of the movement can be furnished by the peasantry just as effectively as by the industrial proletariat.

Ch'en Yün's account is particularly valuable for his enumeration of certain minimum core beliefs which the Communist must accept. "First of all," he states, "it is necessary to understand the pattern of historic development of human society and have a firm faith in the inevitable realization of a Communist society in the future." In other words, the Hegelian belief in a redemptive History lies at the very heart of the faith. The Communist, like the Marxist in general, must feel that he is operating within a definite pre-established plan of history—a plan which can be discerned in both its past and future developments by those properly equipped to have such knowledge, and a plan which finally culminates in an ideal society. Unlike other Marxists, however, the Communist believes that this plan can finally be realized only by the Party, which is, as it were, a living church incarnating the historic will; it alone is equipped to discern the unfolding plan of history from moment to moment and to act on this knowledge. We are thus not surprised to find that the catalogue of virtues prescribed by Ch'en and Liu for CCP members all cluster about the cardinal virtues of devotion and loyalty to the Party.

It is implied throughout that the Party is, in a sense, a living entity which transcends its human cells. The Party member's dedication to the Party is therefore a dedication to a supra-human being. It is not pointed out, however, that this being can act, think, and plan only through the minds of concrete individuals, and that the assumed infallibility of the Party remains incarnate in the Party leadership so long as that leadership maintains itself in power. The Party member's spirit of self-sacrifice must thus rest not only on his faith in the Party as an abstract entity, but also on his faith that the Party leadership at any given time is the proper embodiment of this entity.

Another point which neither article dwells on is the fact that a Communist Party does not rely entirely on the virtuous conduct of its members. The sanction of force lurks always around the corner. It is of course true that the CCP in its New Democracy phase has been strikingly unusual in this respect. Having taken the leadership of the Chinese revolutionary movement, it has been able to draw on the enthusiastic devotion of young believers, eager to help save China by patterning their lives on the image of the model Communist. To the extent that the Party has been able to rely on such devotion, it has been able to keep the potential sanction of force well in the background.

In brief, then, these articles of Ch'en and Liu demonstrate that at the very height of the Yenan period the CCP was determined to maintain its basic Leninist principles of organization in all their pristine vigour within the Party, at the same time that it stood for the national united front in Chinese politics and impressed foreign observers as being more gradualist than revolutionary in its day-to-day programme.

28. CH'EN YÜN: HOW TO BE A COMMUNIST PARTY MEMBER
(May 30, 1939)

I. QUALIFICATIONS FOR PARTY MEMBERSHIP

The CCP is the vanguard of the Chinese proletariat. If (it) is to be so, one of the most important conditions is that it retain the purity of its membership. Accordingly, the question of the qualifications for joining the Party must be a constant preoccupation of the Party. To win members for the Party is the duty and constant task of every CP member. Accordingly, the question of the qualifications for Party membership must be thoroughly understood by every comrade of our Party.

1. *Who May Join the CP?*

According to Article II of the CCP Constitution, the following is stipulated regarding the question of qualifications for Party membership:

"Anyone who subscribes to the programme and Constitution of the CI and the CCP, enters one of the Party organizations and works with great energy in it, obeys all the resolutions of the CI and the Party, and pays Party dues regularly, may become a Party member."

The nature of the Party and the composition of the membership are closely linked to the question of qualifications for Party membership. In building up the Party, the question of the significance and function of Party membership occupies a very important place. It is, therefore, no surprise that it was precisely this question which aroused vehement argument and caused a serious split in opinion at the Second Congress of the Social-Democratic Labour Party of Russia as early as 1903. [p. 68] It was to become the basic point of difference between Lenin and the Mensheviks.

Lenin maintained that: "Only one who subscribes to the Party programme, pays Party dues and participates personally in one of the Party organizations, may become a Party member."

But the provision drafted by the Menshevik Martov was: "Anyone who subscribes to the Party programme, pays Party dues and regularly supports the Party under the leadership of some Party organization may become a Party member."

According to the policy of Lenin, only those who actually participate in the organization, unreservedly obey the organization and are willing to devote themselves heart, body, and soul to the mission of the Party of Communism may become CP members. Lenin fought against Martov in order to establish his principles of Party organization, resolutely opposing Martov's proposal that persons be admitted to Party membership without actual participation or even the intention to participate but merely by giving sympathy or support outside the (Party) organization. This 100 per cent opportunist viewpoint not only obliterates the distinction between Party and class, but also changes the nature of the Party, degrading it to [the status of] a labour union or students' federation, making the Party "sink into a sea of sympathizers and opens the door for unstable, wavering, and opportunist elements" (Lenin). Thus the participation in a specific organization of the Party and positive work for the Party are the minimum requirements for each Party member.

Emphasizing the principle of Lenin, the Bolsheviks established their own fighting Party—a Party which was thoroughly Marxist and harmonious in ideology and organization. This event had a great international significance, establishing the fundamental principle of Party organization for Communist Parties throughout the world. If the CCP has become, during the eighteen years of struggle, a heroic, fighting, powerful party, it is because, at its First National Congress [1921], it fought against Li Han-chün's Menshevist legalism and laid down the foundation of the Party organization in accordance with Leninist principles [p. 69].

With the great expansion of our Party membership today, this Leninist principle of membership has assumed an even more important significance. The tendency on the part of certain individual members of our Party to leave their posts or their work without Party permission must be corrected.

2. *Every Party Member Must Subscribe to the Party Programme. This Does Not Mean, However, That He Must Have An Expert Knowledge of the Party Programme*

Though at present the CCP does not yet have its own complete written Party programme, it nevertheless shares the general programme of Communist Parties throughout the world (the programme of the CI) and its own minimum programme (such as the policies of various Congresses and the Ten Great Policies [for anti-Japanese Resistance and National Salvation, 1937]). Acceptance of the Party programme is a prerequisite for admission to the Party. This does not, however, mean that an expert knowledge of the Party programme is a *sine qua non*; for only one who has received a thorough ideological training can be an expert on the Party programme. If applicants for

Party membership, especially workers and peasants, are required to have an expert knowledge of the Party programme and Constitution before they are admitted to the Party, then not only will we have to reject many revolutionary elements of excellent quality among the candidates, but we will deny the Party's responsibility to train its members.

3. CP Members Must Not Only Participate Actively in the Struggle Against Japan, But Must Also Struggle for Communism

Not every person who engages actively in the anti-Japanese war can become a Party member. In order to request admission into the CP, he must subscribe to the Party programme and be willing to dedicate himself to the Communist cause of the liberation of the proletarian class and the whole of mankind. Therefore, the absorption of members into our Party should be based on a constant and systematic spread of propaganda concerning Communism and the Party programme among the masses, and on a careful observation and selection of the more progressive elements among the masses.

II. THE COMPOSITION OF PARTY MEMBERSHIP [p. 70]

The CCP is the vanguard of the proletariat and is organized by the awakened and progressive elements of the proletariat. But for the Party to be the vanguard of the proletariat there must be constant and systematic adjustment in the composition of our Party membership.

1. We Must, First of All, Strengthen the Representation of Superior Elements of the Working Class in the Party

The CP is the vanguard of the proletariat: "It must, therefore, first of all absorb (into the Party) all the superior elements of the working class" (Stalin), and systematically strengthen the proletarian core of the Party. This is a question of paramount importance for our Party organization.

The strengthening and expansion of the working-class elements in our Party has a great significance, especially at the present stage. The comparative weakness of Party work in the urban workers' movement, the unprecedented suppression of the working class in the past, and the occupation of large industrial cities (by Japan) during the war, have further aggravated the suffering and hardships of the Chinese working class. The increasing unemployment of huge numbers of workers and their dispersion throughout the country further increase the Party's tasks in absorbing workers into the Party. In cities, the Party must first concentrate on the absorption of workers as Party members, and in rural areas the Party should pay particular attention to the absorption of workers who have drifted from cities to villages, as well as hired farm hands and handicraftsmen. We can thus broaden the proletarian base of the Party, activate the workers to play a central role in the war of resistance, and strengthen the leadership of the workers over the vast masses of peasants and urban petty bourgeoisie.

It should be pointed out, however, that the CP is not a "labour party", but "an organized vanguard of the proletariat, the most advanced form of its class organization". Therefore, not all workers can join the Party, but only those superior elements who are most conscious, active, and faithful to the working-class mission.

2. *The Party Must Pay Attention to Poor Peasants and Intellectual Elements*

China is not an advanced capitalist country, but a backward semi-colonial and semi-feudal country. In such [p. 71] a country, there exist vast masses of poverty-stricken, revolutionary peasants. They live in an environment of suffering and suppression of all kinds, resulting in their support of the CP and their unflinching fight against imperialism and feudalism under the leadership of the CP. Historical experience has amply vindicated the mighty role of the peasantry in the revolution; the poor peasants must remain, and will remain, the most powerful ally of the proletariat in the further progress of the revolution. Thus it is absolutely essential to absorb the active elements among the peasantry into the Party in great numbers, thus furnishing us with a social base of rural proletarians and poor peasants in the rural areas.

Similarly, the petty-bourgeois intelligentsia in a semi-colonial and semi-feudal China also may play an important role in the revolutionary movement; it has been proved in the course of our revolutionary movement in the past and in the course of the present anti-Japanese war that many of them [the intelligentsia] have been able to fight heroically for a correct political cause. Due to their cultural level and political consciousness, they have served as a necessary bridge between the Party and the masses. Our Party should absorb a great number of revolutionary intellectual elements who are capable of dedicating themselves to Communism and the proletarian mission. At the same time, experience teaches us that we must emphasize the absorption into the Party of the more revolutionary and poorer elements among the intelligentsia. These revolutionary and poor intellectual elements differ from the intelligentsia in general. Their poor living conditions make it easier for them to approach the Party. Furthermore, they are closer to the lower strata of society and their thinking and manner of life are closely linked to the poor masses. Thus they constitute ideal recruits for the expansion of the Party among the intelligentsia.

3. *The Party Should Pay Particular Attention to Women Workers and the Poor, Revolutionary Women of the Petty-Bourgeois Class—Peasant Women and Women Intellectuals*

Women constitute one-half of the population of China. Without women's participation in the revolution, the revolution cannot succeed. The number of women members in the Party [p. 72] is too small at present, primarily because not enough attention has been paid by the Party to the absorption of women Party members. We must oppose the excuse offered by some CP members for neglecting their duty of introducing women members: namely, that there is little chance for contact between men and women in Chinese society. All CP members, particularly women members, must regard the expansion of female membership as one of their important tasks. The Party must today emphasize (the task) of absorbing into its ranks revolutionary peasant women and women intellectuals in great numbers. The Party must regard this as a part of its regular activity and see to it that the political consciousness and the cultural level of its women members are enhanced through training and work.

4. *All Party Members Must Struggle for the Communist Cause of the Proletariat*

Workers are the foundation of the Party, and the Party must pay particular attention to the strengthening of the worker elements in our organization. Nevertheless, the Party will not refuse to admit people of other class origins who have undergone the training of daily economic struggle and of the revolutionary movement. They must, however, give up their former unproletarian, anti-Communist viewpoint and subscribe to the programme and Constitution of the Party before they can be admitted to the Party. Accordingly, the Party is firmly opposed to any viewpoint that does not insist on the purity of Party composition or the strengthening of its proletarian core, thus degrading the Party to a "national revolutionary alliance" of all classes.

III. THE PROCEDURE FOR ADMISSION TO PARTY MEMBERSHIP, RESTITU-
TION OF PARTY MEMBERSHIP, OR RENEWAL OF MEMBERSHIP

1. *Established Procedure*

For a new member to be admitted to the Party he must be sponsored by a (Party) member or members in accordance with Party provisions and current rules: for workers and hired farm hands, one sponsor; for a petty bourgeois, two sponsors; for those who leave other political parties to join our Party, three sponsors—approved by a Party group and [p. 73] *chih-pu* [Party cell] and certified by a higher Party committee. Those who have once belonged to other political groups must be approved by the district Party committee, the Central Branch Bureau, or the CC [of the CCP] (before they can be admitted into the Party).

2. *Rules on Restitution of Party Membership or Rejoining the Party*

The questions of restitution of Party membership and of rejoining the Party are to be dealt with in accordance with the decision of the CC and the nature of the circumstances. There are four basic principles:

(1) Those who have severed Party relations for a lengthy period but have nevertheless continued to work for the Party and whose status can be vouched for by members of the Party may be reinstated.

(2) Those who have severed Party relations for a lengthy period and claim to have continued their work for the Party, but are unable to produce Party members as witnesses, may rejoin the Party if they now possess the necessary qualification for Party membership. Reinstatement can be effected when witnesses are produced.

(3) All those who have had a long record of Party work but who have separated from the Party for a considerable time (up to one or two years) without committing any anti-revolutionary acts and have since been reinstated, shall not have the years of their absence included in counting their Party seniority.

(4) All those who have severed their relations with the Party for a long time without committing any acts harmful to the interests of the revolution and now possess the necessary qualifications for Party membership may be readmitted as new members after a considerable period of investigation.

As to those (former Party members) who have committed acts of political betrayal, no readmission into the Party is permissible.

IV. PARTY MEMBERS ON PROBATION

1. *Regulations on Duration of Probation* [p. 74]

The length of the probationary period varies with the class origin of the new Party member. At present the probationary periods tentatively decided upon by the CC [for various classes] are as follows: workers and hired farm hands, no probationary period; poor peasants and handicraftsmen, one month; revolutionary students, intellectuals, lower strata civil servants and white-collar workers, middle peasants, revolutionary soldiers, three months; other classes, six months, but this period can be prolonged under special circumstances. (See "Resolution of the CC on Expansion of Party Membership", March 15, 1938.)

2. *The Functions of the Probationary Period, the Duties of the Sponsors, and the Procedure and Criteria for Induction as a Party Member in Good Standing*

When non-workers join the Party, a certain probationary period is mandatory. The probationary period is used for education and checking. The Party should, in accordance with specific local conditions, give Party education to the members on probation, elevate their political level to that of a regular Party member by training them in Marxist-Leninist ideology, assign them specific work, and educate them through work. At the same time, during the probationary period, the Party should study the new member's personality and determine, by checking his personal history and other particulars, whether the candidate's political ideology, Party work, and devotion to the Party qualify him for Party membership; this is a preparatory step for his formal induction as a Party member.

Each new Party member must be recommended by a sponsor politically responsible for him. The sponsor bears an unfailing responsibility to the Party for the person he recommends. He should not only carefully observe what is expressed in the actions and words of the recommended person, but should also positively and patiently help and educate him in matters of politics and in his activities. The manner in which he fulfils this task can serve as a test of the responsibility and devotion to the Party of the member in question.

The criteria for induction as a Party member: the Party should rely upon the results of the training and investigation of the member on probation during the probationary period, in determining whether he has an adequate ideological understanding of the Party as well as a proper devotion to Communism and to his proletarian mission, and whether he has been constantly active in work and faithful to the Party in all his words and actions—it is by such patient methods that the Party is able to judge his preparedness to be a regular Party member. If the answer is affirmative, then with the approval of the group and cell and the endorsement of a Party committee at a higher level (he may become a regular Party member) through the regular procedure [p. 75]. When circumstances permit, a ceremony of induction may be carried out by the Party committee in accordance with concrete local conditions.

Thus induction into Party membership does not depend on the fulfilment of a probationary period, but is decided according to the candidate's degree of understanding of the Party. If, at the end of the probationary period, the necessary requirements for regular membership are not fulfilled (the probationary period) may be extended. The length of the extension should be equal to the original probation period. If found necessary, however, the probationary membership in the Party may be annulled. However, the extension of the probationary period should not be ordered lightly, as in the case of those who extend the probationary period for ten or twenty days as a measure of intra-Party punishment, etc.

As to young Party members, generally those under sixteen years of age are not eligible for Party membership. Those above sixteen may be recommended as members on probation; and those over eighteen may become regular Party members. But those under eighteen who already possess Party membership are to be allowed to retain their Party membership and are not to be dismissed or suspended.

3. The Rights and Obligations of Party Members on Probation

Party members on probation should carry out the work assigned by the Party, pay Party dues, and receive adequate Party training, which may take the form of studying certain Party documents and getting political and military training. Generally, Party members on probation have the right to speak at Party meetings, but do not have the right to vote. When one recommends a person for Party membership, he may first propose the candidate's name; after interviews and investigations by the cell, the formal recommendation will be made. In intra-Party work, members on probation are not eligible to serve as cell staff or group chairmen. However, under special circumstances, exceptions may be made to the above stipulation, as in cases where a new cell is being organized or a great majority of the cell are members on probation.

Members on probation are not eligible to attend certain Party meetings nor to read confidential documents of the Party.

V. THE CRITERIA FOR A CP MEMBER [p. 76]

1. *The Life-long Struggle for Communism*

The CP is a party fighting for the complete liberation of mankind as well as for Communism and its proletarian mission. Therefore a CP member who is willing to dedicate himself to the Communist cause must not only fight for Communism, but also formulate a revolutionary view of life which will lead him to fight relentlessly for the realization of Communism. But how can one formulate and consolidate one's view of life? First of all, it is necessary to understand the pattern of historic development of human society and have a firm faith in the inevitable realization of a Communist society in the future. That is to say, a CP member should, on the basis of his class consciousness, his practical revolutionary experience, and his understanding of Marxism, grasp thoroughly the historic position and role of the proletariat in society, comprehend the interests of the proletariat and its liberating mission, and clearly discern the immediate policies and goal of the CP and its members. Only thus can he firmly formulate his view of life, follow it throughout his life, and struggle to the end for the realization of his convictions. At the same time, every member of the CCP should thoroughly understand that the Chinese revolution is a long, hazardous task, and that on the winding, treacherous path of revolution, a revolutionary must be prepared for prolonged hardship and set-backs; he must also be prepared at a critical moment to sacrifice his very life. Therefore, every CP member should not only have an unwavering faith in the realization of Communism, but also be resolved to fight to the very end, undaunted by either sacrifices or hardships, for the liberation of the working class, the Chinese nation, and the Chinese people.

2. *The Interests of the Revolution Above All*

Our Party is a political party aiming at the complete liberation of the proletariat of China, the entire Chinese nation and people, and the establishment of a Communist society; thus, the interests of the nation and the people and those of the Party are identical. [p. 77] CP members are fighters for a Communist mission under the leadership of the Party. Thus the interests of a Party member are identical with those of the nation, the people, and the Party. Every Party member should give his unlimited devotion to the nation, to the revolution, to our class, and to the Party, subordinating individual interests to those of the nation, the revolution, our class, and the Party.

However, in the course of revolutionary work as well as Party work, the individual interests of Party members may come into conflict with those of the Party. At such a time, every Party member should fall back on his unlimited devotion to the revolution and the Party, sacrifice unhesitatingly his individual interests and bow to the over-all interests of the revolution and the Party. (He must) put the interests of the revolution and the Party in the first place and deal with all individual issues on the principle that revolutionary and Party interests stand above all others. He must not place individual interests above those of the revolution and the Party.

"The interests of the revolution and the Party above ALL" is not an empty phrase. The Party not only demands that Party members understand this phrase, but also emphatically calls on every Party member to carry out this motto resolutely and unhesitatingly in practical life and in every concrete act of daily life. Only when our Party has members who are willing to sacrifice everything for the interests of the revolution and the Party can the successful accomplishment of the revolution by the Party be assured.

3. *Obey Party Discipline, Keep Party Secrets*

In the course of the Party's fighting experience during the past eighteen years, it has been proved that discipline is the guarantee of the execution of the Party line. In the past it was only by overcoming the Ch'en Tu-hsiu-Li-san line as well as the anti-revolutionary political line and sabotage of Chang Kuo-t'ao and others that we were able to assure the carrying out of our revolutionary mission at various stages, and the formation of the anti-Japanese, national united front as well as the prosecution of the present anti-Japanese war. From now on the Party must continue to insist on such discipline, "in order to consolidate the Party, overcome new handicaps, and win fresh victories" (resolution of the [Enlarged] Sixth Plenum [November 1938] of the CC of the CCP). Therefore, it is the duty of every CP member to observe Party discipline resolutely and conscientiously. He should not only struggle with the tendencies that tend to undermine Party discipline, but should also struggle hard with his own words and actions which may tend to endanger Party discipline, in order to become [p. 78] a model in observing Party discipline. Do not think that merely stating one's support of, and voting for, the Party line at meetings or in the presence of the masses are enough for observing Party discipline; it is far from adequate. A good Party member who truly and conscientiously maintains discipline proves this discipline by his actions and dealings in the concrete issues of daily life. He shows himself to be a model in his resolute observation of the iron discipline of the Party.

The strengthening of our revolutionary power and the enhancement of the prestige of the CP have forced enemy agents, traitors, and anti-Communist elements to redouble their efforts to destroy the CP. Therefore, in Party work, the importance of secret work is by no means lessened. On the contrary, the Party should particularly strengthen its secret work, tighten discipline in secret work, and fight against any lack of vigilance regarding secret work. The Party must point out that there has been an extremely dangerous tendency in Party headquarters in certain areas to think that secret work may be slackened under present circumstances. Every Party member should not forget the lessons learnt from bloody experiences of the past resulting from the negligence of secret work. For the preservation of our strength in the war of resistance, and in order to assure the successful accomplishment of our revolutionary and Party mission, every Party member must greatly increase his political alertness. Every Party member must strictly observe discipline in the Party's secret work, and fight against all dangerous tendencies that tend to neglect or destroy the secret work of the Party. Any issue that is prohibited from being made public by the Party should never be revealed to the public without permission; any confidential matter which it is unnecessary to discuss with other Party members should not be talked about carelessly among other Party members. Any act that tends to destroy the secret work of the Party must be punished by Party discipline, even to the point of expulsion from the Party.

4. Carry Out (Party) Resolutions in the Face of All Obstacles

It is not enough for a CP member to support the resolutions of the Party verbally; it is his duty to carry out those resolutions with determination and put these resolutions into practice in his actions. In carrying out Party resolutions, it is sometimes inevitable that certain difficulties [p. 79] and set-backs may be encountered. CP members must overcome such handicaps with an unflinching and unbending spirit. Performing Party work passively like an indifferent employee is absolutely impermissible. The Chinese revolution is a task that involves tedious, prolonged struggles. One of the characteristics of the CCP is its indomitable spirit of sacrifice and struggle. Every CCP member must possess this hard-fighting spirit if he is to inherit and glorify the splendid tradition of the Party.

A CP member should not only be devoted to Party resolutions in his daily work, but must also remain faithful to the revolution and Party resolutions at trying and critical moments; faithful to the revolution and Party resolutions not only when there is close supervision by the Party, but also when there is none; (he must) carry out Party resolutions determinedly not only in the hour of victory but also in the hour of defeat. Only when one has a determined and stubborn heroic spirit can one be called a good CP member.

5. A Model for the Masses

The greater the political influence and the higher the prestige of the Party, the more will the working class and the masses expect from our Party members. Because they are CP members, the vanguard trusted by the masses, the masses expect of them a great deal more than they do from others. The masses often evaluate our Party by the acts of our Party members. The Party member must at all times and places create a favourable impression on the masses by his deeds, so as to create greater faith in, and higher respect for, our Party.

The [Enlarged] Sixth Plenum of the Party [Central Committee, in November 1938] called on all Party members to conduct themselves in an exemplary fashion, in the war of national liberation:

"(Party members) in the Eighth Route Army and the New Fourth Army should serve as models of heroism in warfare and as models in the execution of orders, in their discipline, in political work, and in (maintaining) internal unity and solidarity. The CP members, in their relations with friendly parties and armies [i.e. at this time, the KMT and Nationalist forces] must stand firmly for (national) unity and solidarity, as well as for the policy of a united front. They should serve as models in carrying out their war duties. The words (of a Party member) should be made good in his deeds, and his deeds should be thoroughly carried out; he must be modest in manner, sincere in discussing problems and working with friendly parties and armies, [p. 80] (so as to) become a model in inter-party relations within the united front. In government work, CP members should be absolutely honest, free from nepotism, and serve as examples in working hard with little reward. In the mass movement, CP members must be the friends of the people, not their ruling officials; tireless instructors, not bureaucratic politicians. CP members at all times and places should never let their own individual interests take precedence. Individual interests must be subordinated to those of the nation and of the masses. Thus, selfishness, laziness, corruption, and vanity are (traits) to be most deplored. The spirit of altruism, enthusiasm, service, and hard work should be regarded as the worthy goal."

Every CP member should, as a true model Party member, respond enthusiastically to the above summons in the concrete deeds of his daily life.

A model CP member is also characterized by his strict, immutable viewpoint whenever revolutionary interests or issues which concern the nation and the people (are at stake). No threat nor bribe must shake him in his determination. Anyone who abandons his revolutionary and Party stand, disqualifies himself as a CP member.

There are in the history of the CCP many examples of members who fought for the cause of Communism unrelentingly in the face of every type of adversity and demonstrated their high devotion to the Party as well as to the revolution, under threats and temptations. Thousands and tens of thousands of sterling Party members and leaders have heroically sacrificed their lives at the fighting front, on the execution ground, and in prisons. They have demonstrated to the toiling masses of China and of the world the noble spirit of the sterling children of the Chinese race, and their glorious deeds will shine eternally. They are models for all revolutionaries. The members of our Party should not only revere them, but also follow in their footsteps.

6. *Training and Study* [*hsüeh-hsi*, p. 81]

Revolution is a stupendous and trying undertaking and the conditions of the Chinese revolution and the revolutionary movement are particularly complex and kaleidoscopic; the reason why the CP is able to control, under changing and complex circumstances, the great revolutionary movement and guide it towards victory is because it possesses a revolutionary ideology. Accordingly, a CP member must understand this revolutionary ideology; then he can find a way out of highly complex situations; he can work out his course in the ever-changing (revolutionary) movement, and can carry out his revolutionary assignments successfully. Unless he does so, he will lose his way and direction in the midst of his complicated and ever-changing revolutionary environment. He will be unable to work independently and will fail to carry out correctly the assignments and resolutions of the Party. Thus every CP member must learn through work whenever and wherever possible, elevate his political and cultural level, increase his revolutionary knowledge, and deepen his political vision.

In view of our current situation, what must we study?

(1) Our Party is a fighting Marxist-Leninist Party; we must study, above all, the theories of Marx, Engels, Lenin, and Stalin in order to train ourselves to become truly powerful CP members with distinct Party characteristics. (The purpose of) our study is to grasp the essence of Marxism-Leninism, and learn its viewpoint and method of approaching issues, while avoiding dogmatism.

(2) (We) must study the history and current political situation of China; otherwise we will be unable to formulate the tasks and methods of our present revolutionary work [p. 82].

(3) (We) should study military affairs and technique, particularly guerrilla warfare. Today, "militarization of Party members" has become a fighting slogan for the entire Party.

(4) A Party member whose cultural level is low should before all else spend a lengthy period learning characters and reading books and newspapers to elevate his cultural level. Only the elevation of his cultural standard will make it possible for him to improve his political understanding.

(5) It is even more important, however, (for a CP member) to learn through practical work and (learn) from the masses whenever and wherever possible. The experiences and lessons acquired through practical work in the mass struggle are our best text-books.

Self-criticism is a most valuable instrument of learning for a CP member, and an acceptance of Party criticisms with humility is requisite to the progress of a Party member. A good Party member should accept and understand every criticism from the Party in a sincere and cheerful manner in order to correct his own errors.

Self-satisfaction or unwillingness to learn are the enemies of learning. We are opposed to the tendencies of "egotism" and "self-glorification" as well as to the lack of self-confidence and determination on the part of Party members in their learning. A CP member seldom has an opportunity to sit in a classroom for a lengthy period. It is thus necessary that he should squeeze out time from his busy schedule to study by himself. For this, a persevering spirit is essential.

Our slogan for CP members is "learn, learn, and learn again". The entire Party must respond enthusiastically to the slogan adopted by the Sixth Plenum of the CC: "For oneself, learn persistently; for others, instruct tirelessly!"

Only one who fills the above six qualifications deserves to be called a good CP member without soiling the great and glorious status of CP membership.

29. LIU SHAO-CH'I: ON THE TRAINING OF A COMMUNIST PARTY MEMBER (August 7, 1939) [extract]

The Individual Interests of the CP Member are to be Subordinated Unconditionally to the Interests of the Party [p. 83]

A CP member must not only clearly determine his Communist philosophy of life and his world view, but must also explicitly determine the correct relationship between his individual interests and the interests of the Party. The Marxist principle is that the interests of the individual are subordinate to the interests of the Party, the interest of the part is subordinate to the interest of the whole, the short-range interest is subordinate to the long-range, and the national interest is subordinate to the international.

The CP is a political party representing the proletariat. The CP has no interest or aim aside from the interest of the liberation of the proletariat. However, the final liberation of the proletariat must also be the final liberation of all mankind. . . .

. . . Therefore, the individual interests of the Party member are subordinate to the interests of the Party, which means subordinate to the interests of class and national liberation, of Communism and of social progress.

The test of a CP member's loyalty to the Party and to the task of the revolution and Communism is his ability, regardless of the situation, to subordinate his individual interests unconditionally and absolutely to those of the Party. . . .

. . . [He] should see that his own individual interests are completely identical with Party interests, to the extent that they are fused. When conflicts arise between the interests of the Party and the individual, he can without the slightest hesitation or feeling of compulsion submit to Party interests and sacrifice individual [interests]. . . .

If there are only the interests and objectives of the Party and Communism in the Party member's ideology, if he has no independent, individual objectives separating him from the Party, nor any selfish calculations, if he is truly unselfish:

(1) It is possible for him to possess excellent Communist moral virtues. . . .

(2) It is possible for him to have the greatest courage. . . .

(3) It is possible for him to excel in the study of Marxist-Leninist theory and methods, observe problems with quick penetration and recognize actuality. . . .

(4) He can also be sincere, straightforward, and happy. . . .

(5) It is also possible for him to have the greatest self-respect and self-esteem, and, under the over-all premise of the interests of the Party and revolution, he can be broad-minded, tolerant, and go out of his way to be of help to others, even, when necessary, enduring insults and ill-treatment without "feelings of resentment and hatred"

Comrades! The CP member should possess the greatest and noblest human virtues. At the same time he should adopt a strict and clear Party and proletarian standpoint (the Party and class spirit). Our moral stature is great precisely because it is proletarian and Communist. This moral stature is not built on a foundation which is re-actionary and protects the interests of a few individuals and exploiters, but on the progressive foundation of proletarian interests and the interests of the final liberation of mankind, of the salvation of the world from oppression, and the building of a happy, beautiful Communist world. . . .

When necessary, "sacrificing one's own life to complete one's virtue" and "giving up life to attain righteousness" are considered the most natural thing by most CP members. . . .

The CP does not only represent the interests of each individual Party member, but also represents the long-range interests of all workers and the [p. 88] liberation of mankind. The Party interest is not merely the concentrated expression of the interests of individual Party members, but also of the interests of all workers and of mankind's liberation. . . .

The CP member has his individual interests and individual development, but at certain times contradictions can arise between these interests and the interests of the Party. At such times, it is demanded that the Party member unconditionally sacrifice his individual interests but not sacrifice the interests of the Party (no matter what the situation or pretext) to serve the individual. At the same time, the interests and development of the Party encompass the individual interests and development of the Party member. . . .

[p. 89] This is one aspect, one to which our individual Party members should turn their attention. But there is another aspect.

Although the general interests of the Party encompass the individual interests of the Party member, they cannot always completely encompass them and cannot and should not destroy the individuality of the Party member. The Party member is always faced with certain personal questions which he must attend to himself, and he must furthermore develop himself on the basis of his own individuality and specialties. Thus, in spheres where Party interests are not transgressed, the Party permits the Party member to establish his own individual and family life and to develop his individuality and specialties. In addition, the Party assists, under all possible conditions, the development of the individuality and specialties of the Party member (which are beneficial to the Party) and gives him suitable work and working conditions, as well as rewards, etc. When possible, the Party also looks after and protects the Party member's indispensable personal interests; for example, by giving him the opportunity for education and learning, curing him when sick and solving his family problems, and even sacrificing some Party work, when necessary, to protect its members. However, this is also for the interest of the whole Party, because the Party's task cannot be accomplished if minimum living conditions, working and educational conditions for our comrades are not safeguarded, so that they will work with ease and enthusiasm. This is something to which responsible persons in the Party must turn their attention in dealing with the problems of Party members. This is another aspect of the general problem.

Examples of Erroneous Ideological Concepts Within the Party

What are the fundamentally incorrect ideological concepts which may be held by comrades in the Party? Without attempting to be systematic, I will cite the following:

First, people joining our Party not only come from the various classes of society, but have differing objectives and motives. Many members enter the CP to attain such great objectives as the realization of Communism and the liberation of the proletariat and mankind. Yet there are some who join the Party for other [ulterior] reasons and to attain other objectives. . . .

Second, certain Party members still retain an ideology of comparatively strong individualism and selfishness.

This individualism is expressed in the following ways: in resolving various concrete questions, certain persons put their individual interests first and the interests of the Party in a subordinate position, or worry about personal gain and loss and calculate their individual interests. Or they utilize public means to gain personal advantage, relying on Party work to attain certain personal objectives. . . .

This selfish individualism is often expressed in unprincipled disputes in [p. 93] the Party and in the errors of clique struggle, sectarianism, and particularism. It is also expressed in actions which wilfully damage and show disrespect for Party discipline. . . .

The particularism which exists in the Party differs from this individualism. It arises most often when comrades only see the interests of their particular unit, see their own part of a job but not the whole, and fail to see the work done by another unit. . . .

Third, vainglory, individual heroism, exhibitionism, etc., still persist to a greater or lesser degree in the concepts of not a few comrades. . . .

Comrades! The CP member must not be self-satisfied and proud as an individual. . . .

. . . We are opposed to individual heroics and exhibitionism, but not to the Party members' desiring progress, for this is the CP member's most precious quality. But a progressive attitude which is proletarian and Communist and one which is individualistic are two different things. The former searches for truth, upholds the truth, and fights most effectively for the truth; it is characterized by its unlimited future for advancement and progressiveness. The latter, even for the individual, is of an extremely limited nature in progressiveness and has no future. . . .

[p. 97] Of course—and I reiterate here—in assigning work to Party members, Party leaders should pay attention to the differing circumstances of individual Party members, assign them work suitable to their individuality, play up their strong points, and encourage their enthusiasm for progress. However, a Party member cannot take this as a reason for refusing to accept the work assigned to him by the Party.

Fourth, there are some in the Party who strongly reflect the ideological concepts of the exploiting classes and often use methods meant to be used against the enemy in dealing with comrades and in dealing with intra-Party problems. They completely lack the great devoted and sincere Communist, proletarian spirit of mutual assistance and solidarity. . . .

[p. 98] They obviously reflect the concept of the exploiting classes in decay, because all exploiters, in order to develop their own position, are bound to harm others. The capitalists want to enlarge their own property or avoid bankruptcy in time of [economic] crisis, and they must trample on many lesser capitalists and cause countless workers to starve. The landlords want to develop their own position, and they must exploit the peasants and cause many to lose their land. . . .

Fifth, bureaucratism still exists in our Party and in various organizations (I shall, if the opportunity arises, discuss this problem later). Some individual comrades are still "petty-minded", find fault with small details and do not recognize the larger issues, and so on. They do not possess the noble spirit and vision of Communism and cannot see the over-all situation, but they are intensely interested in the trivial things before their noses. . . .

In addition, the rashness and wavering of the petty bourgeoisie and the destructiveness of the lumpenproletariat and bankrupt peasants are also reflected in the concepts of some comrades, but we will not enumerate them here. In short, within our Party, not only the Communist ideology, which represents the great and determined proletariat, is reflected, but some comrades reflect, to a greater or lesser extent, non-proletarian ideologies and even the ideologies of the decaying exploiting classes. Sometimes these ideologies are concealed and only expressed in minor individual, everyday problems, and sometimes they develop and systematically show themselves in various questions of principle, in important political questions, and in the intra-Party struggle. . . .

Sources of Various Erroneous Ideological Concepts in the Party

Why do these undesirable things still exist in our enlightened Party? I believe that the reason is very simple. Our Party did not materialize out of thin air, but was produced in reality from Chinese society. Although our Party members are generally fine Chinese men and women and the vanguard of the Chinese proletariat, they still come from all parts of Chinese society, and still live in present-day society. This contemporary Chinese society is still filled with the influences of the exploiters, with selfishness and self-interest, hidden scheming, bureaucratism, and other evils. We have many good Party members who are not easily influenced by these things, but some Party members bring with them, or reflect, in our Party the evils of society. Is there anything strange about this? (It is) just like finding mud on the body of one who creeps out of the mire and who often has to stay in the mire. Is there anything strange about that? This is not strange, but unavoidable. On the contrary, it would be strange if these evils did not exist in the CCP. How could an evil society produce a CP completely devoid of evils? . . .

Thus, in the struggles within and outside the Party, we reform society and gradually eradicate all that is dark and backward in society, and at the [p. 105] same time we reform our Party and Party members, resolve the contradictions in the Party, and make our Party members healthy and strong. . . .

[p. 106] *The Intra-Party Struggle and Attitudes Towards Erroneous Ideological Concepts in the Party*

Because of the influence of the exploiting classes, the complexity of elements in the working class, and because of the complexity of elements in our Party today, ideological differences, as well as differences in viewpoint, habit, taste, and feeling have arisen among individual members of our Party. . . .

[p. 107] Thus, the crux of the problem is not the existence of differing ideological concepts within the Party nor the existence of divergencies in opinion, [though] these certainly exist. The crux of the problem is the manner in which the contradictions within the Party are to be resolved, how did these divergencies come into existence, and (the manner in which) incorrect and non-proletarian ideological concepts are to be overcome. Obviously, these contradictions can be resolved, divergencies overcome, and incorrect and non-proletarian concepts defeated only through intra-Party struggle. As Engels said: "Contradictions can never be concealed for long by anyone at any time, they must be resolved through struggle". . . .

The first attitude is to rejoice at the defects, errors, and undesirable characteristics of our Party. . . .

The second attitude is to tolerate, accept, and learn certain erroneous thoughts and (follow) bad examples in order to satisfy personal schemes and desires. . . .

The third attitude is to be unconcerned with the defects, errors, and the various unhealthy phenomena in the Party and allow them to develop freely. . . .

The fourth attitude is that of deep hatred for those who exhibit these errors, defects, and those with incorrect concepts. . . .

The fifth attitude is the one which we should adopt. It is in contradiction to the four attitudes listed above. (1) We must first recognize and differentiate the various phenomena, ideological concepts, diverging opinions and proposals within the Party, [asking ourselves] which are correct and beneficial to the long-range interests of the Party and the revolution, and which are incorrect and harmful to the long-range interests of the Party and revolution; or (whether) both sides of an argument are wrong and a third view or proposal is correct. After level-headed discernment and examination, we should decide on a clear attitude of our own and take our stand on the correct side. [We should] not follow blindly or worship idols. (2) [We should] learn, promote, and extol all good models of conduct and correct spirit in the Party, support all correct proposals and opinions, and not follow bad examples nor allow ourselves to be influenced by incorrect ideological concepts. (3) [We should] not adopt [the point of view of] liberalism, but should struggle uncompromisingly with ideas and [p. 110] proposals which are erroneous in principle and with all evil phenomena in the Party, so that these errors and phenomena can be continuously overcome. [We] should not let things get out of hand and permit these errors and evil phenomena to develop and harm Party interests, nor should we be afraid of this kind of intra-Party struggle. (4) However, an attitude which is neither mechanical nor categorical, combines an uncompromising definiteness in principle and lively forms and methods of struggle with a spirit of tolerance and persuasion, and in the long-range struggle, educates, criticizes, conditions, and reforms those comrades whose thought is not incurably erroneous. Those with this attitude concretely and appropriately promote the necessary thought struggle in the Party on all questions of principle at all times, but do not struggle wildly in the Party, in a manner which is subjective, mechanical, and psychopathic, nor are they fond of struggling. (5) In the intra-Party struggle [we should] consolidate the Party, strengthen Party discipline and authority, mete out organizational punishment to those elements within the Party which have proved incurable, even expelling them from the Party, and in this manner [we] achieve health and consolidation for the Party. This is the attitude which all good, progressive Party members should adopt. Of the five attitudes above, only the fifth is a correct, bolshevik attitude . . . we often fail to carry out self-criticism formally, earnestly, and with a true sense of responsibility; (we often) fail to expose the various errors, defects, and all desirable phenomena in the Party, and correct and eliminate them. Criticism from the bottom up is especially deficient, and we must develop greatly in this respect. However, there is a considerable amount of irresponsible, irregular, and cowardly criticism and expression of dissatisfaction concerning this or that individual, this or that event, as well as considerable behind-the-back discussion and chit-chat in the Party. . . .

Self-criticism is necessary to us not for the destruction of [Party] authority, the destruction of Party discipline, or the weakening of Party leadership, but for the enhancement of Party authority, the reinforcement of Party discipline, and the strengthening of the Party's leadership. . . .

. . . Fundamentally, it is in the struggle against various dark forces within and without the Party that we reform the world and mankind, and at the same time reform our Party and ourselves. The intra-Party struggle is a reflection of the class struggle outside the Party. In the class struggle outside the Party—in the revolutionary struggle of the broad masses—the Party is tempered, developed, and strengthened; at the same time, the Party achieves consolidation and unity in the intra-Party struggle and gives planned, correct, powerful leadership to the revolutionary struggle of the broad masses. It is therefore fundamentally incorrect and of benefit to the enemy to adopt the attitude of liberalism towards various errors, defects, and undesirable phenomena in the Party, to attempt to blot out divergencies in principle in the Party, to evade the intra-Party struggle, to conceal the Party's internal contradictions or to exhibit negligence; because they are in contradiction to the rules of development of the class struggle and to our basic viewpoint of reforming the world and mankind through struggle. It is therefore also incorrect to separate the intra-Party struggle from the class struggle outside the party—from the revolutionary movement of the broad masses—and transform it into empty talk; because the Party cannot be tempered, developed, or strengthened if it is separated from the revolutionary struggle of the broad masses. Yet it is also incorrect to carry things to the other extreme and adopt a categorical attitude towards all comrades who have errors or defects (which are) not incurable, to carry on the intra-Party struggle mechanically, or to subjectively manufacture intra-Party struggles within the Party. Because this is also injurious to the Party, it gives the enemy an opportunity to mount an attack on our Party. This also runs completely counter to the rules of the Party's development. Loyal comrades in the Party who have committed errors should not be utterly denounced from the start; instead they should be persuaded, educated, and tempered with a friendly, sympathetic attitude, and only when absolutely necessary should they be publicly attacked and expelled. Of course, we cannot allow anyone to harm the Party's interests, and we must take precautions lest opportunists, spies, Trotskyites, and two-faced elements take advantage of every opportunity to harm the Party's interests. . . .

. . . We should not ourselves speak thoughtlessly to harm other comrades, [p. 120] but should endure the words of others which harm us. . . .

In general, our ideological training is our fundamental training to become loyal, pure, progressive, model Party members and cadres. We should: (1) from the learning of Marxism-Leninism and the actuality of the revolution, establish our own Communist philosophy of life and world view, establish our own determined Party and class stand. (2) On the basis of Communism's philosophy of life and world view, and a determined Party standpoint, examine all of our own thoughts and actions, correct all our incorrect thoughts, and at the same time observe problems as well as other comrades from this position. (3) Make constant use of appropriate forms and attitudes in struggling with [p. 121] the various incorrect ideological concepts in the Party, especially the ideologies influencing the present revolutionary struggle. (4) Hold ourselves strictly in check in thought, speech, and action; primarily by the adoption of strict standpoints and principles in regulating (ourselves) in political thought, speech, and action which are related to the present revolutionary struggle. In this regard, even petty matters (such as individual life and attitude) deserve our attention. But aside from questions of principle and vital political questions, we should not be excessively strict with our comrades, and should not meticulously find fault with them in petty matters.

Comrades! In brief, this is the fundamental ideological training of the Party member.

COMMENTARY Q. LEADERSHIP OF THE MASSES AND THE INTELLECTUALS

These two resolutions (documents nos. 30 and 31), passed by the CC late in 1939, illustrate aspects of CCP policy from which the Party has derived much strength.

Concerning the first document, on policy towards the masses, three comments are in order:

(1) The theories and operating techniques used by the CCP in its work among the "broad masses" constitute one of the main reasons why the Chinese Communists, although surrounded by hostile forces, outnumbered and greatly inferior in material strength, were able to resist the Japanese during the Sino-Japanese war and afterwards to vanquish the KMT. For twenty years, from 1927 to 1947, the Communist forces under Mao Tse-tung developed their guerrilla tactics as the core of their military strategy; and no guerrilla warfare can be effectively carried out without considerable support from the peasantry. P'eng Te-huai, second in command of the Communist

armies during the war against Japan, epitomized this situation in the widely-quoted saying, "the people are water, the Eighth Route Army are fish; without water, the fish will die".

(2) The major methods adopted by the CCP to win the support of the peasantry during the war of resistance were to encourage their active participation in local administrative work through popular elections, to improve their material welfare by reductions of rent, interest, and taxes, and to educate, indoctrinate, and stimulate them through popular organizations, cultural movements, and social reforms. Before the CCP was in power, the general discontent of the people towards the KMT régime could be skilfully exploited by these means.

(3) Suspicion of the KMT is clearly discernible in various passages of document no. 30, even though there was no formal conflict with the KMT in 1939. Amidst the talk of "consolidating the united front", there are repeated warnings against "the danger of anti-Communism" and "unexpected incidents detrimental to the Party".

In document no. 31 we see one reason why the CCP has been able to win the sympathy, and often the active support, of many Chinese intellectuals, especially the students. Realizing the great weight of the intellectuals' influence in a country where illiteracy is so high, the CCP has made vigorous and effective efforts to "absorb" them by propaganda, training, and work programmes. During the Sino-Japanese war, thousands of students braved many dangers, including those of the KMT secret police, to enrol in the schools at Yenan or to serve as cadres in the agrarian reform movement and in the Communist forces. Their enthusiasm did not keep them from presenting the CCP with a considerable problem of assimilation—many of the students in this war-time adventure possessed in a marked degree those traits of wilful individualism which have usually been called "typically Chinese". The CC directive of 1939 printed below shows a disillusioned realism concerning these foibles; note the references to the need of intellectuals "capable of bearing hardship" and of cadres (Party workers) "capable of handling the intellectuals". The task of assimilation, in short, was to transform "liberal" intellectuals, often boys or girls of well-to-do background from Westernized universities, into disciplined cadre workers devoted to the cause of the revolution and of the Party. For this they really had to "revolutionize themselves". The CC directive also called for the careful cultivation and organization of "non-party intellectuals who are sympathetic towards us". Many such persons are in Peking today.

30. DECISION OF THE CC ON THE WORK OF PENETRATING THE MASSES (November 1, 1939)

(1) The CP must further rely on the masses, and must penetrate into and work among the masses in order to overcome any possible danger of capitulation [to Japan] or of anti-Communism, to consolidate the united front, to fight for continued resistance against Japan and for more democracy in political life, and to prepare for the counter-attack. Otherwise [without penetration into the masses] it is impossible for us [to attain these goals]. Similarly, it is only by the penetration of CP activities among the masses and by winning the support of the multitudinous masses that we shall be able to forestall unexpected losses to the Party and to the war of resistance, in case any act of capitulation or move against the Communists or other unexpected incident should take place. Otherwise we will not be able to prevent such losses. The mass activities carried on under the leadership of the CCP have made considerable progress since the beginning of the war of resistance, resulting in the expansion of our armed forces, formation of guerrilla bases, the growth of progressive elements in the country, and more than two years of sustained war against Japan. At the same time, however, certain seriously erroneous tendencies still exist. They are: (a) a tendency to stress united front activities among the upper strata and to neglect activities among the lower strata of the masses. Many leading organs of the Party either entirely omit mass activities from their agenda, and neglect to guide the lower echelons regarding mass activities, or else carry on few discussions and issue few directives on the subject. Many cells as well as Party members have become alienated from the masses, some do not engage in mass activities, and some are entirely ignorant of how to carry on work among the masses. (b) In some places where the groundwork has been laid for mass activities, many leading organs of the Party have failed to carry on discussion or issue directives regarding methods of intensifying such mass activities, thus leaving matters in a stagnant state. The CC urges the various Party units to correct these erroneous tendencies immediately and make all Party members realize that only by relying even more heavily on the masses and only by activities which penetrate the masses can the CP overcome the dangers of our present political situation, win the victory in the war of resistance, and prevent unexpected losses to the Party as well as to the war of resistance as the result of some untoward incident detrimental to the Party or the war of resistance.

(2) In the areas ruled by the KMT, the leading organs of various Party units must study the local situation and guide the lower units down to the cell in carrying on mass activities among workers, peasants, and petty bourgeoisie. We must utilize government laws and regulations already extant and methods permitted by local custom, do everything possible to draw the Party cell close to the workers, peasants, and bourgeoisie of the area in question, organize them step by step and lead them in political, economic, and cultural reform movements which will prove beneficial to the masses themselves as well as to the war of resistance. We should be content even to begin with very minor reforms. As for lower local administrative units (*pao-chia* and *lien-pao*), local cultural organizations (primary schools and educational associations), local economic organizations (co-operatives, etc.), local military forces (self-defence corps and *min-t'uan*) —every effort should be made to place their control in the hands of CP members, leftist elements, or the more impartial elements of the gentry. All activities should be carried out on the basis of a united front of local leftist elements and impartial elements of the gentry, to the extent permitted by local conditions, and with a view to keeping the Party's strength intact as well as keeping it in reserve without destruction for a long period. In the KMT areas the mass activities of the Party must be carried on by using every possibility of public and legal activity in order to make progress and obtain results; at the same time, organizational work of the Party should be kept strictly secret, for only thus can it be preserved and consolidated. It is necessary to differentiate strictly between the public and secret work of the Party, and there should be adequate co-ordination between the two in order to avoid a repetition of the failure of work in the white [KMT] areas during the civil war days [before 1937]. Accordingly, all CP members in the KMT areas should utilize every possible access to public, legal action, step by step and on the basis of long-range plans, without laxity and yet not with recklessness nor impetuosity, without confusing the secret and public activities of the Party, and work for the organization, education, and improvement of living conditions of the masses. Let the quality of our work among the masses furnish the major criterion for judging the Party's work in any given locality. Party units or members who do not understand, nor get close to, nor concern themselves with, the masses, are simply not good Party units and members. The above principles also apply to work in occupied areas, except that special conditions must be taken into consideration.

(3) In the areas where the Eighth Route Army and the New Fourth Army are operating, drastic economic and political reforms beneficial to the multitudinous anti-Japanese masses should be carried out. In the areas of economic reform we must carry out reductions of rent and interest rates, abolish exorbitant taxes, and improve the workers' welfare. Reforms that are already in force must be re-examined to see to what degree they are being carried out. Those reforms not yet carried out must be effected at once. In the area of political reform, a popular electoral system must be put into practice. All who obstruct the mass movement, particularly the landlord class, must gradually be excluded from the various administrative bodies and a policy of isolating them be adopted, on the basis of mass support for such a measure. Only the workers, peasants, anti-Japanese intellectuals, and those who are not opposed to the mass movement may participate in the government. Special attention should be paid to the local administrations of *ch'ü*, *hsiang* and *ts'un* [districts, groups of villages, and villages], because it is easy for the landlord and undesirable elements to hide in the *ch'ü*, *hsiang* and *ts'un* administrations pretending to be anti-Japanese. In this way we cause political power to be democratized among the masses. Yet this should not prevent us from promoting a united front—up to a certain point—with all impartial elements of the gentry as well as with landlords and merchants who can still be helpful to us in the anti-Japanese war. For example, we should encourage them to contribute money, grain, and weapons in the fight against Japan and maintain all necessary connections with them. All members of local administrative organs and political and economic agencies set up by these various administrative units must be carefully examined by the various Party units. As to local popular organizations, Party members should go deeply among the masses and lead the mass movement to fight for their own welfare and gradually organize the large majority of the masses into unions, peasant associations, women's leagues, youth corps, children's leagues, and people's militia (self-defence army, youth vanguard) to fight against Japan as well as to effect the improvement of living conditions and the enhancement of cultural standards. These popular organizations bear a great responsibility in educating the people and mobilizing their fighting enthusiasm. The local Party unit must carefully check the work of the popular organizations. The Party cell must make these mass activities the foundation of all its activities, and each cell should be the nucleus of the masses in every village or town as well as the propagandist, organizer, and leader of all mass movements and

mass struggles. The political commissars and the political departments of the Eighth Route Army and the New Fourth Army have the duty of rendering active assistance to the above-mentioned administrative work and mass activities. They [the political commissars and political departments] should also instruct the officers and soldiers of the Eighth Route Army and the New Fourth Army not to commit any acts which would alienate them from the masses, not to show any disrespect to the local Party or administrative organs or local popular organizations, but by all means to correct any erroneous tendency to regard the administrative organs and popular organizations as the army's quartermaster offices. The local Party organs and the political department of the army should, from time to time, summarize their experiences in carrying on mass activities and use the conclusions to guide the lower units in carrying on their activities.

(4) At the present stage, the CP should carefully study living conditions, sentiments, and demands of the masses and, on the basis of the above principles, should gradually proceed to organize them and educate them, leading them to a better life and mobilizing their activities, always in accordance with the demands of different circumstances, times, and specific slogans. For such mass activities are of decisive significance in overcoming the danger of capitulation and anti-Communist moves. To enable us to consolidate the CP and to build up an ideologically, politically, and organizationally strong bolshevik CCP based on nationwide mass support, it is necessary that we penetrate into the masses and lead them to carry on a sustained and hard struggle. The CC hopes that Party headquarters at all levels and all Party members will pay particular attention to this point.

31. DECISION OF THE CC ON THE ABSORPTION OF INTELLECTUAL ELEMENTS (December 1, 1939)

(1) In its prolonged and cruel war of national liberation, in its glorious struggle to build a new China, the CP must know well how to attract the intellectual elements before it will be able to organize an overwhelming resistance force, to organize the tens of millions of the peasant masses, and to promote the revolutionary cultural movement as well as develop the united front. Without the participation of the intellectuals, victory in the revolution will be impossible.

(2) In the past three years our Party and our army have made great efforts in the matter of absorbing intellectuals and have in fact absorbed a large number of revolutionary intellectuals into the Party,

the army, and government administrative work, and have had them participate in the cultural and mass movements and in the development of the united front. These have been tremendous achievements. However, certain troops have not yet realized the importance of intellectuals. On the contrary, they still have a mentality of fear and rejection towards intellectuals. Many schools that we have established still do not dare to enlist young students *en masse*. Many local Party units are still reluctant to admit intellectuals into the Party. These phenomena are a result of ignorance regarding the significant role played by intellectuals in our revolutionary mission, of a failure to appreciate the difference between intellectuals in colonial or semi-colonial countries and intellectuals in capitalist countries, the difference between intellectuals who serve the landlords and the bourgeoisie, and those who serve the proletariat and peasantry, the seriousness of the attempt being made by the bourgeois political party to win the intellectuals away from us, as well as the seriousness of the methods being employed by the Japanese imperialists to bribe and drug Chinese intellectuals, and particularly the favourable fact that our Party and army have already produced cadres who are capable of handling the intellectuals. The failure to grasp these factors has resulted in certain wrong tendencies with regard to the problem of intellectuals.

(3) Henceforth, attention should be paid to the following points:

(a) All Party units in combat areas and in the Communist armies should strive to induce large numbers of intellectuals and semi-intellectuals to join our army, enter our schools, and work in our government. Those intellectuals and semi-intellectuals who are loyal, willing to fight the Japanese, and capable of bearing hardship should be absorbed by various means. We should train them through fighting and work and let them serve in the army, in the government, and among the masses. Also those intellectuals who possess the necessary qualifications should be admitted into the Party on the basis of concrete conditions. As for those who are unable or unwilling to join the Party, we should establish smooth working relations with them and lead them to co-operate with us.

(b) In the adoption of this policy of absorbing intellectuals *en masse*, we should undoubtedly completely reject those sent over to us by the enemy or the bourgeois political party, and disloyal elements should also be rejected. A strict stand should be adopted in rejecting such elements. [Treacherous] elements which may have already infiltrated into our Party, army, or government, should be ousted on an individual basis in accordance with the evidence. However, no suspicion should be cast on those intellectuals who are comparatively loyal, and the anti-revolutionary elements should be carefully watched to prevent conspiracies on their part against the innocent.

(*c*) Intellectuals and semi-intellectuals who are useful in various degrees and who are more loyal should be given appropriate work, trained adequately, and led gradually to correct their weaknesses in the course of our sustained struggle, in order to enable them to revolutionize themselves, to adopt a truly mass point of view, and to get along harmoniously with the veteran Party members and cadres as well as with the Party members of worker or peasant stock.

(*d*) Those cadres who are opposed to the participation of intellectuals in their work, especially those cadres who are in the key units of the army, should be persuaded to realize the necessity of absorbing intellectuals to participate in such activities. At the same time, cadres of workers and peasants should be effectively encouraged to hasten their education and raise their own cultural standards in order that the "intellectualization" of worker-peasant cadres and the inculcation of intellectuals with a worker-peasant mass point of view may be achieved at the same time.

(*e*) The above principles also apply basically to combat areas and occupied areas. However, more careful screening with regard to loyalty should be employed when admitting intellectuals into the Party, for the greater protection of Party organs. As for the vast numbers of non-party intellectuals who are sympathetic towards us, appropriate liaison should be established with them, and they should be organized to participate in the heroic anti-Japanese and democratic struggle, in the cultural movement, and in the work of the united front.

(4) Our comrades must realize that a correct policy towards the intellectuals is one of the prime conditions for the success of the revolution. The wrong attitude of our Party in many places and in many military units on the problem of intellectuals during the period of the agrarian revolution[1] should never be repeated in the future. The training of intellectuals of the proletarian class cannot be accomplished without utilizing the intellectuals of the present society. The CC expects that Party headquarters at various levels and all Party members will pay close attention to this question.

Commentary R. The Economic Effort

This resolution (document no. 32), passed by the CC almost four years after the outbreak of the Sino-Japanese war, indicates that economic pressure, resulting from both the Japanese and the KMT blockades, had made its weight felt. The CCP was already well versed in political organization and propaganda. Now it felt the necessity of putting more emphasis on economic and technical work.

The references in this directive to Party personnel who "look down on economic and technical affairs . . . and are reluctant to carry on economic and technical activities or try to bargain when such work is assigned to them . . ." show that the Chinese Communists, though disciples of Marxist materialism, were not immune to the century-old tendency of Chinese literati to shun manual labour. The contradiction between firmly entrenched social mores and the needs of the modern age is clearly reflected in this instance.

In the end the CCP achieved considerable success in coping with its economic problems during and immediately after the Sino-Japanese war. In the later stages of the war the Liberated Areas became more nearly self-sufficient in such essential commodities as grain, cloth, and matches. Prices of staple commodities were kept under control; and inflation, though not absent, was much milder than in KMT areas. This preliminary experience in economic administration has received a severe testing since the take-over of the cities.

Our selection of documents in this volume on the Party line devotes relatively little attention to economic affairs. But it should never be forgotten, in analysing the sources of Chinese Communist strength, that one of their major appeals to the Chinese people has been their promise and performance in meeting the urgent economic needs of everyday life—whether by war-time food production drives or by post-war efforts to curb inflation.

32. DECISION OF THE CC ON THE PARTICIPATION OF PARTY MEMBERS IN ECONOMIC AND TECHNICAL WORK (May 1, 1941)

(1) We must explain to the whole Party that various types of economic and technical work are an indispensable part of our revolutionary activities. They are concrete revolutionary work. Some Party organizations and Party members who possess only a narrow and abstract understanding of our revolutionary work or even look down on economic and technical work, considering it to be without serious political significance, should be corrected in their erroneous views.

(2) We must explain that both ideological training and participation in practical work are essential duties of every Party member. In the revolutionary movement the members of the CP, a party which directs

an army and a political administration, should not "engage exclusively" in ideological work (though there can and should be a small group that engages solely in ideological studies) and stand apart from practical work, nor engage solely in practical work and ignore ideological studies completely. Thus the tendency to use ideological studies as an excuse for not participating in practical work, and that of burying oneself in practical work without taking some time out for ideological studies, should both be corrected.

(3) Every Party member should perform unconditionally the work assigned to him by the Party, and (the attitude of) some Party members who are reluctant to carry on economic and technical activities, or try to bargain when such work is assigned to them, should be corrected.

(4) All Party members who serve in the economic and technical areas must learn from both non-party and Party experts. It is their duty to learn sincerely and to familiarize themselves with their work, in order to promote the progress of our work of reconstruction in various areas and to see to it that each Party member acquires the necessary technical skills for earning an independent living in society.

(5) The Party must strengthen its leadership among Party and non-party members who participate in economic and technical work, promote their progress in political training, and assist them in every way possible.

Secretariat, CC

Commentary S. The Reaffirmation of Leninist Discipline

Liu Shao-ch'i has been widely regarded as the leader of a "pro-Russian" group within the CCP leadership. Whatever may be the truth of this supposition he is noted as a chief theoretician of the Chinese Party. His essay *On the Intra-Party Struggle* is an important link in the series of documents issued by the CCP in the early 1940s under the name of *Documents on the Correction of [unorthodox] Tendencies (Cheng-feng wen-hsien)*. The movement for the "Correction of [unorthodox] tendencies" was probably launched with the aim of rallying and reconsolidating the forces of Chinese Communism in order to overcome the blurring and unsettling effects of the united front strategy. It may also have been launched with a view to preparing the Communist movement for the contingency of a possible disintegration of the united front at some time in the future. Essentially it involved a reclarification of basic Chinese Communist positions on all matters of doctrine and organization. It re-emphasized certain perennial core elements of the Communist tradition, and also clarified the New Democracy line in various spheres of activity. By thus clarifying Party positions on all issues, the CCP leadership could more easily separate the sheep from the goats—i.e. separate "right and left opportunists" from faithful followers of the Party line.

The movement concerned itself with three types of tendencies: (1) in learning, (2) in the Party, and (3) in art and literature. But at the heart of the whole movement there lay the question of proper Party organization and Party discipline. For so long as the basic Leninist principles of Party organization are not accepted, incorrect tendencies in other spheres of Communist activity are an ever-present possibility. Thus Mao Tse-tung constantly insists on "objectivity" in applying Marxist-Leninist doctrine to concrete Chinese realities. But the norm of what is objective and what not, must be fixed by the Party leadership, just as in many churches the correct interpretation of the Scriptures is always fixed by ecclesiastic authority. The proper understanding of the Leninist concept of the Party lies at the very heart of the whole *Cheng-feng* movement.

Viewed in this light, Liu Shao-ch'i's essay emerges as one of the basic texts of the whole movement, since it attempts to define, in detail, the proper attitude of the Communist towards his Party in one of its most important spheres of activity, namely, the intra-Party struggle.

What is meant by "intra-Party struggle"? In the first place, it must be noted that struggle within the Party is not regarded as a deplorable phenomenon. On the contrary, Liu's whole essay is designed to distinguish proper methods of struggle from improper methods. In Liu's own words, "Intra-Party struggle is absolutely necessary to maintain the Party's purity and independence." Secondly, "intra-Party struggle" is not an open debate which aims at the attainment of truth as its end-product. It is rather a struggle aimed at freeing the Party from infection by incorrect views and wrong attitudes. The Party already possesses the truth and the task of the struggle is to bring into the open incorrect tendencies within the Party and then to eliminate them. The intra-Party struggle is thus a method of strengthening Party uniformity and decidedly not a method of encouraging independent views.

There is an assumption underlying Liu's essay that the Party is proceeding down the central beam of History and that all divergencies represent a straying away from the beam. As Liu insists, the Party's direction is not down a middle way between left and right, but is the only way. All other directions are simply false.

Contrary to Liu's claim, however, the CCP has not in fact proceeded down a "straight path" in the course of its history, but has, on the contrary, made many sharp turns. It is therefore quite possible that a Party member who was thoroughly devoted to the Party line in the Soviet period of the early 1930s, and who stubbornly clings to that line, may find himself a "left opportunist" in the New Democracy period of the early 1940s. Heresies are thus likely to emerge in any quarter. The only ultimate criterion of Party loyalty is the disciplined acceptance of the Party line at any given moment, no matter how that line may shift. It can be seen that the tasks of intra-Party struggle are unending.

Liu's main purpose is to point out certain pitfalls and excesses which are to be avoided in the course of intra-Party struggle. The struggle, he insists, must be a struggle of principles and not of personalities. It must concern matters of basic principle and not matters of tactic, where legitimate difference of opinion is possible. Such forms of "unprincipled" struggle represent "leftist" excesses. On the other hand, to gloss over real differences of principle out of personal considerations is one of the typical excesses of "rightism". The true area of intra-Party struggle lies between the Scylla of "leftism" and the Charybdis of "rightism". Also to be avoided is any tendency to wash the Party's linen in circles outside of the Party.

In this document for Party members, Liu has not even begun to deal with some of the real difficulties involved. For example, he draws a sharp line between struggle on matters of principle and "struggle against Mr. X and Mr. Y". But how, then, does he propose to deal with the type of attack which uses the façade of "principle" when its essential motive is an attack on Mr. X and Mr. Y? A skilled dialectician who has an aversion for Mr. X can generally prove that Mr. X has been "incorrect" on some matter of principle, since the principles are often highly ambiguous to begin with. Again, Liu draws a distinction between struggle on matters of principle and on matters of "everyday administrative affairs", where compromise is possible. Marxism-Leninism, it is true, has always insisted on this distinction in the abstract, but it has generally failed to draw a clear line of demarcation between these two spheres in practice. The Party leadership may at any time choose to consider that some matter of "administrative affairs" is actually a matter of principle. The lower echelons can never be sure. Time and again in the world Communist movement, lower functionaries have reached compromises on what appeared to be "administrative affairs" only to find that they had really compromised on basic matters of principle.

To Liu, however, such difficulties do not arise from universal human tendencies. They are, rather, the result of the fact that either the Party membership is not sufficiently enlightened in Party doctrine or the Party has become infected by impure influences from "non-proletarian" classes. These evils can be cured either by eliminating the impure influences or by providing the membership with a more thorough education in Party doctrine.

One of the most significant passages in the whole essay appears at the very end where Liu Shao-ch'i discusses the proper relationship between the various levels of the Party hierarchy in the intra-Party struggle. Here the authoritarian, hierarchical concept of intra-Party relations becomes most evident.

In general, this essay *On the Intra-Party Struggle* is designed to reassert the Leninist nature of the CCP. At the same time the document does reflect the atmosphere of the New Democracy period in its strong emphasis on moderation and on methods of persuasion in dealing with deviant tendencies. Where possible, Liu urges that deviators be won back to orthodoxy by conciliatory methods and by having the heterodox see the error of their ways. Here, too, Chinese Communism, in its New Democracy form, seems to have represented an unusual tendency in the world Communist movement as a whole, where the "intra-Party struggle" had come to be conducted in an atmosphere of unmitigated terror. How long the Chinese Communist Party can maintain these features remains to be seen.

33. LIU SHAO-CH'I: ON THE INTRA-PARTY STRUGGLE
(July 2, 1941) [extract]

I. INTRODUCTION

[p. 153] Comrades! Recently we have raised in the Party the problem of strengthening the Party spirit among Party members. I have heard that the CC has passed a resolution on this question and that we shall be able to obtain it before long. In order to strengthen the Party spirit among Party members, we have to develop a series of concrete struggles in thought so that all types of undesirable tendencies transgressing that spirit will be opposed. But what is to be considered the correct method of developing the struggles in thought within the

Party and what is to be considered the incorrect method? This is the question I would now like to discuss. . . .

[p. 154] Everyone knows that our Party is a party of the proletariat, that it leads the broad masses to battle. . . . The Party and the proletariat have been constantly encircled by the power of the non-proletarian classes: the big and petty bourgeoisie, the peasantry, and even the remnants of feudal forces. These classes, either struggling against the proletariat or in alliance with it, have infiltrated, through the unstable elements within the Party and proletariat, to their heart, and constantly influenced them in ideology, living habits, theory, and action. This, then, is the source of all erroneous, evil tendencies within the Party. It is the social origin of all opportunism within the Party and also the source of the intra-Party struggle.

The intra-Party struggle is a reflection of the struggle outside the Party.

Since the day of its origin the Party has not only fought enemies outside the Party, but has also fought the non-proletarian influences of enemies within the Party. The two struggles are to be distinguished, but both are necessary and, in class substance, they are the same. If the Party does not engage in the second struggle, if it does not constantly carry out a struggle to oppose all undesirable tendencies within the Party, does not constantly reject all non-proletarian ideology and overcome "left" and right opportunism, then non-proletarian ideology and "left" and right opportunism will be able to develop in the Party and influence and guide the Party. . . .

[p. 155] This intra-Party struggle is primarily the struggle in thought, the contents of which are divergencies and mutual opposition in principles of thought. In the Party, even though divergencies and mutual opposition among the comrades can lead to political divergencies and even, under certain conditions, unavoidably lead to divergencies concerning Party organization, the struggle in thought remains its basic substance and content. Therefore an intra-Party struggle which does not contain divergencies in principles of thought, but only embodies personal attacks among the comrades without principle, is a struggle without principle and without content. Within the Party this type of struggle—without principle and without content—is entirely unnecessary. It harms the Party and should be carefully avoided by Party members.

Intra-Party struggle is absolutely necessary to maintain the Party's purity and independence, to guarantee that Party activities are carried on the line which represents the highest interests of the proletariat, and to maintain the Party's proletarian substance. With this aim, the intra-Party struggle must proceed in two directions, advance on two fronts. [This is] because enemy thought influences the Party from two directions, because it attacks the Party from the right and from the "left", because it is manifested in the Party as right and "left" opportunism. Therefore, [in] the intra-Party struggle, [we] must oppose right opportunism and at the same time oppose "left" opportunism. We must struggle against both, and only then will we be able to maintain the proletarian substance of our Party. . . .

[p. 156] Comrade Stalin said, "Only if we struggle for this or that principle, for this or that objective to be established, or to be chosen in attaining this (other) objective . . . only in this way can (we) overcome the contradictions. In everyday administrative questions and in purely practical questions, compromise can and must be made with those within the Party who hold differing views. But if these questions involve divergence in principle, then no compromise or 'middle' way will bring about a solution. In questions of principle, there is not and cannot be a 'middle' way; either these principles become the foundation of Party work, or those (principles) become the foundation of Party work. In questions of principle, the 'middle' way is the 'way' of the shut-off mind, the 'way' of denying divergencies, the 'way' of degradation and death in Party thought. The policy of the 'middle' way is not our policy, but the policy of a political party which is withering and daily approaching putrefaction. Such a policy cannot but turn a party into an empty, bureaucratic organ, separated from the working masses, and, like a wooden idol, with no function whatsoever. Certainly this way is not our way."

He also said, "In the process of overcoming its various intra-Party contradictions, our Party develops and consolidates itself."

Here then lies the necessity for the intra-Party struggle. . . .

II. SPECIAL CONDITIONS IN WHICH THE CCP WAS FOUNDED AND TENDENCIES IN THE INTRA-PARTY STRUGGLE

First: [p. 160] The CCP was established after the [Russian] October Revolution and after the Russian Bolshevik [Party] had already achieved victory and become a living model. Therefore, from the beginning, it was under the guidance of the CI and was established according to the principles of Lenin.

Second: From the beginning, in thought and in organization, the

CCP has not been influenced by the Second International of the European social-democratic parties.

[p. 161] *Third:* China has not gone through the period of the "peaceful" development of capitalism, such as was experienced in Europe, which allowed the working class to engage in a peaceful parliamentary struggle, nor does China have Europe's class of labour aristocracy.

Fourth: A comparatively large segment of the membership of the CCP comes from the petty-bourgeois class and peasantry, and there are also some lumpen [proletariat] elements. This is the social foundation for "left" and right opportunism in the CCP.

Because of the above four conditions, our Party's development has, in the subjective sense, been, from the beginning, according to the principles and way of Lenin. A great many Party members can recite the organizational principles of the Bolshevik Party from memory. The traditions and practices of the social-democratic parties are not to be found in our Party. As a consequence, we have travelled a straight path. From the time of its organization our Party has had self-criticism and thought-struggle, democratic-centralism, and strict organization and discipline. It has not allowed the existence of factions, and has rigorously opposed liberalism, autonomous unionism, and the tendencies of the Economists,[1] etc. Because of this, a systematic theory of right opportunism in organization has not yet been raised openly in the Party. . . .

However, the special conditions and circumstances of the period in which the CCP was established gave rise to two influences; one was good and enabled us, at the very beginning, to establish a Leninist CCP which, subjectively, followed strictly the principles of Lenin, for from the outset the Party [growth] was accompanied by rigorous self-criticism and intra-Party struggle which enabled it to progress rapidly and acted as a force motivating the Party's progress. But there was another influence which [p. 162] often caused our comrades to go to another extreme and commit another error, an influence which frequently caused the intra-Party struggle to become violent and excessive, to go beyond limits and move towards "left" deviation. . . .

A great many comrades mechanically and erroneously conceive of the principles of Lenin as absolutes. They think that a high degree of centralism in Party organization precludes democracy within the Party, that the necessity for an intra-Party struggle precludes peace within the Party, that the Party's position as the highest form of proletarian organization, leading all other proletarian mass organizations in political affairs, precludes the independent nature of trade unions and other organizations of the workers and toiling masses, that unified, iron discipline destroys the individuality of Party members and their initiative and creativity. . . .

[p. 163] Many comrades do not understand that the intra-Party struggle is a struggle in principle; a struggle to uphold one principle or another, to establish one battle objective or another, to select one method or another of attaining the battle objective. They do not understand that in questions of everyday administrative affairs, in questions of a purely practical nature, compromises can and should be made with those in the Party holding different views. They do not know nor understand that in questions of principle, in questions of selecting battle objectives, and in questions of the selection of methods for the attainment of these battle objectives, they should struggle uncompromisingly with those in the Party holding different views. . . .

Many comrades do not understand the nature of principles or questions of principle, or the nature of questions of the Party's strategical plan and tactical line, nor how to grasp these principles and the difference in questions of strategical plan and tactical line to carry out the struggle. Their theoretical level and political experience are still extremely low, and they cannot grasp these highly important questions and fight for them. However, they mechanically remember that it is necessary to carry out struggle within the Party and that it is wrong not to struggle. Although they cannot grasp these important questions nor raise a question from principle, they still want to struggle. Accordingly, able only to grasp individual phenomena and individual questions, they proceed to carry on a struggle and argument, without principle or content with those in the Party holding different views, and thus create disunity, mutual opposition, [p. 164] and organizational divergencies among our comrades. This undesirable condition in the intra-Party struggle exists in our Party.

What has been described above is a deviation in the struggle within the CCP; in our Party it is a deviation of special seriousness (although it also exists in foreign parties). It is a case of the intra-Party struggle being carried too far, going beyond limits, travelling to another extreme—"left" opportunism in the intra-Party struggle and in Party organization (precluding democracy in the Party, precluding a harmonious peace based on principles in the Party, precluding the relative independence of trade unions and other mass organizations, and denying the Party member's individuality, his initiative and creativity).

It has been produced under the special environment and special conditions of the CCP. . . .

[p. 165] Thus the following three deviations may be said to exist in the intra-Party struggle in the CCP: (1) Liberalism and Compromise-ism; (2) mechanical and excessive intra-Party struggle, the "left" opportunism in Party organization and in intra-Party struggle; and (3) unprincipled disputes and struggles within the Party. . . .

III. MANIFESTATIONS OF MECHANICAL AND EXCESSIVE STRUGGLE
    WITHIN THE PARTY

Comrades! Today I shall not speak on liberalism, the first of the [p. 166] three deviations in the Party struggle described above. . . . I only wish to point out that the tendency towards liberalism in the Party has recently had an appreciable development, that in many respects it has already become a principal tendency in the intra-Party struggle, and that the development of thought struggle in the Party has been insufficient. Thus many erroneous tendencies and undesirable phenomena have not received timely correction and Party discipline has gradually relaxed. This is very undesirable. It is to be attributed to the fact that recently a great number of intellectual elements and new Party members have entered the Party, bringing with them to the Party strong bourgeois, liberal ideas. Ideologically, politically, and organizationally, they have not been tempered by the iron discipline of the proletariat. At the same time, some comrades, who have in the past committed the errors of "left" deviation and carrying the intra-Party struggle to excess, now turn around and commit the errors of right deviation and liberalism. During the long period of the united front, the possibility of the bourgeoisie influencing the Party has also increased. Counter-revolutionary elements hidden in the Party have used every method to develop and support liberalism within the Party, and as a consequence the tendency towards liberalism developed. It is a tendency which must be strictly opposed in the struggle to strengthen the Party spirit. . . .

[p. 167] Where is mechanical and excessive struggle in the Party manifested? It is manifested in the following instances:

[p. 168] *First:* in local and army Party units, "struggle meetings" are frequently held. They are even held in such non-party bodies as government organs and mass organizations. These meetings are arranged beforehand so that the principal object is not to discuss work, but to attack certain men, not to struggle primarily against "issues", but against individuals, not to struggle against incorrect thoughts and principles, but against certain persons. The object of the so-called "struggle against Mr. X or Mr. Y" is to attack certain comrades who are in error. The "struggle meetings" are in essence courts of justice for comrades, in which the principal object is not the resolution of questions on the basis of thought, but, through organizational processes, to suppress those comrades who dare to hold divergent views of their own (without any certainty that these views are really incorrect), or those comrades who upset the applecart. In a great majority of the cases where attacks are launched against individuals in "struggle meetings", organizational conclusions are the result. It is quite clear that such a method of struggle is incorrect. . . .

[p. 169] *Second:* the mechanical and excessive form of intra-Party struggle is also manifested in the following conditions: some comrades think that the more savage the intra-Party struggle, the better; the more grave the manner in which the questions are raised, the better; the more mistakes discovered, the more names called, the more blame laid on others, the sharper the criticism, the more severe and rude the method and attitude of criticism, the better . . . and if the words are louder, faces longer, and the fangs sticking out farther . . . they are considered to be better and "most revolutionary". In the intra-Party struggle and self-criticism [such people] do not endeavour to do what is suitable, do not weigh their opinions or stop when they have gone far enough; they struggle on with no limit. It is clear that this attitude is also entirely incorrect.

Third: Some comrades do not yet understand that the intra-Party struggle is basically a struggle in thought, and that only if unanimity is obtained in thought can it then be maintained and strengthened in political affairs, organization, and activities in the Party. Only after questions are resolved on the basis of thought and principle can they then be resolved in organization and Party activities. However, it is not an easy matter to obtain unanimity and resolve questions in thought and principle, to overcome the false principles held by others, to correct their false principles, to transform their thoughts, and correct their [p. 170] long-cherished principles, views, and prejudices. Nor can this end be reached by simple means, whether they be a few words, the struggle meeting method, or simply coercion and force. This end can be achieved only through persevering persuasion and education, and complex struggles by rather prolonged education, struggle, and actual revolutionary work. . . .

[p. 171] *Fourth:* [The fourth case] is a failure to distinguish between the methods to be employed in the struggles within and outside the Party. Some comrades take the methods of the intra-Party struggle and use them mechanically in mass organizations and organs outside the Party, and use the methods of the intra-Party struggle in the struggle of non-Party cadres and masses; some other comrades use the methods of the struggle (which is carried on) outside the Party, the methods of struggle against the enemy and oppositional elements in struggling with their own comrades; they use the methods used against the enemy and opposition and apply them against comrades in the Party. All [p. 172] incitements to dissension and cunning schemes are used. Administrative procedures—investigation, arrest, imprisonment, and trial—are also put to use in the intra-Party struggle. For example, the ultra-"leftist" errors committed by some comrades engaged in the liquidation of traitors were mostly the result of failure to distinguish strictly between the struggles within and outside the Party, a confusion of the intra-Party thought struggle and the work of liquidation of traitors. There are frequently enemies cunningly hidden within the Party; to expose and expel this hidden enemy from the Party it is necessary to carry on a struggle based on actual facts. But this struggle and the educational struggle which must be carried on against Communist Party members who commit errors are two entirely different matters. The struggles within and outside the Party are closely connected, but the methods and forms are different.

There are also some comrades (as a matter of fact, they can no longer be called comrades) who openly avail themselves of and rely on resources outside the Party to engage in the intra-Party struggle and threaten and blackmail the Party. For example, some rely on certain of their achievements, on the troops they command or their weapons, on their mass support or certain of their connections in the united front, to carry on a struggle against the Party and higher organs and threaten them (so as to make them) accept their demands and views; they propagandize and agitate for independence from the Party. Or some take advantage of non-Party, and even bourgeois and enemy newspapers and magazines and various conferences, to criticize the Party and carry on a struggle against higher Party organs and certain comrades and cadres. Obviously this error is as grave as that committed by those who rely on the power of the Party to coerce, dominate, and oppress the non-Party masses, and engage in extortion and blackmail against men outside the Party. Such men struggle against the Party from a position outside the Party; although they still bear the name of CP members, they have already completely divorced themselves from the Party stand and become Party oppositionists.

Fifth: Within our Party a great many questions are being or have been settled in conferences; this is an excellent thing. Yet, in individual organizations, many conferences are held for which the work of preparation, [p. 173] investigation, and research has not been done beforehand, and many controversies and arguments often spring up. Also in all conferences, the task of forming conclusions invariably falls on the highest responsible person attending, and these conference conclusions amount to resolutions; here a great many defects also often arise. In some conference debates, I have seen the commissars [*chih-tao-yüan*] or secretaries of the cells, or other responsible comrades eventually had to form the conclusions [of the discussion]. Yet some responsible comrades themselves have neither a grasp of the situation, nor a clear understanding of the issue; however, they are compelled to form the conclusions; if they do not, they cannot hold that responsible post. Since these responsible comrades have to form the conclusions, there are some who are extremely distressed, break out in a sweat, and make very rough conclusions; these conclusions then amount to resolutions and determine events. This procedure naturally gives rise to a great many errors. Some comrades who do not yet have a firm grasp of questions, are still unwilling to make this fact clear when they make decisions, unwilling to request a period for consideration and research or time to ask higher echelons for instruction. In order to save face and maintain their position, they claim that they do have a firm grasp of the situation, and make decisions carelessly, and the results are often incorrect. Such a situation should also be corrected. . . .

The above are some of the important manifestations of the mechanical and excessive form of intra-Party struggle.

I have naturally cited the worst examples above, and I do not mean to say that they have been universally prevalent in the past and present [p. 174] intra-Party struggle. Yet these forms certainly do exist in the intra-Party struggle, and at one time in the past they dominated the Party and were the principal forms of the intra-Party struggle.

What have been the results in the Party of this type of incorrect and inappropriate intra-Party struggle? The following unfavourable results have been produced:

First: It has assisted the development of patriarchalism in the Party. Under this form of intra-Party struggle, individual leaders and leading organs have oppressed many Party members so that they did not dare speak or criticize. It has created a dictatorship [*tu-tuan*] of individuals or minorities within the Party.

Second: On the other hand, it has assisted the development of extreme democratic tendencies and liberalism within the Party. A formal kind of peace and unity have been manifested in the Party, for many comrades ordinarily do not dare speak or criticize. But once the continued concealment of contradictions becomes impossible, once the situation becomes serious and mistakes are exposed, they criticize and fight recklessly; opposition, schism, and organizational troubles develop in the Party, and it is difficult to settle them. This, then, is the reverse side of the system of Party patriarchalism.

Third: The influence (of this type of struggle) has been to make the correct establishment of intra-Party democratic-centralism difficult, and intra-Party democracy abnormal, irregular, or extremely deficient.

Fourth: It has obstructed the development of enthusiasm, initiative, and creativity on the part of Party members, and has weakened their spirit of responsibility towards the Party and their work. Comrades under its influence do not dare take positive responsibility, do not dare work or create freely, and do not examine and study problems and conditions carefully. It cultivates their tendency to depend on bureaucratic procedure and be yes-men.

Fifth: It has assisted the development of party sectarianism, the development of an unprincipled factional struggle among Party members and the creation of a state of mind which fears criticism and conflict. In certain Party members it has cultivated the attitude of "taking care of oneself", and the attitude that "one affair more is worse than one less".

Sixth: It gives Trotskyite spies and counter-revolutionary elements all the more opportunity to destroy the Party and gives the counter-revolution [p. 175] all the more excuses with which to attack the Party. Trotskyite spies take special advantage of contradictions in the Party and incorrect intra-Party struggles to further their activities for the destruction of the Party, and try to win over those who have been reprimanded and are dissatisfied with the Party. . . .

For a rather long period, these excessive and mechanical forms in the intra-Party struggle have been creating abnormalities in Party life and causing the Party great losses. Despite the fact that the highest leading organs of the Party have already corrected their errors and these forms do not now dominate the struggle being conducted throughout the Party, these forms still have not been corrected in certain middle and lower level or in certain individual organs; they are still more or less commonly existent. . . .

IV. ON THE UNPRINCIPLED INTRA-PARTY STRUGGLE

Comrades! I am now going to speak on another deviation in the intra-Party struggle—the unprincipled struggle within the Party. The prevalence of this phenomenon is especially common and grave within the CCP. Although the so-called "gossip movement" exists in foreign Communist Parties, I think it probably is not so serious abroad as in the CCP. . . .

[p. 176] What are the unprincipled disputes and struggles in the Party?

I consider the following instances of dispute and struggle within the Party to be without principle; that is, they run counter to those common stands and principles which promote the interests of our Party and the proletarian revolution.

First: Some comrades do not raise questions and struggle with other comrades from a Party standpoint or for the sake of the interests of the entire Party, but do so from the standpoint of individual or fractional interests. This is to say, the stand from which they engage in the intra-Party struggle is incorrect. As a consequence, their views on problems and their solutions and methods in dealing with them are also incorrect. Only if their individual or minority interests are benefited do they give approval or support in dealing with a matter. If their individual or minority interests are not benefited, they stand in opposition and do not give their approval. They are unconcerned with the interests of the Party or the revolution and put these in a place of secondary importance. . . .

[p. 177] *Second:* Some comrades provoke conflicts and disputes within the Party, not to improve the Party, but with the opposite purpose in mind or other motives. This purpose is incorrect and the struggle they provoke is also without principle. For example, some comrades foment disputes in the Party and struggle with their comrades to show off, improve their position, save face, or even to vent their hatred and seek revenge. They upset their comrades' work and plans and wreck the order and solidarity of the Party, but fail to give their attention to prevailing circumstances and conditions. Such are the characteristics of this form of unprincipled struggle.

[p. 178] *Third:* Some comrades do not start from a basis of principle in raising questions for acceptance or rejection by the Party. It is only on the basis of their own feelings, likes and dislikes, that they raise questions and struggle, only for the emotional release of the moment or for the soothing of their ruffled tempers, that they revile others and give vent to their anger. This is also a form of struggle without principle. Some comrades, because their experience is limited or their theoretical level low, cannot raise questions for debate on the basis of principle. It is only on particular or miscellaneous questions, questions of a purely practical nature, or everyday administrative questions, which do not involve principle, that they debate with absolute obstinacy. But since this does not involve general questions of principle it is also an unprincipled form of struggle which should not be insisted on. . . .

The fourth (instance) is to engage in the intra-Party struggle unscrupulously or without observing organizational procedures, to befriend or attack comrades in an unprincipled way, provoking dissension, betraying or secretly scheming against comrades, or not speaking to a man's face, but speaking wildly behind his back, irresponsibly criticizing the Party, spreading unfounded opinions, circulating rumours, telling lies, and calumniating others.

The cases cited above are all examples of the struggle without principle. Next, there are also some comrades who infuse certain elements of unprincipled struggle into the struggle concerning principles, or who, under the protective banner of a struggle concerning principles, engage in a struggle which is without principle. In addition, there are some comrades who pay special attention to the quarrels between certain persons, or to the discordant relations between certain persons, instead of the substance of their controversy.

[p. 182] What are the origins of the unprincipled and the mechanical and excessive struggle within the Party? They spring from the following sources:

First: The generally low theoretical level of comrades in the Party and, in many respects, the insufficiency of their experience. For a long time, a leadership and "centre" for the entire Party have actually not materialized and the leadership and the "centre" in the various localities have, up to the present, materialized to only a very slight degree.

[p. 183] *Second:* The petty-bourgeois elements within the Party are strong and the rashness and madness of the petty-bourgeois, and the peasant petty-bourgeois spirit of revenge have constantly influenced the intra-Party struggle.

Third: The democratic life within the Party is not normal, a spirit of objective, mutual discussion of problems among the comrades has not developed, and the tendency to judge and decide problems in a crude, subjective manner is still prevalent to a serious degree.

Fourth: Opportunist elements have infiltrated into the Party, and a certain opportunist psychology exists in a group of comrades within the Party. In order to prove their own "bolshevization" they often intentionally go a little to the "left", thinking that "left" is better than right, or they attack others in order to raise their own prestige.

Fifth: Trotskyite spies and counter-revolutionary elements have infiltrated the Party, making use of the intra-Party struggle to sabotage the Party. Under the cover of the Party banner, traitorous Trotskyite elements often deliberately attack certain comrades, and after the attack still other traitorous Trotskyite elements absorb the comrades who thus have been attacked into the Trotskyite group as traitors. . . .

V. [p. 184] HOW TO CARRY OUT THE INTRA-PARTY STRUGGLE

Comrades! The question before us now is already quite clear, that is, what is the correct and appropriate way to carry out the intra-Party struggle? . . .

First: Our comrades must realize at the outset that the intra-Party struggle is a most serious and responsible matter. It must be carried out with a grave and responsible attitude and certainly not in a slip-shod manner. In carrying out (the struggle) we must first of all base ourselves completely on a correct Party stand, a public spirited, unselfish stand, which is completely in the interest of the Party, for the progress of [Party] work, and of assistance to other comrades in correcting their errors and understanding problems. We must ourselves first see things clearly, see the problems clearly, carry out systematic investigation and research, and at the same time carry out the struggle in a well-organized, well-guided, and prepared manner.

Our comrades should know that you can only correct others' mistakes if you yourself first adopt a correct stand, and you can only rectify the heterodoxy in others if you yourself are first completely orthodox. "You must first rectify yourself, then you can rectify others." . . .

Second: [p. 185] Comrades should understand that the intra-Party struggle is the struggle between differing thoughts and differing principles and (come from) the mutual opposition between thoughts and differing principles in the Party. It is completely necessary that clear boundaries be drawn in thoughts and [p. 186] principles. But in organization, in the methods of struggle, in attitudes of speech and criticism, there should be the least possible opposition, the greatest possible use of moderate forms in discussion and debate. . . .

Opposition in (matters of) thought and principle, and the least possible opposition in questions of organization and method: this is the correct way which we should adopt in the intra-Party struggle. A great many comrades' errors consist of the following tendencies: on one hand, they do not (develop) clear-cut opposition and divergence in thought and principle, and on the other hand they oppose and struggle confusingly on (questions of) organizational operation and on the methods of the struggle. . . .

[p. 187] *Third:* Criticism of Party organization, Party members, and Party work should be appropriate and measured. Bolshevik self-criticism has its bolshevik toleration. Excessive criticism, the exaggeration of others' mistakes, and baseless accusations are all wrong. It is not true that the fiercer the intra-Party struggle, the better; it should have appropriate limits and seek a suitable level. Both "excessive" and "insufficient" (struggle) are undesirable. . . .

Fourth is the general cessation of the holding of struggle meetings both within and outside the Party. (We) should point out defects and errors through the summation and checking of [our] work. We should first (direct our energy) "against things", and afterwards "against persons". . . .

[p. 188] *Fifth:* A comrade who is being criticized or punished must be given every possible opportunity to state his case. When testimony is given against a comrade and when organizational decisions are being made, the comrade himself should ordinarily be informed and the decisions should be made in his presence. When the comrade does not accept the decision, the case should be referred, after debate, to higher authorities. (In all cases where non-acceptance is voiced after the punishment is announced, the Party organization should appeal, even for those who do not wish to appeal.) No Party organization can forbid a comrade who has received punishment to appeal to higher echelons. . . .

After debate has been concluded on questions of thought and principle [p. 189] it is possible to pass a majority decision even if final unanimity has not been reached in the Party. After majority decisions have been made, minority comrades who still hold different views have the right to maintain these views under the condition that they follow the majority strictly in matters of organization and action.

If a certain number of low ranking Party committees or comrades request that higher ranking Party committees or leading organs call an appropriate meeting for the examination of Party work, the higher Party committees should call the meeting and carry out the examination if possible.

Sixth: A clear line should be drawn between the intra-Party and extra-Party struggles, yet at the same time an appropriate relationship should be established. The methods of the intra-Party struggle should not be carried over to the struggle outside the Party, and the methods of the extra-Party struggle should not be carried over to the intra-Party struggle; even less should forces and conditions outside the Party be used to struggle within and intimidate the Party. All Party members must be strictly attentive and cautious lest hidden Trotskyite spies and counter-revolutionary elements take advantage of contradictions and the struggle within the Party to carry on activities ruinous to the Party. In the intra-Party struggle, Party members should take care not to be utilized by these elements. This can be avoided only if all strictly observe Party discipline and engage correctly in the intra-Party struggle.

Within the Party, only a legal struggle is permitted; only a struggle in thought is permitted. Any type of struggle contrary to the Party Constitution and Party discipline is not to be tolerated.

Seventh is the prohibition of unprincipled intra-Party disputes.

(1) If any Party member has an opinion on the leading organs of the Party or on any Party organization, he can raise the issue and criticism only to the proper Party organization. He is not permitted to speak irresponsibly among the masses.

(2) If any Party member has an opinion on another Party member or on a responsible man in the Party, he can only express criticism to their faces or in certain organizations. He is not permitted to gossip loosely.

(3) If any Party member or low ranking committee has an opinion of a high ranking Party committee, it can only be expressed to high ranking [p. 190] Party committees, or a request can be made to call a meeting for examination, or a charge can be made to the higher ranking committees. They are not permitted to speak wildly or transmit (the controversies) to the lower ranks.

(4) If any Party member discovers that another member is acting incorrectly and in such a way as to endanger Party interests, he must report to the proper Party organization; there may be no covering up or mutual screening.

(5) All Party members should support correct influences and orthodoxy- and oppose incorrect influences and all heterodox speeches and

actions. They should seriously reprimand those Party members who like to gossip, broadcast, discover people's secrets, or spread rumours. Leading organs of the Party should issue orders as the occasion demands, forbidding Party members to discuss certain questions.

(6) As the occasion demands, leading organs at every level should talk with those comrades who like to gossip or engage in unprincipled disputes, and give correction, issue warning, or other punishments.

(7) Party committees at all levels should respect the opinions raised by every comrade. They should call meetings regularly, discuss questions, investigate work, and give Party members opportunity to fully express their views.

Unprincipled disputes should be generally forbidden, without a judgment as to which is right and which is wrong. Because they are without principle, there is no right or wrong involved which can be judged.

When we endeavour to settle an unprincipled dispute among our comrades, we should certainly not be content to make a decision based on the dispute itself, but should examine and summarize the relevant work, and indicate future tasks, direction of work, the general line, plans, etc., directly and on principle. Within the framework of these summaries, tasks, courses, lines, and plans, we should criticize the comrades' incorrect views, then afterwards solicit their views to find whether or not they still differ. If they still differ, it has become a dispute in principle, and an unprincipled dispute among comrades has been raised to the level of principle. If the comrades have no difference of opinion on principle, then they should be requested to unite under these summaries, tasks, and courses, and struggle [p. 191] unanimously for their complete fulfilment. Comrades should be asked to avoid all other questions that are without principle. They should settle unprincipled disputes by starting from a summary of past work, solving the present tasks, then promoting the work at hand. Unprincipled disputes cannot be settled otherwise. We certainly should not adopt the attitude of judges in deciding unprincipled disputes, which will not be solved in this manner. If the decision is not made appropriately, both sides will be dissatisfied and the dispute will continue. . . .

In brief, the intra-Party struggle consists basically of divergencies and struggle in thought and principle. All in the Party should reason, clear up the issues, and have some line of reasoning to speak about. Otherwise it is wrong. If lines of reasoning are thrashed out, there is nothing which cannot be done well and easily. In the Party, we should cultivate the spirit of reasoning. The standards by which to judge the correctness or incorrectness of a line of reasoning are the interest of the struggle being carried on by the Party and the proletariat, the submission of the partial interest to the interest of the whole, and the submission of the short-range interest to the long-range interest. All reasoning and all proposals which are in the interest of the struggle of the Party and proletariat—in the long-range interest of the struggle of the entire Party and proletariat—are correct. Those which are detrimental to these interests are all incorrect. . . .

A bolshevik is reasonable, a supporter of the truth, a person who understands reason and is able to be reasonable with others in an agreeable manner; he is not an aggressively unreasonable, irrational fighter.

[p. 193] Comrades! These are the methods I have proposed for carrying on the intra-Party struggle.

I believe that our comrades should follow these methods in carrying on the intra-Party struggle, in opposing the various incorrect tendencies within the Party, and in examining the Party spirit of individual Party members and especially of (Party) cadres. The further strengthening of our Party in thought and organization: this is our goal.

COMMENTARY T. THE CHENG-FENG MOVEMENT

The following three speeches of Mao Tse-tung, all made in the first half of 1942, laid down the basic principles of the *Cheng-feng* movement—a programme for the correction of unorthodox tendencies in the various spheres of CCP activity, in which several thousand CCP members and officials received formal ideological training at Yenan. Some of the central themes of this movement had already appeared in earlier writings and speeches such as Mao Tse-tung's *On the New Democracy* (January 1940, see document no. 24), in his *Reform Our Learning*[1] (May 1941), in a resolution of the CC on the strengthening of Party character (July 1941),[2] and in Liu Shao-chi's *On the Intra-Party Struggle* (July 1941, see document no. 33). These materials help us to understand and appraise not only the highly influential *Cheng-feng* movement itself, but also the doctrinal development of "Maoism" during the Yenan period.

The first two speeches (documents no. 34 and 35) point out three areas of "incorrect Party tendencies": in thought, in intra-Party relations and relations with people outside the Party, and in speech and writing. According to Mao, unorthodox tendencies in learning take the form of subjectivism; in the Party, that of sectarianism; and in literature, that of formalism. In Mao's speech on literature and art (document no. 34), questions of standpoint, attitude, and audience, the relation of work and learning, and the functions of literature and art are critically examined from a Marxist point of view.

The broad background of the *Cheng-feng* movement may be seen in the following three sectors:

(1) *The problem of unorthodox thought.* Ever since the outbreak of the Sino-Japanese war on July 7, 1937, the CCP had suffered from an increasing shortage of trained (especially ideologically trained) personnel. This was a result both of expanding personnel in the enlarged guerrilla areas and of losses through war-time casualties. A few hundred trained cadres turned out at Yenan each year were quickly swallowed up in the vastness of the country. The sudden influx of new Party members had created tensions between the old and new comrades and made for an increase in careerism and unorthodoxy. Evidently some Party members, especially among the new recruits, had interpreted the spectacular shifts of the united front period to mean that the concepts of Western liberalism could be imported into the CCP itself. On the other hand, other more doctrinaire Party members were disturbed by the shift from the ideology of the Soviet period and by what seemed to them to be discrepancies between the Marxist texts and the actual practices of the CCP, particularly with regard to the relations between proletariat and peasantry and between Communism and the growing nationalism of the period. Liu Shao-ch'i had expressed the uneasiness of the Party leadership in his speech *On the Intra-Party Struggle* (document no. 33 above) when he said, "Recently a great number of intellectual elements and new Party members have entered the Party, bringing with them to the Party strong bourgeois, liberal ideas. Ideologically, politically, and organizationally they have not been tempered by the iron discipline of the proletariat. . . ." Thus also the artists of Red China were reminded by Mao that "All culture, or literature and art, belong to some one definite class, some one definite party, i.e. some one definite political line. Art for art's sake, art which transcends class or party, art which stands as a bystander to, or independent of, politics, does not in actual fact exist." (See document no. 36, sec. III.)

(2) *The problem of the Sinification of Marxism.* The accumulated effect of war-time nationalism was also clearly manifest in the *Cheng-feng* movement. Mao Tse-tung in document no. 34 says, "If we have only read this theory [of Marx, Engels, Lenin, and Stalin] but have not used

it as a basis to study the historical reality and the revolutionary reality and have not created our own specific theory in accordance with China's practical needs, then it would be irresponsible to call ourselves Marxist theorists." A similar remark was made by Mao in his speech, *Reform Our Learning* in May 1941, that "Youths of seventeen or eighteen are taught [in the cadres' school at Yenan] to digest *Das Kapital* and the *Anti-Dühring*. As a result, an abnormal psychology is created among the students, who lose interest in Chinese problems and neglect the directives of the Party. They only worship the words passed on to them by the teachers, holding them to be dogma that will remain forever valid." In short, it had become evident that Marxist theory could not be effective in China unless applied very practically to Chinese conditions.

This ideological trend towards the sinification of Marxist dogma was paralleled by the war-time concentration on all-out national resistance to Japan, for the sake of national freedom rather than for revolution as such. The united front inculcated patriotism. After 1936 the term "Soviet", used during the Kiangsi period of 1928–35, had been dropped and the Red Army had become in common parlance the Eighth Route Army. The Marx-Lenin Institute at Yenan was renamed the "Lu-hsün Academy". "Foreign formalism" was attacked as one of the major ills in literature and art. When Mao Tse-tung was asked "whether the Communists are Chinese first or Communist first", he replied: "Without a Chinese nation there could be no CCP. You might just as well ask 'What is first, children or parents?'"[3] No less a person than Po I-po, member of the CC and Vice-Chairman of the North China People's government, has been quoted as saying in 1948 that "the *Cheng-feng* (movement) taught us that the CCP must have its own principles. It was not necessary that we travel the same road as the Soviet Union".[4] Whether such examples represent sinification of the CCP by a sort of osmosis and in a qualitative sense, or were mere changes of terminology for tactical purposes, they seem clearly to reflect the far-reaching influence of a sentiment of nationalism which affected the CCP during the Sino-Japanese war. The assimilation of this vigorous sentiment within the Party's ideological framework was a problem comparable to that of assimilating bourgeois intellectuals.

(3) *Problems of intra-Party morale*. The *Cheng-feng* movement also served to carry out intra Party reforms and tighten Party discipline. The *Decision on the CC's resolutions and Comrade Mao Tse-tung's report concerning the correction of three unorthodox tendencies*, adopted by the

Propaganda Bureau of the CC on April 3, 1942, calls the movement a "spiritual revolution" and states that "All the organizations and schools should thoroughly study and vigorously discuss the above [*Cheng-feng*] documents. . . . Everyone should think hard and penetratingly about his own work and thought and life. The same applies to the examination of other people. . . . The responsible heads of various departments (both Party and administration) should, after studying and discussing these documents, think about the work of the department and its personnel. Also they should exchange views with others, map out plans to check departmental work, proceed to do so according to plan, and then draw conclusions as to how the work could be improved. . . ."[5] Thus the *Cheng-feng* movement was developed as a catalytic procedure to invigorate Party and organizational activities. The CC *Decision on methods of leadership*, dated June 1, 1943, states that "the experience of the *Cheng-feng* movement in 1942 proves that in the correction (of unorthodox) tendencies in every (organizational) unit, it is necessary to form a nucleus of some positive elements centring around the head of the administrative unit in (of charge) the *Cheng-feng* process. This leading core must maintain a close relationship with the masses who participate in the learning (process). Only thus can the goals of the *Cheng-feng* movement be successfully accomplished. . . ."[6]

What are the criteria for members of this "leading core", this élite which is both the head and the backbone of the movement? The same document specifies that "standards for this leading core should be the four criteria for cadres proposed by Dimitrov, i.e. unlimited devotion, close relationship with the masses, ability for independent work, and observation of discipline".[7] It is noteworthy that two of these four requirements (the first and the last) demand the submission of the individual to the Party line. Thus the *Cheng-feng* movement reasserts the motif already noted so often in this volume—the Lenist concept of the Party as a highly centralized, highly disciplined élite.

34. MAO TSE-TUNG: CORRECTING UNORTHODOX TENDENCIES IN LEARNING, THE PARTY, AND LITERATURE AND ART[1]
(February 1, 1942)

(Lecture delivered at the opening day ceremonies of the Party Academy,[2] February 1, 1942.)

Today is the opening day of the Party School. I congratulate the School on the success [of its establishment].

Today I wish to discuss the problem of our Party spirit.

Why must there be a revolutionary party? There must be a revolutionary party because our enemies still exist; furthermore there must be not an ordinary one, but a communist revolutionary party. For if there were no such revolutionary party of the nature of the CP, the complete overthrow of the enemy would be impossible. For the overthrow of the enemy, our ranks must be in order, we must all march in step, our troops must be seasoned, and our weapons fit. Unless these conditions are fulfilled, the enemy will not be overthrown.

What problems still face our Party? (It is a fact that) the general line of the Party is correct and unquestionable, and that our Party work has produced results. We have several hundred thousand Party members; in complete unity with the people, they are engaging in a bitter and decisive struggle against the national enemies. Such a spirit of heroic sacrifice, as well as (our) achievements in the service of the people, can be seen by all and cannot be doubted.

Well, then, does our Party still face problems, or have shortcomings? I say that there are still problems, still shortcomings, and in a certain sense these problems are rather grave.

What are these problems? (They arise because), in the minds of some comrades, several points are not entirely correct or orthodox.

What are these points? There is the question of thought, the question of the intra-Party and extra-Party relations, and the question of speech and writing. In these three respects some of our comrades have still not eliminated unorthodox tendencies. This is to say, our spirit of learning, our Party spirit, and our literary spirit are still not correct. We call the incorrect spirit in learning, subjectivism, the incorrect spirit in the Party, sectarianism, and the incorrect spirit in literature, Party formalism. These incorrect tendencies do not fill the heavens like the north wind in winter, and subjectivism, sectarianism and Party formalism are no longer at present the ruling tendencies. They are merely adverse and deviational drafts of air out of the air-raid shelters. (Laughter.) However, that we still have these tendencies in our Party is bad. We must plug these shelters, and the entire Party must do the work of plugging up. Our Party School must also participate. These three deviational trends, subjectivism, sectarianism, Party formalism all have their historical origins. Although these views do not rule the entire Party, nevertheless they still constantly vex and harass us. Therefore, we must reform and resist them; we must analyse and clarify them, and we must study them.

These, then, are our duties: anti-subjectivism to reform the tendencies in education, anti-sectarianism to reform the tendencies in the Party, and anti-formalism to reform the tendencies in literature.

If we are to accomplish the task of vanquishing the enemy, we must complete the task of reforming these tendencies within the Party. Tendencies in education are at the same time tendencies in Party education; tendencies in literature are at the same time tendencies in Party literature. Thus, both are Party tendencies. If our Party's tendencies are completely orthodox, the people of the entire nation will learn from us, and people outside the Party with these incorrect tendencies, if only they are of goodwill, will learn from us, and the correction of their mistakes will influence the entire nation. Only if the ranks of the CP are in good order, if we are all in step, if our troops are seasoned and our weapons fit, then no matter how powerful the enemy, he cannot escape defeat at our hands.

I shall now discuss subjectivism.

Subjectivism is an unorthodox tendency in learning. It is anti-Marxist-Leninist and cannot co-exist with the CP. What we need is a Marxist-Leninist spirit in learning. This spirit in learning is not only a spirit in the schools, but in the entire Party as well. It is a problem of the mode of thinking in the leading organs, in all the cadres and among all Party members. It is a problem of the orientation towards Marxism-Leninism and of the working orientation of the comrades throughout the Party. Since it is of this nature, the problem of the spirit in learning is of exceptional and primary importance.

At the present time confused concepts are prevalent on questions, for example, as to what is a theorist, or an intellectual, or the relation between theory and practice, and so forth.

The first question is whether the theoretical level of the Party is high or low. A large number of books on Marxism-Leninism have been translated recently and also read. This is excellent. But can we therefore say that the Party has attained a high theoretical level? Certainly our level is somewhat higher than it was in the past. Yet in view of the rich experience of the Chinese revolutionary movement, progress on the theoretical front has been extremely inadequate. Comparing the two, the theoretical level is unusually low and backward. In general our theory has not kept pace with revolutionary experience, not to say that theory should have run ahead of it. We have not yet raised this rich experience to its necessary theoretical level. We have not yet raised all or even the most important practical questions of the revolution, through examining them, to the theoretical level. Look at Chinese economics, politics, military affairs, and culture. How many of us have created theories (concerning these fields) which are worthy to be called theories, which possess a scientific form and closely knit structure, which are not mere skeletons of theories?

This is especially true in economic theory. One hundred years have elapsed since the Opium War, yet in regard to the development of Chinese capitalism, no theoretical work which is truly scientific and in accord with the realities of Chinese economic development has been produced. In the matter of Chinese economics, can we say then that the theoretical level is already high? Can we say that our Party already has economic theorists who are up to standard? This truly cannot be said.

Can we claim that we possess theoreticians just because we have read a great many books on Marxism-Leninism? We cannot say this either. Marxism-Leninism is the theory Marx, Engels, Lenin, and Stalin created on the basis of actual facts, and it consists of general conclusions derived from historical and revolutionary experiences. If we have only read this theory, but have not used it as a basis to study the historical reality and the revolutionary reality, have not created our own and specific theory in accordance with China's practical needs, then it would be irresponsible to call ourselves Marxist theorists. If one acts in the role of a CCP member, but is so accustomed to looking at Chinese problems that one cannot see them, looks every day and sees nothing, puts on glasses and still sees nothing, if one sees only the complete works of Marx, Engels, Lenin, and Stalin on the shelf, then one's achievement on the theoretical front is poor indeed. If we only know how to recite Marxist economics or philosophy, reciting from the first to the tenth chapters until they are overcooked, (laughter) but are completely unable to apply them, can we then be considered Marxist theorists? I should say not. It would really be better if there were fewer such "theorists". If a man read ten thousand volumes by Marx, Engels, Lenin, and Stalin, and read each volume a thousand times so he could recite every sentence from memory, he still could not be considered a theorist.

What type of theorist do we need? We need theorists who base their thinking on the standpoints, concepts, and methods of Marx, Engels, Lenin, and Stalin, who are able to explain correctly the actual problems issuing from history and revolution, who are able to give a scientific interpretation and theoretical explanation to the various problems of Chinese economics, politics, military affairs, and culture.

Such is the type of theorist we need. To be this type of theorist, one must truly understand the substance of Marxism-Leninism, and its standpoints, concepts, and methods. He must be able to apply them in profound and scientific analyses of China's actual problems so that he can discover the laws of their development. This is the type of theorist we really need.

The CC has just issued a resolution summoning our comrades to learn first the application of Marxism-Leninism's standpoints, concepts, and mode of thinking, then to engage in serious research on Chinese history, in research on Chinese economics, politics, military affairs, and culture,[3] and then to create theories, after examination and research have been done on each problem. This is the responsibility we shoulder.

Our Party School should not be content merely to read the doctrines of Marxism-Leninism, but should be able first to master, and then to apply them. Application is the sole object of this mastery. Now that we use percentages to calculate grades, what grade should you be given if you read ten thousand books a thousand times each but were completely unable to apply them? I would say that not even one per cent should be given. (Laughter.) However, if you are able to apply the concepts of Marxism-Leninism in explaining one or two actual problems, you should receive commendation as having accomplished something. The more numerous, the more universal and profound your explanations, the higher your achievement. Our Party School should now adopt this standard in judging a man's observations on Chinese problems after he has studied Marxism-Leninism. There will be some who see clearly, some who do not, some who are able to see, some who are not; superior and inferior, good and bad should be classified according to these distinctions.

What about the problem of the so-called "intelligentsia"? Because our China is a semi-colonial, semi-feudal country and its culture is undeveloped, the intelligentsia is of special value. The CC has passed a resolution on intellectual elements in order to win over the great number of intelligentsia. It is quite correct that an attitude of welcome be adopted towards them, if only they are revolutionary and willing to participate in the war of resistance. But as a result of this (welcome), the intelligentsia has been glorified and the local bumpkins are handicapped. We consider it entirely necessary to hold the intelligentsia in esteem, for without a revolutionary intelligentsia, the revolution cannot succeed. However, we know that there are many intellectuals who consider themselves very learned and who make a great display of their knowledge, not realizing that this attitude is harmful and obstructs their progress. One truth that they should realize is that a great many so-called intellectuals are actually exceedingly unlearned, and that the knowledge of the workers and peasants is sometimes somewhat greater than theirs. At this someone may say, "Aha! You're turning this upside down. It's a mass of confused words!" (Laughter.) But, comrades, don't get excited. What I say is to a certain extent reasonable.

What is knowledge? From ancient times down to the present, there have been only two types of knowledge: one type is knowledge of the struggle in production; the other is knowledge of the class struggle, in which is included knowledge of the national struggle. What knowledge is there aside from this? There is none. Natural science and social science are nothing but the crystallization of these two types of knowledge. Philosophy is a generalization and summary of natural science and social science. Aside from these, there is no other type of knowledge.

Now we shall take a look at those students who graduate and leave their schools where they have been completely isolated from the practical activities of society. In what position do they find themselves? A man studies through from grade school to university, graduates, and is then considered learned. Yet, in the first place, he cannot till the land; second, he has no trade; third, he cannot fight; fourth, he cannot manage a job—in none of these fields is he experienced nor does he have the least practical knowledge. What he possesses is merely book knowledge. Would it be possible to regard such a man as a complete intellectual? It would be very difficult, and at the most I would consider him a half-intellectual, because his knowledge is still incomplete. What is comparatively complete knowledge? All comparatively complete knowledge is formed in two stages: the first is that of knowledge through immediate perception; the second is knowledge through reason. Knowledge through reason is a higher stage of development of knowledge through immediate perception. In which category does the book knowledge of students fall? Even if we suppose that the book contains nothing but truths, it is still theory drawn from the experience of one's predecessors in the struggle of production and the class struggle, and not knowledge drawn from one's own personal experience. It is absolutely necessary that (students) obtain this (theoretical) knowledge, but they should realize that, for them, this knowledge is inverted, backwards, one-sided; it has been proved by others, but still not verified by them. They should know that it is not at all difficult to obtain this type of knowledge, that it is even extremely easy. In comparison, the cook's task in preparing a meal is difficult. To create something ready to eat, he must use a combination of wood, rice, oil, salt, sauce, vinegar, and other materials. This is certainly not easy, and to cook a good meal is all the more difficult. If we compare the tasks of the cook at the North-west Restaurant and the cooks in our homes, we find a great difference. If there is too much fire the food will burn, too much salt, and it will be bitter. (Laughter.) Cooking food and preparing dishes is truly one of the arts. But what about book knowledge? If you do nothing but read, you have only to know three or five thousand characters, learn to thumb through a dictionary, hold some book in your hand, and receive millet from the public. Then you nod your head contentedly and start to read. But books cannot walk, and you can open and close a book at will; this is the easiest thing in the world to do, a great deal easier than it is for the cook to prepare a meal, and much easier than it is for him to slaughter a pig. He has to catch the pig . . . the pig can run . . . (laughter) . . . he slaughters him . . . the pig squeals . . . (Laughter.) A book placed on a desk cannot run, nor can it squeal. (Laughter.) You can dispose of it in any manner you wish. Is there anything easier to do? Therefore, I advise those of you who only have book knowledge and as yet no contact with reality, and those who have had few practical experiences, to realize their own shortcomings and make their attitudes a bit more humble.

How can half-intellectuals be transformed into intellectuals with a title corresponding to reality? There is only one way: to see that those with only book knowledge become practical workers engaged in practical tasks, and see that those doing theoretical work turn to practical research. In this way we can reach our goal.

On hearing this, some people would lose their tempers and say, "According to your interpretation, Marx was also a half-intellectual." I would answer that it's quite true that, in the first place, Marx could not slaughter a pig and, secondly, he could not till a field. But he did participate in the revolutionary movement and also carried out research on commodity production. Millions see and use these commodities every day, but overlook them. Only Marx studied them in every aspect and scrutinized them from all angles, exhibiting none of the carelessness we show in reading the *History of the Communist Party of the Soviet Union*. He analysed the actual development of commodity production and derived a theory from observations of universally existent phenomena. He did personal research on natural science, history, and the proletarian revolution, and created the corresponding theories of dialectical materialism, historical materialism, and proletarian revolution. Thus Marx is to be regarded as a complete intellectual. The difference between him and the half-intellectual is that he participated in an actual revolutionary movement and carried on research and investigation by turning to a reality which was all-inclusive. This type of all-inclusive knowledge is called theory. Our Party needs a great many comrades who can do this type of work. At present many of our comrades are capable of doing such theoretical research, and for the most part they are intelligent and able and promising. We should prize these comrades and value them highly, but their orientation must be correct and past mistakes must not be repeated. They must cast off dogmatism and not stop at reading books.

There is only one type of true theory: that which is derived from the observation of objective reality and proved by objective reality. Nothing else can measure up to the theory of which we speak. Stalin has argued that theory divorced from reality is empty. An empty theory is useless, incorrect, and must be rejected. We must single out those who delight in discussing such empty theories and put them to shame. Marxism-Leninism, derived from objective reality and tested by objective reality, is the most correct, scientific, and revolutionary truth. But many read Marxism-Leninism as dead dogma, thereby obstructing their own theoretical development, and harming themselves and their comrades.

On the other hand, mistakes are also apt to happen if those comrades who are engaged in practical work make an incorrect application of their experience. It is quite true that such men have had a great deal of experience and should be valued highly. But there is great danger if they are satisfied with their experience. They should realize that the greater part of their knowledge is gained from immediate perception and is limited, and that they fall short when it comes to reasoning and universal knowledge, that is to say, they fall short in theory. Thus their knowledge too is also comparatively incomplete. Yet without comparatively complete knowledge it is impossible to accomplish the revolution.

Seen in this way, there are two types of incomplete knowledge. One is knowledge taken ready-made from books, and even Marxist-Leninist books can leave a man empty in his thinking. Another type of knowledge is overweighted on the side of immediate perception and is limited; it has not developed into something rational and universal. Both types are one-sided, and only if they are combined can something worth while and comparatively complete be produced.

However, if our workers' and peasants' cadres are going to study theory, they must first study culture, for if there were no culture, Marxism-Leninism could not be absorbed. At the appropriate time, after culture has been studied thoroughly, they can study Marxism-Leninism. When I was a youth, I did not attend any Marxist-Leninist school; I studied a mass of things like, "Confucius said, 'Is it not pleasant to study your lessons and practice them constantly?'" (Laughter.) I learned to read in just this way. For example, I learned the characters for "to study" and can now use them in "studying" Marxism-Leninism. Moreover, people do not study Confucius now, but the new vernacular literature, history, geography, and general knowledge in the natural sciences. Studied thoroughly, these cultural lessons are applicable everywhere. Our Party's CC is now vigorously urging the workers' and peasants' cadres to engage in cultural studies, because after these are studied, politics, military affairs, and economics can all be studied. Otherwise, even though they have a wealth of experience, the workers' and peasants' cadres will still not be able to advance to the stage where theorizing is possible.

Thus if we are anti-subjectivist, we must see that the two types of persons described above develop in those spheres where they are deficient; we must see that these two types combine. Only if those with book knowledge develop in practical spheres will it be possible for them to go beyond their books; only then will it be possible for them to avoid the error of dogmatism. Men with working experience have to study theory and take their reading seriously; only then will it be possible for them to raise their experience to the level of reason and synthesis, the level of theory. Only then will it be possible for them to avoid classifying their partial experience as universal truth and avoid the error of empiricism. Dogmatism and empiricism are both forms of subjectivism, though they arise from two different extremes.

There are thus two types of subjectivism in our Party. One type is dogmatism, the other empiricism. Both see only one side and not the entire picture. If you ignore this one-sidedness, if you do not understand its shortcomings, nor make reforms, it will be easy for you to travel the path of error.

Of these two types of subjectivism in our Party, the one which is most dangerous now is still dogmatism. For it easily assumes the guise of Marx-Engels-Lenin-Stalinism, frightens the workers' and peasants' cadres and captures the local hayseeds for service as personal servants, and it is difficult for the workers' and peasants' cadres to see through its mask. It can also frighten innocent youths and make them captive. If we conquer dogmatism, we can see to it that cadres with book knowledge develop a willingness to associate with cadres with experience and engage in the study of practical matters. It will be possible to produce many good workers who combine experience and theory, and it will be possible to produce many true theorists. If we conquer dogmatism, comrades with experience can obtain good teachers and rise to the level of theory, thus avoiding the error of empiricism.

In addition to the two muddled terms, "theorist" and "intellectual", there is a phrase we read every day, "the union of theory and practice", which still has a confused meaning for many of our comrades. Every day they speak of "union", but on the contrary, they actually mean "separation", for they take no steps towards "union". How can Marxist-Leninist theory and the reality of the Chinese revolution be united? Take the common saying, "To shoot an arrow, have a target"—[*yu ti, fang shih*]. Arrow [*shih*] means arrow [*chien*], and target [*ti*] means target [*pa*]. [Mao here gives the colloquial words for a classical quotation.] In shooting the arrow, you must have a target to aim at. The relation between Marxism-Leninism and the Chinese revolution is the same as between the arrow and the target. However, some comrades are shooting arrows without a target, shooting them at random. Such people can easily harm the revolutionary cause. Some comrades merely take the arrow in hand, twist it back and forth, and say again and again in praise, "excellent arrow, excellent arrow", but are never willing to shoot it. This type of person is an antique connoisseur who has hardly any relationship with the revolution. The arrow of Marxism-Leninism must be used to hit the target of the Chinese revolution. If it were otherwise, why would we want to study Marxism-Leninism? Is it because we have not digested our millet that we read a book to relieve indigestion? Why has our Party School decided to study Marxism-Leninism? If this problem is not clearly understood, the theoretical level of the Party can never be raised nor can the Chinese revolution succeed.

Our comrades must understand that we do not study Marxism-Leninism because it is pleasing to the eye, nor because it has some mystical value, like the doctrines of the Taoist priests who ascend Mao-shan [*Chü-yung, Kiangsu*] to learn, so they can subdue the devils and evil spirits. Marxism-Leninism has no decorative value, nor has it mystical value. It is only extremely useful. It seems that, right up to the present, quite a few have regarded Marxism-Leninism as a ready-made panacea: once you have it, you can cure all your ills with little effort. This is a type of childish blindness, and we must start a movement to enlighten these people. Those who regard Marxism-Leninism as religious dogma show this type of blind ignorance. We must tell them openly, "Your dogma is of no use", or to use an impolite phrase, "Your dogma is less useful than excrement." We see that dog excrement can fertilize the fields, and man's can feed the dog. And dogmas? They can't fertilize the fields, not can they feed a dog. Of what use are they? (Laughter.) Comrades! You know that the object of such talk is to ridicule those who regard Marxism-Leninism as dogma, to frighten and awaken them, to inculcate in them a correct attitude towards Marxism-Leninism. Marx, Lenin, Engels, and Stalin have repeatedly said, "our doctrine is not dogma; it is a guide to action". Of all things, these people forget this most important sentence. Theory and practice can be combined only if men of the CCP take the standpoints, concepts, and methods of Marxism-Leninism, apply them to China, and create a theory from conscientious research on the realities of the Chinese revolution and Chinese history. If we merely verbalize about union but do not practice union in our actions, we can talk for a hundred years and still not benefit. Since we are opposed to subjective and *ex-parte* views on problems, we must break through the subjective and one-sided nature of dogmatism.

This is what I have to say today about anti-subjectivism as a means of reforming the entire Party's educational tendency. Now we come to the problem of sectarianism.

After twenty years tempering, our Party is not now dominated by sectarianism, but remnants of intra-Party and extra-Party sectarianism do exist. Intra-Party sectarianism tends to produce internal friction and hinders the unification and consolidation of the Party. Extra-Party sectarianism tends to produce friction with the outside and hinders the Party's task of consolidating the entire nation. The Party's great task of consolidating the comrades of the entire Party and the people of the entire nation cannot be carried out freely without obstruction unless the evil roots of these two tendencies are removed.

What are the remnants of intra-Party sectarianism? The following are the principal types.

First is the clamour for independence. A group of our comrades see only particular interests and fail to see the interest of the whole.

They invariably lay special and inappropriate emphasis on the particular work under their own management and expect the interest of the whole to bow to their particular interest. They do not understand the system of Party democratic centralism. They do not realize that a CP not only requires democracy, but it requires centralization even more. They have forgotten the system of democratic centralism in which the minority obeys the majority, the lower ranks obey the higher ranks, the particular obeys the universal, and the entire Party obeys the CC. Chang Kuo-t'ao clamoured to the CC about independence; his clamouring led to a rebellion against the Party and his joining the KMT secret police. Li Li-san clamoured about independence to the CI, and as a result committed the error of the "Li Li-san line". Although what we speak of here is not as extreme and serious as the sectarianism of Li Li-san and Chang Kuo-t'ao, it is still something to be guarded against. We must eradicate all tendencies towards disunity. If Party members are to promote a sense of concern for the whole, each one of them must take the interest of the whole Party as a point of departure in every specific task and every time they speak, write, or act. Absolutely no opposition to this principle is to be tolerated.

It is often impossible to divorce these men who clamour for independence from their "individual-firstism". They are often incorrect on the question of the relationship between the individual and the Party. Although they speak with respect for the Party, they actually place the individual first and the Party second. Comrade Liu Shao-ch'i speaks about the type of man with especially long hands who is quite able to look after his own interests. But what about the interests of others and of the entire Party? This is a matter of no great concern to him, and he says, "What is mine is mine, what is yours is also mine." (Laughter.) About what do such men clamour? About their reputation, their positions, and their vanity. When they manage a particular enterprise, they clamour about independence, and with these objectives in mind form close relations with some people and create friction with others, they boast, adulate, and pull strings, thus injecting the vulgar spirit of the political parties of the bourgeoisie into the CP. Such men suffer from the effects of hypocrisy. I think that we must do things with complete sincerity; it is fundamentally impossible to accomplish anything in this world without a sincere attitude. What is a sincere man? Marx, Engels, Lenin, and Stalin are sincere men; scientists are sincere men. What is a hypocrite? Trotsky, Bucharin, and Chang Kuo-t'ao were great hypocrites; Li Li-san was also hypocritical. Men who clamour about independence for the sake of their individual and particular interests are also hypocrites. All who are crafty, who manage things with an unscientific attitude, or who consider themselves calculating or clever, are in fact exceedingly stupid, and all come to no good. Students in our Party School certainly must give their attention to this problem. We must not fail to establish a centralized, unified Party, purified of fractional or unprincipled struggles. We must see that the marching order of the entire Party is regular and uniform, and that it struggles towards a common objective. It is absolutely necessary that we oppose individualism and sectarianism.

Relations between the cadres who came from outside districts and local cadres must be consolidated, and both must oppose factional tendencies. Because a great many of the anti-Japanese war bases were established only after the arrival of the Eighth Route and New Fourth Armies, the work in many places was developed only after the arrival of the "outside" cadres. Because of this, great attention must be given to the relations between "outside" and local cadres. It must be understood that, under such conditions, the war bases can only grow strong, and our Party can only take root in these bases, if there is solidarity and unanimity between the "outside" and local cadres and only when the latter are trained on a large scale and promoted; otherwise it will be impossible. Both "outside" and local cadres have their merits; both also have their defects. They must learn the merits of each other, and so rectify their own shortcomings; only then can there be progress. The "outside" cadres must certainly be somewhat inferior than the local cadres in their detailed knowledge of the (local) conditions and their relations with the masses. Take my case as an example. I came to northern Shensi five or six years ago, yet I cannot compare with comrades like Kao Kang in my knowledge of conditions here or in my relations with people of this region. No matter what progress I make in investigation and research, I shall always be somewhat inferior to the northern Shensi cadres. Those of our comrades who go to Shansi, Hopei, Shantung, and the other anti-Japanese war bases must certainly give their attention to this problem. What is more, there also are distinctions between "outside" and "local" cadres within one section of a single war base, because of the different stages of development of the regions within the war base. Cadres from comparatively advanced regions which go to comparatively backward regions are a type of "outside" cadre for that area and must pay special attention to the problem of assisting the local cadres. Thus, generally speaking, wherever "outside" cadres assume the responsibility of leadership, they should receive the greater part of the blame if poor relations develop with the local cadres. Thus the responsibility of the most important leaders is all the greater. At present, not enough attention is being given to this problem. There are some comrades who regard the local cadres lightly and laugh at them. "What do the local people understand? The bumpkins!" Such a person, completely misjudging the importance of the local cadres, could never understand their merits, nor could he understand his own shortcomings, and therefore he adopts the incorrect attitude of sectarianism. All the "outside" cadres must cherish, protect, and give constant assistance to the local cadres. They must not ridicule or attack them. Naturally, the local cadres must study the merits of the "outside" cadres; they must rid themselves of unsuitable and narrow points of view, in order to find complete, undivided unity with the "outside" cadres, to become one with them and avoid the tendencies of sectarianism.

The same applies to the relations between the working cadres in the army and the local work cadres. Both must be in complete and consolidated unanimity and oppose sectarian tendencies. Army cadres must assist the local cadres and the local cadres must assist the army cadres. In case of conflict, each must make allowances for the other, and both must engage in exacting self-criticism. Under ordinary circumstances, in cases where the military cadres actually occupy a leading position, primary responsibility must rest with the military cadres if poor relations develop with the local cadres. The problem is very important. The military cadres must first be made to understand their own responsibility so they will take a humble attitude towards the local cadres. Only then can smooth progress be made in the military and developmental work in the war bases.

The same also applies to relations between various army units, localities, and working departments. Here also the particularistic tendency to consider only oneself and disregard others must be opposed. This "particularism" has the following characteristics: not sending cadres on request, or sending inferior men as cadres, exploiting one's neighbours and completely disregarding other organs, localities, and men. This shows a complete loss of the spirit of Communism. "Particularism" is characterized by a disregard for the over-all picture and a complete lack of concern for other organs, localities, and people. Those who have this attitude must receive intensive education if they are to understand that it is a factional tendency and will be a danger to the Party if it continues to develop.

The relations between old and new cadres present still another problem. Since the war of resistance began, our Party has experienced a vast expansion and large numbers of new cadres have been produced. This is excellent. At the Eighteeth Congress of the Communist Party of the Soviet Union, Comrade Stalin said in his report, "The old cadres were invariably few in number, too few considering the number necessary. Moreover, as a result of a natural law of the universe, they have gradually begun to wither and die." Here he is explaining the circumstances affecting the cadres, and, on the other hand, he is explaining natural science. If we do not have unanimous co-operation between the old and numerous new cadres in our Party, our task will not be completed. Old cadres must therefore welcome the new cadres with great earnestness and give them their attention. Certainly the new cadres have defects. They have not participated in the revolution for long and lack experience. There are still those among them who have not stopped dragging in the tails of undesirable concepts of the old society, the remnants of liberal concepts of the petty bourgeoisie. But these defects can be gradually eliminated through training and revolutionary conditioning. Their (the new cadres') merit, just as Stalin said, is that they have a sharp and sensitive perception on new matters, and consequently a high degree of enthusiasm and spirit. In just these respects some of the old cadres are lacking. The old and new cadres must respect one another, learn from one another, firmly maintain their merits and remedy their shortcomings, so they can unite and consolidate as one team and carry out their tasks together. Sectarian tendencies must be opposed. In ordinary circumstances, in those cases where the principal responsibility for leadership is assumed by the old cadres, they must accept principal blame if poor relations develop with the new cadres.

The relations referred to above, between parts and the whole, individuals and the Party, "outside" and local cadres, army and local cadres, army unit and army unit, locality and locality, this working department and that, are all intra-Party relations. In all these relations the spirit of Communism must be promoted and sectarian tendencies opposed, so that the ranks of the Party may be in good order, our steps uniform, and our fighting objectives attained. This is an extremely important problem, which must be thoroughly resolved if we are to reform the Party tendencies. If we do not want to be subjectivistic, but wish to apply the Marxist-Leninist spirit of seeking the truth by reference to facts, we must sweep aside the remnants of sectarianism in the Party and advance the Party to a position of complete and consolidated unity, taking as a point of departure the elevation of Party interests above individual and particular interests.

The remnants of sectarianism must be destroyed in intra-Party relations, but they must also be destroyed in the Party's external relations, for this too is a Party tendency which needs correction. It is not possible to defeat the enemy by merely uniting the comrades of the entire Party. The people of the entire nation must also be united. Only then will it be possible to defeat the enemy. For twenty years we have been engaged in the vast and arduous task of uniting the people of the nation. Since the war of resistance started, our achievements in this task have been even greater than before, but this is not to say that all comrades have a correct spirit nor that all are free of sectarian tendencies. It would be untrue to say this, for a group of our comrades possess this tendency, some of them to a serious extent. Many comrades delight in speaking to non-Party men with an exaggerated air of self-importance. They look down on others and belittle them, and are unwilling to respect others or understand their merits. This is a sectarian tendency. These comrades grow proud instead of modest after learning a few Marxist-Leninist phrases, invariably claiming that others are worthless, not realizing that they themselves really only half understand. There is one truism our comrades must grasp: the number of Party members is always small compared to the number of people outside the Party. If there is one CP member to every one hundred people, then the whole country of 450,000,000 would have 4,500,000 Party members. Granting that such a large membership could be attained, the CP members would still constitute but one per cent of the population, and ninety-nine per cent would be non-members; so on what grounds can we not co-operate with non-Party men? We have an obligation to co-operate with all who are willing and able to co-operate with us; we have absolutely no right to reject them. Yet some Party members do not understand this principle. There are no grounds whatsoever for looking down on and even rejecting those who are willing to co-operate with us. Did Marx, Engels, Lenin, or Stalin give us such grounds? No, on the contrary, they invariably exhorted us not to cut ourselves off from the masses, but to ally ourselves closely with them. Has the CC of the CP given us such grounds? No, not one of the resolutions passed by the CC states that we may isolate ourselves by cutting our ties with the masses. On the contrary, it has always called for close relations with the masses, not alienation. There is therefore no basis whatsoever for any action leading to alienation from the masses. The source of trouble is the sectarian thought created by some of our comrades. Because this type of sectarianism is still a serious problem with some of the Party members and still obstructs the execution of Party policy, we must carry out a large-scale programme of intra-Party training. We must start with our cadres, making sure that they truly understand the gravity of the problem, making sure that they understand that it will be absolutely impossible to defeat the enemy and attain our revolutionary objectives if Communists do not ally themselves with cadres and persons outside the Party.

All sectarian thoughts are subjective and incompatible with the actual needs of the revolution. Thus, in opposing sectarianism, we must also oppose subjectivism.

The problem of Party formalism will be discussed at another meeting. Party formalism is something which conceals filth. It is the manifestation of subjectivism; it is harmful and does not benefit the cause of the revolution. It must therefore be wiped out. Today I cannot discuss it in full, but I shall discuss it next time.

If we are going to oppose subjectivism, we must propagate materialism and the dialectic method. Yet there are still many comrades in the Party who pay no attention at all to the propagation of materialism or dialectics. Some even remain at ease while others spread subjectivism. These comrades think they believe in Marxism, but still make no effort to propagate materialism. When they see or hear something subjective, they do not think it over and criticize it. This is not the attitude of a CP member; this is the reason why many of our comrades take in the poison of subjective thought and develop signs of numbness. We must therefore initiate a movement of enlightenment in our Party which will liberate our comrades' spirits from the darkness of subjectivism and dogmatism, and summon them to resistance against subjectivism, sectarianism, and Party formalism. These things are a great deal like Japanese goods, because the enemy, hoping that we will continue to be shrouded in darkness, is the only one willing that we keep these undesirable products. We must therefore call for resistance against them as we do against Japanese goods. We must resist everything characterized by subjectivism, sectarianism, and Party formalism. We must not allow them to take advantage of the low theoretical level of the Party to put their wares up for sale; we must make it difficult for these tendencies to sell their commodities on the market. To attain this objective we have to sharpen our comrades' sense of smell; each article must be smelled to see if it is good or bad. Only then can a decision be made whether to accept or reject it. CP members must ask "why?" about everything, examine it carefully in their minds, and ask whether it conforms with reality. They certainly must not follow blindly. They must not promote servitude.

Lastly, in opposing subjectivism, sectarianism, and Party formalism, two principles must be observed. The first is, "Punish the past to warn the future", and the second, "Save men by curing their ills". Past errors must be exposed with no thought of personal feelings or face. We must use a scientific attitude to analyse and criticize what has been undesirable in the past so that more care will be taken in later work, and so this work will be better performed. This is the meaning of "Punish the past to warn the future". But our object in exposing errors and criticizing shortcomings is like that of a doctor in curing a disease. The entire purpose is to save the person, not to cure him to death. If a man has appendicitis, the doctor performs an operation and the man is saved. If a person who commits an error, no matter how great, does not bring his disease to an incurable state by concealing it and persisting in his error, and if in addition he is genuinely and honestly willing to be cured, willing to make corrections, we will welcome him so that his disease may be cured and he can become a good comrade. It is certainly not possible to solve the problem by one flurry of blows for the sake of a moment's satisfaction. We cannot adopt a brash attitude towards diseases in thought and politics, but (must have) an attitude of "saving men by curing their diseases". This is the correct and effective method.

I have taken the opening of the Party School today as an occasion to speak on many things, and I hope our comrades will give them their consideration. (Great applause.)

35. MAO TSE-TUNG: OPPOSING PARTY FORMALISM[1]
(February 8, 1942)

Comrade K'ai Feng has just spoken on the purpose of today's meeting. I now intend to discuss the manner in which subjectivism and sectarianism use Party formalism as their propaganda tool and form of expression. If we oppose subjectivism and sectarianism but do not at the same time eradicate Party formalism, they still have a place to hide. If we destroy Party formalism, at the same time subjectivism and sectarianism will be checkmated. It necessarily follows that when a complete exposé is made of the monsters' original form—"(when the) rats run in the street, everyone screams, 'hit them'"—the two monsters can be easily exterminated.

If a man's writing is characterized by Party formalism but he alone reads it, the problem is still unimportant. If he gives it to a second person to read, then its importance has already doubled in comparison, and it is harmful to a significant degree. If in addition he pastes it on the wall, has it mimeographed, publishes it in a newspaper, or prints it as a book, the problem becomes serious and many people can be affected. But persons whose writing is characterized by Party formalism, always intend that many others read their work. Without fail, such conditions must be exposed and eliminated.

Party formalism is identical with the foreign formalism which Lu Hsün opposed in the past. Why do we call it Party formalism? We do this because in addition to a foreign spirit, it also has a little rustic spirit. Ah, it is a new creation! Who says we have not had any creative workers? Here's one right here! (Laughter.) Party formalism has already had a long history within our Party, and especially during the civil war period when it sometimes became a very serious problem.

From the historical point of view, Party formalism is a reaction against the May Fourth [1919] movement.

What does this mean?

In general, during the period of the May Fourth movement men with new ideas opposed the classical style [wen-yen] and promoted Pai-Hua, opposed the old dogmas and promoted science and democracy. All this was quite correct. At the time, the movement was lively, vigorous, progressive, and revolutionary. At the time, the ruling class, without exception, taught Confucian dogmas to the students and compelled people to believe in a set of Confucian doctrines as religious dogma. All writers used the classical style. At that time, the writings and teachings of the ruling class and their collaborators, irrespective of form or content, were all characterized by formalism and dogmatism. That was the old formalism, the old dogmatism. One great achievement of the era of the May Fourth movement was that it exposed the ugliness of the old formalism and old dogmatism and summoned the people to rise against them. The May Fourth movement did not stop at this achievement, but also had, closely related with it, the great merit of opposing imperialism. But opposition to the old formalism and dogmatism was one of its great achievements. However, later there came into existence foreign formalism and foreign dogma. Some men in our Party then developed this foreign formalism and foreign dogmatism into subjectivism, sectarianism, and Party formalism. These then were the new formalism and the new dogmatism, which have been deeply and firmly rooted in the minds of many of our comrades, so that today great energy must be expended in carrying out the work of reform. Seen in this way the movement of the May Fourth period, which was lively, vigorous, progressive, revolutionary, and opposed to the feudalistic old formalism and old dogmatism, was developed by some to its extreme and opposite form to become the new formalism and new dogmatism. It became petrified, not lively and vigorous; reactionary, regressive; and instead of being revolutionary it has become an obstruction to the revolution. This is to say that foreign formalism, Party or new formalism and the new dogma are the antithesis of the original character of the May Fourth movement.

But the May Fourth movement itself also had defects. Many leading figures of the time still did not possess the Marxist spirit of criticism. The method they employed was, in general, still the method of the capitalist classes, in other words, a formalistic method. It was quite correct for them to oppose the old formalism and old dogma, and promote science and democracy; but they did not apply the critical spirit of dialectical materialism and historical materialism to the contemporary situation, history, or things foreign: (according to them) what was bad, was completely bad, bad in every way; what was good, was absolutely good, good in every way. This method of viewing problems formalistically then affected the later development of the movement.

The May Fourth movement had two main streams of development. One group inherited the scientific and democratic spirit of the May Fourth movement and re-formed it on the basis of Marxism. This was the work of CP members and certain non-Party Marxists. Another group travelled the path of the bourgeoisie; this was the right wing, the development of formalism towards the right. But neither was there unanimity within the CP, where there was also a group which went to the extreme, and not having a firm grasp on Marxism, it committed the errors of formalism. These are subjectivism, sectarianism, and Party formalism, the development of formalism towards the left. Viewed in this way, Party formalism is, in one way, a reaction against the positive factors in the May Fourth movement, and, in another, a heritage continuation and development of the negative factors in the May Fourth movement; it is not an accidental product. It is to our benefit to understand this.

If the opposition in the May Fourth movement to the old formalism and the old dogmatism was revolutionary and necessary, then our criticism of the new formalism and new dogmatism is also revolutionary and necessary. If in the May Fourth period we had not opposed the old formalism and the old dogmatism, the mind of the Chinese people would not have been emancipated from its bondage and China would have no hope for independence and freedom. Still, no more than a start in this task was made during the time of the May Fourth movement. If the people of the whole country are going to divorce themselves entirely from the control of the old formalism and old dogmatism, it is still necessary to expend a great deal of energy, and it still remains a great task in the programme of revolutionary reform. Today, if we do not oppose the new formalism and new dogmatism, the mind of the Chinese people will be bound by the chains of another form of extremeness. Have we not all seen the great harm done by foreign formalism and foreign dogmatism? There is a section (of course it is only a section) of comrades in our Party who have taken in the poison of Party formalism and committed the error of dogmatism. If they do not rid themselves of this poison and this error, a lively, vigorous revolutionary spirit cannot arise. The undesirable habit of an incorrect attitude towards Marxism cannot be wiped out, and true Marxism cannot have widespread propagation and development. Then we will not be able to launch an effective struggle against the influence of the old formalism and the old dogmatism on the whole nation and the influence of foreign formalism and foreign dogmatism on a great many people. Then (we) will not be able to obtain our objective—the destruction and annihilation of these things.

Subjectivism, sectarianism, and Party formalism are necessary to the exploiting classes, but not to the proletariat. Within our Party, these are reflections of petty-bourgeois mentality. China is a country with an extremely broad petty bourgeoisie; our Party is surrounded by this class and it produces a great many of our Party members. To a greater or lesser degree they cannot help dragging the tail of this petty-bourgeois class into the Party. If the emotional and one-sided nature of the revolutionaries of petty-bourgeois origin is not brought under control and re-formed, subjectivism and sectarianism are very easily produced. One manifested form of these is foreign formalism or foreign dogmatism.

The task of destroying and sweeping away these conditions is not an easy one. It must be properly done, which means that a reasonable explanation must be given. If the reasoning is good, if it is to the point, it can be effective. The first method in reasoning is to give the patients a powerful stimulus, yell at them, "you're sick!", so the patients will have a fright and break out in an over-all sweat; then, they can be carefully treated.

Now I am going to analyse the harmful aspects of Party formalism. I will imitate the style of stylistic writers of the "eight-legged essay",[2] fighting poison with poison. So we shall call this essay "The Eight Great Charges".

The first charge against Party formalism is "Lengthy Empty Phrases, Words Without Substance." Some of our comrades delight in writing long articles, articles which have not a thing to them and are really like "the foot-bindings of a lazy old woman, long and foul smelling". Why do they have to write at such length? And with such emptiness? There is only one explanation: they do not want the articles to be read by the masses. Because they are long and empty, the masses shake their heads when they see them; how could you expect them to read them? They are of no use except to take advantage of the naïve people, spread bad influences, and create evil practices among them. Last year, on June 22 [1941], the Soviet Union became engaged in a great war, yet on July 3 Stalin delivered a speech which was only as long as an editorial in our *Liberation Daily*. Had it been written by one of our old gentlemen, good heavens, (the speech) would have contained at least one hundred thousand words. Now the whole world is in a stage of great war, and we must learn the ways in which articles can be written briefly and lucidly. Although there has as yet been no fighting in Yenan, our troops nevertheless are fighting at the front every day; and those in the rear are also weighted down with work. If writings are too long, who is going to read them? Some comrades at the front also delight in writing long reports. They write them with great effort, and send them in, intending that we read them. But (do we) dare read them? Since they are bad when long and empty, are they then good if short and empty? No. We should prohibit all writing which contains only empty words. But the first and principal thing to be considered is that the lazy old woman's long, foul-smelling foot-bindings be hurriedly thrown in the privy. Perhaps someone will say, "But isn't *Das Kapital* also long?" What shall we then do? It's easy; just read it carefully. Two common expressions go, "Sing the song of the mountain you are on", and, "Look over the dishes before you eat, take the measurements before you cut the garments." Regardless of what you do, act according to the circumstances; this also applies to writings and speeches. What we oppose is the formalistic tune, with "Length Empty Phrases, Words Without Substance." This does not mean that everything short is to be considered good. In war-time, there is certainly a demand for short writings, but there is a special demand for writings with content. What is most unnecessary and the thing to be most opposed, is the writing filled with words without substance. The same applies also to speeches. We must have no more speeches which are the mouthing of empty phrases, words without substance.

The second charge against Party formalism is "Making a False Show of Authority to Instil Terror." Some types of Party formalism not only contain lengthy empty phrases, but also give a false show of authority and deliberately instil terror, an attitude which contains a deadly poison. The mouthing of empty phrases and words without substance can still be considered childish, but making a false show of authority to instil terror is not only childish but knavish. Lu Hsün criticized this attitude when he said, "Insult and intimidation are certainly not fighting." That which is scientific does not at any time fear criticism, because science is the truth, it does not fear refutation. On the other hand, subjectivism and sectarianism, as displayed in Party formalistic writings and speeches, are deeply afraid of refutation and show extreme cowardice; henceforth they rely on a false show of authority to instil terror, on the calculation that, faced with this intimidation, others will shut their mouths, and they can then "return to court in victory". This false show of authority cannot reflect the truth, but is detrimental to it. Truth does not assume false authority to instil terror; in word and action it is nothing but extremely honest and sincere. Hitherto, two phrases have appeared constantly in our writings and speeches; one is, "struggle savagely", and the other is, "attack mercilessly". It is entirely necessary to use such means in dealing with the enemy and with opposition thought, but it is a mistake to use them in dealing with our own comrades. Quite often, as is stated in the fourth section of the conclusion of the *History of the Communist Party of the Soviet Union*, enemies and opposition thought do sneak into the Party. Without doubt, a savage and merciless attack must be adopted as a means against these persons and types of thought, for the undesirable elements are using these means against the Party. If we persist in being lenient with them, we fall into their trap. But we cannot use the same means in dealing with comrades who unwittingly commit errors. With such comrades we must make use of criticism and self-criticism. This is the method referred to in the fifth section of the conclusion of the *History of the Communist Party of the Soviet Union*. But no matter whom you deal with, a false show of authority to instil terror is in all cases undesirable. Because the strategy of terror is not of the slightest use against the enemy; against our comrades it only does harm. It is the device usually adopted by the exploiting classes or by the lumpenproletariat. The proletariat has no need of such methods. For them only one weapon is sharp and effective: a stern and militant scientific attitude. The CCP does not rely on intimidation for nourishment: it relies on truth, on arriving at the truth by a verification of facts and on science. It goes without saying that the idea of attaining fame, position, or "vitamins" through a false show of authority is even baser. In general, all organs which make decisions and issue directives, and all comrades who write articles or deliver speeches, must always rely on truth and utility. Only when they do this can the revolutionary victory be attained. All other means are useless.

The third charge against Party formalism is, "Shooting Without a Target, Disregarding the Objective." A few years ago I saw the following slogan on the Yenan city wall, "Workers and Peasants Unite and Gain Victory in the War of Resistance." The thought behind the slogan is not at all bad, but in the expression for "workers" [lit. work-men *kung-jen* 工 人], the second stroke in the character for "work" [*kung* 工] was not written straight; it was twisted twice and was written: 工 . As to the character for "men" [*jen* 人], three short strokes were added on the right foot, thus: 人 . There is no doubt that this esteemed comrade was a student of the ancient literati. However, for him to write this on the Yenan city wall in war-time is beyond comprehension. Probably his avowed object was to make sure that people would not read the slogan, otherwise it would be very difficult to explain. If a CP member really intends to engage in propaganda, he must study his audience. He must figure out who will read or hear his writing, speech, conversation, and characters. Otherwise it is the same as deciding that others should not read or hear him. There are many who invariably think that what they write and say is quite understandable. Actually it is nothing of the sort, for what they speak or write is Party formalism. How could people understand? The point of the proverb, "To play the lute to the cow", is to ridicule the listener. If we discard this thought and substitute the idea of respecting the audience, what we have left is the idea of ridiculing the one who plays the lute. What is the purpose in playing carelessly without considering the audience? This is all the more true in the case of Party formalism, which simple cries like a crow, yet is bent on squawking out to the masses. We study the target before we shoot, and play the lute after considering the audience. Should we write articles and make speeches without considering the readers and the audience? We cannot become intimate with our friends, no matter who they are, if we do not understand each other's minds, if we do not know each other's thoughts. A propagandist who does not investigate, study, and analyse the objective of his propaganda, but merely carries on carelessly, will never make the grade.

The fourth charge against Party formalism is, "Insipid Language (empty) like a Tramp." What Shanghai people call a *pi-san* [tramp or vagrant] is very much like a person who practises our Party formalism, dry, shrivelled, extremely unpleasant to see. If in a writing or speech, the same few clichés are repeatedly used, like the "style of students", without any lively, vigorous expressions, is not this language insipid and repulsive like a *pi-san*? At seven, persons enter primary school, at ten or more, middle school, and at twenty or more, they are graduated from a university. Since they have not yet had contact with the masses, it is excusable if their language is poor in expression and extremely simple. But we are a revolutionary party, working for the masses, and if we, too, do not learn the language of the masses, (we will) not manage things well. Many of our comrades now engaged in propaganda work still have not learned this language and their propaganda is completely insipid. Few enjoy reading their writings, and few enjoy hearing their speeches. Why must we learn the language, and why must we devote great effort to learning it? Because language is something we cannot master at our ease. It cannot be done without working diligently. First, the people's language must be learned. The people's language is very rich in expression; it is lively and vigorous and presents life as it is. Many of us have not mastered it, and as a consequence, in writing articles and giving speeches, we do not use lively, vigorous, really effective language; we only have a few varicose veins. These writings and speechs are unhealthy like the *pi-san*, so lean and unpleasant to view. Second, foreign languages must be learned. Foreign languages are certainly not foreign formalism. It is only when Chinese appropriate their forms crudely that they become moribund foreign formalism. We must not transplant foreign languages crudely, but must absorb those good elements in them which are appropriate to our work. Because the Chinese language is not sufficient for our use, many (expressions) in our language now are absorbed from foreign (countries). Take as an example the cadre meeting which is being held today. The two characters *kan-pu* (cadre) have been learned from abroad.[3] We still have to absorb many, many fresh things from foreign countries, but we should not only absorb their progressive theories, but also their fresh terminology. For example, in a speech on the Soviet Constitution, Stalin spoke of the "Party and non-party alliance". We have absorbed this phrase into the administrative platform of the Shensi-Kansu-Ninghsia Border Region, interpreting it as "the practice of democratic co-operation between Communist Party members and non-party men". There are many examples like it. All in all, we must absorb a great many good elements from foreign countries. Third, we must study the ancient language. The present language of the people has been in large part inherited from the language of the past. The treasure vault of the ancient language can still be excavated, and we should absorb any element therein which still has life, then use it to enrich our writings, speeches, and conversation. We of course firmly oppose the use of classical quotations which are already dead; that much is certain. But things which are good and in accord with reason should still be absorbed. At present, men who have taken in too much of the poison of Party formalism refuse to accept anything from the language of the people, languages of foreign countries or that part of the ancient language which is useful; nor are they willing to study them painstakingly. At the Eighteenth Congress of the Communist Party of the Soviet Union Stalin said, "A group of our comrades have lost their feeling for fresh things." Some of our comrades are also like this and there are many fresh things which they do not see. This defect must be cured. What is a propagandist? Not only are teachers propagandists, journalists propagandists, writers and artists propagandists. All our work cadres are also propagandists. Take the military commanders as an example. They do not issue manifestos to the public, but they have to speak to the soldiers and deal with the people. If this isn't propaganda, what is it? As soon as a man talks with another man he is engaged in propaganda work. If he is not mute, he always will have a few words to say. Therefore, our comrades must all study languages. In studying various languages (they must) pay special attention to the language of the people. In studying the language of the people, (they must pay) special attention to the language of the workers, peasants, and soldiers and the masses. If we do not study the language of the masses, we cannot lead the masses.

The fifth charge against Party formalism is, "Categorizing (thoughts) Like Drugs in a Chinese Medicine Shop." If you take a look in a Chinese medicine shop, you see many shelves of drawers in the medicine counter. On each shelf is pasted the name of the drug: *Tang-kuei, Shou-ti, Ta-huang, Mang-hsiao*—everything you need. This method has also been mastered by our comrades. In writing articles, giving speeches, writing books, and writing reports, I, II, III, IV come first; next, 1, 2, 3, 4 [both of these series are in Chinese characters]; then *chia, i, ping, ting*; after that, *tzu, ch'ou, yin, mao* [characters in the traditional sexagenary cycle].[4] Then you still have A, B, C, D, and a, b, c, d. And there are still the arabic numerals, lots of them! Fortunately, the ancients and foreigners have created many symbols for us, so we can open a Chinese medicine shop without effort. If an article is filled with symbols, but states no problem, analyses no problem, and solves no problem, and neither proposes nor opposes, after much verbiage it is still a Chinese medicine shop—without real content. I am not saying that the characters *chia, i, ping,* and *ting* cannot be used, but I am saying that this is the wrong approach to a problem. At present, many comrades enthusiastically engage in the method of opening a Chinese medicine shop, yet it is really the most low-class, childish, and banal method. This method is the method of formalism, classifying issues and things according to their outer labels, but not according to their inner relationships. If one utilizes this method of simply classifying according to outer labels, so that a mass of mutually unrelated concepts is used in organizing an article, speech, or report, he is playing a game with concepts. He may also get others to play this game, and they will not use their heads in considering problems, will not think about the essence of issues and things, but will be satisfied with a *chia-i-ping-ting* arrangement of phenomena. What is a problem? A problem is simply a contradiction in facts. Wherever there is an unresolved contradiction, there is a problem. When you meet a problem, you have to support one side and oppose the other. You have to bring the problem forward for consideration. In bringing forward a problem you have first to do a general examination and research on the two basically contradictory sides of the problem, and only then can you understand the nature of the contradiction. This is the process of discovering the problem. General examination and research can discover and set up the problem, but they still offer no solution. To solve the problem you must do the work of examination and research systematically and thoroughly. This is the process of analysis. Analysis must also be used in setting up the problem, otherwise, seeing a mass of confused and muddled phenomena, you cannot know where the problem, i.e. the inconsistencies, lie. The process of analysis we speak of now means the process of systematic and thorough analysis. Often, when a problem is raised but cannot be solved, it is because the inter-relationship of facts has not yet been exposed, that is to say because the process of systematic and close analysis has not yet been utilized. It follows then that you cannot discover the two basically contra-dictory sides of the problem, which themselves produce and develop many secondary contradictions. In that case, the character of the problem is not yet clarified, and (you) still can neither do the work of synthesis nor solve the problem successfully. If a writing or speech is important and of a guiding nature, it should raise some problem, then provide an analysis, and after that a synthesis which clarifies the nature of the problem and proposes a solution. This cannot be achieved by the method of formalism. Because the childish, low-class, banal, empty-headed methods of formalism are rampant in our Party, they must be unmasked. Then only can people learn to apply the methods of Marxism in examining, raising, analysing, and solving problems. Then only shall we be able to manage things well and our revolutionary tasks be successful.

The sixth charge against Party formalism is, "Irresponsibility Which Does Universal Harm." What has been discussed above is, on the one hand, caused by infantilism, and on the other by inadequate assumption of responsibility. Take washing the face as an example. We must wash our faces every day; many do not stop at washing their faces once; and after washing their faces they still have to take a look in the mirror and engage in some examination and research (loud laughter), afraid it has not been properly done. You all can see what a sense of responsibility they have! If we will only show the same responsible attitude in writing articles and giving speeches as in washing our faces, it will be all right. If your writing or speech is unpresentable, do not present it. (You) should know that it is going to influence the thought and actions of others! Although it is not commendable if, by chance, a man fails to wash his face for a day or two, and it is certainly not a pretty sight if a few dirty spots remain on the face after washing, yet still there is really no great danger involved. It is different in writing articles and giving speeches, where the sole purpose is to influence others, yet our comrades are very careless in this respect. This is reversing the importance and unimportance of things. In writing articles and giving speeches, many comrades do not want to do research or preparation beforehand. After the articles are written, they are not re-read a few times like looking in the mirror after washing the face, but are released carelessly. The result is "writing a thousand words in one stroke, but away from the subject by ten thousand miles". Even though he looks like a talented scholar, he actually does harm everywhere. This bad habit of possessing an inadequate sense of responsibility must be corrected.

The seventh charge against Party formalism is, "Polluting the Party, Harming the Revolution." The eighth is, "Spreading (Propaganda) Which Damages the Nation and Harms the People." The meaning of these two charges is self-evident and there is no necessity of much explanation. The point of all this is that if the Party formalism is not reformed, if it is allowed to develop, the consequences can become very serious. What is hidden in Party formalism is the poison of subjectivism and sectarianism. If this poison spreads, it will do harm to the Party and disease the nation.

The eight sections above constitute our declaration of war against Party formalism.

Party formalism is not only inapt to manifest a revolutionary spirit; it can very easily cause the suffocation of the revolutionary spirit. If the revolutionary spirit is to develop, Party formalism must be cast aside, and lively, vigorous, fresh, effective forms in the spoken and written language must be adopted. Although these forms have already been produced, they are not yet enriched and have not yet reached a universal development. After we have destroyed foreign and Party formalism, new forms in the spoken and written language can become rich and reach a universal development, and the Party's revolutionary mission also will be advanced.

Party formalism is not only present in writings and speeches, but also in meetings. "First, the meeting opens; second, the reports; third, discussion; fourth, conclusions; fifth, adjournment." If everywhere and always, whether large or small, all meetings had to run according to this dead procedure, would not that also be Party formalism? In giving "reports" at meetings, it is usually, "(1) International; (2) Internal; (3) Border Areas; (4) Local." Meetings often last from morning to evening and a man with nothing to say also gives a speech; if he does not, he would be, as it were, failing his comrades. Never does he look at practical conditions, but, to the last, sticks to the old petrified forms and customs. Isn't it also necessary to correct this situation?

At present, many comrades are advocating nationalization (*min-tsu-hua*), use of the scientific spirit (*k'o-hsüeh-hua*), and popularization (*ta-chung-hua*). This is excellent. But this word "hua" means complete transformation, head to tail, inside and out. There are some who have not yet brought about the "slightest" change, and yet here they are calling for "transformation". So I advise these comrades to make these "slight changes" first, then make "transformations". Otherwise, they will remain as before, undivorced from dogmatism and Party formalism. This is known as "high standards, low performance; great ambition, sparse talent"—nothing good will come of it. Thus, those who speak of popularization, but really identify themselves with the few had better take heed. If, one day, a member of the "masses" meets him on the road and says, "Please, sir, let me see how you popularize", he will be stuck. If he not only advocates popularization verbally, but also wants to practise it, then he must actually learn from the people. Otherwise he will never be "transformed". Some, who call every day for popularization, cannot speak even three sentences of the people's language. It is easy to see that they have not set their minds on learning from the people. As before, their intention is to identify themselves with the few.

At today's meeting a pamphlet has been distributed, entitled *A Guide For Propaganda*. It contains four articles. I exhort you, comrades, to read them several times.

The first article, taken from the *History of the Communist Party of the Soviet Union*, tells how Lenin did the propaganda work. In it are explained the circumstances under which Lenin wrote propaganda leaflets:

"Under Lenin's guidance, the St. Petersburg League of Struggle for the Emancipation of the Working Class was the first body in Russia that began to unite socialism with the workers' movement. When a strike broke out in some factory, the League of Struggle, which through the members of its groups was kept well posted on the state of affairs in the industries, immediately responded by issuing leaflets and socialist proclamations. These leaflets, which exposed the oppression of the workers by the factory-owners, explained how the workers should fight for their interests, and set forth the workers' demands, they exposed completely the stark truth about the ulcers of capitalism, the poverty-stricken life of the workers, their intolerably hard working day of twelve to fourteen hours, and their utter lack of rights. They also put forth appropriate political demands in these leaflets."

Here he is very "well posted". He "exposes everything".

"At the end of 1894, Lenin, with the collaboration of the worker Babushkin, wrote the first agitational leaflet of this kind and an appeal to the workers of the Semyannikov Works in St. Petersburg who were on strike."

In writing a leaflet one should consult with comrades who are familiar with the actual conditions. Otherwise, even Lenin would not be able to write. Lenin thus wrote leaflets and did his work on the basis of examination and research.

"Each such leaflet bolstered greatly the morale of the workers, for they saw that the socialists were helping and supporting them."

Are we followers of Lenin? If the answer is "yes", we must work in the spirit of Lenin. We must do things Lenin's way, not "mouthing empty phrases, words without substance", not "shooting the arrow without a target, disregarding the objective", and not "egotistic, boastful chattering".

The second article is taken from Dimitrov's report to the Seventh Congress of the CI [July–August 1935]. What did Dimitrov say?

"We must learn to talk with the masses, not in the language of book formulas, but in the language of fighters for the cause of the masses, whose every sentence, whose every idea reflects the thoughts and sentiments of millions.

"If we do not learn to speak the language which the masses understand, they will not be able to assimilate our decisions. We do not always know how to speak simply, concretely, in images which are familiar and intelligible to the masses. We are still unable to discard those clichéd abstract formulas which we have learned by rote.

"Actually, if you look through our leaflets, newspapers, resolutions and platforms, you will see that they are written in a language and style so erudite that they are difficult for even our Party functionaries to understand, let alone the rank-and-file workers."

What do you think of this? Is not this a penetrating diagnosis of our disease? It is quite true, China has Party formalism, and so do other countries. It is evidently a universal malady. (Laughter.) But we must act according to Comrade Dimitrov's directions, and quickly effect a cure of our own disease.

"Each one of us must assimilate the following elementary rule and make it a law, a Bolshevik law: when writing or speaking always have in mind the rank-and-file worker who must understand you, must believe in your appeal and be ready to follow you. You must always have in mind those for whom you write, and those to whom you speak."

This is the prescription given us by the CI for the cure of our disease, and it must be followed. This is the "law".

The third article is selected from the *Collected Works of Lu Hsün*. It is his letter in reply to the *Pei-tou* [Big Dipper] Periodical Society discussing (the subject) "How to Write". What does he say? In all, he offers eight rules for writing. Here I have selected a few of them for discussion.

The first is, "Pay attention to all types of phenomena. Observe meticulously. Do not write immediately after only a glance."

He says, "Pay attention to everything", not only to some matters while ignoring others. He says "Observe meticulously", not with only one eye or half an eye. Does this apply to us? Don't we go just contrary to his advice? Don't we "write immediately, after only a glance"?

The second is, "When you cannot write, don't persist in writing."

How does this apply to us? Isn't it just as if we had nothing in our bellies, yet were determined to go to stool? Taking the pen and "persisting in writing", without examination or research, is evidence of an irresponsible attitude.

The fourth is, "After you have finished (writing), read (your manuscript over) at least twice. Do your utmost to be pitiless in striking out unnecessary words, sentences, and paragraphs. Condense the materials of a novel into a sketch, but never take the materials of a sketch and stretch them into a novel."

Confucius advocated "thinking twice (before you act)"; Han Yü also spoke of "action derived from thought". This was said under the conditions of feudal society. Today the situation and problems are very complex; it is not enough to think over certain situations even three or four times. Lu Hsün said, "Read (your manuscript over) at least twice." And at the most? He didn't say. I think that it does no harm to read over an important writing ten times or more, revise it painstakingly, and only then publish it. Writings are reflections of objective reality. Since reality is complex and complicated, you must study your facts repeatedly, then only can the reflection be accurate. To proceed in this matter carelessly and lightly is not to know the ABC of writing.

The sixth is, "Do not artificially create adjectives, etc., which are incomprehensible to everyone but yourself." We have "artificially created" too many things, and they are invariably "incomprehensible" to everyone. Sentences sometimes run forty to fifty characters long and are filled with "incomprehensible adjectives". A great many who loudly support Lu Hsün are actually disobeying him!

The last article is the discussion at the Sixth Plenum of the CC, CCP, on the nationalization of propaganda. The Sixth Plenum took place in 1938. At that time we said, "If you speak of Marxism apart from the special characteristics of China, it is only abstract and empty Marxism." That is to say, that a CP member living in China who divorces himself from the actual needs of China in speaking of Marxism is a false Marxist, even though he reads ten thousand Marxist books a thousand times. Such a "Marxist theorist" is a false theorist, like "a mouse getting on to a weighing-hook—he lends himself weight".[5] [To quote the Sixth Plenum further]:

> "Foreign formalism must be done away with. Empty abstract tunes must remain unsung. Dogmatism must be given a rest. For them must be substituted a fresh, lively Chinese spirit and style which the Chinese common people like to hear and see. To separate the substance of internationalism and the form of national-ism is the approach of those who do not have the slightest understanding of internationalism; so we must take these two and integrate them closely. Certain serious shortcomings harboured by our rank and file in connection with this problem must be strictly eradicated."

Although the eradication of foreign formalism has been called for here, some comrades still advocate it in practice. Although silence has been requested on empty, abstract tunes, some comrades persist in singing them frequently. Although a cessation of dogmatism has been called for, some comrades still call it forth. In summary, there are many who act as if the decisions of the Sixth Plenum are just wind past the ear, as if they were intentionally opposing these decisions.

The CC has now resolved that foreign formalism, Party formalism, dogmatism, etc., must, without fail, be abandoned. That is why I am here to speak at such great length. I hope that our comrades will consider this speech carefully and analyse it. Moreover, each must analyse himself; each must weigh his own self carefully. Consult with your sweethearts, your intimate friends, and the comrades around you on matters which you have thought out clearly, and cure your own disease thoroughly. This is our hope.

36. MAO TSE-TUNG: SPEECH MADE AT THE FORUM ON
LITERATURE AND ART AT YENAN (May 2 and 23, 1942) [extract]

Comrades! I have asked you all to come together for a conference today [p. 267] to exchange opinions about, and study the proper relationship between, literary and artistic work and revolutionary work in general, and to seek the proper development of revolutionary literature and art and their greater co-operation with other revolutionary work, so that we may crush our national enemies and fulfil the work of national liberation.

The various fronts of our struggle for the liberation of the Chinese people may be grouped into two: the civil and the martial [i.e. the ancient Chinese contrast between *wen* and *wu*, "literary" and "military", etc.]; they are the cultural front and the military front. We must rely on armed troops to conquer the enemy, but this in itself is not enough. A cultural army is also indispensable for uniting ourselves and conquering the enemy. This cultural army has materialized in China since May Fourth [1919], it has helped the Chinese revolution, and has caused a gradual decrease in the territory dominated by a feudalistic and slavish culture which has yielded to imperialistic encroachments.

Literature and art have been an important and highly effective part of the cultural front since the May Fourth (movement). During the civil war the revolutionary literature and art movement showed great development and in its over-all [p. 268] direction was consistent with the Red Army's struggle of that period, although in actual work the two were fighting isolatedly, due to the separation of the two brother armies by the reactionaries. Since the war of resistance a great number of revolutionary literature and art workers have come to Yenan and every other anti-Japanese base. This is a very good thing. However, merely coming to these bases is not the same as identifying oneself with the people's movement in the bases. If we would push forward the revolutionary work, we will have to make these two become completely identified with each other.

The purpose of our meeting today is to make literature and art become a constructive part of the whole revolutionary machine; to use it as a powerful weapon for uniting and educating the people and for crushing and destroying the enemy, as well as to help the people wage the struggle against the enemy with one heart and one mind. What are some of the problems which must be solved in order to achieve this aim? They are the problems of standpoint, attitude, audience, work, and study.

The problem of standpoint. We adopt the standpoint of the proletariat and the people. The CP members must also adopt the standpoint of the Party, of Party spirit and Party policies. Are there any of our literature and art workers who lack clear and exact understanding on this problem? I think so. Many comrades have frequently lost their own correct standpoint.

The problem of attitude. Following the question of one's standpoint, there arises the problem of the concrete attitudes we are to adopt towards various concrete issues and matters. For example, are we to sing praises or expose defects? These are problems of attitude. Which do we actually need? I say we need both. The question lies in who their recipient is to be. There are three kinds of people—enemies, friends, and ourselves, meaning by the latter the proletariat and its vanguard—and each one must be treated differently. Should we "sing the praises" of the enemy, the Japanese fascists, and all other enemies of the people? Decidedly not, because they are all the worst kind of reactionaries. In technical skills they may have some good points, such as their good weapons. But good weapons held in their hands are reactionary ones. The mission of our armed forces is to capture their [p. 269] weapons and turn those weapons around to crush them. The mission of our cultural forces is to expose the enemy's brutality, his deception, and his certain future defeat, to encourage the troops and people to be of one heart and one mind in resisting the Japanese, and resolutely beat down the enemy. . . . On the other hand, we must certainly praise the masses of the people, the labour and struggle of the people, the army of the people, and the party of the people. The people also have some defects; among the proletariat there are still many who cling to petty-bourgeois ideas, many peasants and petty bourgeois who have backward ideas. These are the burdens under which they are struggling, and we must unceasingly, patiently teach them and help them to get rid of those burdens so that they can stride forward. . . .

The problem of audience is the problem, for whom are literature and art? In the Border Area and every anti-Japanese base in North and Central China, this problem is different from that in the [KMT] rear areas or in Shanghai before the war. In the Shanghai period, the recipients of revolutionary works of literature and art were for the most part students, office workers, and shop employees. In the [KMT] rear areas during the war, the sphere has become a little wider, but basically it is still these same types, because the government there has kept the workers, peasants, and soldiers away from the revolutionary literature and art. In our bases it is completely different. The audience for works of literature and art in our bases is made up of the workers, peasants, and soldiers and their Party, political and military cadres. There are also students in our bases, but these students also are different from the old-style students. They are either experienced cadres or cadres to be. [p. 270] All kinds of cadres, soldiers in the army, workers in the factory, peasants in the village will read books and newspapers if they can read. If they cannot read, they will see plays, look at pictures, sing songs, or listen to music. They, then, are the audience for our works of literature and art. . . .

Since the audience for literature and art is made up of the workers, peasants, soldiers, and their cadres, there arises the problem of understanding and knowing them thoroughly. But in order to understand them and know them thoroughly, understand and know thoroughly every detail, understand and know thoroughly every kind of person among them, in the Party and administrative organizations, in the villages, in the factories, in the Eighth Route Army, and the New Fourth Army, one must work very hard. Our literature and art workers must do their own work, but this work of understanding men and knowing them thoroughly must take first place. What was the status of our literature and art workers previously with regard to this? I say that previously they lacked thorough knowledge, lacked understanding, and were heroes without a place to use their weapons. What did they not know thoroughly? They did not know the people thoroughly. The literature and art workers did not know thoroughly the characters in their own works or their audience and were sometimes even very unfamiliar with them. They did not know thoroughly the workers, peasants, soldiers or their cadres. . . .

In this respect I can say a word about my own experience in the transformation of my feelings. I started out as a student, and in school developed the habits of a student. It did not seem proper for me to do even a little bit of hard work such as carrying my own baggage, in front of a whole crowd of students who were unable to shoulder a load or pick up a heavy weight. At that time I felt that the only clean people in the world were the intellectuals, and the workers, peasants, and soldiers were all comparatively dirty. I could wear the clothes of other intellectuals because I thought they were clean, but I did not want to wear the clothes of the workers, peasants, or soldiers because I felt they were dirty. After the revolution when I joined in with the workers, peasants, and soldiers, I gradually came to know them thoroughly and they too gradually came to know me. At this time, and only then, did I basically outgrow those bourgeois and petty-bourgeois sentiments which the bourgeois school had taught me. At this time I compared the unreconstructed intellectuals with the workers, peasants, and soldiers, and felt that the intellectuals not only were in spirit unclean in many places, but their bodies too were unclean. The cleanest ones still were the workers and peasants—even taking into account that their hands were black and their feet covered with cow dung, they were still cleaner than the bourgeoisie, big and small. This then is what is meant by outgrowing one's sentiments and changing from one class to another. If our intellectual literature and art workers who have come from the ranks of the intelligentsia would make their own works welcomed by the masses, they must transform and completely reconstruct their own thoughts and feelings. . . .

The last problem is one of study. I mean by this the study of Marxism-Leninism and of society. To speak of oneself as a revolutionary writer of Marxism-Leninism, especially a Party member writer, one must have a general knowledge of Marxism-Leninism. However, there are some comrades today who are deficient in its basic concepts. For example, one of the basic concepts of Marxism-Leninism is that the objective determines the subjective, that is to say, [p. 272] the objective reality of the class struggle and national struggle determines our thoughts and feelings. Yet there are some comrades who try to turn this around, who say everything must develop from "love". Now how about love? In a class society there is only class love. Yet these comrades want to look for some kind of super-love that transcends classes; an abstract love, as well as abstract freedom, abstract truth, abstract human nature, etc. This clearly indicates that these comrades have been deeply influenced by the bourgeoisie. They must liquidate this influence to the very core, and must humbly study Marxism-Leninism. Literate-and-art workers must study creative works of literature and art, it is true, but Marxism-Leninism is a science which all revolutionaries must study, and workers in literature and art cannot be an exception. . . .

Conclusion. May 23, 1942. . . .

Now then what is the heart of our problems? I think basically our problem lies in serving the masses and how to serve them. If this problem remains unsolved or is solved only inadequately, this may keep our literature and art workers from being attuned to their own environment and responsibilities, and bring them up against a whole string of problems, both external and internal. In my Conclusion, I shall take this problem [that of serving the people] as the core and explain it, at the same time discussing some of the problems related to it. . . .

I. THE FIRST PROBLEM: FOR WHOM ARE OUR LITERATURE AND ART? . . .

[p. 275] We have said that the new stage of Chinese culture today is a proletarian-led, anti-imperialistic, anti-feudalistic culture of the people. Everything belonging to the true people now definitely comes under the leadership of the proletariat; and everything which comes under the leadership of the bourgeoisie cannot belong to the people. Naturally the new literature and art of the new culture are the same. We do not refuse to utilize the old forms of the feudalistic and bourgeois classes for our own ends, but when these old forms have come into our hands, have been reconstructed, and have had new content added to them, they become a revolutionary thing for the service of the people.

Now, then, what are the people? The greatest mass of the people, those who constitute more than ninety per cent of the total population, are the workers, peasants, soldiers, and petty bourgeoisie. Therefore our literature and art are first of all for the workers, for they are the class which leads the revolution; secondly, they are for the peasants, for they are the most numerous, most firm ally in the revolution; thirdly, they are for the workers and peasants who are armed, i.e. the Eighth Route Army, New Fourth Army, and other people's armed units, for they are the main strength of the struggle; and, fourthly, they are for the petty bourgeoisie for they also are an ally in the revolution and are able to co-operate with us in the long run. These four types form the greatest part of the Chinese nation, and form the most extensive mass of the people. We must also co-operate with the landlord and bourgeois classes who are resisting the Japanese. They, however, do not favour the democracy of the broad masses, and both have a literature and an art which are for themselves. Our literature and art are not created for them, and they for their part reject it.

Our literature and art, then, must be for the above-mentioned four types, of whom the most important are the workers, peasants, and soldiers. The petty-bourgeois class is comparatively small, its revolutionary determination is comparatively weak, and it has had a greater degree of cultural upbringing than the workers, peasants, and soldiers.

Therefore our literature and art are first and foremost for the workers, peasants, and soldiers and secondly for the petty bourgeoisie. . . .

Many comrades, because they themselves are petty-bourgeois intellectuals, find their friends only in the intellectual camp, and use their powers of observation to study and describe that side. If this sort of research and description adopts the standpoint of the proletariat, then it is all right. But they do not do this, or, at least, not completely. They take their stand among the petty bourgeoisie and create their works as a self-expression of the petty-bourgeois class. We have seen this sort of thing in quite a few works of literature and art. . . .

[p. 278] We encourage the revolutionary writers and artists actively to get close to workers, peasants, and soldiers, and allow them complete freedom to create genuine revolutionary literature and art. Therefore this problem is nearing solution here. But a near solution is not the same as a complete and penetrating solution. We say that in order to solve this problem completely and penetratingly, we must study Marxism-Leninism and society, that is to say, a living Marxism-Leninism which is completely applicable to the mass livelihood and mass struggle, and not the Marxism-Leninism of the books. If we transfer the Marxism-Leninism of the books to the masses and achieve a living Marxism-Leninism, there will no longer be sectarianism. . . .

II

Having solved the problem of for whom we are working, we can now take up the next problem of how to go about working for them. To use the words of our comrades, shall we put our utmost strength into elevating [standards] or popularizing? [Mao here raises the problem of quality *v.* quantity]. . . . The elevation comes only from the foundation of the workers, peasants, and soldiers, from the present level of their culture and the foundation of their literature and art in their budding stage. Furthermore (our aim) is not to raise them to the level of the feudal class, bourgeoisie, or petty bourgeoisie, but to elevate them along the direction of their own progress. This then brings up the duty of learning from the workers, peasants, and soldiers. Only by proceeding from them will we be able to be correct in our understanding of popularization and elevation and be able to find a correct relationship between the two.

What is the source of both popularization and elevation? No matter what the literary and artistic quality of a work may be, taken in an ideological form, they are all the result of the reflection and processing of the people's life on human minds. Revolutionary literature and art, then, are the result of the reflection and processing of the people's life on the minds of revolutionary writers. The resources of literature and art which are actually contained in the life of the people are things in their raw form, rough and crude things, but, at the same time, extremely life-like, rich, and basic things. By comparison they are superior to all literature and art in the polished form and are the only inexhaustible source for such literature and art. . . .

Popularizing is a popularizing among the people; elevating, too, is an [p. 282] elevating of the people, and this sort of elevation is not formed out of thin air or behind closed doors, but is on a popular base. It is determined by the popularization, but at the same time gives direction to the popularization. Now to speak of China alone, the development of the revolution, and that of the revolutionary culture are not even, but by fits and starts. In one place there has been the work of popularization and also that of elevation resting on the basis of popularization, while in other places the work of popularization has not yet begun. Therefore, the experience of one place can and should be utilized in other places to give guidance to the work and reduce the amount of travelling on detoured roads. On an international plane, too, the experiences, provided they be good, of foreign countries, especially the Soviet Union, have a function in guiding us in the work of popularization and elevation. However, the whole guiding function of elevating work should not be arbitrary transplanting, which will only have a destructive function.

Besides the elevation which directly serves the needs of the masses, there is still another kind which indirectly serves them. This is the elevation serving the needs of the cadres. . . .

III

Having established that our literature and art are for the people, we can go on to discuss the problem of their relationship within the Party, that is to say, the relationship between the Party's literary and artistic work and the work of the Party as a whole; also the problem of their relationship outside the Party, that is to say, the relationship between the Party's literary and artistic work and the non-Party literary and artistic work—the problem of the united front of literature and art.

Let us first speak about the first problem. In the world of today, all culture or literature and art belong to some one definite class, some one definite party, i.e. some one definite political line. Art for art's sake, art which transcends class or party, art which stands as a by-stander to, or independent of, politics, does not in actual fact exist. Since art is subordinate to class and party in a society which has classes and parties, it must undoubtedly follow the political demands of those classes and parties, must follow the revolutionary period. If it deviates from these, it will deviate from the basic needs of the masses. Proletarian literature and art are one part of the entire proletarian revolutionary cause: as Lenin says, "a screw in the whole machine". Therefore, the literary and artistic work of the Party has a definite and set position in the Party's entire revolutionary work. Opposition to this sort of arrangement will certainly lead to dualism or pluralism, and its real nature will resemble Trotsky's "Marxist politics, bourgeois art". We do not favour over-emphasizing the importance of literature and art, but also we do not favour under-estimating their importance. Literature and art are subordinate [p. 286] to politics, but in turn also wield a great influence over them. Revolutionary literature and art are a part of the whole revolutionary cause. . . .

If we do not have literature and art in their broadest, most universal sense, the revolution cannot carry on, cannot be victorious. It is erroneous not to recognize this point. Furthermore, when we say literature and art follow politics, by politics we mean class politics, mass politics, and not that of a small number of politicians. Politics, no matter whether revolutionary or counter-revolutionary, is a struggle of class against class; it is not the activity of a small number of individuals. The struggle of ideas and the struggle of art, especially revolutionary ideas and art, must follow the political struggle, because only through politics can they express, in concentrated form, class and mass needs. The revolutionary politicians, the political specialists who understand revolutionary political science or political art, are the leaders of the millions of mass politicians; their duty lies in concentrating and extracting the opinions of those mass politicians, and then in giving them back to the masses, to become accepted and practised by the masses. They are not those aristocratic-typed, so-called "politicians" who wishfully create behind closed doors [i.e. out of touch with the actual conditions], who pretend to be wise, and who say only that they have the right [to political activity]. This is the basic distinction between the proletarian and propertied class politician, and also the basic distinction between the proletarian and propertied class politics. It is also erroneous not to recognize this point and to narrow down or vulgarize proletarian politics and politicians.

Let us now speak about the problem of a united front in the world of literature and art. Literature and art follow politics. China's most fundamental political problem today is that of resisting Japan. Therefore, on this point the Party's literature and art workers must unite with all the writers and artists outside the Party (from Party sympathizers and petty-bourgeois writers and artists on down to bourgeois and landlord class writers and artists). Next they must unite on the point of democracy. Since there are some writers and artists who will not agree on this point, the range of [p. 287] accord here narrows down a little. Next they must unite on a point which is a special problem in the world of literature and art—that of literary and artistic style. We advocate proletarian realism, but there are some who will not acquiesce in this, with the result that the range of accord will probably become still smaller. There may be unity on one problem, but on another there may be struggle and criticism. . . .

IV

One of the most important methods of struggle in the world of literature and art is literary and artistic criticism. . . .

Literary and artistic criticism has two standards, political and artistic. According to the political standard, everything promoting [p. 288] unity in the war of resistance, encouraging the masses to be of one heart and one mind, opposing shirking and stimulating progress, is good or comparatively good. Everything failing to promote unity in the war, encouraging the masses to be of divided hearts and minds, opposing progress, and drawing the people into shirking, is bad or comparatively bad. In the final analysis, are the good and bad which we speak of here to be looked at from the point of view of motivation (subjective aspiration) or from that of effect (social application)? Idealists emphasize motivation and disregard effect. Mechanistic materialists emphasize effect and disregard motivation. But we, unlike these two, as dialectical materialists advocate the unity of motivation and effect. The motivation acting for the masses and the effect welcomed by the masses are inseparable; we should keep them united. Motivation which serves the individual or the limited group is no good; neither is that which, while serving the masses, lacks an effect (which is) welcome or advantageous to the masses. When we examine the subjective aspirations of a writer, that is whether or not his motive is correct and good, we do not look at his words but look at the effect of his activity (his work) produced in the social masses. Social application is the standard by which to examine subjective aspirations; the effect is the standard for examining the motivation. Our literary and artistic criticism must not have sectarianism. Under the great principle of unity in the war of resistance we must allow the inclusion of literary and artistic works representing every kind and sort of political attitude. However, our criticism will be firm upon our principle and standpoint. We must give severe judgment to all works of literature and art that are anti-national, anti-scientific, anti-masses, and anti-Communistic in viewpoint, because these so-called works of literature and art, their motivation and effect, all harm the unity of the war (effort).

According to artistic standards, everything having comparatively high artistic quality is good or comparatively good; and everything having comparatively low artistic quality is bad or comparatively bad. This sort of distinction, naturally, also requires a glance at the social application. There are almost no writers or artists who do not consider their own works to be excellent. Our criticism ought to allow the free competition of every kind and sort of work of art, but if we supply correct criticism according to scientific standards of art, we can make comparatively low-grade art gradually become elevated to a high-grade art, and make art which is not suitable to the needs of the mass struggle (even though it may be very high-grade art) change into an art which does meet these needs. This also is absolutely necessary.

[p. 298] There is a political standard, there is an artistic standard; what is the relationship between the two? Politics is not synonymous with art, nor is a general view of the world synonymous with the methodological theories of artistic creation. We not only do not recognize abstract and eternal political standards, but also do not recognize such standards for art. Every class society and every separate class within that society has different political and artistic standards. But no matter what kind of class society or what kind of separate class within that class society it may be, it always puts the political standard first and artistic standard second. The bourgeois class always rejects the proletarian works of literature and art, no matter how high their standard may be. The proletarian classes must also reject the reactionary political nature of the bourgeois works of literature and art, and assimilate their art only in a critical manner. It is possible for some things (which are) politically, basically reactionary to have a certain artistry, for example the fascist literature and art. However, the more artistic a work which is reactionary in content, the more harmful does it become to the people and the more it ought to be rejected. The common characteristics in the literature and art of the exploiting classes in their period of decline are the inconsistencies between their reactionary political content and their artistic form. Our demand, then, is a unity of politics and art, a unity of content and form, and a unity of revolutionary political content and an artistic form of as high a standard as possible. Works of art which are deficient in artistry, no matter how advanced they are politically, will not have any force. For this reason, we oppose works of art whose content is harmful and also oppose the so-called "slogan type" tendency which only considers the content and not the form. We must carry on this twofold struggle in the problem of literature and art.

These two tendencies exist among many of our comrades. There are many comrades who have a tendency to neglect artistic skill, and so they must pay heed to the elevation of artistic skill. But now something which has become more of a problem lies, I think, in the political sphere. Some comrades are deficient in basic general political knowledge, and so have developed all sorts of muddled ideas. . . .

v

. . . Among our comrades there are still many defects such as idealism, foreign dogmatism, utopianism, empty talk, slighting of actuality, and alienation from the masses, and we need a solid, serious movement to correct the unorthodox tendencies. . . .

Since we must identify ourselves with the new era of the masses, we must thoroughly solve the problem of the relationship between the individual and the masses. Two lines from one of Lu Hsün's poems [entitled *Tzu-ch'ao*, "Self-ridicule"]: "With drawn brows I disdainfully face the stares of thousands as I gladly submit myself as a cow for the suckling child" should become our motto. The "thousands" are the enemy, and we must not submit to any enemy, no matter how brutal and wicked. The "suckling child" is the proletariat and the people. All the CP members, all the revolutionists, and all the revolutionary artists and writers must follow Lu Hsün's example and be the "cow" of the proletariat and the people, and serve (them) humbly and devotedly until death. The intellectuals must identify themselves with the masses, and must serve the masses. This process may, in fact it definitely will, produce much suffering and friction. But if everyone is resolved, these demands upon us can be met.

What I have talked about today are only a few of the basic problems of direction in our literature and art movement. There are still many other [p. 297] concrete problems which must continue to be studied in the future. I have faith that the comrades will, with determination, march in this direction. I have faith that the comrades during the process of correcting the unorthodox tendencies and during their long period of study and work in the future will indubitably succeed in changing the face of themselves and their work; in creating many excellent works which will be enthusiastically welcomed by workers, peasants, soldiers, and the people; and in advancing the literature and art movement of our bases and of the entire country to a glorious new stage.

COMMENTARY U. THE CLIMAX OF THE YENAN PERIOD

The revised Party Constitution was passed at the Seventh National Congress on June 11, 1945, at Yenan, at the very end of the momentous decade of the Yenan period. Its provisions appear to reflect a number of trends which deserve further study.

Since this Constitution of 1945 superseded the previous one passed on July 9, 1938, at the Sixth National Congress of the CCP in Moscow, a comparison of the two texts is of interest.[1] In the absence of a more thorough study, the following points in the two Constitutions may be noted: in form the revised Constitution is more elaborate, having 70 articles as against 52 in the 1928 version (although the latter has 15 chapters and the revised version only 11, chapters on the various organs of the CCP being grouped into larger but fewer sections). Three new chapters are added in the 1945 text, on the Duties of Members, Rights and Privileges of Members, and Underground Party Organizations. Another addition is the Preamble of about three printed pages, in which it is significantly and explicitly stated that "the ideas of Mao Tse-tung, the combined principles derived from the practical experiences of the Chinese revolution", are added to Marxism-Leninism as the "guiding principles of all its (the Party's) work".

Certain outstanding features of the new Constitution may be summarized as follows:

(1) *Increased centralization of power.* For example: (*a*) "Prior to their determination by the CC, the local and other Party organizations or their responsible officers shall discuss questions of a national character only among themselves, or submit their proposals respecting such questions to the CC. In no case shall they make a public announcement of their views or decisions . . ." (article 25). (*b*) The creation

of the post of Chairman of the CC, who is stipulated to be concurrently the Chairman of the Central Political Bureau and of the Central Secretariat (article 34). (*c*) The number of members of the Provincial Congresses is to be approved by the CC or its representative organs (article 40); the CC has the right to disapprove the elections of secretaries and members of the standing committees of the Provincial and Regional Party Committees, which in turn hold the right to disapprove the elections of secretaries of the local, municipal, and district Party committees (articles 40 and 48); while the stipulation in the old text that "the Provincial Party Committee is the highest Party organ in a Province" is conspicuously absent in the revised version. (*d*) The Party Congresses at various levels are held at longer intervals; for example, the old provision that a National Congress is to be held every year (article 35) is changed to read (article 29) that it is to be held every three years. (This latter provision has not been observed, there having been no National Congress of the CCP since June 1945.) Since the Congresses on various levels are the superior controlling bodies of the Party Committees on their respective levels, the longer the interval between the convocation of Congresses, the more power is actually vested in the Party Committees. (For changes in the schedules of meetings for provincial, regional, local, county, municipal, and district Congresses, compare articles 22 and 28 in the old text with articles 40 and 47 in the revised version.) (*e*) The regular and alternate members of the CC may be dismissed from the CC or even from Party membership by a decision of two-thirds of the CC membership (article 65). The regular plenary session of the CC meets every six instead of every three months, and is convoked by the Central Political Bureau (article 33). All this serves to heighten directly or indirectly the authority of the Central Political Bureau and of the Chairman of the CC, who is, of course, also the Chairman of the Central Political Bureau.

(2) *Greater weight given to rural areas.* In Chapter VI of the revised text, entitled "The basic organization of the Party", article 50 stipulates that "where there are more than fifty regular and probationary members in a village, or more than 100 regular or probationary members in a factory . . . a principal Party cell may be established . . ." (see also article 51), whereas in the 1928 text, factories and unions are invariably given priority over villages. In the article on "The tasks of the cell", the old text states that "the tasks are to link the workers and peasants . . . by Communist propaganda and agitation . . . to discuss their demands from the viewpoint of the revolutionary class

struggle . . . to absorb them (so they may) participate in the general revolutionary struggle of the proletariat in China and abroad" (article 18); whereas the revised version reads ". . . to unite the masses closely with the Party . . . to carry on propaganda and organizational work among the masses with a view to carrying out the Party programmes and the decisions of higher Party organs . . . constantly to watch, and reflect to the higher Party authority, the aspirations and demands of the masses . . ." (article 52). These differences in emphasis on the various classes in China, whether due to tactical expediency or to a genuine shift of view, seem clearly to show the effect of the Sino-Japanese war, during which the sentiment of nationalism grew so strong.

(3) *More emphasis on "intra-Party democracy"*. Three new articles (66, 67, and 68) added to the revised Constitution call for the Party organs to be "careful in hearing the case of an appellant and in analysing his offence in the light of the circumstances in which it (the error) was committed. . . ." They also provide more channels for appeal. The new text stipulates that the resolutions of the Party Representatives' Conferences at central, provincial, and regional levels must have the approval of their corresponding Congresses (articles 30 and 45), also that "the leading organs of all levels of the Party shall be established through elections", and "the leading organs of all levels of the Party shall submit periodic reports to the organizations by which they are elected" (articles 14 (a) and (b)). In view of the nature of "democratic centralism", no conflict need be imagined between these procedural devices for the activity of lower organs concerning high policy and the ultimate fact of policy control at the top. Control committees at all levels are also provided for in the new Constitution.

(4) The revised Constitution mentions neither the CI nor the CY, whereas the old text mentions the former sixteen times as the supreme authority and guiding hand of the CCP, and devotes its last chapter to the latter. The conspicuous absence of these two organizations in the new text may be explained by the simple fact that they no longer were in existence in 1945.[2] But it is not without interest to note also that such phrases as "to participate in the revolutionary struggle of the international and Chinese proletariat" are omitted in the new document. This seems to reflect the shift of the CCP's domestic propaganda line during the united front period.

37. CONSTITUTION OF THE CHINESE COMMUNIST PARTY
(June 11, 1945)

The CCP is the organized vanguard of the Chinese working class, the highest form of its class organization. Standing for the interests of the Chinese nation and people, its task in the present stage is to struggle for the realization of the New Democracy in China. Its ultimate aim is the realization of Communism in China.

The CCP takes the theories of Marxism-Leninism and the combined principles derived from the practical experience of the Chinese revolution—the ideas of Mao Tse-tung—as the guiding principles of all its work; it denounces any one-sided tendencies towards dogmatism and empiricism. The CCP is based on the dialectical and historical materialism of Marxism, accepting with critical attitude its historical heritage both in China and in other countries, and denouncing any idealistic or mechanistic-materialistic conception of the world.

Because the present Chinese society, except in the new democratic Liberated Areas, remains semi-colonial and semi-feudal; because the dynamic forces of the Chinese revolution are the working class, the peasant class, the petty bourgeoisie, and other democratic elements; because a powerful CCP is already in existence; and because of present international conditions, the Chinese revolution in the present stage must take the form of a new bourgeois-democratic revolution—that is, an anti-imperialist, anti-feudal, new democratic revolution of the masses under the leadership of the proletariat. This revolution has extensive allies at home and abroad. Therefore, the tasks of the CCP in the present stage are: internally, to organize and unify the Chinese workers, peasants, petty bourgeoisie, intelligentsia, and all anti-imperialist and anti-feudal elements and national minorities on its side; and, externally, to unite with the world proletariat, with all oppressed peoples, and with all those nations which treat us with equality—to struggle for the emancipation of the Chinese nation from foreign imperialist aggression, the liquidation of the feudal oppression of the masses, the establishment of an independent, free, democratic, united, and prosperous and strong new democratic federated republic based on the alliance of all revolutionary classes and free union of all races, and to struggle for the realization of world peace and progress.

In the future stage of the Chinese revolution, after the complete victory of the national and democratic revolution in China, the task of the CCP will be to struggle, by necessary steps, according to the requirements of China's social and economic development and the will of her people, for the realization of socialism and Communism in China.

In China, a semi-colonial and semi-feudal country with a vast area and a huge population but not yet a unified country, there is, on the one hand, a heroic and fighting revolutionary tradition among the masses of the people, particularly the workers and peasants; but, on the other hand, there are especially powerful obstacles along the revolutionary path. Because of these conditions the Chinese revolutionary struggle is complicated, and it must, for a very long time, find primary expression in armed struggle. Before the victory of the revolution in the key cities, it will be pre-eminently important to consolidate the villages as a revolutionary base and it will also be necessary for the Party to undergo a long period of patient work among the popular masses. Based on all these characteristics of the Chinese revolution, the CCP must therefore, on the long road of Chinese revolution, be very bold, well experienced, and always alert to mobilize and organize the great masses to overcome all difficulties and avoid all dangers in its path, so that it may march towards its goal while continually training its rank and file.

In its revolutionary struggle the CCP must endeavour to establish itself as the core of all revolutionary mass organizations and of the revolutionary organizations of the nation. It must carry on a solemn struggle against everything of internal or external origin which threatens to undermine the unity of the working class, the alliance of all revolutionary classes, and other revolutionary tasks.

Within its ranks the CCP cannot tolerate the existence of right or left opportunism. It must wage an uncompromising but effective struggle within the Party against opportunists, surrenderists, and adventurists, and must expel from Party membership all those who are obstinate in their errors, in order to maintain unity among the rank and file.

The CCP should not conceal its own mistakes or the shortcomings committed in its work. It should use the methods of criticism and self-criticism constantly to rectify its own mistakes and shortcomings, and should educate its own Party members and staff to correct their own mistakes speedily. It objects to egotism, to being afraid to acknowledge its own mistakes, and to fear of criticism and self-criticism.

CCP members must possess the spirit of whole-hearted and undivided service to the Chinese people; they must have close co-operation with the masses of workers, peasants, and other revolutionary elements, and must constantly consolidate and expand this co-operation. Every Party member must realize the harmony of interests between the masses and the Party, and the identity between being responsible to the Party and the people. He must listen carefully to the voice of the people and to understand their pressing needs, and must help them become organized to struggle for the attainment of these needs. Every Party member must be determined to learn from the masses, while at the same time tirelessly educating them and developing their mass consciousness with revolutionary spirit. The CCP must constantly guard against the danger of being alienated from the masses and must prevent and liquidate within its rank and file such incorrect tendencies as "tailism", dictatorialness, isolationism, bureaucracy, and militarism that will cause its alienation from the masses.

The CCP is a unified, combat organization, built on the principle of democratic centralism, and held together by the discipline which all Party members must observe conscientiously and voluntarily. The strength of the CCP rests on its solidarity, unified will, and integral action. The Party cannot tolerate any internal action which deviates from its programme and Constitution or is detrimental to discipline; it cannot tolerate any demand for autonomy within the Party, factionalism, or two-faced deeds which pretend to obey the Party while opposing it in practice. The CCP must constantly purge from its ranks those who violate the programme, Constitution, and discipline of Party membership, and who are incorrigible in their mistakes.

The CCP asks that every Party member carry on his work positively, in the spirit of self-sacrifice, so that its programme and resolutions can be realized, and the complete liberation of the Chinese nation and the Chinese people achieved.

Chapter I

MEMBERSHIP

Article 1. Those who accept the programme and Constitution of the Party, participate in the activities of its organizations, comply with its resolutions and pay membership fees, may become members of the Party.

Article 2. Party members shall perform the following duties:

(*a*) Endeavour to raise the degree of their consciousness and study the basic ideas of Marxism-Leninism and of Mao Tse-tung's thought.

(*b*) Observe Party discipline strictly, participate positively in the political life of the Party and in the nation's revolutionary movements, carry out actively the Party's policies and the resolutions of Party organs, and struggle to overcome all internal and external phenomena detrimental to the interests of the Party.

(*c*) Serve the masses, strengthen the tie between the Party and the masses, understand and reflect speedily the needs of the masses, and explain the policies of the Party to the masses.

(*d*) Observe exemplarily the disciplines of the revolutionary government and revolutionary organizations, be proficient in one's own work, and set examples for the people in all revolutionary undertakings.

Article 3. Party members shall enjoy the following rights and privileges:

(*a*) Participation in free and practical discussions on the enforcement of the policies of the Party, either in Party meetings or in Party publications.

(*b*) The right to elect and be elected for office within the Party.

(*c*) Submission of suggestions or statements to any organ of the Party, up to the CC.

(*d*) Criticism of the work of any member at Party meetings.

Article 4. Only those persons are eligible for Party membership who are eighteen years of age or over. All persons seeking admission into the Party shall individually comply with the admission procedures according to the following sections:

(*a*) Applications for membership by workers, coolies, hired farm hands, poor peasants, urban paupers, and revolutionary soldiers shall require the recommendation of two regular Party members. The application shall be decided upon at a plenary meeting of the Party cell and be approved by the district Party committee, or a corresponding committee. New members shall undergo a probationary period of six months before they become regular members.

(*b*) Application for membership by middle peasants, salaried employees, intellectual elements, and professionals shall require the recommendation of two regular Party members, one of whom must be a regular member of one year's standing. The application shall be decided upon at a plenary meeting of the Party cell, and be approved by the district Party committee, or a corresponding committee. The probationary period for such new members shall be one year before they become regular members.

In areas where the revolution has only recently been developed, the CC or its representative organ, or the provincial Party organization or regional Party committee, may establish temporary regulations with regard to the qualifications of sponsors and the probationary period of new members as provided in sections (*a*) and (*b*).

(*c*) Applications for membership by persons who have any other social background than provided for in sections (*a*) and (*b*) shall require the recommendation of two regular Party members, one of whom must be a regular member of three years' standing. The application shall be decided upon at a Party cell plenary meeting and approved by a *hsien* or district Party committee, municipal Party committee, or other committee corresponding to the *hsien* Party committee. The probationary period for such members shall be two years before they become regular members.

(*d*) Applications for membership by persons who have withdrawn from another party in which they were ordinary members shall require the recommendation of two regular Party members, one of whom must be a member of three years' standing. The application shall be decided upon at a Party cell plenary meeting and approved by the *hsien* Party committee, or its equivalent. If the applicant was a responsible officer of his former party, his application shall require the recommendation of two regular Party members, one of whom must be a member of five years' standing. The application shall be decided upon at a Party cell plenary meeting and be approved by the provincial Party committee, or its equivalent. (If the applicant was an important responsible officer of his former political party, his application requires the approval of the CC.) The probationary period for such new members shall be two years before they become regular members.

Article 5. In special circumstances, committees of the *hsien* or higher level, or a corresponding Party committee shall have authority to decide directly on the membership of individual applicants.

Article 6. The sponsors shall be responsible for representing faithfully to the Party the ideology, character, and background of the applicant; and before making their recommendation they shall carefully explain to the applicant the Constitution, programme, and policies of the Party.

Before deciding upon and approving the membership application, the Party committee shall designate a working Party member to interview the applicant carefully, and must conduct a serious investigation of the applicant.

Article 7. The purpose of the probationary period is to provide preliminary training for probationary members, and to ensure the

Party organization of a chance to observe the political character of such members in the light of their activities.

The duties and rights and privileges of probationary members are similar to those of regular members, except that they do not possess the right to elect, to be elected, and to vote.

Article 8. The promotion of probationary members to the status of regular members at the termination of the probationary period shall be decided upon at a Party cell plenary meeting, and approved by the higher Party committee by which the original application was approved, or its corresponding organs.

The probationary period may be lengthened or shortened by the appropriate Party committee.

If observation of the probationary member indicates that he is not qualified to join the Party, his probationary membership may be invalidated.

Article 9. The seniority of a member is determined by the date on which he acquires the status of a regular member.

Article 10. If a regular or probationary member is transferred from the area of one Party organization to another, he shall be considered a regular or probationary member of the latter organization.

Article 11. Regular or probationary members who wish to withdraw from the Party shall make formal application to the Party cell, which will be acted upon at a plenary cell meeting where his name shall be eliminated, and reported to the higher Party committee for its records.

Article 12. A regular or probationary member of the Party who, without justifiable reason, has failed to participate in the work of the Party continuously for a period of six months, or to carry out the work assigned him, or to pay membership fees, shall be considered to have voluntarily withdrawn from Party membership; the revocation of his membership shall be decided upon at a plenary meeting of the Party cell and reported to the higher Party committee for its records.

Article 13. The expulsion of regular or probationary members shall take effect after the question has been carefully discussed and decided upon at the Party cell plenary meeting and approved by the higher Party committee.

Under special circumstances, Party committees higher than the cell may decide upon the expulsion of regular or probationary members, but it will take effect only after the approval of the next higher committee.

Chapter II

THE STRUCTURE OF PARTY ORGANIZATION

Article 14. The Party structure is organized on the principle of democratic centralism. The principle of democratic centralism is centralism based upon democracy, and democracy under centralized leadership. Its basic conditions are as follows:

(*a*) The leading organs of all levels of the Party shall be established through elections.

(*b*) The leading organs of all levels of the Party shall submit periodic reports to the organizations by which they are elected.

(*c*) Individual members shall obey the Party organizations to which they belong; the minority shall obey the majority; lower organizations shall obey higher organizations; all organizations shall uniformly obey the CC.

(*d*) Party discipline shall be strictly observed and Party decisions shall be enforced unconditionally.

Article 15. Organizations of the Party shall be established on the basis of the localities or branches of production to which the members belong.

The organizations which take over-all charge of Party activities in a certain locality shall be deemed higher than the individual Party organizations within the locality.

Article 16. The system of Party organization shall be as follows:

(*a*) On the Chinese national level, there shall be a National Congress of the Party, a Central Committee, and a National Conference of Party Representatives.

(*b*) On the provincial, border region and local levels, respectively, there shall be: Provincial Congresses, Provincial Party Committees, and Provincial Conferences of Party Representatives; Border Region Congresses, Border Region Party Committees, and Border Region Conferences of Party Representatives; and Local Congresses, Local Party Committees, and Local Conferences of Party Representatives.

(*c*) On the Hsien level, there shall be Hsien Congresses, Hsien Party Committees, and *Hsien* Conferences of Party Representatives.

(*d*) On the municipal level, there shall be Municipal Congresses, Municipal Party Committees, and Municipal Conferences of Party Representatives.

(*e*) On the urban or rural district level, there shall be District Congresses (or District Plenary Party Meetings), District Party Committees, and District Conferences of Party Representatives.

(*f*) In each factory, mine, village, enterprise, street, company of the army, public organization, or school, there shall be a Plenary Party Meeting, a Party Cell Committee, and a Conference of Party Cell Representatives.

Article 17. The authority at the various levels of Party organization shall be: in the Party cell, the Plenary Meeting; in districts, *hsien*, municipalities, localities, border regions and provinces, the Congress; for the whole Party, the National Congress. When these are not in session, the committees elected by them are the supreme authorities at the various levels of Party organization.

Article 18. The leading organs at the various levels of the Party organization shall be established through election, where possible. Only if it is impossible, because of environmental or other restrictive conditions, to hold general meetings of Party members for direct elections, may the leading organs be elected by the Conferences of Party Representatives, or be appointed by the higher authorities.

Article 19. The election of Party committees at the various levels shall be conducted according to nomination lists by secret ballot or open vote. The right of electors to criticize or change any of the nominees is guaranteed.

Article 20. Party committees at the various levels may call cadres' meetings and meetings of active members to transmit and discuss important decisions of higher Party organs or to study or prepare for their own work.

Article 21. Before decisions have been reached regarding the policy of the Party and various problems [of the Party], all Party members may freely and practically discuss them, and express their own opinions, within Party organs and in Party meetings. But once decisions have been adopted they shall be obeyed, and enforced unconditionally.

Article 22. The leading organs at the various levels of Party organization shall conduct their activities in accordance with the principle of intra-Party democracy so that the revolutionary positiveness and constructiveness of its members may be developed and Party discipline strengthened. Party discipline shall be enforced self-consciously rather than mechanistically, so that the leading organs may perform their functions effectively and the system of centralism may be solidly constructed on a democratic basis. But the leading organs of the various levels of Party organization, in performing their functions, shall not violate the principle of centralism within the Party. Democratic criticism within the Party, which is legitimate and beneficial for centralized action, shall not be misconstrued as anarchistic deviation (such as autonomy and extreme democracy).

Article 23. To ensure that the principle of intra-Party democracy shall be enforced in a manner helpful to the undertakings of the Party; that there will be no danger of weakening combat morale or solidarity of the Party in case of emergency; that there will be no possibility for any conspirator, renegade, or factionalist to utilize the principle of democracy to injure or divide the activities of the Party; and that no small minority will be able to take advantage of the unawareness in thinking of the overwhelming majority to attain its private ends, the broad and general consideration, discussion, and examination of Party policies on the national or local scale shall be conducted only under the following conditions:

(*a*) They shall be conducted when time permits, that is to say, when the objective conditions are not critical; and

(*b*) They shall be based on the resolutions of the CC or of local leading organs of the Party; or

(*c*) They shall be conducted only on the proposal of more than one-half of the members of the lower organizations, or on the proposal of the higher authority.

Article 24. Party organizations at the various levels shall ensure that all publications under their direction propagate the resolutions and policy decisions of the central or higher organizations.

Article 25. Prior to their determination and announcement by the CC, local and other Party organizations, or their responsible officers, shall discuss questions of a national character only among themselves, or submit their proposals respecting such questions to the CC. In no case shall they make a public announcement of their views or decisions. Local Party organizations shall have the right to make decisions concerning questions of a local character, but they are not to be inconsistent with the decisions of the CC or higher organizations.

Article 26. The establishment of any new Party organization must be approved by its immediately higher authority.

Article 27. To facilitate the direction of local Party work, the CC may, according to the requirements of the situation, establish a Central Bureau or Central Branch Bureau with jurisdiction over several provinces or border regions. Such Central Bureau or Central Branch Bureau is the representative organ of the CC; it shall be appointed by, and be responsible to, the CC. These representative organs of the CC may be dissolved or amalgamated whenever they are found to be no longer necessary.

Article 28. To facilitate the conduct of their practical work, Party committees of the various levels may, according to the requirements of the situation, establish different departments or committees for the administration of Party affairs, propaganda and education, military and economic matters, or mass movements. Such departments or committees shall perform their respective functions under the unified leadership of the Party committees of the various levels.

To perform certain temporary or special work, Party committees of the various levels may establish appropriate temporary working committees or departments.

Chapter III

THE CENTRAL ORGANIZATION OF THE PARTY

Article 29. The National Congress shall be determined and convened by the CC. Ordinarily, it shall meet once every three years; but in special circumstances the CC may either postpone it or call it in advance.

The CC shall call the National Congress if local Party organizations representing more than one-half of the membership of the Party request it.

The National Congress, to be constitutional, must be attended by delegates representing more than one-half of the membership of the Party.

The number of delegates to the Congress, and the procedure for their election, shall be determined by the CC.

Article 30. The National Congress shall have the following functions:

(*a*) To hear, deliberate upon, and approve the reports of the CC or other central organizations;

(*b*) To adopt or amend the programme and constitution of the Party;

(*c*) To determine the basic guiding principles and policies of the Party; and

(*d*) To elect the CC.

Article 31. The number of members of the CC shall be determined, and they shall be elected by the National Congress. Vacancies in the CC shall be filled by alternate members in due order.

Article 32. The CC shall represent the Party in maintaining relations with other political parties or groups, and shall be responsible for establishing all of the organizations of the Party, directing their activities, and allocating human and financial resources.

Article 33. Plenary Sessions of the CC shall be convened by the Central Political Bureau once every six months. The Central Political Bureau may either postpone or call them in advance, as the situation warrants. Alternate members of the CC shall have the right to speak at Plenary Sessions.

Article 34. The Central Political Bureau, the Central Secretariat, and the Chairman of the CC shall be elected at the Plenary Sessions of the CC.

Between Plenary Sessions of the CC, the Central Political Bureau shall be the central directing organ of the Party and shall direct all its work.

The Central Secretariat shall perform the routine functions of the CC under the Central Political Bureau.

The Chairman of the CC shall serve concurrently as Chairman of the Central Political Bureau and Chairman of the Central Secretariat.

The CC, according to the requirements of the (Party) work, shall establish Departments of Organization, Propaganda, and other departments; the Military Affairs Committee, the Party Publication Committee, and other committees; and other working organs to administer the different functions of the central authorities under the direction and supervision of the Central Political Bureau, the Central Secretariat, and the Chairman of the CC.

Article 35. In the intervals between National Congresses, the CC may call National Conferences of Party Representatives from various local Party committees for the consideration and determination of current questions of Party policy.

Article 36. Members of the National Conference of Party Representatives shall be elected at a meeting of the National Committee, which shall consist of the Provincial, Border Region, and other Party Committees immediately subordinate to the CC. The number of representatives to the conferences shall be determined by the CC.

The quorum of the National Conference of Party Representatives shall consist of representatives of more than one-half of the Provincial and Border Region Party Committees.

Article 37. The National Conference of Party Representatives shall have the power to remove regular or alternate members of the CC who are found to be incapable of performing their duties, and to elect part of the alternate members of the CC. But the regular or alternate members removed from, and the new alternate members elected to, the CC by such a conference shall not exceed one-fifth of the total number of regular and alternate members of the CC at one time.

Article 38. The resolutions adopted by the National Conference of Party Representatives, and the removal or election of regular or alternate members of the CC by it, shall require the approval of the CC.

After approval by the CC, the resolutions adopted by the National Conference of Party Representatives shall be enforced by all Party organs.

Chapter IV

PARTY ORGANIZATIONS IN PROVINCES AND BORDER REGIONS

Article 39. Provincial or Border Region Congresses and Provincial or Border Region Party Committees shall be under the direction of the CC or its representative organs.

Article 40. Provincial and Border Region Congresses shall be called once every two years by the Provincial or Border Region Party Committees. In special circumstances the Provincial or Border Region Party Committees may either postpone (such Congresses) or call them in advance. But they must be convened by the Provincial or Border Region Party Committees if more than one-half of the lower Party organizations request, or on the proposal of the CC or its representative organ.

The number of members of the Provincial or Border Region Congresses, and the procedure for their election, shall be determined by the Provincial or Border Region Party Committees, with the approval of the CC or its representative organ.

Article 41. Provincial or Border Region Congresses shall hear, deliberate upon, and approve the reports of the Provincial or Border Region Party Committees or other Party organs of the province or border region; they shall deliberate upon and determine the problems and activities of the Provincial or Border Region organizations, and shall elect the Provincial or Border Region Party Committees and the delegates to the National Congress.

Article 42. The standing committee, secretary, and deputy-secretary of the Provincial or Border Region Party Committee shall be elected at the Plenary Session of the Provincial or Border Region Party Committee and shall administer its routine affairs. Secretaries and members of the standing committees of Provincial and Border Region

Party Committees must be approved by the CC. The secretary must be a Party member of five years' standing.

Plenary Sessions of the Provincial or Border Region Party Committees shall be held at least twice every year.

Article 43. Provincial or Border Region Party Committees shall enforce within their jurisdiction the resolutions adopted by the National Congress and the CC, and shall establish all Party organs, allocate the human and financial resources of the Party, and direct the activities of party nuclei in non-party organizations outside the Party.

Article 44. In the intervals between sessions of Provincial or Border Region Congresses, the Provincial or Border Region Party Committees may summon the representatives of local, *hsien*, or other Party committees directly under them to Provincial or Border Region Conferences of Party Representatives to deliberate upon and determine various questions affecting the work within their jurisdiction.

Provincial or Border Region Conferences of Party Representatives shall have the power to remove and elect a part of the members of the Provincial or Border Region Party Committees, but such number shall in no case exceed one-fourth of the total.

Article 45. Resolutions adopted by Provincial or Border Region Conferences of Party Representatives, and the removal or election of members of Provincial or Border Region Party Committees by them, shall require the approval of the Provincial or Border Region Party Committee.

Chapter V

PARTY ORGANIZATIONS IN
LOCALITIES, HSIEN, MUNICIPALITIES, AND DISTRICTS

Article 46. Party organizations and their working methods in localities, *hsien*, municipalities, and districts are similar to the organization and working methods of Party organizations in the provinces and border regions as set out in the preceding chapter. They shall be subject to the direction of their respective superior organs.

Article 47. Congresses in localities, *hsien*, municipalities, and districts shall be held once every two years. In intervals between congresses, Conferences of Party Representatives may be held.

Article 48. Local and Hsien Party Committees shall hold Plenary Sessions at least four times yearly. Municipal and District Party Committees shall hold Plenary Sessions at least monthly.

Members, secretaries and deputy-secretaries of Local, Hsien, Municipal, and District Party Committees shall be approved by the higher Party organization. Secretaries of Local, Hsien, and Municipal Party Committees shall be elected from Party members of more than three years' standing. Secretaries of District Party Committees shall be Party members of more than one year's standing. In areas where the revolution has only recently developed, the regulations concerning the seniority of members to hold office may be modified with the approval of the Provincial or Border Region Party Committee.

Chapter VI

THE BASIC ORGANIZATIONS OF THE PARTY

Article 49. Party cells are the basic organs of the Party. A Party cell shall be established in a factory, mine, village, enterprise, street, company of the army, public organization, school, etc., where there are three or more Party members. Where the Party members thereof are less than three, they shall join the nearest adjoining Party cell.

The establishment of Party cells shall be approved by the Hsien or Municipal Party Committee.

Article 50. Where there is a relatively large membership, the members shall be organized under the Party cell committee into small groups on a natural, residential, or vocational basis. Each group shall elect a leader; a deputy-leader shall be elected when necessary.

Where there are more than fifty regular and probationary members in a village, or more than one hundred regular or probationary members in a factory, public organization, or school, a principal Party cell may be established, under which members shall be organized into a number of branch Party cells according to their residence, section of factory, department of public organization, or class of school. Branch Party cells shall enjoy the same privileges as ordinary Party cells.

Article 51. In large villages or towns, factories, public organizations, and schools where there are more than five hundred regular and probationary members, there may be established, through election, with the approval of the Provincial or Border Region Party Committee, a village committee, factory committee, public organization committee, or school committee, under which members shall be organized into different Party cells according to residence, section, department, or class.

Article 52. Party cells shall unite the masses closely with the Party. Party cells have the following functions:

(*a*) To carry on propaganda and organizational work among the masses with a view to carrying out the Party programmes and the decisions of higher Party organs.

(*b*) Constantly to watch and reflect to the higher Party authority the aspirations and demands of the masses, to pay close attention to the political, economic, and cultural life of the masses, and to organize them for the solution of their own problems.

(*c*) To absorb new members, to collect Party membership fees, to examine and decide upon admissions to membership, and to enforce Party discipline among the Party members.

(*d*) To educate the Party membership and organize members for learning.

Article 53. At its general membership meeting, the Party cell shall elect the cell committee, which shall administer its routine functions. The tenure of the Party cell committee shall range from six months to one year. The number of members of the Party cell committee shall be determined by the size of the Party cell membership, with a minimum of three and a maximum of eleven. A secretary shall be elected by the committee; a deputy-secretary may be elected in case of necessity. The distribution of functions among other members of the committee shall be determined according to practical needs.

Where a Party cell has no more than seven members, there shall be elected only a secretary, or a secretary and deputy-secretary and there shall be no Party cell committee.

Chapter VII

UNDERGROUND ORGANIZATIONS OF THE PARTY

Article 54. In areas where it is impossible for the Party to maintain legal existence or conduct open activities, the structural forms and working methods of the underground organizations shall be especially prescribed by the CC in directives based on the Party Constitution. Where the provisions of this Constitution cannot be applied literally to the structural forms and working methods of underground organizations, they shall be applied with modifications.

Article 55. Underground organizations of the Party shall be even more careful (than provided in the Constitution) in considering the admission of new members. New members shall be required to comply only with those admission procedures which are practicable under secret conditions.

Chapter VIII

CONTROL ORGANS OF THE PARTY

Article 56. A central control committee and local control committees may be established whenever the CC deems it necessary.

Article 57. The central control committee shall be elected by the Plenary Session of the CC. All local control committees shall be elected at the plenary sessions of the local Party committees with the approval of the higher organ.

Article 58. The duties and powers of the central and local control committees shall be to decide upon or review punishments and deal with complaints from Party members.

Article 59. The control committees of the various levels of Party organization shall perform their functions under the direction of their respective Party committees.

Chapter IX

PARTY NUCLEI IN ORGANIZATIONS OUTSIDE THE PARTY

Article 60. In government organizations, labour unions, peasants' associations, co-operatives, and other mass organizations in which three or more Party members hold responsible positions, there shall be established Party nuclei. The duty of the Party nucleus shall be to direct the work of the members in the leading organ in the organization to work for the purpose of strengthening the Party's influence and carrying out the Party's programmes.

Article 61. There shall be a secretary in each Party nucleus. Where the Party nucleus has ten or more members, a Party nucleus staff may be established to conduct the routine work. The Party nucleus staff and secretary are designated by the Party committee to which the nucleus belongs.

Article 62. Party nuclei in organizations outside the Party at the various levels shall be under the direction of the corresponding Party committees, and shall enforce their decisions. Party committees on the various levels may include leading personnel of key Party nuclei to participate in their meetings.

Chapter X

REWARDS AND PUNISHMENTS

Article 63. Party members and Party organizations which, in the performance of their tasks, display their complete loyalty to the interests of the Party and the people, set themselves as models in maintaining the discipline of the Party and of the revolutionary government, manifest distinguished and constructive resourcefulness in executing the Party programme and the policies and decisions of the CC and higher organs in the course of Party work, and win over the sincere support of the popular masses, shall be rewarded.

Article 64. Those who fail to execute the resolutions of the CC and higher organs, or violate the constitution and discipline of the Party, may be punished by Party organs of the various levels according to the concrete situation in the following ways:

(*a*) The punishments to be imposed on entire organizations shall be: censure; partial reorganization of the leading organ; dissolution of the leading organ and appointment of a temporary leading organ; and dissolution of the whole organization and the re-registration of its members.

(*b*) The punishments to be imposed on individual Party members shall be: personal advice or warning; public advice or warning; cancellation of assigned duties; subjection to Party surveillance; and expulsion from Party membership.

Article 65. If a regular or alternate member of the CC commits any act which seriously offends against Party discipline, the CC shall have the power to deprive him of his regular or alternate membership; but the expulsion shall require a two-thirds vote of the CC.

Article 66. When punishment is imposed on a Party organization or an individual Party member, the Party organization or member shall be informed of the reasons for the punishment. If the Party organization or member so punished has any objection to the punishment, proceedings may be instituted and petition may be filed for reconsideration and appeal to the higher organ. The Party committees of the various levels shall transmit such petitions without delay, and in no case shall they be withheld.

Article 67. Expulsion from Party membership is the most severe punishment within the Party. In deciding upon and approving such punishment, Party organs of the various levels should maintain a high degree of caution, and be careful in hearing the case of the appellant and in analysing the offence in the light of the circumstances in which it was committed.

Article 68. The Party's positive aim of reward and punishment for Party members is to educate them and the masses, including the members rewarded or punished. It is by no means intended to encourage exhibitionism or to enforce any principle of mere punitivism within the Party. To reward Party comrades who have distinguished records is to create good practices within the Party and to set up models among the members. To criticize or impose punishment upon comrades who commit offences is a method of correcting past errors and guarding against future errors, of curing malfeasance and saving regenerate individuals.

Chapter XI

FINANCES

Article 69. The revenues of the Party are derived from membership dues, proceeds from all kinds of production and enterprises operated by the Party, and outside contributions.

Article 70. Membership fees for regular and probationary members shall be determined and enforced by the Provincial or Border Region Party Committees, or other corresponding Party Committees.

SEC. VII. THE POST-WAR PERIOD (1945–50)

COMMENTARY V. THE RETURN TO THE CITIES

After the point reached in the preceding document, at the end of the Yenan period and the united front war against Japan, we pass over in this volume the series of events so largely connected with the effort of the United States to act as mediator in forestalling the ruinous CCP-KMT civil war of 1946–50. The Marshall mission of 1946 and other negotiations are documented in the White Paper on *United States Relations with China*, issued by the Department of State in August 1949. In these negotiations the CCP line remained essentially that of coalition government (see document no. 27). In what follows, space permits us to note only the major developments in the

CCP line after the coalition programme finally broke down into an all-out struggle for power. In this period the most spectacular development in policy was the shift from countryside to city, announced just as the CCP military predominance was becoming plainly established in the spring of 1949.

The Second Session of the Seventh Plenum of the CC, CCP, was held between March 16 and 23, 1949, at Shih-chia-chuang in Hopei province about six weeks after the occupation of Peking by the Communist forces under General Lin Piao. The Session made it plain that the CCP was now at a momentous turning-point—from an insurgent group based on rural areas it was becoming the ruling power of a vast subcontinent, including some ten cities each with a populace of over one million.

The major points of significance in the resolutions of March 1949, as reported by the New China News Agency,[1] may be summarized as follows: First, the Plenum reaffirmed the conditions for peace with the KMT government at Nanking which had been laid down by Mao Tse-tung in his statement entitled *On Peace in China* made on January 14, 1949.[2] The eight conditions proposed by Mao were: "(1) punish war criminals; (2) abrogate the bogus constitution [which had been passed by a National Assembly at Nanking at Christmas-time, 1946, without the participation of the CCP]; (3) abolish the pretended legitimacy of the (KMT) power [this meant that the KMT was no longer to be considered the legitimate holder of political power]; (4) reform all reactionary armies in accordance with democratic principles; (5) confiscate bureaucratic capital; (6) reform the agrarian system; (7) abrogate treaties of national betrayal; (8) convoke a political consultative conference without the participation of reactionary elements, establish a democratic coalition government, take over all power from the Nanking KMT reactionary government and its lower levels of government."

Second, the Plenum reiterated the CCP demand for the convocation of a new political consultative conference and the establishment of a coalition government of "democratic parties and groups, people's organizations, and democratic personages". This heralded the establishment of a national administration with the CCP as the core, and served as an inducement to the other anti-KMT parties and groups to join the new government. This step was part of a CCP political offensive, aimed at attracting as many followers as possible for the stupendous tasks of defeating the KMT régime and of post-war reconstruction.

THE RETURN TO THE CITIES

Third, the Plenum sought to warn Party members against cockiness and complacency on the eve of national victory, and exhorted them to "maintain their humble, cautious, unproud, unirritable, and hard-struggle style of work".

The pith of the resolution, however, lies in a fourth objective, "to shift the centre of gravity of Party work under the present situation from rural areas to the cities". In the main, two approaches can be made in analysing this epic decision—from its political aspect and from its economic aspect.

Politically, the decision to put more emphasis on urban areas reflects the continuous attempt of the Party hierarchy to reconcile the Marxist theory of leadership by the urban proletariat with the fact that the CCP came to power mainly through the support and the strength of the peasantry. Mao Tse-tung himself states in his *On Coalition Government* (see document no. 27, 2 (*b*)) that "peasants are the basic foundation of a democratic China". P'eng Chen, a member of the CC and the Political Bureau, made a typical statement in a speech to the Land Conference of the Shansi-Chahar-Hopei Border Region at the end of 1947, that "the historical mission (of the CCP) at present is to lead the peasantry to eliminate feudalism completely (through agrarian revolution) and to vanquish Chiang Kai-shek".[3] One Western observer estimated that, at the end of 1944, ninety-three per cent of the CCP members (who totalled some 1,200,000 at that time) were new ones who had joined after 1937, and nine out of ten were peasants.[4] Nevertheless, the Party line had always maintained that "the workers shall retain their leadership of the peasantry" (Lenin)[5] and "the peasants could not have defeated the landlords without the leadership of the workers" (Stalin);[6] it was natural that the CCP, now at last about to rule millions of urban workers, should publicly announce its emphasis on urban areas.

Quite aside from this long-term political consideration, immediate economic factors were even more decisive in the shift from village to city. The CCP plainly realized the problems involved in taking over the cities and the millions of clerical and managerial personnel, soldiers, and other non-productive elements in the former KMT areas. Faced with the probable extension of the fighting area, and with increasing demands for reconstruction, rehabilitation, and relief, the new régime could not expect to meet its requirements as before, i.e. mainly from agricultural income. To avoid inflation the régime would need either (1) an increase of industrial production, or (2) an inflow of capital and consumer's goods obtained through foreign investments or loans, or through exports. Land reform, as the prime policy of the CCP during the war, had been an effective weapon for promoting social reform, increasing incentives among the peasantry, and winning the support of the majority of the rural community. But no government of all China could hope to increase agricultural productivity substantially without biotechnical improvements as well as other long-range programmes such as urban and rural industrialization, population control, and the like. For example, from data published by the CCP[7] it appears that the total grain production in the Shensi-Kansu-Ninghsia Border Region had increased about eighty per cent from 1937 to 1940 during a period when the cultivated areas increased only about thirty per cent. On the other hand, one American expert estimates that technological improvements in agriculture alone —such as artificial fertilization, improved seeds, mechanization, better tools, pest control, plant and animal breeding, etc.—would double the yield per acre in China.[8] But in any case, these and other improvements, such as better methods in marketing (specifically in standardization, storage, transportation, distribution, and salesmanship) and a modern credit system (through rural banking, co-operatives, loan programmes, etc.), are all dependent on industrial developments and on the type of trained personnel that are generally found in the cities.

Although the Second Session of the Seventh Plenum officially pronounced the shift of Party emphasis to the cities, it should be noted that the Marxist-Leninist emphasis on industrialism and on the model of planned industrialization provided by the Soviet Union had always been part of the living creed of the CCP, even in the hinterland. Never for a moment had the official line given up the intention of converting China into an industrialized state as soon as opportunity allowed. We have no reason to assume that simply because the CP under its Maoist leadership realized that the peasantry alone provided the dynamic base for a revolution, it had therefore renounced this ultimate aim which lies at the very heart of the Marxist-Leninist-Stalinist world view. The Party had never become a peasant party in terms of the ultimate aims of its leaders. Hence the recapture of the cities merely furnished the Party with an opportunity to begin to implement one of its perennial aims. In Jen Pi-shih's speech to the New Democratic Youth League on April 11, 1949, the goal of the CCP in its industrialization programme was said to be "to increase the proportion of industrial production from about ten per cent in the total national income to between thirty and forty per cent in ten to fifteen years".[9]

38. RESOLUTIONS OF THE SECOND SESSION OF THE SEVENTH PLENUM OF THE CC (March 23, 1949)

The Second Session of the Seventh Plenum of the CC, CCP, was successfully concluded in the vicinity of Shih-chia-chuang, [Hopei] after meeting for eight days.

The Plenum was attended by thirty-four CC members and nineteen alternates; twenty CC members and alternates were absent.

Chairman Mao Tse-tung made a work report to the Plenum. The work of the Central Political Bureau, from the First Session [of the Seventh Plenum] in June 1945 up to the present, was ratified by the Plenum, which held that the leadership of the CC had been correct. The Plenum approved the proposal initiated by the CCP for convoking a new Political Consultative Conference without the participation of reactionary elements and establishing a Democratic Coalition Government jointly with democratic parties and groups, people's organizations, and democratic personages.

The Plenum also ratified Chairman Mao Tse-tung's statement of January 14, 1949, and the eight-point peace terms put forward by him as the basis for peace negotiations with the Nanking KMT reactionary government and any other KMT regional governments and military blocs.

The Second Session of the Seventh Plenum stressed the discussion of the question of shifting the centre of gravity of Party work under the present situation from the rural areas to the cities.

The Plenum pointed out that because of the disparity between the people's strength and that of the enemy, from the failure of the Great Chinese Revolution in 1927 up till now, the centre of gravity of the Chinese people's revolutionary struggle had been in the countryside, gathering force in the countryside and using it to encircle the cities and then to capture the cities. Under the leadership of Chairman Mao Tse-tung, the Party had united the broad masses of the labouring people and had carried out this policy of utilizing the countryside to encircle the cities. History has proved that this policy was entirely necessary, totally correct, and completely successful.

But the period for using this way of working has now ended. The period has now begun for working from the cities to the countryside [and for leading the countryside from the cities].[1] Without doubt, attention must be paid both to the cities and to the countryside. Without doubt, it is necessary to link up closely the relations between the cities and the countryside, between workers and peasants, and between industry and agriculture. The countryside must certainly not be cast aside and attention be paid merely to the cities. Anyone who thinks this way is entirely mistaken. But the centre of gravity of Party work must be placed on the cities.

The Plenum pointed out that the Party must do its utmost to learn how to lead the urban population to struggle successfully, and to learn how to administer and build up the cities. In leading the struggle of the urban population, the Party must rely on the working class, rally the other labouring masses, win over the intelligentsia, and win over as many as possible of the petty bourgeoisie and liberal bourgeoisie and their representative personages who can co-operate with the CCP, stand on the same front, and so conduct a firm struggle against the imperialists, KMT reactionaries, bureaucratic capitalists, and vanquish them step by step.

The Plenum was of the opinion that the key point in administering and building up the cities is the rehabilitation and development of industrial production: first, the production of public-owned enterprises; second, that of private enterprises; and, third, handicraft production. Other urban work such as organizational work of the Party, constructive work in governmental organs, trade union work, work of various popular organizations, public security work, cultural and educational work, etc., should serve this central work of rehabilitating and developing industrial production.

The Plenum called on all Party comrades to devote all their energy to learning the techniques and management of industrial production; and to learn commercial, banking, and other work closely related to production. It further warned that if the Party is ignorant in production work, fails to learn production work quickly, is unable to rehabilitate and develop production as quickly as possible and unable to attain actual achievement, improving, first of all, the workers' livelihood and improving the livelihood of the people in general, then the Party and the people cannot maintain their régime, cannot hold their ground and will fail.

The Second Session of the Seventh Plenum pointed out that the people's democratic dictatorship led by the proletariat and based on worker-peasant alliance demands that the CCP earnestly unite all the working class, all the peasantry, and the vast number of revolutionary intelligentsia as the leading forces and foundation of this dictatorship. At the same time, it demands that the CCP unite as much as possible the representative figures of the petty bourgeoisie and liberal bourgeoisie, their intellectuals and political parties and groups, who can co-operate with the CCP, in order jointly to overthrow the reactionary forces within the country, overthrow the imperialist forces, and swiftly rehabilitate and develop production, thereby creating the condition for the steady transforming of China from an agricultural country into an industrial country and from a new democratic state into a socialist state.

The Plenum called on the whole Party to establish a policy of long-term co-operation in thought as well as in work with democratic personages outside the Party. On this question, (we) should oppose both the attitude of unprincipled compromise and the closed-door or insincere attitude that obstructs solidarity between the Party and democratic personages outside the Party. As the nationwide victory of the Chinese revolution, which is of great international significance, will soon arrive, the Second Session of the Seventh Plenum emphatically warned all Party comrades not to be proud and self-satisfied, and not to be softened by other people's unprincipled flatteries. The Plenum pointed out that the Chinese revolution is of great significance but the winning of the nationwide victory of the revolution is only the first step in (our) work. The revolutionary road that lies ahead is even longer and its work even greater and more arduous. The Plenum called on all Party comrades to continue to retain their humble, cautious, unproud, unirritable and hard-struggle style of work so as to exert greater efforts in building a new China after defeating the counter-revolutionary forces.

The Plenum considers that although the economic heritage of China is backward, the Chinese people are brave and industrious. Because of the victory of the Chinese people's democratic revolution, the establishment of the People's Democratic Republic and the leadership of the CCP, in addition to the aid of the powerful world-wide anti-imperialist front headed by the Soviet Union, the tempo of economic construction in China will not be slow, but will possibly be rather fast. A prosperous and strong China will soon come into being. There is no basis at all for a pessimistic point of view regarding the economic revival in China.

COMMENTARY W. THE NEW PHASE OF POWER

Mao Tse-tung's pronouncement of July 1, 1949, *On the People's Democratic Dictatorship*, marks the completion of the enormous shift from the period of some twenty-seven years, during which the CCP was an opposition party striving towards power, to the period in which the CP has become, in effect, the established régime. The Party's basic tenets, it is true, still lie today (1950) within the limits of the New Democracy theory. But there have been certain shifts in emphasis and certain additions which accurately reflect the fact that the Party has crossed the great divide into an entirely new phase.

Mao's statement is divided into two parts, the first consisting of an essay on the history of modern China and of the CCP; and the second consisting of a clarification of the Party's views on certain basic issues now confronting it. The latter section is in the form of a series of rather exasperated replies to a number of annoying objections raised against Communist policies by a fictitious opponent. We shall not here enter into a detailed consideration of the first section, since it is a typical example of the schematic simplifications of orthodox Communist historiography. It is, however, an extremely significant section, since it provides a convenient survey of the point of view from which modern Chinese history must now be written, at least so long as the "People's Democratic Dictatorship" remains the basic element of the CCP line.

In the second section, Mao first takes up with his mythical opponent the question of foreign policy, and defiantly pronounces his now famous policy of "leaning to one side". In certain quarters this pronouncement has been taken as final and irrefutable proof that any conflict between Chinese Communism and the Kremlin is simply out of the question. While it is not the purpose of this commentary to decide whether such a conflict is or is not possible, we would suggest that Mao's pronouncement cannot be taken as conclusive evidence either way. It is not that we need doubt his sincerity, for there can be little doubt that by predilection he leans to the Soviet side. It is with that side that he shares a community of beliefs in terms of which he seeks a sanction for his own power. We need not even doubt that he would prefer to conceive of the world as neatly divided between "a socialist camp" and an "imperialist camp". The point is that conflicts within the Communist world are likely to arise not in the area of emotional commitment but in the area in which conflicts of power interests arise. There can be no doubt that Tito would also prefer to remain in the "socialist camp". But just as laissez-faire liberalism had assumed that all conflicts of interest would be automatically regulated by the market mechanism, so does Leninism comfortably assume that, within the Communist world, power relations will be settled by some sort of pre-established harmony. The fact that Lenin did not anticipate conflicts of power within a Communist world, and the fact that his disciples share this belief, does not necessarily prevent the emergence of such conflicts. Real problems are not exorcised simply by being ignored. There may, of course, be many other factors which may prevent the emergence of a conflict between a Communist China and Moscow, but Mao's pronouncement about "leaning to one side" cannot be accepted as the final word on the subject.

In the area of domestic policy the "People's Democratic Dictatorship" is designed to adapt the theory of the "New Democracy" to a new situation. The notion of "Democratic Dictatorship" is of course not essentially new. The phrase appears in the "New Democracy" and can ultimately be traced back to Lenin's theory of the "Democratic Dictatorship of Workers and Peasants". In Lenin's view such a state would be democratic because it would represent the interests of the overwhelming majority of the (Russian) people. It would be a dictatorship because it would be directed against the reactionary classes. Since the "Democratic Dictatorship" was never realized in Russia, Lenin was never forced to face the question of how a dictatorship—a régime which enforces a single and uniform policy—can be based on a coalition of parties which presumably represent the interests of diverse classes. He himself hints that such a dictatorship is likely to be unstable and of short duration.

During the Yenan period, Mao Tse-tung's use of the phrase "Democratic Dictatorship" was heavily weighted on the side of its "democratic" aspects. During this period the problem of the CCP was to induce an actually separate political force of independent and minor-party elements to co-operate with the CP. Now, however, virtually all final power, as distinct from the many important public functions and government jobs being performed by non-Communists, is concentrated in the hands of the CP. The weight has thus definitely shifted to the side of "dictatorship"—to a definite emphasis on a single, uniform policy. The dictatorship is, to be sure, presumably a dictatorship of four classes, all of which are represented in the new government by a variety of political groups.

How, then, does the new régime meet the problem raised above; that is, the problem of maintaining a dictatorship based on a coalition? The answer is simple. It is merely asserted that the "People's Democratic Dictatorship" must have "the leadership of the working class" (by "the working class" is meant, of course, the CP). Evidence would indicate that the word "leadership" indicates nothing less than the fact that total effective power and complete political initiative now lie with the CP. Even if we assume that the present unanimity of all political groups in the People's Consultative Council at Peking reflects sincere conviction, is it probable that any of them will be allowed to develop separate policies of their own in the future?

It thus seems more than likely that in the realm of political power the theories of the "New Democracy" and even of the "People's Democratic Dictatorship" no longer correspond to any reality. In the realm of economic relations, however, they still reflect the régime's policy of maintaining private property in land and a sector of privately owned industry. We have every reason to credit Mao's sincerity when he tells us that in view of China's feeble industrial development, China must still "utilize all urban and rural factors of capitalism which are beneficial". The actualities of the present Chinese situation appear to correspond most closely to the situation in the Soviet Union during its New Economic Policy phase (1921–7)—a phase in which the CP monopolized political power but granted the peasantry and the nepmen a certain limited economic function. While such may be the actuality, however, Mao maintains a line of continuity with the "New Democracy" as well as the appearance of a unique theoretical development by granting other political groups a place in the new régime's administrative structure. Furthermore, in China's present feeble state, he also manages to rally to his new régime forces which might otherwise have remained neutral or sullenly hostile.

The "People's Democratic Dictatorship" also provides a criterion for distinguishing the friends and foes of the new régime. At first glance, it appears to be a clear-cut division along class lines. The four classes which make up the "people", that is, the proletariat, the peasantry, the petty bourgeoisie, and the national bourgeoisie, are on the side of the government. All others are, of course, "reactionaries". The clarity of this distinction may well be deceptive. Actually, the words "people" and "reactionaries" may be subject to a much more flexible interpretation than might appear in terms of literal class definitions. It is quite conceivable that an industrial worker, who proves obdurate in clinging to incorrect opinions, may turn out to be a tool of reaction. It is also conceivable that a former "bureaucratic capitalist" who zealously and conscientiously clings to the Party line, may become a genuine representative of the "people". Ultimately, the power of class imputation rests with the CP, and beneath all class criteria there lurks the very old criterion of support of, or opposition to, the state. This does not preclude the possibility that purely class-criteria may be used on occasion. But it does indicate that the categories of "people" and "reactionaries" are more flexible than they appear on the surface.

39. MAO TSE-TUNG: ON THE PEOPLE'S DEMOCRATIC DICTATORSHIP (July 1, 1949)
(In Commemoration of the Twenty-eighth Anniversary of the CCP)

This date, the first of July 1949, shows that the CCP has passed through twenty-eight years. Like a man, it has its childhood, youth, manhood, and old age. The CCP is no longer a child, nor is it a youth in his teens; it is an adult. When a man reaches old age he dies; it is the same with a (political) party. When classes are eliminated, all the instruments of class struggle, political parties and the state apparatus, will, as a result, lose their functions, become unnecessary and gradually wither away; and their historical mission accomplished, (mankind) will move to a higher plane of human society. We are just the opposite of the political parties of the bourgeoisie. They are afraid to talk of the elimination of classes, state authority, and party, while we openly declare that we struggle hard precisely for the creation of prerequisites (which will) achieve the elimination of these things. The CP and the state authority of the people's dictatorship constitute such prerequisites. Anyone who does not recognize this truth is no Communist. Young comrades who have just joined the Party and have not read Marxism-Leninism may not yet understand this truth. They must understand this truth before they can have a correct world outlook. They must understand that all mankind have to go through the process of eliminating classes, state authority, and party; the question is only one of time and conditions. The Communists in the world are more intelligent than the bourgeoisie in that respect. They understand the law governing the existence and development of things. They understand dialectics and thus see farther ahead. The bourgeoisie do not welcome this truth because they do not want to be overthrown by the people. To be overthrown—as in the case of the KMT reactionaries who are being overthrown by us at present or of Japanese imperialism which was overthrown by us along with peoples of various countries in the past—is painful and is inconceivable to the persons overthrown. But for the working class, labouring people, and Communists, the question is not one of being overthrown but of working hard and creating conditions for the natural elimination of classes, state authority, and political parties, so that mankind will enter the era of universal fraternity. We have here touched on the perspectives of the progress of mankind in order to explain the following questions.

Our Party has passed through twenty-eight years. Everybody knows that (they were) not passed peacefully but amid difficult surroundings. We had to fight against enemies at home and abroad, and within and outside the Party. We owe thanks to Marx, Engels, Lenin, and Stalin, who gave us weapons. These weapons are not machine-guns but Marxism-Leninism.

Lenin in his book *"Left Wing" Communism—An Infantile Disorder*, written in 1920, described how the Russians sought for revolutionary theory. After several decades of hardships and tribulations they eventually discovered Marxism. There are many things which are the same or similar between China and Russia before the October Revolution. The feudal oppression was the same. The economic and cultural backwardness was similar. Both countries were backward, China even more backward. Progressive people endured hardships and struggled to seek the revolutionary truth, so as to bring about national recovery; this was the same (in both countries).

[Influence from the West][1]

After China's defeat in the Opium War of 1840, progressive Chinese underwent countless tribulations seeking for the truth from the Western countries. Hung Hsiu-ch'üan,[2] K'ang Yu-wei,[3] Yen Fu,[4] and Sun Yat-sen represented this group of people who sought for truth from the West before the birth of the CCP. At that time, all Chinese who sought for progress read every book that contained any fresh Western teaching. The number of students sent to Japan, England, America, France, and Germany was staggering. Great efforts were made to learn from the West: in the nation the imperial examination system was abolished and schools established, (such measures) multiplying like bamboo shoots after rain. What I learned in my youth consisted of such things. These constituted the culture of Western bourgeois democracy, or so-called new school of learning, which included social doctrines and natural sciences of that time as opposed to the culture of China's feudalism, or so-called old school of learning. For quite a long time people who learned the new knowledge were confident that it was sure to save China. Apart from people of the old school, very few of the new school expressed doubt. To save the country, the only way was to enforce reforms, and to enforce reforms, the only way was to learn from foreign countries. Of the foreign countries at that time only the Western capitalist countries were progressive. They had successfully established their modern bourgeois states. The Japanese got good results by learning from the West, therefore the Chinese also wanted to learn from the Japanese. To the Chinese of that time, Russia was backward and very few people wanted to learn from her. This was how the Chinese learned from foreign countries during the period from the forties of the nineteenth century to the beginning of the twentieth century.

[October Revolution and China]

Imperialist aggression shattered the Chinese dream of learning from the West. They wondered why the teachers always practised aggression against their pupils. The Chinese learned much from the West, but what they learned could not be put into effect. Their ideals could not be realized. [Many struggles, including the Revolution of 1911, had all failed.][5] Meanwhile, conditions in the country worsened day by day, and the environment was such that the people could not live. Doubt sprang up, it grew and developed. The First World War shook the whole world. The Russians carried out the October Revolution, creating the first socialist country in the world. Under the leadership of Lenin and Stalin the revolutionary energy of the great Russian proletariat and labouring people, which had lain hidden and could not be seen by foreigners, suddenly erupted like a volcano. The Chinese and all mankind then began to look differently at the Russians. Then, and only then, did there appear for the Chinese an entirely new era both in ideology and in living. The Chinese found the universal truth of Marxism-Leninism which holds good everywhere, and the face of China was changed.

It was through the introduction of the Russians that the Chinese found Marxism. Before the October Revolution the Chinese not only did not know Lenin and Stalin, but also did not know Marx and Engels. The gunfire of the October Revolution sent us Marxism-Leninism. The October Revolution helped the progressive elements of the world and of China to use the world outlook of the proletariat as the instrument for perceiving the destiny of the country, and for reconsidering their own problems. Travel the road of the Russians —this was the conclusion. In 1919, the May Fourth movement took place in China, and the CCP was formed in 1921. In his moment of despair Sun Yat-sen came across the October Revolution and the CCP. He welcomed the October Revolution, welcomed Russian help to China, and welcomed the co-operation of the CCP. Sun Yat-sen died [March 1925] and Chiang Kai-shek came into power. During the long period of twenty-two years [since 1927] Chiang Kai-shek has dragged China into hopeless straits.

During this period the anti-fascist Second World War, with the Soviet Union as its main force, defeated three big imperialist powers, weakened two other big imperialist powers, leaving only one imperialist country in the world—the United States of America, which suffered no loss. However, the domestic crisis in America is very grave. She wants to enslave the entire world and she aided Chiang Kai-shek with arms to slaughter several millions of Chinese. Under the leadership of the CCP, the Chinese people, after having driven away Japanese imperialism, fought the people's war of liberation for three years and gained a basic victory. Thus the civilization of the Western bourgeoisie, the bourgeois democracy, and the pattern of the bourgeois republic all went bankrupt in the minds of the Chinese people. Bourgeois democracy has given way to the people's democracy under the leadership of the proletariat, and the bourgeois republic has given way to the people's republic. A possibility has thus been created of reaching socialism and Communism through the people's republic, of attaining the elimination of classes and universal fraternity. K'ang Yu-wei wrote the book *On Universal Fraternity* [*Ta-t'ung shu*], but he did not, and could not, find the road to it. The bourgeois republic has existed in foreign countries but cannot exist in China, because China is a country oppressed by imperialism. The only (way for us) is to travel the road of the people's republic under the leadership of the proletariat and attain the elimination of classes and universal fraternity.

[*The Birth of the Communist Party*]

All other things had been tried and had failed. Of those who yearned for other things, some had fallen, some had awakened to their mistake, and others are in the process of changing their minds. Events developed so swiftly that many people felt surprised and the need to learn anew. This state of mind is understandable, and we welcome such a well-intentioned attitude, that asks to learn things anew.

Having learnt Marxism-Leninism after the October Revolution, the vanguard of the Chinese proletariat established the CCP. Following this, it entered into the political struggle and had to travel a zigzag path for twenty-eight years before it could gain a basic victory. From the experiences of twenty-eight years, just as from the "experiences of forty years" as Sun Yat-sen said in his will, a common conclusion has been reached, namely: "The firm belief that to attain victory we must awaken the masses of the people and unite ourselves in a common struggle with those peoples of the world who treat us on the basis of equality" [quoted from Sun's famous testament]. Sun Yat-sen had a different world outlook from us, and started out from a different class standpoint in observing and dealing with problems, but in the twenties of the twentieth century, on the problem of how to struggle against imperialism, he arrived at a conclusion which was fundamentally in agreement with ours.

Twenty-four years have elapsed since Sun Yat-sen's death, and under the leadership of the CCP, Chinese revolutionary theory and practice have made big forward strides, fundamentally changing the realities of China. Up to the present, the Chinese people have gained the following two major and basic [lessons of] experiences: (1) (We must) awaken the masses in the country. This is to unite the working class, the peasant class, the petty bourgeoisie, and national bourgeoisie[6] into a national united front under the leadership of the working class, and develop it into a state of the people's democratic dictatorship led by the working class with the alliance of workers and peasants as its basis. (2) (We must) unite in a common struggle with those nations of the world who treat us on the basis of equality and with the people of all countries. This is to ally ourselves with the Soviet Union, to ally ourselves with all the New Democratic countries, and to ally ourselves with the proletariat and the broad masses of the people in other countries, to form an international united front.

["You Lean to One Side"]

"You lean to one side." Precisely so. The forty years' experience of Sun Yat-sen and the twenty-eight years' experience of the CCP have taught us to believe that in order to win and to consolidate the victory we must lean to one side. The experiences of forty years and twenty-eight years, respectively, show that, without exception, the Chinese people either lean to the side of imperialism or to the side of socialism. To sit on the fence is impossible; a third road does not exist. We oppose the Chiang Kai-shek reactionary clique who lean to the side of imperialism; we also oppose the illusion of a third road. Not only in China but also in the world, without exception, one either leans to the side of imperialism or to the side of socialism. Neutrality is mere camouflage and a third road does not exist.

"You are too provocative." We are talking of dealing with domestic and foreign reactionaries; that is, imperialists and their running dogs, and not of any other people. With regard to these people [foreign and domestic reactionaries], the question of provocation does not arise, for whether (we are) provocative or not makes no difference to their being reactionaries. Only by drawing a clear line between reactionaries and revolutionaries, only by exposing the designs and plots of the reactionaries, arousing vigilance and attention within the revolutionary ranks, and only by raising our own morale while subjugating the arrogance of the enemy—can the reactionaries be isolated, conquered, or replaced. In front of a wild beast you cannot show the slightest cowardice. We must learn from Wu Sung [one of the 108 heroes in the famous Chinese novel *All Men Are Brothers*, who killed a tiger with bare hands] on the Ching-yang ridge. To Wu Sung, the tiger on the Ching-yang ridge would eat people all the same whether they were provocative or not. You either kill the tiger or are eaten by it; there is no third choice.

"We want to do business." Entirely correct. Business has to be done. We only oppose domestic and foreign reactionaries who hamper us from doing business, and do not oppose any other people. It should be known that it is no other than imperialists and their lackeys—the Chiang Kai-shek reactionary clique—who hinder our doing business with foreign countries and even hinder our establishing diplomatic relations with foreign countries. Unite all forces at home and abroad to smash the domestic and foreign reactionaries and then there will be business, and the possibility of establishing diplomatic relations with all foreign countries on the basis of equality, mutual benefits, and mutual respect of territorial sovereignty.

[International Assistance]

"Victory is also possible without international assistance"—this is an erroneous conception. In the era when imperialism exists, it is impossible for the true people's revolution of any country to win its own victory without assistance in various forms from the international revolutionary forces, and it is also impossible to consolidate the victory even when it is won. The great October Revolution was thus won and consolidated, as Stalin has told us long ago. It was also in this way that the three imperialist countries were defeated and the new democratic countries established. This is and will be the case with the People's China at present and in the future. Let us think it over; if the Soviet Union did not exist, or there had been no victory in the anti-fascist Second World War, [no defeat of German, Italian, and Japanese imperialism][7] and especially for us, no defeat of Japanese imperialism, if the various new democratic countries had not come into being, and no rising struggles of the oppressed nations in the East, if there had been no struggles of the masses of people in the United States, Britain, France, Germany, Italy, Japan, and other capitalist countries against the reactionary cliques ruling over them, and if there were no sum-total of these things, then the reactionary forces bearing down on us would surely be many times greater than they are at present. Could we have won victory under such circumstances? Obviously not; it would also be impossible to consolidate the victory (even) when it was won. The Chinese people have had much experience in this matter. The remark made by Sun Yat-sen before his death, that alliance must be made with the international revolutionary forces, reflected this experience long ago.

[*Aid from Anglo-American Governments*]

"We need the assistance of the British and American governments." This is also a childish idea at the moment. At present the rulers in Britain and the United States are still imperialists. Would they extend aid to a people's state? If we do business with these countries or suppose these countries would be willing in the future to lend us money on terms of mutual benefit, what would be the reason for it? It would be because the capitalists of these countries want to make money and the bankers want to earn interest to relieve their own crisis; that would be no aid to the Chinese people. The Communist Parties and progressive parties and groups in these countries are now working to bring about business (relations), and even to establish diplomatic relations with us. This is well meant; it means to help us, and it cannot be regarded in the same light as the acts of the bourgeoisie in these countries. During his lifetime Sun Yat-sen repeatedly appealed to the imperialist countries for aid. The outcome was futile, and instead he met with merciless attacks. In his lifetime Sun Yat-sen received international aid only once, and that was from the U.S.S.R. The reader can refer to the will of Dr. Sun Yat-sen, in which he did not ask the people to look and hope for aid from imperialist countries, but earnestly bade them "to unite with those peoples of the world who treat us on the basis of equality". Dr. Sun had had the experience; he had been duped. We must remember his words and not be duped again. Internationally we belong to the anti-imperialist front headed by the U.S.S.R., and we can look for genuine friendly aid only from that front, and not from the imperialist front.

[*People's Democratic Dictatorship*]

"You are dictatorial." Dear sirs, you are right; that is exactly what we are. The experience of several decades, amassed by the Chinese people, tells us to carry out the people's democratic dictatorship. That is, the right of reactionaries to voice their opinions must be abolished and only the people are allowed to have the right of voicing their opinions.

Who are the "people"? At the present stage in China, they are the working class, the peasant class, the petty bourgeoisie, and national bourgeoisie. Under the leadership of the working class and the CP, these classes unite together to form their own state and elect their own government (so as to) carry out a dictatorship over the lackeys of imperialism—the landlord class, the bureaucratic capitalist class, and the KMT reactionaries and their henchmen representing these classes —to suppress them, allowing them only to behave properly and not to talk and act wildly. If they talk and act wildly their (action) will be prohibited and punished immediately. The democratic system is to be carried out within the ranks of the people, giving them freedom of speech, assembly, and association. The right to vote is given only to the people and not to the reactionaries. These two aspects, namely, democracy among the people and dictatorship over the reactionaries, combine to form the people's democratic dictatorship.

Why should it be done this way? Everybody clearly knows that otherwise the revolution would fail, and the people would meet with woe and the State would perish.

"Don't you want to eliminate state authority?" Yes, but we do not want it at present, we cannot want it at present. Why? Because imperialism still exists, the domestic reactionaries still exist, and classes in the country still exist. Our present task is to strengthen the apparatus of the people's state, which refers mainly to the people's army, people's police, and people's courts, for the defence of the country, and the protection of the people's interests; and with this as a condition, to enable China to advance steadily, under the leadership of the working class and the CP, from an agricultural to an industrial country, and from a New Democratic to a Socialist and Communist society, to eliminate classes and to realize the state of universal fraternity. The army, police, and courts of the state are instruments by which classes oppress classes. To the hostile classes the state apparatus is the instrument of oppression. It is violent, and not "benevolent". "You are not benevolent." Just so. We decidedly will not exercise benevolence towards the reactionary acts of the reactionaries and reactionary classes. Our benevolence applies only to the people, and not to the reactionary acts of the reactionaries and reactionary classes outside the people.

The (function of the) people's state is to protect the people. Only when there is the people's state, is it possible for the people to use democratic methods on a nationwide and all-round scale to educate and reform themselves, to free themselves from the influence of reactionaries at home and abroad (this influence is at present still very great and will exist for a long time and cannot be eliminated quickly), to unlearn the bad habits and ideas acquired from the old society and not to let themselves travel on the erroneous path pointed out by the reactionaries, but to continue to advance and develop towards a Socialist and Communist society accomplishing the historic mission of completely eliminating classes and advancing towards a universal fraternity.

The methods we use in this field are democratic; that is, methods of persuasion and not coercion. When people break the law they will be punished, imprisoned, or even sentenced to death. But these are individual cases and are different in principle from the dictatorship over the reactionary class as a class.

[*Future of the Reactionaries*]

After their political régime is overthrown the reactionary classes and the reactionary clique will also be given land and work and a means of living; they will be allowed to re-educate themselves into new persons through work, provided they do not rebel, disrupt, or sabotage. If they are unwilling to work, the people's state will compel them to work. Propaganda and educational work will also be carried out among them, and, moreover, with care and adequacy, as we did among captured officers. This can also be called "benevolent administration", but we shall never forgive their reactionary acts and will never let their reactionary activity have the possibility of a free development.

Such re-education of the reactionary classes can only be carried out in the state of the people's democratic dictatorship. If this work is well done the main exploiting classes of China—the landlord and bureaucratic capitalist classes—will be finally eliminated. (Of the exploiting classes) there remain the national bourgeoisie among many of whom appropriate educational work can be carried out at the present stage. When socialism is realized, that is, when the nationalization of private enterprises has been carried out, they can be further educated and reformed. The people have in their hands a powerful state apparatus and are not afraid of the rebellion of the national bourgeois class.

The grave problem is that of educating the peasants. The peasants' economy is scattered. Judging by the experience of the Soviet Union, it requires a very long time and careful work to attain the socialization of agriculture. Without the socialization of agriculture, there will be no complete and consolidated socialism. And to carry out the socialization of agriculture a powerful industry with state-owned enterprises as the main component must be developed. The state of the people's democratic dictatorship must step by step solve this problem (of the industrialization of the country). The present article does not intend to deal with the economic problem, so I shall not discuss it in detail.

In 1924 a well-known manifesto was passed by the KMT First National Congress, which was directed personally by Sun Yat-sen and participated in by Communists. The manifesto stated: "The so-called democratic system in countries of modern times is often monopolized by the bourgeois class and turned into an instrument for oppressing the common people. But the democracy of the KMT belongs to the people in general and is not the private possession of a few." Except for the question of who is to lead whom, the democracy mentioned here, when viewed as a general political programme, is consistent with the people's democratic dictatorship practised at present by us. [If to the state system, which is only allowed to be the common possession of the common people and not the private possession of the bourgeoisie, is added the leadership of the working class, this state system is that of the people's democratic dictatorship.][8]

Chiang Kai-shek betrayed Sun Yat-sen and used the dictatorship of the bureaucratic capitalist class and the landlord class as an instrument for oppressing the common people of China. This counter-revolutionary dictatorship remained in force for twenty-two years, and not until now has it been overthrown by the Chinese common people under our leadership.

["Dictatorship" and "Totalitarianism"]

The foreign reactionaries who vilify us for carrying out "dictatorship" and "totalitarianism" are in fact the very people who are carrying out dictatorship and totalitarianism of one class, the bourgeoisie, over the proletariat and other people. They are the very people referred to by Sun Yat-sen as the bourgeois class in countries of modern times who oppress the common people. Chiang Kai-shek's counter-revolutionary dictatorship was learnt from these reactionary fellows.

Chu Hsi, a philosopher of the Sung dynasty [A.D. 960–1260], wrote many books and said many things which we have forgotten, but there is one sentence we have not forgotten and this is "Apply to anyone the method he has first used on others." This is what we are doing. That is, to apply to imperialism and its lackeys, the Chiang Kai-shek reactionary clique, the same method with which they treated others. Simply this and nothing else!

The revolutionary dictatorship and the counter-revolutionary dictatorship are opposite in nature. The former learns from the latter. This process of learning is very important, for if the revolutionary people do not learn the methods of ruling over counter-revolutionaries, they will not be able to maintain their régime, which will be overthrown by the reactionary cliques at home and abroad. The reactionary cliques at home and abroad will then restore their rule in China and bring woe to the revolutionary people.

The basis of the people's democratic dictatorship is the alliance of the working class, peasant class, and the urban petty-bourgeois class, and is mainly the alliance of the working class and the peasant class because they constitute eighty to ninety per cent of the Chinese population. It is mainly through the strength of these two classes that imperialism and the KMT reactionary clique were overthrown. The passing from New Democracy to Socialism mainly depends on the alliance of these two classes.

[The Leadership of the Working Class]

The people's democratic dictatorship needs the leadership of the working class, because only the working class is most far-sighted, just and unselfish and endowed with revolutionary thoroughness. The history of the entire revolution proves that without the leadership of the working class, the revolution is bound to fail, and with the leadership of the working class, the revolution is victorious. In the era of imperialism no other class in any country can lead any genuine revolution to victory. This is clearly proved by the fact that the Chinese national bourgeoisie had led the revolution many times and each time had failed.

The national bourgeoisie is of great importance at the present stage. Imperialism is still standing near us and this enemy is very fierce. A long time is required for China to realize true economic independence and become free from reliance on imperialist nations. Only when China's industries are developed, and she no longer depends economically on powerful nations, can there be real independence. The proportion of China's modern industry in the entire national economy is still very small. There are still no reliable figures at present, but according to certain data it is estimated that modern industry only occupies about ten per cent of the total productive output in the national economy of the whole country. To cope with imperialist oppression, and to raise our backward economic status one step higher, China must utilize all urban and rural factors of capitalism which are beneficial and not detrimental to the national economy and the people's livelihood, and unite with the national bourgeoisie in a common struggle. Our present policy is to restrict capitalism and not to eliminate it. But the national bourgeoisie cannot be the leader of the revolutionary united front and should not occupy the main position of state power. This is because the social and economic status of the national bourgeoisie has determined its feebleness; it lacks foresight, lacks courage, and in large part fears the masses.

Sun Yat-sen advocated "awakening the masses" or "helping the peasants and workers". Who is to awaken and help them? Sun Yat-sen meant the petty bourgeoisie and the national bourgeoisie. But this is in fact not feasible. Sun Yat-sen's forty years of revolutionary work was a failure. Why? The reason lies precisely here, in that in the era of imperialism it is impossible for the bourgeoisie to lead any true revolution towards success.

Our twenty-eight years are entirely different. We have plenty of invaluable experience. A party with discipline, armed with the theories of Marx, Engels, Lenin, and Stalin, employing the method of self-criticism, and linked up closely with the masses; an army led by such a party; a united front of various revolutionary strata and groups led by such a party; these three are our main (lessons of) experience. They all mark us off from our predecessors. Relying on these three things, we have won a basic victory. We have traversed tortuous paths and struggled against rightist and leftist opportunistic tendencies within the Party. Whenever serious mistakes were committed in these three matters, the revolution suffered set-backs. The mistakes and set-backs taught us and made us wiser. Thus we were able to do better work. Mistakes are unavoidable for any party or person, but we ask that fewer mistakes be committed. When a mistake is committed, correction must be made, the quicker and the more thoroughly the better.

[*First Step of the 10,000-Mile March*]

Our experience may be summarized and boiled down into one single thing, namely, the people's democratic dictatorship based on the alliance of workers and peasants led by the working class (through the CP). [This dictatorship must unite in concert with international revolutionary forces.][9] This is our formula, our main experience, our main programme.

In the twenty-eight long years of the Party we have done only one thing, and that is, we have won the basic victory. This is worth celebrating, because it is the people's victory and a victory in a large country like China. But there is plenty of work before us, and, as on a march, what work has been done in the past is like the first step on a ten-thousand-mile long march. Remnants of the enemy have still to be wiped out, and the grave task of economic reconstruction still lies before us. Some of the things with which we are familiar will soon be laid aside, and we are compelled to tackle things with which we are unfamiliar. This means difficulty. The imperialists are positive that we are incapable of tackling our economic work. They look on and wait for our failure.

We must overcome difficulties, and must master what we do not know. We must learn economic work from all who know the ropes (no matter who they are). We must acknowledge them as our teachers, and learn from them respectfully and earnestly. We must acknowledge our ignorance, and not pretend to know what we do not know, nor put on bureaucratic airs. Stick to it, and eventually it will be mastered in a few months, one or two years, or three or five years. At first some of the Communists in the U.S.S.R. also did not know how to do economic work, and the imperialists also waited for their failure. But the CP of the Soviet Union won. Under the leadership of Lenin and Stalin they not only could do revolutionary work but also reconstruction work. They have already built up a great and brilliant socialist state. The CP of the U.S.S.R. is our best teacher from whom we must learn. [The international and domestic situation is favourable to us.][10] We can rely wholly on the weapon of the people's democratic dictatorship to unite all people throughout the country, except the reactionaries, and advance steadily towards the goal.

COMMENTARY X. THE NEW GOVERNMENT

As we reach the final rise to power of the Chinese Communist movement, it becomes increasingly difficult to evaluate, or even survey, its record. The political sentiments of the day and the closing of one after another channel of contact make observation difficult if not impossible and judgment correspondingly difficult and faulty. Since our emphasis throughout this volume has been placed on the historical development of the Party line, we conclude with the most portentous, perhaps, of all CCP documents, the stated basis of the new régime which has finally emerged from thirty years of revolutionary effort.

A long preparatory phase preceded the adoption of the *Organic Law of the Central People's Government* by the first session of the Chinese People's Political Consultative Conference (PPCC) on September 27, 1949. As early as May 1, 1948, the CC of the CCP had called on the "various democratic parties and groups, people's organizations, and leaders of society to convoke quickly a new Political Consultative Conference to discuss and effect the convocation of a People's Congress (National Assembly) and to establish a democratic coalition government".[1] From August 1 to November 25, 1948, representatives of various parties, groups, and organizations had held numerous meetings and had agreed on the general basis for convening a new People's Political Consultative Conference (not a mere revival of the PCC which met at Chungking in 1946). On June 15, 1949, the Preparatory Committee of the PPCC was formally set up at Peiping, consisting of 134 delegates from 23 parties or groups. After about three months' preparatory work, the PPCC itself was convened on September 21, 1949, at Peiping, with 585 delegates and 77 alternate delegates including representatives from 14 parties, 9 regional delegations, 6 military groups, 16 organizational groups, plus 75 specially invited delegates. The Conference, which lasted ten days, took the following action: (1) it passed the *Organic Laws* of the Central People's Government (see document no. 40) and of the PPCC, and the *Common Programme* of the PPCC; (2) it fixed the capital at Peking and selected the national flag; (3) it elected Mao Tse-tung Chairman of the Central People's Government (CPG) and picked 6 vice-chairmen and 56 members of the CPG committee; and (4) it elected 180 members of the national committee of the PPCC.

There are a number of significant features in this *Organic Law* which states the basic principles of the new government:

Article 1 defines the nature of the new state: the working class is to lead the People's Republic of China, and the CCP assumes the role of the vanguard and core of the working class. This means, in effect, that the People's Republic is led by the CCP, or, in realistic terms, that the Central People's Government is the administrative arm of the Party.[2]

Although a People's Congress is to be convened some time in future to be the supreme legislative organ of the nation, neither the Organic Law of the CPG nor the Organic Law of the PPCC contains any provisions concerning tenure of office by the government heads or their dismissal or replacement in case of delinquency, disability, or death. The CPG Committee and its Chairman are empowered, among other things, to (1) legislate, interpret, and promulgate laws; (2) approve, abrogate, or revise treaties and agreements with foreign countries; and (3) appoint and dismiss the chairman and members of the Supreme People's Court and the Procurator General (article 7). The State Administrative Council and its Chairman (Premier) are responsible not to any legislative body but to the CPG Committee (article 14). These provisions illustrate the high degree of "centralism" in the present People's Government.

In the actual administration of affairs, four Committees and thirty Ministries are set up. The large number of ministerial posts is said to be necessary to carry out specific economic tasks, an explanation which is attested by the fact that fifteen of the thirty ministerial posts are connected with economic affairs.

The emphasis laid on information is seen in the setting up of three agencies: the Information Bureau, the News Bureau, and the Publication Bureau, in addition to the Ministry of Culture and the Ministry of Education. An examination of the membership of the CPG Committee shows that out of fifty-six seats Communists occupy thirty-one, a comfortable majority. Out of thirty ministerial posts thirteen are headed by non-Communists, but almost all the key ministries are headed by CCP members.

40. ORGANIC LAW OF THE CENTRAL PEOPLE'S GOVERNMENT OF THE PEOPLE'S REPUBLIC OF CHINA (September 27, 1949)

Passed by the First Plenary Session of the Chinese People's Political Consultative Conference on September 27, 1949.

Chapter One

GENERAL PRINCIPLES

Article 1. The People's Republic of China is a State of the People's Democratic Dictatorship, led by the working class, based on the alliance of workers and peasants, and rallying all democratic classes and various nationalities within the country.

Article 2. The Government of the People's Republic of China is a government of the people's congress system based on the principle of democratic centralism.

Article 3. Prior to the convocation of the All-China People's Congress through universal suffrage, the plenary sessions of the Chinese People's Political Consultative Conference shall exercise the functions and powers of the All-China People's Congress, enact the Organic Law of the Central People's Government of the People's Republic of China, elect the Central People's Government Council of the People's Republic of China and vest this Council with the power of exercising state authority.

Article 4. The Central People's Government Council represents the People's Republic of China in international relations, and assumes leadership of the state authority at home.

Article 5. The Central People's Government Council shall set up the State Administrative Council as the highest executive organ for state administration; shall set up the People's Revolutionary Military Council as the organ of supreme military command of the state; and shall set up the Supreme People's Court and the People's Procurator-General's Office as the highest judicial and supervisory organs of the state.

Chapter Two

THE CENTRAL PEOPLE'S GOVERNMENT COUNCIL

Article 6. The Central People's Government Council shall consist of a Chairman and six Vice-Chairmen of the Central People's Governmen and fifty-six Council members elected by the first session of the Chinese People's Political Consultative Conference and a Secretary-General elected by and from the Central People's Government Council.

Article 7. The Central People's Government Council exercises the following jurisdiction in accordance with the Common Programme enacted by the first session of the Chinese People's Political Consultative Conference:

(1) Enactment and interpretation of the laws of the state, promulgation of decrees and supervision of their execution.

(2) Determination of the administrative policies of the state.

(3) Annulment or amendment of the decisions and orders of the

State Administrative Council, which are contrary to the laws and decrees of the state.

(4) Ratification, abrogation or amendment of treaties and agreements concluded by the People's Republic of China with foreign countries.

(5) Dealing with the question of war and peace.

(6) Approval or revision of the state budget and final accounts.

(7) Promulgation of the acts for general amnesty and special pardon.

(8) Instituting and awarding of orders and medals and conferring of titles of honour of the state.

(9) Appointment or dismissal of the following government personnel:

(a) Appointment or dismissal of the premier and deputy premier and members of the State Administrative Council; secretary-general and assistant secretaries-general of the State Administative Council; chairman, vice-chairmen, and members of the various committees and commissions; ministers and vice-ministers of the various ministries; president and vice-presidents of the Academy of Sciences; director and assistant directors of various administrations; and manager and assistant managers of the bank.

(b) Appointment or dismissal or ratification of the appointment or dismissal on the recommendation of the State Administrative Council of the chairman, vice-chairmen, and main administrative personnel of various administrative areas and various provincial or municipal people's governments.

(c) Appointment or recall of the ambassadors, ministers, and plenipotentiary representatives to foreign states.

(d) Appointment or dismissal of the chairman, vice-chairmen, and members of the People's Revolutionary Military Council, the commander-in-chief, deputy commander-in-chief, chief of staff and deputy chief of staff of the People's Liberation Army, and the director and vice-director of the general political department.

(e) Appointment or dismissal of the chief justice, associate chief justices and committee members of the Supreme People's Court, the procurator-general, vice-procurators-general, and committee members of the People's Procurator-General's Office.

(10) Preparation for and convocation of the All-China People's Congress.

Article 8. The chairman of the Central People's Government shall preside over the meetings of the Central People's Government Council and direct the work of the Central People's Government Council.

Article 9. The vice-chairmen and secretary-general of the Central People's Government shall assist the chairman in the discharge of his duties.

Article 10. The Central People's Government Council shall hold bi-monthly meetings convened by the chairman. The chairman may convene the meeting earlier or postpone it when necessary upon the request of more than one-third of the members of the Central People's Government Council or upon the request of the State Administrative Council. More than half of the Council members are required to form a quorum and all resolutions shall be passed with the concurrence of over one-half of the members present at the meeting.

Article 11. The Central People's Government Council shall have a general office and may set up other subordinate working organs when necessary.

Article 12. The organizational regulations of the Central People's Government Council shall be enacted by the Central People's Government Council.

Chapter Three

THE STATE ADMINISTRATIVE COUNCIL

Article 13. The State Administrative Council shall consist of a premier, a certain number of deputy premiers, a secretary-general, and a certain number of members appointed by the Central People's Government Council.

Members of the State Administrative Council may concurrently hold posts as chairmen of the various committees or commissions or as ministers of ministries.

Article 14. The State Administrative Council is responsible and accountable to the Central People's Government Council. When the Central People's Government Council adjourns, the State Administrative Council shall be responsible and accountable to the chairman of the Central People's Government.

Article 15. The State Administrative Council shall exercise the following jurisdiction on the basis and in pursuance of the Common Programme of the Chinese People's Political Consultative Conference, laws, and decrees of the state and the administrative policies stipulated by the Central People's Government Council:

(1) Issue decisions and orders and verify their execution.
(2) Annul or amend the decisions and orders of committees, ministries, commissions, academy, administrations, and bank, and all levels of the government, which are contrary to the laws and decrees of the state and the decisions and orders of the State Administrative Council.
(3) Submit bills to the Central People's Government Council.
(4) Co-ordinate, unify, and direct the inter-relations, the internal organization and the general work of committees, ministries, commissions, academy, administrations, and bank and other subordinate organs.
(5) Direct the work of local people's governments throughout the country.
(6) Appoint or dismiss, or ratify the appointment or dismissal of the main administrative personnel of the *hsien* and municipal level and above, which are not included in Article 7 (9) (*b*).

Article 16. The premier of the State Administrative Council shall direct the affairs of the Council. The deputy premiers and the secretary-general of the State Administrative Council shall assist the premier in the discharge of his duties.

Article 17. The State Administrative Council shall hold weekly meetings convened by the premier. The premier may convene the meeting earlier or postpone it when necessary, or upon the request of over one-third of its members. Over half of the members of the State Administrative Council are required to form a quorum, and resolutions shall be passed with the concurrence of over one-half of the members present at the meeting.

The decisions and orders of the State Administrative Council shall come into force with the signature of the premier or with the counter-signatures of the heads of the committees, ministries, commissions, academy, administrations, and bank concerned.

Article 18. The State Administrative Council shall set up a Committee on Political and Legal Affairs, a Committee on Finance and Economics, a Committee on Culture and Education, a Committee on People's Supervision, and the following ministries, commissions, academies, administrations, and banks which shall direct their respective departments of state administration:

Ministry of Interior, Ministry of Foreign Affairs, Information Administration, Ministry of Public Security, Ministry of Finance, People's Bank, Ministry of Trade, Maritime Customs Administration, Ministry of Heavy Industry, Ministry of Fuel Industry, Ministry of

Textile Industry, Ministry of Food Industry, Ministry of Light Industries (not belonging to the above-mentioned four categories), Ministry of Railways, Ministry of Posts and Telegraphs, Ministry of Communications, Ministry of Agriculture, Ministry of Forestry and Land Reclamation, Ministry of Water Conservancy, Ministry of Labour, Ministry of Culture, Ministry of Education, Academy of Sciences, News Administration, Publications Administration, Ministry of Public Health, Ministry of Justice, Legal Commission, Commission on the Affairs of Nationalities, and Commission on Overseas Chinese Affairs.

The Committee on Political and Legal Affairs shall direct the work of the Ministry of Interior, the Ministry of Public Security, the Ministry of Justice, the Legal Commission, and the Commission on the Affairs of Nationalities.

The Committee on Finance and Economics shall direct the work of the Ministry of Finance, the Ministry of Trade, the Ministry of Heavy Industry, the Ministry of Fuel Industry, the Ministry of Textile Industry, the Ministry of Food Industry, the Ministry of Light Industries, the Ministry of Railways, the Ministry of Posts and Telegraphs, the Ministry of Communications, the Ministry of Agriculture, the Ministry of Forestry and Land Reclamation, the Ministry of Water Conservancy, the Ministry of Labour, the People's Bank, and the Maritime Customs Administration.

The Committee on Culture and Education shall direct the work of the Ministry of Culture, the Ministry of Education, the Ministry of Public Health, the Academy of Sciences, the News Administration, and the Publications Administration.

In order to carry out their work, the Committees may issue decisions and orders to the Ministries, the Commissions, the Academy, the Administrations, or the Bank under their direction and other subordinate organs, and verify their execution.

The Committee on People's Supervision is responsible for the supervision of the execution of duties by government institutions and government functionaries.

Article 19. The Ministries, Commissions, Academy, Administrations, and Bank may issue decisions and orders within their jurisdiction and verify their execution.

Article 20. The State Administrative Council shall have a secretariat to deal with day-to-day work and take charge of the files, archives, and seal of the State Administrative Council, etc.

Article 21. The organizational regulations of the State Administrative Council and the Committees, the Administrations, and Bank and the secretariat shall be enacted or ratified by the Central People's Government Council.

Article 22. The Central People's Government Council may, when necessary, decide on the increase or reduction of the number or merging of the committees, ministries, commissions, academy, administrations, the people's bank, and the secretariat.

Chapter Four

THE PEOPLE'S REVOLUTIONARY MILITARY COUNCIL

Article 23. The People's Liberation Army and other people's armed forces throughout the country shall come under the unified control and command of the People's Revolutionary Military Council.

Article 24. The People's Revolutionary Military Council shall have a chairman and a certain number of vice-chairmen, and a certain number of council members.

Article 25. The organization of the People's Revolutionary Military Council and its administration and command shall be determined by the Central People's Government Council.

Chapter Five

THE SUPREME PEOPLE'S COURT
AND THE PEOPLE'S PROCURATOR-GENERAL'S OFFICE

Article 26. The Supreme People's Court is the highest judicial organ of the country, and is responsible for the directing and supervising of the judicial work of all the judicial organs of the country.

Article 27. The Supreme People's Court shall have a chief justice, a certain number of associate chief justices, and a number of committee members.

Article 28. The People's Procurator-General's Office has the greatest responsibility for the strict observance of the laws on the part of all government institutions and government functionaries as well as nationals of the country.

Article 29. The People's Procurator-General's Office shall have a procurator-general, a certain number of vice-procurators-general, and a certain number of committee members.

Article 30. The organizational regulations of the Supreme People's Court and the Office of the People's Procurator-General shall be enacted by the Central People's Council.

Chapter Six

RIGHTS OF AMENDMENT AND
INTERPRETATION OF THIS ORGANIC LAW

Article 31. The right of amendment of the Organic Law of the Central People's Government belongs to the plenary session of the Chinese People's Political Consultative Conference, or to the Central People's Government Council when the People's Political Consultative Conference is not in session. The right of interpretation of the Organic Law belongs to the Central People's Government Council.

CONCLUDING COMMENTS

Having selected a narrow fraction of Chinese Communist literature for translation above, and added broad generalizations in our commentaries, we feel in no position to evaluate the Chinese Communist revolution in a few words, however well chosen. The American penchant for labelling foreign political situations "Good" or "Bad" has not served us well in our past relations with China and is hardly more useful when applied to Communism. The old classical phrase *Chih-chi chih-pi, pai-chan pai-sheng* ("Know yourself, know the other side; in a hundred battles, win a hundred victories") applies to us with particular force today: given our basic distaste for the theory and methods of world Communism, it is essential that we understand its points of strength in foreign lands.

Certain basic points we believe emerge from the preceding sections. In the first place, the Chinese Communist movement has risen to power in a country where great revolutionary changes were obviously bound to occur in any case. Given the general movement of revolution in all aspects of Chinese life from about 1895 to 1919, the problem of the Comintern and the CCP in the early 1920s was not, How can we start a revolution in China? but rather, How can we capture and control the leadership of the great revolution which is already so plainly under way? As experts in the revolutionary art, the Russians and their Comintern agents set to work with vigour and enthusiasm. But perhaps because they believed revolution to be a predictable science rather than a political art, their first effort to capture the Nationalist revolution from within in the 1920s ended in disaster. Their chief success was in creating the Chinese Communist Party. Yet the Comintern influence upon the fortunes of the CCP in the period through Li Li-san's leadership was often pernicious, and the subsequent rise of Mao Tse-tung in the early 1930s does not seem to have been planned in Moscow.

Fortunately for Moscow, Mao seems to have found the ideology of Marxism-Leninism to be quite as useful as Stalin found him. The need for a new universal view of human history had become urgent in Modern China. The efforts to remake Confucianism, in the period of the 1898 reforms, and the efforts to synthesize Chinese and Western principles, made by scholars like Liang Ch'i-ch'ao and politicians like Sun Yat-sen, had all proved inadequate. Caught in the transition between old and new, East and West, China has had some characteristics of an ideological vacuum and others of an ideological melting-pot. The resulting intellectual confusion has inhibited political unification. In this situation the great strength of Marxism-Leninism has been its emphasis on disciplined ideological organization; for it not only calls for revolution on a vast scale, but demands a highly centralized concentration of power. The doctrine and methods of party discipline, as evidenced for example in the *Cheng-feng* movement, have been a priceless asset to revolutionists working with cadres of rather individualistic intellectuals in the limitless and crowded expanse of the Chinese countryside.

Another strong point of Marxism-Leninism in this context has been its emphasis on thorough-going change. The Chinese Communists have been conducting a political rebellion in a country which had grown utterly tired of the destructive power-struggles among warlords. Mere aspiration to the responsibility of power was no longer an adequate sanction for an armed rebellion. Nor did the political ideal of national unity and international equality remain an adequate sanction for holding power, as Chiang Kai-shek finally discovered. The superficial urban developments of industrialization and general modernization have also been insufficient to meet China's needs. Behind and below all these things the Chinese revolution has called for profound changes in the social, economic, political, and cultural life of the peasant masses. It is indeed ironic that the Communist movement in the 1920s took so long to achieve a full realization of this fact. Paradoxically, it was only by breaking away in practice from what had previously been a basic dogma of Marxism-Leninism—namely, the belief that a Communist Party must have an urban proletarian base—that Communism finally became effective in China. Yet in the end Marxism-Leninism has proved its efficacy for this broad purpose by providing the emotional dynamic to inspire persistent revolutionary effort, the sociological analysis to guide it, and the doctrinal discipline to keep it under control—up to the seizure of power.

These comments in the preceding two paragraphs have of course referred to the period now closed, when the CCP was rising to power. Since the circumstances of the Party have become so different since the take-over, it is quite possible that features which lent strength to the movement in the past may prove less beneficial to it in the future. For example, the ideological discipline of Marxism-Leninism may operate in such a way as to inhibit needed creativity or innovation in the effort at China's reconstruction. Similarly, Marxist-Leninist orthodoxy may be used to support a political status quo and freeze China's political evolution in a mould desired by the holders of power in the Party. This evil picture of conservative dictatorship may be the inseparable obverse of the revolutionary coin.

What stresses and strains can we expect to see develop during the onward course of the Chinese Communist movement? The vilification which has been increasingly heaped upon the United States, so as to cast this country in the role of a long-time mortal enemy of the Chinese people, suggests that the connection between Russian and Chinese Communism—in other words, the problem of national Communism in China—is a major preoccupation in Moscow and also in Peking. Fear of America undoubtedly exists and is also needed as a means to keep China and Russia together, now that the Japanese invaders and the Kuomintang régime have successively served their purpose as the national popular enemies within China. The potentialities of national Communism ("Titoism") in China are beyond our capacity to assess here. In the long run it seems doubtful that Chinese nationalism can be suppressed or stultified, yet in the short term the totalitarian methods of Communist indoctrination and manipulation may accomplish more than we expect, and Chinese patriotic sentiment may for long find its expression within the Moscow orbit.

Western observers in contact with the Chinese Communists in the Yenan period were generally impressed with their egalitarian spirit and sincere reformist zeal, which shone by comparison with Communist power-holders elsewhere. The Yenan Communists were plainly to be described as agrarian reformers who simultaneously espoused Communism. From such descriptions and from certain Russian statements of the time have arisen the later charges that the Yenan Communists were depicted, erroneously, as "*mere* agrarian reformers". We doubt that many serious students of Chinese Communism were ensnared by this phrase. The controversy over it has tended to overlook the fact that agrarian reform and Communism in its early stages are entirely compatible. The important element to note, behind this argument over epithets, is the distinctive Chinese spirit which was manifest at Yenan. This particular quality which seemed to put Chinese Communism in a special category is something we have not attempted to describe in this limited documentary volume. The documents, after all, come from a world of discourse dominated by Marxism-Leninism. The present volume has been based on this assumption: while there has been a great deal of excellent material written regarding the practical impact of Chinese Communism on the masses and its unique flavour, little attempt has so far been made to study the movement through some of its more significant Party documents. The documents of course lend themselves to a concentration on the ideological and internal-political history of the Chinese Communist Party. Our primary focus, consequently, has been the Party itself and not the impact of the Party on the masses. We have not dwelt at length on the details of the truly original evolution of Chinese Communism in its Maoist development, although frequent reference has been made to this originality—the peasant orientation, the emphasis on persuasion rather than force, and the like. Indeed we suggest that the bare bones of Mao's doctrinal exposition actually failed to do justice to the original flavour of the movement during the Yenan period.

The real question is, however, where are we to seek the roots of Mao's originality? We would suggest that they lie in the realm of what might be called *realistic statesmanship*, and that in his treatment of doctrine Mao Tse-tung has not been a whit more or less original or "scientific" than Stalin. Realistic statesmanship, as we understand the term, denotes the ability to grasp the salient facts of a given political situation and to act upon them without allowing one's perception of these facts to be blocked by doctrinaire blinders. Examples of such realistic statesmanship can be found in all times and places and, while it may share certain features in common with what we call the scientific method, on the whole it is something quite different. For example, while a statesman may often break out of the strictures of a certain doctrine in his action, he very often finds it neither necessary nor expedient to acknowledge the fact; but a scientist on the other hand is presumably under compulsion to change his hypotheses when he finds them inadequate to explain newly discovered facts. Thus we find that both Mao and Stalin in their Party lines resort to the expedient of stressing certain elements of doctrine and under-playing others, and of deliberately concealing new facts behind the façade of old phrases. A truly scientific attitude towards Marxism-Leninism on the part of Mao would have obliged him to acknowledge that certain basic premises of Marxism-Leninism, as he found it, had been disproved by his experience in China—for example, that the peasantry must be led by some other economic class before it can effect a revolution, or that a Communist Party must maintain its bonds with an urban proletariat if it is to continue to exist as a Communist Party. Instead, Mao persists at Yenan in maintaining that the peasantry is, in fact, being led by the urban proletariat; he persists in his insistence that the

Communist Party in the hinterland of Yenan is the vanguard of the proletariat.

This assertion of orthodox doctrine, in the period when Chinese Communism seemed to be least in touch with the U.S.S.R., gives us no basis for expecting a doctrinal split between Peking and Moscow.

For Americans the most interesting problem is that of the relation between the CCP and the non-Communist intellectuals in Communist China. The chief fruit of the American investment in missionary education and humanitarian good works in China during the last century has been the modern-minded Western-trained academic and professional personnel who still form a major portion of the Chinese upper class. There is no prospect today that these individuals will be able to form a third force or a political alternative to the CCP as the holder of final power. But their present position and future prospects should be both instructive and of melancholy interest to us. The fate of these intellectuals, and of their formerly pro-Western or "liberal" political views, has an important bearing on the efficacy of the traditional Western ideology in its modern application to Asia.

The Uses of Non-Communists

The position of these intellectuals and administrators today represents only the latest phase in the Chinese Communists' use of non-Communists, which has been a striking feature both of their rise to power and of their present government at Peking. The ideological basis for this use of non-Communists has been the strategy of alliance, the united front, or coalition. It is noteworthy that the great successes of the CCP have been achieved on this general basis of working with others—the rapid growth during the period of the KMT alliance from 1923 to 1927, the far greater expansion during the war-time united front from 1937 to 1945, and the recent post-war success in enlisting the great body of Chinese intellectuals under the coalition banner of the Central People's Government at Peking. This enlistment of intellectuals, it should be noted, has gone hand in hand with a similar absorption of former warlords and military governors, both processes being obvious expedients of the transitional take-over period.

The actual extent of this CCP success in securing non-Communist support is hard for the Western public to realize. The Communist record elsewhere gives no assurance that a coalition in which a Communist Party is the dominant partner will not break down in a series of purges, resulting in the final elimination of independent, minor-party, non-Communist elements from the political scene. Revolutions of all sorts, Communist or otherwise, have shown an inveterate tendency to go through a series of phases in which power is progressively concentrated in the hands of a few, and we may be sure that the revolution in China is not yet at an end. Nevertheless, we must judge developments in China on a factual basis and not merely by our presuppositions. We should note and ponder the fact that within the ranks of Chinese Communism in the New Democracy period—as opposed to Russian Communism in the same years—there is almost no record of the destruction of certain comrades by the Party or by other comrades, through the means of official purges leading to execution or by mysterious assassinations or disappearances. Moral suasion or reindoctrination appear to have taken precedence over violence as the means of settling intra-Party disputes. In this and many other respects the experience of Europe or of Russia may be an inadequate guide to the future of China's ancient society. Traditional traits and ways may persevere among the Chinese people with extraordinary tenacity. Today the esteem given the scholar is still such a trait; and this no doubt accounts in part for the CCP effort to win over and work with the intellectuals, even though Mao Tse-tung has evidenced little but contempt for the traditionally bookish scholars of the past.

The fact is that nearly every leading citizen among the modern Chinese intelligentsia, with the exception of a certain number who had become identified with the Nationalist government, appears to have given a degree of moral support to the new Peking régime. The great body of modern Chinese professors and non-political administrators who were trained in the United States, Britain, and France must be included in this category—sociologists, philosophers, economists, and political scientists as well as industrial specialists, engineers, agronomists, and other technicians. Thus the intellectuals with the highest degree of Western contact and training, men of international repute formerly well known for their liberal and libertarian beliefs, are among the present collaborators with Chinese Communism. As of 1950 they hold high positions in the central and local administrations, continue in charge of leading academic and scientific institutions, and take part in public life and the process of government. All this may change. But it is a truly startling phenomenon which deserves more than passing consideration. The most advanced stratum of the Chinese upper class, the people most like ourselves, appear to have gone over to Communism.

One explanation which comes immediately to mind is the circumstance of the political overturn in China. The Kuomintang having become utterly discredited by its post-war record, the intelligentsia felt themselves increasingly in opposition to it, and therefore actually threatened by it. Many expected Chiang Kai-shek's secret police to make their exit by staging a blood bath among the liberals. Not a few actually fled to the Communist areas for self-preservation. Others were patriotically attracted by the CCP's promise of a united, peaceful, strong nation; still others admired its taking responsibility for the planned salvation of the Chinese people. The inflation, the unpopular civil war effort of the Nationalists, the material and psychological insecurity of life in the cities during the years 1946–8, all prepared the Chinese public generally to welcome the Communists, with the attitude that nothing could be worse than the Kuomintang. Consequently the Communist take-over was followed by a honeymoon period of relief and hope.

This may account for the intellectuals' acquiescence in the new régime, coupled with the fact that personal safety, concern for one's family, and the hope of a better future all dictate an attitude of acceptance rather than open opposition. Yet something more is needed to explain the enthusiasm and active support which have been widely manifested among the intelligentsia.

The Ideological Victory of Communism

This more positive element in the situation is not far to seek: we believe the Communist success with the scholar class is in part a genuine achievement of ideology, a victory for the Communist creed as outlined in some of the preceding documents. Not that Western-trained Chinese intellectuals have become fanatical converts to Marxism-Leninism. But they have in a great many cases seen merit in the practices of the CCP and have in large part subscribed to its theories and explanations of its programme. Increasingly they seem to have accepted the Party line as a valid picture of the modern world.

Here again it is plain that many factors enter into the situation: the contact of Chinese intellectuals with Communism has had a long history as well as a very intense present. Historically it is significant that the Kuomintang got its start mainly in South and Central China and among the overseas Chinese, who were least involved in the imperial régime. In its early days the Nanking government was never very highly esteemed by the literati of China's academic capital, Peiping (Peking). On the other hand, it was two leading professors of the Peking National University (Peita)—Ch'en Tu-hsiu and Li Ta-chao—who led the way in founding the Chinese Communist Party. These men had been leaders in China's intellectual renaissance (which was possible at Peking only after the Manchu empire had shuffled from the scene), and the CCP can rightly trace its lineage to the famous student movement of May 4, 1919, which originated at Peita. Some of the students and professors who participated in that historic and patriotic outburst, but have never become Communists, are in positions of honour in Peking today. Chinese scholars who are aware of China's modern intellectual tradition can easily feel that the wheel of revolution has come full circle, back to the Peking universities and the intelligentsia among whom the movement began.

Against this background it has been possible for the CCP to claim an historic bond with China's modern intelligentsia, which has not been lessened by the fact that so many university students have joined the movement since 1937. It was not at all whimsical for the Communists to say in 1948 that their first act on returning to Yenching University, the leading Protestant institution at Peking, would be to have an alumni reunion.

In the present period the CCP has of course used every means to cement its ties with the scholar class, whose specialized competence is one of the rarest and most essential commodities in the country. Setting up a nationwide administration without the help of the educated few would be unthinkable. Chinese Communism cannot wait for a generation, as the early Manchu rulers did, before they enlist the more active co-operation of the literati. Consequently in addition to the use of non-CCP personnel in the government administration, a multitude of organizations for youth, for students, for the training of cadres have been set up to mobilize China's educated or partly educated manpower. The plethora of study groups and discussion sessions which serve as the channel for the indoctrination of Marxism-Leninism-Maoism among this élite has been widely noted. Under Communism everyone is always in a meeting. Meanwhile the development of those two concomitants of the Communist dogma —thought control and police control—appears to have paralleled this overt organization of the intellectuals' ideas and enthusiasm. The dry stereotypes of the controlled press offer thin fare. But against propaganda and the secret police, the individual is powerless.

Are the non-Communist intellectuals of China, having no choice but to accept the Communist régime, able to accept its doctrines by a process of rationalization or intellectual compromise? Compromise, it may be suggested, is an old Chinese custom, and scholars have always had to be the appendages and civil servants of the régime of the day.

Such an explanation is too simple. It may be true for many scholarly time-servers, in which China has not been lacking. But it does not give us an adequate understanding of the large body of modern Chinese intellectuals of integrity and high ideals who are here in question. These are the scholars who would not collaborate with Japan, who trekked across the plains and over the mountains to the far south-west for the duration of the Sino-Japanese war, who refused to accept the bullying of Chiang Kai-shek's party organizers in the CC clique of the KMT, and who starved in the academic shanty-towns of Kunming and Chungking for nearly a decade, waiting for the time when their talents could again be useful for the salvation of China. Communist subversion of these men and women is not likely as a result purely of intimidation, however subtle and long-continued. The apparent Communist conversion of so many of them is, we suggest, a very important achievement in the ideological sphere.

Background of the Ideological Victory

Let us therefore note briefly the set of ideas which Mao Tse-tung has put so persuasively before his compatriots of the scholar class. (They are perhaps best summed up in his *On Coalition Government*.) Leaving aside the jargon and the ambivalent gimmicks of Marxism-Leninism, this view of the world asserts, first, that China's salvation lies in "liberating" the great mass of the populace from their many ills, that this stupendous task can be accomplished only under strong, far-seeing, and centralized leadership, and that the CCP and its ideology offer the only hope of such leadership. The external forces of evil ("Feudalism" and "Imperialism") can be overcome in this cause only by exorcising the inner evil of unorthodoxy within the CCP and its coalition of loyal allies, so as to build a strong united Chinese nation. Thus the elemental appeals of nationalism and of democratic concern for one's fellow men are closely identified with the Communist cause, its dogma, and its discipline. As one factor in this identification we should note that the Leninist theory of imperialism has long found wide acceptance in Modern China—Chiang Kai-shek himself devoted much of *China's Destiny* in 1943 to proving that China's ills have stemmed mainly from the unequal treaties and the economic and military aggression visited upon China by the capitalist Western powers through the treaty ports. During the last thirty years there has been a growing conviction in China that the Leninist view of international relations is essentially true, a belief which naturally prepares one to follow Leninism in general.

Once the revolutionary leadership of the CCP is acknowledged, it is difficult not to accept its methods. After all, have they not finally succeeded against great odds? The Communist claim to foreknowledge of the process of history could hardly be more credible than on the aftermath of a successful thirty-year struggle for power which began from nothing but a body of ideas, and now encompasses all China. Meanwhile the final clincher in the argument has been the exemplary conduct of the Communist armies and Party workers. Judged by actions rather than words, the Party members in the early take-over period impressed many observers with their selfless devotion to their cause, their concern for the masses, and their practical assiduity, energy, and honesty.

By this combination of ideas and circumstances, we suggest, the non-Communist intellectuals in Peking have wound up under the red banner, seeing no other hope for China, no better channel for their own contributions to the national welfare, no preferable course to follow. But they accept Communist totalitarianism not merely for lack of anything better, but also because they are impressed by its performance and its promises.

When we look to the past for a genuine alternative to this development, we must note that American support of the Kuomintang, in the effort to facilitate reforms which would make it preferred by the Chinese people, did not succeed in this effort. Without venturing to debate the pros and cons of Unites States post-war policy in China, we suggest that our ability to affect the Chinese domestic scene was more sharply limited than we realized. In a country as ancient, sprawling, and densely populated as China it was not possible for the alternative to Communism to be imported largely from outside through foreign aid. Therefore when Chiang Kai-shek, after twenty years, finally lost the Mandate of Heaven (popular moral support or at least, acquiescence), we were unable to restore it to him. Western liberal democracy, the American way of life, had no adequate opportunity to compete for the leadership of the Chinese revolution. In going over to Communism the Western-trained intellectuals of China have now acknowledged this unhappy fact. A régime based on Communist principles would be far below the level of political freedom and civil liberties to which Americans are accustomed, but when it first came into power the Communist-led coalition government at

Peking seemed like a great improvement over the régimes which had preceded it, both in its over-all plans for meeting China's problems and in its active attack upon them.

Through these unhappy developments the American people are now left face to face with a Communist China, but without the strong common bond which formerly existed between us and the modern educated leadership of that country. Like them, we are face to face with Communism, but on opposite sides of the Communist fence. This is not a pleasant prospect from either side, for the documents translated above, selected for their typical quality, indicate no diminution but rather an increase in the strength of the Leninist principles of Chinese Communist organization.

The Potentialities of Totalitarianism

The "democratic centralism" of the CCP means that power is actually concentrated at the top. The outward shows of "democratic" assemblies, discussions, and elections—novel and spirited though they may be—inevitably tend to become meaningless ritual, not the institutions of genuine democracy. Unlike Sun Yat-sen, Chairman Mao does not envisage a limited "period of tutelage" (such as the KMT proclaimed from 1928 to 1946), as a stage on the road to a more full participation of the people in their own government. The CCP asserts, on the contrary, that under the Organic Law of the Central People's Government, democracy is already established; the only prospect of future political improvement must come from the advent of socialism and the eventual millenium of the "withering away" of the state. Meanwhile the separation of the Chinese people into the four classes of the coalition or the "people", on the one hand, and the "reactionaries", on the other, is neither scientific nor objective but sets the stage, as in other Communist lands, for the maltreatment and liquidation of entire groups of citizens. The much-advertised freedoms of the "people" (who do not include all "citizens" but only those who are not "reactionaries") are plainly to be enjoyed only on a controlled basis. Education in our sense is in danger of being prostituted and becoming indoctrination, news and public information have already given way to propaganda, and the individual seems likely to lose his freedom both of action and of thought. The ideological and institutional structure of Chinese Communism, in short, is totalitarian. It subjects the individual to the state power and its elaborate apparatus. Orthodoxy of thought and deed must be preserved in such a state, and can be enforced. We need not labour the point. Chinese Communism brings to the Chinese people the same grim prospect as Communism elsewhere—all the possibilities of slave labour on a massive scale for the state, of the coercion, torture, and destruction of obdurate personalities, of children informing upon parents, and neighbour spying upon neighbour. These possibilities are inherent in the further application of the Marxism-Leninism which has thus far so effectively inspired the revolutionary victory of the CCP. Such evils are evidently the price of "socialist construction" and national strength under this system.

This foreboding, based in large part on the performance of Marxist-Leninist Communist Parties elsewhere in the world, may or may not be fully realized in China. It is not impossible that Mao Tse-tung may go down in Chinese annals as a notorious successor to the First Emperor of the Ch'in, the tyrant who indeed unified China in 221 B.C., but who also burned the books, built the Wall by forced labour, condemned the scholars, and has been excoriated by them ever since. We do not know. The fact remains that Mao and his colleagues now hold power in a way that is not subject to institutionalized checks, as is the power in a democracy. The performance of their régime is therefore more dependent on its own morale and esprit de corps than on its legal institutions and procedures. If the régime cannot secure and keep the moral support of China's upper classes, particularly the intelligentsia, it will have little alternative but to become a police state.

It therefore remains a question whether China's "New Democracy" can be more Chinese than Communist. The tolerance and patience shown by the Mao leadership in the Yenan period and on other occasions, its apparent reasonableness, gradualness, and humanitarian concern for the common people, are part of a sterner and more ruthless creed which claims a monopoly on truth, wisdom, and final power. The Chinese political tradition offers some precedent for esteeming moderation and moral sense as the highest virtues of a ruler. But it sets no real bar to despotism. And totalitarianism in Asia as elsewhere is not a mere revival of things past but a new invention of modern times.

The Relationship to Moscow

The strength of the Marxist-Leninist ideology as one of the sinews of the Chinese Communist movement favours a continuing and close relationship with the Soviet Union. There is as yet no firm evidence that Mao Tse-tung had ever visited Moscow before 1949, but his allegiance to the Russian view of world history can be heavily documented and a significant proportion of his principal colleagues have had Moscow training. Chinese and Russian Communism are tied together by a complex tissue of doctrines and beliefs, nourished from the same sources and aimed at the same general ends.

From the point of view of the Chinese people, on the other hand —as distinct from their new leaders—the geographical distance and differences of language and culture between Russia and China are reinforced by an irreducible difference in national identity. This is the basis for a continuing Chinese nationalism which seems likely to form a continuing bar to the actual incorporation of the Chinese state administratively within the Soviet Union. Chinese-Russian relations must thus remain within the realm of politics and cannot be handled purely as a matter of administration. The Moscow-Peking relationship necessarily has some of the characteristics of an axis or partnership between senior and junior partners.

Consequently the doctrines and desires of Russian and Chinese Communists at the two ends of the axis may have to be adjusted to the continuing historical realities of Russo-Chinese relations. Indeed, Communist China's avowed commitment to the "Soviet camp" should not be taken as ultimate proof that possibilities of conflict are non-existent. The Communist fiction that within the Soviet orbit all possible conflicts of power and policy are simply avoided by some sort of pre-established harmony has been amply shattered by the phenomenon of Titoism. While Chinese Communism may be totally committed to the melodramatic view of the world as divided between an "imperialist camp" and a "socialist camp", certain questions remain unanswered nevertheless. Do the Soviet Union and Communist China have the same ultimate conceptions of what relationships shall obtain between the members of the Soviet camp? Do the Soviet Union and Communist China have the same ultimate conception of China's role in Asia? It is in these areas that the possibilities of future conflict lie, however unreserved may be Mao Tse-tung's emotional commitment to the policy of "leaning to one side".

Meanwhile for the United States, Britain, and the other Western democracies who face a progressive exclusion from contact with the Chinese people, the ideological success of Marxism-Leninism as one component of the Chinese Communist revolution poses a fundamental challenge: Is the Western ideological approach to revolution in Asia indeed bankrupt? Or can we by a more vigorous effort to understand Asia's problems make our faith in personal and intellectual freedom, and our capacity to produce material abundance and social welfare, politically effective in the Asiatic scene?

This raises the further question: Can we find a common ground with the peoples of Asia by making it plain, in deed as well as word, that we do not want them to "lean to one side", either side, but merely to stand upright?

This volume was completed in June 1950. Since then, with Chinese intervention in the Korean war, the government at Peking has gone a long way towards realizing the potentialities of totalitarianism, which we described above (pp. 481–2) as being inherent in the structure of Communist power.

REFERENCE NOTES

Note. These references are arranged in the same order as our interlarded documents (1 to 40) and commentaries (A to X), as listed in the *Table of Contents.* For full form of citations, see *Bibliography B.*

COMMENTARY A:

1. See, for example, Hatano Kanichi, "Chūgoku Kyosantō oyobi Kōgun" (The CCP and the Red Army), in *Shina Nenkan* (China Year-book), 1935, pp. 1600–3.
2. Mif, p. 24.
3. Ch'en Tu-hsiu, p. 4; Hua Kang, p. 447; Ssu-ma Hsien-tao, *Pei-fa hou chih ko-p'ai ssu-ch'ao* (Intellectual currents among political parties after the Northern Expedition), p. 44.
   On the Russian side, Ch'en Tu-hsiu's account of the birth of the "bloc within" is given general confirmation by a letter which Karl Radek wrote to the Sixth Congress of the Comintern in 1928. See dossier no. 6, Trotsky Archives, Houghton Library, Harvard University.
4. The phrase is Lenin's. It appears throughout his *"Left-wing" Communism— An Infantile Disorder* (April 1920).
5. *Fourth Congress of the Communist Internationale*, London, 1923, pp. 222–3. Also *Bericht über den IV. Kongress der Kommunistischen Internationale*, Hamburg, 1923, pp. 140–1.

DOCUMENT NO. 1:

1. Chao Ping-chün, henchman of Yüan Shih-k'ai, served as Premier from 1911 to 1913; resigned when he was found to have been one of the plotters of the assassination of the KMT leader, Sung Chiao-jen (March 1913); and died in 1914.

COMMENTARY B:

1. See, for example, S. C. Tsui, "Influence of the Canton-Moscow Entente upon Sun Yat-sen's Political Philosophy".
2. Isaacs, p. 61; also Ch'en Tu-hsiu, p. 4.

DOCUMENT NO. 3:

1. The last part of this sentence in the original Chinese text as found in *Tung-fang tsa-chih*, vol. xx, no. 2, reads *"ping yuan yü-i tsan-chu"*. The *North China Herald* version, "and can count on the support of Russia", distorts the meaning of this Chinese clause.

DOCUMENT NO. 4:

1. On the warlord intrigues of this period, see Ch'ien Tuan-sheng, *The Government and Politics of China*, Cambridge, 1950, pp. 75–6, and H. F. MacNair, *China in Revolution*, Chicago, 1931, ch. IV.

COMMENTARY D:

1. *Hsiang-tao*, no. 191, March 12, 1927; *Chung-yang fu-k'an*, no. 7, March 28, 1927; *Chinese Correspondence*, no. 8, May 15, 1927 (a modified English version); *Revolutsionnyi Vostok*, no. 2, 1927.
2. *International Press Correspondence*, no. 11, February 3, 1927, p. 232.
3. See M. N. Roy, *Revolution and Counterrevolution*, pp. 481-4, 516-21, 548-9 (note).
4. Edgar Snow, *Red Star*, p. 161.
5. See *International Press Correspondence*, vol. VII, no. 11, p. 231.
6. ibid., vol. VI, no. 90, p. 1583.
7. See Lenin, *Oeuvres Complètes* (Paris, 1935), vol. VIII, p. 235; *Saemtliche Werke* (Wien-Berlin, 1929), vol. VII, p. 377; *Ausgewaehlte Werke* (Wien-Berlin, 1933), vol. VI, p. 391.

COMMENTARY E:

1. See *Bolshevik*, nos. 23-4, December 21, 1927, p. 105; also *Chinese Correspondence*, vol. II, no. 7, May 8, 1927, p. 2.
2. *International Press Correspondence*, vol. VII, no. 11, February 3, 1927, p. 231.
3. ibid., no. 27, April 28, 1927, p. 544.
4. Snow, *Red Star*, pp. 161-2; also, M. N. Roy, *Revolution and Counterrevolution*, p. 481.
5. See Roy, pp. 481-4, 516-21, 548-9.
6. See Stalin's speech of April 5, 1927, as quoted by Isaacs, p. 185.

COMMENTARY F:

1. Ch'ü Ch'iu-pai, *Chung-kuo ko-ming yü Chung-kuo Kung-ch'an-tang* (The Chinese revolution and the Chinese Communist Party), p. 66.
2. Li Ang, *Hung-se wu-t'ai* (The Red Stage), Chungking, 1942, p. 18.
3. *International Press Correspondence*, no. 41, July 14, 1927, p. 899.
4. Ch'ü Ch'iu-pai, p. 66.
5. See Li Ang, p. 20.
6. *International Press Correspondence*, no. 72, November 4, 1926, p. 1251.
7. ibid., no 48, August 18, 1927, p. 1076.
8. P'eng Shu-chih, *Kung-tang lien-hsi hui-i t'an-hua* (Speech at the joint session of the CP) September 1929; also Harold Isaacs, *The Tragedy of the Chinese Revolution*, pp. 341-5.
9. Edgar Snow, *Red Star*, p. 162.
10. P'eng shu-chih as above, no. 8.

DOCUMENT NO. 9:

1. The Chinese text says "January 25", but has been corrected after checking with another Chinese text translated from Russian by Ssu Mei (pseudonym of Chang Wen-t'ien). This date (January 25) is obviously wrong because the resolution mentions the Fifth National Congress which was held in April and May 1927.
2. Our text says "nationalism" (*min-tsu*) instead of "democracy" (*min-ch'üan*), but has been corrected according to Ssu Mei's text.
3. We follow Ssu Mei's text, which omits a negative here.

COMMENTARY G:

1. *International Press Correspondence*, December 12, 1928.
2. See the Political Resolution of the Enlarged Plenum of the CC, November 14, 1927.

DOCUMENT NO. 13:

1. "Political struggle" (*cheng-chih tou-cheng*), when used by the Communists, usually means the effectuation of Party policy, the exposure, condemnation, and correction of unorthodox tendencies and deviating elements, and purification of the Party.
2. The "Kiangsu Affair" refers to the disbandment of the Kiangsu Provincial Executive Committee of the CCP because its members planned to stage a coup by occupying the headquarters of the General Labour Federation of Shanghai, in September 1927, which ended in failure and other "deviations". The "Shun-chih Affair" refers to the dismissal of two CC members by the Political Bureau, after a premature insurrection in October 1927, at Shun-chih and other districts in Hopei, had failed. This expulsion, though done without constitutional grounds, was approved by the Plenum.

COMMENTARY I:

1. Isaacs, p. 403.
2. See *Chung-kuo Kung-ch'an-tang chung-yang wei-yuan-hui kao t'ung-chih shu* (CC, CCP, letter to all comrades), November 16, 1930 (microfilm from Hoover Library); also Isaacs, pp. 408–9.

DOCUMENT NO. 16:

1. This CI letter, the text of which is not available, is mentioned by Harold Isaacs, *The Tragedy of the Chinese Revolution*, in footnote 16 to ch. xix, which reads: "Resolution on the Chinese Question, by the Political Secretariat of the ECCI, July 23, 1930", *Truth* (*Shih-hua*), October 23, 1930.

COMMENTARY J:

1. Lenin, *Saemtliche Werke* (Wien-Berlin, 1929), pp. 270–80.
2. A middle peasant was defined as one who received fifteen per cent or more of his total income from hired labour or tenants (see Jen Pi-shih, *Agrarian Reforms in Communist Areas*, January 1948).
3. Yakhontoff, *The Chinese Soviets*, pp. 130–2.
4. *Rätechina*, p. 621. (This is a collection of official documents of the Soviet period, published in Moscow, 1934.)
5. ibid., pp. 622–3.
6. ibid., Part II, *passim*. Also Isaacs, pp. 418–19.
7. Snow, *Red Star*, p. 186.

DOCUMENT NO. 17:

1. For the basis of our textual changes from Yakhontoff's version, see under *Bibliography A*.

DOCUMENT NO. 19:

1. For the basis of this translation see under *Bibliography A*.

COMMENTARY K:

1. We do not attempt to settle the question whether the Chinese Communists championed the united front before or after the Comintern did so. The declaration of the CC, CCP, of July 24, 1933, "On the Fifth Suppression Campaign", indicates clearly that as of that date the CCP still adhered —at least *officially*—to the CI strategy of the time, that is, to the "united

front from below". On the other hand, an article by Dorothy Woodward on Mao in the *New Statesman and Nation*, January 15, 1949, suggests the possibility that the CCP was pressing for a united front with the Fukien rebels in late 1933 and that it was Comintern intervention which prevented the formation of this united front (which would have been one of the New Democracy type). This would explain Dimitrov's statement at the Seventh CI Congress of July–August 1935, congratulating the CCP on having taken the initiative in the formation of a united front. It would also lend meaning to Mao's statement noted above in *Commentary J,* that the CCP defeat in Kiangsi was due in part to the lack of a united front with the Fukien rebels late in 1933.

2. Mao Tse-tung, "Struggle for the winning of tens of millions of the masses to participate in the anti-Japanese national united front", *Hsüan-chi,* vol. II, p. 11.

3. Mao Tse-tung, "On the question of the future of the revolution", ibid., vol. II, p. 26–7.

COMMENTARY M:

1. Mao's principal ideological statement just preceding *On New Democracy* was *The Chinese Revolution and the Chinese Communist Party (Chung-kuo ko-ming yü Chung-kuo Kung-ch'an-tang)* of November 15, 1939.

2. Wang Ming, speech made at the Seventh ECCI Plenum, 1935.

DOCUMENT NO. 24:

1. For the textual basis of our extract and its omissions, see under *Bibliography A.*

COMMENTARY O:

1. On this complex subject see the State Department White Paper, Annexes 40 and 41, for KMT and CCP statements of September 15, 1944; also printed in the *China Handbook 1937–1945*, Macmillan, New York, 1947, pp. 81–94. Communist statements of the period from March 1944 to March 1945 were published in English in *Kuomintang-Communist Negotiations*, New China News Agency, Yenan, October 1945, 195 pp.

DOCUMENT NO. 26:

1. This is the name used by the Japanese Communist leader outside Japan. His original name was Nozaka Sanji, but he is now known under the name of Nozaka Sanzo. Another name used by him is Nozaka Tetsu. For Japanese characters, see *Glossary.*

2. An asterisk indicates the person is dead as of May 1950. Ch'en T'an-ch'iu's death was reported in an article in *Hua-ch'iao jih-pao* some time in February 1950.

COMMENTARY P:

1. Lenine, V., "Thèses sur la question agraire", *Oeuvres Complètes,* vol. XXV, p. 319.

DOCUMENT NO. 31:

1. The "Agrarian revolution period" (*t'u-ti ko-ming shih-ch'i*) usually refers to the Kiangsi Soviet period and early Yenan period before the cessation of land confiscation in 1938.

DOCUMENT NO. 33:

1. The Economists were a school of Marxists in Russia in the late nineteenth century who felt that socialists should concentrate their efforts on carrying forward the economic struggle of the workers by promoting unionization. They were thus opposed to the diversion of energy to political activities, arguing that since political change follows from economic change, the socialist must concentrate his effort in the area which counts.

COMMENTARY T:

1. *Cheng-feng*, pp. 44–51; *Hsüeh-hsi*, which we translate here as "Learning", means the process, attitude, and institution of study, or the procedures of learning, rather than knowledge itself.
2. ibid., pp. 122–5.
3. Stein, p. 118.
4. Belden, p. 67.
5. *Cheng-feng*, p. 2.
6. ibid., p. 262.
7. ibid., pp. 145–6.

DOCUMENT NO. 34:

1. "Literature and art" is translated from the Chinese term *wen-i*, which in this instance includes *wen-hsüeh* (literature) and *i-shu* (art). In ordinary usage *wen-i* means simply "literature".
2. Details about this Party School are not available. Shan-pei kung-hsüeh (The North Shensi Academy), which was established soon after the Sino-Japanese war began in July 1937, was called by some sources the Party School at that time. This Academy gave short-term training (about two months) to students who were sent out to various areas as cadre workers after graduation. Classes varied from 200 to 600 (at least in 1938). The Party School mentioned in document 34 could be an expansion of the Shan-pei kung-hsüeh.
3. "Culture", translated from the Chinese term *wen-hua*, has its usual meaning here, the same as in Western parlance. But *wen-hua* as used by the Chinese Communists has a second meaning of the knowledge of reading and writing or literacy on its lowest level.

DOCUMENT NO. 35:

1. "Party formalism" is translated from the Chinese term *tang pa-ku*. *Pa-ku* literally means the "eight-legged" essay style traditionally used by classical scholars in the imperial examinations. After the May Fourth movement (1919), when that style fell into disuse, the term came to refer to any stereotyped form of writing. In this case it is the over-formal style developed by the Communists in reports, speeches, notices, etc., that Mao Tse-tung is cautioning against—gobbledygook or jargon.
2. ibid.
3. The term "cadre" was originally taken into Russian from French and used in its primary meaning of a small military organizational unit or group which formed a nucleus for training other military groups. Gradually cadres came to be used in other fields and the term took on the meaning of any organizational unit functioning in the interests of the Communist Party. When the term was taken into Chinese, the characters *kan-pu*

were adopted from Japanese. It has come to denote either a small group or, more commonly, an individual. A *kan-pu* is a worker, not necessarily a CP member (although quite possibly one), but certainly someone highly enthusiastic about the principles for which the Party stands. Imbued with this enthusiasm and with some training in a particular field, he goes out to work in the Party, in politics, factories, the army, villages, or schools, in other words, in every kind of activity in modern Chinese society. The CP membership is confined to a highly select group, but the cadre workers through whom they reach the masses form a vast network throughout Communist China.

4. These two series of Chinese characters known as the "ten heavenly stems" (*t'ien-kan*) and "twelve earthly branches" (*ti-chih*) are used in China to indicate numerals as well as to designate, in rotational combination, the sixty years of the Chinese cycle.

5. Mao here makes a pun by quoting a proverb in which the word *ch'eng* for a weighing hook can also mean "to praise oneself".

COMMENTARY U:

1. Sambō, pp. 200–14.
2. The CI was formally dissolved in June 1943. The name of the CY (of China) seemed to have disappeared from CCP publications and announcements after the Sino-Japanese war in 1937. The New Democratic Youth League, with Liao Ch'eng-chih as Chairman, held its First Congress on April 11, 1949.

COMMENTARY V:

1. *Hua-ch'iao jih-pao* (*The China Daily News*), April 1, 1949, p. 2 and p. 5.
2. *China Digest*, vol. v, no. 7, January 25, 1949, p. 4.
3. P'eng Chen, "Land Redistribution and Reorganizational Work", *Ch'un-tang*, p. 18.
4. Stein, p. 146.
5. Stalin, p. 32.
6. Werner, p. 150.
7. Shan-Kan-Ning (see *Bibliography B*), pp. 43–4.
8. Winfield, p. 294.
9. Jen Pi-shih, p. 24.

DOCUMENT NO. 38:

1. The bracketed phrase does not appear in the Chinese text in *Hua-ch'iao jih-pao* April 1, 1949, p. 2, but appears in the English version published by the *China Digest*—evidently an interpolation for the *China Digest*'s English-reading audience.

DOCUMENT NO. 39:

1. We retain in brackets the headings evidently inserted by the editors of the *China Digest*.
2. Hung Hsiu-ch'üan: leader of the Taiping Rebellion.
3. K'ang Yu-wei: one of the first Chinese advocates of constitutional monarchy and leader of the famous reform movement of 1898.
4. Yen Fu: a pioneer translator in introducing Western philosophical works into China, including T. H. Huxley's *Evolution and Ethics and Other Essays* and Adam Smith's *Wealth of Nations*.

5. This bracketed sentence evidently was interpolated in the *China Digest* translation.
6. "National bourgeoisie" when used by the CCP refers to "bourgeoisie who neither belong to the realm of bureaucratic capitalists nor have any affiliation with foreign imperialists".
7. The bracketed statement evidently was inserted by the editors of the *China Digest* in their English translation.
8. ibid.
9. ibid.
10. ibid.

COMMENTARY X:

1. *Jen-min shou-ts'e*, 1950, section 1, p. 10.
2. For a cogent appraisal of the new administrative structure and its policies, see the articles by Professor Steiner, *Bibliography B*.

BIBLIOGRAPHY A:
LIST OF DOCUMENTS TRANSLATED

Note: This list gives bibliographical data on each of the forty documents presented in the text above. In addition to noting the library source of rare items, we have indicated discrepancies found between different versions of certain documents, and have also noted briefly the nature of passages which we have omitted from certain documents for purposes of condensation. The object in each case has been to identify our sources, some of which are decidedly rare, and to aid future research by indicating the use that has been made of each item.

1. *Chung-kuo Kung-ch'an-tang ti-i-hui tui shih-chü hsüan-yen* 中國共產黨第一回對時局宣言 (First manifesto of the CCP on the current situation), June 10, 1922; taken from a translation into English from Russian, made at the University of California at Los Angeles, mimeographed, single-spaced, 7 pp., by kindness of Professor Arthur Steiner; this translation was checked by A. E. Khodorov with the Russian text from which the translation was made, which is to be found in *Novyi Vostok*, no. 2, 1922, pp. 606–12; a number of minor changes have been made by us; Chinese text not available.

2. *Chung-kuo Kung-ch'an-tang ti-erh-tz'u ch'üan-kuo tai-piao ta-hui hsüan-yen* 中國共產黨第二次全國代表大會宣言 (Manifesto of the Second National Congress of the CCP), July 1922; translated from a Japanese version published in *Shina ni okeru Kyōsan undō* 支那に於ける共産運動 (The Communist movement in China), pp. 95–7, a work published by the Nippon gaiji kyōkai (Japanese Foreign Affairs Association), Tokyo, 1933, 401 pp. (Library of Congress, Orientalia-Japanese 363.822 N237); Chinese text not available.

3. *Sun Chung-shan Yüeh-fei kung-t'ung hsüan-yen* 孫中山越飛共同宣言 (Joint manifesto of Sun Yat-sen and A. Joffe), January 26, 1923; the usual English version of this brief statement, widely reprinted by numerous authors over the years, was taken from the English translation of *The North China Herald*, February 3, 1923, p. 289, which is, however, faulty; our present version is translated from the Chinese text in *Tung-fang tsa-chih* 東方雜誌 (The Eastern Miscellany), vol. XX, no. 2, January 25, 1923, pp. 10–11.

4. *Chung-kuo Kung-ch'an-tang ti-san-tz'u ch'üan-kuo tai-piao ta-hui hsüan-yen* 中國共產黨第三次全國代表大會宣言 (Manifesto of the Third National Congress of the CCP), June 1923; translated from *Hsiang-tao* 響導 (The Guide), official organ of the CCP, no. 30, June 20, 1923, p. 228; secured on microfilm from the Hoover Library, Stanford, Cal.

5. *Sun Chung-shan tui t'an-ho Kung-ch'an-tang ch'eng-wen chih p'i-shih* 孫中山對彈劾共產黨呈文之批示 (Sun Yat-sen's comments on an accusation against the CP); a partial translation of Sun Yat-sen's marginal autograph comments on a petition presented to him on December 3, 1923, by eleven members of the KMT branch in Kwangtung province, making charges against the CCP. See *T'an-ho Kung-ch'an-tang liang ta yao-an* 彈劾共產黨兩大要案 (Two important cases on the impeachment of the CP), published by the Kuo-min-tang chung-yang chien-ch'a wei-yuan-hui 國民黨中央監察委員會 (The Central Control Committee of the KMT), Nanking, September 1927, 30 pp. This thin volume reproduces in photographic facsimile the petition dated December 3, 1923, and Sun's holograph comments, with title page by Hu Han-min 胡漢民 and preface by Wu Ching-heng 吳敬恒, dated July 1927 (Harvard-Yenching Library).

6. *Chung-kuo Kung-ch'an-tang ti-ssu-hui tui shih-chü hsüan-yen* 中國共產黨第四回對時局宣言 (Fourth manifesto of the CCP on the current situation), January 1925; translated from a Japanese version in *Shina Kyōsantō undōshi* 支那共產運動史 (History of the Chinese Communist movement), pp. 91–2, a work

published by Sambō hombu 参謀本部 ([Japanese] General Staff), Tokyo, 1931, 382 pp. (Library of Congress, Orientalia-Japanese 370.378, 363.908 (22)); Chinese text not available.

7. Mao Tse-tung 毛澤東 , *Hu-nan nung-min yün-tung k'ao-ch'a pao-kao* 湖南農民運動考察報告 (Report on an investigation of the peasant movement in Hunan), February 1927; translated from *Mao Tse-tung hsüan-chi* 毛澤東選集 (Selected Works of Mao Tse-tung), vol. I, edited by Chin-Ch'a-Chi jih-pao she 晉察冀日報社 (Shansi-Chahar-Hopei Daily), and published by Chin-Ch'a-Chi New China Book Company, May 1944, pp. 117–18; this edition consists of 5 volumes, 29 items, and 723 pp. (Harvard-Yenching Library).

8. *Chung-kuo Kung-ch'an-tang ti-wu-tz'u ch'üan-kuo tai-piao ta-hui chüeh-i-an chai-yao* 中國共產黨第五次全國代表大會決議案摘要 (Resolutions of the Fifth National Congress of the CCP [May 1927], résumé); the first part, "On the Revolutionary Movement", has been translated from *Shina Kyōsantō no kaikan* 支那共產黨の概觀 (A general survey of the CCP), published by Sambō hombu 参謀本部 ([Japanese] General Staff), 84 pp., Tokyo, 1929 (?), pp. 35–6; the second part, "On Agrarian Policy", has been translated from Okubo Yashushi 大久保泰 , *Chūkō san-jūnen* 中共三十年 (Thirty Years of the CCP), 382 pp., Tokyo, 1949, pp. 80–4 (Harvard-Yenching Library); Chinese texts not available.

9. *Chung-yang chih-hsing wei-yuan-hui kao ch'üan-t'i tang-yuan t'ung-chih shu* 中央執行委員會告全體黨員同志書 (Circular letter of the CC [CCP] to all Party members), August 1927; translated from microfilm of *Chung-kuo ko-ming* 中國革命 (The Chinese revolution), January 1933, pp. 149–205 (Hoover Library, Stanford, California). Another Chinese text is entitled *Chung-kuo Kung-ch'an-tang pa-yueh (1927) hui-i hsüan-yen* 中國共產黨八月 (1927) 會議宣言 (Manifesto of the August [1927] Conference of the CCP), published by the Sun Yat-sen University, Moscow, 1927, p. 48; an editor's note on the last page by Ssu Mei 思美 (pseud. of Chang Wen-t'ien 張聞天) states that "this letter is translated from Russian, because

of the unavailability of the original Chinese text. After this round-about way, some differences with the original text are inevitable . . ." (Library of Congress, Orientalia-Chinese E351-C45).

The following is a table showing the major discrepancies found after comparing the two texts. The text published in *Chung-kuo ko-ming* and translated in this volume is called Text I; and the text translated into Chinese from Russian by Ssu Mei is called Text II. Except in two instances where Text II seems to make better sense (see last page of translation), whenever discrepancies appear Text I has been followed as the primary source.

TEXT I	TEXT II
No passages are underlined	Section headings and certain passages are underlined
Heading for section I: Introduction	Heading for section I: To All CP Members
Heading for section V: The CCP and the KMT	Heading for section V: Materials on the August Conference
p. 163, l. 7: June 19	p. 12, l. 9: 23 (no month given)
p. 171, l. 2: Eighth Enlarged Plenum of the ECCI	p. 18, l. 21: Ninth Enlarged Plenum of the ECCI
p. 172, l. 11: January 1927	p. 20, l. 3: February 1927
p. 173, l. 7: Seventh Congress of the Hunan Provincial Party Committee	p. 20, l. 16: Sixth Congress of the Hunan Provincial Party Committee
p. 173, l. 10: Petty bourgeois leaders of the KMT	p. 21, l. 21: The Central (Government) of the KMT
p. 174, l. 11: Excessive actions in Wuhan	p. 21, l. 8: Excessive actions in the peasant movement in Hunan
p. 187, l. 3: June 30	p. 32, l. 8: July 3
p. 206: Text ends with the words "final victory."	p. 48, l. 4–5: adds another sentence after the words "final victory"— "and bring about the noble and shining triumph of the great Chinese Revolution."

10. *Pa-ch'i chin-chi hui-i i-chüeh-an* 八七緊急會議議決案, (Resolutions of the August 7 Emergency Conference), August

1927; translated from *Shina ni okeru Kyōsan undō* 支那に於ける 共産運動 (The Communist movement in China), pp. 133–8; published by the Nippon gaiji kyōkai (Japanese Foreign Affairs Association), Tokyo, 1933, p. 401 (Library of Congress, Orientalia-Japanese 363.822 N237); Chinese text not available.

11. *Ti-liu-tz'u tai-piao ta-hui cheng-chih wen-t'i chüeh-i-an* 第六 次代表大會政治問題決議案 (Political resolution of the Sixth National Congress [of the CCP]), September 1928; translated from mimeographed pamphlet, *Chung-kuo Kung-ch'an-tang ti-liu tz'u tai-piao ta-hui chüeh-i-an* 中國共產黨第六次代表大 會決議案 (Resolutions of the Sixth National Congress of the CCP), of which the table of contents is as follows:

	TOTAL PAGES
1. Political resolution	27
2. Resolution on the peasant movement	11
3. Resolution on the land question	23
4. Resolution on the labour movement	17
5. Resolution on the women's movement	10
6. Resolution on the CY movement	5
7. Present tasks in propaganda work	7
8. Resolution on the organizational question in the Soviet régime	22
9. Draft resolution on CCP organization	9

Title page also in Russian: Resoliutsii VI C'ezda kitaiskoi kommu-nistcheskoi partii (Resolutions of the Sixth National Congress of the CCP), Izdanie, KUTK [i.e. Komunisticheskii Universitet Trudya-shchikhsya Kitaia, Communist University for Chinese Toilers], paper cover, mimeographed, Moscow, 1928 (Library of Congress, Orientalia-Chinese E312.9 A111).

12. *Ti-liu-tz'u tai-piao ta-hui kuan-yü nung-min yün-tung chüeh-i-an* 第六次代表大會關於農民運動決議案 (Resolution of the Sixth National Congress [of the CCP] on the peasant movement), September 1928, 11 pp.; translated from the same pamphlet as no. 11 above.

13. *Erh-chung ch'üan-hui ti chüeh-i yü ching-shen* 二中全會的決議與精神 (The resolutions and spirit of the Second Plenum of the CC), July 9, 1929; translated from a pamphlet *Chung-Kung chung-yang ti erh-tz'u ch'üan-t'i hui-i ts'ai-liao* 中共中央第二次全體會議材料 (Materials of the Second Plenum of the CC of the CCP), of which the full table of contents is as follows:

The title page of this pamphlet states that it was published by Chung-kuo wen-t'i yen-chiu-yuan 中國問題研究院 (Research Institute on the Chinese Question), Moscow, 1930; paper cover, mimeographed, 137 pp.; Russian data on last page: Steklographia KUTK [i.e. Komunisticheskii Universitet Trudyashchikhsya Kitaia, Communist University for Chinese Toilers], Moscow, Volkhowka, 16, Moskublit 2072, KUTK V.4, T.600 copies, 1930 (Library of Congress, Orientalia-Chinese E351-C46).

14. Li Li-san: 李立三, *Ko-ming kao-ch'ao yü i-sheng ho shu-sheng ti shou-hsien sheng-li* 革命高潮與一省和數省的首先勝利 (The new revolutionary rising tide and preliminary successes in one or more provinces), June 11, 1930; translated from Chinese text in

microfilm from Hoover Library; see *Hung-ch'i* 紅旗 (The Red Flag), no. 121, special issue, July 19, 1930, pp. 1–4 (Hoover Library).

15. *Shao Shan pao-kao—San-chung ch'üan-hui ts'ai-liao ti chiu-hao* 少山 報告 — 三中全會材料第九號 (Shao Shan's Report—Reference item number nine of the Third Plenum of the CC[CCP]), September 24, 1930; extracts of salient sections have been made from the revised version of an English translation by Chi Wen-shun 紀文勛 and Robert North of the Hoover Institute, which has been compared with the original pamphlet, dated January 3, 1931, 9 pp., secured in microfilm from the Hoover Library; a number of changes have been made in the translation.

For reference we note here our major omissions and their pagination in the original Chinese text: Editorial note by Shao Shan (Chou En-lai, p. 1); The deepening crisis of international capitalism, and of international relations (I.1; p. 1); The consolidation of the Soviet Union and the decline of capitalism (I.3; p. 1); Warlord and peasant wars; Soviet power as against the National Assembly (II.3; p. 2); Union of hired farm hands and the poor peasant corps (III.2 [5]; p. 5); Call for mutinies in warlord armies (III.3 [5]; p. 7); Youth and women (III.3 [6]; p. 7); The minorities problem (III.3 [7]; p. 7); Problems of the revolutionary transformation (V.2; p. 9); Opposition to erroneous notions of the revolutionary transformation according to the Three People's Principles and Trotskyism (V.3; p. 9).

16. *Chung-Kung chung-yang k'uo-ta-ti ti-ssu-tz'u ch'üan-t'i hui-i i-chüeh-an* 中共中央擴大的第四次全體會議議決案 (Resolution of the Enlarged Fourth Plenum of the CC of the CCP), January 1931; revised from an English translation by Chi Wen-shun and Robert North which has been compared with the original pamphlet, entitled *Chung-kuo Kung-ch'an-tang chung-yang wei-yuan-hui k'uo-ta-ti ti-ssu-tz'u ch'üan-t'i hui-i i-chüeh-an* and dated January 1931, 4 pp.; secured in microfilm from the Hoover Library; a number of changes have been made in the translation.

17. *Su-wei-ai kung-ho-kuo hsien-fa* 蘇維埃共和國憲法 (Constitution of the Soviet Republic), November 1931; English

translation taken from appendix, p. 217, of Victor A. Yakhontoff, *The Chinese Soviets*, Coward-McCann, Inc., New York, 1934, 296 pp., acknowledged in footnote on p. 217: "Courtesy of the International Publishers" (see their publication, *Fundamental Laws of the Chinese Soviet Republic*); this translation has been checked with the Japanese version in *Shina ni okeru Kyōsan undō* (The Communist movement in China), pp. 347–52, see under Doc. 10 above; subsequently, having found a Chinese text in the volume *Su-wei-ai Chung-kuo* (Columbia University Library, see Bibliography B below), pp. 37–44, we have been able to make a number of corrections in the faulty English translation thus far available.

18. *Su-wei-ai kung-ho-kuo t'u-ti-fa*　蘇維埃共和國土地法 (Land Law of the Soviet Republic), November 1931; English translation taken from the appendix, p. 223, in Yakhontoff, *The Chinese Soviets*, see under Doc. no. 17 above, acknowledged as "Courtesy of the International Publishers"; this translation has been checked with the Japanese version in *Shina ni okeru Kyōsan undō* (The Communist movement in China), see under Doc. no. 10 above, pp. 353–7; having subsequently found a Chinese text in *Su-wei-ai Chung-kuo*, pp. 107–11 (noted under the preceding item, no. 17), through the courtesy of Professor C. M. Wilbur, we have been able to make a number of textual corrections in the hitherto faulty English translation.

19. Mao Tse-tung　毛澤東, *Tui ti-erh-tz'u Su-wei-ai ch'üan-kuo tai-piao ta-hui ti pao-kao*　對第二次蘇維埃全國代表大會的報告 (Report to the Second All-China Soviet Congress), January 22, 1934; extract of salient sections made from English translation in appendix of Yakhontoff, *The Chinese Soviets*, as in no. 17–18 above, pp. 249–83, acknowledged in footnote on p. 249: "As it appeared in the *Chinese Workers' Correspondence*, Shanghai, vol. 4, no. 11, March 31, 1934, without any correction or changes. The above organization is an official news agency of the CCP. (Courtesy of Miss Agnes Smedley)"; this translation has been checked with the Japanese version in *Shina Sobieto undō no kenkyū*　支那ソヴエト運動の研究 (A Study of the Chinese Soviet movement), published by the Tōa

keizai chōsa kyoku (Economic Research Bureau of East Asia), Tokyo, 1935, 459 pp., see pp. 357–402 (Library of Congress, Orientalia-Japanese 302.676, 363.807 (22)); subsequently checked with Chinese text found in the volume *Chih-yu Su-wei-ai neng-kou chiu Chung-kuo* (Only the Soviet can save China), pp. 13–100 (see under Bibliography B below), which enabled us to correct the faulty English translation hitherto available. The last-named source states that its text is taken from the central organ of the Soviet area, *Tou-cheng* 鬥爭 (Struggle), no. 66.

For reference we note the following sections omitted in our extract and their pagination in Yakhontoff, *The Chinese Soviets*: KMT offensives against Soviet area (pp. 253–5); Red Army (pp. 256–8); Penal reforms in Soviet area (p. 262); Soviet labour policy (pp. 262–6); Soviet financial policy (pp. 269–71); Soviet economic policy (pp. 271–3; Soviet culture (pp. 273–6); Soviet marriage laws (p. 276); Soviet nationalities policy (pp. 276–7); Military tasks of the Soviets (pp. 277–8); Red Army reforms (pp. 278–9); Economic tasks of the Soviets (pp. 279–80).

20. *Chung-kuo Kung-ch'an-tang k'ang-Jih chiu-kuo shih ta kang-ling* 中國共產黨抗日救國十大綱領 (The ten great policies of the CCP for anti-Japanese resistance and national salvation), August 15, 1937; translated from the appendix of *T'ung-i-chan-hsien hsia ti Chung-kuo Kung-ch'an-tang* 統一戰線下的中國共產黨 (The CCP in the united front [period]), edited by Kuo-chi shih-shih yen-chiu-hui 國際時事研究會 (Research society on international affairs), published by I-pan shu-tien 一般書店, Hongkong, January 1938, 94 pp., see pp. 91–4.

21. *Chung-kuo Kung-ch'an-tang wei kung-pu Kuo-Kung ho-tso hsüan-yen* 中國共產黨為公佈國共合作宣言 (The CCP's public statement on KMT-CCP co-operation), September 22, 1937; translated from the appendix of *T'ung-i-chan-hsien hsia ti Chung-kuo Kung-ch'an-tang*, see no. 20 above, pp. 89–91; our present translation differs in a number of minor points from the English translation which has appeared successively in *Finance and Commerce*, Shanghai, September 29, 1937, p. 252; Lawrence K. Rosinger, *China's Wartime*

Politics 1937–44, Princeton, 1944, pp. 96–7; and the Department of State, *United States Relations with China*, Washington, August 1949, pp. 523–4.

22. Mao Tse-tung 毛澤東, *Kuo-Kung liang-tang t'ung-i-chan-hsien ch'eng-li hou chung-kuo ko-ming ti p'o-ch'ieh jen-wu,* 國共 兩黨統一戰線成立後中國革命的迫切任務 (Urgent tasks of the Chinese revolution since the formation of the KMT-CCP united front), September 29, 1937; translated from *Mao Tse-tung hsüan-chi*, see no. 7 above, vol. II, pp. 43–77.

23. *Chung-yang kuan-yü Chung-Kung shih-ch'i chou-nien chi-nien hsüan-ch'uan kang-yao* 中央關於中共十七週年紀念宣傳 綱要 (Propaganda outline issued by the CC on the seventeenth anniversary of the CCP), June 24, 1938; translated from *K'ang-chan i-lai chung-yao wen-chien hui-chi, 1937–42* 抗戰以來重要文件 彙集 *1937–42* (A compendium of important documents since [the outbreak of] the War of Resistance, 1937–42), issued by the Chung-Kung chung-yang shu-chi-ch'u 中共中央書記處 (Secretariat of the CC, CCP), Yenan, 1942, 223 pp., see p. 55; this volume contains 67 important documents of the CCP from July 8, 1937, to July 7, 1942 (Harvard-Yenching Library).

24. Mao Tse-tung 毛澤東, *Hsin-min-chu chu-i lun* 新民主主 義論 (On the New Democracy), January 19, 1940; extract of salient sections of an English translation printed by Sharaf Athar Ali, New Age Printing Press, Bombay, India, reprinted in United States Congress, House of Representatives, Committee on Foreign Affairs, Subcommittee no. 5—National and International Movements, *Report: The Strategy and Tactics of World Communism*, Supplement III, Country Studies, C. *Communism in China*, appendix B, "Mao Tse-tung, *China's New Democracy*", pp. 67–91 (U.S. Government printing office, Washington, 1949, 105 pp.); checked with Chinese text, *Hsin-min-chu chu-i lun* (On the New Democracy), published by Chieh-fang she 解放社 (Liberation [Emancipation] News Agency), Yenan, March 1946, 65 pp.; also checked with an English translation published by the New Century Publishers, New York, with an introduction by Earl

Browder, entitled *Mao Tse-tung's "Democracy"*, and with a digest in English issued by the Chinese News Service, with a preface by Lin Yutang, New York, 1947, 24 pp.; and also checked with mimeographed notes "On the English translations of Mao Tse-tung's *New Democracy*" by Michael Lindsay, 1947, 7 pp.; on the basis of these various checkings, a number of minor textual changes have been made.

For reference we note major omissions in our condensation and their pagination in the original Chinese text: Political conditions before and after the May 4 Movement (pp. 15–18); Why a bourgeois dictatorship is impossible in China (pp. 25–30); Differences between the *San-min chu-i* (The Three People's Principles) of Dr. Sun Yat-sen and Communism (pp. 36–7); The old *San-min chu-i* (pp. 44–6); The four stages of the cultural revolution (pp. 52–8).

25. *Chung-yang kuan-yü k'ang-Jih ken-chü-ti t'u-ti cheng-ts'e ti chüeh-ting,* 中央關於抗日根據地土地政策的決定 (Decision of the CC on land policy in the anti-Japanese base areas), January 28, 1942; translated from *K'ang-chan i-lai chung-yao wen-chien hui-chi,* see no. 23 above, pp. 188–92.

26. Reports on the Seventh National Congress of the CCP, April 1945; translated from news despatches of the Hsin-hua she (New China News Agency) on the Seventh National Congress appearing in *Ch'i-ta wen-hsien* 七大文獻 *Chung-kuo Kung-ch'an-tang ti-ch'i-tz'u ch'üan-kuo tai-piao ta-hui wen-hsien* 中國共產黨第七次全國代表大會文獻 (Documents of the Seventh National Congress of the CCP), published by Chieh-fang she 解放社 (Liberation [Emancipation] News Agency), June 1945, 180 pp., see pp. 1–7 and last 6 pp. (Harvard-Yenching Library).

27. Mao Tse-tung 毛澤東, *Lun lien-ho cheng-fu* 論聯合政府 (On Coalition Government), April 24, 1945; extract of salient sections from an English translation printed by "The Culture Supply Co.", Chefoo, China; title page: *On Coalition Government, Report to the 7th Congress of the Chinese Communist Party at Yenan*, by Mao Tse-tung, December 1946, 96 pp.; checked with the Chinese text, Mao Tse-tung, *Lun lien-ho cheng-fu*, published by the Chieh-fang she, May 1945,

98 pp., and with another English version issued by the New China News Agency dated August 1945, 150 pp.; after these checkings, a number of changes have been made.

Major omissions and their pagination in the original Chinese text: History of the anti-Japanese war (pp. 10–15); The KMT areas (pp. 25–6); Comparison of the liberated and the KMT areas (pp. 27–9); Who undermines the war of resistance and endangers the country? (pp. 29–31); Call for complete annihilation of the Japanese (pp. 52–3); The KMT one-party dictatorship to be replaced by a coalition government (pp. 53–7); Call for unification of the Chinese people (pp. 59–61) and for the creation of a people's army (pp. 61–4); Tasks in KMT areas (pp. 84–6) and in (Japanese) occupied areas (pp. 86–7).

28. Ch'en Yün 陳雲, *Tsen-yang tso i-ko Kung-ch'an-tang-yuan* 怎樣做一個共產黨員 (How to be a Communist Party member), May 30, 1939; translated from *Cheng-feng wen-hsien* 整風文獻 (Documents on the correction of unorthodox tendencies), pp. 67–82; this important volume contains 30 items, including important speeches of Mao Tse-tung, major decisions of the CC, CCP (all belonging to the period 1939–42 except for 1 item in 1929 and another in 1937), and 9 translations of articles by Lenin, Stalin and Dimitrov; edited by Chieh-fang she 解放社 (The Emancipation [Liberation] News Agency), Yenan, published by Hsin-hua shu-tien 新華書店 (New China Book Company), Shansi-Chahar-Hopei branch, Kalgan, March 1946, 297 pp. (Harvard-Yenching Library).

29. Liu Shao-ch'i 劉少奇, *Lun Kung-ch'an-tang-yüan ti hsiu-yang* 論共產黨員的修養 (On the training of a Communist Party member), August 7, 1939; extract of salient sections from an English translation made by Boyd R. Compton of the Far Eastern Institute, University of Washington, Seattle, Wash.; this translation has been checked with the Chinese text in *Cheng-feng wen-hsien*, see no. 28 above, pp. 83–121, with certain changes.

For reference we note the following major omissions and their pagination in the original Chinese text: Obligations of Party members (pp. 89–90); Reasons for basic ideological errors in the Party (pp. 90–2);

Party members should be unselfish in contrast to the exploiters and imperialists (pp. 95–6; 98–100); Sources of ideological errors in the Party (pp. 102–4); Stalin on contradictions within the CP (pp. 105–6); Different attitudes towards shortcomings of the CCP (pp. 107–8; 110–17); On the intra-Party struggle (pp. 118–19); Unprincipled disputes opposed (p. 120).

30. *Chung-yang kuan-yü shen-ju ch'ün-chung kung-tso ti chüeh-ting* 中央關於深入羣眾工作的決定 (Decision of the CC on the work of penetrating the masses), November 1, 1939; translated from *K'ang-chan i-lai chung-yao wen-chien hui-chi*, see no. 23 above, pp. 111–12.

31. *Chung-yang kuan-yü hsi-shou chih-shih fen-tzu ti chüeh-ting* 中央關於吸收知識份子的決定 (Decision of the CC on the absorption of intellectual elements), December 1, 1939; translated from *K'ang-chan i-lai chung-yao wen-chien hui-chi*, see no. 23 above, pp. 113–14.

32. *Chung-yang kuan-yü tang-yüan ts'an-chia ching-chi ho chi-shu kung-tso ti chüeh-ting* 中央關於黨員參加經濟和技術工作的決定 (Decision of the CC on the participation of Party members in economic and technical work), May 1, 1941; translated from *K'ang-chan i-lai chung-yao wen-chien hui-chi*, see no. 23 above, p. 161.

33. Liu Shao-ch'i 劉少奇, *Lun tang-nei tou-cheng*, 論黨內鬥爭 (On the intra-Party struggle), July 2, 1941; extract of salient sections taken, with some minor revisions, from a translation made by Boyd R. Compton, Far Eastern Institute, University of Washington, Seattle; checked with Chinese text in *Cheng-feng wen-hsien*, see no. 28 above, pp. 153–93.

Major omissions and their pagination in the original Chinese text: What Marx, Engels, and Lenin accomplished for the world proletariat (pp. 156–60); Examples of mechanical and excessive intra-Party struggle (pp. 166–7); Meaning of the "struggle meetings" (pp. 168–9); Errors in the intra-Party struggle (pp. 170–1; 176–7); The nature and content of "principle" (pp. 179–82); Self-criticism (pp. 183–4; 185); Nature and content of "reasoning" (p. 192).

34. Mao Tse-tung 毛澤東, *Cheng-tun hsüeh-feng tang-feng wen-feng* 整頓學風黨風文風 (Correcting unorthodox tendencies in learning, the Party, and literature and art), February 1, 1942; taken, with some minor revisions, from an English translation made by Boyd R. Compton, Far Eastern Institute, University of Washington, Seattle; checked with Chinese text in *Cheng-feng wen-hsien,* see no. 28 above, pp. 7–24.

35. Mao Tse-tung 毛澤東, *Fan-tui tang pa-ku* 反對黨八股 (Opposing Party formalism), February 8, 1942; taken, with minor revisions, from an English translation made by Boyd R. Compton, Far Eastern Institute, University of Washington, Seattle; checked with Chinese text in *Cheng-feng wen-hsien,* see no. 28 above, pp. 25–40.

36. Mao Tse-tung 毛澤東, *Tsai Yen-an wen-i tso-t'an-hui shang ti chiang-hua,* 在延安文藝座談會上的講話 (Speech at the forum on literature and art at Yenan), May 2 and May 23, 1942; extract of salient sections from an English translation made by Mrs. Adele Austin Rickett, Peking; checked with Chinese text in *Cheng-feng wen-hsien,* pp. 267–97.

Major omissions and their pagination in the original Chinese text: For whom are literature and art? (pp. 273–4); The weaknesses of the petty-bourgeoisie (p. 276); Sources and raw materials of literature and art (pp. 279–81); The question of popularization (pp. 282–5); Fallacies in literary and art criticism (pp. 289–94); Struggle against non-proletarian, especially petty-bourgeois, ideology (pp. 294–6).

37. *Chung-kuo Kung-ch'an-tang tang-kang,* 中國共產黨黨綱 (Constitution of the CCP), June 11, 1945; the revised version of an English translation made at the University of California, Los Angeles, mimeographed, single-spaced, 16 pp., with title page: "Constitution of the CCP—adopted by the Seventh National Party Congress, Yenan, June 11, 1945; translated under the supervision of, and edited by, H. Arthur Steiner, Professor of Political Science, University of California at Los Angeles, copyright, 1949"; checked with the Chinese text in *Chung-kuo Kung-ch'an-tang yü Kung-ch'an-tang-yüan,* 中國共產黨與共產黨員 (The CCP and the Communist Party

members), edited by the Hung-mien 紅棉 (Red Cotton) Publishing Company, published by the Hsin-min-chu 新民主 (New Democracy) Publishing Company, Hongkong, April 1948, 80 pp.; a number of changes have been made.

38. *Erh-chung ch'üan-hui chüeh-i-an* 二中全會決議案 (Resolutions of the Second [session of the Seventh] Plenum of the CC), March 13, 1949; taken from an English translation of the New China News Agency published in the *China Digest* (*Chung-kuo wen-chai* 中國文摘), vol. V, no. 12, April 5, 1949, Hongkong, pp. 3–5; after checking with the Chinese text published in *Hua-ch'iao jih-pao* 華僑日報 ("China Daily News"), New York, April 1, 1949, pp. 2 and 5, a number of changes have been made. The *China Digest* heading "Second Plenary Session of the CC of the Seventh CCP Congress" is misleading; the above Chinese heading taken from *Hua-ch'iao jih-pao* is also incorrect.

39. Mao Tse-tung 毛澤東 , *Lun jen-min min-chu chuan-cheng,* 論 人民民主專政 (On the People's Democratic Dictatorship), July 1, 1949; taken from an English translation of the New China News Agency published in the *China Digest* (*Chung-kuo wen-chai*), vol. VI, no. 7, July 13, 1949, Hongkong, pp. 3–8; checked with and revised according to the Chinese text published in *1950 Jen-min nien-chien* 一九五〇人民年鑑 (People's Year Book, 1950), edited by Shen Sung-fang 沈頌芳 , Ta-kung Book Store, Hongkong, January 1950, pp. *ting* 1–12.

40. *Chung-yang jen-min cheng-fu tsu-chih-fa* 中央人民政府組 織法 (Organic Law of the Central People's Government), September 27, 1949; taken, with minor changes, from an English translation of the New China News Agency published in the *China Digest*, vol. VII, no. 2, October 19, 1949; checked with the Chinese text published in *1950 Jen-min nien-chien*, see no. 39 above, pp. *ting* 23–8.

BIBLIOGRAPHY B: LIST OF WORKS CITED

Note: This is an alphabetic list of sources (mainly concerning the Chinese Communist movement) which are cited in our Reference Notes, many of which are referred to several times in this volume. It is not meant to be a bibliography on Chinese Communism.

Belden, Jack, *China Shakes the World*, Harper and Brothers, New York, 1949, 524 pp.

Bolshevik, see *Pu-erh-sai-wei-k'o.*

Ch'en Tu-hsiu, *Kao ch'üan-tang t'ung-chih shu* 告全黨同志書 (A Letter to all Party comrades), December 10, 1929, 16 pp. (Hoover Library).

Cheng-feng: Chieh-fang she 解放社 , comp., *Cheng-feng wen-hsien* 整風文獻 (Documents on the correction of [unorthodox] tendencies [in learning, the Party, and literature and art]), revised edition, published by Hsin-hua 新華 Book Company, Shansi-Chahar-Hopei branch, Kalgan, March 1946, 297 pp.

Chih-yu Su-wei-ai neng-kou chiu Chung-kuo 只有蘇維埃能夠救中國 (Only the Soviet can save China), cover bears seal of CEC, Chinese Soviet Republic, n.p., 1934, 112 pp., preface by K'ang Sheng康生 , printed in Russian on back: "Publication No. 2493, Polygrafkniga, A series of collected works on Soviet China, No. 2. Publishing house for foreign workers in the Soviet Union." The Columbia University copy is stamped as originally distributed through "Giu Guo Sh Bao 'Au Secours de la Patrie' " 救國時報社 (i.e. *Chiu-kuo shih-pao*, lit. National salvation times), 7, Rue Commines, Paris-3. Professor C. M. Wilbur kindly brought this volume to our attention (Columbia University Library).

China Digest, Chung-kuo wen-chai 中國文摘 , China Digest Association, Hongkong, January 1948 to January 1950.

Chinese Correspondence (the English-language organ of the CEC of the left-KMT at Wuhan, 1927), no. 8, May 15, 1927.

Ch'un-tang: *Wei ch'un-chieh tang ti tsu-chih erh tou-cheng* 為純潔黨的組織而鬥爭 (Struggle for the purification of Party organization), a collection of 12 items on Party purification first published in late 1947, Cheng-pao she 正報社 , Hongkong, January 1948, 85 pp.

Chung-yao jen-wu: *Chung-Kung chung-yao jen-wu* 中共重要人物 (Important personalities of the CCP), author unknown, Min-chien 民間 Publishing Co., Peiping, 1949, 32 pp.

Ch'ü: Ch'ü Ch'iu-pai 瞿秋白 , *Chung-kuo ko-ming yü Chung-kuo Kung-ch'an-tang* 中國革命與中國共產黨 (The Chinese revolution and the Chinese Communist Party), Moscow, 1928, 116 pp. (Library of Congress, Orientalia-Chinese E351 C52).

Dallin, David J., *Soviet Russia and the Far East*, Yale University Press, New Haven, 1948, 389 pp.

Engels, Friedrich, *Herr Eugen Dühring's revolution in Science* (Anti-Dühring), International Publishers, New York, 1935, 421 pp.

Epstein, Israel, *The Unfinished Revolution in China*, Little, Brown and Company, Boston, 1947, 442 pp.

Fairbank, John King, and E-tu Zen Sun, *Chinese Communist Publications, an annotated bibliography of materials in the Chinese Library at Harvard University*, mimeographed, Russian Research Center, Harvard University, February 1948, 122 pp.

Fundamental Laws of the Chinese Soviet Republic with an Introduction by Bela Kun, International Publishers, New York, printed in Great Britain by Western Printing Services Ltd., Bristol, 1934, 87 pp.

Hatano: Hatano, Kanichi 波多野乾一 , *Sekishoku Shina no kyūmei*, 赤色支那の究明 (A study of Red China), published by Daitō 大東 Publishing Co., Tokyo, 1941, 384 pp. (Library of Congress).

Hsiang-tao chou-k'an 響導週刊 (The Guide Weekly), no. 191, March 12, 1927, microfilm (Hoover Library).

Hua-ch'iao: *Hua-ch'iao jih-pao* 華僑日報 ("China Daily News"), published in New York, various issues 1948–50.

Hua Kang 華崗 , *1925–1927 Chung-kuo ta ko-ming shih, 1925–7* 中國

大革命史 (History of the Great Chinese Revolution 1925–7), Ch'un-keng 春耕 Book Co., Shanghai, 1932, dated at end of book: "manuscript finished in March 1930", 561 pp.

Hua-shang pao: *Hua-shang pao shou-ts'e* 華商報手冊 (Hua Shang Daily News Handbook), Hua-shang pao tzu-liao-shih 華商報資料室, Hongkong, 1949, 368 pp.

Hua Ying-shen 華應申 *Chung-kuo Kung-ch'an-tang lieh-shih chuan* 中國共產黨烈士傳 (Biographies of Martyrs of the CCP), Hsin-hua 新華 Book Co., Shantung, 1947, 224 pp.

Inprecor: *International Press Correspondence*, organ of the Executive Committee of the Communist Internationale, Moscow, 1925–35 10 vols., many thousand pages.

Isaacs, Harold R., *The Tragedy of the Chinese revolution*, Martin Secker and Warburg, Ltd., London, 1938, 502 pp.

Jen-min shou-ts'e, 1950, 人民手冊 *1950* (The People's Handbook, 1950), published by Ta-kung pao 大公報, Shanghai, January 1950, 7 sections, 142 pp.

Jen Pi-shih, *Agrarian Reform in Communist China* (English translation, mimeographed, of a speech made by Jen Pi-shih on January 28, 1948), 24 pp.

K'ang-chan: *K'ang-chan i-lai chung-yao wen-chien hui-chi 1937–42* 抗戰以來重要文件彙集 *1937–42*. (A compendium of important documents since the outbreak of the war of resistance, 1937–42), compiled by the Secretariat of the Central Committee of the Chinese Communist Party, n.p., 1942, 223 pp.

Kautsky, Karl, *Die Agrarfrage, ein übersicht über die Tendenzen der modernen Landwirthschaft und die Agrarpolitik der Sozial demokratie*, Stuttgart, 1902, 451 pp.

Kuo-wen chou-pao 國聞週報 (The Kuo-wen Weekly), vol. V, nos. 1 and 2, January 1928.

Lenine, Vladimir Il'ich, *Oeuvres Complètes*, Editions Sociales Internationales, Paris, 1935, 25 vols.

Lenin, V., *Selected Works*, Foreign Language Publishing House, Moscow, 1942, 2 vols.

Li Ang 李昂, *Hung-se wu-t'ai* 紅色舞台 (The Red Stage),

Sheng-li 勝利 Publishing Co., Kwangtung Branch, Ch'ü-chiang (Kukong), Kwangtung, 1942, 184 pp. (Library of Congress).

Lindsay, Michael, *Notes on the English Translations of Mao Tse-tung's "New Democracy"*, mimeographed, 1946, 7 pp.

Lu Hsün 魯迅 (Lusin or Lu Hsin), *Lu Hsün san-shih-nien chi* 魯迅 三十年集 (Lu Hsün's collected writings during thirty years), compiled by Lu Hsün hsien-sheng chi-nien wei-yuan-hui 魯迅 先生紀念委員會 (Lu Hsün memorial committee), published by Lu Hsün ch'üan-chi ch'u-pan she 魯迅全集出版社 Shanghai, 1947, 20 vols.

Mao, Hsüan-chi: *Mao Tse-tung hsüan-chi* 毛澤東選集 (Selected Works of Mao Tse-tung), Hsin-hua 新華 Book Co., Shantung, 1944, 5 vols., 888 pp.

Marx, Karl, *Das Kapital*, vol. I, Modern Library, Random House, New York, 1906, 870 pp.

Marx, Karl, *Selected Works*, edited by I. B. Lasker, Foreign Languages Publishing House, Moscow, 1946 (Library of Congress).

Mif, Pavel, "Kitaiskaia kompartiia v kriticheskii dni" (The CCP in critical days), *Bolshevik*, December 31, 1927, 24 pp., microfilm (Hoover Library).

Nippon gaiji: Nippon gaiji kyokai 日本外事協會 (Japanese Foreign Affairs Association), comp., *Shina ni okeru kyōsan undō* 支 那に於ける共産運動 (The Communist movement in China), Tokyo, 1933, 401 pp.

P'eng Shu-chih, *Kung-tang lien-hsi hui-i t'an-hua* 共黨聯席會 議談話 (Speech at joint session of the CP), September 12, 1929 (?), 25 pp.

Pu-erh-sai-wei-k'o 布爾塞維克 (*Bolshevik*), nos. 23–44, December 21, 1927 (Hoover Library).

Rätechina (also published in Russian in 1934 as Johanson i Taube, *Soviety v Kitae* [Soviets in China]), translated from German, Partiinoe Izdatyel'stvo, Moscow, 1934, 518 pp.

Revolyutsionnyi Vostok, no. 2, 1927.

Roy, M. N., *Revolution and counterrevolution in China*, Renaissance Publishing Company, Calcutta, India, 1948, 672 pp.

Sambō: Sambō hombu　参謀本部　*Shina kyōsantō no gaikan*　支那
共産党の概観 (A general survey of the CCP), Tokyo, 1929 (?),
84 pp. (Library of Congress).

Shen Sung-fang 沈頌芳 , ed., *I-chiu-wu-ling jen-min nien-chien* 一九五〇
人民年鑑 (People's Year Book 1950), Ta-kung Book
Company, Hongkong, 1950, 5 sections, 363 pp.

Shen-Kan-Ning: *Shan-Kan-Ning pien-ch'ü cheng-fu kung-tso pao-kao 1939–
1941* 陝甘寧邊區政府工作報告 *1939–1941*. (Work re-
port of the Shensi-Kansu-Ninghsia Border Region Government,
1939–41), published by Shan-Kan-Ning pien-ch'ü cheng-fu
wei-yüan-hui 陝甘寧邊區政府委員會 (Shensi-Kansu-
Ninghsia Border Region Government Committee), Yenan, July
1931, 134 pp.

Shina Nenkan 支那年鑑 (China Yearbook), Tōa Dōbunkai
東亞同文會 , Tokyo, 1935, 1703 pp.

Snow, Edgar, *Red Star Over China*, Modern Library edition, New York,
1938, 529 pp.

Soviety v Kitae, see *Rätechina*.

Stalin, Josif, *Leninism*, International Publishers, New York, 1942,
479 pp.

Stalin, Josif, *Selected Writings*, International Publishers, New York,
479 pp.

Stein, Gunther, *The Challenge of Red China*, McGraw-Hill Book Co.,
Inc., New York, 1945, 490 pp.

Steiner, H. Arthur, "Mainsprings of Chinese Communist Foreign
Policy", *American Journal of International Law*, vol. 44, no. 1 (January
1950), pp. 69–99; "Chinese Communist Urban Policy", *American
Political Science Review*, vol. XLIV, no. 1 (March 1950), pp. 47–63.

Su-wei-ai Chung-kuo 蘇維埃中國 (Soviet China), cover bears
seal of CEC, Chinese Soviet Republic, n.p., 1933, 223 pp., preface
by Wang Ming 王明 dated September 27, 1933. Probably published like the volume *Chih-yu Su-wei-ai* . . . , listed above, by the
Publishing house for foreign workers in the Soviet Union, Moscow.
The Columbia University copy is stamped as originally distributed
through "Giu Guo Sh Bao 'Au Secours de la Patrie' " 救國時

報社 (i.e. *Chiu-kuoshih-pao*, lit. National salvation times), 7, Rue Commines, Paris-3. Professor C. M. Wilbur found and sent us this volume (Columbia University Library).

Sun Wen 孫文 (Sun Yat-sen 孫逸仙), *Tsung-li ch'üan-chi* 總理全集 (Complete collected works of the Director-General [of the KMT]), ed. by Hu Han-min 胡漢民 , Shanghai, 1930. 4 collections (chi 集) and 5 volumes.

Teng Chung-hsia 鄧中夏 , *Chung-kuo chih-kung yün-tung chien-shih* 中國職工運動簡史 (A short history of the Chinese labour movement), published by Chieh-fang-she, distributed by Hsin-hua 新華 Book Co., Yenan, May 1, 1943, 287 pp. Preface to the 2nd edition dated 1942; "word from the Author" dated 1930, Moscow; Appendix includes a life of Comrade Teng Chung-hsia, p. 282 et seq.

Tōa: Tōa keizai chōsa kyoku 東亞經濟調查局 ([Japanese] East Asia Economic Research Bureau), *Shina Sobieto undō no kenkyū* 支那ソヴエリ運動の研究 (A study of the Chinese Soviet movement), Tokyo, 1935, 459 pp. (Library of Congress).

Tsui, S. C. (Ts'ui Shu-ch'in) 崔書琴 , "Influence of the Canton-Moscow Entente upon Sun Yat-sen's Political Philosophy", *Chinese Social and Political Science Review*, vol. 18, no. 1, April 1934, pp. 96–145.

Trotsky, Leon, *Problems of the Chinese Revolution*, Pioneer Publishers, New York, 1932, 432 pp.

T'u-kai: Liu Shao-ch'i 劉少奇等 and others, *T'u-kai cheng-tang tien-hsing ching-yen* 土改整黨典型經驗 (Typical experiences in [the work of] land reform and Party purification), a collection of 9 items from late 1947 to early 1948, published by Chung-kuo ch'u-pan she 中國出版社 , Hongkong, April 1948, 58 pp.

T'u-ti ko-ming: *Chung-kuo Kung-ch'an-tang yü t'u-ti ko-ming* 中國共產黨與土地革命 (The CCP and the agrarian revolution), a collection of 12 items on the land policy of the CCP, published by Cheng-pao she 正報社 , Hongkong, n.d. (probably 1948), 78 pp.

Watanabe, Shigeo 渡邊茂雄 , *Shō Kaiseki to Mō Shitaku* 蔣介

石と毛澤東　(Chiang Kai-shek and Mao Tse-tung), published by Kōdan She　講談社　, Tokyo, 1941, 239 pp.

Werner, Morris Robert (editor), *Stalin's Kampf—Joseph Stalin's Credo—written by himself*, Jarrolds Publishers, Ltd., London, 1940, 295 pp.

White Paper: U.S. Department of State, *United States Relations with China—with Special Reference to the Period 1944–1949*, U.S. Government Printing Office, Washington, D.C., August 1949, 1054 pp.

Winfield, Gerald, *China, The Land and the People*, William Sloane Associates, Inc., New York, 1948, 437 pp.

Yakhontoff, Victor A., *The Chinese Soviets*, Coward-McCann Inc., New York, 1934, 292 pp.

GLOSSARY

Note: This glossary contains abbreviations, names of Chinese persons, names of organizations or organizational units, and a selection of vocabulary phrases and special terms commonly used in Chinese works concerning Communism and derived by us from the above texts—all arranged in one single alphabetic list of Wade-Giles romanizations followed by characters. All this need not concern the general reader. It is offered merely to aid those who already read Chinese, but who may not be acquainted with the special lingo, abbreviated references, and clichés developed in the Chinese Communist movement. The organizational names, vocabulary phrases, and special terms are in italics; * indicates a deceased person. We have included only personal names to be found in the text above, without attempting to present biographical data concerning them nor to list any but the most common variant names, pseudonyms, or aliases.

Boku Ichiu 朴一禹

CC (see *Chung-yang wei-yüan-hui*)

CCP (see *Chung-kuo Kung-ch'an-tang*)

CEC (see *Chung-yang chih-hsing-wei-yüan-hui*)

Chan-tou ti 戰鬥的 (Fighting, combative)

Chang Chi-ch'un 張際春

Chang Hsüeh-liang 張學良

Chang Kuo-t'ao 張國燾 (Chang T'e-li 張特立)

Chang Lan 張瀾

Chang Shao-cheng* 張紹錚

Chang T'ai-lei* 張太雷

Chang Ting-ch'eng 張鼎承

Chang Tso-lin* 張作霖

Chang Tsung-hsün 張宗遜

Chang Tung-sun 張東蓀

Chang Tzu-p'ing	張資平	
Chang Wen-t'ien	張聞天	(alias Lo Fu 洛甫 and Ssu Mei 思美)
Chang Yün-i	張雲逸	
Ch'ang-cheng	長征	(The Long March [of the CCP, 1934–5])
Chao Chen-sheng	趙振聲	
Chao Kuo-chün	趙國鈞	
Chao Ping-chün*	趙秉鈞	
Chao Shih-yen	趙世炎	(alias Shih Yang 施洋)*
Chao Yung	趙容	(alias K'ang Sheng 康生)
Ch'e-ti	澈底	(Thorough, complete)
Chen-li	真理	(Truth, truism)
Ch'en I	陳毅	
Ch'en Keng	陳賡	
Ch'en Kung-po*	陳公博	
Ch'en Ming-shu	陳銘樞	(Ch'en Chen-ju 陳真如)
Ch'en Po-ta	陳伯達	(Ch'en Pai-ta)
Ch'en Shao-min, Miss	陳少敏	
Ch'en Shao-yü	陳紹禹	(alias Wang Ming 王明)
also Ch'en Shao-yü	陳韶玉	
Ch'en T'an-ch'iu*	陳潭秋	
Ch'en Tu-hsiu*	陳獨秀	(Ch'en Shih-an 陳實菴)
Ch'en Wang-tao	陳望道	
Ch'en Yen-nien*	陳延年	
Ch'en Yu-jen	陳友仁	(Eugene Ch'en)*
Ch'en Yü	陳郁	
Ch'en Yün	陳雲	(Alias of Liao Ch'eng-yün 廖程雲)
Cheng-chih	政治	(Politics, political)
Cheng-chih chü (see Chung-yang cheng-chih-chü)	政治局	
Cheng-chih tou-cheng	政治鬥爭	(Political struggle)
Cheng-ch'üan	政權	(Régime, political power)
Cheng-ch'üeh	正確	(Correct, right)

Cheng-feng yün-tung	整風運動	(Movement for correction of [unorthodox] tendencies—[in learning, the Party, and literature])
Cheng-lun	爭論	(Argument, controversy)
Cheng-pien	政變	(Coup d'état, coup)
Cheng-tang	政黨	(Political party, party)
Cheng-tun san-feng hsüeh-feng, tang-feng, wen-feng	整頓三風 學風,黨風,文風	(Correcting the three [unorthodox] tendencies in learning, the Party and literature)
Cheng Wei-shan	鄭唯善	
Cheng-wu yüan	政務院	(State Administrative Council)
Ch'eng-pan chu-i	懲辦主義	(Punitivism)
Ch'eng-shih hsiao-tzu-ch'an chieh-chi	城市小資產階級	(Urban petty bourgeoisie)
Ch'eng-shih tzu-ch'an chieh-chi	城市資產階級	(Urban bourgeoisie)
Ch'eng Tzu-hua	程子華	
Chi-chi fen-tzu	積極份子	(Active elements)
Chi-hsieh ti	機械的	(Mechanical)
Chi-hsieh wei-wu lun	機械唯物論	(Mechanical materialism)
Chi-hui chu-i	機會主義	(Opportunism)
Chi-hui chu-i che	機會主義者	(Opportunist)
Chi-lü	紀律	(Discipline)
Ch'i Hsieh-yüan*	齊燮元	
Ch'i-yeh	企業	(Enterprise, industry)
Chia-chang chih	家長制	(Patriarchal system, patriarchism)
Chiang Kai-shek 蔣介石 (Chiang Chieh-shih, Chiang Chung-cheng 蔣中正)		
Chiang Kuang-nai	蔣光鼐	
Chiao-t'iao chu-i	教條主義	(Dogmatism)
Chiao-yü	教育	(Education, educate, train)

Chieh-chi	階級	(Class)
Chieh-chi fen-hua	階級分化	(Class differentiation)
Chieh-chi tou-cheng	階級鬥爭	(Class struggle)
Chieh-ch'üan chu-i	極權主義	(Totalitarianism)
Chieh-fang	解放	(Liberation, emancipation, to liberate, to emancipate)
Chieh-fang ch'ü	解放區	(Liberated Area[s])
Chieh-lun	結論	(Conclusion)
Chieh-ts'eng	階層	(Class, group)
Chieh-tuan	階段	(Stage, period)
Chien-hsi	奸細	(Spy, saboteur)
Chien-tsu chien-hsi	減租減息	(Reductions of rent and interest rate)
Ch'ien-chin fen-tzu	前進份子	(Progressive elements)
Ch'ien-chin ti	前進的	(Progressive)
Chih-kung yün-tung	職工運動	(Labour movement)
Chih-min-ti	殖民地	(Colony or colonial)
Chih-pu	支部	(Cell—basic unit of the Party)
Chih-pu tai-piao hui-i	支部代表會議	(Conference of Party Cell Representatives)
Chih-pu wei-yüan-hui	支部委員會	(Cell Committee)
Chih-shih fen-tzu	知識份子	(Intellectual elements, intelligentsia)
Chih-tao chi-kuan	指導機關	(Directing organ[s], leadership, leading organ[s])
Chih-tao-yüan	指導員	(Commissar [usually in the Communist forces])
Chih-ts'ai	制裁	(Disciplinary measure)
Chih-tu	制度	(System)
Chih-wei (For *Chih-pu wei-yüan-hui* or *Chih-pu wei-yüan-hui wei-yüan* 支部委員會 委員)	支委	
Ch'ih-se hsien-feng tui	赤色先鋒隊	(Red Vanguard)

Ch'in-lüeh	侵略	(Aggression, invade)
Ch'in Pang-hsien	秦邦憲	(alias Po Ku 博古)*
Ching-chi	經濟	(Economy, economic)
Ching-chueh-hsing	警覺性	(Vigilance, alertness, watchfulness)
Ching-shen	精神	(Spirit)
Ching-yen	經驗	(Experience)
Ching-yen chu-i	經驗主義	(Empiricism)
Ch'ing-hsü	情緒	(Sentiment, feeling)
Chiu-ch'a tui	糾察隊	(Workers' guards, Workers' militia, pickets)
Chiu-cheng	糾正	(To correct)
Chou En-lai	周恩來	(alias Wu Hao 伍豪 also Shao Shan 少山)
Chou Fu-hai	周佛海	
Chou Tso-jen	周作人	
Chu Ch'ing-lai*	諸青來	
Chu-hsi	主席	(Chairman)
Chu Hsi*	朱熹	
Chu Hsüeh-fan	朱學範	
Chu-kuan	主觀	(Subjective)
Chu-kuan chu-i	主觀主義	(Subjectivism)
Chu P'ei-te*	朱培德	
Chu Te	朱德	(Chu Teh)
Chuan-cheng	專政	(Dictatorship)
Chung-chien lu-hsien	中間路線	(The middle way, middle path)
Chung-ch'üan-hui 中全會 (For *Chung-yang wei-yüan-hui ch'üan-t'i hui-i*)		
Chung-hsin	中心	(Central, prime)
Chung-Kung (For *Chung-kuo Kung-ch'an-tang*)	中共	
Chung-kuo Kung-ch'an-tang	中國共產黨	(The Chinese Communist Party)
Chung-nung	中農	(Middle peasants)

Chung-wei 中委 (For *Chung-yang wei-yüan-hui* or *Chung-yang wei-yüan-hui wei-yüan*)

Chung-yang 中央 (For *Chung-yang wei-yüan-hui*)

Chung-yang cheng-chih-chü 中央政治局　(Central Political Bureau —Politburo)

Chung-yang chih-hsing wei-yüan-hui 中央執行委員會　(Central Executive Committee)

Chung-yang chü 中央局　(Central Bureau)

Chung-yang fen-chü 中央分局　(Regional Bureau of the CCP)

Chung-yang jen-min cheng-fu 中央人民政府　(Central People's Government)

Chung-yang jen-min cheng-fu wei-yüan-hui 中央人民政府委員會　(Central People's Government Council)

Chung-yang shu-chi ch'u 中央書記處　(Central Secretariat)

Chung-yang wei-yüan-hui 中央委員會　(Central Committee [in some contexts actually the Political Bureau of the CC])

Chung-yang wei-yüan-hui ch'üan-t'i hui-i 中央委員會全體會議　(Plenum of the Central Committee)

Chung-yang wei-yüan-hui wei-yüan 中央委員會委員　(Member of the Central Committee)

*Ch'ü Ch'iu-pai** 瞿秋白

Ch'ü-hsiao chu-i 取消主義　(Liquidationism)

Ch'ü-hsiao p'ai 取消派　(Liquidationists)

Ch'ü tai-piao hui-i 區代表會議　(District Conference of Party Representatives)

Ch'ü tai-piao ta-hui 區代表大會　(District Congress)

Ch'ü-wei 區委 (For *Ch'ü wei-yüan-hui* or *Ch'ü wei-yüan-hui wei-yüan*)

Ch'ü wei-yüan-hui 區委員會　(District Committee)

Ch'ü wei-yüan-hui wei-yüan 區委員會委員　(Member of District Committee)

Ch'üan-kuo tai-piao hui-i 全國代表會議 (National Conference of Party Representatives)

Ch'üan-kuo tai-piao-ta-hui 全國代表大會 ([National] Congress)

Ch'üan-kuo tsung-kung-hui 全國總工會 (National Federation of Labour)

Ch'üan-li 權利 (Right[s], privilege[s])

Ch'üan-tang fei-ch'ang hui-i 全黨非常會議 (Extraordinary or Emergency Conference of the Party)

Ch'üan-t'i hui-i 全體會議 (Plenary Session)

Ch'üan-tsung 全總 (For *Ch'üan-kuo tsung-kung-hui*)

Chüeh-i-an 決議案 (or *I-chüeh-an* 議決案) (Resolution[s], decision)

Chüeh-tui chu-i 絕對主義 (Absolutism)

Chün-cheng wei-yüan-hui 軍政委員會 (Military and Political Committee, Highest regional administrative organ)

Chün-fa 軍閥 (Warlords, militarists)

Chün-fa chan-cheng 軍閥戰爭 (Warlords' warfare, warlord's imbroglios, fighting among the warlords)

Ch'un-chung 羣衆 (The masses)

Ch'un-chung t'uan-t'i 羣衆團體 (Mass organizations)

CI (For *Kung-ch'an kuo-chi* or *Ti-san Kuo-chi*)

CY (For *Kung-ch'an chu-i ch'ing-nien-t'uan*)

ECCI (For *Kung-ch'an kuo-chi chung-yang chih-hsing wei-yüan hui*)

Erh-wu chien-tsu 二五減租 (Twenty-five per cent rent reduction)

Fa-hsi-szu 法西斯 (Fascist, Fascism)

Fan ko-ming 反革命 (Counter-revolutionary, counter-revolution)

Fan-ti 反帝 (For *Fan ti-kuo-chu-i*)

Fan ti-kuo-chu-i 反帝國主義 (Anti-imperialist, anti-imperialism)

Fan-tung-p'ai	反動派	(Reactionary[ies])
Fang-chen	方針	(Policy, guiding principle, programme, course, direction)
Fang Chih-min*	方志敏	
Fang-hsiang	方向	(Direction)
Fang Lin	方霖	
Fei chieh-chi-hua ti	非階級化的	(Class-alienated, rejected by one's class)
Fen-hsi	分析	(Analyse, analysis)
Fen-tou	奮鬥	(Struggle, fight)
Feng-chien	封建	(Feudal)
Feng-chien chu-i	封建主義	(Feudalism)
Feng-chien yü-tu	封建餘毒	(Feudal remnants)
Feng Kuo-chang*	馮國璋	
Feng-t'ou chu-i	風頭主義	(Exhibitionism)
Feng Yü-hsiang*	馮玉祥	
Fu-chu-hsi	副主席	(Vice-chairman)
Fu-nung	富農	(Rich peasant[s])
Fu-t'sung	服從	(Obey)
Han-chien	漢奸	(Traitor)
Han Lin-fu	韓麟符	
Han Yü*	韓愈	
Hei-an shih-li	黑暗勢力	(Dark forces, evil forces)
Ho Ch'ang*	賀昌	
Ho Chien*	何鍵	
Ho-fa chu-i	合法主義	(Legalism)
Ho K'o-ch'üan	何克全	(alias K'ai Feng 凱豐) ⟨
Ho Liu-hua	何柳華	(Alias of Liao Ch'eng-chih)
Ho Lung	賀龍	
Ho Meng-hsiung*	何夢雄	
Ho Shu-heng*	何叔衡	
Ho-tso	合作	(Co-operation, co-operate)
Ho-tso she	合作社	(Co-operative[s])

Hou-pu	候補	(Alternate, probational)
Hsi Chung-hsün	習仲勲	
Hsi-sheng	犧牲	(Sacrifice)
Hsia-chi chi-kuan	下層機關	(Lower organs)
Hsia Hsi*	夏曦	
Hsia-ts'eng	下層	(Lower strata, lower layer)
Hsiang Chung-fa*	向忠發	
Hsiang Ying*	項英	
Hsiao Chin-kuang	蕭勁光	
Hsiao K'o	蕭克	
Hsiao-nung ching-chi	小農經濟	(Small peasant economy)
Hsiao-tsu	小組	(Group—subdivision of a cell)
Hsiao tsu-chih	小組織	(Clique, sect; lit., a small organization)
Hsiao tzu-ch'an chieh-chi	小資産階級	(Petty bourgeoisie)
Hsiao Yao-nan*	蕭耀南	
Hsien	縣	(County or District)
Hsien-chin fen-tzu	先進份子	(Advanced elements, progressive elements)
Hsien-feng-tui	先鋒隊	(Vanguard)
Hsien tai-piao hui-i	縣代表會議	(County or District Conference of Party Representatives)
Hsien tai-piao ta-hui	縣代表大會	(County or District Congress)
Hsien-wei (For *Hsien wei-yüan-hui* or *Hsien wei-yüan-hui wei-yüan*)	縣委	
Hsien wei-yüan-hui	縣委員會	(County or District Committee)
Hsien wei-yüan-hui wei-yüan	縣委員會委員	(Member of County or District Committee)
Hsin Chung-kuo	新中國	(New China)
Hsin-min-chu chu-i	新民主主義	(New Democracy)
Hsin-ssu-chün	新四軍	(The New Fourth Army)

Hsin-yang	信仰	(Belief, faith, conviction)
Hsing-shih	形式	(Form)
Hsing-shih	形勢	(Situation, condition)
Hsiung Hsi-ling	熊希齡	
Hsü Hsiang-ch'ien	徐向前	
Hsü K'o-hsiang	許克祥	
Hsü Pei-hung	徐悲鴻	
Hsü Shih-ch'ang*	徐世昌	
Hsü Shu-cheng*	徐樹錚	
Hsü T'e-li	徐特立	(Hsü Mou-hsün 徐懋循)
Hsüan-ch'uan	宣傳	(Propaganda, propagandize)
Hsüan-ch'uan kung-tso	宣傳工作	(Propaganda work)
Hsüan-yen	宣言	(Manifesto, public statement)
Hsüeh-hsi	學習	(Learn, learning, training)
Hsün-ling	訓令	(Directives, instructions)
Hu Han-min*	胡漢民	
Hu Shih	胡適	(Hu Shih-chih 胡適之)
Hu Wen-chiang*	湖文江	
Hua Kang	華崗	
Hua Ying-shen	華應申	
Huang K'o-ch'eng	黃克誠	
Huang-se kung-hui	黃色工會	(Yellow union[s]—rightist union[s])
Hui-i	會議	(Conference, council)
Hung-chun	紅軍	(Red Army)
Hung Hsiu-ch'üan*	洪秀全	
I-pien tao	一邊倒	(Leaning to one side)
I-wu	義務	(Duty, obligation)
Jao Shu-shih	饒漱石	
Jen Cho-hsüan	任卓宣	(alias Yeh Ch'ing 葉青)
Jen-min cheng-hsieh ch'üan-kuo wei-yüan-hui 人民政協全國委員會		(National Committee of the People's Political Consultative Council)

Jen-min cheng-chih hsieh-shang hui-i	人民政治協商會議	(People's Political Consultative Council)
Jen-min ko-ming chün-shih wei-yüan-hui	人民革命軍事委員會	(People's Revolutionary Military Council)
Jen-min ta-chung	人民大眾	(The people, the masses)
Jen Pi-shih*	任弼時	
Jen-sheng-kuan	人生觀	(Philosophy of life)
Jen-wu	任務	(Tasks)
Jih-ch'ang sheng-huo tou-cheng	日常生活鬥爭	(Daily economic struggle)
Kai-liang chu-i	改良主義	(Reformism)
Kai-tsao	改造	(Reform, remould)
Kai-tsu-p'ai	改組派	(Reorganizationist group)
K'ai Feng	凱豐	(Alias of Ho K'o-ch'üan)
Kan-pu	幹部	(Cadre, either an individual or a small group; often but not necessarily, a CP member)
Kang-ling	綱領	(Policy, programme, plank)
Kang-yao	綱要	(Outline, essentials)
K'ang-Jih	抗日	(Anti-Japanese)
K'ang Sheng	康生	(Alias of Chao Yung)
*K'ang Yu-wei**	康有為	
Kao-ch'ao	高潮	(Rising tide, upsurge)
Kao Ch'ung-min	高崇民	
Kao Kang	高崗	
Kao Yü-han	高語罕	
KMT (For Kuo-min-tang)		
Ko-chi tang-pu	各級黨部	(Party headquarters on all levels, all Party branches)
Ko-jen chu-i	個人主義	(Individualism)
Ko-jen ying-hsiung chu-i	個人英雄主義	(Vainglorious individualism, egotism)
Ko-ming	革命	(Revolution, revolutionary)
Ko-ming hsien-feng	革命先鋒	(Vanguard of the revolution)

Ko-ming kao-ch'ao	革命高潮	(Revolutionary rising tide)
K'o-chüan tsa-shui	苛捐雜稅	(Exorbitant taxes and irregular [excessive] levies)
K'o-hsüeh t'ai-tu	科學態度	(Scientific attitude)
K'o-kuan	客觀	(Objective, objectivity)
K'o-neng hsing	可能性	(Possibility)
K'ou-hao	口號	(Slogan[s])
Ku Chu-t'ung	顧祝同	
Ku-nung	僱農	(Hired farm hand[s])
Ku Shun-chang	顧順章	
Ku Ta-ts'un	古大存	
Ku-yung ping-shih	僱傭兵士	(Mercenary soldier[s])
K'u-li	苦力	(Coolie)
Kuan Hsiang-ying*	關向應	
Kuan-liao chu-i	官僚主義	(Bureaucratism)
Kuan-liao tzu-pen-chia	官僚資本家	(Bureaucratic capitalist[s])
Kuan-nien	觀念	(Concept, idea)
Kuan-nien hsing-t'ai	觀念形態	(Ideology)
Kuang-ta ch'ün-chung	廣大羣眾	(Broad masses, multitudinous masses)
Kung-ch'an chu-i	共產主義	(Communism)
Kung-ch'an chu-i ch'ing-nien-t'uan	共產主義青年團	(Communist Youth Corps —CY)
Kung-ch'an kuo-chi	共產國際	(The Communist or Third International, Comintern —CI)
Kung-ch'an kuo-chi chung-yang chih-hsing wei-yüan-hui	共產國際中央執行委員會	(Central Executive Committee of the Communist International—ECCI)
Kung-chü	工具	(Tool, instrument, pawn)
Kung-hui	工會	(Union)
Kung-jen ch'ün-chung	工人羣眾	(Working masses)
Kung-jen yün-tung	工人運動	(Workers' movement)
Kung-ku	鞏固	(Consolidate)
Kung-liang	公糧	(lit., Public grain—i.e. tax in kind)

Kung-nung ko-ming	工農革命	(Workers' and peasants' revolution)
Kung-nung-ping	工農兵	(Workers, peasants, and soldiers)
Kung-nung-ping tai-piao hui-i	工農兵代表會議	(Council of workers', peasants', and soldiers' deputies)
Kung-shih	公式	(Formula)
K'ung Fu-tzu*	孔夫子	(Confucius)
Kuo-chi (For *Kung-ch'an kuo-chi* or *Ti-san kuo-chi*)		
Kuo-chi chih-wei-hui (For *Kung-ch'an kuo-chi chung-yang chih-hsing-wei-yuan-hui*)		
Kuo-huo	過火	(Excessive, extreme)
Kuo Miao-ken	郭妙根	
Kuo-min ta-hui	國民大會	(National Assembly)
Kuo-min-tang	國民黨	(The Nationalist Party [of China])
Kuo-nan	國難	(National crisis, national emergency)
Kuo-yu hua	國有化	(Nationalization)
K'uo-ta ch'üan-t'i hui-i	擴大全體會議	(Enlarged plenum)
Lao-tung ying-hsiung	勞動英雄	(Labour hero)
Li Ang	李昂	(pseudonym?)
Li-ch'ang	立場	(Stand)
Li Chi-shen (sen)	李濟琛	
Li Fu-ch'un	李富春	
Li Han-chun	李漢俊	
Li Hsien-nien	李先念	
Li-i	利益	(Interest[s], advantage[s])
Li Li-san	李立三	(Li Lung-ch'i 李隆郅 alias Pai Shan or Po Shan 柏山)
Li-liang	力量	(Strength, force)
Li Lieh-chün*	李烈鈞	

Li-lun	理論	(Theory, theories)
Li-lun-chia	理論家	(Theorist[s])
Li-shih wei-wu lun	歷史唯物論	(Historical materialism)
Li Ta	李達	
Li Ta-chao*	李大釗	(Li Shou-ch'ang 李守常)
Li Wei-han	李維漢	(alias Lo Mai 羅邁)
Li Yü	黎玉	
Li Yüan-hung*	黎元洪	
Liang Shih-ch'iu	梁實秋	
Liao Ch'eng-chih	廖承志	(alias Ho Liu-hua 何柳華)
Liao Ch'eng-yün	廖程雲	(alias Ch'en Yün 陳雲)
Liao Chung-k'ai*	廖仲凱	
Lieh-ning chu-i	列寧主義	(Leninism)
Lieh-shen	劣紳	(Bad gentry)
Lien-ho chan-hsien	聯合戰線	(United front)
Lien-ho cheng-fu	聯合政府	(Coalition government)
Lien-kung 聯共 (For *Su-lien kung-ch'an-tang* 蘇聯共產黨)		
Lien-meng	聯盟	(Alliance, league)
Lin Feng	林楓	
Lin Hsiang-ch'ien*	林祥謙	
Lin Piao	林彪	(Lin Yü-yung 林育蓉)
Lin Tsu-han	林祖涵	(Lin Po-ch'ü 林伯渠)
Lin Wei-min*	林偉民	
Lin Yü-t'ang	林語堂	
Ling-tao	領導	(Lead, leadership)
Ling-tao chi-kuan	領導機關	(Leading organ[s], leadership)
Liu Ch'ang-sheng	劉長勝	
Liu Chih-tan	劉志丹	(Tzu-tan 子丹)*
Liu Chün-shan	劉峻山	
Liu Hsiao	劉曉	
Liu Hua*	劉華	
Liu Jen-ching	劉仁靜	
Liu Lan-t'ao	劉瀾濤	
Liu Ning-i	劉寧一	

Liu Po-ch'eng	劉伯承	
Liu Shao-ch'i	劉少奇	
Liu T'ieh-ch'ao*	劉鐵超	
Liu Tzu-chiu	劉子久	
Liu Wen-sung	劉文松	
Lo Fu	洛甫	(Alias of Chang Wen-t'ien)
Lo I-nung*	羅亦農	
Lo I-yuan*	羅綺園	
Lo Jui-ch'ing	羅瑞卿	
Lo Jung-huan	羅榮桓	
Lo Mai	羅邁	(Alias of Li Wei-han)
Lo Ping-hui	羅炳輝	
Lu-hsien	路線	(Line)
Lu Hsün	魯迅	(Lusin, Lu Hsin)*
Lu Ting-i	陸定一	
Lü Cheng-ts'ao	呂正操	
Lung-tuan	壟斷	(Monopoly, monopolize)
Ma Chün*	馬駿	
Ma En Lieh Shih	馬恩列史	(Marx, Engels, Lenin, and Stalin)
Ma-k'o-ssu-chu-i	馬克斯主義	(Marxism)
Ma-Lieh chu-i	馬列主義	(Marxism-Leninism)
Mai-pan	買辦	(Compradore[s])
Mang-tung chu-i	盲動主義	(Putschism, adventurism, literally blind-actionism)
Mao-hsien chu-i	冒險主義	(Adventurism)
Mao-hsien chu-i che	冒險主義者	(Adventurist)
Mao Tse-tung	毛澤東	(Jun-chih 潤芝)
Mao Tse-tung ssu-hsiang	毛澤東思想	(Mao Tse-tung's thought, idea of Mao Tse-tung)
Meng Ch'ing-shu	孟慶樹	(Mme. Ch'en Shao-yü)
Meng-sai wei-k'o tang	孟塞維克黨	(Menshevik Party)
Mi-mi kung-tso	秘密工作	(Secret Work)
Mi-shu-chang	秘書長	(Secretary-General)
Min-chu	民主	(Democracy, democratic)

Min-chu chi-chung chih	民主集中制	(Democratic centralism)
Min-chu ko-ming	民主革命	(Democratic revolution)
Min-ch'üan chu-i	民權主義	([Sun Yat-sen's] Principle of Democracy or People's Rights)
Min-sheng chu-i	民生主義	([Sun Yat-sen's] Principle of People's Livelihood)
Min-tsu chu-i	民族主義	([Sun Yat-sen's] Principle of Nationalism)
Min-tsu ko-ming	民族革命	(National revolution)
Min-tsu t'ung-i chan-hsien	民族統一戰線	(National united front)
Min-tsu tzu-ch'an chieh-chi	民族資產階級	(National bourgeoisie [Bourgeoisie who are neither bureaucratic capitalists nor capitalists who affiliate with foreign imperialists])
Min-tsu tzu-chüeh	民族自決	(Self-determination)
Min-t'uan	民團	(People's corps, militia)
Ming-ling chu-i	命令主義	(Dictatorialness)
Mo-fan	模範	(Model, exemplar, exemplary)
Mo-shou	沒收	(Confiscate, confiscation)
Mou	畝	(Unit in Chinese land measurement, about one-sixth of an acre)
Mu-piao	目標	(Goal, target, aim)
Nei-chan	內戰	(Civil war)
Nei-jung	內容	(Content, substance)
Nieh Jung-chen	聶榮臻	
Nozaka Sanzo	野坂參三	(Original name Nozaka Sanji 野坂參次 , outside Japan, he called himself Okano Susumu 岡野進 , also Nozaka Tetsu 野坂鐵)

Nu-li	努力	(Endeavor)
Nung-min	農民	(Peasant[s])
Nung-min chiu-kuo hsieh-hui	農民救國協會	(Peasant Association for National Salvation, a term used during the Sino-Japanese War)
Nung-min hsieh-hui	農民協會	(Peasant Association)
Nung-min i-shih	農民意識	(Peasant mentality)
Pa-kung	罷工	(Strike[s])
Pa-lu chün	八路軍	(The Eighth Route Army)
Pai Shan	柏山	(or Po Shan, alias of Li Li-san)
Pai-se k'ung-pu	白色恐怖	(White terror)
P'ai-pieh	派別	(Clique, sect)
Pan chih-min-ti	半殖民地	(Semi-colonial)
Pan feng-chien	半封建	(Semi-feudal)
Pao-kao	報告	(Report)
Pao-tung	暴動	(Insurrection, uprising, revolt)
Pei-fa	北伐	(The Northern Expedition, 1926-7)
Pei-p'an	背叛	(Betray, betrayal)
Pen-wei chu-i	本位主義	(Particularism — thinking only of one's own unit or department but disregarding the organization as a whole)
Peng-k'uei	崩潰	(Collapse)
P'eng Chen	彭真	
P'eng Pai*	彭湃	
P'eng Shu-chih	彭述之	
P'eng Te-huai	彭德懷	
P'i-p'an	批判	(Criticism, criticize)
P'i-p'ing	批評	(Criticism, criticize)
Piao-chun	標準	(Standard, criterion)
Pieh-san	癟三	(Tramp, vagrant—a Shanghai colloquialism)

Pien-cheng fa	辯証法	(Dialecticism)
Pien-cheng wei-wu lun	辯証唯物論	(Dialectical materialism)
Pien-ch'ü	邊區	(Border Area, Border Region)
Pien-ch'ü tai-piao hui-i	邊區代表會議	(Border Region Conference of Party Representatives)
Pien-ch'ü tai-piao ta-hui	邊區代表大會	(Border Region Congress)
Pien-ch'ü wei-yüan-hui	邊區委員會	(Border Region Committee)
Pien-ch'ü wei-yüan-hui wei-yüan	邊區委員會委員	(Member of Border Region Committee)
Pien-wei (For Pien-ch'ü wei-yüan-hui or Pien-ch'ü wei-yüan-hui wei-yüan) 邊委		
P'in-nung	貧農	(Poor peasants)
P'ing-teng	平等	(Equality, equal)
Po-hsüeh 剝削 (or Po-hsiao)		(Exploit, exploitation)
Po-hsüeh chieh-chi	剝削階級	(Exploiting class)
Po I-po	薄一波	
Po Ku*		(Alias of Ch'in Pang-hsien)
P'o-huai	破壞	(Destroy, destruction, sabotage)
Pu cheng-ch'üeh	不正確	(Erroneous, incorrect, wrong, unorthodox)
Pu-erh-sai-wei-k'o hua	布爾塞維克化	(Bolshevization)
Pu p'ing-teng	不平等	(Inequality, unequal)
Pu-tuan ko-ming	不斷革命	(Permanent revolution)
San-min chu-i	三民主義	(Three People's Principles [of Sun Yat-sen])
San-san chih	三三制	(Three-thirds system — a system practised by the CCP during the Sino-Japanese War, giving one-third of administrative posts to KMT, one-third to CCP members, and one-third to nonparty members)

Shan-pei kung-hsüeh	陝北公學	(North Shensi Academy)
Shang-chi chi-kuan	上級機關	(Higher organs)
Shang-ts'eng	上層	(Upper strata, upper layer)
Shao Li-tzu	邵力子	
Shao Shan	少山	(Alias of Chou En-lai)
She-hui	社會	(Society, social)
She-hui chu-i	社會主義	(Socialism, socialistic)
She-hui huà	社會化	(Socialize)
Shen Hung-lieh	沈鴻烈	
Shen Sung-fang	沈頌芳	
Shen Tse-min*	沈澤民	
Shen Yen-ping	沈雁冰	(Nom de Plume: Mao Tun 茅盾)
Sheng-ch'an	生產	(Production, produce)
Sheng-huo t'iao-chien	生活條件	(Living conditions)
Sheng tai-piao hui-i	省代表會議	(Provincial Conference of Party Representatives)
Sheng tai-piao ta-hui	省代表大會	(Provincial Congress)
Sheng-wei (For *Sheng wei-yüan-hui* or *Sheng wei-yüan-hui wei-yüan*)	省委	
Sheng wei-yüan-hui	省委員會	(Provincial Committee)
Sheng wei-yüan-hui wei-yüan	省委員會委員	(Member of Provincial Committee)
Shih Ch'eng-t'ung	施承統	
Shih-chi kung-tso	實際工作	(Practical work)
Shih-ch'i	時期	(Period)
Shih-chieh-kuan	世界觀	(Weltanschauung, world view)
Shih-chien	實踐	(Practice, actuality, practical)
Shih-hua	實話	(True words)
Shih-ming	使命	(Mission, task)
Shih-pai chu-i	失敗主義	(Defeatism)
Shih tai-piao hui-i	市代表會議	(Municipal Conference of Party Representatives)

Shih tai-piao ta-hui	市代表大會	(Municipal Congress)
Shih-t'ai-lin chu-i	史太林主義	(Stalinism)
Shih-wei (For *Shih wei-yüan-hui* or *Shih wei-yüan-hui wei-yüan*)	市委	
Shih-wei-yüan-hui	市委員會	(Municipal Committee)
Shih wei-yüan-hui wei-yüan	市委員會委員	(Member of the Municipal Committee)
Shih Yang*	施洋	(Alias of Chao Shih-yen)
Shih-yueh ko-ming	十月革命	(The October Revolution [1917])
Shu-chi	書記	(Secretary)
Shu She-yü	舒舍予	(Nom de Plume: Lao She)
Shui-p'ing	水平	(Level)
Soong Ching-ling		(See Sung Ching-ling)
Su Chao-cheng*	蘇兆澂	
Su-ch'ing	蕭清	(Liquidate, clear up)
Su-lien kung-ch'an-tang	蘇聯共產黨	(Communist Party of the Soviet Union)
Su-wei-ai	蘇維埃	(Soviet)
Su Yü	粟裕	
Sun Chung-shan 孫中山 (Sun Wen, Sun I-hsien 孫文孫逸仙)*		(Sun Yat-sen)
Sun Lieh-ch'en*	孫烈臣	
Sung Chiao-jen*	宋教仁	
Sung Ching-ling	宋慶齡	(Mme. Sun Yat-sen)
Sung Jen-ch'iung	宋任窮	
Ssu-jen ch'i-yeh	私人企業	(Private enterprise)
Ssu Mei		(Alias of Chang Wen-t'ien)
Ta-tao	打倒	(Down with . . .)
Ta-to-shu	大多數	(Majority)
Ta-t'ung shu	大同書	(Title of book by K'ang Yu-wei)
Tai-piao hui-i	代表會議	(Conference of [Party] Representatives)

Tai-piao ta-hui	代表大會	(Congress)
Tai Tou-yüan	戴斗垣	
T'an Chen-lin	譚震林	
T'an Cheng	譚政	
T'an P'ing-shan	譚平山	
Tang-chang	黨章	(Party constitution, Party regulations)
Tang-chi	黨籍	(Party membership)
Tang-kang	黨綱	(Party programme, Party constitution)
Tang-nei	黨內	(Intra-Party, within the Party)
Tang pa-ku	黨八股	(Party formalism: [*pa-ku* was originally the essay style used by pre-Chinese-renaissance scholars in stereotyped examinations])
Tang-pu	黨部	(Party headquarters)
Tang ti ling-tao chi-kuan	黨的領導機關	(Leading Party organs, Party leadership)
Tang-t'uan	黨團	(Party organizations)
Tang-wei (See *Tang wei-yüan-hui* or *Tang wei-yüan-hui wei-yüan*)	黨委	
Tang wei-yüan-hui	黨委員會	(Party committee)
Tang wei-yüan-hui wei-yüan	黨委員會委員	(Member of Party Committee, Party Commissioner)
Tang-yuan	黨員	(Party member)
T'ang Meng-hsiao	唐孟瀟	(See T'ang Sheng-chih)
T'ang Sheng-chih	唐生智	(T'ang Meng-hsiao)
T'e-tien	特點	(Characteristics, special features)
Teng Chung-hsia*	鄧中夏	
Teng Fa*	鄧發	
Teng Hsiao-p'ing	鄧小平	

Teng Tzu-hui	鄧子恢	
Teng Ying-ch'ao	鄧穎超	(Mme. Chou En-lai)
T'eng Tai-yüan	滕代遠	
Ti-chu	地主	(Landlord[s])
Ti-fang	地方	(Locality, local)
Ti-fang tai-piao hui-i	地方代表會議	(Local Conference of Party Representatives)
Ti-fang tai-piao ta-hui	地方代表大會	(Local Congress)
Ti-fang wei-yüan-hui	地方委員會	(Local Committee)
Ti-fang wei-yüan-hui wei-yüan	地方委員會委員	(Member of Local Committee)
Ti-hsia tsu-chih	地下組織	(Underground organization)
Ti-jen	敵人	(Enemy)
Ti-kuo chu-i	帝國主義	(Imperialism)
Ti-san kuo-chi	第三國際	(The Third or Communist International, or Comintern—CI)

Ti-wei (For *Ti-fang wei-yüan-hui* or *Ti-fang wei-yüan-hui wei-yüan*)

T'i-hsi	體系	(System)
T'iao-chien	條件	(Condition, factor)
T'iao-ho chu-i	調和主義	(lit., "compromise-ism", i.e. the doctrine of, belief in, or tendency to, compromise)
Tien-nung	佃農	(Tenant farmer)
T'o-hsieh	妥協	(Compromise)
T'o-li	脫離	(Alienate)
T'o-p'ai	托派	(Trotskyites)
T'o-lo-ssu-chi p'ai	托洛斯基派	(Trotskyites)
Tou-cheng	鬥爭	(Struggle, fight)
T'ou-hsiang chu-i	投降主義	(lit., "surrender-ism", i.e. the doctrine of, belief in, or tendency to, surrender)

Ts'ai Ch'ang	蔡暢	(Mme. Li Fu-ch'un)
Ts'ai Chen-te	蔡振德	
Ts'ai Ho-shen*	蔡和森	
Ts'ai T'ing-k'ai	蔡廷楷	
Ts'ao K'un*	曹錕	
Ts'e-lüeh	策略	(Strategy, tactics, policy)
Tseng Ching-ping	曾鏡水	
Tseng Shan	曾山	
Tso Ch'üan*	左權	
Tso-ch'ing mao-hsien chu-i	左傾冒險主義	(Leftist adventurism)
Tso-ch'ing wei-hsien	左傾危險	(Danger of leftist deviation)
Tso-ch'ing yu-chih-ping	左傾幼稚病	(Leftist infantile disorder)
Tso-feng	作風	(Spirit, working style, characteristics)
Tso-p'ai	左派	(Left wing, leftist)
Tso-t'an-hui	座談會	(Forum, discussion meeting)
Ts'o-che	挫折	(Set-back, defeat)
Ts'o-wu	錯誤	(Error, mistake)
Ts'o-wu ti	錯誤的	(Erroneous, mistaken, wrong)
Tsou-kou	走狗	(Running dog, lackey)
Tsu-chih kung-tso	組織工作	(Organizational work)
Tsui-kao jen-min chien-ch'a shu	最高人民檢查署	(Bureau of Procurator General)
Tsui-kao jen-min fa-yüan	最高人民法院	(People's Supreme Court)
Tsung-fa ssu-hsiang chih-tu	宗法思想制度	(Patriarchal system, patriarchalism)
Tsung pa-kung	總罷工	(General strike)
Tsung-p'ai chu-i	宗派主義	(Sectarianism)
Tsung-shu-chi	總書記	(Secretary-General)
Tsung-ti lu-hsien	總的路線	(General line, overall line)
Tu-ts'ai	獨裁	(Dictatorship, dictatorial)
T'u-hao lieh-shen	土豪劣紳	(Village bosses and bad gentry)

T'u-ti ko-ming	土地革命	(Agrarian revolution)
T'u-ti wen-t'i	土地問題	(Land question)
Tuan Ch'i-jui*	段琪瑞	
T'uan-chieh	團結	(Solidarity, to unify)
T'uan-t'i	團體	(Organization)
Tung-li	動力	(Sources of power, dynamic power)
Tung Pi-wu	董必武	
Tung-yao	動搖	(Vacillate, vacillation, wavering)
Tung-yao fen-tzu	動搖份子	(Wavering elements)
T'ung-chih	同志	(Comrade)
T'ung-chih	統治	(Rule, to rule)
T'ung-chih chieh-chi	統治階級	(Ruling class)
T'ung-i chan-hsien	統一戰線	(United front)
Tzu-ch'an chieh-chi	資產階級	(Bourgeoisie)
Tzu-ch'ao	自嘲	(Self-ridicule)
Tzu-pen-chia	資本家	(Capitalist[s])
Tzu-pen chu-i	資本主義	(Capitalism, capitalist)
Tzu-wo p'i-p'an	自我批判	(Self-criticism)
Tzu-yu	自由	(Freedom, liberty, free)
Tzu-yu chu-i	自由主義	(Liberalism)
Tzu-yu chu-i che	自由主義者	(Liberal)
Wan I	萬毅	
Wan-ku-p'ai	頑固派	(Diehards, reactionaries)
Wan-sui	萬歲	(Long live . . .)
Wang Chen	王震	
Wang Chia-hsiang	王稼祥	
Wang Ching-wei*	汪精衛	
Wang Jo-fei*	王若飛	
Wang Ming	王明	(Alias of Ch'en Shao-yü)
Wang Shou-tao	王首道	
Wang Ts'ung-wu	王從吾	
Wang Wei-chou	王維舟	
Wei-hsin lun	唯心論	(Idealism)

Wei-pa chu-i	尾巴主義	(Tailism—passive trailing behind the masses in contrast to active leadership; from Russian Chvostizm)
Wei-wu lun	唯物論	(Materialism)
Wei-wu shih-kuan	唯物史觀	(Historical materialism)
Wei-wu pien-cheng-fa	唯物辯證法	(Materialist dialectics)
Wei-yüan-hui	委員會	(Committee)
Wen-hua	文化	(Culture, sometimes used by the CCP to indicate the knowledge of reading and writing, or literacy on its lowest level)
Wen-hua shui-p'ing	文化水平	(Cultural level)
Wen-i	文藝	(Abbreviation for *Wen-hsüeh* 文學 and *i-shu* 藝術 , i.e. literature and art, literary)
Wen-t'i	問題	(Question, problem)
Wu-ch'an chieh-chi	無產階級	(The proletariat)
Wu-ch'i	武器	(Weapon)
Wu Ching-heng	吳敬恆	(Chih-hui 吳稚暉)
Wu Chün-sheng*	吳俊陞	
Wu-lan-fu	烏蘭夫	(Yün Tse 雲澤)
Wu P'ei-fu*	吳佩孚	
Wu-ssu yün-tung	五四運動	(The May 4 [1919] Movement, the date of inception of the Chinese student movement of 1919, taken to represent the whole nationalistic and cultural renaissance of the period)
Wu Yü-chang	吳玉章	
Ya-p'o	壓迫	(Oppression, oppress)
Yang Chih-tse	楊致澤	

Yang Hu-ch'eng*　　　楊虎城

Yang pa-ku　　　　　洋八股　　　(Foreign formalism, cp.
　　　　　　　　　　　　　　　　　　Tang pa-ku)

Yang P'ao-an*　　　　楊豹安

Yeh Chien-ying　　　　葉劍英

Yeh Ch'ing　　　　　葉青　　　　(Alias of Jen Cho-hsüan)

Yeh T'ing*　　　　　葉挺

Yen-chung　　　　　嚴重　　　　(Grave, serious)

Yen Fu*　　　　　　嚴復

Yen Hsi-shan　　　　閻錫山

Yen-lun tzu-yu　　　　言論自由　　(Freedom of speech)

Yen Yung-ch'iu*　　　晏容秋

Yin-su　　　　　　　因素　　　　(Factor, element)

Yu-chi chan-cheng　　　遊擊戰爭　　(Guerrilla warfare)

Yu-ch'ing　　　　　　右傾　　　　(Rightist deviation, right-
　　　　　　　　　　　　　　　　　　ist)

Yu-ch'ing wei-hsien　　右傾危險　　(Danger of rightist devia-
　　　　　　　　　　　　　　　　　　tion)

Yu-min wu-ch'an chieh-chi　游民無產階級　(Lumpenproletariat)

Yu-p'ai　　　　　　　右派　　　　(Right wing, rightist)

Yü-chou-kuan　　　　宇宙觀　　　(Cosmology, world out-
　　　　　　　　　　　　　　　　　　look)

Yü Fang-tan*　　　　于方丹

Yü Shu-te　　　　　于樹德

Yüan Shih-k'ai*　　　袁世凱

Yüan-tse　　　　　　原則　　　　(Principle)

Yün Tai-ying*　　　　惲代英

Yün Tse (Wu-lan-fu)

Yün-tung　　　　　　運動　　　　(Movement)

INDEX

CONRAD BRANDT, Associate Fellow of St. Antony's College, Oxford University, has previously taught at the University of California, Berkeley, and at Harvard University. He is currently an advisor on Chinese history for Encyclopaedia Britannica.

BENJAMIN I. SCHWARTZ is Professor of History and Government at Harvard University and a Research Associate at the East Asian Research Center at Harvard. He is the author of *Chinese Communism and the Rise of Mao,* and his most recent publication is *In Search of Wealth and Power: Yen Fu and the West.*

JOHN K. FAIRBANK has taught since 1936 at Harvard, where he is Frances Lee Higginson Professor of History and Director of the Center for Asian Studies. His book with S. Y. Teng, *China's Response to the West: A Documentary Survey 1839–1923,* is Atheneum paperback number 44.

Atheneum Paperbacks

HISTORY

HISTORY—ASIA

Atheneum Paperbacks

4730 / 12

Atheneum Paperbacks

STUDIES IN AMERICAN NEGRO LIFE

Atheneum Paperbacks

THE NEW YORK TIMES BYLINE BOOKS

THE ADAMS PAPERS

ECONOMICS AND BUSINESS

PHYSICAL SCIENCES AND MATHEMATICS

Atheneum Paperbacks

HISTORY—AMERICAN—1900 TO THE PRESENT